Robert Meersman   Tharam Dillon
Pilar Herrero (Eds.)

On the Move to Meaningful Internet Systems: OTM 2010 Workshops

Confederated International Workshops and Posters:
AVYTAT, ADI, DATAVIEW, EI2N, ISDE
MONET, OnToContent, ORM, P2P-CDVE
SeDeS, SWWS and OTMA
Hersonissos, Crete, Greece, October 25-29, 2010
Proceedings

 Springer

Volume Editors

Robert Meersman
Vrije Universiteit Brussel (VUB), STAR Lab
Bldg G/10, Pleinlaan 2, 1050 Brussel, Belgium
E-mail: meersman@vub.ac.be

Tharam Dillon
Curtin University, Digital Ecosystems and Business Intelligence
Institute (DEBII), EU4, De Laeter Way, Bentley, 6102 Australia
E-mail: t.dillon@curtin.edu.au

Pilar Herrero
Universidad Politécnica de Madrid, Facultad de Informática
Campus de Montegancedo S/N
28660 Boadilla del Monte, Madrid, Spain
E-mail: pherrero@fi.upm.es

Library of Congress Control Number: 2010938295

CR Subject Classification (1998): C.2, H.4, D.2, H.3, C.2.4, I.2

LNCS Sublibrary: SL 3 – Information Systems and Application, incl. Internet/Web
and HCI

ISSN   0302-9743
ISBN-10   3-642-16960-0 Springer Berlin Heidelberg New York
ISBN-13   978-3-642-16960-1 Springer Berlin Heidelberg New York

springer.com

© Springer-Verlag Berlin Heidelberg 2010
Printed in Germany

Typesetting: Camera-ready by author, data conversion by Scientific Publishing Services, Chennai, India
Printed on acid-free paper   06/3180

Volume Editors

Robert Meersman
Tharam Dillon
Pilar Herrero

AVYTAT 2010

Javier Cámara
Carlos E. Cuesta
Howard Foster
Miguel Angel Pérez-Toledano

ADI 2010

Olivier Curé
Stefan Jablonski
David Thau

DATAVIEW 2010

Sara Comai
Moira Norrie
Alessandro Bozzon

EI2N 2010

Giuseppe Berio
Qing Li
Kemafor Anyanwu
Hervé Panetto

ISDE 2010

Alok Mishra
Jürgen Münch
Deepti Mishra

MONET 2010

Patrizia Grifoni
Fernando Ferri
Irina Kondratova
Arianna D'Ulizia

OnToContent 2010
Paolo Ceravolo
Majed Ayyad
Mustafa Jarrar
Andreas Schmidt

ORM 2010
Terry Halpin
Herman Balsters

P2PCDVE 2010
Laura Ricci
Largo Bruno Pontecorvo

SeDeS 2010
Yan Tang
Jan Vanthienen
Yannis Charalabidis

SWWS 2010
Tharam S. Dillon
Ernesto Damiani
Elizabeth Chang
Paolo Ceravolo
Jaipal Singh

OTMA 2010
Peter Spyns
Anja Schanzenberger

General Co-chairs' Message for OnTheMove 2010

The OnTheMove 2010 event in Hersonissos, Crete, during October 24-29, further consolidated the growth of the conference series that was started in Irvine, California, in 2002, and held in Catania, Sicily, in 2003, in Cyprus in 2004 and 2005, in Montpellier in 2006, in Vilamoura in 2007 and 2009, and in Monterrey, Mexico in 2008. The event continues to attract a diversified and representative selection of today's worldwide research on the scientific concepts underlying new computing paradigms, which, of necessity, must be distributed, heterogeneous and autonomous yet meaningfully collaborative. Indeed, as such large, complex and networked intelligent information systems become the focus and norm for computing, there continues to be an acute and ever increasing need to address and discuss face to face in an integrated forum the implied software, system and enterprise issues as well as methodological, semantic, theoretical and application issues. As we all realize, e-mail, the Internet and even video conferences are not by themselves sufficient for effective and efficient scientific exchange.

The OnTheMove (OTM) Federated Conferences series has been created to cover the scientific exchange needs of the community/ies that work in the broad yet closely connected fundamental technological spectrum of Web-based distributed computing. The OTM program every year covers data and Web semantics, distributed objects, Web services, databases, information systems, enterprise workflow and collaboration, ubiquity, interoperability, mobility, grid and high-performance computing.

OTM does not consider itself a so-called multi-conference but instead is proud to give meaning to the "federated" aspect in its full title: it aspires to be a primary scientific meeting place where all aspects of research and development of Internet- and intranet-based systems in organizations and for e-business are discussed in a scientifically motivated way, in a forum of (loosely) interconnected workshops and conferences. This ninth edition of the OTM Federated Conferences event therefore once more provided an opportunity for researchers and practitioners to understand and publish these developments within their individual as well as within their broader contexts. To further promote synergy and coherence, the main conferences of OTM 2010 were conceived against a background of three interlocking global themes, namely, "Cloud Computing Infrastructures," "The Internet of Things, or Cyberphysical Systems," "(Semantic) Web 2.0 and Social Computing for the Enterprise."

Originally the federative structure of OTM was formed by the co-location of three related, complementary and successful main conference series: DOA (Distributed Objects and Applications, since 1999), covering the relevant infrastructure-enabling technologies, ODBASE (Ontologies, DataBases and Applications of SEmantics, since 2002), covering Web semantics, XML databases and ontologies, and CoopIS (Cooperative Information Systems, since 1993), covering the application of these technologies in an enterprise context through, for example, workflow systems and knowledge management. In 2007 the IS workshop (Information Security) was added to try covering also the specific issues of security in complex Internet-based information systems. Each of the main conferences specifically seeks high-quality contributions and encourages researchers to treat their respective topics within a framework that incorporates jointly (a) theory, (b) conceptual design and development, and (c) applications, in particular case studies and industrial solutions.

Following and expanding the model created in 2003, we again solicited and selected quality workshop proposals to complement the more "archival" nature of the main conferences with research results in a number of selected and more "avant-garde" areas related to the general topic of Web-based distributed computing. For instance, the so-called Semantic Web has given rise to several novel research areas combining linguistics, information systems technology and artificial intelligence, such as the modeling of (legal) regulatory systems and the ubiquitous nature of their usage. We were glad to see that seven of our successful earlier workshops (ADI, EI2N, SWWS, ORM, OnToContent, MONET, ISDE) re-appeared in 2010 with, in some cases, a fourth or even fifth edition, often in alliance with other older or newly emerging workshops, and that no fewer than four brand-new independent workshops could be selected from proposals and hosted: AVYTAT, DATAVIEW, P2PCDVE, SeDeS. Our OTM registration format ("one workshop buys all") actively intends to stimulate workshop audiences to productively mingle with each other and, optionally, with those of the main conferences.

We were also most happy to see that once more in 2010 the number of quality submissions for the OnTheMove Academy (OTMA, formerly called Doctoral Consortium Workshop), our "vision for the future" in research in the areas covered by OTM, took off again and with increasing success. We must thank the team of collaborators led by Peter Spyns and Anja Schanzenberger, and of course the OTMA Dean, Erich Neuhold, for their continued commitment and efforts in implementing our unique interactive formula to bring PhD students together. In OTMA, research proposals are submitted for evaluation; selected submissions and their approaches are (eventually) presented by the students in front of a wider audience at the conference, and intended to be independently and are extensively analyzed and discussed in public by a panel of senior professors.

As said, all four main conferences and the associated workshops shared the distributed aspects of modern computing systems, and the resulting application pull created by the Internet and the so-called Semantic Web. For DOA 2010, the primary emphasis stayed on the distributed object infrastructure; for ODBASE 2010, it became the knowledge bases and methods required for enabling the use of formal semantics; for CoopIS 2010, the focus as usual was on the interaction of such technologies and methods with management issues, such as occur in networked organizations, and for IS 2010 the emphasis was on information security in the networked society. These subject areas overlap in a scientifically natural fashion and many submissions in fact also treated an envisaged mutual impact among them. As for the earlier editions, the organizers wanted to stimulate this cross-pollination by a "shared" program of famous keynote speakers around the chosen themes: we were quite proud to announce Wil van der Aalst, T.U. Eindhoven, The Netherlands, Beng Chin Ooi, National University of Singapore, Michael Brodie, Chief Scientist, Verizon, USA, and Michael Sobolewski, Polish-Japanese Institute of IT, Poland.

We received a total of 223 submissions for the four main conferences and 127 submissions in total for the workshops. The numbers are about 5% lower than for 2009. Not only may we indeed again claim success in attracting an increasingly representative volume of scientific papers, many from the USA and Asia, but these numbers of course allow the Program Committees to compose a high-quality cross-section of current research in the areas covered by OTM. In fact, the Program Chairs of the CoopIS 2010 conferences decided to accept only approximately one paper from every five submissions, while ODBASE 2010 and DOA 2010 accepted about the same number of papers for presentation and publication as in 2008 and 2009 (i.e., average one paper out of three to four submitted, not counting posters). For the workshops and IS 2010 the acceptance rate varied but the aim was to stay consistently at about one accepted paper for two to three submitted, and subordinated of course to scientific quality assessment. As usual we have separated the proceedings into three volumes with their own titles,two for the main conferences and one for the workshops, and we are most grateful to the Springer LNCS team in Heidelberg for their professional suggestions and meticulous collaboration in producing the files for downloading on the USB sticks.

The reviewing process by the respective Program Committees was again performed very professionally, and each paper in the main conferences was reviewed by at least three referees, with arbitrated e-mail discussions in the case of strongly diverging evaluations. It may be worthwhile to emphasize that it is an explicit OTM policy that all conference Program Committees and Chairs make their selections completely autonomously from the OTM organization itself. Like last year, paper proceedings were on separate request and order this year, and incurred an extra charge.

The General Chairs are once more especially grateful to the many people directly or indirectly involved in the set-up of these federated conferences. Few people realize what a large number of individuals have to be involved, and what a huge amount of work, and in 2010 certainly also financial risk, the organization of an event like OTM entails. Apart from the persons in their roles mentioned above, we therefore wish to thank in particular our eight main conference PC Co-chairs: CoopIS 2010: Herve Panetto, Jorge Cardoso, M. Brian Blake; ODBASE 2010: Alejandro Buchmann, Panos Chrysanthis, York Sure; DOA 2010: Ernesto Damiani, Kai Hwang. And similarly the 2010 IS, OTMA and Workshops PC (Co-)chairs: Javier Cámara, Carlos E. Cuesta, Howard Foster, Miguel Angel Pérez-Toledano, Stefan Jablonski, Olivier Curé, David Thau, Sara Comai, Moira Norrie, Alessandro Bozzon, Giuseppe Berio, Qing Li, Kemafor Anyanwu,

Hervé Panetto (again), Alok Mishra, Jürgen Münch, Deepti Mishra, Patrizia Grifoni, Fernando Ferri, Irina Kondratova, Arianna D'Ulizia, Paolo Ceravolo, Majed Ayyad, Terry Halpin, Herman Balsters, Laura Ricci, Yan Tang, Jan Vanthienen, Yannis Charalabidis, Ernesto Damiani (again), Elizabeth Chang, Gritzalis Stefanos, Giles Hogben, Peter Spyns, Erich J. Neuhold and Anja Schanzenberger. Most of them, together with their many PC members, performed a superb and professional job in selecting the best papers from the harvest of submissions. We are all grateful to our supremely competent and experienced Conference Secretariat and technical support staff in Antwerp, Daniel Meersman, Ana-Cecilia, and Jan Demey, and last but certainly not least to our editorial team in Perth (DEBII-Curtin University) chaired by Houwayda El Fawal Mansour. The General Co-chairs acknowledge with gratitude the academic freedom, logistic support and facilities they enjoy from their respective institutions, Vrije Universiteit Brussel (VUB), Curtin University, Perth, Australia, and Universitad Politécnica de Madrid (UPM), without which such an enterprise would not be feasible. We do hope that the results of this federated scientific enterprise contribute to your research and your place in the scientific network... We look forward to seeing you again at next year's event!

August 2010

Robert Meersman
Tharam Dillon
Pilar Herrero

Organization

OTM (On The Move) is a federated event involving a series of major international conferences and workshops. These proceedings contain the posters presented at the OTM 2010 conferences and the papers presented at the OTM 2010 workshops, consisting of 12 workshops, namely: AVYTAT (Adaptation in serVice EcosYsTems and ArchiTectures), ADI (AMBIENT DATA INTEGRATION), DATAVIEW (DATA Visualization and Integration in Enterprises and on the Web), EI2N (Enterprise Integration, Interoperability and Networking), ISDE (Information Systems in Distributed Environment), MONET (MObile and NEtworking Technologies for social applications), OnToContent (Ontology Content), ORM (Fact-Oriented Modeling), P2P CDVE (P2P Collaborative Distributed Virtual Environments), SeDeS (Semantic and Decision Support), SWWS (Semantic Web and Web Semantics) and OTMA (On The Move Academy).

Executive Commitee

General Co-chairs

Robert Meersman	VU Brussels, Belgium
Tharam Dillon	Curtin University of Technology, Australia
Pilar Herrero	Universidad Politécnica de Madrid, Spain

AVYTAT 2009 PC Co-chairs

Javier Cámara	INRIA Rhône-Alpes, France
Carlos E. Cuesta	Rey Juan Carlos University, Spain
Howard Foster	Imperial College London, UK
Miguel Angel Pérez-Toledano	University of Extremadura, Spain

ADI 2010 PC Co-chairs

Olivier Curé	Université Paris Est, France
Stefan Jablonski	University of Bayreuth, Germany
David Thau	University of California Davis, USA

DATAVIEW 2010 PC Co-chairs

Sara Comai	Politecnico di Milano, Italy
Moira Norrie	ETH Zürich, Switzerland
Alessandro Bozzon	Politecnico di Milano, Italy

EI2N 2010 PC Co-chairs

Giuseppe Berio	University of South Britain, France
Qing Li	Tsinghua University, P.R. China
Kemafor Anyanwu	North Carolina State University, USA
Hervé Panetto	Nancy University, France

ISDE 2010 PC Co-chairs

Alok Mishra	Atilim University, Turkey
Jürgen Münch	Fraunhofer Institute for Experimental Software Engineering, Germany
Deepti Mishra	Atilim University, Turkey

MONET 2010 PC Co-chairs

Patrizia Grifoni	IRPPS, Italy
Fernando Ferri	IRPPS, Italy
Irina Kondratova	NRC Institute, Canada
Arianna D'Ulizia	IRPPS, Italy

OnToContent 2010 PC Co-chairs

Paolo Ceravolo	Università degli Studi di Milano, Italy
Majed Ayyad	NextLevel Technology Systems Ramallah, Palestine
Mustafa Jarrar	Birzeit University, Palestine
Andreas Schmidt	FZI, Germany

ORM 2010 PC Co-chairs

Terry Halpin	LogicBlox, Australia and INTI Education Group, Malaysia
Herman Balsters	University of Groningen, The Netherlands

P2P CDVE 2010 PC Co-chairs

Laura Ricci	Università degli Studi di Pisa, Italy
Largo Bruno Pontecorvo	Università degli Studi di Pisa, Italy

SeDeS 2010 PC Co-chairs

Yan Tang	STARLab, Vrije Universiteit Brussel, Belgium
Jan Vanthienen	Katholieke Universiteit Leuven, Belgium
Yannis Charalabidis	National Technical University of Athens, Greece

SWWS 2010 PC Co-chairs

Tharam Dillon   Curtin University of Technology, Australia
Ernesto Damiani   Milan University, Italy
Elizabeth Chang   Curtin University of Technology, Australia
Paolo Ceravolo   Milan University, Italy
Jaipal Singh   Curtin University of Technology, Australia

OTMA 2010 PC Co-chairs

Peter Spyns   Vrije Universiteit Brussel,Belgium
Anja Schanzenberger   University of Applied Sciences Augsburg,
                           Germany

Publication Chair

Houwayda Elfawal Mansour   DEBII, Australia

Publicity-Sponsorship Chair

Ana-Cecilia Martinez Barbosa   DOA Institute, Belgium

Logistics Team

Daniel Meersman   Head of Operations
Ana-Cecilia Martinez Barbosa
Jan Demey

AVYTAT 2010 Program Committee

Dharini Balasubramaniam   Juan Manuel Murillo
Carlos Canal   Sascha Ossowski
Sorana Cîmpan   Jennifer Pérez
Pedro J. Clemente   Pascal Poizat
Laurence Duchien   Pilar Romay
José Luiz Fiadeiro   Gwen Salaün
Rogerio de Lemos   Houman Younessi
Tommi Mikkonen   Yijun Yu

ADI 2010 Program Committee

Christoph Bussler Olivier Curé   Sascha Mueller
Mathieu D'aquin   Erich Ortner
Wolfgang Deiters   Riccardo Rosati
Stefan Jablonski   Kurt Sandkuhl
Robert Jeansoulin   François Scharffe
Roland Kaschek   David Thau
Myriam Lamolle
Richard Lenz

DATAVIEW 2010 Program Committee

Marco Brambilla
Irene Celino
Emanuele DellaValle
Roberto De Virgilio
Flavio Maria De Paoli
Martin Gaedke
Michael Grossniklaus

Suzanne Little
Juan Carlos Preciado
Beat Signer
Giovanni Toffetti Carughi
Raluca Paiu
Marco Winckler

EI2N 2010 Program Committee

Giuseppe Berio
Peter Bernus
Nacer Boudjlida
Luis M. Camarinha-Matos
J. Cecil
Vincent Chapurlat
David Chen
Adrian Curaj
Michele Dassisti
Charlotta Johnsson
Andres Garcia Higuera
Ricardo Gonçalves
Ted Goranson
John Gotze
Roland Jochem
Georgios Kapogiannis
John Krogstie
Qing Li
Peter Loos
Juan-Carlos Mendez
Istvan Mezgar

Arturo Molina
Yannick Naudet
Ovidiu Noran
Angel Ortiz
Hervé Panetto
Jin Woo Park
Michaël Petit
Wolfgang Prinz
Czeslaw Smutnicki
Aurelian M. Stanescu
Michael Sobolewski
Janusz Szpytko
Pat Turner
Bruno Vallespir
François B. Vernadat
Georg Weichhart
Lawrence Whitman
Milan Zdravkovic
Xuan Zhou

ISDE 2010 Program Committee

Amar Gupta
Allen E. Milewski
Anil Kumar Tripathi
Barbara Carminati
Bernard Wong
Cagatay Catal
Charles Wallace
Cigdem Gencel

Darja Smite
Deo Prakash Vidyarthi
Ian Allison
Ita Richardson
Jeffrey Carver
Juan Garbajosa
Jukka Kääriäinen
June Verner

Kassem Saleh
Liguo Yu
Ali Babar
Mahmood Niazi
Nilay Oza
Nils. B. Moe
Nik Bessis

Pierre F. Tiako
Orit Hazzan
Qing YAO
Silvia Abrahao
Srini Ramaswamy

MONET 2010 Program Committee

Kevin C. Almeroth
Frederic Andres
Russell Beale
Yiwei Cao
Tiziana Catarci
Richard Chbeir
Karin Coninx
Simon Courtenage
Juan De Lara
Anna Formica
C.-C. Jay Kuo
Peter Leijdekkers
Stephen Marsh
Rebecca Montanari
Michele Missikoff
Nuria Oliver

Marco Padula
Manish Parashar
Andrew Phippen
Nitendra Rajput
Tommo Reti
Ahmed M. Safwat
Nicola Santoro
Tim Strayer
Henri Ter Hofte
Thanassis Tiropanis
Yoshito Tobe
Riccardo Torlone
Mikael Wiberg
Adam Wojciechowski

OnToContent 2010 Program Committee

Abder Koukam
Alessandro Oltramari
Antonio Zilli
Barry Smith
Christophe Roche
Davy Monticolo
Domenico Talia
Eva Blomqvist
Fabio Vitali
Federica Paci
Trichet Francky
Geert Poels
Karl Reed

Ling Feng
Marcello Leida
Martin Hepp
Michael Brown
Miguel Sicilia
Vincenzo Maltese
Philippe Cudré-Mauroux
Riccardo Albertoni
Robert Tolksdorf
Silvie Spreeuwenberg
Stijn Heymans

ORM 2010 Program Committee

Herman Balsters
Scott Becker
Linda Bird
Anthony Bloesch
Peter Bollen
Lex Bruil
Andy Carver
Matthew Curland
Dave Cuyler
Necito Dela Cruz
Olga De Troyer
Gordon Everest
Ken Evans
Pat Hallock
Terry Halpin
Stijn Hoppenbrouwers
Mike Jackson
Mustafa Jarrar

Marijke Keet
Tony Morgan
Maurice Nijssen
Baba Piprani
Erik Proper
Ron Ross
Gerhard Skagestein
Deny Smeets
Silvie Spreeuwenberg
Peter Spyns
Kurt Stirewalt
Serge Valera
Jan Vanthienen
Jos Vos
Theo van der Weide
Joost van Griethuysen

P2P CDVE 2010 Program Committee

Laura Ricci
Fabrizio Baiardi
Ranieri Baraglia
Abdennour El Rhalibi
Stefano Ferretti
Behnoosh Hariri
Stephan Krause
Alberto Montresor

Raffaele Perego
Marco Roccetti
Gregor Schiele
Domenico Talia
Arno Wacker
Shun Yun Hu

SeDeS 2010 Program Committee

Frode Eika Sandnes
Saiful Akbar
Weihua Li
José Fernán Martínez
Yue Liu
Jiehan Zhou
Peter Spyns

Zhiwen Yu
Johan Criel
Bin Guo
Ying Liu
Dimitris Askounis
Luke Chen

OTMA 2010 Program Committee

Galia Angelova	Chengfei Liu
Christoph Bussler	Erich J. Neuhold
Paolo Ceravolo	Hervé Panetto
Jaime Delgado	Anja Schanzenberger
Ling Feng	Peter Spyns
Avigdor Gal	Maria Esther Vidal
Alfred Holl	Adam Wierzbicki
Frédéric Le Mouël	

Supporting and Sponsoring Institutions

OTM 2010 was proudly supported or sponsored by Vrije Universiteit Brussel in Belgium, Curtin University of technology in Australia, Universidad Politechnica de Madrid in Spain, Object Management Group, and Collibra.

Table of Contents

On the Move 2010 Keynotes

Posters and Industry Papers of the COOPIS 2010 International Conference

Posters

Agents/ Industry Panel

Posters of the DOA 2010 International Conference

Posters of the ODBASE 2010 International Conference

Workshop on Adaptation in serVice EcosYsTems and ArchiTectures (AVYTAT 2010)

Adaptation in Service-Oriented Architectures

Workshop on Ambient Data Integration (ADI 2010)

Ambient Intelligence and Reasoning

Data Integration Approaches

Modeling in ADI

Industrial Enterprise Interoperability and Networking

Workshop on Information Systems in Distributed Environment (ISDE 2010)

Process Management in Distributed Information System Development

Distributed Information Systems: Implementation Issues

Workshop on MObile and NEtworking Technologies for social applications (MONET 2010)

Improving Social Networking: Service-Oriented Architectures, Location-Based Services, and Multimodality

Adaptive Issues and Solutions in Networking and Mobile Applications

Workshop on Ontology Content (OnToContent 2010)

Ontology Engineering

Ontology in Social Entreprise

Workshop on Fact-Oriented Modeling (ORM 2010)

Data Integration

Master Data Management and Metamodeling

Extensions to Fact-Oriented Modeling

Logic and Derivation

Patterns in Input Data and Data Models

Workshop on P2P Collaborative Distributed Virtual Environments (P2P CDVE 2010)

Workshop on Semantic and Decision Support (SeDeS 2010)

Workshop IFIP on Semantic Web and Web Semantics (SWWS 2010)

On The Move Academy (OTMA 2010)

Position Papers

Technical Papers

OTM'10 Keynote

Beng Chin Ooi

Beng Chin Ooi, National University of Singapore (NUS)

Short Bio

Beng Chin is Professor of Computer Science at School of Computing, at the National University of Singapore (NUS). He obtained his BSc (1st Class Honors) and PhD from Monash University, Australia, in 1985 and 1989 respectively. His research interests include database performance issues, indexing techniques, multimedia and spatio-temporal databases, P2P systems and advanced applications, and cloud computing. His current system projects include BestPeer, P2P based data management system, and epiC, a data-intensive cloud computing platform.

He has served as a PC member for international conferences including ACM SIGMOD, VLDB, IEEE ICDE, WWW, SIGKDD and Vice PC Chair for ICDE'00, 04,06, co-PC Chair for SSD'93 and DASFAA'05, PC Chair for ACM SIGMOD'07, and Core DB track PC chair for VLDB'08. He is the Editor-in-Chief of IEEE Transactions on Knowledge and Data Engineering (TKDE), and a trustee member of VLDB Endowment Board. He is the recipient of ACM SIGMOD 2009 Contributions award.

Talk

"Supporting OLTP and OLAP Queries on Cloud Platforms"

MapReduce-based systems have been widely used for large-scale data analysis. Although these systems achieve storage-system independence, high scalability, and fine-grained fault tolerance, their performance have been shown to be unsatisfactory.It has also been shown that MapReduce-based systems are significantly slower than Parallel Database systems in performing a variety of analytic tasks. Some attribute the performance gap between MapReduce-based and Parallel Database systems to architectural design. This speculation yields an interesting question: Must a system sacrifice performance to achieve flexibility and scalability? Consequently, we conducted an in-depth performance study of MapReduce in its open source implementation, Hadoop. We identified various factors that have significant performance effect on the system. Subsequently, based on what we have learned, we propose a new architectural design as an attempt to support both OLTP and OLAP queries on Cloud platforms. I shall describe some of our ongoing work in this talk.

R. Meersman et al. (Eds.): OTM 2010 Workshops, LNCS 6428, p. 1, 2010.
© Springer-Verlag Berlin Heidelberg 2010

OTM'10 Keynote

Michael Brodie

Chief Scientist, Verizon, USA

Short Bio

Dr Michael Brodie is Chief Scientist of Verizon Services Operations in Verizon Communications, one of the world's leading providers of communications services. Dr Brodie works on large-scale strategic Information Technology opportunities and challenges to deliver business value from advanced and emerging technologies and practices. He is concerned with the Big Picture, core technologies and integration within a large scale, operational telecommunications environment.

Dr Brodie holds a PhD in Databases from the University of Toronto and has active interests in the Semantic Web, SOA, and other advanced technologies to address secure, interoperable web-scale information systems, databases, infrastructure and application architectures. Dr Brodie has authored over 150 books, chapters and articles and has presented over 100 keynotes or invited lectures in over 30 countries.

Dr Brodie is a member of the USA National Academies Committee on Technical and Privacy Dimensions of Information for Terrorism Prevention and other National Goals. He is an Adjunct Professor, National University of Ireland, Galway (2006-present) and Visiting Professor, Curtin University of Technology, Perth, Australia (2009). He chairs three Advisory Boards Semantic Technology Institutes International, Vienna, Austria (January 2007 present); Digital Enterprise Research Institute, National University of Ireland (2003-present); Semantic Technology Institute, Innsbrck, Austria (2003-present); and is a member of several advisory boards - The European Research Consortium for Informatics and Mathematics (2007 present); School of Computer and Communication Sciences, cole Polytechnique Fdrale de Lausanne, Switzerland (2001 present); European Unions Information Society Technologies 5th, 6th and 7th Framework Programmes (2003-present); several European and Asian research projects; editorial board of several research journals; past Board member of research foundations including the VLDB Endowment (Very Large Data Bases, 1992 - 2004), and of the Advisory Board of Forrester Research, Inc. (2006-2008). He is on the Advisory Board of Chamberlain Studios (2006-present).

Talk

"Over The Moon: Data Integration's Essential Challenges"

R. Meersman et al. (Eds.): OTM 2010 Workshops, LNCS 6428, pp. 2–3, 2010.

To understand and communicate reality, man simplifies his perception of reality by creating models that are necessarily simpler than reality. For an Information System and its supporting databases to fulfill their requirements, the databases are modeled by radical simplification of reality by identifying those aspects of reality that are essential to the intended perception, i.e., those that are relevant to the requirements, and eliminating all other aspects; and representing the essential properties of those aspects in terms that meet the requirements within the perceptual and modelling limits of the human modeler.

Data modelling involves human designers using a database design methodology together with data modelling tools, e.g., Entity-Relational (ER) and Relational, based on data models, e.g., ER and Relational, and implemented using a relational DBMS. To be more precise, data modelling is an integral component with Information Systems design and development that involves additional methodologies, models, e.g., workflow, and implementation information, e.g., workflow engines, application servers, and web servers. The design, development, and operation of an Information Systems and its databases in dependent on all of the methodologies, models, and tools. For simplicity, we limit this discussion to the design, development, and operation of databases; even though the requirements, loosely referred as the semantics, of the intended perception can be represented anywhere in the Information System - in the databases, the processes, or the application code.

Just as two or more human perceptions of the same or overlapping aspects of reality are unlikely to be identical, so are two or more databases representing overlapping aspects of reality unlikely to be identical. Different databases are designed and developed at different times, to meet different requirements, by different people with different understandings of reality, using different tools, and different methodologies. Hence, two or more different perceptions or databases are typically distinct and are relatively incomplete, inconsistent, and potentially conflicting.

Over time, business, legal, and other requirements have led to the need to represent the real world more precisely in Information Systems. Large-scale integration beyond the scale of most applications necessarily brings in real requirements that prevent the application of simplifying assumptions normally used to solve theses problems (as lower scale). It is likely that as modelling requirements become increasingly complex and as scale of integration grows, this complexity will arise for future Information Ecosystems and the conventional techniques will no longer work.

EI2N'10 - Keynote

Michael Sobolewski

Polish-Japanese Institute of Information Technology, Warsaw, Poland

Short Bio

Michael Sobolewski received his Ph.D. from the Institute of Computer Science, Polish Academy of Sciences. He is the Principal Investigator of the SORCER Lab (SORCERsoft.org) focused on research in distributed service-centric metacomputing. Currently he is a World Class Collaborator at the Air Force Research Lab (AFRL), WPAFB/USA and a Visiting Professor at the Polish Japanese Institute of IT, Warsaw, Poland. Before, he was a Professor of Computer Science, Texas Tech University and Director of SORCER Lab from 2002 till 2009. Now he is engaged in development of Algorithms for Federated High Fidelity Engineering Design Optimization applying his innovative SORCER solutions at AFRL.

While at the GE Global Research Center (GRC), 1994-2002, he was a senior computer scientist and the chief architect of large-scale projects funded by the United States Federal Government including the Federated Intelligent Product EnviRonment (FIPER) project and Computer Aided Manufacturing Network (CAMnet). Also, based on his web-based generic application framework he developed seventeen successful distributed systems for various GE business components. Before his work at GE GRC he was a Research Associate at the Concurrent Engineering Center (CERC) and and Visiting Professor at Computer Science Department, West Virginia University (1998-1994). At CERC/WVU he was a project leader for knowledge-based integration for the DARPA Initiative in Concurrent Engineering (DICE).

Prior to coming to the USA, during 18-year career with the Polish Academy of Sciences, Warsaw, Poland, he was the Head of the Pattern Recognition and Image Processing Department, the Head of the Expert Systems Laboratory, and was engaged in research in the area of knowledge representation, knowledge-based systems, pattern recognition, image processing, neural networks, object-oriented programming, and graphical interfaces. He has served as a visiting professor, lecturer, or consultant in Sweden, Finland, Italy, Switzerland, Germany, Hungary, Slovakia, Poland, Russia, and USA.

Talk

From the very beginning of networked computing, the desire has existed to develop protocols and methods that facilitate the ability of people and automatic processes across different computers to share resources and information across

R. Meersman et al. (Eds.): OTM 2010 Workshops, LNCS 6428, pp. 4–5, 2010.

different computing nodes in an optimized way. As ARPANET began through the involvement of the NSF to evolve into the Internet for general use, the steady stream of ideas became a flood of techniques to submit, control, and schedule jobs across enterprise systems. The latest in these ideas are the grid and cloud, intended to be used by a wide variety of different users in a non-hierarchical manner to provide access to powerful aggregates of distributed resources. Grids and clouds, in the ideal, are intended to be accessed for enterprise computation, data storage and distribution, and visualization and display, among other applications without undue regard for the specific nature of the hardware and underlying operating systems on the resources on which these jobs are carried out. In general, grid and cloud computing is client-server computing that abstract the details of the server awayone requests a service (resource), not a specific server (machine). However, both terms are vague from the point of view of computing architectures and computing models and referring to "everything that we already do".

The reality at present, however, is that service-centric grids are still very difficult for most users to access, and that detailed and low-level programming must be carried out by the user through command line and script execution to carefully tailor jobs on each end to the resources on which they will run, or for the data structure that they will access. This produces frustration on the part of the user, delays in the adoption of enterprise techniques, and a multiplicity of specialized enterprise-aware tools that are not, in fact, aware of each other which defeats the basic purpose of the grid or cloud. Most enterprise programs are still not written in metaprogramming languages but line by line in conventional compiled languages or scripting languages as decades ago. The current state of the art is that these conventional programs and scripts can provide instructions of a metaprogramming language with a relevant operating system handling the service grid as its metaprocessor. However, there are presently no acceptable metaprogramming methodologies to program, deploy, and dynamically federate these services for a metaprogram securely and efficiently with fault detection and recovery. In this presentation the emerging protocol neutral SORCER using service-object oriented architecture with its exertion-oriented networking and its exertion-programming model is contrasted with the service protocol-oriented architecture (e.g. OGSA, CORBA, RMI) that limits us to one fixed wire protocol.

First-Step toward Energy-Aware Adaptive Business Processes

Cinzia Cappiello, Maria Grazia Fugini, G.R. Gangadharan,
Alexandre Mello Ferreira, Barbara Pernici, and Pierluigi Plebani

Politecnico di Milano - Piazza L. da Vinci, 32 - Milan, Italy
{last_name}@elet.polimi.it

Abstract. Energy saving has been mainly focused on techniques to extend the products longevity or to virtualize physical resources. On the contrary, less attention has been paid on the applications that run on the machines and that also contribute to the energy consumption. In this paper we introduce an approach for defining *energy-aware adaptive business process* co-design.

In our previous work [1], we have proposed a novel energy-aware resource allocation mechanisms and policies for business process-based applications. These mechanisms were intended to minimize the energy consumption of the process, infrastructure, and control layer of a data center. Also, we have presented a new energy efficiency metric for a single service, which maps directly the relationship between energy consumption and execution time [2]. The goal here is to propose an approach for defining *energy-aware adaptive business process* (E-BP) co-design. E-BPs are characterized in terms of properties, defined at design-time, that are related to the energy consumption of resources like processor and storage. Through an annotation of resource usage, the BP can run in different modes, in particular in an energy efficient way. Namely, we enable the analysis of the resource usage by the BP given the same functionalities and keeping being in the range of accepted response times, the BP can be more energy efficient.

As shown in Figure 1, our system architecture is composed of three different layers. The *infrastructure layer* includes all the physical energy-hungry equipments installed in the IT service center, either they are running our considered application or not. *Middleware layer* is responsible to manage virtual resource reservation, workload distribution, and resource monitoring. Finally, the *application layer* includes the BPs that embraces software services. The model also includes an *Energy-aware allocation controller*. This module, driven by a set of ECA (Event Condition Action) rules defined by the designer, is in charge of modifying the allocation of the resources during the execution of the BP through an energy-aware process co-design. As a consequence, the objective of the designer is to find the best solution able to manage the clash between consumption and performance. Our approach aims at validating the choices made at design time and at proposing suitable methods to react in case any adjustment is required.

According to the power consumed by each device and the resources assigned to the components at the different layers, we can obtain the real energy consumption

R. Meersman et al. (Eds.): OTM 2010 Workshops, LNCS 6428, pp. 6–7, 2010.

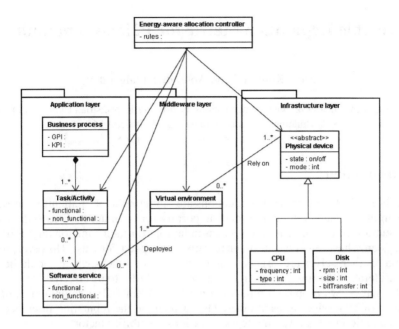

Fig. 1. System architecture

E_{BP}. Since several instances of the same process might be executed and each of them might consume energy differently, E_{BP} depends on the average power consumption over the average process instance duration. *Energy leakage* allows measuring the amount of resources which are not used towards the achievement of the BP goals. In fact, it is defined as the difference between the actual energy consumption E_{BP} related to the process execution and the estimated one $\overline{E}_{BP}$. When leakage is detected, adaptation strategies may combine less quality, less functionality and resource reallocation. In addition, the strategies may be applied at design-time (application layer), run-time (middleware layer) or both, being mainly based on the collected log information by the middleware layer.

Acknowledgment. Part of this work has been funded by the European Commission within the Green Active Management of Energy in IT Service centers (GAMES) FP7 project.

References

1. Ardagna, D., Cappiello, C., Lovera, M., Pernici, B., Tanelli, M.: Active energy-aware management of business-process based applications. In: Proceedings of the ServiceWave (2008)
2. Ferreira, A.M., Kritikos, K., Pernici, B.: Energy-aware design of service-based applications. In: Baresi, L., Chi, C.H., Suzuki, J. (eds.) ICSOC-ServiceWave 2009. LNCS, vol. 5900, pp. 99–114. Springer, Heidelberg (2009)

Credible Reputation Metric for P2P e-Communities

Eleni Koutrouli and Aphrodite Tsalgatidou

Department of Informatics & Telecommunications, National & Kapodistrian University of Athens,
T.Y.P.A. Buildings, Panepistimiopolis 157 71 Ilisia, Athens, Greece
{ekou,atsalga}@di.uoa.gr

1 Introduction

Peer-to-Peer (P2P) systems and applications are attracting a lot of attention nowadays, as they mimic human communities and support useful community. Due to their social and decentralized nature, trust plays an essential role for their functionality. P2P reputation systems have emerged in order to satisfy this need for trust. However, reputation systems themselves are targets of multiple kinds of attacks which should be taken into consideration during the design of the former in order to be effective.

In this paper[1] we propose a reputation mechanism for P2P e-communities of entities which offer services to each other. The focus is on the reputation inference algorithm (reputation metric) which integrates various credibility factors.

2 P2P Reputation Systems Credibility Requirements

A P2P reputation system comprises entities that play interchangeably the roles of *trustor, trustee* and *recommender*. The *trustor* is an entity which wants to make a *trust decision* regarding whether to participate or not in a *transaction* with another entity, the *trustee*. The *recommender* is the entity that provides the trustor with a *recommendation*, that is information regarding the trustworthiness of the trustee. To make a trust decision the trustor tries to predict the future behaviour of the trustee by estimating the trustee's *reputation* based on to its own earlier experience with the trustee and / or by acquiring *recommendations* from other entities. A recommendation is either a *rating* for a single transaction, or an *opinion* formed by the outcome of several transactions.

Entities participating in reputation systems can distort the credibility of the latter in various ways, such as by giving **unfair recommendations** either deliberately (*bad mouthing*) [1] or not and by **changing their behaviour strategically** (*oscillating behaviour*) [2]. In order to mitigate these attacks we considered the following requirements, which have been pointed out in [3]: 1. The *formation of opinion-based recommendations* should take into consideration the number of the aggregated recommendations and their recency. The *confidence* that the recommender has for its recommendation should also be estimated and provided to the trustor. 2. *Credibility of recommender* should be tracked. 3.The algorithm used for *reputation calculation* should take into account both direct and indirect transactional information, as well as the recency of recommendations and the confidence that can be placed on recommendations and on direct experience.

---

[1] This work has been partially funded by the European Commission under contracts FP7-249120 and FP6-4559 for projects ENVISION and SODIUM.

R. Meersman et al. (Eds.): OTM 2010 Workshops, LNCS 6428, pp. 8–9, 2010.

3 Reputation Inference Formulae[2] and Simulation Results

$$DirectRep_{A,B} = \frac{1}{\sum e^{-Dt}} \sum_{i=1}^{n} e^{-Dt} TransEval_{t_i,B}$$

$$IndirectRep_{A,B} = \sum_{\rho=1}^{k} \frac{RecRep_{\rho}*(RecommendationValue_{\rho,B} * Conf_{\rho,B})}{k}$$

$$OverallRep_{A,B} = \alpha * Conf_{A,B} * DirectRep_{A,B} + (1-\alpha) * IndirectRep_{A,B}$$

$$Conf_{A,B} = NT * (1 - Dev_{A,B}) * e^{-Dt}$$

$$NT = \begin{cases} 1, & if\ n \geq N \\ \frac{n}{N}, & otherwise \end{cases}$$

$$Dev_{A,B} = \sum_{i=1}^{n} \frac{|TransEval_{t_i,B} - DirectRep_{A,B}|}{n}$$

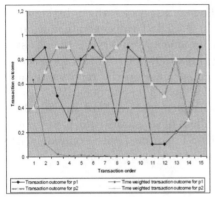

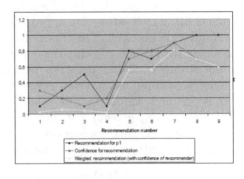

Fig. 1. Time Weighting of Transaction Outcome Values for p1 and p2

Fig. 2. Weighting Recom. Values with Confidence of Recommender.

4 Conclusions

We propose a reputation metric which integrates various sources of information by assigning weights that express their importance. By incorporating confidence and the time decay function, we aim at dealing with *strategic changes of transactional behaviour*. Keeping track of recommendation reputation helps against *bad mouthing* attacks. Our reputation metric is dynamic because of the time considerations on one hand and the possibility to use different weights for direct and indirect reputation.

References

[1] Dellarocas, C.: Immunizing Online Reputation Reporting Systems Against Unfair Ratings and Discriminatory Behaviour. In: Proc. of 2nd ACM Conference on Electronic Commerce (2000)

[2] Duma, C., Shahmehri, N., Caronni, G.: Dynamic Trust Metrics for Peer-to-Peer Systems. In: Proc. of 2nd Intl. Workshop on P2P Data Management, Security and Trust, pp. 776–781 (2005)

[3] Ruohomaa, S., Kutvonen, L., Koutrouli, E.: Reputation Management Survey. In: Proc. of 2nd Intl. Conference on Availability, Reliability and Security (ARES 2007), pp. 103–111 (2007)

---

[2] All values are in the range [0,1] Confidence is estimated based on the number of evaluated transactions (*NT* factor) and the volatility of the evaluated values (*Dev* factor).

A Tool for QoS Probability Distribution Estimation of Web Service Compositions

Huiyuan Zheng, Jian Yang, and Weiliang Zhao

Department of Computing, Macquarie University, NSW 2109, Australia
{huiyuan.zheng,jian.yang,weiliang.zhao}@mq.edu.au

1 Introduction

In this paper, we develop a QoS DIstribution Estimation Tool: QoSDIST for service compositions. QoSDIST has the following functions which distinguish it from existing QoS estimation approaches: (1) QoSDIST can generate much more accurate QoS probability distributions for component Web services than existing methods [1]; (2) When estimating the QoS probability distribution for a service composition, QoSDIST does not put any constraints on the representation of the QoSs of component Web services, i.e., the QoS of a component Web service can be in single value, discrete values with frequencies, standard statistical distribution, or any general distribution regardless of its shape, which can not be done by any existing approaches; (3) QoSDIST can deal with commonly used composition patterns, including loop with arbitrary exit points.

2 Proposed Method

2.1 QoS Probability Distribution Generation for Web Services

We adopt Gaussian Kernel Density estimation approach to generate QoS probability distributions for Web services. Compared with existing methods' fitting a QoS sample with a well known QoS probability distribution, the method used in this paper does not rely on assumptions that the data are drawn from a given probability distribution. This property makes this method more robust than existing Web services' QoS generation methods.

2.2 QoS Probability Distribution Estimation for Service Compositions

We design a calculation approach which can compute QoS for service compositions. We assume that the QoS of Web services are independent of each other. The QoS metric for a component Web service can be represented by a constant value or a probability distribution, which can either be a well known statistical probability distribution or a general probability distribution.

3 Evaluation

3.1 QoS Distribution Generation Result for Web Services

In Figure 1, solid lines represent the QoS distributions generated by QoSDIST. It can be seen that QoS distributions obtained by QoSDIST are able to represent

R. Meersman et al. (Eds.): OTM 2010 Workshops, LNCS 6428, pp. 10–11, 2010.

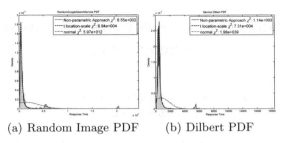

(a) Random Image PDF   (b) Dilbert PDF

Fig. 1. QoS Probability Distributions for Web Services

the real QoS distributions for Web services while standard statistical distributions (t location-scale and normal distributions) do not have this ability.

3.2   QoS Distribution Estimation Result for Service Compositions

It can be seen from Figure 2 that the calculated QoS distributions by QoSDIST fit the simulation results quite well for all the four composition patterns. This result indicates that QoSDIST is able to calculate the precise QoS distributions for a service composition even though the QoSs of its component Web services are represented by nonstandard QoS distributions.

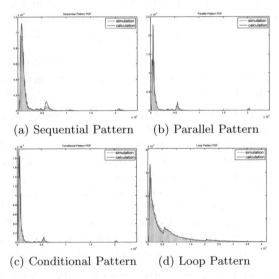

(a) Sequential Pattern   (b) Parallel Pattern

(c) Conditional Pattern   (d) Loop Pattern

Fig. 2. QoS Probability Distributions for Composition Patterns

Reference

1. Rosario, S., Benveniste, A., Haar, S., Jard, C.: Probabilistic qos and soft contracts for transaction-based web services orchestrations. IEEE Transactions on Services Computing 1(4), 187–200 (2008)

Methodologies of Support to the Execution of Risk Management

Luís Nascimento[1,2], André Vasconcelos[1,2], Pedro Sousa[2], José Alegria[3], and Alberto Mendes[3]

[1] Center for Organizational Design and Engineering, INESC Inovação. Rua Alves Redol 9, 1000-029 Lisboa, Portugal
[2] Instituto Superior Técnico, Universidade Técnica de Lisboa. Av. Rovisco Pais 1, 1049-001 Lisboa, Portugal
[3] Portugal Telecom, Av. Álvaro Pais 2, 1649-041 Lisboa, Portugal
{luis.batista,andre.vasconcelos}@ist.utl.pt,
pedro.sousa@link.pt, {jose-alegria,alberto-m-mendes}@telecom.pt

1 Introduction

There are several guidelines to the risk management. During the last quarter of 2009 was even published the ISO 31000, which proposes itself to be the real standard (unanimously recognized as such) to the risk management. However any of these guidelines supports the execution of itself. So, its full execution becomes frequently impossible with the actual organizational reality, many times characterized by significant architectural heterogeneities, cultural differences, and enormous disparities from a business process point of view.

We choose as test-bed, because of its generality, the ISO 31000 [1], and directly related with two activities of its risk management process arise the two execution challenges detailed and justified below:

- The common lack of holistic organizational representations does not allow the construction and maintenance of full organizational knowledge [2]. Therefore, the challenge, at this level, materializes itself in the following: *how to infer and establish the target context, in order to properly support the sequent activities of the process, if there isn't a full knowledge of this context?*
- Generally, organizations are also not prepared to be observed and controlled, and as such, when we try to collect status information, this constitutes a huge effort, since this information either does not exist, or if it exists it is intractable, due to both, its quantity, or its presentation [3]. Therefore, there is one more execution challenge: *how to identify, analyze, and evaluate efficiently risk events with thois panorama?*

These two execution challenges are clearly related with the execution of the activities Establishing the Context and Risk Assessment, respectively. The other activities of the process depend firstly of the full execution of these two. So, *the aim of this work is to propose an execution methodology that helps to overcome these challenges.*

2 Solution Proposal

To address the first execution challenge, what we propose is the development of the adequate cartography work using architectural meta-models that can support the

R. Meersman et al. (Eds.): OTM 2010 Workshops, LNCS 6428, pp. 12–13, 2010.
© Springer-Verlag Berlin Heidelberg 2010

representation of full enterprise architectures. These are the ones that are better formatted to represent the internal and external relations of the organizational ecosystems. The meta-models of the CEOF [4] and of the ArchiMate [5] are two good examples. To the second execution challenge, given the typical large sets of data to treat and the multidimensional nature that characterizes each data item, we propose the application of multidimensional techniques of analysis. We suggest the ROLAP server Mondrian[1] to deal with the two typical variables of risk, the probability and impact [6], in an approach risk event by risk event.

These two proposals are oriented to the resolution of the each one of the challenges identified, and integrated, constitutes the methodology that is the goal of this investigation. Its functional dynamic is based on the complementarity of the proposals. The cartography work developed has two main goals: the first is support the construction of a knowledge base about the context, the other is to provide the dimensions that contemplate the architectural items of the cubes developed in the multidimensional analysis methods.

3   Conclusion

The goal of the investigation was met! We proved that the methodology has potential to support the execution of risk management in the activities Establishing the Context and Risk Assessment. The application of the methodology in a real context, submitting it to the treatment of the technological risk, namely to the unavailability event, not only let us to prove its potential in this case, but also let us note its generality. If the methodology will be provided with data relative to other events, or to other types of organizational risks, it will operate normally. Furthermore, the data manipulated and produced by the organizations in the generality of its activities has a lot of attributes (time reference, geographic reference, accountability reference, among others) which is one of the primordial conditions to the application of the multidimensional analysis methods.

References

1. ISO 31000:2009 - Risk management – Principles and guidelines
2. Tribolet, J.: Organizations, People, Processes and Knowledge: from the reification of the human being as a component of knowledge to the knowledge of organizational self. Sistemas de Informação Organizacionais. Sílabo Editora (November 2005)
3. Jauk, G.: Intrusion Detection with Mondrian and Snort. VDM Verlag Dr. Müller Aktiengesellschaft & Co. KG (2009) ISBN 978-3-639-14052-1
4. Vasconcelos, A., Sousa, P., Tribolet, J.: Enterprise Architecture Analysis - An Information System Evaluation Approach. Enterprise Modelling and Information Systems Architectures 3(2) (December 2008) ISSN 1860-6059
5. Lankhorst, A.: Enterprise Architecture at Work: Modelling Communication and Analysis. Springer, Heidelberg (December 2005) ISBN-10 3-540-24371-2
6. Degraeve, Z., Nicholson, N.: Risk: How to make decisions in an uncertain world. Format Publishing (2004) ISBN-10 1903091365

---

[1] http://mondrian.pentaho.org/

Financier-Led Asset Lease Model

Xiaohui Zhao, Samuil Angelov, and Paul Grefen

Information Systems Group
Department of Industrial Engineering & Innovation Sciences
Eindhoven University of Technology
5600MB, Eindhoven, The Netherlands
{x.zhao,s.angelov,p.w.p.j.grefen}@tue.nl

Nowadays, the business globalisation trend drives organisations to spread their business worldwide, which in turn generates vast asset demands. In this context, broader asset channels and higher financial capacities are required to boost the asset lease sector to meet the increasing asset demands [1, 2]. In this background, with the reliable financial sources and extensive information channels, financiers are expected to take the pivot role in integrating world-wide asset information with the help of advanced cooperative information systems [3, 4]. As reported by Leasing World [5], the mass market possesses vast asset lease demands that are unexplored by current lease industry. Different from conventional lease customers, the customers of the mass market prefer to lease assets with a limited volume for a short period. Furthermore, these requests substantially vary in terms of geographic locations, desired asset packages, bundled services, financial assistances, etc. Unfortunately, these customer requests do not match with the business of traditional asset lease industry. To cater for the asset demands of the mass market, this section presents a financier-led asset lease model and the operations of the employed virtual asset network. In this model, the financier acts as the proxy for customers to access the various assets and services of the virtual asset network. By integrating the asset information and asset related services of these companies, a virtual asset network can be established as a pool of various assets and related services. Through an open-access 'portal', customers can choose and design their service requests from a wide range of asset types, pick-up locations, usage periods, asset modifications, payment plans, etc. The financier is responsible for analysing and aggregating these requests, as well as seeking optimal service outsourcing solutions. Thus, this model offers customers the access to worldwide distributed assets with flexible customisation options. Different from traditional finance lease models, customers bypass the contact with asset vendors yet receive the integrated services from the financier.

The virtual asset network creates a highly dynamic business environment, where different companies can join or quit the network from time to time, and the provided services and assets are also changing frequently. Such dynamics call for substantial supports for information and business integration supports, such as electronic contracting, cross-organisational monitoring, dynamic service publishing and integration, etc. As the asset information proxy and service integrator, the financier fully depends on the assets and services of the virtual asset network to serve customers' asset lease requests through service outsourcing. Yet, the environmental dynamics make it very difficult for the financier to predefine service outsourcing plans. Thus, the financier

R. Meersman et al. (Eds.): OTM 2010 Workshops, LNCS 6428, pp. 14–15, 2010.
© Springer-Verlag Berlin Heidelberg 2010

has to continuously adjust the service outsourcing schedule to adapt to environmental changes. Besides, such service outsourcing selections are further complicated by diverse asset configurations, service dependencies, etc. Choices of current service outsourcing selection may result in various consequences to future selections, and this makes that each service outsourcing selection a chain of a series of selections. Aiming to tackle this issue, we have analysed the service outsourcing behaviours in this new asset lease model, and proposed an adaptive scheduling mechanism. This mechanism enables the financier's decision making system to learn the environmental dynamics automatically and use this knowledge to arrange and adjust service outsourcing schedules.

This financier-led asset lease model considerably shifts up the asset availability, accessibility and scalability with the help of the virtual asset network. Compared to traditional asset lease models, this financier-led asset lease model benefits the financier, customers, asset vendors and related companies in different aspects.

In this model, the financier gains a dominant position in the asset leasing market. The direct financial support and abundant asset services, provided by the financier, will attract a large number of clients from the mass market. This large client group in turn helps the financier achieve more profits, higher asset utilisation, better finance flow efficiency, more rebates from vendors, etc.

The virtual asset network provides customers with a convenient access to worldwide available assets. In addition, with its strong financial capability, the financier can offer very flexible lease schemes, payment plans, etc., such as pay per use, hourly rental, relay rental, etc. (in addition to conventional long-term lease contracts with purchase option). Further, a customisable payment method (e.g., unified currency for the payment of multiple leases in different countries) is another example for the potential benefits for the global business extension of small companies.

Asset providers and service providers can benefit from the extra customer group attracted by the financier. This will certainly enhance the turnover of asset providers and service providers. In addition, the reliable financial guarantees from the financier consolidate the capital liquidity of asset providers and service providers.

The reported work is conducted in the context of collaboration between the Information Systems Group, Department of Industrial Engineering and Innovation Sciences, Eindhoven University of Technology, and De Lage Landen, a global provider of asset-based financing services.

References

[1] Larsen, G.: Model-driven Development: Assets and Reuse. IBM Systems Journal 45(3), 541–554 (2006)
[2] Ziemba, W.T., Mulvey, J.M.: Worldwide Asset and Liability Modeling. Cambridge University Press, Cambridge (1998)
[3] Khanna, A.: Straight through Processing for Financial Services. Elsevier, Amsterdam (2008)
[4] Luftenegger, E., Angelov, S., van der Linden, E., Grefen, P.: The State of the Art of Innovation-Driven Business Models in the Financial Services Industry, Beta Report, Eindhoven University of Technology (2010)
[5] FLA sees 2009 as Pivotal Year (2009), http://www.leasingworld.co.uk

Continuous MapReduce for In-DB Stream Analytics

Qiming Chen and Meichun Hsu

HP Labs, Palo Alto, California, USA
Hewlett Packard Co.
{qiming.chen,meichun.hsu}@hp.com

Abstract. Scaling-out data-intensive analytics is generally made by means of parallel computation for gaining CPU bandwidth, and incremental computation for balancing workload. Combining these two mechanisms is the key to support large scale stream analytics.

Map-Reduce (M-R) is a programming model for supporting parallel computation over vast amounts of data on large clusters of commodity machines. Through a simple interface with two functions, map and reduce, this model facilitates parallel implementation of data intensive applications. In-DB M-R allows these functions to be embedded within standard queries to exploit the SQL expressive power, and allows them to be executed by the query engine with fast data access and reduced data move. However, when the data form infinite streams, the semantics and scale-out capability of M-R are challenged.

To solve this problem, we propose to integrate M-R with the continuous query model characterized by Cut-Rewind (C-R), i.e. cut a query execution based on some granule of the stream data and then rewind the state of the query without shutting it down, for processing the next chunk of stream data. This approach allows an M-R query with full SQL expressive power to be applied to dynamic stream data chunk by chunk for continuous, window-based stream analytics.

Our experience shows that integrating M-R and C-R can provide a powerful combination for parallelized and granulized stream processing. This combination enables us to scale-out stream analytics "horizontally" based on the M-R model, and "vertically" based on the C-R model.

The proposed approach has been prototyped on a commercial and proprietary parallel database engine. Our preliminary experiments reveal the merit of using query engine for near-real-time parallel and incremental stream analytics.

1 Introduction

To effectively handle the scale of analytical tasks in an era of information explosion, partitioning data and applying computation to data partitions in parallel is the key. The concept of Map-Reduce (M-R) essentially comes from supporting large-scale parallel data-intensive computation [6,9,16].

1.1 The Issues

Due to the massive growth of data volume and the pressing need for low latency, we need to relax the *load-first analyze-later* legacy of data warehousing and focus on

R. Meersman et al. (Eds.): OTM 2010 Workshops, LNCS 6428, pp. 16–34, 2010.
© Springer-Verlag Berlin Heidelberg 2010

stream analytics for delivering BI solutions within actionable time windows. Thus we start with integrating stream processing capability into the query engine, which, however, requires us to deal with infinite incoming data, to apply a SQL query to the data chunk by chunk falling in consecutive time windows, and to trace the execution states and application context continuously for supporting sliding window based, history sensitive operations. Meeting all these requirements is challenging since they are conflict wrt the existing query engine.

The next issue is to scale-out In-DB stream processing through parallel computation. As we know, the parallel database engine can over-perform the disk based platform for M-R computations because the parallel query processing relies on in-memory pipeline to shuffle data from the *map* phase to the *reduce* phase [9]. However, to processing data streams, each M-R node needs to deal with infinite stream data, which constitutes to another kind of scalability problem. From either semantics or performance point of view, to solve this problem requires chunk-based incremental computation. In fact, this is also required by the window semantics of stream processing.

We envisage that integrating M-R like parallel computation and chunk-based incremental computation will provide a powerful combination not only for compromising the above situation but also for scaling out In-DB, continuous analytics on streamed data.

1.2 The Prior Art

Recently In-DB stream processing infrastructure has been increasingly investigated [5,11,15], for its advantage in exploiting the full SQL expressive power and DBMS functionality as compared with the current generation of data stream processing systems built from scratch independently of the database engine [1,2,12].

The parallel database engine has been compared with the disk-based M-R platform, such as Google M-R and Hadoop M-R; the result shows that the former can shuffle the *map* results in memory, rather than storing them back to the disk, thus provide significant performance gain [6,10]. Support In-DB M-R is also in-line with the effort of pushing data-intensive analytics down to the data management layer for fast data access and reduced data transfer [6]. Recently several In-DB M-R platforms have been developed such as Greenplum [13], Aster and HP Neoview [14].

Although M-R is designed for handling vast amount of data through parallel computations over data partitioned to multiple server nodes, the data at each server node are assumed to be bounded. In order to support the BI applications on dynamically collected data streams, the current In-DB M-R must be extended for handling unbounded data. Further, since stream processing is typically window based, we believe extending In-DB M-R for processing the incoming data chunk by chunk, is the right direction. These issues have not been appropriately studied.

The combined benefits of In-DB analytics, M-R and stream processing may not be achieved using the current generation of stream processing systems or so-called iterative M-R systems, since in the first place they are generally not In-DB systems but stand-alone systems built outside of the database engine; next, these systems, even some are SQL based [11,15], adopt workflow like services for launching operations once and once again for chunk-wise data manipulation; all these lead to significant overhead in inter-platform communication and data transfer.

To scale-out In-DB stream analytics in terms of *parallel computation* through M-R, and scale-out M-R in terms of *incremental computation*, the real challenge is how to handle chunk-wise In-DB M-R in terms of continuous queries directly executable by the query engine; however, to the best of our knowledge, this has not been addressed so far.

1.3 The Solution

We introduce a new paradigm for scalable stream analytics which is characterized by the combination of the parallel computation on partitioned data streams and the granule-based incremental computation on each data stream partition. We push stream analytics down to the parallel DBMS for leveraging data management functionality and gaining data access efficiency, and extend the query engine for providing the above parallel and incremental stream processing capability.

- We support In-DB M-R for parallel analytics which exploits the SQL expressive power and leverages the existing parallel database functionality.
- We extend the query engine for "just-in-time" stream processing in terms of continuously analyzing the stream data before they are stored on the disk. We support the granule-based stream processing semantics in terms of the Cut-Rewind (C-R) query model, namely, cut a query execution based on some granule ("chunk") of the stream data (e.g. a tuple or set of tuples cut by a time boundary or other types of boundary) and then rewind the state of the query without shutting it down, for processing the next chunk of stream data. This mechanism well fits in the window based data manipulation nature of stream processing. It allows a query to be executed cycle by cycle for processing the unbounded stream data chunk by chunk, while retaining the application context (e.g. data buffered with UDFs) continuously across the execution cycles for dealing with sliding-window oriented history sensitive operations.
- We integrate M-R and C-R to provide a powerful combination for scaling out In-DB continuous analytics "horizontally" based on the M-R model, and "vertically" based on the C-R model.

The proposed mechanisms have been integrated into HP Neoview - a commercial and proprietary parallel database engine. Our preliminary experiments have revealed the merit of using query engine to enable near-real-time and data intensive parallel stream processing, and proven that the integration of M-R and C-R can bring the platform support to data-intensive stream analytics to a new level.

The rest of this paper is organized as follows: Section 2 outlines our In-DB M-R approach; Section 3 discusses the *cut-and-rewind* approach that underlies the cycle-based continuous query model for in-DB stream analytics; Section 4 illustrates the power of combining M-R and C-R for scaling out stream analytics both "horizontally" and "vertically"; Section 5 concludes the paper.

2 Support Map-Reduce on Parallel Database Engine

The concept of M-R comes from supporting computation on partitioned data in parallel. Originally the M-R infrastructure is built on a cluster of servers hosting a distributed file system; as shown in Fig 1, it takes two computation functions

$$map: (k, v) => (k',v')^*   reduce: (k', v')^* => (k', v'^*)$$

and executes them in parallel, such that each *map* function is applied to a set of key-value tuples (k,v) and transforms it into a set of tuples of a different type (k',v'); then all the values v' are re-partitioned by k' and each *reduce* function aggregates the set of values v' with the same k'.

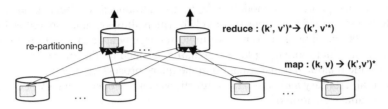

Fig. 1. Map-Reduce computation model

With M-R, the user only needs to provide a *map* function and a *reduce* function while the system interaction and parallel execution are handled by the platform. Such ease of adapting contributes to the taking-off of M-R.

2.1 In-Database Map-Reduce

A parallel database engine, such as HP Neoview, is built on a cluster of interconnected server nodes; each node can hold multiple query processing servers which are either query executors (ESP) or data processor (DP2). A DP2 is responsible for retrieving data from the database, as well as for certain local query processing. The ESPs cooperatively carry out parallel query processing by exchanging and merging partial results. In M-R computation, typically a *map*() is handled by a DP2 and/or an ESP, and a *reduce*() is handled by one or more ESPs. Re-grouping the *map* results to perform *reduce* is made by re-partitioning data. This is shown in Fig 2.

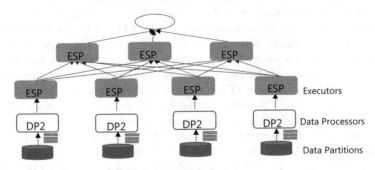

Fig. 2. Parallel database engine

The correspondence between M-R and parallel query processing has been observed [6,10]. The strengths of parallel SQL engines include integrated schema management, declarative query language, rich optimization, and adaptive workload management, which are missing from the file system based M-R platforms. The combination of parallel query processing and M-R computation can benefit both – enriching M-R through schema management and optimization that do not exist in today's M-R engines, expanding the reach of the M-R to sophisticated data management, as well as enriching the capability of parallel database engines for reaching general analytics computation.

In order to support M-R model in SQL, we introduced a special kind of UDFs called Relation Valued Functions (RVFs) [7], which allows a function, either for *map*, *reduce* or other computation, to receive tuple-set arguments and to return a tuple-set, in order to carry out more complex computation defined on the entire input relations, and to provide relational transformation in the query processing pipeline.

In general, arbitrary *map* and *reduce* functions can be coded as an RVF, and the M-R is the parallel execution of

SELECT ... FROM f_{reduce} (f_{map} (...));

where f_{map} returns *map* results, and f_{reduce} takes the results of f_{map}, possibly materialized as a set of accumulators, and provide global aggregation. The *reduce* function may fall in two cases:

- the *reduce* is expressed by standard SQL aggregate functions as seen in the above example, or by system honored User Defined Aggregate (UDA) functions; in this case the *reduce* as *aggregate-groupby* can be handled by the parallel query engine naturally;
- the *reduce* function is user defined but neither a SQL aggregate nor a UDA; in this case it must be registered as a REDUCE function, and the parallel query engine must be extended to support *group-by* on such a function.

2.2   In-DB Map Reduce Example

We shall use an example to show how the M-R computation can be naturally expressed in SQL with UDFs running on a parallel database system. This example is about vehicle exhaust emission analysis, where the sensors are infrared absorption analyzers for measuring the concentration of CO, CO_2, H-C and NO in the vehicle exhaust emissions passing through the sampling cells. The exhaust emission is measured by *ppm* (*parts per million*, convertible to percentage). The readings of these sensors form the input data of our system. We generated the simulation data for an urban area with a large number of vehicles. In this section a snapshot of the readings is taken into account as a bounded data source. In the next section we take into account the continuity of readings as unbounded stream data.

One goal of the exhaust emission analysis is to determine the centroids of the areas with concentrated air pollutions. We treat this problem as a simplified single-iteration clustering problem, i.e. given k initial centroids based on the past experience, geographically re-assign each vehicle with exhaust emission exceeding a given threshold to the closest centroid, and based on such re-grouping to calculate the new location of each exhaust emission centroid as the mean location of its member vehicles. For illustrative purpose we adopt the single-iteration computation of the popular k-means algorithm to approximate the moving of the emission centroids, which can be expressed by the following query.

```
SELECT cid AS new_emmision_centroid, AVG(X) AS cx, AVG(Y) AS cy FROM
    (SELECT v.x AS X, v.y AS Y,
                nearest_centroid (v.x, v.y, 'SELECT cid, cx, cy  FROM Emission_centroids') AS cid
    FROM Vehicle_locations v  WHERE v.CO > CO_threshold AND ...) r
    GROUP BY cid;
```

where the vehicle emission data are stored in table *Vehicle_locations* [*vid*, *x*, *y*, CO, CO_2, H-C, NO ...], the existing centroids data are retrieved from table *Emission_centroids* [*cid*, *cx*, *cy*, ...], the new centroids are returned by the query. Executed on a parallel database, the above query is executed in the M-R style:

- *Map*: finding nearest cluster centroids of every vehicle *vid* and assigning *vid* to that cluster; i.e. from the *x*, *y* location of each tuple in the relation *Vehicle_locations*, compute its distances to all centroids in relation *Emission_centroids*, and assign its membership to the closest one, resulting the tuples with schema [*x*, *y*, *cid*], each representing the nearest centroid, *cid* , of the vehicle at the *x*, *y* location.
- *Reduce*: re-computing the set of new centroids, each as the geometric *mean* of all the vehicle locations assigned to that cluster.

To draw an analogy to SQL query, *map* is analogous to the clause for generating the nearest centroid for each vehicle (row), and *reduce* is analogous to the aggregate function AVG() that is computed over all the rows with the same group-by attribute. On a parallel database, the *Vehicle_locations* table is hash partitioned by *vid* over multiple server nodes, and the *map* function for assigning the nearest centroids is applied to these data partitions in parallel, each yields a local portion of result-set; these result sets are automatically re-partitioned by *cid* for the parallel *reduce* computation in the aggregation / group-by phase. The same relational interface of RVFs and relational operators allows them to be invoked compositionally in a query for integrating the *map* function and the *reduce* function in a single SQL query. The above M-R query is executed tuple by tuple wrt the vehicles, but having all centroids loaded in the RVF *nearest_centroid* () initially only once [6,7].

Fig 3 shows how the parallel plan of this query, where Locations data are hash partitioned, and centroids are replicated to multiple nodes to be processed parallelly by the RVF instances for finding nearest centroids (*map*); new centroids are computed by groupby-aggregate (*reduce*); re-partitioning *map* results are automatically handled by the parallel database engine by means of the standard exchange operator.

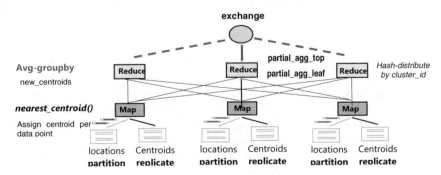

Fig. 3. Map-Reduce on parallel database

2.3 In-Database Map-Reduce Performance

We tested our in-DB M-R approach on a commercial and proprietary parallel data-base engine – HP Neoview. The test environment is set-up on a HP Neoview parallel database cluster with 8 server nodes and 16 disks. Our experiments show its proven scalability in data size and in applications, and superior performance compared with using a conventional non-M-R, ad-hoc query. The comparison result is illustrated in Fig 4.

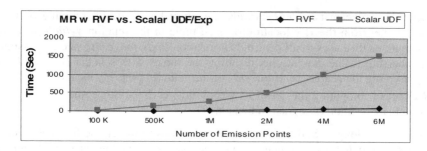

Fig. 4. One iteration clustering performance using Map-Reduce and RVF vs. using regular UDF and SQL expression on parallel database

We also compared In-DB M-R computation and the disk-based Hadoop M-R com-putation. Our experience has proven that the pipeline from *map* to *reduce* is the major bottleneck of many M-R applications running on the disk based M-R platforms; and using parallel query engine can dramatically reduce the overhead for storing the *map* results back to disks (provided these results can be pipelined or fit in the memory). The comparison of running the above query on 1M vehicle locations and 100 cen-troids using In-DB M-R and using Hadoop platform is shown in Fig 5.

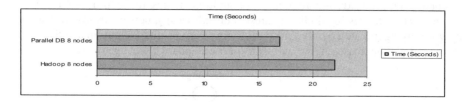

Fig. 5. Parallel in-DB Map-Reduce execution over-performs Hadoop

In general, M-R scales out data intensive applications by data partitioning and par-allel computation; In-DB M-R allows the *map* and *reduce* functions to be embedded within a query to exploit the SQL expressive power, and executed by the query engine with fast data access and reduced data move. However, when the data form infinite streams, the semantics and scale-out capability of M-R is challenged by the lack of chunk-wise incremental computation.

3   A Continuous Query Model for Chunk-Wise Stream Processing

In this section we turn our focus to a special kind of continuous query applying to stream data chunk by chunk, with the motivation of supporting granule-based In-DB M-R for stream processing.

There exist several differences between the conventional query processing and the stream processing. First, a query is defined on bounded relations but stream data are unbounded; next, stream processing adopts window-based semantics, i.e. processing the incoming data chunk by chunk falling in consecutive time windows, but the SQL operators are either based on one tuple (such as filter operators) or the entire relation; further, stream processing is also required to handle sliding window operations continuously across chunk based data processing; and finally, endless stream analytics results must be continuously accessible along their production, under specific transaction semantics.

However, a query engine should be extensible for stream processing since the per-tuple based query processing forms the similar dataflow pipeline seen in stream processing. Based on this potential, we advocate an extended SQL model that unifies queries over both streaming and static relational data, and a new architecture for integrating stream processing and DBMS to support continuous, "just-in-time" analytics with window-based operators and transaction semantics. These requirements have motivated us to introduce the following solutions.

- We start with providing unbounded relation data to feed queries continuously, by using function-scan instead of table-scan, to turn captured events into unbounded sequence of relation tuples without first storing them on disk. We develop UDF shells [6,7] to deliver operators with stream semantics (e.g. moving average, notification) that are not available in conventional SQL.
- We propose the cycle-based query model, and support it in terms of the *cut-and-rewind* mechanism, namely, cutting a query execution based on some granule ("chunk") of the stream data (e.g. in a time window), and then rewinding the state of the query without shutting it down, for processing the next chunk of stream data. This mechanism, on one hand, allows applying a query continuously to the stream data chunks falling in consecutive time windows, within a single, long-standing query; on the other hand, allows retaining the application context (e.g. data buffered with UDFs) continuously across the execution cycles to perform sliding-window oriented, history sensitive operations.
- We further support the cycle-based transaction model with *cycle-based* isolation and visibility.

3.1   Processing Stream Using Continuous Query

We use extended function-scan to fuel queries continuously with unbounded stream data. The first step is to replace the database table, which contains a set of tuples on disk, by the special kind of table function, called Stream Source Function (SSF) that returns a sequence of tuples to feed queries without first storing on disk. A SSF can listen or read data/events sequence and generate stream elements tuple by tuple continuously. A SSF is called multiple, up to infinite, times during the execution of a continuous query, each call returns one tuple. When the end-of-cycle event or condition is seen, the SSF signals the query engine to terminate the current query execution cycle.

We rely on SSF and query engine for continuous querying on the basis that "as far as data do not end, the query does not end", rather than employing an extra scheduler to launch a sequence of one-time query instances. The SSF scan is supported at two levels, the SSF level and the query executor level. A data structure containing function call information, hFC, bridges these two levels. hFC is initiated by the query executor and passed in/out the SSF for exchanging function invocation related information. We use this mechanism for minimizing the code change, but maximize the extensibility, of the query engine.

One important characteristics of stream processing is the use of stream-oriented history-sensitive analytic operators such as moving average or change point detection. This represents a different requirement from the regular query processing that only cares about the current state. While the standard SQL engine contains a number of built-in analytic operators, stream history-sensitive operators are not supported. Using UDFs is the generally accepted mechanism to extend query operators in a DBMS. A UDF can be provided with a data buffer in its function closure, and for caching stream processing state (synopsis). Furthermore, it is also used to support one or more *emitters* for delivering the analytics results to interested clients in the middle of a cycle, which is critical in satisfying stream applications with low latency requirement.

We use UDFs to add window operators and other history sensitive operators, buffering required raw data or intermediate results within the UDF closures. A scalar UDF is called multiple times on the per-tuple basis, following the typical FIRST_CALL, NORMAL_CALL, FINAL_CALL skeleton. The data buffer structures are initiated in the FIRST_CALL and used in each NORMAL_CALL. A window function defined as a scalar UDF incrementally buffers the stream data, and manipulates the buffered data chunk for the required window operation. Although we aim to process stream data chunk by chunk, our continuous query model, to be described later, allows the query instance to remain alive across chunk-wise query evaluation; thus the UDF buffer is retained between query cycles to have the data states traceable continuously (we see otherwise if the stream query is made of multiple one-time instances, the buffered data cannot be traced continuously across cycle boundaries). As a further optimization, the static data retrieved from the database can be loaded in a window operation initially and then retained in the entire long-standing query, which removes much of the data access cost as seen in the multi-query-instances based stream processing.

3.2 Cycle-Based Continuous Query Model

Our proposed continuous model is defined as follows: given a query Q over a set of relations $R_1,..,R_n$ and an infinite stream of relation tuples S with a criterion C for cutting S into an unbounded sequence of chunks, e.g. by every 1-minute time window,

$$<S_{C0}, S_{C1}, ..., S_{Ci}, ...>$$

where S_{Ci} denotes the *i-th* "chunk" of the stream according to the chunking-criterion C. S_{Ci} can be interpreted as a relation. The semantics of applying the query Q to the unbounded stream S plus the bounded relations $R_1,..,R_n$ lies in

$$Q\ (S,\ R_1,..,R_n) \rightarrow\ < Q\ (S_{C0},\ R_1,..,R_n),\ ...\ Q\ (S_{Ci},\ R_1,..,R_n),\ ...\ >$$

which continuously generates an unbounded sequence of query results, one on each *chunk* of the stream data.

Our goal is to support the above semantics using a continuous query that runs cycle by cycle for processing the stream data chunks, each data chunk to be processed in each cycle, in a single, long-standing query instance. In this sense we also refer to the *data chunking criterion* C as the *query cycle specification*. The cycle specification can be based on time or a number of tuples, which can amount to as small as a single tuple, and as large as billions of tuples per cycle. The stream query may be terminated based on specification in the query (e.g. run for 300 cycles), user intervention, or a special end-of-stream signal received from the stream source.

A significant advantage of the unified model lies in that it allows us to exploit the full SQL expressive power on each data chunk. The output is also a stream consisting of a sequence of chunks, with each chunk representing the query result of one execution cycle. While there may be different ways to implement our proposed unified model, our approach is to generalize the SQL engine to include support for stream sources. The approach enables queries over both static and streaming data, retains the full SQL power, while executing stream queries efficiently.

3.3 Cut-and-Rewind (C-R)

To support the cycle based execution of stream queries, we propose the *cut-and-rewind* query execution model, namely, cut a query execution based on the cycle specification (e.g. by time), and then rewind the state of the query without shutting it down, for processing the next chunk of stream data in the next cycle.

Under this *cut-and-rewind* mechanism, a stream query execution is divided into a sequence of *cycles*, each for processing a chunk of data only; it, on one hand, allows applying a SQL query to unbounded stream data chunk by chunk within a single, long-standing query instance; on the other hand, allows the application context (e.g. data buffered within a User Defined Function (UDF)) to be retained continuously across the execution cycles, which is required for supporting sliding-window oriented, history sensitive operations. Bringing these two capabilities together is the key in our approach.

Cut. *Cutting* stream data into chunks is originated in the SSF at the bottom of the query tree. Upon detection of end-of-cycle condition, the SSF signals *end-of-data* to the query engine through setting a flag on the function call handle, that, after being interpreted by the query engine, results in the termination of the current query execution cycle.

If the cut condition is detected by testing the newly received stream element, the *end-of-data* event of the current cycle would be captured upon receipt of the first tuple of the next cycle; in this case, that tuple will not be returned by the SSF in the current cycle, but buffered within the SSF and returned as the first tuple of the next cycle. Since the query instance is kept alive, that tuple can be kept across the cycle boundary.

Rewind. Upon termination of an execution cycle, the query engine does not shut down the query instance but *rewinds* it for processing the next chunk of stream data.

Rewinding a query is a top-down process along the query plan instance tree, with specific treatment on each node type. In general, the intermediate results of the standard SQL operators (associated with the current chunk of data) are discarded but the application context kept in UDFs (e.g. for handling sliding windows) are retained. The query will not be re-parsed, re-planned or re-initiated.

Note that rewinding the query plan instance aims to process the next chunk of data, rather than re-deliver the current query result; therefore it is different from "rewinding a query cursor" for re-delivering the current result set from the beginning. For example, the conventional cursor rewind tends to keep the hash-tables for a hash-join operation but our rewind will have such hash-tables discarded since they were built for the previous, rather than the next, data chunk.

As mentioned above, the proposed *cut-and-rewind* approach has the ability to keep the continuity of the query instance over the entire stream while dividing it to a sequence of execution cycles. This is significant in supporting history sensitive stream analytic operations, as discussed in the previous section.

3.4   Query Cycle Based Transaction Model

One problem of the current generation of DSMSs is that they do not support transactions. Intuitively, as stream data are unbounded and the query for processing these data may never end, the conventional notion of transaction boundary is hard to apply. In fact, transaction notions have not been appropriately defined for stream processing, and the existing DSMSs typically make application specific, informal guarantees of correctness.

However, to allow a hybrid system where stream queries can refer to static data stored in a database, or to allow the stream analysis results (whether intermediate or final) to persist and be visible to other concurrent queries in the system in a timely manner, a transaction model which allows the stream processing to periodically "commit" its results and makes them visible is needed.

Commit Stream analytics Cycle by Cycle. Conventionally a query is placed in a transaction boundary. In general, the query result and the possible update effect are made visible only after the commitment of the transaction (although weaker transaction semantics do exist). In order to allow the result of a long-running stream query to be incrementally accessible, we introduce the cycle-based transaction model incorporated with the *cut-and-rewind* query model, under which a stream query is committed one cycle at a time in a sequence of "micro-transactions". The transaction boundaries are consistent with the query cycles, thus synchronized with the chunk-wise stream processing. The per-cycle stream processing results are made visible as soon as the cycle ends. The isolation level is Cycle based Read Committed (CRC). To allow the cycle results to be continuously visible to external world, regardless of the table is under the subsequent cycle-based transactions, we enforce record level locking.

We extended both SELECT INTO and INSERT INTO facilities to support cycle-based transaction semantics. We also added an option to force the data to stay in memory, and an automatic space reclaiming utility should the data be written to the disk.

Continuous Persisting. In a regular database system, the queries with SPJ (Select, Project, Join) operations and those with the update (Insert, Delete, Update) operations are different in the flow of resulting data. In a SPJ query, the destination of results is a query receiver connected to the client. In a data update query, such as insert, the results are emitted to, or synched to, the database.

In stream processing, such separation would be impractical. The analytic results must be streaming to the client continuously as well as being stored in the database if needed for other applications to access. Therefore, we extended the query engine to have query evaluation and results persisting integrated and expressed in a single query. This two-receiver approach makes it possible to have the results both persisted and streamed out externally.

Certain intermediate stream processing results can be deposited into the database from UDFs. To do so the UDF must be relaxed from the read-only mode, and employ the database internal query facility to form, parse, plan and execute queries efficiently.

3.5 An Example of Using Cycle-Query for Continuous Stream Analytics

We extend the simulated vehicle exhaust emissions monitoring example by taking into account the continuous readings rather than a snapshot of readings.

We assume that each car is equipped by a GPS for positioning its x, y location and the urban district it is in, as well as an infrared absorption analyzer for measuring the concentration of CO, CO_2, H-C and NO in its exhaust emission; the position and emission of each car is read every 30 seconds (0.5 minute) and each reading constitutes an event with attributes *vid, time* (in seconds), *x*, *y*, and the emission rate of CO, CO_2, H-C and NO in *ppm*.

The events are read, and the streaming tuples with timestamps are generated by the stream source function, *SSF_exhausts(time-window, cycles)*, where "*time-window*" is specified by minutes; "*cycles*" is the number of cycles the query is supposed to run. For example, *SSF_exhausts(1, 180)* delivers the tuples falling in every minute (60 seconds) to be processed in one execution cycle, for 180 cycles (3 hours). Setting parameter "*cycles*" to 0 allows the query to run infinite cycles.

We measure the average emissions in every minute and report, in every minute and in each district, the moving average in the past 10 minutes, in terms of the following cycle-based continued query.

```
SELECT p.minute, p.district,
    exhaust_moving_avg(p.district, p.minute, p.avg_emmision) AS past_10m_avg_emission
FROM (
    SELECT s.minute AS minute, s.district AS district, AVG(s.emission) AS avg_emission
    FROM (
        SELECT FLOOR(time/60)::integer AS minute, district,
                comp_exhaust(CO_ppm, CO2_ppm, HC_ppm, NO_ppm,
                        'SELECT * FROM comp_rules')  AS emission
        FROM SSF_exhausts (1, 0)) s
    GROUP BY minute, district ) p;
```

This query repeatedly applies to the data chunks falling in 1-minute time-windows, and rewinds the specified, up to infinite, times. We assume that the composite exhaust is calculated by the RVF *comp_exhaust* based on the dynamic readings and the static relation "comp_rules". As shown in Fig. 6, from the global querying perspective,

- the sub-query with alias *s* calculates the emissions from the readings;
- the sub-query with alias *p* yields the average emissions for every minute and in every district; overall, the SQL aggregate function is computed chunk by chunk with no context carried over from one chunk to the next;
- the dimensioned moving average in the past 10 minutes is calculated by the UDF *exhaust_moving_avg()*; this function buffers the past per-minute average for accumulating the 10-minute moving average; since the query is only rewound but not shut down, the buffer sustains continuously across query cycles - exactly the advantage of cut/rewind over shutdown/restart.

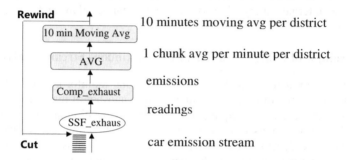

Fig. 6. Air pollution assessment from car emission readings with chunk-wise stream processing

We chose to test the cut-and-rewind approach conceptually on a single database node on HP xw8600 with 2 x Intel Xeon E54102 2.33 Ghz CPUs and 4 GB RAM, running the PostgreSQL also extended with the proposed capability, for proof-of-concept. The test data are supplied in the following two modes: the stress test mode where the data are read by the SSF from a file continuously without following the real-time intervals (continuous input); and the real-time mode where the data are received from a data driver outside of the query engine with real-time intervals.

In cycle-based stream processing, the remaining time of query evaluation after the input data chunk is cut, called Post Cut Elapsed Time (PCET), is particularly important since it directly affects the delta time for the results to be accessible after the last tuple of the data chunk in the cycle has been received.

Fig 7 shows the query time, as well as the PCET, for processing each 1-minute data chunk. It can be seen that the PCET (the blue line) is well controlled around 0.2 second, meaning that the maximal response time for the segment toll results, as measured from the time a cycle (a minute) ends, is around 0.2 second.

With real-time input, the events (car position reports) are delivered by a data driver in real-time with additional system-assigned timestamps. The query runs cycle by cycle on each one-minute data chunk. Fig 8 shows the maximal toll notification response time in each of the 180 1-minute windows.

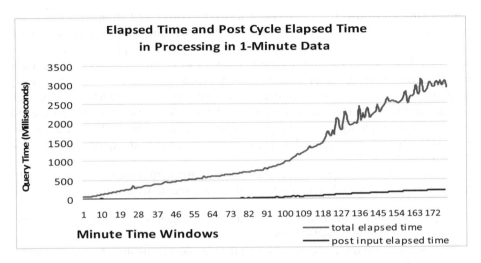

Fig. 7. Query time as well as PCET on the data chunk falling in each minute time window

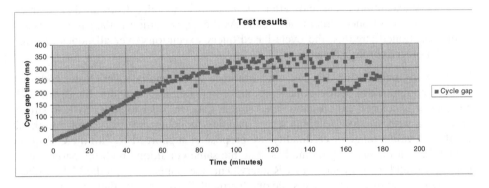

Fig. 8. Maximal toll notification response time in consecutive one-minute time windows

4   Map-Reduce and Cut-Rewind: The Powerful Combination

BI generally covers the whole computation chain from event streams to analysis results and business decisions. This lays a base for us to integrate In-DB M-R and stream processing. However, embedded in a one-time SQL query, the M-R computation cannot rely on the conventional query engine to roll over unbounded input data. Then if an additional middleware layer is introduced for performing an M-R query iteratively on the data chunks, several kinds of performance penalty would be incurred, including the overhead of repeated query setup/teardown and static data loading, as well as the extra cost of data copying and moving between the query engine and the middleware. It also causes the loss of continuity in tracking the application context, e.g. the data cached in the UDF closures, which is required by history sensitive operations such as the moving average calculation.

We solve the above problem based on the combination of M-R and C-R.

Cut-Rewind a Parallel Query. To explain how to extend the C-R approach to a parallel query engine for stream processing, let us review the parallel query execution process. A SQL query is parsed and optimized into a query plan that is a tree of operators. In parallel execution multiple instances of certain sub-query, called fragments, are distributed to the participating query executors and data processors on multiple machine nodes. On each sub-query tree processed at a machine node, the scan operator at the leaf of the tree gets and materializes a block of data, to be delivered to the upper layer tuple by tuple. The global query execution state is kept in the initial site. At the end of query execution, the memory allocated to the query execution instance is de-allocated.

To support C-R on a parallel database, every participating query engine is facilitated with the C-R capability. Collectively they cooperated in the following way.

- Similar to partitioning the input data in a parallel database, the input stream is partitioned over multiple machine nodes.
- The same cut condition is defined on all the partitioned streams. A critical requirement is that if the cycle based continuous querying is "cut" on time window, the stream cannot be partitioned by time, but by other attributes.
- A query execution cycle ends after *end-of-data* is signaled from all data sources, i.e. all the partitioned streams are "cut". As the *cut* condition is the same across all the partitioned streams, the cycle-based query executions over all nodes are well synchronized through data driven.

With the original M-R model, data are partitioned "horizontally" over cluster nodes for parallel computation; while enhancing the computation bandwidth by divide-and-conquer, it is not defined on unbounded stream data. In order to apply M-R to stream processing with window semantics, i.e. mapping-reducing the data chunk by chunk divided by value, range or cardinality, we propose to support M-R with the C-R query model, i.e. cut the *map* input data based on the same condition on all the participating *map* nodes, and then rewind the M-R query. This mechanism allows the M-R application to run cycle by cycle, hence scale out "vertically" over infinite data streams.

Cyclic Map-Reduce for Chunk-wise Stream Processing. As illustrated in Fig. 9, the chunk-wise M-R can be supported by means the cycle-based continuous query under the C-R mechanism.

Overall, the M-R query is applied to unbounded streamed data chunk by chunk according to a certain "cut" condition such as the advance of time window. In parallel execution, the "cut" condition is identical in all the participating *map* nodes and therefore also is used to synchronize their operations.

- At any *map* node, when the *cut* condition is met by checking the incoming data, the SSF at that node signals the *end-of-data*;
- When the SSFs on all the participating map nodes have signaled the *end-of-data*, the map phase of the current query cycle is completed, and the chunk-wise *map* results in multiple nodes are shuffled to the *reduce* sites. Upon the completion of the *reduce* phase, the current query cycle is terminated by the query engine and the M-R query rewinds and rolls to its next execution cycle.

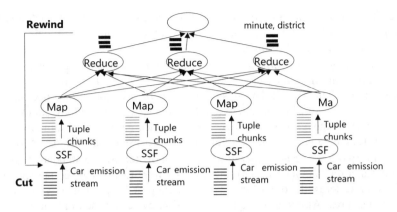

Fig. 9. Combine Map-Reduce and C-R for scaling out stream processing

The semantics of the cyclic M-R on stream can be formalized as below.

- A M-R query Q_{MR} is defined on an infinite stream of relation tuples S and set of relations $R_1,..,R_n$
- A criterion C for cutting each partition of S into an unbounded sequence of chunks, e.g. by every 1-minute time window, $<S_{C0}, S_{C1}, ..., S_{Ci}, ...>$ where S_{Ci} denotes the i-th "chunk" of the stream according to the chunking-criterion C. S_{Ci} can be interpreted as a relation.
- A partition key is given for partitioning S over the server nodes, while $R_1,..,R_n$ are replicated on these nodes;
- The semantics of applying the M-R query Q_{MR} to the partitioned stream S as well as $R_1,..,R_n$ lies in $Q_{MR}(S, R_1,..,R_n) \rightarrow < Q_{MR}(S_{C0}, R_1,..,R_n), ... Q_{MR}(S_{Ci}, R_1,..,R_n), ... >$ which continuously generates an unbounded sequence of M-R query results, one on each *chunk* of the stream data. Note that data partitioning is transparent at this conceptual level.

Compared with scheduling multiple queries/operations by a workflow-like system outside the query engine, which dominates the present stream processing management and some extended M-R framework, benefits gained by the proposed approach include the full SQL expressive power, enhanced semantics in chunk-wise processing and in history-sensitivity, as well as reduced overhead for setup/teardown queries, for loading static data repeatedly, and for IPC or even ODBC oriented data copying/moving.

Extended Example on Parallel DB. We extend the simulated vehicle exhaust emissions monitoring example on the parallel database engine. Conceptually the query shape remains the same. For parallel processing, the car emission stream is hash-partitioned by *vid* to all the *map* nodes but the data are supplied chunk by chunk at each node. As shown in Fig. 10, the query runs cycle by cycle on the parallel database, each cycle for processing the data falling in a one-minute time window. Since the "cut" condition is identical over all the data partitions, it provides the *sync-points* for the overall chunk-wise query evaluation. Shuffling the *map* results for parallel *reducing* is handled by the parallel database engine in the standard way of parallel query processing. In each cycle, the query is executed in the following way.

- On each *map* node, the *SSF_exhausts* is invoked multiple times in each query execution cycle, with each call returns one tuple to fuel the query. It signals the *end-of-data* upon the change of minute.
- The *map* function, comp_exhaust(), is executed in parallel, each derives the composite exhaust emission measure of an input tuple, based on the static relation "comp_rules". This static relation is loaded *only once* initially for processing all the tuples in a cycle, and can sustain over all the cycles due to the long-standing nature of the query instance. It is easy to see performance gain from eliminating repeated loading static data is particularly significant in processing infinite stream data.
- There are two-level *reduce* operations, one conducted by the standard SQL aggregation function AVG() for deriving the per-minute average composite exhaust emission measures; the other further derives the past 10 minutes moving average of these measures. Although the query execution cycle is based on one minute time window, it is possible to buffer the past 10 minutes measures for deriving their moving average, because the query instance is cyclic rewound but never shutdown, the data buffered with that UDF can retain across query cycles in such an "ever green" query instance.
- When all the *map* sites reach the *end-of-data*, the whole query enters the *end-of-data* status, upon the completion of the current execution cycle, the query is rewound and then the next execution cycle preceded. In this way the M-R computation is executed cycle by cycle.

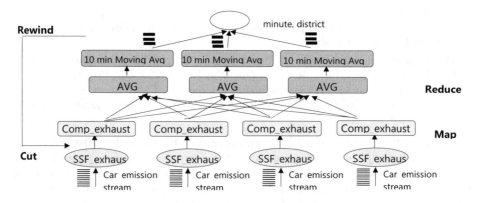

Fig. 10. Air pollution assessment with chunk-wise Map-Reduce stream processing

Integrating M-R in the C-R framework allows the M-R operation to scale out cycle-by-cycle continuously.

5 Conclusions

Pushing data-intensive computation down to the database layer for fast data access and reduced data transfer, and leveraging the parallel execution infrastructure already existent in parallel database engines to support scalable stream analytics, are the key to Live-BI. In this work we address the issue of applying In-DB M-R to streamed data.

In-DB M-R scales out analytics by enhancing the CPU bandwidth, and allows the M-R functions to be embedded within standard SQL queries to exploit the SQL expressive power and DBMS functionalities. However, with the current technology, In-DB M-R cannot scale-out with respect to continuous and infinite stream data.

We tackled this issue by integrating the In-DB M-R model with the C-R query model to support data chunk oriented M-R computation. Under our approach, an M-R application can be applied to the input data chunk by chunk continuously within a single, long-standing query instance. Such a powerful combination enables us to scale-out data intensive stream analytics "horizontally" based on the M-R model, and "vertically" based on the C-R model.

Our experimental results show the superior performance of processing data stream by the query engine parallelly and incrementally. This is because we completely pushed stream processing down to the query engine with efficient direct heap-access and near-zero data copy and move overhead. This is also because we did not introduce any additional middleware platform to manage the windows of stream data and the iteration of M-R, therefore significantly avoid the inter-platform communication and data transfer.

The proposed approach has been prototyped by extending HP's parallel database Neoview. The C-R approach is also implemented on the PostgreSQL engine for proof-of-concept. Our preliminary experience reveals the merit of combining M-R and C-R for scaling out In-DB stream analytics. We plan to take this combination as the core of our new generation Live-BI platform.

References

1. Arasu, A., Babu, S., Widom, J.: The CQL Continuous Query Language: Semantic Foundations and Query Execution. VLDB Journal 2(15) (June 2006)
2. Chandrasekaran, S., et al.: TelegraphCQ: Continuous Dataflow Processing for an Uncertain World. In: CIDR 2003 (2003)
3. Bryant, R.E.: Data-Intensive Supercomputing: The case for DISC, CMU-CS-07-128 (2007)
4. Chandrasekaran, S., et al.: TelegraphCQ: Continuous Dataflow Processing for an Uncertain World. In: CIDR 2003 (2003)
5. Chen, Q., Hsu, M.: Experience in Extending Query Engine for Continuous Analytics, Tech Rep HPL-2010-44 (2010)
6. Chen, Q., Therber, A., Hsu, M., Zeller, H., Zhang, B., Wu, R.: Efficiently Support Map-Reduce alike Computation Models Inside Parallel DBMS. In: Proc. Thirteenth International Database Engineering & Applications Symposium, IDEAS 2009 (2009)
7. Chen, Q., Hsu, M., Liu, R.: Extend UDF Technology for Integrated Analytics. In: Proc. DaWaK 2009 (2009)
8. Chen, Q., Hsu, M.: Data-Continuous SQL Process Model. In: Proc. 16th International Conference on Cooperative Information Systems, CoopIS 2008 (2008)
9. Dean, J.: Experiences with MapReduce, an abstraction for large-scale computation. In: Int. Conf. on Parallel Architecture and Compilation Techniques. ACM, New York (2006)
10. DeWitt, D.J., Paulson, E., Robinson, E., Naughton, J., Royalty, J., Shankar, S., Krioukov, A.: Clustera: An Integrated Computation And Data Management System. In: VLDB 2008 (2008)

11. Franklin, M.J., et al.: Continuous Analytics: Rethinking Query Processing in a NetworkEffect World. In: CIDR 2009 (2009)
12. Gedik, B., Andrade, H., Wu, K.-L., Yu, P.S., Doo, M.C.: SPADE: The System S Declarative Stream Processing Engine. In: ACM SIGMOD 2008 (2008)
13. Greenplum, Greenplum MapReduce for the Petabytes Database (2008),
    http://www.greenplum.com/resources/MapReduce/
14. HP Neoview enterprise data warehousing platform,
    http://h71028.www7.hp.com/enterprise/cache/
    414444-0-0-225-121.html
15. Liarou, E., et al.: Exploiting the Power of Relational Databases for Efficient Stream Processing. In: EDBT 2009 (2009)
16. Yang, H.-c., Dasdan, A., Hsiao, R.-L., Parker, D.S.: Map-reduce-merge: simplified relational data processing on large clusters. In: ACM SIGMOD 2007 (2007)

Approaches towards Dealing with Complex Systems Configuration

Nirmal K. Mukhi

IBM T J Watson Research Center
P.O. Box 704, Yorktown Heights, NY 10598
nmukhi@us.ibm.com

Abstract. This paper describes some challenges facing architects who have to develop solutions operating on distributed virtualized infrastructures. It suggests the use of model-driven deployment and end-to-end monitoring for alleviating some of these problems.

1 Introduction

The creation and delivery of software solutions is in the midst of a sea change. The first part of this change was about the architecture of complex software systems and the now widespread use of service-oriented principles and standard service protocols. The unprecedented levels of interoperability this fosters has, in many respects, broken down long-standing barriers in the way of seamless distributed systems development. Most programmers no longer concern themselves with minutae about how to marshal data and what protocols need to be used to communicate with a remote program, an achievement that has led to far better utilization of the opportunities offered by the Internet and distributed systems in general. The second part of this change is about delivery of software services. Virtualized infrastructures and cloud-based delivery is revolutionizing how software is delivered to the consumer. The burden of maintenance of systems, long an overhead for software consumers, is eliminated in this approach to utility computing. Other benefits include the improved utilization of systems, and the flexibility for consumers to select the quality of service that best reflects their requirements.

While offering many advantages, solutions developed following this new paradigm exhibit two features that challenge systems architects:

- *The Complexity Problem*: The solution typically consists of a large number of software services deployed over a complex virtualized environment. The solution development will depend on a large number of cross-cutting concerns, both functional as well as non-functional. The needs of software services and offerings of the available infrastructure need to be appropriately matched during the design phase and competing requirements need to be resolved. Dependencies between components of the solution might impose additional constraints on the solution design that need to be taken care of. All these factors make the development of such solutions extremely complex.

R. Meersman et al. (Eds.): OTM 2010 Workshops, LNCS 6428, pp. 35–37, 2010.

– *The Evolution Problem*: Once deployed and operational, the system is not
static: the underlying infrastructure may continuously evolve to meet changing needs of the solution. This dynamic aspect may also surface further up
the stack: additional software services may be brought online depending on
the usage profile and nature of the solution. Keeping track of these changes
is extremely important for compliance and defect analysis.

We briefly describe two topics that address these problems. The first is the *model-
driven approach* that attempts to address the complexity problem we outlined
above. The second is the use of *end-to-end monitoring* to continuously track and
record changes to the overall system, which is a promising approach to address
the evolution problem.

2   The Model-Driven Approach

The solutions we refer to consist of multiple layers: hardware systems (real or virtual), software infrastructure (covering operating systems and middleware such
as databases and application servers) and finally services that are composed to
create applications. Model-driven approaches provide solution designers with abstractions and tools that allow them to conceptualize the whole system across
these levels, and build in dependencies and other constraints to reduce the solution space. The desired outcome of the exercise is the determination (and possible
automated configuration) of a consistent set of hardware, middleware and services
that meet the various functional and non-functional constraints, as well as a deployment plan. The reader may refer to [5], [2], [1] for further information on these
approaches. The challenge in applying this technique is in the lack of uniformity
of the systems being configured, as a result of which any modeling tool may not
be able to utilize the configurability offered by the infrastructure (and thus produce a non-optimal deployment plan). Additionally, such models suffer from the
lack of roundtripping, wherein the model and the actual deployment can get out
of sync due to configuration changes that are applied manually. Once this occurs,
the model loses its value as a faithful representation of the solution.

A complementary thread of work to the model-driven approach is *model-based*
in that models are developed to represent abstractions (such as the *business view*
or *IT view*). The goal is to use these models for simulation, dependency analysis,
change management and verification rather transformation of the model into
deployable artifacts.

3   End-to-End Monitoring

As stated, distributed system solutions consist of many separate components,
and one of the principles behind the new paradigm is that these components as
well as the underlying infrastructure can and should change to accomodate new
patterns of use. As an example, a data service accessed by the solution might
need to grow its storage footprint in response to large amounts of data being

stored. Many cloud and Grid infrastructures transparently offer these kinds of facilities. Migration of services from one physical server to another for load balancing purposes is also usually transparently offered. The potential rapidity of change means that it is difficult to develop a comprehensive end-to-end view of the state of the system. While a single system or platform is amenable to comprehensive monitoring, in this context it represents just one of many connected islands within the larger system. The provenance of the system state, i.e. what past actions or events led to the current configuration, is an important aid to maintainence and for various compliance and legal purposes. For example, it is a pre-requisite to verifying that the system complies with service-level agreements. If there is a failure of a disk, the knowledge of what services are affected by the lack of its availability is crucial to remediation and root-cause analysis. In the past, provenance work has been used to capture and maintain the evolution of systems, database information and business data ([4], [7], [3]), but there is potential in its application to monitor distributed system solutions as well. A bottom-up discovery of system resource use to infer impact analysis, described in works such as [6] might also be a promising technique for addressing the evolution problem.

References

1. Adabala, S., Chadha, V., Chawla, P., Figueiredo, R.J.O., Fortes, J.A.B., Krsul, I., Matsunaga, A.M., Tsugawa, M.O., Zhang, J., 0002, M.Z., Zhu, L., Zhu, X.: From virtualized resources to virtual computing grids: the in-vigo system. Future Generation Comp. Syst. 21(6), 896–909 (2005)
2. Chase, J.S., Irwin, D.E., Grit, L.E., Moore, J.D., Sprenkle, S.E.: Dynamic virtual clusters in a grid site manager. In: HPDC 2003: Proceedings of the 12th IEEE International Symposium on High Performance Distributed Computing, p. 90. IEEE Computer Society, Washington (2003)
3. Cheney, J., Chiticariu, L., Tan, W.-C.: Provenance in databases: Why, how, and where. Found. Trends Databases 1(4), 379–474 (2009)
4. Curbera, F., Doganata, Y., Martens, A., Mukhi, N.K., Slominski, A.: Business provenance — a technology to increase traceability of end-to-end operations. In: Meersman, R., Tari, Z. (eds.) OTM 2008, Part II. LNCS, vol. 5332, pp. 100–119. Springer, Heidelberg (2008)
5. Konstantinou, A.V., Eilam, T., Kalantar, M., Totok, A.A., Arnold, W., Snible, E.: An architecture for virtual solution composition and deployment in infrastructure clouds. In: VTDC 2009: Proceedings of the 3rd International Workshop on Virtualization Technologies in Distributed Computing, pp. 9–18. ACM, New York (2009)
6. Magoutis, K., Devarakonda, M., Joukov, N., Vogl, N.G.: Galapagos: model-driven discovery of end-to-end application-storage relationships in distributed systems. IBM J. Res. Dev. 52(4), 367–377 (2008)
7. Muniswamy-Reddy, K.K., Holland, D.A., Braun, U., Seltzer, M.: Provenance-aware storage systems. In: ATEC 2006: Proceedings of the annual conference on USENIX 2006 Annual Technical Conference, pp. 4–4. USENIX Association, Berkeley (2006)

ASSERT4SOA: Toward Security Certification of Service-Oriented Applications

Marco Anisetti[1], Claudio A. Ardagna[1], Franco Guida[2], Sigrid Gürgens[3],
Volkmar Lotz[4], Antonio Maña[5], Claudia Pandolfo[6],
Jean-Christophe Pazzaglia[4], Gimena Pujol[5], and George Spanoudakis[7]

[1] Università degli Studi di Milano, DTI, Crema, Italy
{claudio.ardagna,marco.anisetti}@unimi.it
[2] Fondazione Ugo Bordoni, Roma, Italy
guida@fub.it
[3] Fraunhofer Institute for Secure Information Technology, Germany
sigrid.guergens@sit.fraunhofer.de
[4] SAP Research, Sophia Antipolis, France
{jean-christophe.pazzaglia,volkmar.lotz}@sap.com
[5] University of Malaga, Computer Science Department, Malaga, Spain
{gimena,amg}@lcc.uma.es
[6] Engineering Ingegneria Informatica, Roma, Italy
claudia.pandolfo@eng.it
[7] City University London, Department of Computing, London, UK
G.Spanoudakis@soi.city.ac.uk

Abstract. ASSERT4SOA project proposes machine readable certificates to be used to allow Web service requesters to automatically assess the security properties of Web services (and their providers) as certified by a trusted third party. This vision promises to open up an entire new market for certification services.

1 Introduction

The term "certification" has been used with several different meanings in ICT [2]. Software practitioners can earn a certificate for expertise in a certain hardware or software technology. The maturity of crucial IT processes, such as software development, can be - and is often - certified. Even individual software systems can be certified as having particular non-functional properties, including safety, security, or privacy. The certification of non-functional properties, however, has had only a limited success to this day. Despite the availability of security certification schemes like Common Criteria [5] only a few commercial IT systems (e.g., those developed by highly regulated industries) have earned them.

In this paper we present the vision of ASSERT4SOA, a FP7 STREP project starting October 2010 that will deal with service certification issues. ASSERT4SOA, that builds over a number of research ideas put forward by consortium members [4], is aimed at supporting new certification scenarios, where the security certification of software systems is required and plays a major role.

R. Meersman et al. (Eds.): OTM 2010 Workshops, LNCS 6428, pp. 38–40, 2010.

Current trends in the IT industry suggest that software systems in the future will be very different from their counterparts today, due to greater adoption of Service-Oriented Architectures (SOAs), the wider spread of the deployment of Software-as-a-Service (SaaS), and the increased use of wireless and mobile technologies [6,7]. These trends point to large-scale, heterogeneous ICT infrastructures hosting applications that are dynamically built from loosely-coupled, well-separated services, where key non-functional properties like security, privacy, and reliability will be of increased and critical importance.

In service-based scenarios, certifying software properties will be crucial. Current certification schemes, however, are either insufficient in addressing the needs of such scenarios or not applicable at all (e.g., certificate awarded to monolithic software systems only [1,2]). ASSERT4SOA will fill this gap by producing novel techniques and tools for expressing, assessing, and certifying security properties for complex service-oriented applications, composed of distributed software services that may dynamically be selected, assembled, and replaced within complex and continuously evolving software ecosystems [3,8].

2   ASSERT4SOA Certificates

ASSERT4SOA certification will cover both individual software services and the environment in which they operate at execution time, allowing runtime management of the security, privacy and reliability properties, as well as business processes and applications based on them. ASSERT4SOA certificates will be handled by a dedicated set of newly developed services, collectively referred to as the "ASSERT4SOA architecture", fully integrated within the SOA-based software system lifecycle. The ASSERT4SOA architecture will enable: *i)* backward compatibility of existing certification processes within the SOA context; *ii)* a new ontology-based format for certificates, linking security properties with evidences supporting them; *iii)* runtime certificate-aware service selection based on target assurance level for composite applications.

ASSERT4SOA will support certificate-driven selection of individual services and, in addition, the evaluation of security properties of composite services based on the properties of their individual certified-services. The exploitation strategy of ASSERT4SOA certification scheme is threefold.

- To achieve the desired impact on the software certification community, ASSERT4SOA use cases will cover the whole SOA-based application lifecycle. Also, ASSERT4SOA will be providing methodological guidelines to support accredited certification agencies in the assessment of service-based composite applications.
- To reach out to SOA implementers, ASSERT4SOA will propose a standard ontology-based metadata format to express certified properties and will develop an architecture (components, protocols, and mechanisms) to use certification claims during the main phases of the service-based applications (e.g., deployment, lookup, service call, service composition).

– ASSERT4SOA will equip service-oriented application users with powerful, easy-to-understand mechanisms to assess at runtime the trustworthiness of composite applications. These mechanisms will use the security properties certified during the certification process of individual services; when a composite application will be orchestrated, the ASSERT4SOA infrastructure will compute the global level of assurance resulting from the interactions between the services in the given context.

These three exploitation objectives are incremental and aim to enable the progressive development of a new, service-based certification business ecosystems that will enable all European players - ranging from individual citizens to large businesses - to assess the security of the mission-critical applications they use based on a proven methodology.

3   Conclusions and Outlook

Early implementations of Web services tended to be sandbox-type services open to a small number of business partners with whom a trust relationship was already established. So the effort of understanding and assessing Web services' security properties was often perceived as superfluous. In recent years Web services have increasingly gained acceptance as the technology of choice for implementing inter-organizational business processes. In these situations, partners need additional information concerning the security schemes provided by each service to decide whether to use the service. The ASSERT4SOA vision proposes a machine readable certificate to be used to allow service requesters to assess the security properties of service providers as certified by a trusted third party. This vision promises to open up an entire new market for certification services.

References

1. Alvaro, A., de Almeida, E., de Lemos Meira, S.: Software component certification: A survey. In: Proc. of EUROMICRO 2005, Porto, Portugal (August-September 2005)
2. Damiani, E., Ardagna, C.A., El Ioini, N.: Open Source Security Certification. Springer, Heidelberg (2009)
3. Damiani, E., El Ioini, N., Sillitti, A., Succi, G.: Ws-certificate. In: Proc. of the IEEE SERVICES I 2009, Los Angeles, CA, USA (July 2009)
4. Damiani, E., Maña, A.: Toward ws-certificate. In: Proc. of the ACM SWS 2009, Chicago, IL, USA (November 2009)
5. Herrmann, D.: Using the Common Criteria for IT security evaluation. Auerbach Publications (2002)
6. Papazoglou, M., Traverso, P., Dustdar, S., Leymann, F.: Service-oriented computing: State of the art and research challenges. Computer 40(11), 38–45 (2007)
7. Robinson, J.: Demand for software-as-a-service still growing (May 2009),
   http://www.information-age.com/channels/commsand-networking/
   perspectives-and-trends/1046687/
   demand-forsoftwareasaservice-still-growing.thtml (accessed August 2010)
8. Securing Web Services for Army SOA,
   http://www.sei.cmu.edu/solutions/softwaredev/securing-web-services.cfm
   (accessed August 2010)

Allowing Citizens to Self-compose Personalized Services: A Cloud Computing Model

Lanfranco Marasso[1], Marco De Maggio[2], Valentina Chetta[2], Maddalena Grieco[2], Carla Elia[2], and Salvatore Totaro[2]

[1] Engineering Ingegneria Informatica,
via San Martino della Battaglia, 56
00185Rome, Italy
[2] Centro Cultura Innovativa d'Impresa – University of Salento
Via per Monteroni, sn
73100Lecce, italy
{lanfranco.marasso}@eng.it,
{marco.demaggio,salvatore.totaro}@ebms.unile.it,
{valentina.chetta,maddalena.grieco,carla.elia}@xnetlab.ebms.it

Abstract. This paper presents a Cloud Computing (CC) model designed for the service-to-citizens provided by the Public Administration and investigates the Service Oriented Architecture (SOA) as the suitable architectural approach, scalable and interoperable, to allow anyone to design a desirable service. Together with the extensive use of mashup it shows its ability to allow users to personalize their services.

Citizens, thanks to this flexible model, could self-compose their services in a variety of ways, specifically designed to include people spanning from the so-called digital natives to people minimally experienced with technologies.

Keywords: Cloud Computing , Service Oriented Architecture, service to citizens, distributed resources, future internet services.

1 Introduction

Today's on-demand society assumes nearly universal access to real-time data and analytics in a resilient, secure environment. Anything short of that standard is unacceptable. These demands are being driven by a proliferation of data sources, mobile devices, radio frequency identification systems, unified communications, Web2.0 services and technologies such as mashups.

Cloud Computing enhances effective service delivery and fosters citizen-driven innovation because it allows to respond rapidly to customer needs in a cost-effective way. Public Administration shows today the need to change its perspective to the design and delivery of services, by adopting a citizen-centric approach that fully supports the co-creation of the service experience and involves citizens and other public or private organizations.

This paper presents an innovative Cloud Computing model which relies on the central position of citizens, that can self-compose their services in a variety of ways specifically designed to include people spanning from the so-called digital natives to people minimally experienced with technologies.

R. Meersman et al. (Eds.): OTM 2010 Workshops, LNCS 6428, pp. 41–42, 2010.

2   The Features of a New Service-to-Citizen Model Enabled by Cloud Computing

The new model is intended to provide services that meet citizens preferences and needs aggregating services of different nature, public and private, in a simple way.

Public sector information management is clearly dominated by a "silo" model, the most of the government organizations rely on large stand-alone information systems. The new Cloud Computing model must allow services to be provided by multiple access points, and to be combined in complex *tasks*. The proposed CC model is based upon three different levels:

- the *connectivity level* based on the web, aimed at ensuring that the signals will travel among the cloud nodes in an encrypted and determined way;
- the *signaling level*: the classic client-server architecture now used in the web systems will join a system based on signals and connectors, where each cloud agent will emit signals, all data will travel in the signal standard format and will be directed toward specific connectors exposed by the cloud nodes;
- the *task level*, responsible for establishing a connection between needed cloud nodes in order to achieve a task; at this level, the agency and the citizen must align on the same protocol, although the bundled services depend on other nodes in the cloud.

The deployment of advanced citizen-driven services require the building of an environment in which the service providers, public and private players, can keep their organizational and technological infrastructure. The Service Oriented Architecture (SOA) allows on one side to structure organizational units as self-consistent components that produce and consume value-added services, and on the other side to define technological components to deliver modular services. According to this approach, services are developed and hosted by different providers, described in specific standard interface, published in an accessible registry, and can be requested via standard protocols [2]. The application of the SOA in conjunction to the recently coined concept of mashup enables a web 2.0 approach to service composition, allowing final users to self-create in a simple way ad-hoc services that are tailored on their specific needs. The "mashup" concept refers to the capability of a system to allow users to deal with content (data, information, services) retrieved from external data sources (web services, data store, web application) to create entirely new and innovative services [1]. It represents an easy "user-centric" service composition technology, that could guarantee a wider accessibility and inclusion to all the citizens, reducing the complexity of SOA service composition from elaborated ad hoc models and tools to the simple "drag and drop" action within a web browser.

References

1. Geambasu, R., Gribble, S.D., Levy, H.M.: CloudViews: Communal data sharing in public clouds. In: Hot Cloud 2009 (June 2009)
2. Liu, X., Hui, Y., Sun, W., Liang, H.: Towards Service Composition Based on Mashup. In: IEEE SCW, pp. 332–339 (2007)

Towards Large-Size Ontology Alignment by Mapping Groups of Concepts

Patrice Buche[1,3], Juliette Dibie-Barthélemy[2], and Liliana Ibănescu[2]

[1] INRA - UMR IATE, 2, place Pierre Viala, F-34060 Montpellier Cedex 2, France
[2] INRA - Mét@risk & AgroParisTech, 16 rue Claude Bernard, F-75231 Paris
Cedex 5, France
[3] LIRMM, CNRS-UM2, F-34392 Montpellier, France
Patrice.Buche@supagro.inra.fr,
{Juliette.Dibie,Liliana.Ibanescu}@agroparistech.fr

Abstract. This paper presents a semi-automatic method to map groups of concepts between two ontologies.

1 Mapping Groups of Concepts

After a preliminary work presented in [1], we propose in this paper a new semi-automatic method to align large-size ontologies by reusing existing mappings between groups of concepts. Our method deals with ontologies, a reference one and a source one, which are composed of concepts, properties and axioms, where the axioms specify the range of properties for some concepts. The originality of our method is to map concepts not one-by-one, but groups by groups, using predefined mappings between groups of concepts and the concepts' descriptions by axioms. A group of concepts is defined by restrictions on properties. Given a new group of concepts in the reference ontology, the method finds first the "semantically close" groups to this new group, and then reuses the existing mappings to build the corresponding group of concepts in the source ontology.

Our approach is guided by the application needs and gives a first semi-automatic solution to make the work of the user easier when he/she has to align large-size and different ontologies in which concepts are described by many different properties. This method has been tested on a real application in food safety [2] and the first preliminary experimental results are promising.

2 Related Works

Ontology alignment is an active research area which has been largely studied in the literature (see [3,4]) and many systems have been developed to align ontologies (see the Ontology Alignment Evaluation Initiative[1]). To the best of our knowledge, the problem of finding several to several correspondences between

---

[1] http://oaei.ontologymatching.org/

R. Meersman et al. (Eds.): OTM 2010 Workshops, LNCS 6428, pp. 43–44, 2010.

concepts has not been already addressed. Most work on ontology alignment studies how establishing one to one correspondences between concepts.

The problem of finding alignments between large-size ontologies has been especially addressed by works on ontology partition [5,6]. These works can be compared with ours since the groups of concepts can be considered as a kind of partition of the ontologies, but our method is guided by the existing groups and not by the alignment task, and, its goal is to build groups of concepts. The most close work to ours is the one of [7,8] which proposes to use Partial Reference Alignments (PRA) to partition the ontology into mappable groups. These PRA are subsets of all correct mappings and allow one to reduce the search space, to compute similarities between terms and to filter mapping suggestions. The main difference is that, in our case, the finality of our method is to find mappings between groups of concepts and not between concepts.

3 Conclusion

Our alignment method proposes a first step to map groups of concepts according to existing mappings between groups. The relationship which may exist in the reference ontology between a new group and the existing groups and their mappings plays an important role in the construction of the corresponding new group in the source ontology. Our method uses existing mappings to define new mappings which is an idea classically used in machine learning methods such as in the system GLUE [9]. We will study in which way we can use these methods to improve our algorithm.

References

1. Doussot, D., Buche, P., Dibie-Barthélemy, J., Haemmerlé, O.: Using Fuzzy Conceptual Graphs to Map Ontologies. In: Proceedings of ODBASE 2006. LNCS, vol. 4275, pp. 891–900. Springer, Heidelberg (2006)
2. Buche, P., Dibie-Barthélemy, J., Tressou, J.: Le logiciel CARAT, pp. 305–333. Lavoisier (2006)
3. Euzenat, J., Shvaiko, P.: Ontology Matching. Springer, Heidelberg (2007)
4. Noy, N.F.: Ontology Mapping, pp. 573–590. Springer, Heidelberg (2009)
5. Hu, W., Zhao, Y., Qu, Y.: Similarity-Based Ontology Alignment in OWL-Lite. In: Asian Semantic Web Conference, ASWC, pp. 72–83 (2006)
6. Hamdi, F., Safar, B., Zargayouna, H., Reynaud, C.: Partitionnement d'ontologies pour le passage l'échelle des techniques d'alignement. In: Extraction et Gestion des Connaissances, EGC, pp. 409–420 (2009)
7. Lambrix, P., Tan, H., Liu, Q.: SAMBO and SAMBOdtf Results for the Ontology Alignment Evaluation Initiative 2008. In: Sheth, A.P., Staab, S., Dean, M., Paolucci, M., Maynard, D., Finin, T., Thirunarayan, K. (eds.) ISWC 2008. LNCS, vol. 5318, Springer, Heidelberg (2008)
8. Lambrix, P., Liu, Q.: Using Partial Reference Alignments to Align Ontologies. In: Aroyo, L., Traverso, P., Ciravegna, F., Cimiano, P., Heath, T., Hyvönen, E., Mizoguchi, R., Oren, E., Sabou, M., Simperl, E. (eds.) ESWC 2009. LNCS, vol. 5554, pp. 188–202. Springer, Heidelberg (2009)
9. Doan, A., Madhavan, J., Dhamankar, R., Domingos, P., Halevy, A.Y.: Learning to match ontologies on the Semantic Web. Very Large Data Bases (VLDB) Journal 12(4), 303–319 (2003)

Performance Testing of
Semantic Publish/Subscribe Systems

Martin Murth[1], Dietmar Winkler[2], Stefan Biffl[2], Eva Kühn[1], and Thomas Moser[2]

[1] Institute of Computer Languages, Vienna University of Technology
[2] Christian Doppler Laboratory "Software Engineering Integration for
Flexible Automation Systems", Vienna University of Technology
{mm,eva}@complang.tuwien.ac.at,
{dietmar.winkler,stefan.biffl,thomas.moser}@tuwien.ac.at

Abstract. Publish/subscribe mechanisms support clients in observing knowledge represented in semantic repositories and responding to knowledge changes. Currently available implementations of semantic publish/subscribe systems differ significantly with respect to performance and functionality. In this paper we present an evaluation framework for systematically evaluating publish/subscribe systems and its application to identify performance bottlenecks and optimization approaches.

1 Introduction and Motivation

The application of semantic repositories enables managing highly dynamic knowledge bases [4]. Semantic publish/subscribe mechanisms foster the notification of changes systematically [3]. Registered queries (e.g., using SPARQL) on repositories and individual subscriptions will lead to the notification of individual subscribers initiated by knowledge base updates. Several publish/subscribe mechanisms have been developed in the past, e.g., the Semantic Event Notification System (SENS) [3] due to various application requirements (e.g., focus on functional behavior and performance measures). Nevertheless, a key question is how to evaluate publish/subscribe systems with focus on performance measures efficiently. Several benchmark frameworks, e.g., LUBM [1] [4], focus on the assessment of load, reasoning, and query performance of semantic repositories. However, a standardized approach for evaluating semantic publish/subscribe mechanisms is not yet available. We developed the SEP-BM (Semantic Event Processing Benchmark) framework focusing on two common performance metrics, i.e., *notification time* and *publication throughput*, and implemented a framework for measuring these metrics for semantic publish/subscribe systems [4].

2 SEP-BM Benchmark Framework

Figure 1 presents the concept of the novel benchmark framework consisting of a *benchmark base configuration* and *a benchmark runner*. The benchmark base configuration comprises data sets based on an ontology and 20 query definitions for subscription to test performance measures: The configuration generator provides sequences of publication operations (i.e., scenarios); the reference data generator provides traceability information regarding publication/notification relationships for

R. Meersman et al. (Eds.): OTM 2010 Workshops, LNCS 6428, pp. 45–46, 2010.
© Springer-Verlag Berlin Heidelberg 2010

measurement purposes. The benchmark runner executes the scenarios and performs data analyses, i.e., analyzing notification time and publication throughput.

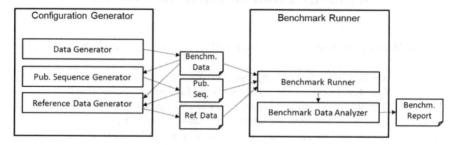

Fig. 1. Benchmark framework components

Focusing on these major success-critical issues regarding publish/subscribe performance we applied a set of defined test scenarios to SENS and an optimized (heuristic-supported) variant. Not surprisingly, the observation of a first SENS [2] prototype (without heuristic optimization) showed a relationship between low notification times and high publication throughput rates for complex reasoning approaches and/or large input data and low selectivity. Based on these findings we developed a heuristics-based optimization mechanism [2] and identified general prerequisites for successful employment of heuristic optimizations, typically leading to performance problems: (a) need for complex reasoning and querying tasks during the evaluation of subscriptions and (b) large input sets and low selectivity of the subscription query statements. See Murth *et al.* for details of SEP-BM Framework and the initial evaluation results [4].

3 Conclusion

According to the initial evaluation the SEP-BM framework [2] helps to (a) enable performance bottleneck detection of publish/subscribe systems, (b) identify root causes of performance bottlenecks and indicate candidate optimization approaches, and (c) support quantifiable performance measurement to evaluate optimization mechanisms.

Acknowledgments. This work has been supported by the Christian Doppler Forschungsgesellschaft and the BMWFJ, Austria.

References

[1] Guo, Y., Pan, Z., Heflin, J.: LUBM: A benchmark for OWL knowledge base systems. Journal of Web Semantics 3(2-3), 158–182 (2005)
[2] Murth, M., Kühn, E.: A heuristics framework for semantic subscription processing. In: Aroyo, L., Traverso, P., Ciravegna, F., Cimiano, P., Heath, T., Hyvönen, E., Mizoguchi, R., Oren, E., Sabou, M., Simperl, E. (eds.) ESWC 2009. LNCS, vol. 5554, pp. 96–110. Springer, Heidelberg (2009)
[3] Murth, M., Kühn, E.: Knowledge-based coordination with a reliable semantic subscription mechanism. In: Proc. 24th ACM Symp. of Applied Computing (SAC) - Special Track on Coordination Models, Languages and Applications, pp. 1374–1380. ACM, New York (2009)
[4] Murth, M., Winkler, D., Biffl, S., Kühn, E., Moser, T.: Performance Testing of Semantic Publish/Subscribe Systems, TU Vienna, Technical Report, IFS:QSE 10/05 (2010), http://qse.ifs.tuwien.ac.at/publication/IFS-QSE-10-05.pdf

Modeling and Use of an Ontology Network for Website Recommendation Systems

Edelweis Rohrer[1], Regina Motz[1], and Alicia Díaz[2]

[1] Instituto de Computación, Facultad de Ingeniería,
Universidad de la República, Uruguay
{rmotz,erohrer}@fing.edu.uy
[2] LIFIA, Facultad de Informática,
Universidad Nacional de La Plata, Argentina
alicia.diaz@lifia.info.unlp.edu.ar

Abstract. The modeling of website recommendation systems involves the combination of many features: website domain, metrics of quality, quality criteria, recommendation criteria, user profile, and specific domain features. When specifying these systems, it must be ensured the proper interrelationship of all these features. In order to ensure the proper relationships of all these features, we propose an ontology network, the `Salus` ontology. This work presents the structure of each of the networked ontologies and the semantic relationships that exist among them[1].

1 The `Salus` Ontology Network

Currently, the development of ontologies to the Semantic Web is based on the integration of existing ontologies [1]. In this work we have followed this approach to develop the `Salus` Ontology used in a Health Website Recommendation System as an ontology network. Our focus is on the different kinds of relationships between the networked ontologies. More precisely, the `Salus` ontology is a network of ontology networks; this means that each component of the `Salus` ontology is itself an ontology network and all of them are related among each other. It is broadly outlined in the Figure 1.

`Salus` networked ontologies are interrelated by four different relations: *isA ConservativeExtention Of*, *mappingSimilarTo* and *isTheSchemaFor*, took from the DOOR ontology [2], and the *uses* relation, defined by us, which describes an extension of a given ontology by importing of individuals from another ontology.

The different specific-domain ontology networks correspond to the different knowledge domains conceptualized by the `Salus` ontology. The *Health* ontology network models the health domain: the *Health* ontology conceptualizes any diseases and the *Specific Health* ontology is a more specific disease. Both ontologies are related by the *isA ConservativeExtentionOf* relation. The *WebSite* ontology

---

[1] Funded by: Salus/CYTED and PROSUL, PAE 37279-PICT 02203 and LACCIR: e-Cloudss.

R. Meersman et al. (Eds.): OTM 2010 Workshops, LNCS 6428, pp. 47–48, 2010.

network conceptualizes the domain of webpages and describes web resources considered in a quality assessment. The *WebSite Specification* ontology plays the role of a metamodel for the *WebSite* ontology (*isTheShemaFor* relation). Its main concepts are *Web Resource* and *Web Resource Property*. A web resource is any resource which is identified by an URL. Web resource properties model the properties attached to a web resource. *Quality Assurance* ontology network conceptualizes metrics, quality specifications and quality assessments, each one in an ontology. The relationship *mappingSimilarTo* exists between the *Quality Assessment* and the *WebSite Specialization* ontologies, in order to define an alignment between Web Resource and Web Content concepts. *Context* ontology network describes user profiles and query resources. The *Context Specification* ontology is a metamodel to the *User Profile* and *Query Situation* ontologies. *Recommendation* ontology network describes the criteria of recommendation for a particular context and quality dimensions, and the obtained recommendation level. The *Recommendation Specification* ontology describes the criterion to make a recommendation. The *Recommendation* ontology models concrete recommendation assessments. This ontology uses the *Recommendation Specification* ontology.

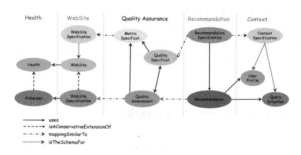

Fig. 1. Salus ontology network

During the execution of the process to recommend websites, the Salus ontology is useful to discover knowledge domain units in the web pages and to support quality and recommendation assessments. In the last cases, it assists in the modeling and specification of a recommendation system and in checking the correctness of the resulting system specification. The population of the Salus ontology is done in three different moments: at the start up of the recommendation system, when performing the quality assessment of a set of webpages and finally, at the execution of recommendation assessments.

References

1. Kleshchev, A., Artemjeva, I.: An analysis of some relations among domain ontologies. Int. Journal on Information Theories and Applications 12, 85–93 (2005)
2. Allocca, C., d'Aquin, M., Motta, E.: Door - towards a formalization of ontology relations. In: Dietz, J.L.G. (ed.) KEOD, pp. 13–20. INSTICC Press (2009)

The Open Innovation Paradigm and the Semantic Web: An Ontology for Distributed Product Innovation

Davor Meersman and Tharam Dillon

Digital Ecosystems and Business Intelligence Institute, Curtin University of Technology,
De Laeter Way, Technology Park 4,
6102 Bentley, Australia
{d.meersman,t.dillon}@curtin.edu.au

Abstract. In this paper we introduce an ontology specifically designed for product innovation. We discuss the specifics and advantages of domain ontology construction for product innovation. We then look at the application of the framework to the scuba diving equipment manufacturing industry domain.

Keywords: open innovation, product ontology, product innovation.

1 Open Innovation and Heterogeneity

The inherent inter-organisational nature of the open innovation paradigm [1] implies a versatility of participating agents and systems, heterogeneous information formats and differing semantics. The problem of product data integration has been addressed by the Semantic Web community by the development of product ontologies. The most important product ontologies today are eClassOWL [2], PRONTO [3], SWOP [4] and GoodRelations [5]. Properties such as product shape, material, colour, family and other manufacturing and sales related concepts are covered, in some ontologies to very great detail. However, in the context of open innovation the main shortcoming of these ontologies is that product, component and property functions are not included. Hence they are to be regarded more as very important and valuable assets in the modelling, manufacturing and commerce process, rather than tools to drive innovation. We would like to argue that for ontologies to be valuable in innovation processes, we need to rethink the entire idea of product ontology.

2 Product Innovation Ontology for Open Innovation

A major conceptual component of our ontology is that product, component and property functions are integrated in a very granular product representation. Besides listing which products have which components and properties, we define which components, which sub-components and even which properties have a certain function. Because the existence of properties in a component is driven by the function they perform, i.e. the fulfilment of initial requirements and in some cases posterior cost considerations, the inclusion of functions and their linkage to products, product components and product properties is crucial in the context of ideation. Why is something there?

R. Meersman et al. (Eds.): OTM 2010 Workshops, LNCS 6428, pp. 49–52, 2010.

Another big difference between a regular product ontology and an ontology geared towards product innovation, is that the entire domain of product application is included in the product innovation ontology, as the usage of the product has a great influence on the reasoning behind feature introduction.

The advantage of using an ontology to represent domain and product knowledge for innovation processes is that the instance level can stay hidden from potentially competitive industry partners. Because the mechanics of product functioning are expressed on the class/property (concept/relation) level, no instance information is shared between users of the ontology. The ontology only really means something to thes users with respect to their own instances in product engineering databases.

The highest level of the ontology features the following classes:

- Actor: any actor using objects in any process in the domain
- Object: products and components used in processes by actors and objects
- Process: any process in the domain, executed by an actor with the use of objects
- Quality: concepts that define how, to what extent, when etc. something happens; properties and functions of objects, actors and processes.

3 Analysis

For the application of the ontology framework we have chosen the scuba equipment manufacturing domain because it is a young, well-defined domain with plenty of domain experts (instructors, service technicians). However there has been a slowdown of the pace of innovation in the sector [6]. There are currently approximately 250 concepts and relations in the ontology, which at the moment equates to about 1500 fact statements. In this paper we will focus on the second stage regulator and how it inter-plays with other classes and relations. The second stage regulator is the part of the breathing apparatus that is held by the diver in his or her mouth. Its main function is to deliver breathing gas tot the diver at ambient pressure.

The components of the second stage regulator often have sub-components. For example the purge dome has a purge button sub-component in Figure 1. In this example we can also see the main function of the purge dome: to protect the diaphragm.

The properties of components are expressed in a variety of ways. Each component has a shape and a material. We have also introduced the shape feature property. These are properties that specify certain features of the shape, such as holes, threads, grooves, etc. In this example the cup shaped purge dome has a hole.

The function of the sub-component 'purge button' of the purge dome is to press the lever that moves the piston. This causes gas to flow in and the regulator to purge.

Although most of the times the component function is the result of an interplay between material, shape and shape features, a shape feature can also have a distinct function. The conceptual difference is that a shape feature inherits material properties and the general function from its parent, but can offer additional specific functions.

A final aspect we want to discuss here is the operation of components versus their general working. We distinguish two roles and co-roles, uses/usedby and operates/operatedby. The difference is that uses/usedby refers to (sub-) component or (sub-)process dependencies and operates/operatedby refers to where components are or can be operated by an actor. This is done out of product engineering considerations.

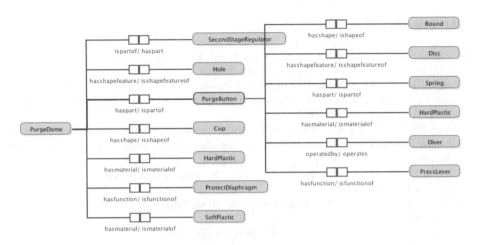

Fig. 1. Purge dome with components, properties and functions

4 Future Work

There are a number of issues that still need to be addressed.

1. We will study the effects (both positive and negative) of a purely semantic approach to an engineering domain that is traditionally diagram driven.
2. The possible level of granularity is virtually endless. We expect that an optimal level will be found only after some iterations of the ontology.
3. The process realm of the ontology currently assumes a best case scenario. However, often functions are in place to prevent (possibly catastrophic) problems. Critical failure processes will be addressed in future work.
4. The component material property will be elaborated further.
5. We will apply the ontology to a more service-oriented environment.
6. We intend to involve end users in a later stage of the research so the entire image of user preference becomes clear within the ontology.

5 Conclusion

In this paper we have introduced an ontology which we believe fills a significant gap in the semantic representation of business: the ideation and innovation process. We have argued that in order to have meaningful product development, the entire product application domain needs to be integrated in the product ontology. We have argued that the inclusion of product, component and property functions is a conditio sine qua non. We have demonstrated that a relevant and meaningful representation of engineering knowledge can be achieved on the class level. Finally, we have discussed various design decisions. In this paper we have illustrated that for ontologies to be valuable in innovation processes, we did need to rethink the idea of product ontology.

References

1. Chesbrough, H., Vanhaverbeke, W., West, J. (eds.): Open Innovation: Researching a New Paradigm. Oxford University Press, Oxford (2006)
2. Hepp, M.: The True Complexity of Product Representation in the Semantic Web. In: Proceedings of the 14th European Conference on Information System (ECIS 2006), Gothenburg, Sweden, pp. 1–12 (2006)
3. Vegetti, M., Henning, G.P., Leone, H.P.: Product ontology: definition of an ontology for the complex product modelling domain. In: Proceedings of the Mercosur Congress on Process Systems Engineering (2005),
   `http://www.enpromer2005.eq.ufrj.br/lng/en/index.php`
   (accessed on: May 26, 2010)
4. Böhms, M.: The SWOP Semantic Product Modelling Approach. In: SWOP project deliverable 23. SWOP (2006),
   `http://www.swop-project.eu/swop-solutions/`
   `semantic-product-modelling-approach/`
   `SWOP_D23_WP2_T2300_TNO_2008-04-15_v12.pdf` (accessed on June 14, 2010)
5. Hepp, M.: GoodRelations: An Ontology for Describing Products and Services Offers on the Web. In: Proceedings of the 16th International Conference on Knowledge Engineering and Knowledge Management, pp. 332–347. EKAW (2008)
6. Gilliam, B.: A Personal Perspective on Dive Innovation: Has the Dive Industry Run Out of Ideas? Undercurrent, Undercurrent, Sausalito, CA (2009),
   `http://www.undercurrent.org/UCnow/articles/`
   `DiveInnovation200903.shtml` (accessed on January 10, 2010)

SMILE – A Framework for Semantic Applications

Jakub Galgonek, Tomáš Knap, Martin Kruliš, and Martin Nečaský*

Department of Software Engineering
Faculty of Mathematics and Physics, Charles University in Prague
Malostranské nám. 25, Prague, Czech Republic
{galgonek,knap,krulis,necasky}@ksi.mff.cuni.cz

Abstract. Even though the semantic web become actual topic of research recently, there are no complex solutions for building semantic
applications yet to our best knowledge. We describe a complex architecture which covers storing, querying, manipulation and visualization
of semantic data in a programmer-friendly way. The architecture is currently being applied in a real-life web portal.

Keywords: semantic, web, RDF, web services, XML.

1 Introduction

In this paper, we briefly describe a framework developed for purposes of a web
portal which will support the community of computer professionals from the
regions of Czech Republic. The portal is a part of *SoSIReCR*[1] project. The main
problem we have solved was that only few user requirements were known at
the design time. These should come during the portal life-time. Therefore, a
flexible approach was taken, so the system could be partially developed by users
themselves. The framework works with an ontology that can be modified by
users and its visualization mechanisms can easily adapt to these modifications.

2 Framework Architecture

Data Model

The model is designed to be adaptable to a constantly changing ontology. Therefore, it treats meta-data as regular data, so users can create new classes or modify
existing ones. Also the presence of meta-data must be optional, so the system
will be able to handle data from domains that are not specified yet.

The data model recognizes two main logical entities: *objects* (real-world objects like *users*) and oriented *links* (relationships between objects). Objects are

---

* This paper was partially supported by the grant SVV-2010-261312 and by Czech
  Science Foundation (GACR), grants no. P202/10/0573 and P202/10/0761.
[1] http://www.sosirecr.cz

R. Meersman et al. (Eds.): OTM 2010 Workshops, LNCS 6428, pp. 53–54, 2010.

instances of `Object` class and links are instances of `Link` class. Both may have flat or structured properties. Users may express their own ontology by creating or modifying subclasses of existing classes. The model supports introspection so the meta-data can be traversed as regular data. Since the data model is closely related to RDF [1], we use an RDF database for data storage.

Service Layer

Although our data storage provides a low level API for accessing the data model, it does not provide a uniform platform–independent way for accessing the data model from various user interfaces, having the scalability and security dimensions in mind. The proposed service layer is implemented on top of *Apache Axis 2* [2], because we were looking for an open source solution (preferably in Java) supporting the latest standards for web services.

For the purpose of the user interface working with the data model, we have designed the set of *database* and *security* web services. The database services encapsulate all the basic operations necessary to retrieve, update, and manage the data model. The security services ensure user authentication.

User Interface

The user interface is also supposed to adapt to the constantly changing ontology. It also has to be universal enough to cover different situations and different ways of application. Therefore, the interface has been designed without reliance on data structure and with declarative approach to data presentations.

The interface implements Model-View-Controller design pattern, where the *model* is built on top of the web services, *view* is realized by XSLT stylesheets and *controllers* are implemented as JavaScript classes. XSLT templates are loosely coupled with classes in data model and they are designed to handle unknown objects, properties, links, etc. Classes that does not have their own template are processed by more generic templates. Therefore, newly created classes can be visualized immediately (not in the best possible way though).

3   Conclusions

We have successfully introduced a new framework which allows programmes easily develop applications for future Web of Data. Our architecture is the first compact attempt to solve this problem to our best knowledge. It covers data storage and manipulation, and it also provides a flexible and programmer-friendly way for their presentation. Even though there are remaining issues to be solved (e.g. network traffic optimizations or system security), the architecture has already proven itself on the SoSIReCR project.

References

1. Manola, F., Miller, E.: RDF Primer, W3C Recommendation (February 2004), http://www.w3.org/TR/2004/REC-rdf-primer-20040210/
2. The Apache Software Foundation: Axis 2, http://ws.apache.org/axis2/

AVYTAT'10 - PC Co-chairs Message

The architectural approach for self-adaptation is one of the most promising lines of current research in the area. This workshop focuses on adaptive systems, supported by open, dynamic architectures, in particular as expressed in the specific case of service ecosystems. In general, it intends to determine the synergies between software architecture and adaptation, and the influence of the underlying structure in self-adaptive properties and attributes. Adaptivity is considered as an architecture-level feature, and therefore it cannot be dissociated from architectural specification.

These are the proceedings for the First International Workshop on Adaptation in Service Ecosystems and Architectures (AVYTAT 2010), held in conjunction with the On The Move Federated Conferences and Workshops (OTM'10), during October 25-29 in Hersonissou, Crete, Greece. This workshop builds on the co-chairs' experience on the topics of software adaptation, dynamic architectures and service-oriented systems, and intends to define the convergence between these strongly related areas.

It was an honor for the workshop to count with a very high-quality Program Committee, composed of world-wide recognized experts in a specialized, and still emergent, research area. Apart from the co-chairs themselves, the committee included four researchers from France, plus four others from the United Kingdom, and six more from Spain, emphasizing the presence of our countries of origin. But it also included researchers from Finland, Australia and the United States, who complemented and enriched our viewpoints with their insightful contributions. These reviewers accepted 50% of the submissions, which ultimately included 60% of those submitted as full papers. We would like to thank the Committee members for their excellent work and invaluable help.

The program of the workshop is structured as a special track session, around the topic "Adaptation in Service-Oriented Architectures". All the papers describe practical works, in which concrete software frameworks are designed -and built- to be able to support adaptation and change. All of them are based on strongly theoretical basis, and their initial experiences are applied to real-world case studies.

The paper by López-Sanz et al. deals with the formalization of the high-level perspective of a model-driven framework for the definition of service-oriented architectures. This results in the translation of their PIM-level models to architectural descriptions in a dynamic ADL, necessary due to the changing nature of service-oriented models. The paper by Cámara et al. describes a generic run-time framework for behavioral adaptation in service systems, based on the description of their protocols. These protocols are described as state machines and supported by common ontologies, such that the behavioral differences between involved elements can be computed and generated as adaptors. This process has been built on top of Jini and AspectJ. Finally, the paper by Pérez-Sotelo et al. describes a complex five-layered generic framework to define service-oriented,

R. Meersman et al. (Eds.): OTM 2010 Workshops, LNCS 6428, pp. 55–56, 2010.

agent-based architectures based on the notions of organization and agreement. In this context, adaptation is provided by self-organizing structures and their emergent behaviors; the paper shows how this process can be driven by pre-defined adaptation patterns, which are included in the framework. In summary, all of them describe promising work, and research which has yet to provide a number of future results.

To conclude, we would like to thank the authors for their submissions, and the OTM chairs and organizers for their support in creating and setting up this workshop.

August 2010

Javier Cámara
Howard Foster
Carlos E. Cuesta
Miguel Ángel
Pérez-Toledano
AVYTAT'10

Formalizing High-Level Service-Oriented Architectural Models Using a Dynamic ADL

Marcos López-Sanz, Carlos E. Cuesta, and Esperanza Marcos

Kybele Research Group
Rey Juan Carlos University
Mostoles – 28933 Madrid, Spain
{marcos.lopez,carlos.cuesta,esperanza.marcos}@urjc.es

Abstract. Despite the well-known advantages of applying the MDA approach, particularly when applied to the development of SOA-based systems, there are still some gaps in the process that need to be filled. Specifically, when modelling the system at the PIM level, we have an architectural description at a high level of abstraction, as it must only comprise technologically independent models. But this architecture cannot be directly validated, as we must transform it into a PSM version before being able to execute it. In order to solve this issue, we propose to formalize the architectural model using Domain Specific Language, an ADL which supports the description of dynamic, adaptive and evolvable architectures, such as SOA itself. Our choice, π-ADL, allows for the definition of executable versions of the architecture; and therefore providing this specification implies having a prototype of the system at the PIM level. This appears as a perfect way of getting an executable yet completely technology neutral version of the architecture. We illustrate this by discussing a real-world case study, in which a service-oriented messaging system is modelled at the PIM level and then specified using its π-ADL counterpart; the result can then be used to validate the architecture at the right abstraction level.

Keywords: Service-Oriented Architecture, Model-Driven Architecture, PIM-level modelling, π-ADL.

1 Introduction

Service orientation has established as leading technological trend due to its advantages for cross-organization integration, adaptability and scalability. As the Service-Oriented Computing (SOC) paradigm [2] is largely considered as the *de facto* solution for emerging information society challenges, many application areas are taking advantage of services. They range from the field of Software Architecture to the definition of software development processes; and, in particular, as a foundation for environments in which dynamism and adaptation are key concerns.

Taking a deeper look at the Software Engineering field we found strategies that benefit from and contribute to the SOC paradigm. The Model-Driven Architecture (MDA) proposal [9], in particular, has been used to develop methods [4] using the principles of SOC and also for the implementation of SOA solutions [3].

R. Meersman et al. (Eds.): OTM 2010 Workshops, LNCS 6428, pp. 57–66, 2010.

However, and despite the well-known advantages of MDA (separation in abstraction levels, definition of automatic transformations between models, model adaptability to multiple domains, etc.), the model-driven approach lacks the ability to define *early* executable versions of the system. Taking into account the separation in CIM, PIM and PSM levels stated by the MDA proposal, it is only at the PSM level when the features of a specific technology are considered. Therefore, it is not possible to get a working prototype until reaching that abstraction level. In this paper we study this problem in the context of SOA-based architectural modelling and within a model-driven methodological framework called MIDAS [2].

The architecture of a software system comprises "*all the components of a system, their relationships to each other and the environment and the principles governing its design and evolution*" [6]. In that sense, the architecture is considered to be a concrete view of the system which corresponds, essentially, with an abstraction of its structure and main behaviour [7].

In previous work we defined the foundations of architectural models supporting all the features of Service-Oriented Architectures (SOA) at the PIM level of abstraction. Considering the role of the architecture in a model-driven framework and the necessity of an early executable version of the system, we have found that using a language from the architectural domain of research might be the best option for overcome those needs. In particular, we have focused π-ADL [10] as a Domain Specific Language (DSL) for the representation of our architectural models.

By providing a correspondence between the concepts gathered in the architectural models at PIM level and their counterparts in a language such as π-ADL, we ensure that, on the one hand, the architectural models are *sound* and, on the other hand, that the architect has at his disposal a toolset for creating a valid executable prototype of the system in early stages of the development process.

The structure of the paper is as follows: Section 2 gives an overview of the basic concepts considered in this paper: π-ADL, MDA and SOA. Section 3 presents a case study used to illustrate the benefits of using π-ADL for describing SOA architectures that represent architectural models at the PIM level of abstraction. Finally, Section 4 discusses the main contributions of this article and some of the future works.

2   Previous Concepts

This article is part of a much broader research effort: the refinement of MIDAS [2], a software development framework based on the MDA principles. The model architecture of this methodology is divided into 3 orthogonal dimensions, describing the abstraction levels (vertical axis), core concerns (horizontal) and crosscutting aspects (transversal); the latter includes the architectural model itself.

The architectural description must cover both PIM (Platform-Independent Model) and PSM (Platform-Specific Model) levels of abstraction, as defined in MDA. As it has been explained in previous work [7], the main reason to make this is that MIDAS follows an ACMDA (*Architecture-Centric Model-Driven Architecture*) approach: it defines a method for the development of information systems based on models and guided by the architecture.

With an architectural view of the system at PIM level, we facilitate the establishment of different PSM-level models according to the specific target platform which are derived from a unique PIM model. However, this has as main drawback the impossibility of having a precise executable version of the system.

2.1 Specification of Service-Oriented Architectural Models

This subsection covers the description of the concepts supporting the architectural modelling and the relationships among them. These concepts are gathered in the metamodel used to define service-oriented architectural models at PIM level in MIDAS. The service metamodel containing the foundations of that model can be seen in Figure 1. Next each of the concepts is briefly explained.

Service Providers
Generally speaking, a SOA is built upon independent entities which provide and manage services. Service providers can be classified into two main groups:

- ✓ **Inner service providers**, which are internal organizations to the system designed. They can be also understood as the part of the software solution whose inner elements are being designed in detail.
- ✓ **Outer service providers,** which are external entities containing services which collaborate with the system to perform a specific task of value for the system but which are not under its control or whose internal structure is not known or valuable for the development of the current architectural model.

The relationship between two service providers appears in the moment that a business need arises and the services involved in its resolution belong to each of them. Because the interconnected elements represent business entities, the relation among them is understood as a '**business contract**'.

Service Description: Identity, Operations and Roles
Our vision of the service concept, at the PIM level, is aligned with that of the OASIS reference model for services [8]. That is, therefore, *the atomic artefact within the architectural modelling that allows the practical support for the system features and business processes identified in higher abstraction layers during the development process.* The main elements that allow the description of a service at the PIM level of abstraction are: the **SERVID**, a **set of operations**, and a **service role**. With these three elements it is enough to clearly model a service within a concrete architectural configuration.

Service Interaction: Contracts and Interaction Patterns
Service interaction is based on the tacit agreement to act in a concrete manner gathered under a contract signed by the participant services.

- ✓ **Service contracts.** Services relate, communicate and interact with each other according to agreed contracts. In the architectural description of the service models, these 'contracts' are understood as connectors, specifying point-to-point relationships between the services that 'sign' those contracts.

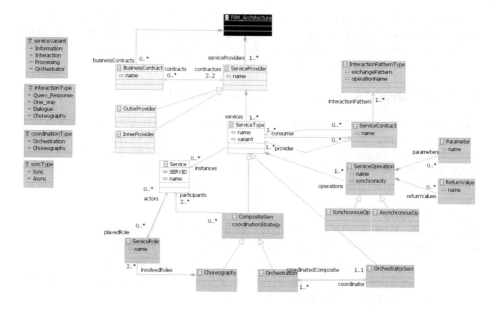

Fig. 1. PIM-level service architectural metamodel

✓ **Interaction Patterns.** These interactions are defined as pairs '*operation name-interaction kind*' establishing a connection between the set of operations available from the provider service and the kind of exchange pattern that will be followed when using that operation. These patterns are reduced to four alternatives. '*One-way*', '*Query/Response*', '*Dialogue*' (in which the concrete protocol can be complex) and '*Choreography*' which will be used in scenarios where several services agree to collaborate to reach a common goal.

Service Composition: Orchestrations and Choreographies

Composition within SOA is accomplished by means of an interactive collaboration among its participants according to a coordination scheme and without constraining the independence of the composed elements. The classification of service composition alternatives is done used to build up the composition:

✓ **Orchestration.** This kind of coordination is founded upon the idea of having a special service in charge of directing the whole compound element. This special service (*OrchestratorServ* in the metamodel) knows the flow of service consumptions that must be done to accomplish the functionality desired.

✓ **Choreography.** This kind of composition represents an interacting environment among equivalent services. This "equivalence" means that there is no service mastering over any other or directing the flow of information.

2.2 π-ADL at a Glance

π-ADL [10] is a language designed for defining software architectures and is formally founded on the higher-order typed π-calculus. π-ADL.NET is a compiler tool for π-ADL, and was predominantly used to validate the case study presented in section 3.

In a π-ADL program, the top level constructs are *behaviours* and *abstractions*. Each behaviour definition results in a separate execution entry point, meaning that the program will have as many top level concurrent threads of execution as the number of behaviours it defines. Abstractions are reusable behaviour templates and their functionality can be invoked from behaviours as well as other abstractions.

The body of a behaviour (or an abstraction) can contain *variable* and *connection* declarations. Connections provide functionality analogous to channels in π-calculus: code in different parts of behaviours or abstractions can communicate synchronously via connections. Connections are typed, and can send and receive any of the existing variable types, as well as connections themselves. Sending a value via a connection is called an output-prefix, and receiving via a connection is called an input prefix.

The *compose* keyword serves the purpose of creating two or more parallel threads of execution within a program and corresponds to the concurrency construct in π-calculus. Another important π-ADL construct is the *choose* block. Only one of the sub-blocks inside a choose block is executed when execution passes into it. Finally, to provide the equivalent of the π-calculus replicate construct, π-ADL provides the *replicate* keyword.

3   Case Study

The selected case study emulates the functionality of a SMPP (Short Message Peer-to-Peer Protocol) [12] gateway system by means of services. SMPP is a telecommunications industry protocol for exchanging SMS messages between SMS peer entities. We focus on the following building blocks and functionalities:

- *Reception Subsystem*: its main purpose is to receive sending SMS requests directly from the user. It contains a single service (*ReceptionService*) offering several useful operations for the user to send SMS texts.
- *Storage Subsystem*: this subsystem stores information related to clients and SMS messages. It comprises two services:
  - *SecureDataService*: performs operations requiring a secure connection.
  - *SMSManagerService*: in charge of managing all the information related to SMS messages (such as status, SMS text) and creating listings and reports.
- *SMS Processing Subsystem*: this subsystem is in charge of retrieving, processing and sending the SMS texts and related information to the specialized SMS server.
  - *SMSSenderService*: Retrieves SMS texts from the Storage Subsystem and sends them to Short Message Service Centres (SMSC).
    DirectoryService: The main task performed by this service is to return the service identifier of the *SMSCenterService* which has to be used to send a SMS to a specific recipient.
- *SMSC (Short Message Service Centre):* this entity represents specialized SMS servers capable to send the SMS texts to a number of recipients. Its functionality is enacted by one service (*SMSCenterService*).

Next, we present a partial formalization of the architectural model with π-ADL, emphasizing the aspects of that provide an adequate solution for our system as well as explaining how the structures and principles of π-ADL are adapted to our vision of PIM-level service architecture:

Representation of a service and its operations. Services represent computing entities performing a specific behaviour within the system architecture and thus they are specified by means of π-ADL abstractions (see Listing 3.1 for the architectural specification of the *ReceptionService*).

Every service abstraction defines its own communication channels through input and output connections. The data acquired and sent by these connections comprises a description of the operation and the data associated to that message. Depending on the operation requested, the service abstraction will transfer the control of the execution to the corresponding operation. The only behaviour associated with the service abstraction is, therefore, that of redirecting the functionality request to the corresponding operation and sending back returning values if any.

Operations, in turn, are also specified by means of abstractions as they encapsulate part of the functionality offered by services. Like any other abstraction used in the description of the service architecture, operation abstractions will receive the information tokens through connections, sending back an answer when applicable.

```
value ReceptionService is abstraction () {
// omitted variable definition
if (input::operation == "sendSMS") do {
  via SendSMS send input::data where {resultConn renames resultConn};
  via resultConn receive result;
  compose { via outConn send result; and  done;     }   }}
```
Listing 3.1. Specification of the *ReceptionService*

In π-ADL communication through the connections is performed synchronously. This means that communication with operations is synchronous. Therefore, the semantics associated with the asynchronous operations are lost since the abstraction will be blocked in a send operation until any other abstraction in the architecture perform a receive operation over that channel. In order to model asynchronous operations, the specification can be placed in one of the sub-blocks of a compose block, with the second sub-block returning immediately with the done keyword.

Representation of contracts. As stated previously, services relate and communicate through contracts. Within the architecture these contracts are active connectors in charge of enabling the message exchange between services according to a specific pattern, represented by means of the programmatic specification of a state machine. Similarly, connectors in π-ADL are represented by means of abstractions.

In a static service environment, in which contracts between services are established at design time, all the information needed by a contract to correctly fulfil its behaviour (message exchange pattern and contractors) is defined and initialized internally within the contract abstraction when the system starts. In dynamic environments however, this is normally accomplished by transferring all the information through the channel opened simultaneously when the abstraction is executed. In both cases, the contract is able to perform the behaviour needed to transfer data requests and results from one service to another from that information.

Listing 3.2 depicts part of the analysis of a state of the message pattern execution. In it, it is shown how, in order to send anything to one of the services connected through the shipping contract, a compose structure should be used: first to send the data through the connection and second to execute the abstraction and unify the connections.

When executing the specification of a service architecture with π-ADL any behaviour defined is carried out as an independent thread of execution. However, in order to be able to perform a coordinated and joint execution, the different abstractions must be linked. Because of the dynamic nature of the service architectures, contract abstractions can be reused as the instances of the services they communicate can vary during the lifecycle of the system. In order to achieve this behaviour, contracts (or more appropriately abstractions performing the contract role) must be able to dynamically instantiate the channel that they have to use to send or receive the data transferred in each moment. To deal with this issue π-ADL defines the dynamic(<connection_name>) operator. This operator represents one of the main advantages for dynamic architecture specification since π-ADL allows the transference of connections through connections.

```
...
if (state::via_SERVID == "S") do{
  compose {
    via outConnectionS send inData;
  and
    via dynamic(input::ServConnGroup(0)::SERVID) send Void
    where {outConnectionS renames inConn,inConnectionS renames outConn};
  }}else do{   via outConnectionC send inData; }
...
```

Listing 3.2. Fragment extracted from the *Shipping* contract

Representation of dynamism. In our case study, In order to send the SMS messages stored on the database, it is necessary to know which specific service should be used. To achieve that behaviour it is essential to be aware of the existence of a specialized service attending to requests from services asking for other services to perform tasks with specific requirements. This represents a dynamic environment since it is necessary to create a communication channel that did not exist at design time but is discovered when the system is in execution (i.e. when the *SMSManagerService* must send the SMS texts to a concrete *SMSCenterService*).

In a service-oriented environment the dynamicity may occur in several scenarios: when it is necessary to create a new contract between services or when the new element to add is another service. In those cases it is mandatory to have a special service in charge of performing the usual operations that occur in dynamic environments, i.e. *link*, *unlink*, *create* and *destroy* of contract abstractions. This service will be the *DirectoryService* that appears in Figure 2.

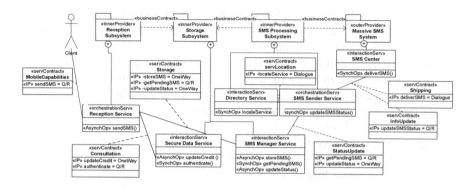

Fig. 2. Architectural model of the SMPP case study

```
value locateService is abstraction (
locationConn:view[inConn:Connection[view[operation:String,data:any]],
input : view[operation : String, data : any],
connSMSCenter: Connection[view[operation : String, data : any]]]){
        requestData = locationConn::input::data;
compose      {
// full description of the message exchange pattern omitted
// prepare and create connector: Shipping
            via Shipping send contractStartInfo;
    and
            clientDataResponse::contractConn = shContractClientConn;
// info about the service operations and semantics of the service
            clientDataResponse::servMetaInfo = "";
            clientResponse::data = clientDataResponse;
            clientResponse::operation = "locateService";
            via locationConn::inConn send clientResponse;
    and     done;             }}
```

Listing 3.3. Specification of the *locateService* operation

Representation of service composition. Coordination among services can be achieved by defining choreographies or orchestrations. Choreographies can be formalized with π-ADL by means of shared connections. Orchestrations, in turn, depend mostly on the code specified inside a unique abstraction belonging to a service playing the role of coordinator of the composition.

In our case study a service taking the orchestrator role is the SMS Sender Service which coordinates the access to the storage subsystem (using the SMS Manager service), the retrieval of the information of the concrete *SMSCenterService* to be used to send the SMS texts by invoking the Directory Service and finally the *SMSCenterService* to complete the desired functionality.

4   Conclusions and Future Works

MDA is one of the current leading trends in the definition of software development methodologies. Its basis lies in the definition of model sets divided in several abstraction levels together with model transformation rules. Observing the principles of the SOC paradigm and its inherent features for system integration and interoperability it is possible to accept MDA as a suitable approach for the development of SOA solutions.

While defining model-driven development frameworks, and MDA-based in particular, the architecture has been demonstrated to be the ideal source of guidance of the development process since it reflects the structure of the systems embedded in its components, the relations among them and their evolution during the lifecycle of the software being developed. In the case of MIDAS, we have defined UML metamodels for the PIM-level view of the architecture.

In this work, and in order to solve the initial lack of early prototypes in MDA-based developments, we have proposed to give a formal definition of the system architecture by means of an ADL. Specifically we have chosen π-ADL because of its support for representing dynamic and evolvable architectures as well as the largely faithful compiler tool available for this language. Moreover, by using a formal representation of the system we can use mathematical formalisms to validate the UML models created for each of the abstraction levels defined within MIDAS.

There are many research lines that arise from the work presented in this paper. One research direction is, given the already defined UML notation and metamodel for the π-ADL language, the definition of transformation rules between the UML metamodel of the architecture at PIM-level and that of the π-ADL language. More research lines include the refinement of the language support for specific SOA aspects such as the definition of choreographies, dynamic and evolvable environments requiring the representation of new types of components and connectors within the system architecture, etc.

Acknowledgements

This research is partially granted by projects MODEL-CAOS (TIN2008-03582) and AT (Agreement Technologies) (CONSOLIDER CSD2007-0022), from the Spanish Ministry of Science and Technology, and by COST AT (COST Action IC0801) from European Union RTD Framework Programme.

References

[1] Broy, M.: Model Driven, Architecture-Centric Modeling in Software Development. In: Proceedings of 9th Intl. Conf. in Engineering Complex Computer Systems (ICECCS 2004), pp. 3–12. IEEE Computer Society, Los Alamitos (April 2004)
[2] Cáceres, P., Marcos, E., Vela, B.: A MDA-Based Approach for Web Information System Development. In: Workshop in Software Model Engineering (2003),
http://www.metamodel.com/wisme-2003/ (retrieved March 2007)
[3] De Castro, V., López-Sanz, M., Marcos, E.: Business Process Development based on Web Services: A Web Information System for Medical Images Management and Processing. In: Leymann, F., Zhang, L.J. (eds.) Proceedings of IEEE International Conference on Web Services, pp. 807–814. IEEE Computer Society, Los Alamitos (2006)
[4] De Castro, V., Marcos, E., López-Sanz, M.: A Model Driven Method for Service Composition Modeling: A Case Study. International Journal of Web Engineering and Technology 2(4), 335–353 (2006)

[5] Gomaa, H.: Architecture-Centric Evolution in Software Product Lines. In: ECOOP'2005 Workshop on Architecture-Centric Evolution (ACE 2005), Glasgow (July 2005)

[6] IEEE AWG. IEEE RP-1471-2000: Recommended Practice for Architectural Description for Software-Intensive Systems. IEEE Computer Society Press (2000)

[7] López-Sanz, M., Acuña, C., Cuesta, C.E., Marcos, E.: Defining Service-Oriented Software Architecture Models for a MDA-based Development Process at the PIM level. In: Proceedings of WICSA 2008, Vancouver, Canada, pp. 309–312 (2008)

[8] Marcos, E., Acuña, C.J., Cuesta, C.E.: Integrating Software Architecture into a MDA Framework. In: Gruhn, V., Oquendo, F. (eds.) EWSA 2006. LNCS, vol. 4344, pp. 127–143. Springer, Heidelberg (2006)

[9] OASIS: Reference Model for Service Oriented Architecture (2006), Committee draft 1.0. from
http://www.oasis-open.org/committees/download.php/16587/
wd-soa-rm-cd1ED.pdf (retrieved Febuary 2007)

[10] OMG: Model Driven Architecture. In: Miller, J., Mukerji, J. (eds.) Document No. ormsc/2001-07-01 , http://www.omg.com/mda (retrieved May 2006)

[11] Oquendo, F.: π-ADL: An Architecture Description Language based on the Higher Order Typed π-Calculus for Specifying Dynamic and Mobile Software Architectures. ACM Software Engineering Notes (3) (May 2004)

[12] Papazoglou, M.P.: Service-Oriented Computing: Concepts,Characteristics and Directions. In: Proc. of the Fourth International Conference on Web Information Systems Engineering (WISE 2003), Roma, Italy, December 10-12, pp. 3–12 (2003)

[13] SMPP Forum: SMPP v5.0 Specification, http://www.smsforum.net/ (retrieved September 2007)

A Framework for Run-Time Behavioural Service Adaptation in Ubiquitous Computing

Javier Cámara[1], Carlos Canal[2], and Nikolay Vasilev[2]

[1] INRIA Rhône-Alpes, France
Javier.Camara-Moreno@inria.fr
[2] Department of Computer Science, University of Málaga, Spain
canal@lcc.uma.es, nikolay.vasilev@gmail.com

Abstract. In Ubiquitous Computing, users interact with multiple small networked computing devices on a daily basis, accessing services present within their physical environment. In particular, the need to discover and correctly access those services as users move from one location to another and the conditions of the environment change, is a crucial requirement in the design and implementation of such systems. This work addresses the discovery and adaptation of services with potentially mismatching interfaces in ubiquitous computing environments, where applications are directly subject to the availability of services which may be discovered or depart from the system's environment at any given moment. In particular, we discuss the design of a framework to enable scalable adaptation capabilities.

1 Introduction

Since the appearance of modern computers, we have shifted from what Mark Weiser once defined as the *Mainframe Age* in which a single computer was shared by many people, to the *Ubiquitous Computing Age* [12], in which a single person commonly interacts with many small networked computing devices, accessing services present within the physical environment. In particular, the need to discover and correctly access those services as the conditions of the environment change, is a crucial requirement in the design and implementation of such systems.

Services are independently developed by different service providers as reusable black boxes whose functionality is accessed through public interfaces. The heterogeneity of service implementations, which are not designed to interoperate with each other in most situations, commonly results in the appearance of mismatch among their public interfaces when they are composed. Specifically, we can distinguish four interoperability levels in existing Interface Description Languages (IDLs): *(i) Signature*. At this level, IDLs (*e.g.,* Java interfaces, WSDL descriptions) provide operation names, type of arguments and return values. Signature interoperability problems are related to different operation names or parameter types between provided and required operations on the different interfaces; *(ii) Protocol* or *behaviour*. Specifies the order in which the operations available on an interface should be invoked. If such orders are incompatible among services, this may lead situations such as *deadlocks* or infinite loops. Notorious examples of behavioural interface descriptions include Abstract BPEL, automata-based

R. Meersman et al. (Eds.): OTM 2010 Workshops, LNCS 6428, pp. 67–76, 2010.

languages such as UML state diagrams, or high-level MSCs; *(iii) Functional* or *Semantic*. Even if service interfaces match at the other levels, we must ensure that they are going to fulfill their expected behaviour. This level of description provides semantic information about services using ontology-based notations such as OWL-S (used in Web Services), which are interesting for service mining; and *(iv) Service*. Description of other non-functional properties like temporal requirements, security, etc.

Software Adaptation [4,13] is the only way to compose services with mismatching interfaces in a non-intrusively manner by automatically generating mediating *adaptor* services able to solve interoperability problems between them at all levels. Particularly, in this work we focus on the protocol or behavioural level, currently acknowledged as one of the most relevant research directions in software adaptation [4,2,10,13]. Most approaches in behavioural software adaptation build adaptors for the whole system at design-time, a costly process that relies on the specific set of services involved in the system. Hence, these techniques (often referred to as static approaches) are not suited for ubicomp environments, since the adaptor would have to be recomputed each time a new service is discovered or departs from the current system configuration. On the contrary, in some recent developments [11,5,7] a composition engine enacts adaptation at run-time. In particular, Cámara et al. [3] addressed run-time adaptation in the specific context of ubicomp environments. However, although this approach lays out the formal foundations of adaptation in such environments, the reference architecture used by the authors (and in general by all the aforementioned run-time approaches) does not consider scalability issues, and includes a single central adaptation unit which performs all the adaptation between all services in the system, something that turns this central node into a performance bottleneck.

Here, we extend the work in [3], providing architectural support for service adaptation in ubicomp environments, where applications are directly subject to the availability of services which may be discovered or depart from the system's environment anytime. In particular, we discuss the design of a framework to enable scalable adaptation capabilities and support of service discovery which considers behavioural information about the services available in the environment.

To illustrate our approach, we will use a running example described in the context of an airport: let us suppose a traveller who walks into an airport with a PDA or a smartphone equipped with a client containing a client application based on the different services which may be accessed through a local wireless network at the airport. First, the user needs to contact his airline and check-in in order to obtain a seat on the flight. This is achieved by approaching a kiosk which provides a local check-in service available to the handheld device. Next, the traveller may browse the duty-free shops located at the airport. The selected shop should be able to access the airport information system in order to check if a passenger has checked-in on a particular flight, and apply a tax exemption on the sale in that case. The payment is completed by means of credit card information stored in the traveller's device.

In the rest of this paper, Section 2 presents our service model and the run-time adaptation process in ubicomp environments. Next, Section 3 discusses the design and implementation of our framework. Finally, Section 4 compares our approach with the related work in the field, and Section 5 concludes.

2   Behavioural Adaptation in Ubiquitous Computing

In this work we use a service interface model [3] which includes both a signature, and a behavioural interface. In order to enable composition with services which are discovered at run-time, we extend the behavioural interfaces with additional information. In particular, our behavioural interface consists of: **(i)** a protocol description (STS); and **(ii)** a set of correspondences between abstract and concrete service operations.

Definition 1 (STS). *An STS is a tuple* (A, S, I, B, T) *where: A is an alphabet that corresponds to message events relative to the service's provided and required operations, S is a set of states, $I \in S$ is the initial state, $B \in S$ are stable states in which the service can be removed from the current system configuration if it is not engaged in any open transactions and, and $T \subseteq S \times A \times S$ is a transition relation.*

Generic Correspondences. Adaptor generation approaches commonly rely on interface mappings that express correspondences between operations names, as well as parameter types and ordering on the different interfaces. However, these mappings can be produced only once the description of the different interfaces is known. In ubicomp environments, this information is only available when services are discovered at run-time. Specifically, when we are describing the protocol of a service to be reused in such systems, we know what the required operations are, but we do not know which specific service implementation is going to provide them, or even the specific name of the concrete operation implementing the required functionality.

Approaches to run-time service discovery use *service ontologies* that describe the properties and capabilities of services in unambiguous, computer-interpretable form. Here, we assume that services available in the environment are exposed using such descriptions, which will be used as a reference to relate service interfaces. For simplicity, instead of using any of the emerging standards for the semantic description of services, we will use in the remainder a notation which abstracts away specific notations for service descriptions such as OWL-S [6].

Definition 2 (Abstract Operation Signature). *An* abstract operation signature *is the name of a generic operation, together with its arguments and return types defined within the context of a service ontology.*

Definition 3 (Abstract Role). *We define an* abstract role *as a set of abstract operation signatures associated with a common task or goal.*

Our model of interface makes explicit correspondences of how labels in the protocol description (STS) are related with generic operations described by the service ontology. To do so, we also rely on vectors (based on synchronous vectors [1]). However, in this application domain, we have to make a distinction between the generic correspondences established in vectors, and what we call *vector instances*, which relate actual service interface operations.

Definition 4 (Vector). *A vector for a service STS (A, S, I, B, T) and an abstract role, is a couple $\langle e_l, e_r \rangle$ where e_l is a label term for A, and e_r is an abstract label term for* *an abstract role. A label term t contains the name of the operation, a direction(?/!), and as many untyped fresh names as elements in the argument type list (placeholders). An* abstract label term *is defined in the context of an abstract role, instead of a service interface.*

Definition 5 (Vector Instance). *A vector instance for a pair of service STSs* $(A_l, S_l, I_l, B_l, T_l)$ *and* $(A_r, S_r, I_r, B_r, T_r)$ *is a couple* $\langle e_l, e_r \rangle$ *where* e_l, e_r *are label terms in* A_l *and* A_r, *respectively.*

Vector instances are obtained from vectors by binding concrete service interface operations at run-time. Specifically, for each vector v, we extract all the other vectors on the counterpart interfaces including abstract label terms corresponding to the same abstract operation signatures.

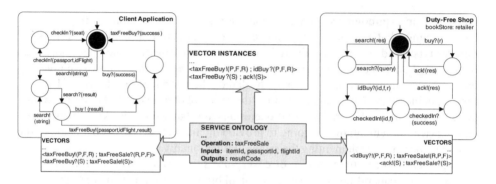

Fig. 1. Protocol STS and vector instantiation example for the client and the store

Fig. 1 depicts an example of vector instantiation between the client and the online store in our case study: concrete interface operations taxFreeBuy and idBuy are related through the taxFreeSale abstract operation in the service ontology. Placeholders P,F, and R are used to relate sent and received arguments between the operations.

Once we have described interfaces and processed vector instantiation, we have to compute the reachability analysis of stable states being given a set of service protocols, and a set of instantiated vectors. A stable state of the system is one, where each of the services in the system is on a stable state. It is only at this point that services can be incorporated or removed, and the system properly reconfigured. To perform this adaptability analysis we use a depth-first search algorithm which seeks stable system states, and stops as soon as a final state for the whole system has been found. If the analysis determines that global stability can be reached, then the execution of the system can be launched (Fig. 2).

3   Framework Architecture

Although the service composition process presented in last section enables interoperability between services with potentially mismatching interfaces at run-time, this

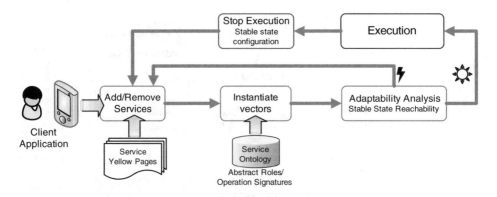

Fig. 2. Overview of the adapted service composition process

process also requires support from an architectural point of view in order to put this approach into practice. Specifically, we can identify two important problems that need to be addressed in order to allow scalable adapted service interaction in ubiquitous computing environments:

- Adaptation. We have to rule out design choices which consider a single central adaptation unit performing all the adaptation between all services in the system. This can quickly turn into a performance bottleneck.
- Service Discovery. Our framework must facilitate the discovery of candidate service implementations for client applications. The discovery mechanism must take into account behavioural descriptions of services. Moreover, we cannot load a single service registry with the task of checking if a service is adaptable for the purposes of a client application at the behavioural level.

In order to provide support for the adaptation process described in the previous section, we have designed a framework that tackles the aforementioned problems. Fig. 3 depicts the architecture of our framework, where we can distinguish the following components:

Client Applications and Service Providers. Both clients and services expose their functionality public interfaces (*Behavioural Interface Descriptions* or BIDs) which describe provided and required operations, as well as a description of their protocol (STS), which are necessary for behavioural adaptation. In the case of service providers, BIDs are accompanied by a thin *proxy component* that is imported to the client side and is used for communication with the service's implementation. A service BID, along with its corresponding proxy is known in our framework as a *service entry*. These entries are used by clients to discover suitable service implementations. Further details about their use can be found in Section 3.1.

Adaptation Manager. In our framework, the adaptation process is performed always at the client's side by a component called *adaptation manager*, which stays in between the client application and the rest of the elements in the environment. This manager consists of two main components: **(i)** the *adaptation engine* in charge of handling all

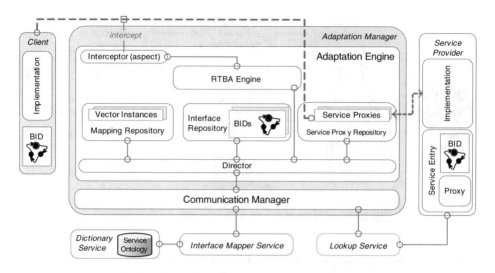

Fig. 3. Framework architecture

adaptation-related tasks. The main subcomponent of the adaptation engine is the *run-time behavioural adaptation engine* (RTBAE for short) where the global stability check and the adaptation algorithms are implemented. In the process of the adaptation other subcomponent - the *interceptor*, implemented as an aspect, is used to notify the RT-BAE when an operation is invoked on the client application or on the *service proxy*. To perform adaptation, the RTBAE needs the client and service BIDs and also appropriate vector instances. The vector instances, along with the BIDs and all service proxies are stored in dedicated components of the adaptation engine, the *mapping*, *interface* and *service proxy repositories*. Finally, the *director* subcomponent is a mediator that is in charge of coordinating all operations within the adaptation engine; and (ii) the communication manager, which is responsible for providing the adaptation manager with all the elements required to perform the adaptation, communicating with the lookup and interface mapper services.

Network Services. The framework also includes a set of network services that enable service discovery and matching: (i) the *Lookup service* performs service matching over the set of service implementations registered in it, determining the set of service entries that match the request criteria of the client. To do this, it uses the client's BID provided by the client's communication manager, and the BID in the service entry of each candidate service, (ii) the *interface mapper service* produces vector instances for the adaptation process using one or more (iii) *dictionary services*, which contain a representation of the valid abstract service types and operations which may be exposed in the environment.

3.1   Framework Component Interaction

Initially, after the lookup service starts up, the dictionary and interface mapper services start up and register with the lookup service (Fig. 4). Afterwards, when the service

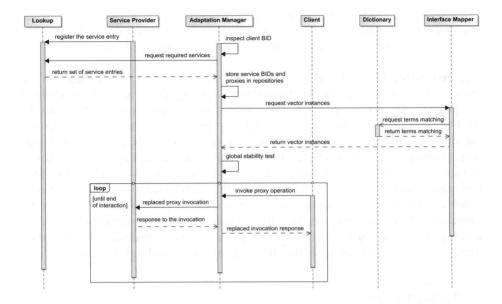

Fig. 4. Dynamics of the process followed for service discovery and adaptation

providers appear in the network, they register with the lookup service sending their service entries.

Service Discovery. When a client enters the network, its associated director stores its BID in the interface repository. The communication manager then queries the lookup service for available service implementations in the network that could provide operations required by the client. This query includes the information in the client's BID. As a result, a list of service entries is sent to the client's communication manager. The list contains only one service for each type required by the client. The director stores for each received service its BID and proxy into their respective repositories. Then, the communication manager bundles the BIDs of the client and the services obtained in the previous matching, and sends them to the interface mapper, which returns the set of vector instances needed for the adaptation. Finally, the director stores them in the mapping repository.

The director extracts the client and required services BIDs from the interface repository and supplies them to the RTBAE, which uses them to execute the global stability analysis in order to ensure that during execution, the system is not going to end up in a deadlock state. If the result from this check is positive, the real adaptation process starts. Otherwise, the RTBAE starts to discard proxies. In the latter case, the director first removes each discarded proxy and BID from their respective repositories, followed by the related vector instances from the mappings repository. Then the communication manager tries to find a replacement service from the discarded type of service. The discarded service entry will not be accepted by the communication manager if the lookup service sends it back again, unless the set of services in the different repositories has changed since the time of the last service entry request. When a replacement service implementation is found, the process starts all over again. When the global stability check succeeds, the framework proceeds with the actual adaptation process.

Adapted Interaction. The adaptation process in our framework implements an extended version of the algorithm presented in [2]. During this process, the interceptor component intercepts all operation invocations in the service proxies and notifies the RTBAE about the invoked operation. The RTBA engine replaces the invocation according to the indications of the RTBAE, which in turn determines the invocation substitutions to apply according to the adaptation algorithm and the message correspondences encoded in vector instances stored into the interface mapping repository. Once the system reaches stable state, the director removes the proxies, BIDs and vector instances which are not needed anymore from the corresponding repositories. If from the current stable state, the client application has all the required service proxies and BIDs to continue operating, the adaptation process starts all over again. Otherwise, the adaptation manager keeps on performing service discovery until this condition is fulfilled.

4   Related Work

So far, there are few proposals in the literature where a composition engine enacts behavioural adaptation at run-time, not requiring the explicit generation of an adaptor protocol description at design-time. Dumas et al. [11] introduce a service mediation engine which interprets an interface mapping obtained at design-time. Internally, this engine relies on an abstract representation of behavioural interfaces as FSMs. The engine manipulates the exchanged messages according to the interface mapping provided (expressed as a set of production rules). It is worth observing that a deadlock is only detected once the current execution of the engine terminates. Hence, deadlocks are only considered as a termination anomaly, but cannot be prevented.

Cavallaro and di Nitto [5] propose an approach to allow the invocation of services at run-time with mismatches at the signature and protocol levels. The authors consider that the user is going to specify the task to be carried out by implementing a service composition with respect to a set of abstract service interfaces, instead of real service implementations, which will only be known at run-time. Their approach includes a framework for service composition which takes a BPEL process specified with respect to a set of abstract services as input. When an abstract service is invoked by the process, the call is forwarded to a proxy for that abstract service, which subsequently forwards the call to the concrete implementation of the service selected at run-time. The actual adaptor is inserted in the communication between the proxy and the concrete service implementation. However, the authors propose to map states and transitions between abstract and concrete service protocols, assuming that protocols have equivalent states and transitions. This is a strong assumption that reduces drastically the number of cases where adaptation can be performed. Indeed, no means are provided to systematically deal with deadlocks in the resulting adaptors.

Moser et al. [7] present a system that allows the monitoring of BPEL processes according to Quality of Service (QoS) attributes, as well as the replacement of partner services involved in the process at run-time. The alternative service replacements can either be *syntactically* or *semantically* equivalent to the original. To enable interoperability, this approach addresses adaptation through the use of special components named *transformers*. These are mediators that compensate interface mismatches between the original service and its replacement by applying transformation rules to incoming and outgoing messages. Both monitoring and adaptation facilities are implemented using AOP. Although this approach enables substitution of services at run-time with a certain degree of adaptation, important behavioural aspects of services are not addressed (e.g., guaranteeing deadlock freedom when services are integrated into the BPEL process).

Finally, Cámara et al. [3] contribute an interface model which relates abstract service types with concrete implementations and an extended version of a run-time adaptation engine that enables behavioural service adaptation at run-time. In this case, behavioural interface descriptions are used to perform adaptability check of the services before they start their (adapted) interaction, ruling out undesired behaviours such as deadlocks or livelocks. Unfortunately, there is no architectural support provided for their approach. Specifically, although the authors mention the possibility of distributing the adaptation process, this point is not addressed and they assume a single centralized adaptation unit which performs all the adaptation of service interactions.

5   Conclusions and Future Work

In this work, we have presented a proposal to support run-time behavioural adaptation in ubiquitous computing environments. In particular, we have discussed the design of a framework that enables run-time service discovery, taking into account behavioural service interface information and transparent adaptation of service interactions. Moreover, we have implemented a prototype of our framework, extending the Java Jini service platform using Aspect-Oriented Programming (AspectJ).

With respect to future work, in the current version of our framework only one service instance of each required type is returned by the dispatcher to the client. This is intended to reduce network traffic, but if the reachability check in the client virtual machine fails, the process of retrieving services would need to restart, consuming too much time and client resources, and potentially causing heavy network traffic. Hence, we think that optimizing the interaction protocol between the client and the dispatcher, as well as the service matching mechanisms is an interesting direction that could represent a noticeable improvement of the framework's performance. Moreover, right now if a service disappears in a non-stable state, the current transaction has to be aborted. In relation with this problem, we aim at enabling reconfiguration, using execution trace equivalence checking in order to replace departing services in the middle of a running transaction.

References

1. Arnold, A.: Finite transition systems: semantics of communicating systems. Prentice Hall International (UK) Ltd., Englewood Cliffs (1994)
2. Cámara, J., Canal, C., Salaün, G.: Composition and run-time adaptation of mismatching behavioural interfaces. Journal of Universal Computer Science 14, 2182–2211 (2008)

3. Cámara, J., Canal, C., Salaün, G.: Behavioural self-adaptation of services in ubiquitous computing environments. In: International Workshop on Software Engineering for Adaptive and Self-Managing Systems, pp. 28–37 (2009)
4. Canal, C., Murillo, J.M., Poizat, P.: Software adaptation. L'Objet 12(1), 9–31 (2006)
5. Cavallaro, L., Nitto, E.D.: An approach to adapt service requests to actual service interfaces. In: Proceedings of Software Engineering for Adaptive and Self-Managing Systems (SEAMS 2008), pp. 129–136. ACM, New York (2008)
6. Coalition, T.O.S.: OWL-S: Semantic markup for web services (2004),
   http://www.daml.org/services
7. Moser, O., Rosenberg, F., Dustdar, S.: Non-intrusive monitoring and service adaptation for WS-BPEL. In: Huai, J., Chen, R., Hon, H., Liu, Y., Ma, W., Tomkins, A., Zhang, X. (eds.) Proceedings of the 17th International Conference on World Wide Web (WWW 2008), pp. 815–824. ACM, New York (2008)
8. Newmarch, J.: Foundations of Jini TM 2 Programming. Apress, Inc., New York (2006)
9. Papazoglou, M.: Service-oriented computing: Concepts, characteristics and directions. In: Fourth International Conference on Web Information Systems Engineering, WISE 2003 (2003)
10. Wang, K., Dumas, M., Ouyang, C., Vayssière, J.: The service adaptation machine. In: ECOWS, pp. 145–154. IEEE Computer Society, Los Alamitos (2008)
11. Wang, K., Dumas, M., Ouyang, C., Vayssiere, J.: The service adaptation machine. In: Proceedings of the 6th IEEE European Conference on Web Services (ECOWS 2008), pp. 145–154. IEEE Computer Society, Los Alamitos (2008)
12. Weiser, M.: Hot topics: Ubiquitous computing. IEEE Computer (1993)
13. Yellin, D.M., Strom, R.E.: Protocol specifications and component adaptors. ACM Trans. Program. Lang. Syst. 19(2), 292–333 (1997)

Towards Adaptive Service Ecosystems with Agreement Technologies

J. Santiago Pérez-Sotelo[1], Carlos E. Cuesta[2], and Sascha Ossowski[1]

[1] Centre for Intelligent Information Technologies (CETINIA)
[2] Kybele Research Group, Dept. Comp. Languages and Systems II
Rey Juan Carlos University
28933 Móstoles (Madrid), Spain
{josesantiago.perez,carlos.cuesta,sascha.ossowski}@urjc.es

Abstract. The growing complexity of software is emphasizing the need for systems that have autonomy, robustness and adaptability among their most important features. Hence, their development and maintenance strategies must be redesigned. Humans should be relieved from an important part of these tasks, which should be performed by systems themselves; self-adaptation can be therefore considered as an architecture-level concern. Service-oriented architectures, and in particular service ecosystems as their more dynamic variant, show a higher degree of adaptivity and flexibility than many other alternatives. In this context, Agreement Technologies (AT) appears as a service-oriented, architecture-aware evolutions of Multi-Agent Systems, which themselves are self-aware structures conceived to solve generic problems. However, they still do not provide mechanisms to change their composition patterns and element types, which are necessary to achieve real self-adaptivity. This work proposes an architectural solution for it: the required dynamism will be supported by an emergent agreement - an evolving architectural structure based on combining predefined controls and protocols. These are handled in the context of the service-oriented, agent-based and organization-centric framework defined by AT, and implemented within the THOMAS platform. This work provides the first architectural abstractions to support this emergent structure. A real-world example showing the interest of this approach is also provided, and some conclusions about its applicability are finally outlined.

Keywords: Self-Adaptation, Adaptive Architecture, Multi-Agent Systems, Agreement Technologies, Service Ecosystem.

1 Introduction

It is well known that in recent years the software systems have grown in complexity. This level of complexity, which may be called "social" according to [8], is leading software designers to rethink the strategy for handling it. Many routine tasks previously deferred to human users are now being handled by systems themselves, including many actions related to the system's own functions. Complex systems are now able to observe themselves, and to adapt its structure and behaviour as necessary.

R. Meersman et al. (Eds.): OTM 2010 Workshops, LNCS 6428, pp. 77–87, 2010.

Therefore, this approach [13] has a global influence on the system, at many levels, leading us to consider self-adaptation as a basic architectural concern [14].

Simultaneously, Multi-Agent Systems (MAS) have been developed as a generic approach in Artificial Intelligence (AI) to solve complex problems. They describe self-aware structures, with learning capacity and conceived to be flexible and to be able to adapt to different situations. Some advanced approaches use the concept of *organizations* to provide further structuring, taking the form of complex agent architectures. However, existing structures still have limitations in order to reach actual self-adaptivity, i.e. having not only the capability to affect their settings, but also their own composition and types.

The proposed approach intends to go beyond more "classic" agent technologies and propose a solution based in service ecosystem with Agreement Technologies (AT) [1][18] to deal with the dynamism. The services are not offered directly through the agents, but through the organizations. The objective is to provide adaptive organizations, and the emphasis is in the coordination mechanism which is also adaptive, independently of how the agents export their services.

The research referred to in this paper can be summarized as the pursuit of three goals: first, the definition of a general platform to identify the underlying *agent-based, service-oriented* and *organization-centric architecture*, leading to the essential platform for AT; second, the introduction of further structure, to make it *adaptive*; and third, the identification of the generic adaptive structure for organizations, in the form of the *agreement* construct, and its evolution. The purpose is to define a generic problem-solving *intelligent* technology, capable of being used in an *open* context, and able to *adapt* to future evolution, supported by a self-organized architecture.

The rest of this paper is structured as follows: in Section 2 a motivating example is presented to illustrate main ideas and the proposed approach, which is defined as service-oriented, organization-centric and agent-based. The following section describes the architecture that provides support to this work - the THOMAS framework [3], which now includes developments at the service level, adapting it to the OSGi [17] platform. The actual framework presents some limitations, for example when adapting according to environment changes, in the structure of organizations, or even when new norms and social relationships are introduced between agents. These restrictions are objectives of the OVAMAH project [19]. Section 4 discusses the core of the approach, in which an adaptive architecture emerges within a MAS. Finally, conclusions and further lines of work are outlined.

2   Motivating Example: Two Scenarios

There are situations when an adaptive architecture would be the best solution to solve complex problems. In order to illustrate a situation like these a motivating example with two scenarios is presented. This example is hypothetical but based in real situations, which are related to a demonstrator currently under development in the AT project [1]: *mobile-Health*. Although the proposed scenarios are closely-related to medical emergencies, they may apply to any crisis situation.

The emergency is a fire in a suburban leisure park. The coordination between the entities involved in the resolution of the crisis has decided that five ambulances and one helicopter are needed, as well as three fire trucks and five police cars. From an organizational point of view all these elements form an organization, namely O1. Considering these scenario in a MAS environment, each actor maps onto an agent. So, fourteen agents will interact in the organization O1.

- *Scenario 1:* the agents come to the crisis area and they must to organize to face the urgency. Each agent has its role, goals and plans, therefore, to become part of the group (organization) negotiations at different levels are needed, as well as to define a coordinated control. Leader election protocols can be used to achieve a preliminary organization. When a group of individuals follows protocols like these they can define implicit structural patterns.
- *Scenario 2:* the organization is already working in the crisis area. One of its essential services (provided by an inside organization, or even an agent) is no longer provided. This can be caused by different reasons, e. g. the agent/organization is urgently required in another emergency, or it can not reach the area due to lack of resources, etc. Given that the organization must first detect that the agent is not available and then finds an alternative solution, replace the essential service by a similar one, for example. This scenario shows how adaptivity requires the reorganization of agents, new system configurations and dealing with coordination problems.

It is clear that organizations are dynamic in both scenarios. Therefore, it is necessary to modify their structures, configurations and coordination. Particularly in an agent-oriented environment, the goal is to achieve an *automatic reconfiguration*. The system must carry out a series of *evolutionary steps* until it finds an optimal point. This can perfectly be a continuous process, as the situation itself evolves. This example justifies why this behaviour could not be completely pre-designed; it should be emergent and the coordination should be achieved inside the architecture, which is essentially a *service ecosystem,* i.e. a set of services which were separately created and must interact and coordinate within a certain context.

The THOMAS platform provides services and facilities to carry out a system reconfiguration, as discussed below. More details about supporting medical emergencies by using a standard MAS and this framework can be found in [6]. However, as mentioned above, in this example organizations have to be dynamic so that the system evolves to an optimal point. This is an actual limitation of THOMAS and its development evolution is reflected in the OVAMAH project [19].

3   An Agent-Oriented Infrastructure to Support Service Ecosystems

As previously noted, the base architecture must support the model defined as service-oriented, organization-centric, and agent-based architecture. Current research in the platform is oriented to achieve a greater capacity and functionality. From this point of view, services are utilized to achieve interoperability, and the main idea is to export the agent system as a system of services. The resulting service ecosystem will be supported, not only technologically, but also methodologically [28]. In the following, a brief description and the evolution of the framework THOMAS – AT MAS is presented.

3.1 A Service-Oriented, Agent-Based Architecture

As the proposed approach is based on service-oriented concepts, the main idea is to export the agent system as a system of services. Although services technology is established and has standards [4][7][15], its methodology and influence on other paradigms (such as agent-oriented architectures) is still under development. The feature of *service discovery* provides flexibility to a service-oriented architecture, but these architectures are strongly bound by their semantics and choreographies. *Mashups* (or web application hybrids) can be considered as exceptions, but they still mean ad-hoc solutions [16].

Service-oriented architectures are able to grow and evolve, by means of service discovery and composition. The inner complexity of this dynamic architecture creates a composite structure in which every member is optional and may have a different origin, but at the same time it plays an explicit role in an intertwined, self-supported environment – effectively, a *service ecosystem*, in which every element is related to every other.

Since the proposed environment must be truly adaptive and dynamic, it requires the use of rich semantic and highly technological capabilities. Therefore, it is considered a wise use of *agents* in a broader context, with an upper layer of services added to provide, in particular, the *interoperability* feature. It is easy to conceive a service to present the operational capabilities of an *agent* or a collection of agents as an *organization*, which in turn provides *services*. Using agents allows the explicit treatment of *semantics*, a *structured coordination*, the use of a methodology to service development, to structure them into *organizations*, and the use of their *learning* capacity, among others characteristics.

Implicit in the definition of MAS is the need to *register* agents in the system, to separate those ones who belong to the architecture from those who do not. The same approach will be used to identify services. To allow their external access, they will be explicitly registered and grouped as part of a service. This service could be later discovered by other entities within the distributed registry of the system.

3.2 The THOMAS Framework

The main concepts are built on top of the THOMAS framework [3] which, including its middleware (Figure 1), is structured in three levels, but they are not strictly layers:

- *Platform Kernel (PK)*. It is the actual kernel of the middleware; includes both the Network Layer and the Agent Management System (AMS) component. It provides all the capabilities of FIPA-compliant architecture [9]. Therefore, at this layer the platform is already an (open) Multi-Agent System.
- *Service & Organization Management*. This is the conceptual level composed of the Organization Management System (OMS) and the Service Facilitator (SF) components.
- *Organization Execution Framework*. It is the "space" where all the computational entities "live" and perform their functions. Agents and their organizations, and the services they offer, are conceptually located in it. Every specific application would be conceived, designed and executed at this abstraction level.

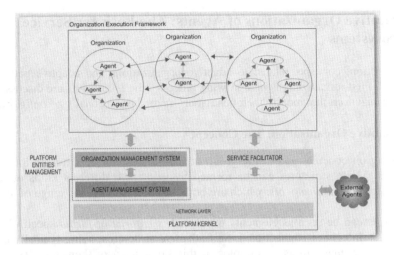

Fig. 1. THOMAS Technical Architecture (inspired on [3])

The *Platform Entities Management* subsystem is layered in turn, AMS and OMS, which are used to provide capabilities to the platform. Refer to [3] for more details.

3.3   Ecosystem Evolution on Top of THOMAS

The framework is under development, currently adapting to OSGi [17] specification. The main idea is to modularize applications into smaller entities called bundles. These entities can be installed, updated or removed on the fly and dynamically, providing the ability to change the system behaviour without ever having to disrupt its operation. The Service Tracker is distinguished among the services provided by this standard, especially for the proposed approach. This service lets tracking other registered services on the platform. It is used to ensure that the services to be provided are still available or not. This service is essential to face the second scenario presented in Section 2.

In a *bundle*-based system, producers of services, as well as consumers, can appear and disappear at any time. The standard provides a tool to facilitate the message passing between two entities belonging to different bundles, the *Whiteboard pattern*. This tool utilizes the service registry to maintain a list of listeners of the system, and delegates to the platform the life cycle control of the event producers and consumers. This control notifies the consumers when a producer disappears, and vice versa.

The current research, which is included as part of the OVAMAH project [19], is extending the objectives of the platform THOMAS. Besides providing the necessary technology for the development of virtual organizations in open environments, it will allow to facilitate dynamic answers for changing situations by means of the adaptation and/or evolution of the organizations. For example, agents forming an organizational unit could create (or remove) another unit, affecting the groups of the system; decide the moment to add or delete norms; the social relationship between roles could change at runtime, the conditions to activate/deactivate, as well as the cardinality of roles; the system topology (given by the relationships) could be changed also at runtime and then validate the changes with objectives and organizational type; the services could be matched to new roles; etc.

4   Adaptive Organizations of Agents: The Basis for Service Ecosystems

In this section, concepts related to adaptive organizations and adaptive patterns are presented. First, organizations in a growing process - the *initiatives* - are discussed; and then, organizations that modify their behaviour - named provisionally *reconfigurations*.

4.1   Adaptive Organization: The Concept

Depending on concrete goals, any group of individuals can be arranged into certain structures. These structures can be formed by using two different kinds of mechanisms: *controls* and *protocols*, which are both based in limiting the range of available actions.

Controls can be seen as elements which either *enforce* or *forbid* specific interactions (or architectural connections). Self-adaptive structures, being typically centralized [2], show many classic examples of this kind: most of them manifest explicit control loops, inspired in *regulators* of classic control theory.

Protocols, which either *enable* or *channel* behaviour, are based on consensus and agreements. They can be described generically as the way to control decentralized (even distributed) structures [16]. Basically, when protocols are present, every agent knows the way to interact with the rest; it is necessary to comply with them to be able to communicate, but at the same time they are also *regulating* the development of the interacting structure itself.

These two mechanisms define a wide spectrum of regulation, in which agent organizations and their architectures are simultaneously harnessed by atomic, unary *controls* (norms, limits, locks, control loops or constraints) and multiple, connective *protocols* (hubs, bridges, channels, or spaces). It is important to note that the purpose of these mechanisms is to "discover" a suitable structure of controls and protocols so that a global structure can emerge. These elements will make possible to define the main inner structures in order to obtain agreement-based organizations. Once a primary structure can be defined, an elemental group emerges as a preliminary organization, which will be referred as *an initiative*.

4.2   Self-organizing Organizations: The Initiative

As previously noted, the controls and protocols can be used to dynamically generate a preliminary organization inside a group of individuals and to generate certain structure (therefore several of them are considered as *generative controls* and *generative protocols*). This structure leads to an organization that grows with the environmental dynamics. In this approach the emergent organization is called *an initiative*: not yet fully established, but still evolving.

Nevertheless, the *initiative* can continue growing and mutating because of its *adaptive* nature, but when it has some *stable* structure, it can be called *organization*. This *stable* structure is achieved when all the participants can afford the necessary agreement in order to gain the objective. This *organization* is then conceptually similar to others in several MAS approaches. The previous paragraph implies three important concepts:

- *An initiative.* It is a preliminary group of individuals (agents) which assemble in a certain structure, generated by a set of controls and protocols, as well as certain associative patterns;
- *An organization.* It is a established group; in our approach, it is dynamically originated from an initiative (though there are also static organizations; once they are created, both kinds are functionally equivalent);
- *An agreement.* It is the act by which an initiative became into a stable organization. In fact, this can be seen as the consensus which is reached between individuals inside the initial "seed" group.

This process can be thought as the system moving to a new state, in which the structure of the "past" is supplanted by a "new" emergent structure. Obviously, this novel structure admits new elements because of the dynamic environment, but now one of its goals is to reinforce its nature, and tends to perpetuate itself.

Considering the motivating example, in first moment it can be thought that some police cars arrive to the crisis area but no one is the leader of the group. They can follow an internal protocol to choose a leader (even hierarchy can be defined as a protocol), and this agreement generates a preliminary organization. When using this kind of protocols - *generative protocols* - some implicit structural patterns can be defined.

An *initiative* can be generated from such patterns, named *agreement patterns*, where the term is used in an architectural sense. They are pre-designed from the required services of an *initiative* and the corresponding semantic refining. Some of them have been already identified, and receive such names as *Façade*, *Mediator*, or *Surveyor*, among others (see Subsection 4.4). It is important to consider that though some of these are typical names for patterns, they are defined in a completely different context; in particular, these are not classic object-oriented patterns, but architectural patterns.

The patterns represent a static structure (a fragment) leading to a dynamic one, the initiative, reaching a stable form, the organization. As already noted, the system is ultimately conceived as a *service-oriented architecture*; so methodologically, our first stable organizations must be conceived as the providers for certain high-level services. Then, these services must be proposed as the starting point for the functional definition of those first organizations.

The functional decomposition of these services will be also used to design the hierarchical structure of organizations. The concept of *service process,* in this context, intends to provide a clear *semantic* perspective of a service's functionality, by describing it as a workflow. Each (high-level) service unfolds into a (semantic) process, which describes the coordination between lower level services. Every service is provided by a low-level organization, providing the structural decomposition from the previous, high-level organization. This process guides the (semantic) definition of any service-oriented organization, and it is used to define the static structures. Moreover, even the dynamic, emergent agreements *must* be consistent with these semantic definitions; so this process provides also a method to discover the required patterns for the *initiatives*. Once again, it has yet to be refined, and the desired methodology has to acquire a definitive form.

4.3 Self-adaptive Organizations as Actual Ecosystems

Concepts related to organizations in a growing process were discussed in the previous subsection, and self-organization is important due to structures construction containing the organizations. Next, other concepts are presented, which are related to changes suffered by organizations that have reached a *quiescent* or safe state for adaptation, in a certain way.

In this case, namely *pure adaptation*, the importance lies in the way that an existing organization has to adapt to a new behaviour. First, it has to realize that a change has occurred, i. e. a change can emerge in an intrinsic way [22], and then it has to adapt itself.

In Section 2, the second scenario is presented when the organization is already working in the crisis area and one essential service is not available. Four alternatives for adaptation have been identified:

- *Case 1* – with no modification of the organization's main objective: a search is made inside the organization, looking for a service similar to that is no longer available. The main idea is the direct replacement of the service.
- *Case 2* – with no modification of main objective: the internal search finds only a service with minimum similarity to which is no longer available. In this case, the responsible for that service must learn to answer as the one that is currently unavailable. A learning process is feasible since this is a MAS-oriented environment. The time spent in this task should be reasonable, according to the scenario characteristics.
- *Case 3* – with no modification of main objective: if the internal search fails, the organization is allowed to make an external search. This case can be considered as a state change of the organization. It comes back to the *initiative* level, which is maintained until reaches a quiescent or safe state, by agreement.
- *Case 4* – with change of the organization's main objective: in this case, the organization is "forced" to modify the objective, or divide it in partials goals. It is not possible to offer the original service.

These four cases are the first to be studied for a real adaptation of the organizations, due to they modify not only the structure but the type of constituent element. More cases like these are expected to develop in the medium term.

4.4 Adaptation Patterns

As already noted, the *agreement patterns* are pre-designed from the required services of an *initiative* and for the corresponding semantic refining.

Particularly, these are *not* classic object-oriented patterns, because they are defined in a different context: they are *architectural patterns*.

According to [23] it is possible to classify the architectural design patterns as follows: monitoring (M), decision-making (DM), or reconfiguration (R) based on their objective. M and DM patterns can also be classified as either creational (C) or structural (S), as defined in [11]. Likewise, R patterns can also be classified as behavioural (B) and structural (S) since they specify how to physically restructure an architecture once the system has reached a quiescent or safe state for adaptation [23]. Three of these patterns have been already identified for the proposed approach, and they are described in Table 1.

Obviously, there are more patterns and not all of them only describe roles. For instance, the *Surveyor Election* defines the protocol (one among many) to decide the next *surveyor*; and *Surveyor Change* describes a protocol to demote the current *surveyor* and forward its knowledge to a new one.

Table 1. Agreement Patterns: architectural design patterns

Name	Category	Description
Façade	M, S	To be able to easily interact with an organization which still lacks a defined structure, some agent has to represent the organization itself in terms of interaction. This agent redirects any incoming communication.
Mediator	R, B	During the emergence process, the organization is not yet established, and data services are probably not working. Some agent must act as a *mediator*, which makes possible to access to data sources, albeit indirectly, and also to perform the necessary (*semantic*) translations.
Surveyor	R, S	During the emergence process, at least one agent must monitor the growing of the initiative itself, both to decide when new elements are inserted, and also when the initiative forms a *stable* organization. It has access to the pattern library and decides when a certain pattern must be triggered.

5 Conclusions and Future Work

This paper has explored structural concepts as the basis of an architectural approach to provide self-adaptivity to software systems. The proposed concept of *initiative* must be considered as a starting point to provide mechanisms to change the composition patterns and element types within such systems.

The required dynamism can be supported by an emergent agreement - an evolving architectural structure, based on combining predefined controls and protocols. These mechanisms are handled in the context of the service-oriented, agent-based and organization-centric framework defined in AT, provided by the implementation in THOMAS platform, the OVAMAH project, and services compatible to OSGi standard.

The key idea is to create an architectural context, in which agents are *coordinated* and *reorganized* by inclusion in preliminary structures –i.e. agreement patterns– and then in stable organizations. The platform described in Section 3, including modifications to be made by the OVAMAH project, provides services and facilities to carry out the system reconfiguration. The proposed concepts it can already be considered as a starting point to establish the necessary structures to achieve actual self-adaptivity. Technologically, the existing work is both FIPA [9] compliant, and also able to interact with Jade [12] agents. Indeed, even when this approach seems promising, these are just the first steps.

Further work will develop and implement variants of this approach, in order to refine it. The concepts are still evolving and the process of defining their limits still continues – but even at this initial stage, the existing fragments of the approach have already proven its utility and expressive power. Current results suggest that the adaptive architecture is indeed feasible because the infrastructure developed can grow just adding new adaptive patterns. The results could fulfil the promise of generalizing the usefulness and extension of the service ecosystem approach, adapting it to new and more agile technologies.

Acknowledgements. This work has been partially funded by Spanish Ministry of Science and Innovation through National Projects *Agreement Technologies* (CONSOLIDER CSD2007-0022), MULTIPLE (TIN2009-13838), and OVAMAH (TIN2009-13839-C03-02); and the European Union RTD Framework Programme, through COST Action *Agreement Technologies* (COST Action IC0801).

References

1. Agreement Technologies (AT) Project (2009),
   http://www.agreement-technologies.org/
2. Andersson, J., de Lemos, R., Malek, S., Weyns, D.: Modeling Dimensions of Self-Adaptive Software Systems. In: Cheng, B.H.C., de Lemos, R., Giese, H., Inverardi, P., Magee, J. (eds.) Software Engineering for Self-Adaptive Systems. LNCS, vol. 5525, pp. 27–47. Springer, Heidelberg (2009)
3. Argente, E., Botti, V., Carrascosa, C., Giret, A., Julian, V., Rebollo, M.: An Abstract Architecture for Virtual Organizations: The THOMAS Project. Technical report, DSIC, Universidad Politécnica de Valencia (2008)
4. Booth, D., Haas, H., McCabe, F., Newcomer, E., Champion, M., Ferris, C., Orchard, D.: Web Services Architecture. W3C WSA Working Group, W3 Consortium (2004)
5. Centeno, R., Fagundes, M., Billhardt, H., Ossowski, S.: Supporting Medical Emergencies by SMA. In: Håkansson, A., Nguyen, N.T., Hartung, R.L., Howlett, R.J., Jain, L.C. (eds.) KES-AMSTA 2009. LNCS, vol. 5559, pp. 823–833. Springer, Heidelberg (2009)
6. Cuesta, C.E., Fuente, P., Barrio, M., Beato, E.: Dynamic Coordination Architecture through the use of Reflection. In: Proc. 16th ACM Symposium on Applied Computing (SAC 2001), pp. 134–140. ACM Press, New York (March 2001)
7. Esteban, J., Laskey, K., McCabe, F., Thornton, D.: Reference Architecture for Service Oriented Architecture 1.0. Organization for the Advancement of Structured Information Standards, OASIS (2008)
8. Fiadeiro, J.L.: Designing for Software's Social Complexity. In: Computer - IEEE Computer Society, pp. 34–39 (2007)
9. FIPA. FIPA Abstract Architecture Specification. Technical Report SC00001L, Foundation for Intelligent Physical Agents. FIPA TC Architecture (2002)
10. Galloway, A.R.: Protocol: How Control Exists after Decentralization. MIT Press, Cambridge (2004)
11. Gamma, E., Helm, R., Johnson, R., Vlissides, J.: Design Patterns: Elements of Reusable Object-Oriented Software. Addison-Wesley Professional, Reading (1994)
12. JADE - Java Agent DEvelopment Framework, http://jade.tilab.com/
13. Kephart, J.O., Chess, D.M.: The Vision of Autonomic Computing. IEEE Computer 36(1), 41–50 (2003)
14. Kramer, J., Magee, J.: Self-Managed Systems: an Architectural Challenge. In: Future of Software Engineering (FOSE@ ICSE 2007), pp. 259–268. IEEE, Los Alamitos (2007)
15. MacKenzie, C., Laskey, K., McCabe, F., Brown, P., Metz, R.: Reference Model for Service Oriented Architecture 1.0. Organization for the Advancement of Structured Information Standards, OASIS (2006)
16. OMA: The Open Mashup Alliance, http://www.openmashup.org/
17. OSGi: formerly known as the Open Services Gateway initiative, now an obsolete name, http://www.osgi.org/

18. Ossowski, S.: Coordination in multi-agent systems: Towards a technology of agreement. In: Bergmann, R., Lindemann, G., Kirn, S., Pěchouček, M. (eds.) MATES 2008. LNCS (LNAI), vol. 5244, pp. 2–12. Springer, Heidelberg (2008)
19. OVAMAH - Organizaciones Virtuales Adaptativas: Técnicas y Mecanismos de Descripción y Adaptación, http://www.cetinia.urjc.es/es/node/353
20. Pérez, J.S., Cuesta, C., Ossowski, S.: Agreement as an Adaptive Architecture for Open Multi-Agent Systems. In: Sistedes (ed.) II Workshop on Autonomic and SELF-adaptive Systems - WASELF 2009. TJISBD, vol. 3(4), pp. 62–76 (2009)
21. Pérez, J.S., Cuesta, C., Ossowski, S.: Agreement Technologies for Adaptive, Service-Oriented Multi-Agent Systems. In: II Workshop on Agreement Technologies WAT – XIII Conferencia de la Asociación Española para la Inteligencia Artificial CAEPIA (2009)
22. Prokopenko, M., Boschetti, F., Ryan, A.J.: An Information-Theoretic Primer on Complexity, Self-Organization, and Emergence. Complexity 15(1),11–28 (2008)
23. Ramírez, A.J., Cheng, B.H.C.: Design Patterns for Developing Dynamically Adaptive Systems. In: ICSE 2010-SEAMS, pp. 49–58 (2010)

ADI'10 - PC Co-chairs Message

Welcome to the 3rd International Workshop on Ambient Data Integration (ADI'10). The workshop was held in conjunction with the On The Move Federated Conference and Workshops (OTM'10), October 25-29, 2010 in Hersonissou, Crete, Greece.

Ambient data integration places an emphasis on integrating data across embedded, context aware, personalized devices that can adapt to rapidly changing environments. Hence, this workshop aims to discuss relevant aspects for the success of data integration systems with the focus on the ubiquity, management and conceptualization of these systems. We expect that ambient issues in data integration are going to challenge system designers for quite some time and significant effort is needed in order to tackle them. This workshop brings together researchers and practitioners to share their recent ideas and advances towards this emerging and important problem.

The program of the full day workshop is composed as follows: 2 talks and 5 papers, that is we have accepted 45% of the papers submitted.

Concerning the talks, Grigoris Antoniou and Antonis Bikakis presented their work on defeasible contextual reasoning in ambient intelligence while Dave Thau gave a presentation on ambient data integration in the context of collaborative collection of data in wild environments. The accepted papers can be partitioned into two groups: data integration approaches and modeling in the context of ADI.

Regarding data integration approaches, the paper by Richard Mordinyi and al is dealing with issues in enterprise data and applications integration and proposes a framework combining two systems for solving these problems. Rosalie Belian and Ana Carolina Salgado presented a context based schema integration process that is applied to a health care application. Finally, the paper written by Bastian Roth and al tackles the issue of data integration. Focusing on scientific applications it distinguishes between materialized and virtual data integration systems and compares available systems based on an evaluation scheme that is introduced.

The modeling papers can be summarized as follows. In their paper, Thomas Buchmann and al present a generic framework, including a complete work flow for provenance and quality control, integration to institutional repositories, and evolution of research data. Ludovic Menet and Myriam Lamolle propose an approach for incremental validation of UML class diagrams based on a set of formally specified rules.

We would like to thank the authors for their submissions, the program committee members for their excellent work, and the conference organizers for their great support to set up the workshop.

August 2010

Olivier Curé
Stefan Jablonski
Dave Thau
ADI'10

R. Meersman et al. (Eds.): OTM 2010 Workshops, LNCS 6428, p. 88, 2010.
© Springer-Verlag Berlin Heidelberg 2010

Defeasible Contextual Reasoning in Ambient Intelligence: Theory and Applications

Antonis Bikakis and Grigoris Antoniou

Institute of Computer Science, FO.R.T.H., Vassilika Voutwn
P.O. Box 1385, GR 71110, Heraklion, Greece
{bikakis,antoniou}@ics.forth.gr

The study of Ambient Intelligence environments and pervasive computing systems has introduced new research challenges in the field of Distributed Artificial Intelligence. These are mainly caused by the imperfect nature of context and the special characteristics of the entities that possess and share the available context knowledge. In such environments, context may be unknown, ambiguous, imprecise or erroneous. Ambient agents are expected to have different goals, experiences and perceptive capabilities and use distinct vocabularies to describe their context. Due to the highly dynamic and open nature of the environment and the unreliable wireless communications that are restricted by the range of transmitters, ambient agents do not typically know a priori all other entities that are present at a specific time instance nor can they communicate directly with all of them.

Motivated by these challenges, we propose a fully distributed approach for contextual reasoning in Ambient Intelligence environments, which combines the virtues of Multi-Context Systems and Defeasible Argumentation. The general approach consists of three models: (a) a representation model, which is a nonmonotonic extension of Multi-Context Systems; according to this, local context knowledge of ambient agents is encoded in rule theories (contexts), and information flow between agents is achieved through defeasible mapping rules that associate concepts used by different contexts; (b) an argument-based reasoning model, in which conflicts that arise from the interaction of mutually inconsistent contexts are captured through attacking arguments, and conflict resolution is achieved by ranking arguments according to a preference ordering on the system contexts; and (c) an operational model in the form of four distributed algorithms for query evaluation, each of which implements a different strategy for conflict resolution. The proposed models have been implemented and evaluated in Ambient Intelligence and Social Networking scenarios, which involve interaction between several different types of stationary and mobile devices communicating through wireless networks.

R. Meersman et al. (Eds.): OTM 2010 Workshops, LNCS 6428, p. 89, 2010.

RDF Containers – A Framework for the Integration of Distributed and Heterogeneous Applications

Richard Mordinyi[1,2], Thomas Moser[2], Martin Murth[1], Eva Kühn[1], and Stefan Biffl[2]

[1] Space-Based Computing Group, Vienna University of Technology, Austria
[2] Christian Doppler Laboratory "Software Engineering Integration for Flexible Automation Systems", Vienna University of Technology, Austria
{firstname.lastname}@tuwien.ac.at

Abstract. Current trends like globalization and virtual enterprises result in an increasing need for on-the-fly integration of distributed applications grown over the past decades and originally not intended for integration and cooperation. In order to enable the collaboration of such applications, aspects of distribution, such as heterogeneous data sources, heterogeneous network technologies and coordination requirements, have to be addressed in the integration process. In this position paper, we introduce a framework, the so-called RDF Containers, for technical and semantic integration of distributed and heterogeneous data sources considering integration requirements. We discuss the benefits and limitations of the proposed framework based on a real-world use case from the e-health domain. The major benefit is that both semantic and technical integration are supported by a single framework, while complexity aspects related to the integration process do not affect the integrated applications.

Keywords: semantic integration, space-based computing.

1 Introduction

Today's communication network technologies offer enough bandwidth and interconnection facilities for the development of applications based on combining well-established distributed applications, resulting in the increasing need for efficient and effective system integration methodologies [1]. Core questions are on the one hand side how to satisfy communication and coordination requirements between technologically different application platforms probably belonging to different autonomously acting enterprises. On the other hand side how to integrate data models across platform and domain boundaries, and finally how software engineers can be supported in designing and implementing distributed applications.

Hence, typical system integration challenges result from both technical heterogeneities, e.g., tools from different sources may use a range of technologies that become expensive and error-prone to integrate in traditional point-to-point ways; as well as from semantic heterogeneities, e.g., project participants may use different terms for common concepts in the application domain [2].

Modern technical integration approaches, such as the Enterprise Service Bus (ESB) concept [1], rely on message-based infrastructures and are capable of abstracting

R. Meersman et al. (Eds.): OTM 2010 Workshops, LNCS 6428, pp. 90–99, 2010.

complexity issues of distributed systems from the application. However, coordination logic (e.g., message ordering or coordination patterns) still remains in the application, hindering the application designers to focus entirely on the application itself [3]. Current alternative solutions for semantic integration like standards for data models [4], data-driven tool integration [5], or complete data transformation [6] work in principle, but pose their own challenges, such as inefficient and complex data access and query definitions, solutions which are not robust enough, or take considerable effort to develop and modify.

In this position paper, we introduce the RDF Containers approach as a platform for technical and semantic integration of distributed and heterogeneous data sources. RDF Containers combine the space based computing paradigm (SBC) for solving technical integration and coordination challenges [7], and the Engineering Knowledge Base (EKB) framework for supporting semantic integration [8]. SBC is a coordination middleware based on concepts of virtual shared memory that explicitly distinguishes between computation and coordination logic. This allows shifting coordination complexities into the middleware layer, thus minimizing the implementation effort for the application developers needed to control these coordination complexities and therefore allows focusing on application development entirely. Additionally, SBC provides mechanisms to abstract issues of technical heterogeneity in distributed systems, and therefore facilitates technical integration [7]. The EKB framework uses ontologies for explicitly modeling common and local concepts as well as mappings between these concepts, thus enabling semantic integration in multi-organizational scenarios. Standards are hard to apply for projects with experts from different organizations, who have independently invested efforts into the development of different kinds of local data standards or notations. The EKB framework allows these experts to use their established and well-known local tools and data models, while additionally providing access to data originating from tools of other organizations within their local tools using local data standards or notations [8, 9].

We discuss the benefits and limitations of RDF Containers based on a real-world use case from the e-Health domain, in which data regarding accident victims is dynamically consolidated from various sources (e.g., hospitals, doctors) and used for the coordination of their treatments. Major benefit of RDF Containers is that both semantic and technical integration are supported by a single framework, while complexity aspects related to the integration and coordination of processes do not affect the integrated applications.

The remainder of this paper is structured as follows: Section 2 summarizes related work on technical and semantic integration. Section 3 identifies the research issues, while section 4 introduces the use-case. Section 5 presents the proposed approach, section 6 discusses the findings, and finally section 7 concludes the paper and presents further work.

2 Related Work

This section summarizes related work on technical and semantic integration.

2.1 Technical Integration

System integration is the task to combine numerous different systems to appear as one big system. There are several levels at which system integration could be performed [10], but there is so far no standardized out-of-the-box solution for an integration process that explains how to integrate arbitrary systems. The limitations of integration over heterogeneous middleware technologies with different APIs, transportation capabilities, or network architecture styles implies the development of static and therefore inflexible wrappers between each combination of middleware technologies, and thus increases the complexity of communication. Traditional approaches for integration of business services can be categorized [1] into: Hub and spoke vs. distributed integration and coupled vs. separated application and integration logic. As an example, the Enterprise Service Bus (ESB) provides the infrastructure services for message exchange and routing as the infrastructure for Service Oriented Architecture (SOA) [11]. It provides a distributed integration platform and clear separation of business logic and integration logic. It offers routing services to navigate the requests to the relevant service provider based on a routing path specification. By relying on its basic functionality of routing messages between individual services, an ESB supports only a very basic type of coordination form. In case services need to coordinate each other in a more complex way in order to achieve a common goal, the complexity of changing coordination requirements cannot be realized in the middleware. Thus, the services themselves need to be adapted, such that by making use of the supported capabilities of an ESB only, the new business goal can be achieved. This implies increased implementation complexity [12], decreased efficiency [3], and higher service development time.

2.2 Semantic Integration

Semantic integration is defined as the solving of problems originating from the intent to share data across disparate and semantically heterogeneous data [2]. These problems include the matching of ontologies or schemas, the detection of duplicate entries, the reconciliation of inconsistencies, and the modeling of complex relations in different data sources. [13] One of the most important and most actively studied problems in semantic integration is establishing semantic correspondences (also called mappings) between vocabularies of different data sources [14]. There are three main categories of semantic conflicts in the context of data integration that can appear: confounding conflicts, scaling conflicts, and naming conflicts. The use of ontologies as a solution option to semantic integration and interoperability problems has been studied over the last 10 years. Noy [15] identified three major dimensions of the application of ontologies for supporting semantic integration: the task of finding mappings (semi-)automatically, the declarative formal representation of these mappings, and reasoning using these mappings.

There exist two major architectures for mapping discovery between ontologies. On the one hand, the vision is a general upper ontology which is agreed upon by developers of different applications. On the other hand, there are approaches comprising heuristics-based or machine learning techniques that use various characteristics of ontologies (e.g., structure, concepts, instances) to find mappings. These approaches are similar to approaches for mapping XML schemas or other structured data [16].

Naturally, defining the mappings between ontologies, either automatically, semi-automatically, or interactively, is not a goal in itself. The resulting mappings are used for various integration tasks: data transformation, query answering, or web-service composition, to name a few. Given that ontologies are often used for reasoning, it is only natural that many of these integration tasks involve reasoning over the source ontologies and the mappings [13].

3 Research Issues

The need for designing and implementing collaborating applications based on distributed and heterogeneous data sources is steadily increasing since today's communication network technologies offer enough bandwidth and interconnection facilities for such applications, as well as because of current trends towards globalization and virtual enterprises [1]. Because of technical and semantic gaps between different stakeholders and platforms, there are limitations to a comprehensive systems integration methodology. Core questions are on the one hand side how to enable communication and coordination between technologically different applications that typically originate from inter-enterprise collaborations, and on the other hand side how to integrate data models across platform and domain boundaries. In both cases, the complexity regarding the integration of such applications should not affect the integrated applications.

Traditional system integration approaches, such as the Enterprise Service Bus (ESB) concept [1], face challenges regarding technical integration and the efforts needed to cope with complexity issues (like cognitive complexity) of coordinating autonomous enterprises; as well as from semantic heterogeneities, e.g., project participants may use different terms for common concepts in the application domain [2].

Based on the limitations of traditional methodologies regarding technical and semantic integration of distributed applications and their heterogeneous data sources, we propose a unified system integration methodology capable of dealing with both technical and semantic heterogeneities. Therefore, we derive the following research issues.

RI-1: Technical Integration taking into account coordination requirements. To what extent do current technical integration frameworks support both the abstraction of heterogeneous network technologies and the flexible coordination of distributed applications?

RI-2: Semantic Integration without the need for a common data schema. Investigate the capabilities of current semantic integration solutions that do not imply the usage of a common data schema (which is hard or even impossible to achieve for well-established applications). How could semantic integration solutions support changes (e.g., new or updated data sources) of available data sources?

RI-3: Effects on integrated distributed applications. How could additional complexity resulting from the integration process itself be hidden from the integrated applications?

We discuss the proposed RDF Containers framework based on a real-world use case from the e-Health domain, in which patient summaries originating from various sources (e.g., hospitals, doctors) should be made available for healthcare authorities in EPS (European Patient Summary) style [17].

4 Use Case

The following use case from the e-Health area describes an extension of the use case defined in TripCom [18], where the development of a Europe-wide information system for the management and exchange of patient data was considered - also referred to as the European Patient Summary (EPS) [17] In the EPS use case, we employed RDF representations of patient data in shared spaces to achieve scalability for discovery of data published in the Internet. The extended use case introduces two additional requirements, describing frequently observed demands in real-world system implementations: (i) data about accident victims needs to be integrated in an ad-hoc manner, thus allowing to provide a consolidated view on the patients' health records within minutes or even seconds, and (ii) it must be possible to spontaneously change the treatments and treatment orders of patients, hence imposing high requirements on the coordination capabilities of the developed system.

Story board: During a trip through the Austrian Alps, a bus collides with a motor vehicle and many of the occupants are seriously injured. The first who arrive at the accident site are several ambulance men, providing first aid to the accident victims. Depending on type and severity of the injury, they request further ambulance cars and medical support. For this purpose, each ambulance man is equipped with a mobile device that can be used to record patient data, required medical support, and to request the transportation to a nearby hospital.

To ensure that the best possible medical treatment can be given to the accident victims, data from multiple and potentially heterogeneous data sources need to be consolidated: a) data from the accident site provided by the ambulance man, e.g., identity of the accident victim, type and severity of the injury, etc.; b) data from the accident victim's health care providers in their home countries, e.g., health records from the victim's general practitioners and specialists, x-ray images, information about allergies or intolerances, etc.; and c) data from the ambulances and the nearby hospitals, e.g., medical equipment and treatment options, availability of operating rooms, medications available in ambulance cars, etc.

The developed information system needs to integrate these data and to provide it to the physicians and clinical personnel of the hospitals. It further needs to determine which ambulance cars can take which injured persons and it has to coordinate the transportation of the victims to the surrounding hospitals. As there are typically not enough ambulance cars available right after an accident, it is also important that the ambulance cars are always used to maximum capacity. For example, slightly injured people should not be transported separately, and ambulance cars with emergency doctors should only transport seriously injured persons. At the hospitals, the accident victims are treated in the order in which they arrive. However, in case of critical injuries, the treatment of certain victims may need to be prioritized. It is therefore necessary that the single departments of a hospital can coordinate the treatment orders, that they can synchronize their most recent treatments, and that they can spontaneously adjust the treatment method when new information is provided.

5 RDF Containers

This section shortly introduces the Space-Based Computing (SBC) paradigm and the Engineering Knowledge Base (EKB) framework, which are combined by the RDF Containers approach described in the third subsection.

5.1 The Space-Based Computing (SBC) Paradigm

SBC explicitly distinguishes between computational and coordination logic, thus moving the complexities of coordination into the middleware layer allowing the application to focus on its business goals. It provides an extensible coordination logic with its main concepts being containers, coordinators, and aspects [3, 12]. Coordinators are Internet addressable resources that contain data (numbers, strings, records etc.) in a structured way. Each container possesses one or more coordinators (FIFO, key, random, vector etc.) that determine the semantic of accessing data. Pre and post aspects can be added to intercept operations on the containers. This allows supporting different architectural styles simultaneously and contributes to efficiently realize new business requirements without influencing the application. Especially, the coordinator concept represents the way how distributed applications coordinate themselves. By means of supporting coordination patterns within the middleware, a) the complexity of coordination can be decreased in the application, and b) allows the efficient coordination of distributed application, since the model explicitly represents business coordination requirements [19].

5.2 The Engineering Knowledge Base (EKB) Framework

The Engineering Knowledge Base (EKB) framework [8] is an ontology-based data modeling approach which supports explicit modeling of existing knowledge in machine-understandable syntax (e.g., knowledge of the EPS domain), with a focus on providing links between local data structures (e.g., English and Austrian National Patient Summaries) support the exchange of information between these local data structures and thus making systems engineering more efficient and flexible. The EKB framework stores the local knowledge in ontologies and provides semantic mapping services to access design-time and run-time concepts and data. The general mechanism of the EKB framework uses common concepts identified beforehand as basis for mappings between proprietary local knowledge and more generic domain-specific knowledge to support transformation between these tools and platforms [8, 9]. Due to the mappings between local ontologies and domain ontology data structures that are semantically equal can be identified, because they are either aligned to the same domain concept or belong to the same tree segment in the concept tree described in the domain ontology [20].

5.3 RDF Containers – Overview and Architecture

The basic architectural model consists of a set of data sources (e.g., triple stores) which conform to different heterogeneous data schemas. In our example, these data sources represent the different National Patient Summaries (NPS), e.g., English and

Austrian patient summaries, which use their own notations. The data sources are geo-graphically distributed across Europe and thus need to be integrated both technically and semantically in order to meet the requirements of the European Patient Summary (EPS) scenario.

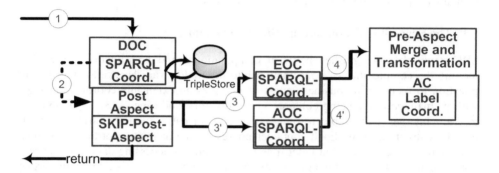

Fig. 1. Overview of the RDF Container Architecture for the EPS Use Case

Figure 1 depicts the architecture and an exemplary workflow of the RDF Contain-ers for the EPS scenario. The architecture primarily consists of a container represent-ing the common concepts of the EPS domain (*Domain Ontology Container-DOC*) and a set of containers representing the local concepts of the different NPSs (*English and Austrian Ontology Container-EOC, AOC*). In order to access the data stored in the data sources (e.g., triple stores), a special *SPARQL Coordinator* has been imple-mented and deployed. This coordinator abstracts various types of data sources that could be queried using SPARQL syntax. The exemplary workflow represents a read operation querying for information (e.g., regarding prior treatments or known aller-gies of a patient) from the available heterogeneous data sources.

As first step, an authorized role performs a query at the *DOC*. The operation pro-vides two parameters: a unique ID identifying the operation itself, and a reference to the *Answer Container AC*. An AC is a container that stores the result of an operation in order to enable the execution of asynchronous operations. The coordinator maps the method call to an SPARQL query and executes it on the deployed TripleStore. The result of this operation indicates that two more additional operations (i.e., by querying the domain ontology the number of the local data sources to be queried, as well as their location identified through their namespace emerges) on national data sources have to be performed. In the second step a post-aspect intercepts the operation which by now also contains the results of its execution on the container. Based on the result set the post aspect realizes that two more operations, on national data sources, have to be performed. Therefore, the post-aspect performs automatically transformed versions of the original query on the English and Austrian NPSs asynchronously us-ing the same parameter for the AC but changed IDs. In a next step the *SKIP-post-aspect* is called, which aborts the operation. However, as in the previous aspect the new operations have been executed in an asynchronous manner, only the operation on the *DOC* has been aborted without having any effects on the two new operations on *EOC* (step 3) and *AOC* (step 3'). Those two containers independently perform the query operations, and based on the specified answer container, they write (steps 4 and 4') the result into the given *AC*. This container contains a pre-aspect that intercepts incoming operations in order to satisfy its two main functionalities. The first one is to wait for all sub-results belonging to the ID (the number of sub-results to wait for is determined by the identified number of local data sources to be queried) of the operation of step 1. The second task of that aspect is to merge the incoming results. The merge operation is performed by means of transformation instructions, so-called T-Maps [20] which describe how a concept can be mapped to another and how data can be manipulated (e.g., merged, transformed). Once the aspect finished manipulating incoming results based on the requirements of the operation of step 1, it writes the final results into the answer container *AC*.

6 Discussion and Conclusion

Current trends in IT like globalization and virtual enterprises result in an increasing need for on-the-fly integration of distributed applications grown over the past decades and originally not intended for integration [1]. Typical system integration challenges result from both technical heterogeneities, e.g., tools from different sources may use a range of technologies that become expensive and error-prone to integrate in traditional point-to-point ways; as well as from semantic heterogeneities, e.g., project participants may use different terms for common concepts in the application domain [2]. In addition, in most modern technical integration approaches, coordination logic (e.g., message ordering or coordination patterns) still remains in the application, hindering the application designers to focus entirely on the application itself [3].

In this position paper, we introduce the RDF Containers approach as a platform for technical and semantic integration of distributed and heterogeneous data sources. RDF Containers combine the space based computing paradigm (SBC) for solving technical integration and coordination challenges [7], and the Engineering Knowledge Base (EKB) framework for supporting semantic integration [8]. We discussed the benefits and limitations of RDF Containers based on a real-world use case from the e-Health domain, in which patient summaries originating from various sources (e.g., hospitals, doctors) should be made available for healthcare authorities in EPS (European Patient Summary) style [17, 18].

RI-1: Technical Integration taking into account coordination requirements. Regarding technical integration issues of the use case, the proposed RDF Containers offer advantages such as a) the efficient implementation of the used coordination patters (e.g., FIFO, LIFO, auction, marketplace); b) the support of both centralized (e.g., server-based) and distributed (e.g., peer-to-peer) integration approaches, which appear transparent to the application designer because of the abstraction capabilities of the SBC paradigm; and c) the support of several different architectural styles (e.g., dataflow, data-centered, implicit invocation), enabling the concurrent and/or exchangeable usage of different technical integration approaches. While discussing the use case scenario, we identified two possible limitations of using the SBC paradigm, namely on the one hand side the possible performance decrease because of the introduction of an additional abstraction layer, and on the other hand side the need for a change of mind regarding traditional application design and implementation.

RI-2: **Semantic Integration without the need for a common data schema.** Regarding semantic integration issues of the use case, the proposed RDF Containers offer advantages such as a) the fact that there is no common data schema needed which all project participants / data sources have to agree on; b) the possibility to define queries of heterogeneous data sources on a domain level without the need to stick to local and proprietary notations or syntax; and c) the automated derivation of transformation instructions of local and proprietary data models based on the identified common concepts and the mappings between these common concepts and the local, tool- and platform-specific concepts. While discussing the use case scenario, we identified two possible limitations of using the EKB framework, namely on the one hand side the initial effort for setting up the EKB framework properly, which may turn out to be too high for small applications, and on the other hand side the additional training effort for IT personnel regarding ontologies.

RI-3: Effects on integrated distributed applications. Additionally, the RDF Containers approach facilitates the architectural design and implementation of distributed applications. This allows shifting coordination complexities into the middleware layer, thus minimizing the implementation effort for the application developers needed to control these coordination complexities and therefore allows focusing on application development entirely. Furthermore, RDF Containers allow domain experts to use their established and well-known local tools and data models, while additionally providing access to data originating from tools of other organizations within their local tools using local data standards or notations [8, 9].

Future work. Future research will include exhaustive empirical evaluation in order to measure the efficiency and robustness of RDF Containers, and additionally the usability of the approach will be evaluated with industry practitioners. We will also investigate advanced data placement and data replication strategies based on extended semantic descriptions of the data (e.g., privacy, performance).

Acknowledgments. This work has been supported by the Christian Doppler Forschungsgesellschaft and the BMWFJ, Austria, and by the Vienna University of Technology, Complex Systems Design & Engineering Lab.

References

1. Chappel, D.A.: Enterprise Service Bus. O'Reilly Media, Sebastopol (2004)
2. Halevy, A.: Why your data won't mix. Queue 3, 50–58 (2005)
3. Kühn, E., Mordinyi, R., Keszthelyi, L., Schreiber, C.: Introducing the concept of customizable structured spaces for agent coordination in the production automation domain. In: 8th Int. Conf. on Autonomous Agents and Multi-Agent Systems, pp. 625–632 (2009)
4. Kruchten, P.: The rational unified process: an introduction. Addison-Wesley, Reading (2000)
5. Hohpe, G., Woolf, B.: Enterprise Integration Patterns: Designing, Building, and Deploying Messaging Solutions. Addison-Wesley Professional, Reading (2004)
6. Assmann, D., Dörr, J., Eisenbarth, M., Hefke, M., Soto, M., Szulman, P., Trifu, A.: Using Ontology-Based Reference Models in Digital Production Engineering Integration. In: 16th IFAC World Congress, Prague, Czech Republic (2005)

7. Mordinyi, R., Moser, T., Kühn, E., Biffl, S., Mikula, A.: Foundations for a Model-Driven Integration of Business Services in a Safety-Critical Application Domain. In: Software Engineering and Advanced Applications, Euromicro Conference, pp. 267–274 (2009)
8. Moser, T., Biffl, S., Sunindyo, W.D., Winkler, D.: Integrating Production Automation Expert Knowledge Across Engineering Stakeholder Domains. In: Int. Conf. Complex, Intelligent and Software Intensive Systems (CISIS 2010), pp. 352–359 (2010)
9. Biffl, S., Sunindyo, W.D., Moser, T.: Bridging Semantic Gaps Between Stakeholders in the Production Automation Domain with Ontology Areas. In: 21st Int. Conf. on Software Engineering and Knowledge Engineering, pp. 233–239 (2009)
10. Balasubramanian, K., Gokhale, A., Karsai, G., Sztipanovits, J., Neema, S.: Developing Applications Using Model-Driven Design Environments. Computer 39, 33 (2006)
11. Papazoglou, M.P., Heuvel, W.-J.: Service oriented architectures: approaches, technologies and research issues. The VLDB Journal 16, 389–415 (2007)
12. Mordinyi, R., Kühn, E., Schatten, A.: Space-based Architectures as Abstraction Layer for Distributed Business Applications. In: 4th Int. Conf. on Complex, Intelligent and Software Intensive Systems (CISIS 2010), pp. 47–53 (2010)
13. Noy, N.F., Doan, A.H., Halevy, A.Y.: Semantic Integration. AI Magazine 26, 7–10 (2005)
14. Doan, A., Noy, N.F., Halevy, A.Y.: Introduction to the special issue on semantic integration. SIGMOD Rec. 33, 11–13 (2004)
15. Noy, N.F.: Semantic integration: a survey of ontology-based approaches. SIGMOD Rec. 33, 65–70 (2004)
16. Bergamaschi, S., Castano, S., Vincini, M.: Semantic integration of semistructured and structured data sources. SIGMOD Rec. 28, 54–59 (1999)
17. Krummenacher, R., Simperl, E., Nixon, L., Cerizza, D., Valle, E.D., Della, E.: Enabling the European Patient Summary Through Triplespaces. In: 20th IEEE International Symposium on Computer-based medical systems, pp. 319–324 (2007)
18. Cerizza, D., Valle, E.D., Francisco, D.D., Krummenacher, R., Munoz, H., Murth, M., Simperl, E.P.-B.: State of the art and requirements analysis for sharing health data in the triplespace (2007), http://www.tripcom.org/docs/del/D8B.1.pdf
19. Mordinyi, R.: Managing Complex and Dynamic Software Systems with Space-Based Computing. Phd Thesis, Vienna University of Technology (2010)
20. Moser, T., Schimper, K., Mordinyi, R., Anjomshoaa, A.: SAMOA - A Semi-automated Ontology Alignment Method for Systems Integration in Safety-critical Environments. In: 2nd IEEE Int. Workshop on Ontology Alignment and Visualization, pp. 724–729 (2009)

A Context-Based Schema Integration Process Applied to Healthcare Data Sources

Rosalie Barreto Belian[1] and Ana Carolina Salgado[2]

[1] Center for Health Sciences/UFPE, 50670-901, Recife, PE, Brazil
[2] Center for Informatics/UFPE, 50732-970, Recife, PE, Brazil
`rosalie.belian@ufpe.br, acs@cin.ufpe.br`

Abstract. Decision-making in healthcare mainly depends on the integration of distributed health information contained in multiple, autonomous and heterogeneous data sources. Many information integration systems have been proposed as a way of offering a concise and uniform view of the distributed data, abstracting out their syntactic, structural and semantic diversities. This paper proposes a context-based schema integration process for a mediator-based information integration system applied to healthcare data sources. The distinguishing feature of this process is to explore and model the contextual information needed for schema-level sense disambiguation in its different steps. This process tackles the semantics of data source schema elements by identifying their meanings and, thereafter, establishing semantic affinities among them. The contextual information is modeled using an ontology-based approach enabling reasoning, reusability and sharing of information.

Keywords: Health, Database integration, Schema and sub-schema, Heterogeneous databases, Database semantics, Context, Ontology design.

1 Introduction

In the recent years, the Web brought new ways of accessing health services and information by health stakeholders. However, a significant part of the decision-making information is fragmented and maintained by healthcare providers and institutions, in their own sites, causing "islands" of data, hampering the execution of health processes [1]. Health information is continuously produced with different purposes, reflecting distinct practices and using different standards/vocabularies. Thus, it is imperative that modern health services use integrated information, acquired from disparate Web data sources, enhancing their users' decision-making capabilities.

The problem of integrating information from distinct data sources is the one of solving its syntactic, structural and semantic heterogeneities providing their users with a uniform view of the distributed data [2]. Many information integration systems rely on a mediator-based approach [3-10] using a global schema to pose user queries and reformulate them to the native local source formats [11].

A **schema integration** process receives a set of data source schemas, with divergent structures and semantics, and produces a single integrated schema, with conformed resulting elements, and a set of inter-schemas mappings [12]. A schema

R. Meersman et al. (Eds.): OTM 2010 Workshops, LNCS 6428, pp. 100–109, 2010.

integration process usually performs the following tasks [12, 13]: i) the preprocessing, that translates schemas into a common format and makes element names comparable; ii) the schema matching and mapping, that produces inter-schema mappings relating semantic similar elements; and iii) the schema merging and restructuring, which groups corresponding elements to produce the integrated schema.

Even in the case of data sources from the same domain, schema integration is usually performed on heterogeneous data sources, requiring that syntactic, structural and semantic heterogeneities be addressed [14, 15, 16]. Therefore, semantic disambiguation is indispensable since, without knowing the meaning of the elements, structural and syntactic methods for integrating schemas are of little use [14].

Schemas and instances drawn from data sources rarely contain explicit semantic descriptions to derive the intended meaning or purpose of a schema element. Implicit semantic information can be obtained from controlled vocabularies and ontologies. A **domain ontology** establishes a common vocabulary for information sharing in a knowledge domain including machine-interpretable definitions of concepts and relations among them [17]. Besides, semantic interpretation is a context-dependent task which requires specific understandings about the shared domain. In this case, **contextual information** should be acquired and taken into account for identifying the meaning of element names, what may provide a more accurate semantic interpretation, allowing restrictions to or changes in the element meaning according to a given context. For example, in healthcare area, we will need domain and contextual knowledge to elucidate the meaning of the "implant" term that may refer to: i) an embryo to become attached in the womb (gynecological context); or ii) some kind of prosthetic material surgically inserted in the body (surgical context).

Context, i.e. the circumstantial elements that make a certain situation unique and comprehensible [18], may be employed as a way to improve decision-making over schema heterogeneity reconciliation. In data and schema integration, a context "contains metadata relating to its meaning, properties (such as its source, quality and precision), and organization" [14] providing useful descriptions about structural, organizational and conceptual issues related to a schema element.

Additionally, schema elements from health data sources are named according to the corporate style and usually need to be preprocessed to become in an appropriate format. Thus, contextual data may be used as auxiliary information to match schema elements and domain ontology terms, in order to retrieve a more approximated term to designate a schema element. For example, the acronym *RA* may be expanded to a number of medical terms: *Rheumatoid Arthritis*, *Renal Artery* or *Right Atrium* depending on the context.

This work proposes a context-based schema integration process, applied to healthcare data sources, whose distinguishing feature is that it explores and models the contextual information required for schema-level semantic disambiguation in its different steps. It was developed for a mediator-based information integration system, adopting the GAV approach and an internal XML-based model to represent data source and mediated schemas [19]. The contextual information was modeled using an ontology-based approach enabling reasoning, reusability and sharing of information. The paper is organized as follow. Section 2 presents a healthcare scenario with its distinct application views. Section 3 presents an overview of the schema integration process. Related work is discussed in Section 4 and, Section 5, our conclusions.

2   A Motivating Scenario

This scenario is related to a second-opinion application that allows members from the healthcare staff to work in a collaborative way, sharing information for discussing patient's diagnosis. Clinical data is kept by each health institution and can be shared through an information integration system (health care data sources: S_1, S_2 and S_3, whose excerpts are depicted in Figures 1, 2 and 3).

Legend: entities - box rectangles, attributes - ellipses, relationships - lozenges

Fig. 1. S_1 Data Source schema (clinical data from a private health organization)

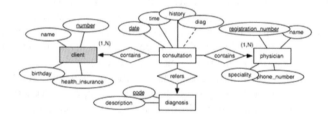

Fig. 2. S_2 Data Source schema (health insurance company and the client's medical treatments)

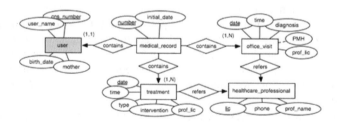

Fig. 3. S_3 Data Source schema (public health institution)

3   The Schema Integration Process - Overview

The proposed process receives native schemas from the local data sources translated to the XML-based internal model which define the tags ENTITY, ATTRIBUTE and RELATIONSHIP to represent these elements [19]. The schema is submitted to a normalization routine which makes orthographical adjustments over its element names allowing further process operations. Thus, the *Lexical Schema Enrichment* (1) produces a set of annotated schemas with the acquired lexical information. The *Semantic Schema Element Clustering* (2) classifies each schema element into their most semantically similar cluster. The resulting set of clusters includes the overall data source schema elements and constitutes the first draft of the integrated schema, being the basis for the *Mediated Schema Generation* (3). This analyses the set of clusters to produce a consistent mediated schema and a set of inter-schema mappings (among mediated and data source schemas). The overall process is detailed in [20].

Context, in our approach, is a set of contextual elements (CE) surrounding a domain entity (DE) which are considered relevant in a specific situation (for example, to solve a semantic conflict between two schema elements in a match operation, we may need take into account the sub-domain CE) [21]. We proposed a context ontology for data integration (DI) [22] that includes contextual information about: data sources, schemas, vocabulary terms (e.g. meanings, semantic relationships and lexical information), users and applications. In addition, domain information is being obtained from the source vocabulary (UMLS, www.nlm.nih.gov/research/umls/) and included in the ontology into the related CEs.

3.1 Lexical Schema Enrichment

The **Spell-check** corrects misspelling problems and expands abbreviations and acronyms. Achieved by performing a language-based matching which aims to find vocabulary terms syntactically similar to a given element name. This matching operation employs element-level schema information and also uses the context ontology as auxiliary source of domain and contextual information. Roughly speaking, this operation is carried out using the following mechanisms: i) ontology classification methods; ii) syntactic-based matching; and, iii) rule-based reasoning.

Ontology classification is used to: confirm the correct spelling of an element name and find the expanded form to abbreviations and acronyms. A string-based matching algorithm is used to find misspelled or abbreviated names. This gives rise to more than one syntactically similar term, which can be selected on the basis of a degree of similarity (string-distance) and using lexical and schematic heuristic-rules [20].

The definition below presents the extended version for the lexical schema annotation. Particularly, were extended only the ENTITY and ATTRIBUTE elements, since the RELATIONSHIP tag identifies the entity names.

Definition 1: The *lexical information annotation* is a tuple *(source_name, assigned_term, description)* that is appended to every ENTITY and ATTRIBUTE elements as an XML *attribute_list* of these elements. Thus, we have defined the following extensions: *source_name*="ontology name": represents the source of the lexical information; *assigned_term*="term name": represents the final term assigned to this element; *description*="text": represents the textual description of the term obtained from the ontology.

Example$_1$: The following tags are an excerpt of the extended "*patient*" entity from S$_1$ (Figure 1) including the lexical information (in bold).

```
<ENTITY name="patient" source_name="umls" assigned_term="patient"
        description="Any person who receives medical attention care or treatment" >
    <ATTRIBUTE name="pat_number" type="xs:integer" cardMin="1" cardMax="1" key="true"
                source_name="umls" assigned_term="patient number" description="patient
                identification"/>
    <ATTRIBUTE name="pat_name" type="xs:string" cardMin="1" cardMax="1" source_name="umls"
                assigned_term="patient name" description="patient name"/>
    <RELATIONSHIP_NAME name="office_visit_patient"/
</ENTITY
```

3.2 Semantic Schema Element Clustering

The clustering algorithm is a linguistic-based one, i.e., it groups similar schema elements using their names and intended meanings. It considers synonym, homonym and subsumption relationships to disambiguate element names in a given clustering operation, which are also used, in addition to the data source and ontology information, to identify four types of inter-cluster relationships: i) *Hypernymy/hyponymy* occurs when one semantic cluster is subsumed to another one (*is-a* relationship); ii) *Meronymy/holonymy* is the general *part-whole* relationship in which a given cluster makes part of a higher level one (*part-of* relationship); iii) *Association* is also a kind of meronymic relationship in which two clusters maintain a semantic connection (*refers-to* relationship); and iv) *Attribution* occurs between two clusters, where one represents an entity and the other, its attribute (*has* relationship).

This sub-process uses the following terminology to define semantic clusters, elements and mappings [20]: SC denotes a set of semantic clusters; Cl$_i$ denotes a given cluster that belongs to the set of semantic clusters; and, Ec$_j$: denotes a schema element from a corresponding data source that is mapped to a given cluster.

Definition 2: Let Cl$_i$ be a *semantic cluster* which is represented by the tuple (Cl_id, meaning, description, {cluster relationships}), where: *Cl_id* is the cluster id; *meaning* is the name which represents the cluster meaning; *description* is an explanation about the cluster meaning; *cluster relationships* are a set of pairs <r$_i$, t$_i$>, where r$_i$ represents a relationship with another cluster and the corresponding type t$_i$, which may be *contains*, *refers-to* or *has*, indicating hypernymy/meronymy, association or attribution.

Definition 3: Let Ec$_i$ be an *element of a cluster* represented by the tuple (Ec_id, element name, description, role, entity, key indication, mapping), where: *Ec_id* is the element id; *element name* is the name of the schema element which is associated to a cluster; *description* is a textual information explaining the element meaning; *role* establishes the role played by the element in the schema (entity or attribute); *entity* is the name of the related entity when it plays the role of attribute in the schema; *key_indication* denotes if an attribute element is the key-element of the given entity; *mapping* establishes an association between a given schema element and a specific semantic cluster. We define mapping = (Cl_id, S_id), where: Cl_id, is a semantic cluster and S_id is the data source identification.

Definition 4: Let SC be a *set of semantic clusters* that contains clusters, schema elements and mappings. Thus the set of semantic clusters is defined as: SC={(Cl$_i$, Cl$_j$,

..., Cl_m), $(Ec_1, .., EC_n)$}. Figure 4 shows a partial representation of the set of clusters generated to the running example depicted in Section 2 (Figures 1, 2 and 3).

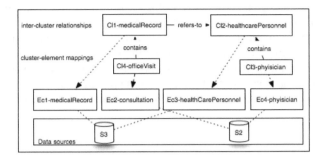

Fig. 4. A partial representation of a set of semantic clusters

The set of semantic clusters in Figure 4 has four clusters Cl_1, Cl_2, Cl_3, Cl_4 and four elements Ec_1, Ec_2, Ec_3, Ec_4 from S_2 and S_3 data sources. Thus, SC={(Cl_1, Cl_2, Cl_3, Cl_4), (Ec_1, Ec_2, Ec_3, Ec_4)}. The Cl_3 semantic cluster groups every data source schema element with meaning physician, and can be exemplified by Cl_3 = (cl_3, physician, "A licensed medical practitioner", {<healthcarePersonnel, contains> <phone, has> <name, has> <professionalCouncil, has> <specialty, has>}). This representation also includes the inter-cluster relationship between Cl_3 and Cl_2: healthcarePersonnel *contains* physician, depicted by the continued line in the diagram. According to Figure 4, the existing cluster-element mappings are (cl_1, s_3), (cl_1, s_2), (cl_2, s_3) and (cl_3, s_2), represented by the dashed lines. Furthermore, Definition 3 can be exemplified by the *physician* element representation: Ec_4 = (ec_4, physician, "Individual legally authorized to practice medicine", entity, none, none, <cl_3, s_2>).

3.3 Mediated Schema Generation

Different from the common methodologies for schema integration that includes merging and restructuring operations in this phase [12], our approach receives and analyses the set of clusters (initial outline of the integrated schema), using contextual information in order to achieve the main tasks below.

Definition of the role played by the mediated schema elements. A semantic cluster may assume the role of an entity or an attribute, depending on which role occurs most frequently in the data source schemas (information obtained from the set of clusters).

Definition of the names of the mediated schema elements. When the cluster is created it is designated with the name of the first clustered element. We have used contextual information to choose an appropriate name for a mediated element through an ontology search operation, which takes into account the set of candidate terms and selects the one that better fits user preferences and application requirements (CEs).

Definition of the resulting relationships. The set of clusters includes only the relationships obtained directly from the data sources. A resulting relationship type is the type of the relationship with the highest number of occurrences in the involved entities. In addition, using the information provided by the ontology, each existing relationship is specialized in order to keep more semantics (translated to is_a, part_of or refers_to by the clustering step). Besides, inheritance inter-clusters relationships can be also identified using ontology information. For example, the *health_professional* cluster was created due to the corresponding element in S_3. In turn, S_1 and S_2 have given rise to the *doctor* cluster. Thus, based on the ontology information, we can infer that *doctor is-a health_professional*. But, this relationship was not previously identified because it does not exist in the data sources. Figure 5 and Table 1, illustrate the resulting mediated schema and the inter-schema mappings generated by this sub-process to S_1, S_2 and S_3 healthcare data sources.

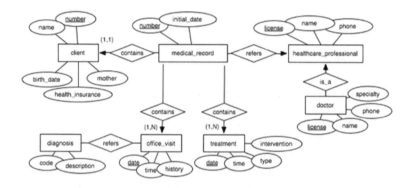

Fig. 5. S_m Mediated schema (graphical representation)

Table 1. Inter-schema mappings excerpt (S_m, S_1, S_2 and S_3)

Entity correspondence assertions
$patient_M \cong patient_1$
$patient_M \cong client_2$
$patient_M \cong user_3$
Attribute correspondence assertions
$patient_M.name_M \cong patient_1.pat\_name_1$
$patient_M.name_M \cong client_2.name_2$
$patient_M.name_M \cong user_3.user\_name_3$
$patient_M.birthdate_M \cong patient_1.age_1$
$patient_M.birthdate_M \cong client_2.birthday_2$

3.4 Implementation Issues and Results

The proposed *Schema Integration Process* was implemented in Java™ programming language and the context ontology was codified in OWL[1] using Protégé[2]. The methods for reasoning and providing access to the ontology information were provided by

---

[1] Web Ontology Language, www.w3.org/TR/owl-features/
[2] Protege 3.2-beta version, protege.stanford.edu/

Jena[3]. Ontology search operations were carried out using W3C/SPARQL[4] query language, which allows obtaining semantic information from the ontology inferred model produced by Jena. For simplicity, the set of clusters is being stored using MySQL (www.mysql.com). But, it will be stored within the ontology in order to better represent cluster elements, and also to increase decision-making capabilities.

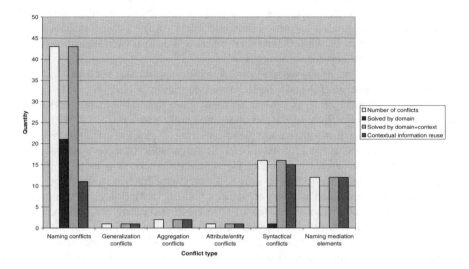

Fig. 6. Preliminary results comparing <u>domain</u> *vs* <u>context+domain</u> executions

We argue that the achievement of this solution is directly related to its effectiveness in resolving schema-level conflicts. Thus, we carried out some preliminary tests in order to characterize the semantic conflicts that were expected to be solved by the schema integration process. Thus, we have compared results from the process execution using *contextual+domain* information in contrast with results obtained only using *domain information*. Figure 6 summarizes the results obtained for each kind of conflict identified in our healthcare data source schemas.

These results were obtained considering: i) the total number of conflicts in each category; ii) the use of *domain* information only; iii) the use of *contextual+domain* information; and iv) the volume of contextual information reused in each category. The latter was measured considering the volume of contextual information that had to be codified to solve certain conflicts. The conflicts in Figure 6 were processed in the order of their appearance, revealing an increasing of knowledge reuse (i.e. the rules previously codified to solve the initial naming conflicts were reused). It is expected, also, that the quality of the ontology content be improved with further executions integrating sources from related domains. We have submitted the resulting mediated schema to a process that evaluates its quality, and proposes the removal of schema redundancies [23].

---

[3] Jena, jena.sourceforge.net/
[4] SPARQL Query Language, www.w3.org/TR/2006/WD-rdf-sparql-query-20061004/

4   Related Work

There are several data integration systems whose approaches use integrated mediated schemas, some of them specially applied to the health domain, such as: AUTOMED, BioMediator, Kontaxis *et al.* and Mork *et al.* [7-10]. While BioMediator and Mork *et al.* create the mediated schema a priori, through a manual process, AUTOMED and Kontaxis *et al.* have presented (semi-) automatic processes. In turn, AUTOMED schema matching approach identifies semantic relationships using metadata acquired from the schema objects, while Kontaxis *et al.* uses WordNet (wordnet.princeton.edu) and UMLS in lexical and semantic analysis.

Considering generic tools, we analyzed semantic approaches used in a number of systems that perform useful tasks for schema integration: Clio/ContextMatch [3, 4], Cupid [5] and Madria *et al.* [6]. Most of them have tackled semantic relationships only using dictionaries/thesauri as auxiliary semantic sources [5, 6]. Besides, just Cupid has presented a normalization task, handling expansion of abbreviation and acronyms, using thesaurus and domain-specific references. In these systems, contextual information was used to: i) locate the schema element as a node of the graph structure (as in Cupid); ii) define a unified context (mediated schema) and a target schema (data sources) used in query transformation (as in Madria *et al.*); and iii) represent contextual schema matches (as in Clio/ContextMatch). We believe that our context model used to address normalization, lexical annotation and meaning disambiguation of schema elements, and also in the mediated schema generation, could provide additional information to solve a number of schema-level conflicts beyond those tackled by the mentioned systems.

5   Concluding Remarks and Future Work

Despite the drawbacks of data integration solutions relying on mediator-based schemas, the solutions address a number of open issues which remain valid for others approaches (e.g. schema mapping generation). In this light, this work presented the application of a context-based schema integration process to real healthcare data sources (acquired from a Brazilian System for Medical 2o opinion). It proposed the usage of domain and contextual information tackling structural and semantic conflicts, which may lead to more precise results in the integration of the data source schemas. Another contribution of this work was the identification of the contextual information relevant to schema integration and particularly to naming conflicts resolution. Furthermore, in a broader way we have identified relevant contextual elements generating a specific ontology to an information integration environment.

The entire process is portable for other domains, requiring a significant effort to acquire the new domain and contextual information (which will decrease in further executions in the same domain). Additionally, the data source schemas must be represented in the internal XML format, as explained in Section 3.

In future developments we intend to tackle: the use of instance-level information, the clustering process optimization and the improvement of the ontology content (e.g. using a generic vocabulary, historical results and mappings).

References

1. Brazhnik, O., Jones, J.: Anatomy of Data Integration. J. Bio. Inform. 40(3), 252–269 (2007)
2. Sheth, A., Kashyap, V.: So Far (Schematically), yet so near (semantically). IFIP TC2/WG2.6 (1992)
3. Chiticariu, L., Hernández, M., Kolaitis, P., Popa, L.: Semi-automatic schema integration in Clio. In: 33rd International VLDB Conference, pp. 1326–1329 (2007)
4. Bohannon, P., Elnahrawy, E., Fan, W., Flaster, M.: Putting context into schema Matching. In: 32nd International VLDB Conference, pp. 307–318 (2006)
5. Madhavan, J., Bernstein, P., Rahm, E.: Generic Schema Matching with Cupid. In: 27th VLDB Conference, Roma, Italy (2001)
6. Madria, S., Passi, K., Bhowmick, S.: An XML Schema Integration and Query Mechanism System. Data & Knowledge Engineering, 266–303 (2008)
7. Zamboulis, L., Martin, N., Poulovassilis, A.: Bioinformatics Service Reconciliation By Heterogeneous Schema Transformation. In: 4th International Conference on Data Integration in the Life Sciences, pp. 89–104 (2007)
8. Donelson, L., Tarczy-Hornock, P., Mork, P., Dolan, C., Mitchell, J., Barrier, M., Mei, H.: The BioMediator system as a data integration tool to answer diverse biologic queries. MEDINFO (2004)
9. Kontaxis, K., Sakellaris, G., Fotiadis, D.: Using XML and controlled vocabularies to achieve unambiguous knowledge acquisition from multiple heterogeneous medical data sources. In: IEEE Conference on Information Technology Applications in Biomedicine (2003)
10. Mork, P., Halevy, A., Tarczy-Hornoch, P.: A model for data integration systems of biomedical data applied to online genetic databases. In: AMIA Annual Symposium (2001)
11. Wiederhold, G.: Mediators in the architecture of future information systems. IEEE Computer 3(21), 38–50 (1992)
12. Batini, C., Lanzerini, M., Navathe, S.: A comparative analysis of methodologies for database schema integration. ACM Computing Surveys 18(4), 323–364 (1986)
13. Rahm, E., Bernstein, P.: A survey of approaches to automatic schema matching. VLDB Journal 10(4), 334–350 (2001)
14. Kashyap, V., Sheth, A.: Semantic and schematic similarities between database objects: a context-based approach. The VLDB Journal 5, 276–304 (1996)
15. Kim, W.: Modern Database Systems: The Object Model, Interoperability and Beyond. ACM Press, New York (1995) ISBN 0-201-59098-0
16. Storey, V.: Understanding Semantic Relationships. VLDB Journal 2(4), 455–488 (1993)
17. Noy, N., McGuiness, D.: Ontology Development 101: A Guide to Creating Your First Ontology, CiteSeer (2001)
18. Dey, A.: Understanding and Using Context. Personal and Ubiquitous Computing Journal 5(1), 4–7 (2001)
19. Lóscio, B., Salgado, A., Galvão, L.: Conceptual Modeling of XML Schemas. In: International Conference on Conceptual Modeling ER (2003)
20. Belian, R.: A Context-based Name Resolution Approach for Semantic Schema Integration. PHD Thesis, Federal University of Pernambuco, Brazil (2008)
21. Vieira, V., Tedesco, P., Salgado, A., Brézillon, P.: Investigating the specifics of contextual elements management: The CEManTIKA Approach. In: Sixth International and Interdisciplinary Conference on Modeling and Using Context, pp. 493–506 (2007)
22. Souza, D., Belian, R., Salgado, A., Tedesco, P.: Towards a Context Ontology to Enhance Data Integration Processes. In: VLDB Workshop on Ontology-based Techniques for Databases in Information Systems and Knowledge Systems, pp. 49–56 (2008)
23. Batista, M., Salgado, A.: Minimality Quality Criterion Evaluation for Integrated Schemas. Journal of Information Assurance and Security 2, 275–287 (2007)

Data Integration Systems for Scientific Applications

Bastian Roth, Bernhard Volz, and Robin Hecht

Chair for Applied Computer Science IV
University of Bayreuth
Universitätsstraße 30
95440 Bayreuth, Germany
bastian.roth@stmail.uni-bayreuth.de
{bernhard.volz,robin.hecht}@uni-bayreuth.de

Abstract. The integration of data stemming from heterogeneous sources is an issue that has challenged computer science research for years – not to say decades. Therefore, many methods, frameworks and tools were and are still being developed that all promise to solve the integration of data. This work describes those which we think are most promising by relating them to each other. Since our focus is on scientific applications, we consider important properties within this domain such as data provenance. However, aspects like the extensibility of an approach are also considered.

1 Introduction

Data integration is an "old" problem which got an extreme boost in the past especially since the amount of data sources was and still is extremely increasing. Many examples of scientific applications nowadays depend on a high volume of reliable data – for instance the prediction of the world climate depends on data that are recorded by weather stations throughout the whole world (including data from satellites and large sensor networks). Despite the existence of standardized formats for data, there are still many heterogeneous sources whose data are needed and therefore a conversion of these data becomes inevitable. Another domain of applications that depend on lots of data and for which also the integration of many heterogeneous sources is a must, is life sciences. In the past, large international networks were formed that solely focus on providing data – GBIF [1] is just one of them.

But also the generation of data raises issues for data integration; usually, research projects generate lots of data – either manually by performing lab experiments or automatically with the help of sensor networks and related technologies. In both cases, data comes with different format and different semantics.

However, while a project is still "alive" (i.e. it has funding) all data are somehow to be related to each other in order to either approve or to refute a hypothesis. At the end of a project, data sets are normally archived in different ways – some are printed out and stored in files, others are burned on a CD or DVD and then stored somewhere; nearly all archival processes are "local", i.e. data are not available to the scientific community beyond the project lifetime. Because of that, initiatives are spreading that either demand research or assist them (e.g. by providing infrastructure and manpower) in preserving data for future use – which basically means to keep data

R. Meersman et al. (Eds.): OTM 2010 Workshops, LNCS 6428, pp. 110–118, 2010.
© Springer-Verlag Berlin Heidelberg 2010

"online". Such initiatives cumulate in international networks for exchanging data or public repositories. But when the transition of data to such a network or repository is to be performed, data conversion – and therefore data exchange or data integration – is an issue since most of the projects are not using the data structures of repositories for storage from the beginning.

Since we (as a research group at the University of Bayreuth) are facing one of aforementioned scenarios nearly on a monthly basis, we were evaluating different systems, frameworks and methods for the integration of data if and how they could help us ease the process of data integration. Sine our use cases involve only the off-line integration of rather "small" amounts of data, we are only considering systems suitable for these scenario; thus, systems which require high-performance equipment or are not obtainable for free are not discussed in this article.

The results of this evaluation are being presented within this paper. Since the quality of data is an important reason whether a certain data source is used for scientific research, our focus is on the ability of the systems to track down changes that were performed on data during the integration process. This problem is referred to as "data provenance" [2, 3]. Since all of the systems – in one or the other way – transform data from one format into the other but they merely support data provenance, it turned out that this feature is of most interest when deciding for one of the solutions.

The remainder of this contribution is structured as follows: Section 2 shortly presents a classification of data integration systems as it can be found in literature. Section 3 explains our evaluation criteria in detail; Section 4 introduces systems and frameworks for data integration which we choose for our evaluation. Section 5 then gives a comparison of these systems and Section 6 finally concludes our contribution.

2 Classification

Data integration frameworks can be classified into materialized and virtual integration systems [4] (cf. Fig. 1). For the first category, data warehouses [5] are the most famous representatives. These systems extract, transform and load data from different sources into a single schema. The so called ETL process [5] automatically updates this global repository in a predefined cycle.

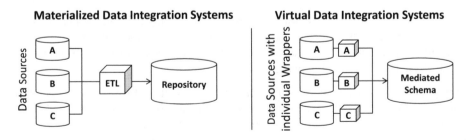

Fig. 1. Data Integration system types

Even though virtual integration systems do have a global schema as well, they do not extract data from the backend systems. The mediated schema functions as a query interface, which transforms queries by means of wrappers into the specialized queries of the original databases at runtime [6]. Afterwards, gained data are formatted and merged according to the global schema being used.

Data warehouses are used in domains where data "freshness" is less important than data completeness and system performance [7]. A manager who is interested in sales figures of the last day would prefer a materialized integration system. By contrast, the weather station which was mentioned in the introduction needs the current data of each sensor to provide an up-to-date storm warning. A virtual integration system like Federated Databases [8] would be the better choice in this scenario. However, both approaches share the integration process (cf. Fig. 2) which is kind of detached from the actual system architecture.

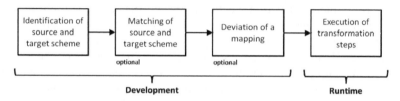

Fig. 2. Common process for data integration

Looking at this process (Fig. 2) a coarse-grained division into two phases can be made, namely *development* and *runtime*. The development phase in the trivial case only needs to identify source and target scheme because both scheme are identical and thus just a simple copy operation is required to integrate data. But normally after the identification task, source and target schema must be matched and an adequate mapping is derived in form of a transformation description that is executed later during the runtime phase. As a matter of fact, matching algorithms do not deliver perfect results such that the match first needs to be checked by a data expert [9]. Therefore, the development phase cannot be run automatically but semi-automatically.

3 Evaluation Criteria

In this paper we mainly concentrate on functionality during the runtime phase, but we also take into account the basic tasks of the development phase. Therefore we decide to compare and evaluate the analyzed frameworks by means of those criteria which are described in the following paragraphs:

a) Support for schema matching, b) Transformation functionality: available operations during runtime phase, c) Extensibility: possibility to add further/specialized operations, d) Variety of data sources and sinks that can be read/written, e) Feasibility to handle composite data, f) Support of distributed computation, g) Support of data provenance and h) Support of data fusion.

The schema matching criterion specifies whether an analyzed system supports schema matching. If one does so, the basic principles of the provided matching strategy are illustrated, e.g. the use of mapping tables and/or ontologies.

Transformation functionality is directly represented by the available transformation operations during runtime phase. These operations can be divided into three overlapping categories of atomic operations. (1) The data flow category contains operations that influence the path of data; prominent examples for such operations are read, write and update which can be judged as mandatory since they are needed to represent a "copy" operation. (2) In data manipulation category, data manipulating operations are placed (e.g. unit conversions). (3) The schema integration category comprises operations that are responsible for direct mediation between source and target schema (e.g. type conversion, renaming of attributes). Nevertheless, some operations like "compare two items" can be put into all three categories; thus, the three categories are overlapping to some extent.

The extensibility criterion refers to the ability for extending the functionality of data integration systems by providing additional or modifying existing operations. But also the possibility to add further source and sink types is part of this criterion even though it can also be accounted to another, the variety of data sources and sinks for which support is already built into the systems. Since normally scientists do not have deep knowledge about the design and implementation of complex information systems, we assume this criterion to also be of importance for the application of a data integration framework in practice. An advanced aspect within the last criteria is the abstraction level of managed data – is there a common schema for data extracted from sources or does data simply "come out" of the source with no information about schema and/or structure. In the latter case, additional meta data needs to be inferred – sometimes automatically, sometimes manually.

Also the support of composite data structures is important; in case a system does not support composite structures but most sources and sinks do, data structures have to be "flattened" at the source and "made composite" again in or before the sink. Additionally, some operations might be easier to implement in case composite data structures are supported.

Distributed computation of transformations contributes to the ability to integrate large amounts of data or such data which require expensive computations to be performed. Then, transformation tasks can be spread out to different machines allowing for balancing work load between cross-linked computers.

Data provenance means, besides recording information about the source of data, active logging of modifications which are executed on data during a transformation [2]. How much the data provenance information helps in ensuring a certain quality within data greatly depends on the method, how data provenance information is being retrieved. Data fusion [6] finally targets at removing duplicates, infer missing values or removing conflicts within data sets by merging multiple records of one and the same real-world object into one.

4 Frameworks

As mentioned in Section 2, data integration frameworks can be classified into systems that provide a materialized view and systems that provide a virtual view.

4.1 Materialized Data Integration Frameworks and Systems

Since one of the working topics of our group are Scientific Workflows, we are often encountering Kepler [10] and Taverna [11] being used also for integrating data; therefore we were investigating these systems too even they were developed for other purposes originally. Although not being pure data integration frameworks, both systems are often mentioned in combination with data integration especially concerning data intensive scientific applications [12]. While Kepler maintains execution and visualization of scientific workflows, Taverna's main focus lies in data processing through orchestration of web services.

Even though data integration is not obviously provided at the first sight, data processing is a significant component of Kepler. Kepler workflows consist of several process steps which are called actors. When accounting for allocated actors, the system provides all transformation functionalities mentioned above besides schema integration operations. Since Kepler is able to call external services from a workflow, in principle it is possible to integrate additional functionality.

The orchestration of web services is the underlying concept of Taverna. Even though Taverna offers basic functionality for data integration like read and write operations on text files, a JDBC-connection and rudimentary XML handling, the integration of third party solutions by connecting to an external web service can be necessary.

By default both frameworks are working at a quite low level of abstraction which can lead to complex configurations of workflows respectively web service orchestrations. But there are several extensions that provide good support for the data integration task, e.g. the CoMaD framework for Kepler that also brings data provenance to Kepler [13].

SnapLogic is a component-based data integration framework for the development of data integration pipelines [14]. The components which realize specific integration functionality are connected to a pipeline within the graphical designer or a domain specific language, called SnAPI. Each component usually expects a list of key-value-pairs which is specifying input and output parameters. Due to this key-value-assignment data additionally get a semantic nature. Thus a higher abstraction level of data processing is reached, because it is no longer necessary to directly work with strings and arrays – like it must be done by using Taverna or Kepler. Suitable wrapper components encapsulate both reading and writing access to different data sources and create / persist a corresponding key-value-pair representation. Even though many use cases can be realized with SnapLogic in a rather easy way, extending it is not easy because up to our knowledge there is no dedicated extension API such that developers are forced to look into the sources of the core program.

4.2 Data Integration Systems for Virtual Data Integration

The LifeDB [15] system with its SQL like query language BioFlow [16] allows for virtual integration of different sources. Within a BioFlow query arbitrary terms of each individual schema of all connected data sources can be used. However, there are two preconditions that must be fulfilled: (1) there is a wrapper for each source and (2) the scheme of sources have to be described with an ontology. Analogous to SQL, a

BioFlow query is translated into a corresponding operator tree which is finally executed by LifeDB. Basically these operators are [17]:

- Semantic Reconciliation Function: detection of a mapping based on ontologies
- Key Discovery Function: automatic detection of primary and foreign keys
- Wrapper Function: encapsulation of different types of data sources

Additionally, BioFlow supports handling composite XML based data. Such data can be queried by a SQL-based language, called Nested Relational SQL. So within a BioFlow query it is possible to select both flat tables and XML fragments simultaneously. However, so far we were not able to spot an implementation of the LifeDB system beside a limited prototype which is also no longer available.

Fusionplex [18] is a virtual integration systems that supports resolving conflicts. Together with HumMer, it is mentioned in [6] as being a promising approach. Although its core attention lies in data fusion, the system is able to support the user during the whole data integration process. However, Fusionplex assumes a global identifier for each real world object, wherefore no outstanding matching and mapping algorithms are integrated in this system.

Foremost, Fusionplex determines the global views that are relevant to the given query. Afterwards, the relevant data sets are loaded from the different sources and are materialized in a temporary repository. Unavailable attributes are filled with null values, whereas unnecessary attributes are not considered. At the end of this process, all tuples are represented in one schema.

Fusionplex considers information about the quality of data sources. This information is required during the attribute-wise fusion process where duplicate objects are reduced by fusing functions to one representation containing only one high-quality value for each attribute. Users are integrated into this process by resolving inconsistencies, evaluating the quality of data sources and the importance of the features. To allow users declaring resolution parameters like average, maximum or something else, Fusionplex introduces a special SQL dialect. Fusionplex uses a relational model internally, but supports other models too, as long as the data is presented in a tabular format.

The Humboldt-Merger system (HumMer) [19] uses a similar approach compared to Fusionplex, which allows fusing data residing in heterogeneous data sources by extending SQL. In contrast to Fusionplex, HumMer does not assume a global identifier for each real world object. Based on a specialized algorithm [20], the system supports semi-automatic matching between heterogeneous scheme. Furthermore duplicate objects are identified and merged into one automatically [19].Users can influence the whole data integration process at any time by altering the proposed mapping, classifying duplicates and defining strategies how data conflicts should be resolved. For this purpose HumMer offers a wizard like interface which requests user input if needed, but uses default settings whenever possible. Schema matching and duplicate detection are triggered automatically using default parameters. Conflict handling is specified on an attribute level by choosing one conflict handling function per column. HumMer can be used in an online mode in which all values are processed consecutively. Therefore, distributed computing is provided conceptually. Also the connection of different data source types like databases, flat files, XML files and webservices are possible [19]. Resolved data conflicts can be undone and resolved manually, so this framework supports the most minimal version of data provenance.

5 System Comparison

Generic schema matching and schema mapping are very important aspects of data integration frameworks. Users should be able to merge data from different and heterogeneous data sources with the most minimal effort. Therefore, similarities in different schemas should be detected automatically by different algorithms and, based on the results, possible transformation strategies should be offered to the user who can use them during the schema mapping phase. Taverna and Kepler do not have any schema matching and schema mapping components, but are able to integrate software solutions from third parties. Composite data structures are supported if they are based on XML. SnapLogic instead uses mapping tables. Because of not providing any schema matching operators, these mapping tables have to be specified for each component manually. Not being able to consider composite data objects is one disadvantage of this table mapping approach.

	Taverna	Kepler	SnapLogic	BioFlow	Fusionplex	HumMer
Schema Matching	No	No	Based on identical names	Based on ontologies	No	Yes
Schema Mapping	No	No	Yes	Yes	Yes	Yes
Schema Integration Operators	Integration of third party solutions	Integration of third party solutions	Yes	Yes	No	Yes
Data Manipulation Operators	Only strings, arrays and lists	Yes	Yes	Yes	No	No
Extensibility	Through web services	Through web services and applications	Only possible with Community Edition	Yes	Possible, but not supported	Possible, but not supported
Variety of data sources and sinks	Through web services	Yes	Yes	Database, XML files, web forms	Yes	Yes
Support of composite data	Based on XML	Based on XML	No	Based on XML	No	No
Shared computation	Web Services	Web Services	yes	Tools can be outsourced	No	Possible, but not supported
Data Provenance	Workflow Provenance	Only with extensions	No	No	No	Rudimental
Data Fusion	No	No	No	No	Yes	Yes
Implementation	Yes	Yes	Yes	Only prototype with very few functionality	Only prototype, no testversion	Only prototype, no testversion

Fig. 3. Summary of our findings

Both SnapLogic and BioFlow include operators for schema integration and data manipulation. While Fusionplex does not provide schema matching and schema mapping, HumMer, in contrast, supports users during the whole data integration process. Schema matching is encouraged by an own algorithm based on finding duplicate data objects by their similar attribute values. Afterwards, a mapping strategy based on schema integration techniques is suggested to the user. Obviously, this algorithm cannot handle heterogeneous arithmetic synonyms. Data manipulation is not mentioned in any reference [19-21].

Furthermore the aspect of extensible functionality of a data integration system should be incorporated. In essence, Taverna and Kepler base their data integration process on orchestration of web services. On that account their functionality could easily be extended by including other web services. In Contrast, the Community Edition of SnapLogic is not suitable for additional functionality because this version is very hard to extend. Bioflow implicates a functionality extension as well. The OntoMatch component can be replaced by more powerful tools. While offering different algorithms for data fusion neither the documentation of Fusionplex nor that one of HumMer tells whether the respective system can be extended with other algorithms. Even if these frameworks do not provide such an interface, both concepts can be extended in principle.

After merging different data sources, support for solving issues that cause inconsistent or corrupted data is necessary. Fusionplex and HumMer beside CoMaD for Kepler are the only data integration frameworks which focus on this topic.

Another important aspect of data integration is data provenance which is supported by a few frameworks in different ways. While HumMer only displays the underlying data source for each data item during the data fusion process, Taverna and Kepler provide a more detailed data provenance by means of extensions. Here, only input and output data and the corresponding transformation process are logged, the detailed operation steps are ignored. However, the CoMaD [13] approach promises to introduce sophisticated data provenance support in Kepler. The results of our evaluation are summarized in Fig. 3.

6   Conclusion

The classification is based on practical experience which we obtained from several projects where data integration was significantly important. Our experience shows that there is no system which is applicable for all kinds of use cases. Kepler and Taverna are mainly meant to be used for modeling and executing scientific workflows. However, services and methods exist that introduce data integration and data provenance in both frameworks. These extensions, if an all-embracing support for data provenance is required, call for modifications that touch the core of each system and by that force developers to re-implement their components in order to include dependencies that are only visible to these customized extensions.

SnapLogic was designed for data integration and additionally supports developers in creating a transformation by providing rudimentary matching and mapping algorithms. Since it also does not support data provenance, it cannot be applied in many scientific scenarios.

LifeDB with BioFlow is a promising approach; however, so far there is only a prototypical application available.

Fusionplex and HumMer are suitable for merging data sources with identical schemas. Beside the integration of data in a global schema both systems support resolving conflicts which are caused by duplicate values.

References

1. GBIF - Global Biodiversity Information Facilit, http://www.gbif.org/ (visited: 2010-07-05)
2. Tan, W.-C.: Provenance in Databases: Past Current and future. Bulletin of the Technical Committee on Data Engineering 32, 3–12 (2007)
3. Simmhan, Y.L., Plale, B., Gannon, D.: A Survey of Data Provenance in e-Science. ACM SIGMOD Record 34, 31–36 (2005)
4. Leser, U., Naumann, F.: Informationsintegration. dpunkt-Verlag, Heidelberg (2006)
5. Bauer, A., Günzel, H.: Data Warehouse Systeme. dpunkt.verlag, Heidelberg (2008)
6. Bleiholder, J., Naumann, F.: Data Fusion. ACM Computing Surveys (CSUR) 41, 1–40 (2008)
7. Hull, R., Zhou, G.: A Framework for Supporting Data Integration using the Materialized and Virtual Approaches. SIGMOD Rec. 25, 481–492 (1996)
8. Sheth, A.P., Larson, J.A.: Federated Database Systems for Managing Distributed, Heterogeneous, and Autonomous Databases. ACM Computing Surveys (CSUR) 22, 183–236 (1990)
9. Bernstein, P., Melnik, S.: Model Management 2.0: Manipulating Richer Mappings. In: ACM SIGMOD International Conference on Management of Data, pp. 1–12. ACM, New York (2007)
10. Kepler, https://kepler-project.org/ (visited: 2010-07-05)
11. Taverna Workflow System: http://www.taverna.org.uk/ (visited: 2010-07-05)
12. Oinn, T., Greenwood, M., Addis, M., Alpdemir, M.N., Ferris, J., Glover, K., Goble, C., Goderis, A., Hull, D., Marvin, D.: Taverna: Lessons in Creating a Workflow Environment for the Life Sciences. Concurrency and Computation: Practice and Experience 18, 1067–1100 (2006)
13. Bowers, S., McPhillips, T.M., Ludäscher, B.: Provenance in Collection-Oriented Scientific Workflows. Concurrency and Computation: Practice and Experience 20, 519–529 (2008)
14. SnapLogic - The DataFlow Company: http://www.snaplogic.org (visited: 2010-07-05)
15. Bhattacharjee, A., Islam, A., Amin, M., Hossain, S., Hosain, S., Jamil, H., Lipovich, L.: On-the-Fly Integration and Ad Hoc Querying of Life Sciences Databases Using LifeDB. In: Bhowmick, S.S., Küng, J., Wagner, R. (eds.) Database and Expert Systems Applications. LNCS, vol. 5690, pp. 561–575. Springer, Heidelberg (2009)
16. Jamil, H., El-Hajj-Diab, B.: Bioflow: A Web-based Declarative Workflow Language for Life Sciences. In: IEEE Congress on Services (SERVICES 2008), pp. 453–460. IEEE, Hawaii (2008)
17. Hosain, S., Jamil, H.: An Algebraic Language for Semantic Data Integration on the Hidden Web. In: IEEE International Conference on Semantic Computing (ICSC 2009), pp. 237–244. IEEE, Berkeley (2009)
18. Motro, A., Anokhin, P.: Fusionplex: Resolution of Data Inconsistencies in the Integration of Heterogeneous Information Sources. Information Fusion 7, 176–196 (2006)
19. Bilke, A., Bleiholder, J., Naumann, F., Böhm, C., Draba, K., Weis, M.: Automatic Data Fusion with HumMer. In: 31st International Conference on Very Large Data Bases (VLDB 2005), Trondheim, Norway, pp. 1251–1254 (2005)
20. Bilke, A., Naumann, F.: Matching Using Duplicates. In: 21st International Conference on Data Engineering (ICDE 2005), Tokyo, Japan, pp. 69–80 (2005)
21. Bleiholder, J., Naumann, F.: Declarative Data Fusion – Syntax, Semantics and Implementation. In: Eder, J., Haav, H.-M., Kalja, A., Penjam, J. (eds.) ADBIS 2005. LNCS, vol. 3631, pp. 58–73. Springer, Heidelberg (2005)

Collaborative Environmental In Situ Data Collection: Experiences and Opportunities for Ambient Data Integration

David Thau

Google, Inc., 1600 Amphitheatre Parkway, Mountain View, CA 94043
thau@google.com

Collaborative environmental in situ data collection occurs when a team of investigators goes into the field together to collect environmental data. These data might be necessary, e.g., for a biodiversity inventory, compilation of a soil density map, or to estimate above-ground forest carbon stocks. Investigators will often arrive at a location and disperse, collecting data, and then compiling it either in the field, or at a later time. Typically, an area will be divided into a set of plots, and within those, subplots. Teams of investigators will visit each of these plots with standardized forms and specialized equipment for collecting the data of interest. For example, in a forest inventory, investigators might collect data about the diameter and species of the trees in the forest, the trees' health, fire damage and soil quality at the plot, proximity to roads, and whether any logging has taken place.

Plots are often hard to reach, involving treks through dense forest, river crossings, and other obstacles. This constrains the types of materials that may be brought into the field. Once in the field, working conditions can be very uncomfortable, constraining the amount of time spent in the field. To minimize the time necessary to collect their data, teams often parallelize data collection. In some cases, each person visits a subplot and records all the data there, and the data are later combined. In other cases, one person is given the task of recording data while the others yell out measurements. Once the data have been collected, they must be validated. This validation includes verifying that numbers are within reasonable ranges, ensuring that recorded species are conceivably located in the given region, and checking the uniqueness of identifiers. Some of this validation may be done in the field, while others, such as checking system-wide identifier uniqueness, require access to database that may not easily be brought into the field.

While most people engaging in collaborative in situ data collection use paper forms to collect their data, the task lends itself to the application of more recently developed technologies, such as PDAs, smart phones, and wireless networks. This talk will provide details about collaborative environmental in situ data collection, and discuss general challenges involved in bringing non-paper-based technology into the field, as well as offer some suggestions for how these difficulties may be mitigated. Most importantly, the talk will present a number of places where ambient data integration may be applied to further reduce the amount of time involved in collecting in situ data. Finally, the talk will conclude by generalizing this work to areas outside of environmental data collection.

R. Meersman et al. (Eds.): OTM 2010 Workshops, LNCS 6428, p. 119, 2010.
© Springer-Verlag Berlin Heidelberg 2010

Incremental Validation of Models in a MDE Approach Applied to the Modeling of Complex Data Structures

Ludovic Menet, Myiam Lamolle, and Chan Le Dc

LIASD, IUT de Montreuil/Université Paris 8,
140 rue de la Nouvelle France,
93100 Montreuil, France
{l.menet,m.lamolle,c.leduc}@iut.uni-paris8.fr

Abstract. In this paper, we propose an incremental validation method in the scope of a Model Driven Engineering (MDE) approach used to develop XML Schema models. The suggested MDE approach is based on an abstraction layer thanks to UML class diagrams, and on a series of transformations allowing the definition of XML Schema models. Our method of validation aims at minimizing model errors and optimizing the process of model checking. So, we introduce the notion of "contexts of validation" allowing the check of the data model sub-parts. We also use the first-order logic to specify the constraints that the models have to verify. A validation of our approach is presented through an application that we developed.

Keywords: MDE, Meta-model, UML, UML Profile, XML Schema, Validation, Validation contexts.

1 Introduction

We can acknowledge that XML [12] has become the standard for exchanging information over the Internet. XML Schema [13] has been defined to describe the structure of an XML document in a more precise way than a simple Document Type Definition (DTD). The use of XML seems to be adapted to the definition of models but it implies an extensive knowledge of this language. A lot of softwares such as Altova XML Spy [1] have been developed to model graphically XML Schema models as trees. These softwares allow optimizing the modeling of XML schemas but each of them proposes a different formalism of representation, thus creating some confusion during the modeling of these schemas. A Model Driven Engineering (MDE) approach appears to be a solution to the difficulties encountered during the modeling of such data structures. The objective of a MDE approach is to move the complexity of an application implementation to the specification of this one. It is then an issue of making an abstraction of the programming language using an abstract modeling process focused on the use of several standards such as MOF [9], OCL [10], UML [11] and XMI [5]. In this way, the works that we have previously lead for integrating a MDE approach were of two types: modeling [8] and transformation of models [6].

In addition, structural consistency and validation processes are important aspects during the definition of data models. The classical approaches of models validation

R. Meersman et al. (Eds.): OTM 2010 Workshops, LNCS 6428, pp. 120–129, 2010.

are focused on checking the whole of a model. In these approaches, when a model is updated, it is necessary to validate the entire model in order to check whether the modification has implied some incoherence in the model's structure. In the case of small models these approaches are suitable; however, in industrials contexts with larger models, they do not. The main cause of this issue is that the informations provided by previous validation processes are not used by the later checking procedures. In this paper we propose the introduction of an incremental validation approach for optimizing the validation of data models. For this purpose we proceed in several steps:

1. Formalization of the UML class diagram meta-model to allow the expression of validation rules,
2. Definition of validation contexts focused on a graph representation,
3. Definition of the incremental validation algorithm,
4. Experimentation and validation of our approach by the development of a specific application.

In the second part of this paper, we will formalize the notion of meta-model as a mathematical object, which allows us defining rules and constraints as logical expressions of the first-order logic. Section 3 describes our incremental validation approach founded on the notion of validation contexts, and also presents an application of it. Section 4 presents our conclusions and future perspectives of this work.

2   Meta-models Formalization

The validation of models is an important step during the modeling process. The first step of our approach consists in formalizing the notion of meta-model. The formalization as a mathematical object will allow us expressing rules and constraints, and performing inferences on a model.

In this section we focus on this formalization and we will apply it on the UML class diagram meta-model.

2.1   Definitions

We formalize the notion of meta-model as being a set of *classes, attributes, references*. We use this notion for defining a meta-model *(MM)* as an 8-uplet that we can describe in the following way: *MM = {MC, P, R, T, MetaClass, PropType, RefType, Super}* where:

- *MC* is the finite set of the meta-classes of the meta-model,
- *P* is the finite set of the properties (attributes) of the meta-model,
- *R* is the finite set of the references (associations) of the meta-model,
- *T* is the finite set of primitives types used in the meta-model,
- *MetaClass* is the function that returns the meta-class of each property and reference,
- *PropType* is the function that associates to each property its primitive type,

- *RefType* is the function that associates to each reference its type of meta-class,
- *PropValue* is the function that associates to each property of a meta-class a value,
- *RefValue* is the function that associates to each reference of a meta-class a value,
- *Super* ⊂ MCxMC is the inheritance relation between the meta-classes of the meta-model. This relation is binary, not reflexive and not symmetric.

According to these definitions we can formalize the UML class diagram meta-model.

2.2   Formalization of the Concept of Class Diagram

Figure 1 presents the simplified UML class diagram meta-model.

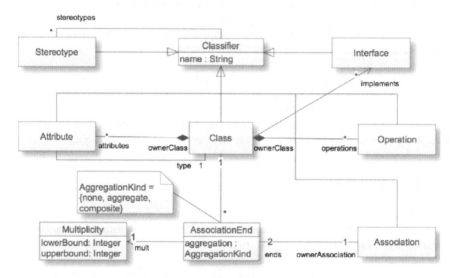

Fig. 1. UML class diagram meta-model

In this work, we exclude from the meta-model notions of *interface* and *operations*. These concepts cannot be represented with XML Schema, and have therefore to be excluded when defining a XML Schema model *via* our UML profile. Barbier and Henderson-Sellers in [3] showed the unsuitability of this meta-modeling using attributes, mainly because of the OCL constraints lacks associated with these attributes (OCL language is an UML sub-set). However Henderson-Sellers [4] precises that the use of OCL in these conditions is not adequate: it only compensates temporarily for the inconsistencies of the language. Yet OCL should be used to express additional constraints rather than as a short-term solution. Moreover very few tools supporting at times partially OCL, we decided to preserve this meta-modeling, and to focus on rules and constraints expressed as formulas of the first-order logic.

From the definitions presented in 2.1, we can formalize the meta-model of UML class diagrams as follows:

MC = {Classifier, Class, Attribute, AssociationEnd, Association, Stereotype, Multiplicity}

P = {name, lowerBound, upperBound, aggregation}

R = {type, ownerClass, attributs, mult, ends, ownerAssociation, superClass, stereotypes}

T = {String, Integer}

MetaClass(name) = {Classifier}

MetaClass(lowerBound) = {Multiplicity}

MetaClass(upperBound) = {Multiplicity}

MetaClass(aggregation) = {AssociationEnd}

PropType(name) = {String}

PropType(aggregation) = {String}

PropType(lowerBound) = {Integer}

PropType(upperBound) = {Integer}

MetaClass(type) = {Attribute}, RefType(type) = {Class}

MetaClass(owerClass) = {Attribute}, RefType(ownerClass) = {Class}

MetaClass(attributes) = {Class}, RefType(attributes) = {Attribute}

MetaClass(mult) = {AssociationEnd}, RefType(mult) = {Multiplicity}

MetaClass(ends) = {Association}, RefType(ends) = {AssociationEnd}

MetaClass(ownerAssociation) = {AssociationEnd}, RefType(ownerAssociation) = {Association}

MetaClass(superClass) = {Class}, RefType(superClass) = {Class}

MetaClass(stereotypes) = {Classifier}, RefType(stereotypes) = {Stereotype}

Super = {(Class, Classifier), (Attribute, Classifier), (Stereotype, Classifier), (Association, Classifier)}

This formalization allows us expressing constraints as formulas of the first-order logic. For example, we want to define a constraint specifying that the *ComplexType* stereotype has to uniquely be defined on elements having as meta-class, the meta-class *Class*. This rule is expressed as the equation (1):

$$\exists \, y, x \mid ((\text{Class}(y, \text{``Stereotype''}) \cap \text{Ref}(x, \text{``stereotype''}, y) \cap \text{Prop}(y, \text{``name''}, \text{``ComplexType''}) \,) \Rightarrow \text{Class}(x, \text{``Class''})) \,. \tag{1}$$

With:

- Class(m_e, m_c) is the predicate such as Class(m_e, m_c) $\Leftrightarrow$ MetaClass(m_e) = m_c,
- Prop(m_e, p, val) is the predicate such as Prop(m_e, p, val) $\Leftrightarrow$ PropValue(m_e, p) = val,

  Ref(m_e, r, val) is the predicate such as Ref(m_e, r, val) $\Leftrightarrow$ RefValue(m_e, r) = val.

3 Incremental Validation of Models Focused on Graphs

Classical approaches of model validation consist in verifying the complete consistency of a model. When a model is modified, it is necessary to validate over the whole model to check whether the modification made may have lead to an inconsistency in the model structure. In this section, we propose to introduce an incremental validation approach to reduce the checking cost by verifying just the part of model involved by the modification.

In an incremental validation approach, two issues are met: (i) What rules have to be checked for each action on the model? (ii) Which parts of the model have to be checked?

The solution to the first question is to consider that, for a given action, a series of rules must be verified. In that matter, a classification of the rules to verify will allow us indicating which rules to validate when a specific action occurs, and not verifying the ones that are not involved by this action.

Concerning the second point, we introduce the notion of *contexts*, which permit, for a given model, knowing the parts of the model that could satisfy or not a rule of validation. Using this mechanism of contexts, we optimize validation process by considering that only the modifications affecting a type of context can involve its verification. Based on these principles, we will set up an incremental validation algorithm.

3.1 Representation of Models as Graphs

Because of their structure adapted to traversal algorithms and of their easy updatability, we chose to represent a model as an oriented graph. The use of a graph allows the partitioning of a model and making inference on its entirety or on its sub-parts. For this, we have to transform the class diagrams in graphs. Figure 2 shows the graph meta-model that we defined to represent a diagram of UML class.

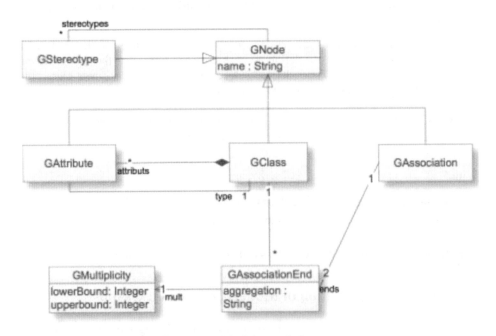

Fig. 2. Meta-model of the graph data structure

The transformation process of a class diagram to a graph must be as simple as possible. So, we define the meta-model so that it would be similar to the meta-model of UML class diagrams.

3.2 Classification of Actions and Rules of Consistency

In the scope of the definition process of data models, we define possible types of actions and categories of consistency rules. We name *events* the set of possible actions/elements combinations. For example, the modification of a class or of a property, the deletion of a reference, etc., represent events.

This typology of actions is used to specify which are the triggering events of a set of rules to check. We define 4 sets of rules, which permit the classification of consitency rules:

- RC is the set of rules defined in a model,
- RC_{CL} is the set of rules defined and applied on an element of *Class* type,
- RC_{Prop} is the set of rules defined and applied on an element of *Property* type,
- RC_{Ref} is the set of rules defined and applied on an element of *Reference* type.

  With $RC = RC_{CL} \cap RC_{Prop} \cap RC_{Ref}$

We use this classification of consistency rules and the graph representation to define the notions of validation contexts.

3.3 Validation Contexts

Our aim is to determine which sub-parts must be checked when an event is triggered in the model. For this, we define the notion of validation context as a set of elements (sub-graphs) to validate linked to a type of event. Hence we define 3 types of validation contexts:

- *Class context*, represents the set of elements depending on an event on a *Class*,
- *Property context*, represents the set of elements depending on an event on a *Property*,
- *Reference context,* represents the set of elements depending on an event on a *Reference* type.

For example, Figure 3 shows the notion of validation context from a graph corresponding to a class diagram representing a publications database.

In this example, the validation context of the class *Author* is composed of the class *Author*, its stereotypes, attributes and associations. The validation context of the association *authors* is composed of the *authors* association, its cardinalities, and the two associated classes, *i.e. Root* and *Author*. The validation context of the attribute *title_id* is composed of the attribute *title_id* and its stereotypes.

So, we define an incremental validation algorithm based on the notions of events and of validation contexts. When an event is triggered, the incremental validation algorithm process runs as follows: (i) Get the contexts associated with the event, (ii) Get the rules of consistency associated with the event, (iii) Validate the contexts depending on this event.

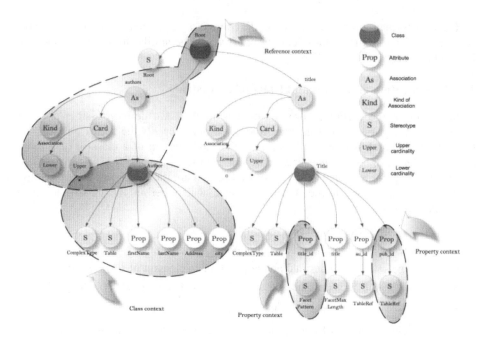

Fig. 3. Example of validation contexts representation

3.4 Application of Our Incremental Validation Approach

In order to apply our approach, we developed a modeling, which allows defining XML Schema models. This tool is based on the CASE (Computer Aided Software Environment) ArgoUML [2]. ArgoUML is an open source UML modeling software. Based on ArgoUML, we developed a module including the UML profile, and import and export functions of XML Schema models. The import function allows generating a UML class diagram from a XML Schema model. The export function allows generating the XML Schema code of a class diagram defined with our UML profile. The validation process of the UML diagrams is also extended in order to integrate our method of incremental validation. Figure 4 shows our incremental validation process that we have introduced in ArgoUML.

Figure 4 presents the link between our validation process, ArgoUML and Racer. We chose the inference engine Racer [14] because it has excellent performances on reasoning, and it defines a Java API, which allows exploiting it through an external application (i.e. ArgoUML in our case). In our validation process, we apply the algorithm that we defined in the previous part. When an event occurs on a model, the validation engine that we created is in charge, in the background, to deal automatically with this event and to validate it. The validation of this event is performed by generating its dependent contexts, and applying rules on the composing elements of these contexts. The set of contexts and rules is transmitted through a Java API to Racer, which is in charge of "reasoning" on the model's parts to validate. The results of the inference process performed by Racer are returned to ArgoUML. We deal with the messages sent by Racer to generate a validation report formulating the possible errors resulting from the event on the model.

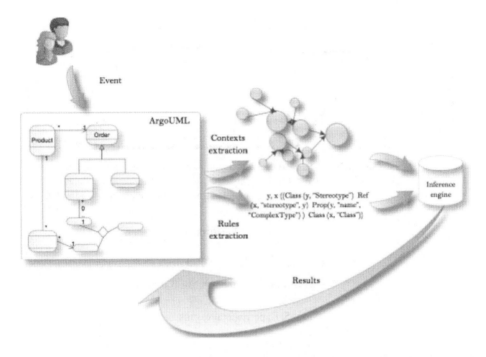

Fig. 4. Incremental validation process

3.5   Experimental Results

In this section, we propose to experiment our incremental validation approach on a model of large scale (about 5000 nodes). In order for the results to be representative, we choose to compare the performances of our incremental validation approach with a classical non-incremental validation. The comparison criteria that we held are: the time for a first validation of a model, the time for a complete revalidation, and the time for a revalidation after completing an insertion, deletion, or modification action on a model (Figure 5). We choose not to consider the aspects associated with themes of memory occupation insofar as these aspects can strongly vary from one machine to another.

When using our approach, our study shows that validation times are drastically reduced, and this for any event produced. In the case of a second validation without modification of the model, our approach reuses the information resulting from the first validation, which allows us to obtain a time reduction in the order of a tenth of the necessary time for a classical validation method. Similarly, when a simple event (insertion or modification) occurs on the model, the following validations are about five to ten times faster. Indeed, our validation algorithm allows detecting which part of the model to validate, so that only these parts are subjects to validate again.

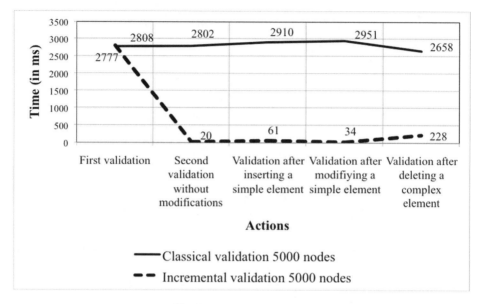

Fig. 5. Experimental results

4   Conclusion

Previously, we introduced the use of a MDE approach to define XML Schema models
([8] and [6]). This approach allowed obtaining an abstraction layer through an UML
profile dedicated to the XML Schema semantic. To move from an abstract level to a
concrete level, we defined mappings and put them into practice via an application that
we developed. We proposed in this paper an incremental approach to validate models,
in order to complete our MDE method. This approach based on notions of validation
contexts and events optimizes processes of validation on large models. Our method
does not provide an automatic correction of potential errors raised in the validation
process, as the user has to manually correct errors that are detected during each event.
To improve our method of validation, it would be interesting to focus our work on
approaches to calculate sets of corrective modifications, which will allow correcting
on an automatic manner the detected errors, or to propose adequate corrections.

References

1. Altova XMLSpy., http://www.altova.com/xmlspy
2. ArgoUML, http://argouml.tigris.org/
3. Barbier, F., Henderson-Sellers, B.: The whole-part relationship in object modelling: A
   definition in cOlOr. Information and Software Technology 43(1), 19–39 (2001)
4. Henderson-Sellers, B.: Some Problems with the UML V1.3 Metamodel. In: 34th Annual
   Hawaii International Conference on System Sciences, Maui, Hawaii, janvier 3-6 (2001)
5. Iyengar S., Brodsky A.: XML Metadata Interchange (XMI) Proposal to the OMG Object
   Analysis & Design Task. Object Management Group, http://www.omg.org.

6. Lamolle, M., Menet, L.: Towards a Bidirectional Transformation of UML and XML Models. In: Proceedings of the 2008 International Conference on E-Learning, E-Business, Enterprise Information System and E-Government, EEE 2008, juillet,, Las Vegas, Nevada, USA, pp. 14–17 (2008)
7. Menet, L., Lamolle, M.: Meta-modelling object: expression of semantic constraints in complex data structure. In: Proceedings of ERIMA 2007, Biarritz, France, pp. 104–108 (2007)
8. Menet, L., Lamolle, M.: Designing XML Pivot Models for Master Data Integration via UML Profile. In: ICEIS 2008, International Conference on Enterprise Information Systems, Barcelone, Spain, juin 12-16, vol. DISI, pp. 461–464 (2008)
9. MetaObject Facility, http://www.omg.org/mof/
10. OMG. Response, to the UML 2.0 OCL (2002),
    http://www.omg.org/docs/ad/02-05-09.pdf
11. Unified Modeling Language, http://www.uml.org
12. Extendible Markup Language (XML) 1.0. W3C XML Working Group (2000),
    http://www.w3.org/TR/REC-xml
13. W3C. XML-Schema Part 1: Structures, 2nd edn. (2004),
    http://www.w3.org/TR/xmlschema-1
14. Haarslev, V., Möller, R.: Description of the racer system and its applications. In: Proceedings of the International Workshop on Description Logics (DL 2001), Stanford, Californie, pp. 132–141 (August 2001)

Towards a Generic Infrastructure for Sustainable Management of Quality Controlled Primary Data

Thomas Buchmann, Stefan Jablonski, Bernhard Volz,
and Bernhard Westfechtel

Institute for Computer Science,
University of Bayreuth
Bayreuth, Germany
{thomas.buchmann,stefan.jablonski,bernhard.volz,
bernhard.westfechtel}@uni-bayreuth.de

Abstract. Collecting primary data in scientific research is currently being performed in numerous repositories. Frequently, these repositories have not been designed to support long-term evolution of data, processes, and tools. Furthermore, in many cases repositories have been set up for the specific needs of some research project, and are not maintained any longer when the project is terminated. Finally, quality control and data provenance issues are not addressed to a sufficient extent.

Based on the experiences gained in a joint project with biologists in the domain of biodiversity informatics, we propose a generic infrastructure for sustainable management of quality controlled primary data. The infrastructure encompasses both project and institutional repositories and provides a process for migrating project data into institutional repositories. Evolution and adaptability are supported through a generic approach with respect to underlying data schemas, processes, and tools. Specific emphasis is placed on quality assurance and data provenance.

1 Introduction

The importance of the management of *primary data* in scientific research is increasingly being recognized. Primary data are collected in an abundant set of research projects. However, severe problems are still faced concerning the long-term management of primary data and provision of these data to research communities.

For example, let us consider biodiversity data. *Biodiversity* is the variation of life forms, and it is often used as a measure for the health of biological systems. By collecting biodiversity data over long time spans, the evolution of biological systems may be traced. Therefore, it is crucial that biodiversity data are managed in a sustainable way.

Biodiversity informatics [1] is considered with the development of methods, infrastructures, and tools for managing biodiversity data. Biodiversity data are managed in numerous *repositories* on different scale levels, including personal, project, institutional, and global repositories. At a global level, *portals* such as GBIF (Global Biodiversity Information Facility [2]) and BioCASE (Biological Collection Access Service

R. Meersman et al. (Eds.): OTM 2010 Workshops, LNCS 6428, pp. 130–138, 2010.
© Springer-Verlag Berlin Heidelberg 2010

for Europe [3]) provide access to biodiversity data which are exported from a huge number of repositories. To facilitate data exchange, various *standards* such as ABCD (Access to Biological Collection Data [4]) or Darwin Core [5] have been developed under the umbrella of TDWG (Biodiversity Information Standards, previously called Taxonomic Database Working Group [6]). Furthermore, several domain-specific *frameworks* for developing biodiversity data management systems are available commercially or in the public domain, e.g., BRAHMS (Botanical Research and Herbarium Management Systems [7]) and BioOffice [8]. Finally, institutions are developing frameworks for in-house use, e.g., the DiversityWorkbench [9] hosted by the SNSB (Staatliche Naturwissenschaftliche Sammlungen Bayerns).

Thus, nowadays biodiversity informatics is a very active field, in which numerous activities are being performed on different levels of scale. However, this does by no means imply that the challenges of biodiversity informatics have already been solved. In the contrary, researchers working in this field are increasingly recognizing that they are facing difficult problems of data management. In particular, current solutions suffer from the following drawbacks:

- *Specific solutions*: Usually, the systems for managing biodiversity data have been written to solve a specific problem of data management in a defined context. These systems cannot be easily adapted to other problem domains.
- *No sustainable management*: Often, project repositories are not maintained after the funding of the project has terminated. Thus, valuable data are lost.
- *Data losses*: Since biodiversity data are spread over numerous repositories, global portals such as GBIF were founded which provide world-wide global access. However, data are exported into such portals with massive loss of data, and the data are not harmonized.
- *Lack of quality control and data provenance*: While large amounts of data may be accessed via global portals, the portals cannot guarantee a defined level of data quality, nor do they support data provenance (i.e., it cannot be traced where the data came from, in which ways they were produced, etc.).
- *No migration path from project to institutional repositories*: Institutional repositories have been set up to bridge the gap between project repositories and global portals by managing biodiversity data which are consolidated and subject to quality control. However, migration of project data into institutional repositories is a laborious process which is not supported by adequate tools.
- *No evolution support*: Biodiversity data are the results of biological research, and as such they are subject to constant change – not only on the level of instances, but also on the level of data schemas. Furthermore, the scientific work processes are changing, as well. Finally, maintaining repositories over a long period has to deal with technological evolution. Current systems are hardly designed for evolution with respect to any of these dimensions.

In this paper, we propose an *infrastructure* for sustainable management of primary data. The proposal is based on experiences which we have gained in a joint research project carried out with biologists in the domain of biodiversity informatics [10], as well as on the analysis of other projects and systems in related domains. In contrast to existing approaches which by the majority stem from the application domains and therefore focus on specific requirements of these domains, we aim at the conception and implementation of a generalizable approach which is determined by the following key characteristics:

- *Generic approach.* The infrastructure is generic such that it may be reused in different scientific domains (including, but not restricted to biodiversity data).
- *Evolution support.* The infrastructure is designed such that it may be adapted to evolving data, processes, and tools.
- *Workflow support.* The scientific work processes for data collection, analysis, and provision are defined explicitly, and their enactment is supported by workflow technology. In this way, processes may be partially automated, and because of their explicit definition they may also be changed more easily.
- *Quality control and data provenance.* Quality control and data provenance [11] are essential functions which need to be considered from the very beginning of the design of the infrastructure.
- *Focus on institutional repositories.* Institutional repositories play a key role in the sustainable management of primary data. Therefore, the infrastructure primarily focuses on the management of institutional repositories.
- *Migration of project data.* The process of migrating project data into an institutional repository is supported by tools which reduce the effort to be invested by project participants and maintainers of institutional repositories. Adequate support for data migration is crucial for populating institutional repositories.

By considering all the requirements of the application domains from the beginning, the proposed infrastructure is capable of supporting all the key characteristics concurrently. That does not mean that our infrastructure can – right from the beginning – be applied in all application domains. It means that this infrastructure can be applied in these application domains after customization. The implementation of the infrastructure is configured in such a way that the customization can be performed. This is guaranteed by leveraging on modern concepts of software, data and process engineering taking into account current research on Scientific Data Management [12].

2 Overview

Figure 1 depicts a very coarse grained overview of the generic infrastructure. The central part of the infrastructure is the *institutional data repository* which contains all kinds of primary data collected in various research projects. To provide easy management of the different data schemas used in these projects, a *generic data model* is used. This generic data model is designed for extensibility and provides sustainable support for existing and future research projects.

The infrastructure comprises a *data integration layer*, which is responsible for data migration from local research projects into the institutional data repository. Concerning data integration, two different approaches are possible: In an *a priori approach* the required data structures are defined by institutional data experts and local project experts, which results in an easy data migration. In case of *a posteriori integration*, an interactive migration process is required.

The *administration workbench* provides essential functions for sustainable management of primary data. *Unique data identification* provides for globally unique identifiers (DOIs) such that primary data can be identified reliably and persistently. To provide access control on critical data, the infrastructure is equipped with appropriate mechanisms for *rights management*. In this way, a researcher can limit the access on the collected data to himself or certain selected users, until the research results are validated and published. Finally, *quality management* is concerned with controlling the quality of primary data. Quality management provides for *data validation* and in particular includes support for *data provenance* such that all primary data may be traced reliably back to their origins.

Primary data stored in institutional data repositories may be *published* in different ways: (1) Publication of the research results on the internet or other channels is possible. (2) The data can also be exported to common data repositories or data sharing networks like GBIF [2], etc. to provide broad distribution of the gathered research results. Please note that the publication of data means assigning a permanent identifier to each data record and providing a suitable resolve service; also, data does remain within the repository in contrast to exporting it which possibly involves a transformation from the internal representation into another format.

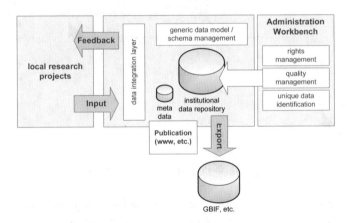

Fig. 1. Architecture

3 Project Data Migration

This section describes the processes needed to migrate data from local research projects into the global institutional data repository. When migrating data, we have to distinguish between two different scenarios: (1) The local research project was set up with a data schema which is a subset of the schema used in the institutional repository, which leads to a straightforward *a priori* integration of the collected primary data and (2) the data schema used in the local research project differs from the one used in the institutional database which requires user interaction of both local and institutional experts when establishing an *a posteriori* matching between the different schemas. Data migration is essential for sustainable management of collected primary data, since local research projects usually are funded only for a certain amount of time. After the funding ends, the local repositories are no longer being maintained which results in loss of valuable data.

Figure 2 depicts the data migration process. Ellipses represent the start and the end of the process, decisions are shown as diamonds. Process steps are depicted as boxes. A black triangle in the bottom right corner indicates a complex step which is refined by a subprocess (not shown). Input data needed for a process step are depicted by boxes above incoming control flow edges, while required roles are shown below the box for the process step itself.

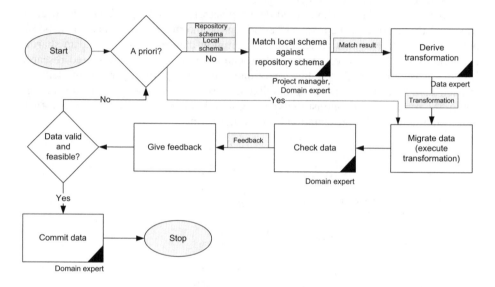

Fig. 2. Project data migration

The difference between a priori and a posteriori integration is the matching process. In order to migrate local research data from projects not using a subset of the generic data model of the institutional repository, a matching between the local schema and the institutional repository schema has to be established. In case of an a priori data integration, the necessary transformation can be described before the local research project starts. This leads to an easy data migration after the project has ended.

The process is described step by step below:

- *Match local schema against repository schema:* In this step experts both from the local research project (depicted by *project manager* in Figure 2) and the institutional repository (*domain expert*) interactively establish a mapping between the local schema and the repository schema in order to avoid data loss when migrating the primary data collected into the local research project. Both roles are needed in order to establish the transformation since each of them knows "their" schema best and thus the match can be performed most efficiently by these two roles.

- *Derive transformation:* In this step, the match result that was created in the previous step is used to derive concrete, i.e. executable, transformation rules. A data expert is required in order to describe the required transformation steps in such a manner that it can be executed in the succeeding step by a transformation framework.

- *Migrate data:* This step uses the transformation that migrates the primary data collected in local research projects into the institutional repository. This transformation can either be created a priori – in case the local research project uses a subset of the generic data model, or in case the generic data model was extended before the project was started to match the specific needs – or a posteriori by performing the steps described above. Please note that the a priori scenario will result in a much less complex transformation than the a posteriori case; thus, the a posteriori scenario is more likely to introduce errors.

- *Check data:* After the primary data was migrated into the institutional repository, a domain expert has to check and validate the results. This is a very important task concerning the overall quality of the data stored in the repository. The data transferred into the repository has to be reliable. Since every new data item transferred into the repository is checked by a domain expert, reliability can be ensured. Additionally, data provenance is being used for tracking changes and recording information about the source of data.

- *Give feedback:* The domain expert produces feedback on the migrated data in terms of quality and plausibility. This feedback is now sent back to the local project. In case of negative feedback the migration process can be restarted either from scratch or by re-using identified correspondences and transformations from the previous run. Especially if the feedback concerns local data structures rather than the quality of local data, the matching between local schema and repository schema has to be redone. However, if there are only a few minor things to fix, the repository administrator can perform correctional tasks interactively with someone from the project. Please note, that the latter case is not shown in Figure 2.

- *Commit data:* If positive feedback was given by the domain expert, the domain expert is now able to commit the data migrated from the local research project into the institutional repository. From this time on, data can be accessed from repository users if and only if the copyright holder of the data has agreed upon publication of his/her data. Please note that permanent identifiers are associated with each data item during the commit action.

4 Challenges

- *generic approach:* Since it is unrealistic to build and establish a common schema for each application domain (e.g. biology, ecology, etc.), a generic infrastructure has to be provided that allows its applicants to define and manage a schema as well as adapt a set of generic tools to this new schema (self-organization). With "managing a schema" we mean that users are empowered to define a schema and evaluate it within the community, e.g., by providing means for measuring access to the schema and allow to drop those parts of a schema which are not used frequently or whose "quality" has been evaluated in a negative sense (e.g. because nobody is using a part of a schema, entering or accessing data of it, ...). However, if the schema evolves, data still needs to be transferred to new structures such that information loss is minimized. While the general infrastructure of a repository for primary research data will more or less remain unchanged when being mapped to other application domains, data schemas are not preserved. Therefore, the support for maintaining a schema which can change constantly is an important feature for the ability to pull in other domains than those the system was designed for on the first run and thus contributes to the sustainability of the overall system.

Using innovative data models (e.g. ontologies), an "expert system" could be built that answers queries not only in the traditional "Google like" manner but also leverages from semantic relationships defined within an ontology for producing result sets that fit queries better. Also, ontologies can be used to guide users when entering data or classifying data within the repository. Altogether, semantic web technologies can contribute to data quality if they are properly and thoroughly applied.

- *workflow support*: Workflows and processes are a commonly accepted means for representing, structuring and controlling complex scenarios. The advantage of workflow technology is especially based on the ability to restructure complex operation series by re-configuration and maybe partial re-definition of a process rather than re-implementing or adapting an application. Standardized processes of a domain, but also self-defined processes can be easily transferred and adapted to the purpose of a repository because of the general high abstraction of workflows from a technical problem domain [13]. Therefore, quality management processes but also other procedures that involve human interaction within a repository (cf. Section 3) should be based on standardized workflow management solutions such as BPEL [14] or BPMN [15].

- *quality control and data provenance*: An important topic within the creation of a new repository is the possibility for integrating functionality that concerns the ensurance of data quality. On one hand, data must be reliable – which means that data are checked, e.g. by community-accepted domain experts. On the other hand, changes having been performed on the data have to be reproducible. A common way for reaching the latter goal is to introduce versioning of data. However, versioning by itself does not provide information about a certain change, i.e., why was the change necessary and how was it performed. Versioning merely tells what has been changed and what was the old value. Being able to tell more about changes is an issue in current research commonly summarized with the term "data provenance" [16, 17]. Also, standards for metadata are, if existing, to be used where applicable.

- *data migration*: From time to time even the best data structure needs to be redesigned and existing data needs to be migrated to new data structures. Also, when transferring data from old research projects into a repository, data migration from the old system into the new one is still an eminent issue. Research in computer science showed in the past years, that, e.g., model management [18] can help to at least partially solve the problems of data integration. Together with support for ontologies and ontology matching algorithms, data migration can be automated to a great extent, even though we consider fully automatic migration unrealistic in the studied application domains.

- *software architecture*: The implementation of a repository for primary research data is a long-term investment. Therefore, frameworks, tools and technologies that are standardized and expected to be available for a long time should be used. Since not every obstacle can be estimated, an approach for the architecture should be used that allows for easy customization of the system. In the past, research in computer science developed such approaches which are all based on modeling an application first and then generating most parts of the final application; e.g., consider the Model Driven Architecture [19, 20]. Beside the approach for developing an architecture, also other factors that are important for modern information systems such as the ability for scaling, a high availability, security, digital rights management and the freedom to operate such a system within a cloud (especially since cloud computing is often advertised as being a technology that ensures long-term support for operating a system) must be built-in properties of a repository. Last but not least, the user interface of such a repository should be accessible from everywhere in the world, independent of any special platform; i.e. it should be running within a browser in the spirit of a Web 2.0 application.

- *evolution*: Evolution is a concern that cuts through all others; especially since the intention is to develop a piece of software that can be operated for a long time, well-defined strategies and methods should be proposed together with the system that tell how the repository and its content can be adapted. However, this needs support within the system itself. Standardized frameworks (e.g. for querying ontologies, evaluating schema matches, workflow modeling and execution, but also for the architecture and – of course – the development lifecycle) together with modern data storage technologies provide such a support and should be used.

5 Conclusion

Our proposal benefits from its clear top-down approach: beginning with the gathering of application requirements and their analysis, a broad architecture for an infrastructure for primary data management is defined. This approach is not driven by the requirements of a single project but is based upon the experience and analysis of many primary data management projects. In this way, a generalizable architecture for a sustainable infrastructure may be achieved which differs considerably from specific solutions having been developed so far for managing primary data.

References

1. Meridith, A.L., James, L.E., Ebbe, N.: Biodiversity Informatics: The Challenge of Rapid Development, Large Databases, and Complex Data (Keynote). In: Proceedings of the 26th International Conference on Very Large Data Bases. Morgan Kaufmann Publishers Inc. Cairo (2000)
2. GBIF - Global Biodiversity Information Facility, http://www.gbif.org/ (visited: 2010-07-05)

3. Berendsohn, W.G., Döring, M., Gebhardt, M., Güntsch, A.: BioCase - A Biological Collection Access Service for Europe. Alliance News 29, 6–7 (2002)
4. Access to Biological Collection Data - version 2.0, http://www.tdwg.org/standards/115/ (visited: 2009-06-20)
5. TDWG, B.I.S.: Darwin Core. Darwin Core Task Group (2009)
6. Biodiversity Information Standards TDWG: http://www.tdwg.org/ (visited: 2010-08-11)
7. Botanical Research and Herbarium Management System (BRAHMS), http://dps.plants.ox.ac.uk/bol/BRAHMS/Home/Default/ (visited: 2010-08-11)
8. BioOffice, http://www.biooffice.at/ (visited: 2010-08-11)
9. DiversityWorkbench, http://www.diversityworkbench.net (visited: 2010-08-11)
10. Triebel, D., Ahlmer, W., Bresinsky, A., Dürhammer, O., Jablonski, S., Kehl, A., Klotz, J., Neubacher, D., Poschlod, P., Rambold, G., Schneider, T., Volz, B., Weiss, M.: Developing a sustainable working platform for gathering biological data in the field. In: International Conference on Biodiversity Informatics (eBiosphere), London, UK (2009)
11. Tan, W.-C.: Provenance in Databases: Past, Current, and future. Bulletin of the Technical Committee on Data Engineering 32, 3–12 (2007)
12. Shoshani, A., Rotem, D. (eds.): Scientific Data Management - ChallengesTechnology and Deployment. Chapman and Hall, CRC (2010)
13. Jablonski, S., Bussler, C.: Workflow Management: Modeling Concepts, Architecture and Implementation. International Thomson Computer Press, New York (1996)
14. Web Services Business Process Execution Language Version 2.0, http://docs.oasis-open.org/wsbpel/2.0/wsbpel-v2.0.html (visited: 2008-11-26)
15. BPMN 1.1 Specification, http://www.omg.org/spec/BPMN/1.1/ (visited: 2008-11-26)
16. Buneman, P., Khanna, S., Wang-Chiew, T.: Why and Where: A Characterization of Data Provenance. In: Van den Bussche, J., Vianu, V. (eds.) ICDT 2001. LNCS, vol. 1973, pp. 316–330. Springer, Heidelberg (2000)
17. Simmhan, Y.L., Plale, B., Gannon, D.: A Survey of Data Provenance in e-Science. ACM SIGMOD Record 34, 31–36 (2005)
18. Melnik, S.: Generic Model Management: Concepts And Algorithms. Springer, New York (2004)
19. Kleppe, A.G., Warmer, J., Bast, W.: MDA Explained - The Practice and Promise of the Model Driven Architecture. Addison-Wesley Longman Publishing Co., Inc, Boston (2003)
20. Stahl, T., Völter, M., Czarnecki, K.: Model-Driven Software Development: Technology, Engineering, Management. John Wiley & Sons, Chichester (2006)

DATAVIEW'10 - PC Co-chairs Message

Welcome to the 1st International Workshop on DATA Visualization and Integration in Enterprise and on the Web (DATAVIEW'10), held in conjunction with the On The Move Federated Conference and Workshops (OTM'10), October 25-29, 2010 in Hersonissou, Crete, Greece.

The increasing availability of machine-consumable data on the web offers developers and end-users new challenging opportunities for data-intensive application development. In such a context, there is an increasing need for theories, methods, and tools that address data integration and visualization, and user interaction. This workshop aims at bringing together researchers and practitioners in the fields of software engineering, web engineering, semantic web, databases, (multimedia) information retrieval and data visualization to discuss the feasibility of using and combining different approaches for creating effective data-intensive web and enterprise applications where the integration, visualization and interaction with data is a main concern.

The program of the half-day workshop includes 5 papers and a final discussion session which is open to all participants and aims at identifying additional requirements needed in order to advance the state of the art in the field by providing novel methods and techniques to existing design and development environments.

The accepted papers cover two main macro-topics: web and enterprise data visualization, and semantic web data integration and visualization.

Web and enterprise data visualization is addressed by three papers: Stefania Leone et al. propose a modular framework for experimentation with ambient wall displays, considering the problem in terms of types of abstract representations of the physical properties of the displays as well as the data to be displayed. The paper from Bozzon et al. provides a conceptual definition of the web search result layout problem for mono-, ambiguous, or multi-domain results. Finally, the work from Avi Wasser and Maya Lincoln discusses an integrated visualization framework for representing business process models according to different views, based on the user requirements of different roles involved in the process definition and consumption.

The topic of semantic web data integration and visualization is covered by paper from Marcello Leida et al. The paper discusses data visualizations for generic ontologies, presenting the major approaches and identifying the problems that prevent these approaches from providing an automatic, dynamic, generic, and flexible ontology visualization tool for analytical purposes.

We would like to thank all the persons who contributed to setting up the workshop: the authors for their submissions, the program committee members for their excellent work, and the OTM team for their great support in the organization of the workshops.

August 2010

Sara Comai
Moira Norrie
Alessandro Bozzon
DATAVIEW'10

R. Meersman et al. (Eds.): OTM 2010 Workshops, LNCS 6428, p. 139, 2010.
© Springer-Verlag Berlin Heidelberg 2010

Framework for Experimentation with Ambient Wall Displays

Stefania Leone, Alexandre de Spindler, and Moira C. Norrie

Institute for Information Systems, ETH Zurich
CH-8092 Zurich, Switzerland
{leone,despindler,norrie}@inf.ethz.ch

Abstract. Ambient walls have been proposed as a means of displaying different forms of awareness information in organisations. The ambient walls that have been developed vary widely in terms of their dimensions as well as the size and type of lights used to make up the display. Typically, the ambient wall is physically constructed and researchers then experiment with different information content and visualisations. We present a framework that supports experimentation with ambient wall displays in terms of, not only the types of awareness information displayed and its abstract representation, but also the physical properties of the display. The framework may be used for the rapid development of applications for specific walls as well as supporting the design of physical walls suited to a specific application.

1   Introduction

Within the field of CSCW (Computer Supported Cooperative Work), researchers have tackled the problem of raising community awareness in order to promote knowledge sharing within an organisation and extend cooperation beyond formal project boundaries. The aim is to make users aware of events and the activities of other members of the community in a manner that does not disrupt their normal working practices. Specific projects can be categorised according to the sources of information displayed and how it is visualised.

Ambient displays embed the information into the physical environment with the intention that the information should be displayed in a way that is, not only non-disruptive, but also calming to the users [1]. These displays may take many physical forms ranging from wall-mounted screens to sculptures and may also involve different senses such as sound and touch instead of, or as well as, sight [2,3]. Aesthetics play an important role in the design of ambient displays and a number of projects have a close link to art either involving artists in the design of the ambient display or visualising information based on artworks [4].

Hello.Wall [5] and Open Wall [6] are examples of ambient displays that use a wall of lights to display awareness information. In both cases, a physical wall was designed and built and then experiments were carried out with different kinds of awareness information and visualisations. We believe that it is important to develop tools to support experimentation with ambient wall displays

R. Meersman et al. (Eds.): OTM 2010 Workshops, LNCS 6428, pp. 140–149, 2010.
© Springer-Verlag Berlin Heidelberg 2010

before building actual physical walls. Further, these tools should be based on general software frameworks that would also support the rapid development of applications for specific ambient walls once constructed. We have developed such a framework and, in this paper, describe the main components together with an example to demonstrate its use and flexibility.

We present the background in Sect. 2 before describing our approach in Sect. 3. An overview of the architecture is given in Sect. 4. Details of the transformation and projection processes are presented in Sect. 5 and the framework itself in Sect. 6. Concluding remarks are given in Sect. 7.

2   Background

Hello.Wall is an ambient display that was developed within the Ambient Agoras project [5]. It is 1.8 metres wide and 2 metres high with 124 light-emitting cells organised in an eight-row array structure. Different light patterns were used to represent different types of information. They also distinguished between public and private patterns to make it possible to communicate personal information to users in a public space. Note that the Hello.Wall was designed to provide notifications as well as awareness and therefore also provided means to detect users and allow them to interact with the wall. Interaction was done through a special ViewPort device carried by users and they defined three communication zones — ambient, notification and interactions — based on the distance of a user to the wall. Experiments were carried out to evaluate how well the Hello.Wall and supporting artifacts could facilitate communication between remote teams. A wall was installed in a lounge space at each of the remote sites and dynamic abstract patterns used to visualise awareness information about the presence, availability and mood of remote users.

The Open Wall was developed as part of the more general SArt project exploring research issues in the intersection of art and software[1]. Open Wall is a wall-mounted display consisting of 96 circuit boards each with a 5 by 5 grid of LEDs. The circuit boards are in turn arranged in a 16 by 6 grid. Each LED can emit light with 99 possible intensities. Once the wall was built, students and also artists experimented with the wall and proposed a wide variety of content designs. A web-based interface allowed designers to easily upload and view content. Although the main focus of the Open Wall project was the design of content rather than the investigation of awareness, a number of the proposals were related to social awareness such as displaying a world canvas of Twitter updates or showing movement within buildings.

Not So White Wall[2] is an interactive wallpaper that uses heat sensitive ink and a resistor matrix to present large scale pixilated images, that slowly change.

Having worked on other awareness projects [7,8], we were interested in investigating the use of ambient walls for displaying various kinds of awareness information. However, we wanted a flexible and low cost way of being able to

---

[1] http://prosjekt.idi.ntnu.no/sart/
[2] http://www.nastypixel.com/prototype/not-so-white-walls

experiment with walls of different sizes and characteristics as well as investigating the use of different information sources and abstract representations. We therefore chose to use projection as a means of simulating a physical wall and developed a framework that allows the characteristics of the display to be configured in many different ways. In addition, one or more information sources can easily be integrated and functions defined that determine how this data will be aggregated and visualised.

3   Approach

In this section, we describe our approach based on experiments that we carried out to investigate the use of ambient wall displays to visualise awareness information about friends. The sources of information were social networking sites such as Twitter[3] and Facebook[4] which offer popular micro-blogging facilities. Using these sites, it is common nowadays for people to frequently broadcast their current status, where they are, and what they think to their community of friends [9]. The idea is to track the status update time and update frequency and display that information on the ambient wall to give the user a feeling of how active their social network is. Two different abstract representations of this, based on different wall configurations, are shown in Fig. 1.

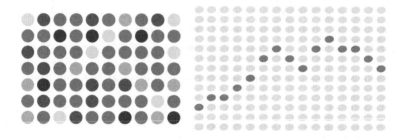

Fig. 1. Wall Screenshot

The representation on the left is effectively a snapshot of the activity level of a user's friends where the dots represent the friends and their light intensities indicate how recently they updated their status. In contrast, the representation on the right is a *dynamic representation* of the aggregated activity level of all of the user's friends displayed as a heartbeat graph. The vertical position of a dot reflects the average activity level at a particular point in time and the set of rows form a sliding time window. The fact that each dot is shifted one row every time a new activity level is added makes the graph move in a manner similar to displays on a heart beat monitor.

To track the activity level of a user's friends, we need to have access to the user's social network and define a metric for tracking the activity level. Facebook

---

[3] www.twitter.com

[4] www.facebook.com

offers an API[5] that allows application developers to access the platform data, such as a user profile and status updates, programmatically. We implemented a data provider application that registers with the Facebook API to be notified about status updates. On a regular basis, for example every hour, a snapshot is created which consists of a tuple of the form *(userid, timestamp)*, where *timestamp* is the time the status of the user with id *userid* was last updated. We define the current activity level of a friend as the timespan between now and the last time a friend's status was updated. This snapshot is sent to the wall framework, where it is stored, processed and eventually displayed on the ambient wall.

To support the development of such applications and experimentation with different abstract representations, our framework allows users to easily integrate one or more data providers, offers an extensible library of transformation functions that can be used and combined in flexible ways to generate the abstract representations and can support different walls through the notion of multiple output channels.

Since a physical wall has a pre-defined set of characteristics such as its overall dimension and the number, shape, size and arrangement of its elements, developers may want to experiment with different characteristics before building it. Therefore, our framework provides an output channel which is able to generate web pages displaying simulated walls. Such a web wall is fully configurable and the developer can specify the size of the wall and of the individual elements as well as the number, shape and arrangement of the individual elements. It can either be displayed using a conventional screen or projected onto an architectural space.

Finally, we note that it is also possible to support other forms of ambient displays that use other senses such as sight, smell, touch and hearing using our framework by simply specifying the appropriate output channel.

4   Architecture

The architecture of our framework is depicted in Fig. 2. The *Wall Framework* is the core of the system and consists of two components, the *Wall Server* and the *Channels*. The *Wall Server* deals with the applications. For every data provider, an `Application` instance is created and associated with a `Function` object transforming the provided data to numerical values visualised on a wall. An extensible set of frequently used transformation and matrix generation functions is available to the developer of wall applications. The application is also associated with a `Configuration` object defining how the numerical values are mapped to the variable characteristics of a wall such as the light intensity, colour, shape or size of its elements. The *Application Manager* is responsible for managing all the applications, functions and configurations. External data providers, depicted on the left, periodically send snapshots that are stored alongside the corresponding application instance.

---

[5] http://wiki.developers.facebook.com/index.php/API

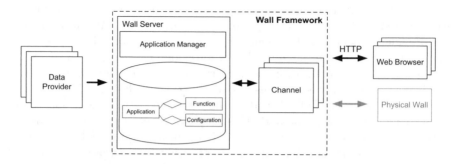

Fig. 2. Architecture

While the wall server manages communication with data providers, a *Channel* handles communication with a wall where the data is visualised. An application is registered with a channel which periodically asks the wall server if a new snapshot has been issued by a data provider. If so, the channel initiates the transformation and mapping process by requesting the latest data to be visualised. It is then responsible for conveying the received data to the wall. If multiple applications are registered with a single channel, then this process is repeated for each one of them. Our framework is extensible in that new output channels can easily be added by implementing a channel interface to handle the channel-specific display on the wall.

For example, the applications illustrated in Fig. 1 could both be registered with a predefined web channel handling the display of web-based wall simulations. This channel provides a URL for each application, to which a web browser may be set in order to view one of the web walls. Therefore, the channel maintains a map that associates applications to URLs. When a client web browser navigates to one of these URLs, the application data is embedded in an HTML document which is returned to the browser.

Note that the channel implementation is highly dependent on the wall properties. In the case of a physical wall, an update component might trigger the transformation process periodically and update the wall display with new matrix data, while, in our example, the wall display is initiated by an HTTP request.

5   Application Development

To develop an application using our framework, a data provider and channel must first be implemented and then a function and configuration defined. In a first step, an application must be created using the wall server which returns a unique identifier referring to the new application. A data provider such as the one providing the activity levels for Facebook friends uses the wall server in order to issue the snapshots that it creates, together with the application identifier. If multiple providers create snapshots for a single application, they all must use the same identifier.

Second, a channel must be provided, which encapsulates the processes of periodically checking for updates with the wall server, retrieving data to be visualised and conveying it to the wall. To integrate a channel into our framework, it must be implemented according to an interface specifying the services that enable applications to be registered and the display process to be started and stopped. When a channel is started, it conveys the data of each registered application to the wall.

Third, the function transforming the snapshot data must be either selected among the ones provided as part of the framework or implemented by the application developer. Then, the mapping of values returned by the function to the format required by the channel must be configured. The function and configuration are attached to the application using the wall server and the application identifier. Finally, the application is registered with the channel and the channel is started.

In the remainder of this section, we describe the transformation and mapping processes in detail. Fig. 3 gives an overview of these processes. On the top left, snapshots are issued by a data provider and stored. In our example, the snapshots consist of a set of tuples containing references to Facebook friends and their activity levels. Generally, a snapshot is a map containing an entry to be visualised for each instance of an application domain entity.

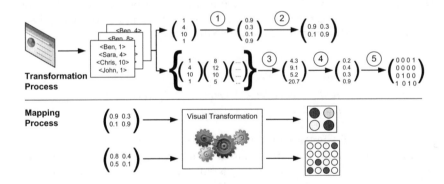

Fig. 3. Transformation and Projection Process

The goal of the transformation process is to first map the entries of one or multiple snapshots to an application-specific value and then to generate a matrix containing a value to be visualised for each wall element. In the case of our first application where the wall elements represent Facebook friends, the activity level of each friend is simply mapped to a value ranging between zero and one, as indicated by the arrow labelled (1). The matrix generation is indicated by the arrow labelled (2). The generated matrix contains the same values as the previous vector, however, arranged so that each matrix entry maps to a wall element.

For the second application, a set of n snapshots S is aggregated as follows. For all i where $0 \leq i \leq n$, the average of all entries contained in S_i is computed and put at position i of the resulting vector. Consequently, the resulting vector contains the average activity levels of each snapshot. This aggregation step is shown in the figure with an arrow labelled (3). Similar to the previous example, the vector containing the averages is then mapped to values between zero and one (4) and finally transformed to a matrix (5).

However, in contrast to the case where each matrix element represents an individual Facebook friend, this time the matrix rows represent a particular snapshot and each row contains a single non-zero entry at the column representing the average activity level. For example, the left-most row represents a snapshot which has a low average activity level. Therefore, there is a value of one at the bottom and all other entries are set to zero. Conversely, the right-most row represents a snapshot with a high level of activity and the non-zero entry is set in the top-most column. As with the previous example, the entries of this matrix have a one-to-one correspondence to wall elements. Consequently, the non-zero entries represent the heart beat graph.

In general, the transformation of snapshots into matrices is a sequence of map, reduce and generative functions applied to the snapshots. The first goal of the transformation process is achieved using an arbitrarily complex sequence of *map* and *reduce* functions. Map functions taking a vector as input produce an output vector. If they are given a set of vectors, they output a set of vectors. In contrast, reduce functions taking a single vector produce a single value whereas sets of vectors are reduced to single vectors. Functions can be composed in arbitrary order to produce the desired output, as long as the signature of a subsequent function matches the output of the preceding function.

$$Map = f(Vector) : Vector$$
$$MapSet = f(Set < Vector >) : Set < Vector >$$
$$Reduce = f(Set < Vector >) : Vector$$
$$ReduceSet = f(Set < Vector >) : Set < Vector >$$

The second step of the transformation proceses consists of generating a matrix by means of *generative* vector-to-matrix functions. Since the final matrix representation contains the entries to be visualised by individual wall elements, its size corresponds to the dimensions of the wall as specified by the configuration associated to the application.

Since we want to support different kinds of wall displays, we make a separation between the matrix representation and the actual output format. While the matrix representation generated by the transformation process only specifies the values to be rendered with the wall elements, the final output matrix of the mapping process contains values of a channel-specific format.

In the lower part of Fig. 3, the two matrices are transformed to different visual representations according to the application configuration. In the case of the web wall, where the matrix entries are rendered to HTML elements, one can specify element shapes, colours and sizes. Each of these properties can either be defined to be static or to be varied according to the matrix values. For the upper representation, the matrix values have been transformed to RGB colour definitions of the form $\#1E457B$ which is dark blue for very active friends,

$\#C6DDFF$ for friends with a lower activity level and $\#F0F7FF$ as a light blue for the least active ones. The element shape and size are static. In the lower example, the element colour is binary and the other characteristics are static.

6 Framework

An application developed using our framework is composed of four components: a data provider which produces snapshots consisting of domain entities and their values of interest, a set of function implementations which will be applied as part of the transformation process, a channel implementation that displays the collected and transformed data as well as a channel-specific configuration.

The framework API offers programmatic access for creating and retrieving applications and storing associated snapshots in the database. Fig. 4 shows the classes forming the API. The ApplicationManager manages applications which are represented as instances of the Application class. Such instances offer the means for the data provider to store snapshots. Using the set(Snapshot) method, the data provider periodically stores a map of the form Map<Object, Object> where entities are mapped to their values to be visualised. Such a map is an instance of the Snapshot class which allows a value to be set for a given entity by means of its set method.

Fig. 4. Framework API

Fig. 5 shows the interfaces and abstract classes that represent the functions of the transformation process and support their composition. Our framework provides a set of map and reduce functions which are applicable to sets and single vectors. Moreover, application developers can implement their own functions according to the interfaces.

In order to provide a composed function, the developer creates a class extending the abstract Composed class which provides the means to add and access child functions. The composed function provided by the developer must implement one of the Map, MapSet and Reduce or ReduceSet interfaces, such that it can

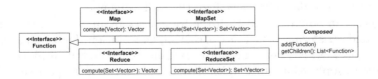

Fig. 5. Interfaces and abstract class definition for the transformation functions

be seamlessly integrated into the transformation process. The implementation of the respective `compute()` method consists of iterating over all child functions, calling their `compute()` methods and returning a result. The return value can either be the result of the last child in the case of a sequential composition or an aggregation over all children results.

The transformation process of an application is configured using the `set-(Function)` method declared by the `Application` class. This method takes a single root function object as an argument. The root function may be a single atomic function or a composed function consisting of children functions which may in turn be atomic or composed.

For the mapping process, the configuration is defined for a specific channel. In the case of a physical wall, the configuration simply defines the mapping of numerical values to light intensity or colour. A web wall is configured in terms of its dimensions, number of elements, their shape, size and colour. In both cases, each of these properties can either be set to be constant or to reflect the values of the matrix representation. If a property should represent a variable value, a translator class is specified. This class must implement a `Translator` interface declaring a single method `translate(float)` which returns a value that can be sent to the wall.

The following XML code shows a configuration for the example application visualising Facebook friend activity levels.

```
<configuration application="Facebook">
  <dimension>
    <rows>13</rows>
    <columns>15</columns>
  </dimension>
  <shape>
    <type>oval</type>
    ...
  </shape>
  <colour>grey</colour>
  <intensity>ActivityLevelTranslator</intensity>
  <url>../ambientApp/facebookAggregatedDisplay</url>
</configuration>
```

The dimension of the wall is set to be a 13 x 15 matrix of oval elements with a fixed size. If the number of entities to be displayed is unknown or even varying in each snapshot, the dimension can be specified as a single float value indicating the ratio of rows to columns. The actual dimensions are then computed at runtime according to the number of entities provided. An `ActivityLevelTranslator` class is specified to define the colour of the wall elements.

Channels can be integrated with the framework by implementing a `Channel` interface and registering an instance of this implementation. The channel interface declares three methods `registerApplication`, `start` and `stop` which are used to register an application, start and stop the display process, respectively. When a channel is started, it will periodically retrieve the output matrix of the registered applications and display the values on the wall. The framework features a built-in web channel which can be accessed using regular web browsers that navigate to the application-specific URL. The URL can be set in the channel configuration file shown above.

7 Conclusion

We have presented a framework that supports the development of applications for ambient wall displays. Our framework is highly configurable and extensible in that information from different sources can be presented on different kinds of ambient displays using a variety of abstract representations. In addition to supporting the development of applications for specific physical wall displays, the flexibility of the framework also makes it ideal for rapid prototyping as part of the design of physical walls.

References

1. Weiser, M., Brown, J.: Designing Calm Technology. PowerGrid Journal 1 (July 1996)
2. Ishii, H., Wineski, C., Brave, S., Dahley, A., Gorbet, M., Ullmer, B., Yarin, P.: ambientRoom: Integrating Ambient Media with Architectural Space. In: Proc. CHI 1998 (1998)
3. Pedersen, E., Sokoler, T.: AROMA: Abstract Representation Of Presence Supporting Mutual Awareness. In: Proc. CHI 1997 (1997)
4. Holmquist, L., Skog, T.: Informative Art: Information Visualization in Everyday Environments. In: Graphite 2003 (Febraury 2003)
5. Streitz, N., Röcker, C., Prante, T., van Alphen, D., Stenzel, R., Magerkurth, C.: Designing Smart Artifacts for Smart Environments. Computer 38(3) (March 2005)
6. Jaccheri, L.: The Open Wall: A Software-Intensive Art Installation. ERCIM News (77) (April 2009)
7. de Spindler, A., Leone, S., Geel, M., Norrie, M.C.: Using Tag Clouds to Promote Community Awareness in Research Environments. In: Proc. CDVE 2010 (2010)
8. Decurtins, C., Norrie, M.C., Reuss, E., Weibel, N.: AwareNews - A Context-Aware Peripheral News and Awareness Display. In: Proc. IE 2008. (2008)
9. Java, A., Song, X., Finin, T., Tseng, B.: Why we twitter: understanding microblogging usage and communities. In: Zhang, H., Spiliopoulou, M., Mobasher, B., Giles, C.L., McCallum, A., Nasraoui, O., Srivastava, J., Yen, J. (eds.) WebKDD 2007. LNCS, vol. 5439, pp. 56–65. Springer, Heidelberg (2009)

A Characterization of the Layout Definition Problem for Web Search Results

Alessandro Bozzon, Marco Brambilla, and Sara Comai

Politecnico di Milano
Dipartimento di Elettronica e Informazione (DEI)
Piazza L. Da Vinci 32,
I-20133 Milan, Italy
{alessandro.bozzon,sara.comai,marco.brambilla}@polimi.it

Abstract. In the last years the user information seeking process on the Web has shifted from document search to object search. Hence, the answers provided by Web search engines cannot consist any more in a mere list of pages. In this paper we consider queries returning *mono-*, *ambiguous*, or *multi-domain results*, where the domain represents a specific field of interests such as *City*, *People*, *Movies*, etc. and we characterize the problem for the definition of the layout of such results. In particular, we describe a conceptual definition of the Web search result layout problem, by identifying: the parameters involved in the layout design, the tuning dimensions available for optimizing the result layout, and the possible strategies that can be adopted for producing such layouts. Finally, we provide an outlook on the possible future research directions on this topic.

1 Introduction and Motivation

Latest years witnessed a huge increase in the amount of produced digital data. As a results, the need arose for applications able to mine in huge repositories and help users in finding information. The most representative example of such application classes are search engines, which rapidly became a key asset in any kind of information system, providing the basic functionalities to support the user information seeking process [6]. As the amount and kind of information grew, user requirements changed, and search engines needed to adapt accordingly. In the context of the Web, for instance, few years sufficed to shift the user information seeking process from document search to the object search and search as a process paradigms [1,8]. This is the effect of two separate trends: on one side, users start looking for information and objects of interest instead of Web pages that describe such objects. Therefore, they expect the search engine of choice to directly satisfy their need. For instance, if the user asks for the temperature in New York City, he expects the search engine to directly find this information, not a list of pages dealing about it. On the other side, as users get confident in the use of search engines, their queries become more and more complex, to the point that their formulation goes beyond what can be expressed with a few

R. Meersman et al. (Eds.): OTM 2010 Workshops, LNCS 6428, pp. 150–159, 2010.

keywords or within a one-shot question. Thus, typically the interaction involves several request and response steps, and answers must consist in something more structured than a list of Web pages [2].

To cope with such new requirements, Web search engines must tailor their algorithms and interfaces to different information *domains*, i.e. semantic fields of interest such as cities, people, restaurants, hotels, movies, and so on. Furthermore, for each domain of interest, result sets can comprise contents of different *types*, such as images, news feeds, videos, web pages, and so on. The *domain*, *content type* and *layout* of the result set must comply with the user expectations according to the *intent* expressed in the query, which can span one or more domains.

Throughout the paper, we will refer to three representative examples of keyword-based queries, to clarify the different issues that arise when addressing the problems of result layout design:

- Query 1: *"Washington D.C."*; this is an example of *mono-domain query*, i.e., a query concerning a single semantic domain, the City domain. The challenge in this case is simply to identify the best mix of result types and visualizations for the specified domain.
- Query 2: *"Washington"*; this is an example of *ambiguous domain query*, i.e., a query that yields multiple semantic domains. Indeed, the query "Washington" may either refer to "Washington D.C." (the capital of the U.S.), to "George Washington" (the first U.S. president), or to the "Washington" state. The main issue associated with this query is to identify the user intent or, when this is not possible, to produce a *diversified result* set (and display) to grant coverage of the most expected intents;
- Query 3: *"rock concert Washington July 2010 good restaurant "*; this is an example of *multi-domain query*, i.e. a query which expresses an information need spanning several domains that are explicitly mentioned in the query. In this case, the query refers to cities, restaurants, and concerts. The main issue associated with this kind of query is to compose a result set (and appropriate layout) of *composed objects*, built by connecting different concepts together.

The results of all these queries are composed by heterogeneous information items, i.e., belonging to different types. For example, different types of information may be returned for the US capital city like maps, news, images, etc. Typically, different result types are produced by different search engines, and then need to be aggregated in an optimal unified layout. Unfortunately, while search result layout appears to be an interesting research field, no attention has been devoted so far to the problem of the automatic display of search results.

In this paper, we propose a conceptual definition of the search result layout problem, by identifying: the parameters involved in the layout design, the tuning dimensions available for optimizing the result layout, and the possible strategies that can be adopted for producing such layouts. In Section 2 we outline the current status of the field; in Section 3 we present our reference framework model; in Section 4 we point out the main design dimensions to consider in the definition of search results layout. Finally, Section 5 draws the conclusions and provides an outlook on the possible future research directions on this topic.

2   Background

The visualization of search results is a core asset for modern search engines, as several studies show that result visualization is accountable for a big part of the perceived quality in the user experience [4]. Different approaches are implemented by the various system, to tackle the problem described in the examples above.

General-purpose Web search engines (e.g. Google, Yahoo! and Bing) now include domain-specific functionalities (e.g. image, video, blog, news, Web page, search) to provide better results, but their performances are limited to the capability of dealing with *mono-domain* and *ambiguous domain queries*: for *Query 1* the engine aggregates results coming from the different domain-specific search engines (e.g., the Local and Image engines so as to show both the map of "Washington D.C."), while for *Query 2*, a general-purpose engine typically performs a result diversification task [7], splitting the result list to include information items related to all the identified domains. The organization of results in the page is then generated, according to a custom, proprietary function that takes into account at least the identified domains, the cardinality of the result sets, and the user profiles. By observing the behaviours of the engines, one can guess that only a few domains are recognized and that custom templates are used for the most common ones.

On the other hand, multi-domain queries are usually not managed correctly by search systems. The only approach that takes into account this issue is Search Computing (SeCo) [3], which recently proposed a set of methods an tools for tackling *explicit* multi-domain queries by automatically joining the results of various search services in order to build a comprehensive answer, integrating relevant pieces of information found in different domains. In Search Computing aggregation is performed at a system level, and a single result list is produced, consisting of *combinations* of results belonging to different domain. Engines like the one provided by SeCo enable the computation of queries like *Query 3*, possibly adding functionalities such as global ranking, top-k result calculation, multiple visualization, and so on.

3   Model of the Search Process

The search process for a typical search engine integrating domain-specific search results can be modeled as shown in Figure 1, and it consists of the following phases:

Query submission: the user submits the query, typically specifying some keywords in a search form. More complex input formats (e.g., structured multi-field forms) convey more information and clearer user semantics, thus easing the job of the search engine in identifying the user intents and the involved domains.

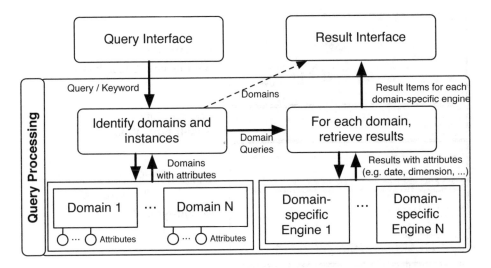

Fig. 1. Overview of a typical query and result presentation process

Query computation: the search engine computes the result of the submitted query. Given the initial query, the engine may identify one or more *domains* the query may refer to.

In our model we assume the presence of a pre-determined set of domains (e.g., City, People, Restaurant, Hotel, etc.), where each domain is characterized by a set of typed *attributes*, describing its properties. Domains may also be organized in taxonomies or ontologies, where domain-to-domain relationships may include generalizations/specializations. or be generic associations (e.g., similarity). We also assume that, given a query, a domain identification service is able to retrieve all the involved domains.

For each identified domain, domain-specific sub-engines are invoked to retrieve the corresponding results. We assume that each sub-engine yields a specific *result-type*, i.e. a physical definition of the underlying domain, where each attribute yields an atomic or composite type. For instance, the *City* domain may be described at a physical level by a *Local* result type composed by attributes such as *name:string, population:float, geoCoordinates:[latitude:float, longitude:float], pictures: {image: url}*.

This model can also include relationships between the *domains* and the *content type-specific engines*, so that, depending on the domain, specific engines may be selected: e.g., for *City* retrieve information of type *Local, Image, Web*, etc.; for *Concert* retrieve information of type *Web, Image, Video, News*, etc.

Result visualization: the user interface shows a subset of the retrieved results, possibly related to different domains. As exemplified in Figure 2 and Figure 3, for each domain, the interface may stress different attributes, so as to enable alternative visualizations. In the following we will focus on this phase, assuming that the set of retrieved domains, result types, and attributes are available.

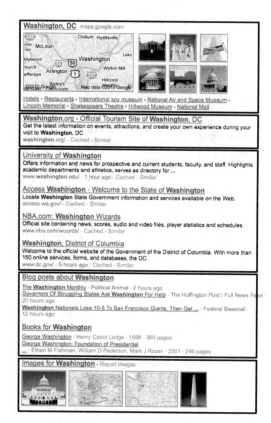

Domain: City
Result-type: Local, Image

Domain: City
Result-type: Web

Domains: City, State, Sport Team, Organizations
Result-type: Web

Domains: City, People, Sport Team
Result-type: Books, Blogs

Domains: People, State
Result-type: Images

Fig. 2. An example of ambiguous domain result list layout for *Query 2*. Source: www.google.com

Domain: Concert   **Domain**: Hotel   **Domain**: Restaurant
Result-Type: Web   **Result-Type**: Web **Result-Type**: Web

Fig. 3. An example of multi-domain result list layout for *Query 3'*. Source: demo.search-computing.org

4   Characterizing the Layout Definition Problem

Defining the final layout of the results is a complex problem, which involves several design decisions and tuning parameters. The following sections will elaborate on the parameters involved in the layout design (Section 4.1), the tuning dimensions available for optimizing the result layout and the possible strategies that can be adopted for producing such layouts (Section 4.2).

4.1   Parameters

The calculation of the page layout for a generic Web search result list is affected by a set of parameters, which can be calculated either off-line (before executing the query) or only at run-time (after the execution of the query). Examples of off-line parameters include:

1. *Relationships between domains*: if a relationship exists between domains, then such association can be exploited to drive the aggregation/distribution of results coming from each domain;
2. *Relationships between result types*: if a relationship exists between different results types, mash-up components may be used: for example, images/videos may be placed within a map. Furthermore, if several attributes belong to the same type, they can be conveyed through a unified view. For instance, if several geographical coordinates are available, they can be shown altogether in the same map.
3. *Relationships between domains and result types*: if a relationship exists between domains and result types, explicit selection heuristics can be used; for instance, the system may assume that a *City* domain is better represented by a *Local* result type and by an *Image* type.
4. *Knowledge about user behaviour*: user studies may reveal information about the behavior of users when exploring a result list page. Several studies highlight the importance of the so-called "golden triangle", that is the left-top part of the page [4]; other studies [5], instead, reveal how users interact with the result items, showing, for instance, that the 6th result in a result page is usually more clicked than the 4th and the 5th; such information can be used to better define the layout of the result page, assigning items to the most appropriate locations;
5. *User profile* : users may specify preferences on the result types to be shown, on the preferred Web page languages, etc. Such information can be used to discriminate among domain specific search engines in the system.

Several run-time parameters impact on the layout decision too, including:

1. The *relevance of the domains* w.r.t. to the query. In ambiguous domain queries, such relevance is the likelihood of the domain for the provided query. For instance, in *query 2,* "Washington" may refer to the city with probability 70%, to George Washington with probability 20%, and to Washington state

with probability 10%. In explicit multi-domain queries, instead, the importance of a domain can be proportional to the number of results it yields for a given query; for instance, *query 3* might return combinations composed of few restaurants but several concerts. In such a case, one may evaluate the informativeness brought by each domain-specific result list, thus privileging, in the final results list, restaurants out of concerts;

2. For each *result type*, the cardinality of the results list, the scoring profile(s) and/or default sorting function(s) of the results with respect to some attribute(s) (like, for example, the number of visualizations or the recency of a video or piece of news);

3. *User context*: the system may try to infer the *user intent* by exploiting contextual informations about the user, such as her location, or her previous queries in her current interaction session. For instance, if the user is currently in Washington and submits *query 2*, the *Local* results may be more important than *Book* ones, as, probably, the user is more interested in getting information about her surroundings.

4.2 Layout Dimensions and Strategies

Off-line and run-time parameters can be exploited to design the layout of the result page.

The layout can be defined at different levels of abstraction: at a **lower level** of abstraction concrete languages for the specification of the layout are taken into account and a wireframe of the page can be defined (as exemplified in Figure 4): at this level, the style of the page is defined, including its structure and look&feel. The different *areas of the page* can be identified both for fixed content (like, e.g., a navigation menu, targeted advertisements, or related queries) and for the dynamic content of the results (that can be possibly organized into columns/rows, like in the central part of Figure 4). Moreover, *formatting* rules for graphic items, like fonts, colors, borders, and margins can be expressed, e.g., by means of Cascading Style Sheets rules or equivalent specifications. Such rules can be defined at page level or, possibly, can be differentiated for result types (e.g., for images, Web links, etc.) or conceptual elements (e.g., a specific style may be defined for domains, a different style can be used to highlight relationships between domains in multi-domain results, etc.).

At a **higher level** of abstraction, conceptual elements like the domains, the result types, and their attributes can be considered: at this level the *positioning* of the dynamically retrieved results is actually defined. The design of the positioning is quite hard, since several options are possible. Such design choices can be taken according to rules expressed as functions of the off-line and run-time parameters described in the previous section. Among the available layout design dimensions, we can identify:

– How many domains should be shown in the first page of the results? In which order? For example, in ambiguous domain queries, the relevance can be considered to determine both the number of domains and their order; in

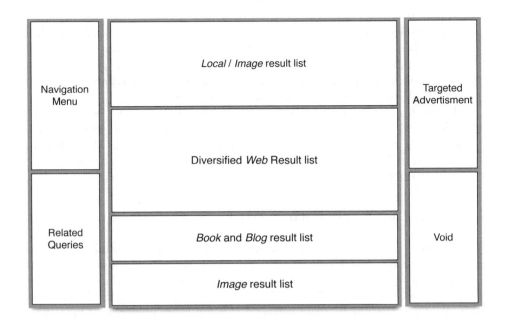

Fig. 4. An example of page layout wireframe for the result page of Figure 2

explicit multi-domain queries the number of instances of each domain and the instances of their relationships may determine such information.

- How much space should be devoted to each domain? Which specific locations of the page may be dedicated to given domains to better reflect their importance in the result list? This might be based on the estimated relevance of the domain w.r.t. the query.
- Given a domain, how many results types should be shown? In which order? How much space should be devoted to each result type? For example, for a given domain, *Web* links, *Images* and *News* are returned; *Images* may be repeated in different locations (e.g., at the top and at the bottom of the page) or with the same fixed space; *Images* are provided before *Web* links for specific domains like Cities, People etc, otherwise they are placed after the *Web* links, etc.
- For each result type, which attributes should be shown to the end user? In which order? For example, for Images only a clickable snapshot may be shown; for Books the title, publisher, and a link may be shown.

Once the dimensions are identified, proper design strategies are required. Such strategies must be adaptive to both off-line and run-time parameters, to better fit the user information needs and the underlying information seeking task. A design strategy consists of several *layout specification rules*, which can be produced:

- *Manually*, when the interface designer holds the experience and the knowledge required to provide a satisfactory user interface;

- *Automatically* inferred from *a-priori knowledge* about the involved *domains*: if quantitative information about the identified domains is available, then such information should be used to drive the layout definition. For instance, if in a multi-domain query a relationship holds between *City* and *Movie*, quantitative information about the cardinality of the relationship can be used to define the order of appearance of the domains.
- *Automatically* inferred from *a-priori knowledge* about the *users*: log mining techniques can be applied to identify the typical user interaction patterns with both *domains* and *result types*. For instance, if the logs show that for the *People* domain a *result type* including pictures is favored, then such a trend should be considered.

5   Conclusions and Future Work

In this paper we have introduced a general framework describing the search process for mono-, ambiguous, and multi- domain queries, where the results are composed by heterogeneous information items, possibly produced by several search engines. For such results one of the challenging problem is the definition of their layout. At this aim we identified a set of possible parameters that may affect the design choices of the layout, classified into off-line and run-time parameters; moreover, we outlined the main layout dimensions that need to be considered in the positioning of the result items.

Current search engines adopt pre-defined strategies for known domains or result types and only focus on mono- and ambiguous domain queries. As future work we plan to define general-purpose algorithms and heuristics to generalize the solution, including all the parameters detailed in Section 4.1. Moreover, we plan to integrate this study with user evaluation, to assess the efficacy of the selected parameters and to measure the effectiveness of the different layouts that can be obtained for the different types of queries.

Acknowledgments. This research is part of the Search Computing (SeCo) project [www.search-computing.org], funded by the European Research Council (ERC).

References

1. Baeza-Yates, R., Raghavan, P.: Next generation web search. In: Ceri, S., Brambilla, M. (eds.) Search Computing. LNCS, vol. 5950, pp. 11–23. Springer, Heidelberg (2010)
2. Bozzon, A., Brambilla, M., Ceri, S., Fraternali, P.: Liquid Query: Multi-domain Exploratory Search on the Web. In: WWW 2010: 19th International Conference on World Wide Web, pp. 161–170. ACM, New York (2010)
3. Ceri, S., Brambilla, M.: Search Computing. LNCS, vol. 5950. Springer, Heidelberg (2010)
4. Hearst, M.A.: Search User Interfaces, 1st edn. Cambridge University Press, Cambridge (2009)

5. Joachims, T., Granka, L., Pang, B., Hembrooke, H., Gay, G.: Accurately interpreting clickthrough data as implicit feedback. In: ACM SIGIR Conference on Research and Development in Information Retrieval (SIGIR), pp. 154–161 (2005)
6. Kuhlthau, C.C.: Inside the search process: Information seeking from the user's perspective. Journal of the American Society for Information Science 42(5-5), 361–371 (1991)
7. Minack, E., Demartini, G., Nejdl, W.: approaches to search result diversification. In: Bernstein, A., Karger, D.R., Heath, T., Feigenbaum, L., Maynard, D., Motta, E., Thirunarayan, K. (eds.) ISWC 2009. LNCS, vol. 5823, Springer, Heidelberg (2009)
8. Nie, Z., Zhang, Y., Wen, J.R., Ma, W.Y.: Object-level ranking: bringing order to web objects. In: WWW 2005: Proceedings of the 14th International Conference on World Wide Web, pp. 567–574. ACM Press, New York (2005)

ProcessGene View: An Integrated Visualization of Business Process Models

Avi Wasser[1] and Maya Lincoln[2]

[1] University of Haifa, Mount Carmel, Israel
awasser@research.haifa.ac.il
[2] ProcessGene Ltd. 10940 Wilshire Bvd., Los Angeles, CA 90024, USA
maya.lincoln@processgene.com

Abstract. One of the main challenges in the field of business process management is creating visibility into the business of organizations. The prevailing approach utilizes conceptual business process modeling as the foundation for creating and managing this visibility. Our approach aims to extend previous academic and industry efforts in this field by suggesting a systematic business process visualization method - featuring the multi-faceted visualization interfaces to an existing process model. Each interface encapsulates the data in a different manner- aiming to serve different user populations as well as different use-cases. To test and illustrate the suggested method we implemented it as an add-on to an off-the-shelf BPM software suite.

Keywords: Business process model visibility, Conceptual models for data visualization and exploration, Interfaces for Web-scale and large-scale data repositories search and exploration.

1 Introduction

During the past decade Business Process Management (BPM) has become a significant research domain, with vast applications in industry [13,2]. One of the main BPM challenges has been creating visibility into the business of organizations [6,10,9,8] and the prevailing approach utilizes conceptual business process modeling as the foundation for creating and managing this visibility - aiming to present the entire business knowledge in a unified environment. Business process models typically encompass a large set of data artifacts of different types, that may include process narratives, diagrams and flowcharts, IT configurations, administrative information such as user change requests and compliance data. These artifacts serve different types of users, at various business scenarios. The extent and diversity of data within the process model on one hand and the diversity of user types (e.g. business users, software developers, solution architects) and usage scenarios on the other hand makes it difficult to visualize the process data and use the model effectively.

Our work aims to present a method for supporting the encapsulation of business process data in an integrative and intuitive visualization model. The method spread the model into different viewpoints that serve as gateways to different

R. Meersman et al. (Eds.): OTM 2010 Workshops, LNCS 6428, pp. 160–169, 2010.

data layers and by that enables users to view the model through different interfaces and to navigate to their required data in a more focused and direct way. The suggested method enables clear integration to a variety of third party systems; in fact to every system that supports SOA. More particularly, the approach can assist both business users and IT implementers in understanding and working with business process models. The innovation of this work is in providing an integrative framework for interfacing with a process model in different ways that are compatible to the different model users and usage scenarios. While each is interface may have been separately discussed in other works and in other contexts, this work is the first attempt to integrate these views in a unified framework.

The paper features the following sections: a review of approaches for BPM visualization (section 2); the business process visualization method (section 3); including an example for suggested visualization interfaces (sections 3.1 to 3.6); and finally conclusions and suggestions for further work (section 4).

2   Related Work

Several previous works have described the typology of business process modeling notations by presenting structural notations for visualizing business process model data [1,7,12,13], but only few previous works have looked in detail into the issue of integrated business process visualization. [4,3] have described a situation in which different users or user roles have different perspectives over business processes and related data, and hence there is a need for a personalized visualization of the business process model. Existing BPM tools and visualization methods generally do not focus at providing mechanisms for building and visualizing differentiated views (e.g. process models are displayed to users in the same way as drawn by the process designer and not as specific subsets that cater the needs of a specific user population). To tackle this inflexibility, previous work has presented a visualization approach, which allows to create personalized process views based on parametrized operations- aiming to reduce or aggregate process information in a desired way[4]. Another approach, proposed a solution for the visualization of large business process specifications and used a set of criteria to produce specifications that exclude less relevant features [11] from the presentation layer.

The relatively small amount of academic research in the topic of business process visualization layers has restricted the development of "business process model visualization science", leaving it mostly to vendors and commercial organizations [5]. Presumably, professionals have developed business process visualization repositories on the basis of experience accumulated through analyzing business activity and implementing IT systems in a variety of industries. These solutions, such as the Oracle Tutor [1] or the SAP solution composer [2], assume a hierarchical process-artifact relationship, when one of the process descriptive

---

[1] http://www.oracle.com/applications/tutor/index.html

[2] http://www.sap.com/solutions/businessmaps/composer/index.epx

artifacts is an indicative pointer to a synthetic ERP environment (e.g. to the Oracle EBS demo[3] environment or to SAP IDES[4]), aiming to visualize, in a rather loose format, how the ERP system can be configured in accordance to relevant segments of business process models. To do that the Oracle suite, for example, relates its processes to a set of application configurations, that function as a foundation for the ERP implementation. These visualizations vary significantly between vendors and we were not able to locate a scientific systematization of visualization interfaces.

Our approach extends the previous academic and industry efforts by suggesting a generalized, systematic business process visualization method - presenting six alternative (but correlated) interfaces to an existing process model, while each interface exposes data artifacts that are encapsulated within this model in a different manner- aiming to serve different user populations and different usage scenarios.

3   The Business Process Visualization Method

The business process visualization method enables the presentation of business process model content through six alternative interfaces, exposing data encapsulated within the process model using different viewpoints (as illustrated in 1). Each such interface is aimed at enabling different types of users to visualize different types of data within an existing business process model in an easy and focused way. In order to demonstrate the suggested interfaces we developed a software prototype that is connected to an off-the-shelf business process management system - the ProcessGene Suite[5].

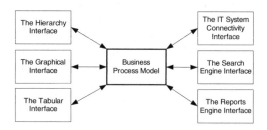

Fig. 1. The business process model visualization interfaces

3.1   The Hierarchy Interface

The *Hierarchy Interface* presents business processes within a business process model in a hierarchical manner. Such presentation creates a hierarchical catalog

---

[3] http://www.oracle.com/applications/e-business-suite.html

[4] http://help.sap.com/SAPHelp_46c/helpdata/EN/af/
fc4f35dfe82578e10000009b38f839/frameset.htm

[5] http://www.processgene.com

of process names in which a user can easily drill down directly to process data and issues of interest. Process names in this interface are ordered in a process tree so that higher process levels can be expanded to reveal their sub-processes (more detailed processes that are aimed at fulfilling the higher-level process goal). For example, the process name: "Human Resource Management" can be found at the first level of the process catalog, and when expanding this process - more detailed processes can are presented, including, for example, the processes: "Recruitment," "Payroll Management," and "Employee Termination Management." A further expansion of the "Recruitment" process exposes more detailed processes, such as "CV Review" and "Candidate Assessment."

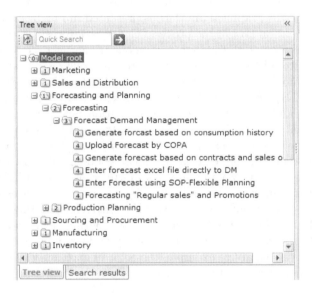

Fig. 2. An example of the Hierarchy Interface

An example of the Hierarchy Interface is presented in Fig. 2. In this example the process tree contains four hierarchy levels. According to this example, one of the highest level (level #1) processes is "Forecasting and Planning". This process is detailed into two level #2 processes "Forecasting" and "Production Planning." A further breakdown of "Forecasting" leads to one level #3 process which is then detailed into six level #4 processes, including the process "Generate forecast based on consumption history."

3.2   The Graphical Interface

The *Graphical Interface* presents the business processes within a process model in terms of execution flows (diagrams), aimed at enabling users to navigate the model using a graphical presentation layer. This interface suits users who are familiar with the terms of graphical representation components and of workflow notations in business process models. This interface is mostly useful when a user is interested in data related to execution flows (e.g. searching for a triggering event of a specific process, or searching for the next activity to be followed by a given one).

Process execution flows in the process model present the activities required for fulfilling the process goal, interconnected to each other to reflect the execution order. Each such execution flow can be connected to other execution flows in the process model - and this connectivity is presented by specifying *triggering* and *continuing* execution flows (meaning - execution flows that are invoked before and after the current execution flow, correspondingly). In addition, some execution flows can also be invoked at the middle of an execution flow. In this case they are connected directly to the execution flow's activities.

An example of the graphical interface is presented in Fig. 3. According to this example the execution flow of the process "Generate forecast based on consumption history" is presented to the user, having one triggering execution flow named "Create new material (item)" (located before the *Start* shape) and one continuing execution flow - "Transfer data to demand management" (located before the *End* shape). By presenting the model in such way, a user can jump between execution flows and navigate to required execution flow segments. This model also works in conjunction with the hierarchical tree and helps to over come some of the tree limitations. For example, in a tree structure it is not possible to show a sequence between tree nodes that are located under different branches. The graphical presentation helps eliminate this shortcoming by pointing to tree nodes that are managed through out the model ("cross-functional processes"), without limiting the use to a certain function (tree branch). This pointing can be carried out without losing the hierarchy structure, by relating each graphical element to its hierarchical position in the model and by adding the branch location as a shape attribute (in the above example, the color of each activity in the diagram represents its hierarchal level in the process hierarchy tree).

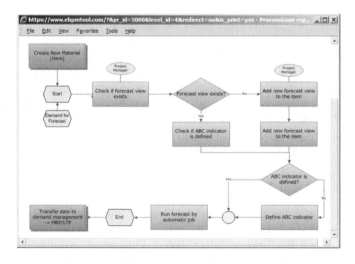

Fig. 3. An example of the Graphical Interface

3.3 The Tabular Interface

The *Tabular Interface* eliminates the complexity of execution flow structures by presenting the process model in a tabular structure and enabling users to navigate its content in a way similar to reading a map or a blueprint. To implement this notion, we use the SAP blueprint format[6], according to which each high-level process (e.g. "Human resource management," "Procurement management," or "Logistics management") is related to a *Horizontal tabular model* which presents a table with level #2 processes - at the beginning of each table row and their level #3 processes - specified along the rest of the row's cells (as illustrated in Fig. 4). Each table row in the high level model is then related to a *Vertical tabular model* in which level #4 processes are detailed in the column of each parent process (see illustration in Fig. 5). This representation of process levels can go on, where each odd process level is represented by a horizontal tabular model and each even process level is represented by a vertical tabular model.

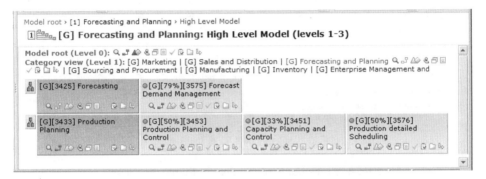

Fig. 4. An example of the horizontal tabular model of the Tabular Interface

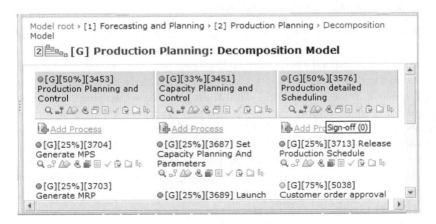

Fig. 5. An example of the vertical tabular model of the Tabular Interface

---

[6] http://www.sap.com

3.4   The Search Engine Interface

The *Search Engine Interface* and the *Reports Engine Interface* enable a more general way of searching the entire process model by specifying keywords. The Search Engine Interface is simpler and is based solely on keywords search, suitable for all kind of model users and most adequate for quick searches. For example, using this interface a user can search for all processes and SAP transactions related to "Forecast" (see Fig. 6).

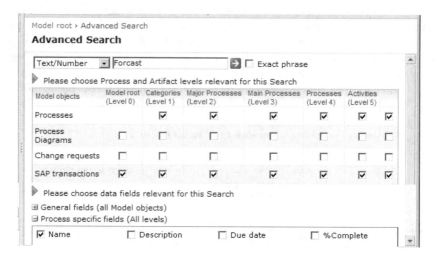

Fig. 6. An example of the Search Engine Interface

3.5   The Reports Engine Interface

The *Reports Engine Interface* enables specifying more complex queries on the model data and structure to explore more precise model segments. This interface is suitable for advanced users that either have prior knowledge of the process model structure or to users that are interested in a more precise segment of the model which is related to several conditions and cross-querying. This interface presents all model components (e.g. processes, diagrams, IT transactions, risks, controls) and their related data fields (e.g. name, description, owner, status). For each such data field it is possible to define constraints in the form of keywords, number ranges and date ranges (see illustration in Fig. 7). To reduce the returned result and focus it according to the user's needs, it is also possible to define which data field will be presented in the report output. This is done using the check-box near each data field.

As a more complex usage scenario, let us examine an use-case in which a user is interested to find out "how order-based decisions are handled by sales representatives". First, he can use the Hierarchy Interface and select the functionality are of his choice. In our example, the user selects a level #1 process, "Order to

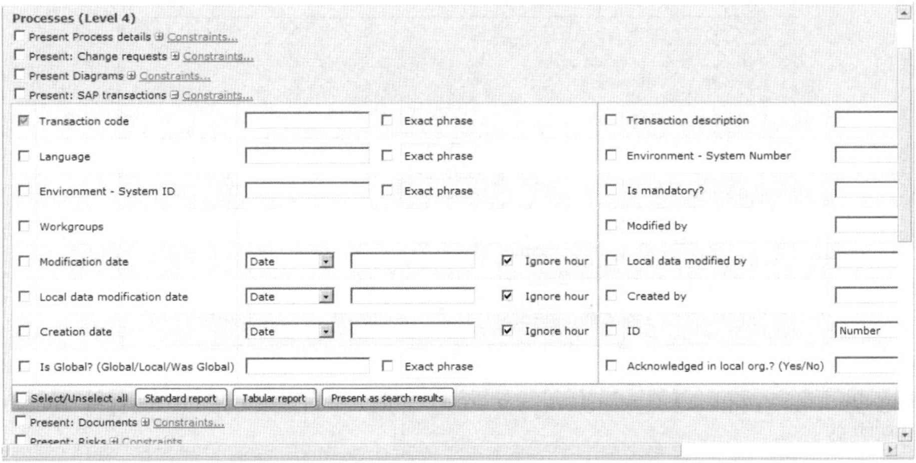

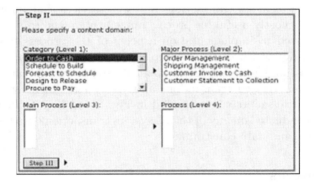

Fig. 7. An example of the Reports Engine Interface

Cash", based on the information that orders can be handled by sales representatives at pertaining lower-hierarchy business processes (e.g. "Order Management" and "Shipping Management") (see illustration in Fig. 8).

Fig. 8. An example of combing the usage of the Hierarchy Interface and the Reports Engine Interface to conduct more complex queries

At the next step, the user defines content requirements for the relevant process artifact and process fields (as illustrated in Fig. 9). Following our example, the user limits the "Name" field to include the string "order," the "Description" field to include the string "decision," and the "Owner" field to include the string "sales." She leaves the "exact phrase" option unchecked in order to retrieve more results. If, in addition, the user is interested only in "new" processes defined in the organization after a new sales strategy was implemented during 2006, she will add to the "Creation date" field the expression: "01-01-2006 - *". On top of these data fields the user can also check other required data fields - in order to include

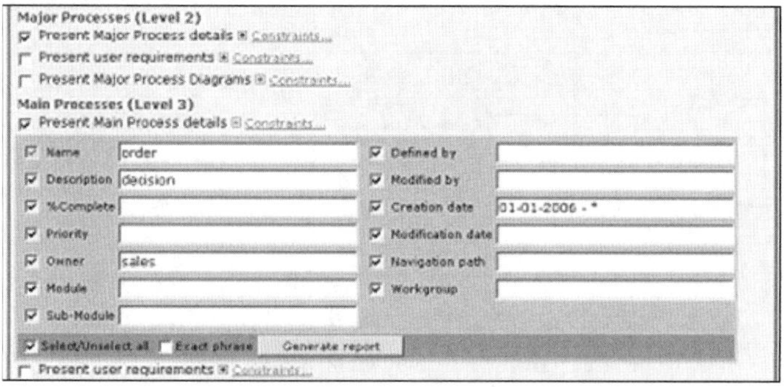

Fig. 9. An example of conducting a more complex query using the Reports Engine Interface

them in the report's output. This example demonstrates how a user without any in-depth understanding of the data structure can extract relevant results for a relatively complex query – solely by using the Reports Engine Interface.

3.6   The IT System Connectivity Interface

The *IT System Connectivity Interface* exposes IT components related to the process model in terms of transactions and web services that implement them. This interface is mostly useful for process implementers and software developers that are interested in implementation aspects of the process model. To dive into the knowledge world of the IT implementation of processes, each process is related to its implementing IT components so that users can either search processes by their related transactions and vise versa. An illustration of such search on SAP transactions is presented in Fig. 6 and Fig. 7. Such search and report can be conducted on any of the IT system transaction data fields involving keywords, range and date constraints.

4   Conclusions

The suggested method aims to extend previous academic and industry efforts by suggesting a generalized, systematic business process visualization method - demonstrating multi-faceted alternative interfaces to an existing process model. Each interface encapsulates the data in a different manner- aiming to serve different user populations as well as different use-cases. This encapsulation facilitates an important tool assisting model users in achieving their goals. We consider this work as a starting point that can already be applied in real-life scenarios, yet several research issues remain open for future work, including: (1) constructing a learning mechanism that will take into account previous user preferences and the user profile and adjust (in real time) the visualization interface; (2) being able to combine several visualizations in one GUI ; and (3) extending the scope of visualization interfaces to support additional business scenarios.

References

1. Becker, J., Rosemann, M., Von Uthmann, C.: Guidelines of business process modeling. Business Process Management, 241–262 (2000)
2. Bhattacharya, K., Gerede, C., Hull, R., Liu, R., Su, J.: Towards formal analysis of artifact-centric business process models. In: Alonso, G., Dadam, P., Rosemann, M. (eds.) BPM 2007. LNCS, vol. 4714, p. 288. Springer, Heidelberg (2007)
3. Bobrik, R., Reichert, M., Bauer, T.: Requirements for the visualization of system-spanning business processes. In: Proceedings of the Sixteenth International Workshop on Database and Expert Systems Applications, pp. 948–954 (2005)
4. Bobrik, R., Reichert, M., Bauer, T.: View-based process visualization. In: Alonso, G., Dadam, P., Rosemann, M. (eds.) BPM 2007. LNCS, vol. 4714, pp. 88–95. Springer, Heidelberg (2007)
5. Fettke, P., Loos, P., Zwicker, J.: Business process reference models: Survey and classification. In: Bussler, C.J., Haller, A. (eds.) BPM 2005. LNCS, vol. 3812, pp. 469–483. Springer, Heidelberg (2006)
6. Hull, R.: Artifact-centric business process models: Brief survey of research results and challenges. In: On the Move to Meaningful Internet Systems: OTM 2008, OTM 2008 Confederated International Conferences, CoopIS, DOA, GADA, IS, and ODBASE 2008 (2008)
7. Herwig, S., Lis, L., Stein, A., Becker, J., Delfmann, P.: Towards increased comparability of conceptual models - enforcing naming conventions through domain thesauri and linguistic grammars. In: ECIS (2009)
8. Lofts, N.: Process visualization: an executive guide to business process design. Wiley, Chichester (2002)
9. Malone, T.W.: The future of work: How the new order of business will shape your organization, your management style, and your life. Harvard Business School Press, Boston (2004)
10. Malone, T.W., Crowston, K., Herman, G.A.: Organizing business knowledge: the MIT process handbook. MIT Press, Cambridge (2003)
11. Streit, A., Pham, B., Brown, R.: Visualization support for managing large business process specifications. BPM 2005, 205–219 (2005)
12. van der Aalst, W.M.P., Barros, A.P., ter Hofstede, A.H.M., Kiepuszewski, B.: Advanced workflow patterns. In: Scheuermann, P., Etzion, O. (eds.) CoopIS 2000. LNCS, vol. 1901, pp. 18–29. Springer, Heidelberg (2000)
13. Weske, M., Van der Aalst, W.M.P., Verbeek, H.M.W.: Advances in business process management. Data and Knowledge Engineering 50(1), 1–8 (2004)

Outlines for Dynamic Visualization of Semantic Web Data

Marcello Leida, Ali Afzal, and Basim Majeed

EBTIC (Etisalat BT Innovation Centre),
Khalifa University - Abu Dhabi Campus
PO Box 127788, Abu Dhabi, UAE
{marcello.leida,ali.afzal}@kustar.ac.ae,
basim.majeed@bt.com
http://www.ebtic.org

Abstract. Ontologies, the data model underpinning the Semantic Web vision, are nowadays widely used to represent data from different origins and of diverse nature, supported by a plethora of tools for the storage and querying of ontologies. However, in the area of information visualization there is still much to be achieved. Several strategies and implementations have appeared over the past years as a result of the increase in publicly available data modelled as Resource Description Framework (RDF). The problem of representing this data using charts, dashboards, maps and so on has become pressing, in particular to prove the value of the Semantic Web to enhance the analysis of business data. In this paper we describe the problem of ontology visualization by presenting the major approaches, focusing on the problems that prevent these approaches from providing an automatic, dynamic, generic and flexible ontology visualization tool for analytical purposes.

Keywords: semantic web, data visualization, ontologies, survey.

1 Introduction

The community supporting the Semantic Web vision [1], is nowadays experiencing a renewed interest especially form outside the pure academic research environment: a growing number of companies is discovering the potential of the ideas behind the Semantic Web; focusing the attention on the advantages that the work done towards the Semantic Web will provide. The idea of the web as a huge knowledge base, composed of highly interconnected graphs, where arcs and nodes have their well-defined, machine understandable semantics is indeed extremely appealing and the growing interest around projects like *Linking Open Data (LOD)*[1] confirms this trend.

Enterprises have sensed the potential improvement of their Business Intelligence (BI) capabilities that the information in the Web could leverage: the use of virtually infinite information in the web that can be coupled with internal

---

[1] http://linkeddata.org/

R. Meersman et al. (Eds.): OTM 2010 Workshops, LNCS 6428, pp. 170–179, 2010.

resources in order to improve the quality of analytical and reporting tools. The increasing interest of Enterprises in areas such as social intelligence confirms this assumption: the work presented in [2] is an example of how information that is not stored or maintained by a company can generate valuable knowledge for the company itself. The main issue that limits the use of the Web as collective knowledge, that can be converted to valuable information for a company, is the effort required to extract such knowledge from various sources (forums, blogs, news, ...) in an effective and reliable way. The data model proposed by the Semantic Web community aims at solving these problems by removing confusion at meta-data level which specifies unequivocally the meaning of data.

The Semantic Web data model is defined using the term Ontology: a concept borrowed from Philosophy which, in the context of IT has been defined as *"formal, explicit specification of a shared conceptualisation"* [3]. This model formally represents concepts, attributes of these concepts, relations between concepts and instances of concepts. The mathematical model is a graph with labeled directed arcs, where meta-data and data share the same model. The main problem with ontological data is the effort required to model information, to perform queries and to visualize results, for people not familiar with the underlying theoretical concepts; this indeed is a strong limit that so far relegated the application of ontologies to a niche of experts. In order to tackle this issue the Semantic Web community has developed tools for producing (e.g. [4]), maintaining (e.g. [5]), and consuming (e.g. [6,7]) Semantic Web data, typically in the form of RDF [8] documents. But even if these tools made Semantic Web technologies more accessible to end-users, there is still much to do before converging to a mature technology that can replace existing ones.

Enterprises are obviously not interested in the properties of a new technology, if these properties do not potentially lead to tangible benefits for the Enterprise itself. This assumption is particularly true in the case of Semantic Web: even though Enterprises understood the potential benefits that semantics can provide, there are still many aspects that are not mature enough, preventing the market from finally shifting to this new paradigm. One of these aspects is the visualization of ontological data: initially visualization of ontologies was merely a way for researchers to display the ontology as a graph, in order to have a clearer picture of the overall structure; but these visualization techniques are not interesting from an Enterprise-user point of view, whose target is to make sense out of numbers. Nowadays, we are witnessing a drastic change in this trend; thanks mainly to the LOD project and the projects funded by UK and US governments to release public data as Linked Data. These developments suddenly made available huge amount of data represented as graphs as well as the tools to store and retrieve such information. Consequently, the need for methods to visualize it efficiently is rising.

Automatic approaches to visualize data have never been seriously taken into account. The main reason can be seen in the ill-defined semantic of data: just a simple list of values can be displayed with several methods (tables, pie-chart, lines, histograms, ...) so imagine the complexity when it comes to displaying a big amount of highly interconnected information. With the introduction of meta-data, it is possible to associate a meaning to a value that a human can understand and make use of, by associating to the meta-data a specific semantic. Now, with the introduction of ontologies and formally defined semantics this meta-data becomes machine understandable. Therefore in this paper we discuss the importance of an automatic or semi-automatic approach to generating flexible data visualizations of generic ontologies. The paper will present in Section 2 the actual state-of-the-art in different visualization techniques that has been used to visualize Semantic Web data, while in Section 3 we present our analysis of the gaps that needs to be filled in order to come to a usable generic approach to data visualization, the paper concludes with Section 4 which outlines future works and our final considerations.

2   Visualization of Ontologies

Several data visualization techniques have been proposed in order to obtain a graphical visualization of Semantic Web data. Generally all the approaches pro-posed can be classified in two major areas: i) techniques to visualize the overall ontological graphs and ii) techniques used to visualize results of SPARQL [9] queries or, more generically, selected parts of the ontology. Since data in the Semantic Web is represented as a graph the first set of approaches is the most natural way to view at ontologies and therefore the first visualization techniques appearing in the Semantic Web research community exploit the *subject, predi-cate, object* pattern to create interactive network-like views of ontologies.

One of the most famous tools in the research community is *Protegé* [10]: a tool that allows to create, load and modify RDF documents. The tool implies a deep understanding of the ontological paradigm so it has not attracted many users outside the Semantic Web domain. However the major factor of success of Protegé is that it is based on a plug-in architecture therefore third-parties can develop additional features that can be easily integrated with the original tool. Many of these plug-ins are focused at the visualization aspects of the ontologies such as *Jambalaya* [11] and *IsaViz* [12]. Besides these two approaches, many other solutions based on graphs, trees, tree maps, crop circles and similar are presented in detail in a survey [13] which extensively describes implementations and different visualization techniques used to visualize the ontological graph. As we already stated in the introductory section, the problem with these techniques is that they are oriented towards a structural visualization of the ontology and they have no practical utility for a typical analyst or an Enterprise-user who expects to work with dashboards, charts and tables.

From a different point of view comes *Simile* [6], a set of projects developed by the MIT to support users in dealing with Semantic Web data, without requiring particular knowledge of the underpinning theoretical framework. Part of this project is *Exibit*, which allows the user to display ontological data in different forms: pie charts, time lines, interactive maps and so on. This is an innovative and completely different approach with respect to the visualization techniques

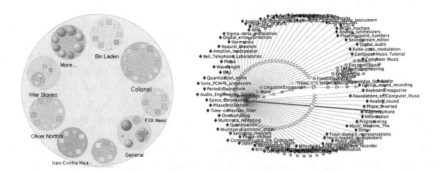

Fig. 1. An example of Crop Circles (left) and the well known Jambalaya plug-in of Protegé (right)

that were available at the time: the data is presented using different views according to user's goals. This is a typical example of visualization approaches that can be used to display the results of SPARQL queries and that nowadays are experiencing an increasing level of interest especially from BI and analytics community; mainly as consequence of the publication, as ontologies, of government data (mainly UK and US) and other data of general interest (GeoNames[2], FOAF[3], DBPEDIA[4], ...) that can be easily linked and retrieved using freely available tools. The possibilities that queries over Semantic Web data offer are extremely powerful because they allow seamless access to multiple data sources at once. As an example consider an ontology representing geographical information (such as GeoNames) and an Enterprise-level ontology modelling customer complaints. With these two data sources it is possible, *with one query*, to obtain for each complaint its geographical location, for example by specifying in the query a join on customer address with the related place in the GeoNames ontology. Once the query results are retrieved imagine the impact, in terms of analysis and reporting, of directly displaying the complaints on a map, this way it will be possible to identify easily the areas where the complaints are concentrated. Moreover imagine the ability to select the complaints referring to broadband customers and to associate them with an ontology modelling operative information of the devices serving these customer (number of connections, bandwidth distributed over a window of time). Now image that in the map by clicking on the corresponding customer's icon, we can display a set of graphs with information about the device so that it is easy to verify if the device is the reason of the complaints. These two simple examples made clear the benefit of using ontologies to model the information and the importance of visualization procedures to make this information easily readable.

Following this trend, the work presented in the *Data-Gov* project [14] is what we consider a bright example of the different ways ontological data returned

[2] http://www.geonames.org/ontology/
[3] http://www.foaf-project.org/
[4] http://dbpedia.org/

by queries can be rendered and proposed to the final consumer: starting from government data publicly available, the authors provide a set of examples where data is retrieved and displayed through meaningful charts, maps and diagrams.

The approach is based on a three-steps process: i) query, ii) transform and iii) visualize. The first step is to create a SPARQL query that is submitted to the SPARQL endpoint service provided by most of the available ontology store platforms [15], the result of the query is transformed by a process (such as a pre-defined XSLT [16] procedure) and the resulting document is submitted to a visualization service such as Exibit or Google Visualization [7]. As is possible to see in Figure 2 a set of linked ontologies modelling different domains of interest (Government, Services, Community, Environment, Linked Data) are displayed in different ways, according to the user's interests. This set of diagrams and charts are very informative from a purely analytical point of view. This approach is a powerful process to transform and represent raw ontological data as meaningful visualizations, understandable by managers and business analysts. Most importantly there is no need to understand the ontological model of the data by the final user.

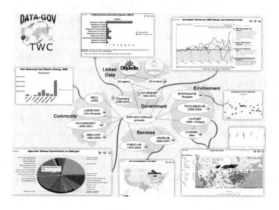

Fig. 2. A set of demo examples on how to display SPARQL query results as appearing in [14]

In the *Data-Gov* project, the authors assume that the queries and the transformation procedures are defined manually by a domain expert: this situation is acceptable in case the queries are always the same and circumscribed to a relatively small set. Moreover in such approach the visualization is static and it can not be dynamically refined. This is a limitation that does not allow the degree of flexibility required by modern BI analysis and furthermore is definitely not acceptable in case of queries that can not be predicted a-priori. According to this last assumption there are other interesting works, showing how the results of unpredictable queries on Semantic Web data can be presented to the user: *Wolfram Alpha*[17] is, among the growing set of Semantic Search Engines, the one that presents the results to the user using mash-ups and faceted browsing capabilities.

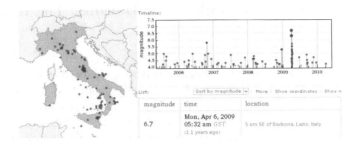

Fig. 3. Result of the query *"timeline of Italian earthquakes"* as returned by *Wolfram Alpha* [17]

Wolfram Alpha is based on a set of templates that provide a faceted visualization of the results: the solution is based on a set of basic components; one for visualizing maps, one for graphs, one for images and one for displaying information into a tabular form. These basic blocks are used to build several different templates which are composed by a set of procedures aimed at extracting data from the right source and displaying it into a faceted page. As it is possible to see in Figure 3, the result of the query *"timeline of Italian earthquakes"* is displayed using maps and graphs, there is a map that displays the location of the earthquakes over the whole Italy and a graph that displays the temporal distribution of the earthquakes against their strength. Even though the visualization of the results of Wolfram Alpha is extremely intuitive and informative, it still entails several limitations: the algorithms recognizes the type of template to use according to the query entered by the user, extracts the results from a set of sources that is known *a-priori* and applies the template to create the visualization.

The problem of the previous approaches is that the visualization is created as result of a query, but it cannot be refined; resulting in a static visualization of the results. This is indeed an important limitation to the expressive power provided by the highly connected nature of the ontologies. Starting from a visualization the user can interact with it, refine it and by exploiting the ontology's connections the user might end up visualizing data that he/she had not initially considered. This is indeed the main problem of using template-based approaches: templates imply knowledge of the data source to display, but due to the nature of Semantic Web, it is not advisable to rely on predefined approaches designed to work with specific ontologies. The original ontology may change, and even in a domain-specific application the user most likely will have to deal with data that was not initially considered. Following this novel trend we can identify Tabulator [18], which is a Semantic Web browser defined as a generic approach to displaying and browsing dynamically Semantic Web data. An outstanding feature of *Tabulator* is that it is able to handle ontologies without any previous knowledge of the ontology's schema, but the visualization is limited to maps and calendar views, so at the moment it does not allow the display of information in charts or other visualization models.

3   From Static to Dynamic Visualizations: The Missing Step

The work presented in the previous Section can be considered as the actual state-of-the-art of visualization techniques for Semantic Web data. For the purpose of BI applications we believe that an approach based on transformation and visualization of query results is the best solution to displaying the *correct* data into *powerful* visualization tools. An approach like the *Data-Gov* project still requires the manual definition of queries and translation procedures; if the first problem can be somehow limited by the use of mash-ups such as Mash-QL [19] or Semantic Web Pipes [20], the manual definition of transformation procedures to visualize every different query executed is not an acceptable solution for the targeted user. A promising approach is the definition of visualization templates, such as *Fresnel* [21]. Fresnel is a declarative approach, based on the idea of *lenses* and *formats*: lenses specify *what* to show and formats define *how* to show it, describing how the data will be formatted for users' visualization. WYSIWYG tools to define Fresnel visualizations are already under advanced development. This is indeed a very powerful solution that can be adopted independently from the definition of the ontology, but is still limited for what is required in our scenario.

Ontologies provide well-defined semantics and therefore they can offer more in terms of understanding of the meaning of data, with respect to traditional data models. This assumption implies that automatic or semi-automatic techniques to create dynamic visualizations according to user intentions are not science fiction anymore. As stated also by the authors in [18], the information describing how the data should be visualized will likely be released with the data itself so that the visualization of previously unknown ontologies will be trivial. But, if the contribution of template-based approach is an important step in this direction, and even assuming that every ontology will be released with this additional information, we still believe that there is a missing step in order to satisfy the requirements of managers and business analysts for a flexible solution.

Template-based approaches are successfully applicable while browsing the ontology, but reporting tools in general most likely will display data as result of a query: each template represents how to display a particular concept or attribute while browsing the graph. However in case of queries it is not specified if the data is in relation with each other and how this influences the way data has to be visualized. As an example consider an ontology representing *customers*, *products* and *orders* and a query that returns the revenue of the orders for every country a customer is located. The result of the query are values from attributes belonging to different concepts, not directly in relation; this will syntactically appear as a list of strings and numbers. Semantically they represents the name of the country and the revenue that the country generated for the Enterprise and, as shown in Figure 4, they can be visualized in several ways all of which are correct. But even in case some Fresnel lenses and selectors have been defined on the resources, these are not informative enough to generate the visualization.

Fig. 4. Two different visualizations from the same result set

We believe that additional information should be provided by the query results and by the visualization libraries in order to automatically or semi-automatically (in case more than one choice is possible) associate the visualization to the query results. This information can be a standardized vocabulary that will be used to annotate the variables returned by the query and the input parameters of the visualization service so that an intermediate process can exploit this information to match the query result with the set of suitable visualization procedures. As a possible approach, we can provide a formal definition of the annotation in order to define hierarchies, common semantics and shared properties within the annotations; a tree structure will be expressive enough for the issue:

```
visual:country  = childOf(visual:label)
```

Ideally this information will be provided by the original ontologies, aligning our proposal with [18], so that the query process will obtain this information from the ontology and use it to annotate the query variables. This assumption implies that during the definition of the ontology the various elements are associated with the suitable node closest to the root of the annotation vocabulary and that the query will use one of the child nodes to annotate the variables of the query:

```
PREFIX ebtic:<http://www.ebtic.org/OTMDemo#>
PREFIX visual:<http://www.ebtic.org/visualAnnotations#>
SELECT ?country AS visual:country ?revenue AS visual:value
WHERE { ?location ebtic:Country ?country.
?customer ebtic:location ?location.
?order ebtic:orderedBy ?customer.
?order ebtic:TotalPrice ?revenue.}
```

An intermediate matching process will filter the entire set of possible visualizations methods by returning only the ones that are coherent with the query result set. This will be done by annotating every visualization method with the allowed set of input. As an example:

```
Map.allowedInput=[visual:country,visual:value]
BarChart.allowedInput=[visual:label,List{visual:value}]
```

A possible definition of the application flow is illustrated in Figure 5 that outlines the steps from the query generation to the visualization of results. The user, interacting with the visualization (e.g. by clicking on points in the graphs) will

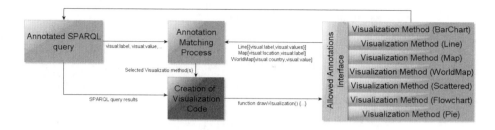

Fig. 5. The application flow of our approach

generate additional SPARQL queries that will lead to different visualizations, emphasising the dynamic aspect of our approach. In conclusion, what is missing in order to implement such a system is an intermediate language allowing query results and visualization methods to understand each other. Results of the queries need to semantically specify which kind of data they represent and on the other hand, visualization methods need to provide information about the kind of data they can handle.

4   Conclusions and Future Work

The Semantic Web vision is becoming a reality day by day. The RDF format is already widely used to model data of different origin and nature. The reasoning and query capabilities have been proven to be efficient and effective. However, from the point of view of data visualization there is still much to be done. The data has to be displayed in a way that generates information for users that do not need to know about the underlying data model. Several visualization strategies and implementations have appeared in the last years. Following the increase of publicly available ontologies, the problem of reporting this data using charts, dashboards, maps and so on became pressing, especially in order to demonstrate the power of the Semantic Web to business analysts and managers. In this paper we described the problem of ontology visualization by presenting the major approaches that are available, focusing on the issues that prevent these approaches from providing a dynamic, generic and efficient ontology visualization tool to final users. We concluded this paper with an outline of a possible solution: a shared vocabulary used to represent useful information for the visualization of ontological elements. Future work on this topic will be the definition of the annotation vocabulary plus a set of examples covering different scenarios.

References

1. Berners-Lee, T.: The Semantic Web. Scientific American (May 2001)
2. Nguyen, D., Thompson, S., Hoile, C.: Hubbub - An Innovative Customer Support Forum. In: BIS Workshops 2008, pp. 55–67 (2008)

3. Gruber, T.: A translation approach to portable ontology specifications. Knowledge Acquisition 5, 199–220 (1993)
4. Bizer, C., Cyganiak, R., Garbers, J., Maresch, O., Becker, C.: The D2RQ Platform v0.7 - Treating Non-RDF Relational Databases as Virtual RDF Graphs
5. Broekstra, J., Kampman, A., van Harmelen, F.: Sesame: A Generic Architecture for Storing and Querying RDF and RDF Schema. In: International Semantic Web Conference, pp. 54–68 (2002)
6. Huynh, D., Mazzocchi, S., Karger, D.: Piggy Bank: Experience the Semantic Web Inside Your Web Browser. In: Gil, Y., Motta, E., Benjamins, V.R., Musen, M.A. (eds.) ISWC 2005. LNCS, vol. 3729, pp. 413–430. Springer, Heidelberg (2005)
7. Google Visualization API, http://code.google.com/apis/charttools/
8. Manola, F., Miller, E.: RDF Primer, http://www.w3.org/TR/rdf-primer/
9. Prud'hommeaux, E., Seaborne, A.: SPARQL a query language for RDF, http://www.w3.org/TR/rdf-sparql-query/
10. Gennari, J.H., Musen, M.A., Fergerson, R.W., Grosso, W.E., Crubzy, M., Eriksson, H., Noy, N.F., Tu, S.W.: The evolution of Protg: an environment for knowledge-based systems development. Int. J. Hum.-Comput. Stud. 58(1), 89–123 (2003)
11. Storey, M., Musen, M., Silva, J., Best, C., Ernst, N., Fergerson, R., Noy, N.: Jambalaya: Interactive visualization to enhance ontology authoring and knowledge acquisition in protege (2001)
12. Pietriga, E.: IsaViz: A Visual Authoring Tool for RDF., http://www.w3.org/2001/11/IsaViz/
13. Katifori, A., Halatsis, C., Lepouras, G., Vassilakis, C., Giannopoulou, E.: Ontology visualization methods - a survey. ACM Comput. Surv. 39(4), 10 (2007)
14. Ding, L., DiFranzo, D., Graves, A., Michaelis, J., Li, X., McGuinness, D.L., Hendler, J.A.: TWC data-gov corpus: incrementally generating linked government data from data.gov. In: WWW 2010, pp. 1383–1386 (2010)
15. Hartig, O., Bizer, C., Freytag, J.: Executing SPARQL Queries over the Web of Linked Data. In: Bernstein, A., Karger, D.R., Heath, T., Feigenbaum, L., Maynard, D., Motta, E., Thirunarayan, K. (eds.) ISWC 2009. LNCS, vol. 5823, pp. 293–309. Springer, Heidelberg (2009)
16. XSLT Transformations, http://www.w3.org/TR/xslt
17. Wolfram Alpha, http://www.wolframalpha.com/
18. Lee, T.B., Chen, Y., Chilton, L., Connolly, D., Dhanaraj, R., Hollenbach, J., Lerer, A., Sheets, D.: Tabulator: Exploring and Analyzing linked data on the Semantic Web, The 3rd International Semantic Web User Interaction Workshop (SWUI 2006) Workshop, Athens, Georgia (November 6, 2006)
19. Jarrar, M., Dikaiakos, M.D.: MashQL: a query-by-diagram topping SPARQL. In: Proceeding of the 2nd International Workshop on Ontologies and Nformation Systems For the Semantic Web, ONISW 2008, Napa Valley, California, USA, October 30-30, pp. 89–96. ACM, New York (2008)
20. Phuoc, D.L., Polleres, A., Morbidoni, C., Hauswirth, M., Tummarello, G.: Rapid semantic web mashup development through semantic web pipes. In: Proceedings of the 18th World Wide Web Conference (WWW 2009), Madrid, Spain (April 2009)
21. Fresnel - Display Vocabulary for RDF, http://www.w3.org/2005/04/fresnel-info/

EI2N'10 & SeDeS'10 - PC Co-chairs Message

After the successful fourth edition in 2009, the fifth edition of the Enterprise Integration, Interoperability and Networking workshop (EI2N'2010) has been organized as part of the OTM'2010 Federated Conferences and is supported by the IFAC Technical Committee 5.3 "Enterprise Integration and Networking", the IFIP TC 8 WG 8.1 "Design and Evaluation of Information Systems", the SIG INTEROP Grande-Rgion on "Enterprise Systems Interoperability" and the French CNRS National Research Group GDR MACS.

Collaboration is necessary for enterprises to prosper in the current extreme dynamic and heterogeneous business environment. Enterprise integration, interoperability and networking are the major disciplines that have studied how to do companies to collaborate and communicate in the most effective way. These disciplines are well-established and are supported by international conferences, initiatives, groups, task forces and governmental projects all over the world where different domains of knowledge have been considered from different points of views and a variety of objectives (e.g., technological or managerial). Enterprise Integration involves breaking down organizational barriers to improve synergy within the enterprise so that business goals are achieved in a more productive and efficient way. The past decade of enterprise integration research and industrial implementation has seen the emergence of important new areas, such as research into interoperability and networking, which involve breaking down organizational barriers to improve synergy within the enterprise and among enterprises. The ambition to achieve dynamic, efficient and effective cooperation of enterprises within networks of companies, or in an entire industry sector, requires the improvement of existing, or the development of new, theories and technologies. Enterprise Modelling, Architecture, and semantic techniques are the pillars supporting the achievement of Enterprise Integration and Interoperability. Internet of Things and Cloud Computing now present new opportunities to realize inter enterprise and intra enterprise integration. For these reasons, the workshop's objective is to foster discussions among representatives of these neighboring disciplines and to discover new research paths within the enterprise integration community. After peer reviews, 6 papers have been accepted out of 12 submissions to this workshop. Prof. Michael Sobolewski (Polish-Japanese Institute of IT, Poland) has been invited as EI2N plenary keynote on "Exerted Enterprise Computing: from Protocol-oriented Networking to Exertion-oriented Networking". In addition to the presentations of the accepted papers, groups have been organized into what E2IN traditionally calls "workshop cafs", to discuss and debate the presented topics. This year discussion enabled putting forward new research related to "interoperability issues in collaborative information systems". These groups reported the results of the respective discussions during a plenary session that was jointly organized with the CoopIS'2010 conference, in order to share the vision for future research on this top domain. The papers published in this volume of proceedings present samples of current research in

R. Meersman et al. (Eds.): OTM 2010 Workshops, LNCS 6428, pp. 180–181, 2010.
© Springer-Verlag Berlin Heidelberg 2010

the enterprise modeling, systems interoperability, services management, cloud integration and, more globally, systems engineering and enterprise architecture domains. Some new architecting principles that has gained currency in the recent past is semantic technique, service oriented architecture and cloud computing with their principles, reference models and technology, and if applied correctly can be an important contributor to the future of interoperable, networked and collaborative enterprises. The success of this complex field also depends on the maturity and coherency of the management of the involved enterprises, a topic covered by the second workshop caf. As a special track of EI2N'2010, SeDeS'2010 is the first international workshop on Semantics & Decision Support. The call for papers saw 12 submissions, among which the Programme Committee has selected 4 papers to be presented at EI2N'2010. The selected papers cover the topics of ontology-based decision making applications in the fields of eGovernment, eLearning, business rule management and Human Resource Management.

It has been a great pleasure to work with the members of the international programme committee who dedicated their valuable effort for reviewing the submitted papers; we are indebted to all of them.

We also would like to thank all authors for their contribution to the workshop objectives and discussions.

August 2010

Qing Li
Hervé Panetto
Giuseppe Berio
Kemafor Anyanwu
EI2N'10 & SeDes'10

Exerted Enterprise Computing: From Protocol-Oriented Networking to Exertion-Oriented Networking

Michael Sobolewski

SORCER Research Group
Polish-Japanese Institute of Information Technology,
Warsaw, Poland
sobol@sorcersoft.org

Abstract. Most enterprise computing programs are still *not* written in metaprogramming languages but rather composed line by line in software programming languages as they were decades ago. These programming languages are poorly suited to expressing enterprise processes targeted at complex, domain-specific and transdisciplinary problems. The current state of the art is that legacy programs and scripts can be used as programming instructions provided by *dynamic service objects*. New metaprograms (programs of programs) require *relevant operating systems* managing service objects as a virtual service *metaprocessor*. However, there are presently no acceptable metaprogramming methodologies to program, deploy, and dynamically federate these relevant service objects into a virtual processor securely and efficiently with fault detection and recovery. In this paper the emerging metacomputing SORCER platform with its federated method invocation and exertion-oriented programming model is contrasted with *service protocol-oriented architectures* (e.g., OGSA, CORBA, RMI) which limit us to one fixed wire protocol, static network configurations, and often restricts us to heavyweight containers (e.g., application servers) for hosting service objects.

Keywords: process expression, metacomputing, service-oriented computing, SOA, dynamic service objects.

1 Introduction

"Computing's core challenge is how not to make a mess of it." Edsger Dijkstra

Computing has evolved over centuries. It is and always has been about processes and process expressions. The creation or activation of process expressions has changed over time as it reflects the continuous change in problems being solved by humans and the languages used. As a current example, UML behavior diagrams allow us to define multiple process expressions that generalize flowchart diagrams which were introduced by Markov in 1954 to represent "algorithms" [15, 5].

As we reach adolescence in the Internet era we are facing the dawn of the metacomputing era, an era that will be marked not by PCs, workstations, and servers, but by computational capability that is embedded in all things around us—virtual

R. Meersman et al. (Eds.): OTM 2010 Workshops, LNCS 6428, pp. 182–201, 2010.

computing services as programming instructions of a virtual metacomputer. The term "metacomputing" was coined around 1987 by NCSA Director, Larry Smarr: "The metacomputer is, simply put, a collection of computers held together by state-of-the-art technology and balanced so that, to the individual user, it looks and acts like a single computer. The constituent parts of the resulting metacomputer could be housed locally, or distributed between buildings, even continents." [16]

In computing science the common thread in all computing disciplines are *process expression* and *actualization of process expression* [5], for example:

1. An *architecture* is an expression of a continuously acting process to interpret symbolically expressed processes.
2. A *user interface* is an expression of an interactive human-machine process.
3. A *program* is an expression of a computing process.
4. A *programming language* is an environment within which to create symbolic process expressions.
5. A *compiler* is an expression of a process that translates between symbolic process expressions in different languages.
6. An *operating system* is an expression of a process that manages the interpretation of other process expressions.
7. A *processor* is an actualization of a process.
8. An *application* is an expression of the application process.
9. A *computing platform* is an expression of a runtime process defined by its programming language, operating system, and processor.
10. A *computer* is an actualization of a computing platform.
11. A *metaprogram* is an expression of a metaprocess, as the *process of processes*.
12. A *metaprogramming language* is an environment within which to create symbolic metaprocess expressions.
13. A *metaoperating system* is an expression of a process that manages the interpretation of other metaprocess expressions.
14. A *metaprocessor* is an actualization of the metaprocess on the aggregation of distinct computers working together so that to the user it looks and operates like a single processor.
15. A *metacomputing platform* is an expression of a runtime process defined by its metaprogramming language, metaoperating system, and metaprocessor.
16. A *metacomputer* is an actualization of a metacomputing platform.
17. *Enterprise computing* is an expression of transdisciplinary enterprise processes.

Obviously, there is an essential overlap between the domains of mathematics and computer science, but the core concerns with the nature of process expression itself are usually ignored in mathematics since mathematicians are concerned with the nature of the behavior of a process independent of how that process is expressed. Computing science is concerned with computing processes and computer science is mainly concerned with the nature of the expression of processes independent of its process. In Fig. 1, the difference between programming and metaprogramming is illustrated where a metaprogram on its metaprocessor is the program of programs on multiple processors.

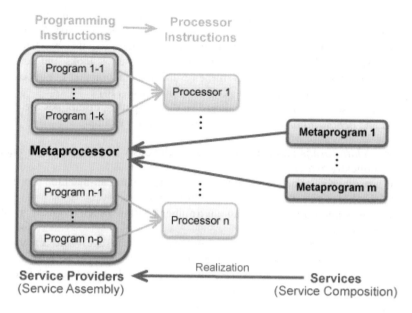

Fig. 1. The programming structure is indicated by yellow colors and the metaprogramming structure by bluish colors. Programming instructions are realized by native processor instructions, but metainstructions by services (with blue outlines) invoking legacy programs (with yellow outlines). Metaprogramming is focused on service compositions and metacomputer engineering on construction of metaprocessors—service assemblies from other services and modules.

Service providers expose existing programs that execute on a network of processors (see Fig. 1) as service types. These service types, e.g. Java interfaces, are implemented by service objects hosted by a provider. The service objects just consume services and provide services from and to each other respectively. Applications are increasingly moving to the network—self aware, autonomic networks that are always fully functional. A service provider exposes multiple interfaces implemented by its service objects that in turn provide instructions for the service-oriented processor (metaprocessor). Most current efforts in service systems are focused on *service-oriented engineering*—constructing metaprocessors by assembling service objects from other services and modules (e.g., OSGi, SCA, BPEL).

Thus, the metaprocessor via its operating system carries access to applications, tools, and utilities, i.e., programs exposed by service objects. Service providers can *federate* with each other dynamically to provide *service collaborations*—to realize a metaprogram—the service-oriented expression of the metaprocess.

The SORCER [20-24] service-oriented system is the enterprise platform based the service-oriented philosophy outlined above. Its architecture is derived from the metaprogramming model with three languages that allow for model-driven programming with service collaborations (Section 3.2). It supports three core neutralities [22]: requestor/provider wire protocol [28], provider implementation, and provider location in the network.

Let's consider the "Hello Service Arithmetic" example. Assume we have three services on the network:

```
f3 = x1 - x2; f4 = x1 * x2; and f5 = x1 + x2
```

which implement three interfaces: Subtractor, Multiplier, and Adder, respectively. We want to program a distributed service that mimics a function composition:

```
f3(f4, f5) and calculate: f3(f4(10.0, 50.0), f5(20.0, 80.0))
```

to get 400.0 as the result of collaboration of three services: f4, f5, and f3. Consider the equivalent service-oriented program (workflow) that can run in SORCER:

```
String arg = "arg", result = "result";
String x1 = "x1", x2 = "x2", y = "y";
Task f3 = task("f3", op("subtract", Subtractor.class),
    context("subtract", in(path(arg,x1), null),
        in(path(arg,x2),null), out(path(result,y),null)));
Task f4 = task("f4", op("multiply", Multiplier.class),
    context("multiply", in(path(arg, x1), 10.0),
        in(path(arg,x2), 50.0), out(path(result,y),null)));
Task f5 = task("f5", op("add", Adder.class),
    context("add", in(path(arg,x1), 20.0),
        in(path(arg,x2), 80.0),out(path(result,y),null)));
Job f1= job("f1",
    job("f2",f4,f5,strategy(Flow.PARALLEL, Access.PULL)),
    f3,
    pipe(out(f4, path(result,y)), in(f3, path(arg,x1))),
    pipe(out(f5, path(result,y)), in(f3, path(arg,x2))));
return value(exert(f1), path("f3", result));
```

The first two lines define the names of the arguments used in this program. Next, three tasks f3, f4, and f5 are declared from which two composite services are declared: f1 and f2. A few metalanguage operators are used in the program to define services: op (short for *operation*) defines the *service operation* by its name in the requested service type, e.g., the operation "subtract" in the Java interface Subtractor.class in f3; operators in, out, and inout specify service input and output parameters by paths in the associative array called context. The expressions that start with the operator task or job are called *exertions*. Exertions specify service compositions and define the *process* by its control *strategy* expressed by the strategy operator in jobs. Service compositions (exertions) define virtual services created from other services. Tasks are elementary services and jobs are compound services in exertion-oriented programming.

The program above defines a function composition f3:

```
f3(f4(x1, x2), f5(x1, x2)),
```

as a SORCER service composition f1:

```
f1(f2(f4(x1, x2), f5(x1, x2)), f3).
```

Task f4 requests operation "multiply" of its arguments "arg/x1" and "arg/x2" by the service Multiplier.class. Task f5 requests operation "add" of its arguments "arg/x1" and "arg/x2" by service Adder.class. Task f3 requests to "subtract" "arg/x2" from "arg/x1" by Subtractor.class where input parameter values are not defined yet. Job f2 requests execution of both f4 and f5 with its process strategy:

strategy (Flow.PARALLEL, Access.PULL))

This means that the component services f4 and f5 of f2 are executed in parallel and the corresponding service objects will not be accessed directly (PUSH) by the SORCER OS. In this case the corresponding service objects will process their tasks via the SORCER shared exertion space (PULL) when they are available to do so [21]. The default control strategy is sequential (Flow.SEQUENTIAL) execution with PUSH access, which is applied to job f2.

Finally the job f1, executes first job f2 and then via data pipes (defined with the pipe operator in f1) passes the results of tasks f4 and f5 on to task f3 for "arg/x1" and "arg/x2" correspondingly. The last statement in the above program exerts the collaboration exert(f1). Exerting means executing the service collaboration and returning the exertion with the processed contexts of all component exertions along with operational details like execution states, errors, exceptions, etc. Then it returns the value of the service collaboration f1 with the path path("f3", result), which selects the value 400.0 from the context of executed task f3 at the path "result". The single service activation, exert(f1), creates at runtime a dynamic federation of required collaborating services with no network configuration. This type of process is referred to as "federated".

The rest of the paper is organized as follows: Section 2 differentiates metacomputing from computing and defines metacomputing concepts used in SORCER. Section 3 presents the SORCER platform with its metaprogramming languages and metaoperating system and Subsection 3.5 illustrates how to implement service-objects to execute the service-oriented program presented above. This is followed by concluding remarks and plans for future work.

2   From Computing to Metacomputing

From the very beginning of networked computing, the desire has existed to develop protocols and methods that facilitate the ability of people and automatic processes to share resources and information across different computing nodes in an optimized way. As ARPANET [14] began through the involvement of the NSF to evolve into the Internet for general use, the steady stream of ideas became a flood of techniques to submit, control, and schedule jobs across distributed systems. The latest in these ideas are the grid [6, 25, 26] and cloud [13], intended for use by a wide variety of different applications in a non-hierarchical manner to provide access to powerful aggregates of resources. Grids and clouds, in the ideal, are intended to be accessed for computation, data storage and distribution, visualization, and display, among other applications, without undue regard for the specific nature of the hardware and underlying operating systems on the resources on which these jobs are carried out. While a grid is focused on computing *resource* utilization, clouds are focused on virtualization. In general, grid and cloud computing are client-server architectures that abstract away the details of the server—one requests a *resource* (service), not a specific *server* (machine). However, both terms are vague from the point of view of computing process expression and relevant programming models and referring to "everything that we already do" by providing various middleware architectures that are not only difficult to use but difficult for the end users to understand.

The concept of "middleware" has remained largely unchanged since client-server computing emerged in the late 1980s. It's software that provides a link between separate software applications or services. Middleware sits "in the middle" between application software that may be executing on different operating systems. Middleware consists of a set of services that allow multiple processes running on one or more machines to interact. The distinction between operating system and middleware functionality is, to some extent, arbitrary. Additional services provided by separately-developed middleware can be integrated into operating systems when needed.

Either middleware or an operating system (OS) is the expression of a process that manages the interpretation of *other process expressions*. Thus, to express a service-oriented (SO) process we need a service-oriented OS, but also we need an *expression of an SO process*. For the latter we need an *SO program* and the corresponding SO processor to *activate it* according to the OS *interpretation*. Thus, the SO process is expressed by three complementing each other process expressions:

1. *expression of an SO process*—the SO program;
2. *management of the service collaboration* representing the SO program—the SO operating system; and
3. activation of the SO collaboration—the SO processor.

Service architectures can be distinguished by the type of application metaprogramming language and related metaoperating system. Most existing service architectures are focused mainly on service provider assemblies at the middleware level (OSGi [OSGi Alliance], BPEL [11], Globus/Condor [26]), but not the metaprogramming by end users. It is reminiscent of the 60s when job schedulers were used while operating systems with high level programming environments were still in the development phases and only low-level application programming for job schedulers was available.

Lack of application metaprogramming languages is the main source of confusion regarding what SO programming is all about. It is still very difficult for most users to create user-defined SO programs. Instead of domain-specific SO programs, detailed and low-level programming must be carried out by the user through command line and script execution to carefully tailor jobs on each end to the resources on which they will run, or for the data structure that they will access. This produces frustration on the part of the user, delays in the adoption of enterprise techniques, and a multiplicity of specialized "enterprise-aware" tools that are not, in fact, aware of each other which defeats the basic purpose of the grid or cloud.

Let's consider, for example, Web Services (WS) [4], OSGi, and Jini [10, 1] architectures. Each is a service architecture but *built for different service semantics*. WS is a service architecture for distributed systems that are built on a static middleware fixed on the XML/WSDL/SOAP/BPEL and running on Application Servers. OSGi is a service architecture (at least by name) for services that are in the same process address space. Jini is a service architecture for distributed systems that is built out of dynamic service objects that are separated by an unreliable network [4]. Each allows allow you to build programs out of collaborating services with detailed programming required. Each has a completely different concept of service that the user has to be familiar with. The major difference is in the type of collaboration you can create and how you can create service collaborations. Also, the unreliable network (Jini) is a very different environment [4] from the single virtual machine (OSGi), or an Application Server used for WS deployment.

Creating a collaboration of services in any of the three environments is easy for neither end users nor developers. Creating collaborations of services coming from all three environments in a uniform way is not possible and no metaprogramming is available that would differ from middleware programming. These environments are mainly focused on metaprocessor but not on three intrinsic layers of SO computing: *SO programming* (metalanguage), *SO management* (middleware), and *SO execution* (dynamic federations of service providers).

Before we delve into the SORCER metacomputing and metaprogramming concepts, the introduction of some terminology used throughout the paper is required:

- A *computation* is a process following a well-defined model that is understood and can be symbolically expressed and physically accomplished (physically expressed). A computation can be seen as a purely physical phenomenon occurring inside a system called a *computer*.
- Computing requires a *computing platform* (runtime) to operate. Computing platforms that allow programs to run require a *processor*, *operating system*, and *programming environment* with related tools to create symbolic process expressions—*programs*. A computation is physically expressed by a processor and symbolically expressed by a program.
- A *distributed computation* allows for sharing computing resources usually llocated on several remote computers (compute nodes) to collaboratively run a single complex computation in a transparent and coherent way. In distributed computing, computations are decomposed into programs, processes, and compute nodes.
- A *metacomputer* is an interconnected and balanced set of compute nodes that operate as a single unit, which is accessible by its computing platform (*metaprocessor*, *metaoperating system*, and *metaprogramming environment*).
- A *metacomputation* is a form of distributed computation (a computation of computations) determined by *collaborating computations* that a metacomputer can interpret and execute. A *service object* selected at runtime by a metaoperating system implements metainstructions that invoke what are usually legacy programs.
- A collection of service providers selected and managed for a metacomputation is called a *virtual metaprocessor*.
- A *metaprogram* is an expression of metacomputation, represented in a *programming language*, which a *metacomputer* follows in processing shared data for a *service collaboration* managed by its *metaoperating system* on its virtual *metaprocessor*.

- A *service object* is a remote object that provides services to other service objects. *Service objects* are identified primarily by service types and typically do not have a lifecycle of their own; any state they do contain tends to be an aggregate of the states of the *local entity objects* that they offer to service requestors. A service object that implements multiple interfaces provides *multiple services*. A *service provider* makes interfaces of multiple service objects available on the network.
- A *service-oriented architecture (SOA)* is a software architecture using loosely coupled service providers. The SOA integrates them into a distributed computing system by means of SO programming. Service objects are made available as independent components that can be accessed without a priori knowledge of their underlying platform, implementation, and location. The client-server architecture separates a client from a server, SOA introduces a third component, a service registry. The registry allows the metaoperating system (not the end user or application) to dynamically find service objects on the network.
- If the application (wire) protocol between requestors and all service providers is predefined and constant then this type of SOA is called a *service-protocol oriented architecture* (SPOA). In contrast, if the communication is based on message passing and the wire protocol can be chosen by a provider to satisfy efficient communication with its requestors, then the architecture is called a *service-object oriented architecture* (SOOA).

Let's emphasize the major distinction between SOOA and SPOA: in SOOA, a proxy object is created and always owned by the service provider, but in SPOA, the requestor creates and owns a proxy which has to meet the requirements of the protocol that the provider and requestor agreed upon a priori. Thus, in SPOA the protocol is always fixed, generic, and reduced to a common denominator—one size fits all—that leads to inefficient network communication with heterogeneous large datasets. In SOOA, each provider can decide on the most efficient protocol(s) needed for a particular distributed application. For example, SPOA wire protocols are: SOAP in Web and Grid Services, IIOP in CORBA, JRMP in Java RMI. SORCER implements its SOOA with the Jini service architecture [10].

The platforms and related programming models have evolved as process expression has evolved from the sequential process expression activated on a single computer to the concurrent process expression activated on multiple computers. The evolution in process expression introduces new platform benefits but at the same time introduces additional programming complexity that operating systems have to deal with. We can distinguish seven quantum jumps in process expression and related programming complexity [22]:

1. Sequential programming (e.g., von Neumann architecture)
2. Multi-threaded programming (e.g., Java Platform)
3. Multi-process programming (e.g., Unix platform)
4. Multi-machine-process programming (e.g., CORBA)
5. Knowledge-based programming (e.g., DICEtalk [19])
6. Service-protocol oriented programming (e.g., Web and Grid Services)
7. Service-object oriented programming (e.g. SORCER)

SORCER introduces an exertion-oriented (EO) programming model with federated method invocation (FMI) in its SOOA. FMI defines the communication framework between three SORCER architectural layers: SO programming, management, and execution.

3 Service-Object Oriented Platform: SORCER

The term "federated" means that a single service invocation with no network configuration creates at runtime a dynamic federation of required collaborating services. SORCER (Service-ORiented Computing EnviRonment) is a federated service-to-service (S2S) metacomputing environment that treats service providers as network peers with well-defined semantics of a service-object oriented architecture (SOOA). It is based on Jini semantics of services [10] in the network and the Jini programming model [3, 1] with explicit leases, distributed events, transactions, and discovery/join protocols. Jini focuses on service management in a networked environment, SORCER is focused on exertion-oriented (EO) programming and the execution environment for exertions (see Fig. 2).

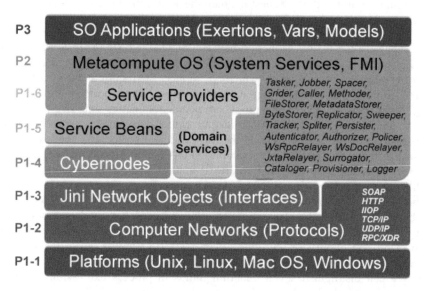

Fig. 2. SORCER layered architecture, where P1 metaprocessor, P1-6 application services, P2 operating system services, P3 programming environment

3.1 Exertion-Oriented Programming

The programming example presented in the Introduction implies that an expression of service (task or job) in the EO declarative language can be written as one line—the feature of functional programming. For example f1 can be rewritten in one line by substituting references to the component exertions by their corresponding expressions.

The operators in the EO language, described in the Introduction, correspond to Java interfaces and classes [20]. The SORCER framework almost entirely designed in terms of Java interfaces. To explain how SORCER works we will refer to a few Java interfaces and classes in the remainder of this paper. For example, operators `task` and `job` return objects that are defined by the `Exertion` interface with corresponding reference implementations: `ServiceTask` and `ServiceJob` respectively. Thus for each EO operator there is a corresponding Java object. To avoid potential confusions of concepts with the dual representation in declarative language and implementation language we will refer to a declarative language concept as defined so far and appending "object" when referring to the corresponding Java type. For example, an "exertion" is an expression in the EO language and an "exertion object" as one implementing the `Exertion` interface.

An *exertion* is an expression of a *service collaboration* realized by both metaoperating system providers (in short *mos-providers*) and application providers (in short *app-providers*). For each exertion the mos-federation is formed *dynamically* to reflect the exertion's recursive service composition and control strategy [23]. The mos-federation manages for the exertion late bindings to the required app-providers in the *dynamically* formed app-federation (exertion's metaprocessor). The app-federation represents *service objects* that implement all exertion operations. Thus, the mos-federation provides the functionality of the SORCER OS (SOS) and the app-federation provides the functionality of the SORCER metaprocessor (SMP).

Please note that exertion objects are entities that encapsulate explicitly *data, operations*, and *control strategy*. SOS uses service compositions, interfaces, and control strategies, but data contexts and corresponding methods are used by SMP. The interfaces are dynamically bound to corresponding service-objects at runtime even to those that have to be provisioned on-demand. The service objects in the app-federation execute the exertion's operations transparently according to the exertion's *control strategy* managed by SOS. The SORCER *Triple Command Pattern* [9] defines federated method invocation (FMI) that integrates SOS with SMP. FMI is presented in more detail in Section. 5.4 [22]

From the SORCER platform point of view, exertions are entities at the *EO programming level*, sos-federations at the *SOS level*, and app-federations at the *SMP level*. Thus, an exertion represents the process of the cooperating SOS and SMP service providers (see Fig. 3).

The primary difference between the sos-federation and the app-federation is *management* and *execution*. The sos-federation and the app-federation distinctions are based on the analogies between the *company management* and *employees*. The top-level exertion refers to the *central control* (the Chairman of the company—binding the top-level exertion to SOS) of the behavior of a *management system* (the Chairman's staff—sos-federation), while the app-federation refers to *the execution system* (the company employees—the service objects) that operates according to execution rules (SORCER FMI), but without centralized control.

The SORCER SOOA consists of three major types of remote objects: service providers, registries, and proxy objects. The provider is responsible for deploying the service on the network, publishing its proxy object to one or more registries, and allowing requestors to access its proxy. Providers advertise their availability on the

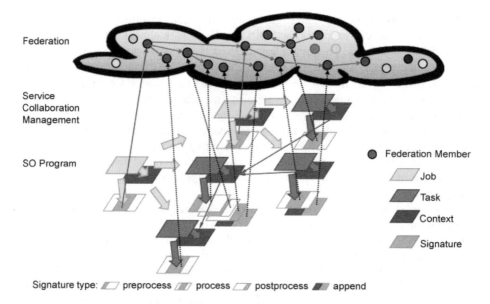

Signature type: preprocess process postprocess append

Fig. 3. Exertions and federations. The top-level exertion with component exertions is depicted below the service cloud. Green arrows between data contexts show data flow (context pipes). The solid red lines indicate late bindings to operating system services. Late bindings to all application services defined by the exertion signatures are indicated by dashed lines. The providers in the cloud, in red color, form the service federation—metaprocessor.

network only while present; registries intercept these announcements and cache proxy objects to the provider services. The requestor (e.g., exertion) discovers registries and then looks up proxies by sending queries to registries and making selections from the available service types. Queries contain search criteria (defined by the op operator) related to the type and quality of service. Registries facilitate searching by storing proxy objects of services and making them available to requestors. Providers use discovery/join protocols to publish services on the network; requestors use discovery/join protocols to obtain service proxies on the network. SORCER uses Jini discovery/join protocols to implement dynamic service management for its SOS and SMP. Exertion objects are requestors capable of dynamically finding sos-providers, for example dynamically looking up or provisioning on-demnd Taskers and Jobbers that in turn manage corresponding app-federations.

A task object is an elementary command managed by a SOS provider of the Tasker type. A Tasker can provide a single service by itself or can manage a small-scale federation for the same data context used by all providers in its federation. A job object is defined hierarchically in terms of tasks and other jobs, including control flow exertions [22]. A job object is a composite command managed by rendezvous providers of Jobber, Spacer, or Cataloger type managing hierarchical large-scale collaborations.

The exertion's data, called a *data context* [20], describes the data that Taskers work on. A data context, or simply a *context*, is an associative array that describes service provider ontology along with related data. A provider's ontology is controlled by the provider vocabulary that describes data structures in a provider's namespace within a specified service domain of interest. A requestor defining an exertion has to comply with that ontology as it specifies how the context data is interpreted and used by the provider. The notion of context is derived from the knowledge representation scheme called percept calculus [19]. Thus, data context can be used as a knowledge base the same way it is used in the DICEtalk platform [19] or as a var-oriented model presented in Section 3.2.

3.2 Var-Oriented Programming

The fundamental principle of functional programming is that a computation can be realized by composing functions. Functional programming languages consider functions to be data, avoid states, and mutable values in the evaluation process in contrast to the imperative programming style, which emphasizes changes in state values. Thus, one can write a function that takes other functions as parameters, returning yet another function. Experience suggests that functional programs are more robust and easier to test than imperative ones.

Not all operations are mathematical functions. In nonfunctional programming languages, "functions" are subroutines that return values while in a mathematical sense a function is a unique mapping from input values to output values. The SORCER var-oriented (VO) framework allows one to use functions, subroutines, or coroutines in the same way. Here the term *var* is used to denote a mathematical function, subroutine, coroutine, or any data (object).

VO programming is a programming paradigm that treats any computation as the triplet: *value, evaluator*, and *filter* (VEF). Evaluators and filters can be executed locally or remotely, sequentially or concurrently. In particular, evaluators and filters can be considered as exertions, service providers, or conventional programs as indicated by green arrows in Fig. 4. The paradigm emphasizes the usage of *evaluators* and a *pipeline of filters* to define the variable value. Semantics of a *var*, whether it's a mathematical function, subroutine, coroutine, or just a value (object) depends on the evaluator type and pipeline of filters used with the variable. VO programming allows for exertions to use vars in data contexts. Alternatively, data contexts (implementing `Context` interface) with specialized structures of vars, called *VO models,* can be used for enterprise-wide metacomputing. Three VO analysis models: *response, parametric*, and *optimization* have been studied already.

The variable evaluation strategy is defined as follows: the associated current evaluator determines the variable's raw value, and the current pipeline of filters returns the output value. Multiple associations of evaluator-filter can be used with the same var (multifidelity). Evaluator's raw value may depend on other var arguments and those vars in turn can depend on other argument vars and so on. This var dependency chaining is called VO composition and provides in SORCER the integration framework for all possible types of computations represented by various types of evaluators including exertion evaluators.

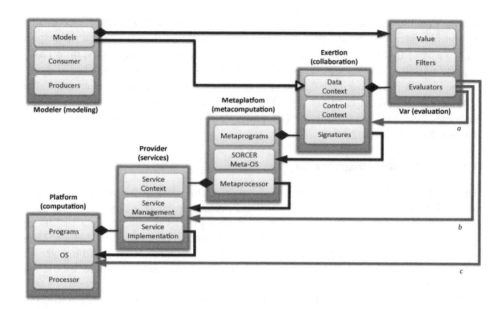

Fig. 4. SORCER computing abstractions: model, evaluation, collaboration, and computation. Arrows indicate associations, diamonds indicate compositions, the hollow arrow generalization, and arrows in green color indicate various ways of var evaluation.

The same evaluator with different filters can be associated with many vars. The modular VFE triplet structure of vars and reuse of evaluators and filters, including exertion evaluators with context filters, in defining VO-oriented models is the key feature of VO programming that complements SO programming with local computations.

VO models support *multidisciplinary* (vars from other models), and *multifidelity* (multiple evaluators per var) computing and are called *amorphous* models. For the same VO model an alternative set of evaluators (another fidelity) can be selected at runtime to evaluate a new particular version ("shape") of the model and quickly update the related process in the right evolving direction.

3.3 SORCER Operating System

The SORCER OS (SOS) allows executing service-oriented program and by itself is the service-oriented system. The overlay network of the services defining the functionality of SOS is called the *sos-federation* and the overlay network of application-specific services is called the *app-federation* (see Fig. 2). The *metainstruction set* of the SORCER metaprocessor consists of all operations offered by all services in the service federation—the union of the sos-federation and the app-federation. Thus, an EO program is composed of metainstructions with its own control strategy per service composition and data context representing the shared metaprogram data. Service signatures (instances of Signature type) correspond to op operators that specify operations of collaboration participants in the app-federation. Each signature primarily is defined by a service type, operation in that interface, and a set of optional attributes. Four types of signatures are

distinguished: PROCESS, PREPROCESS, POSTPROCESS, and APPEND. A PROC-
ESS signature—of which there is only one allowed per exertion—defines the dynamic
late binding to a provider that implements the signature's interface. The data context
[20] describes the data that tasks and jobs work on. An APPEND signature defines the
context received from the provider specified by this signature. The received context is
then appended in runtime to the existing data context. The resulting context is then
processed by PREPROCESS, PROCESS, and POSTPROCESS operations of the exertion. Appending a data context allows a requestor to use network shared data in runtime
not available to the requestor when the exertion is declared. SOS allows for an exertion
to create and manage a service collaboration and transparently coordinate the execution
of all component exertions within the assembled federation. Please note that these metacomputing concepts are defined differently in traditional grid computing where a job is
just an executing process for a submitted executable code with no federation being
formed for the executable—the executable becomes the single service itself.

An exertion can be activated, it means its *collaboration exerted*, by invoking the
exert operation on the exertion object:

$$\texttt{Exertion\#exert(Transaction) : Exertion,}$$

where a parameter of the Transaction type is required when a transactional semantics is needed for all participating nested exertions within the parent one. Thus,
EO programming allows us to execute an exertion and invoke exertion's signatures on
collaborating service objects indirectly, but where does the service-to-service communication come into play? How do these services communicate with one another if
they are all different? Top-level communication between services, or the sending of
service requests, is done through the use of the generic Servicer interface and the
operation service that all SORCER providers are required to provide:

$$\texttt{Servicer\#service(Exertion, Transaction):Exertion.}$$

This top-level service operation takes an exertion object as an argument and gives
back an exertion object as the return value.

So why are exertion objects used rather than directly calling on a provider's method
and passing data contexts? There are two basic answers to this. First, passing exertion
objects helps to aid with the network-centric messaging. A service requestor can send
an exertion object implicitly out onto the network—Exertion#exert()—and
any service provider can pick it up. The receiving provider can then look at the signature's interface and operation requested within the exertion object, and if it doesn't
implement the desired interface or provide the desired method, it can continue forwarding it to another service provider who can service it. Second, passing exertion
objects helps with fault detection and recovery. Each exertion object has its own
completion state associated with it to specify if it has yet to run, has already completed, or has failed. Since full exertion objects are both passed and returned, the user
can view the failed exertion to see what method was being called as well as what was
used in the data context input that may have caused the problem. Since exertion objects provide all the information needed to execute the exertion including its control
strategy, the user would be able to pause a job between component exertions, analyze
it and make needed updates. To figure out where to resume an exertion, the executing

provider would simply have to look at the exertion's completion states and resume the first one that wasn't completed yet. In other words, EO programming allows the user, *not programmer* to update the metaprogram on-the-fly, what practically translates into creating new interactive collaborative applications at runtime. Applying the inversion principle, SOS executes the exertion's collaboration with dynamically found, if present, or provisioned on-demand service objects. The exertion caller has no direct dependency to service objects since the exertion uses only service types (interfaces) they implement.

Despite the fact that any Servicer can accept any exertion, SOS services have well defined roles in the S2S platform (see Fig. 2):

a) Taskers – accept service tasks; they are used to create application services by dependency injection (service assembly) or by inheritance (subclassing `ServiceTasker` and implementing required service interfaces);
b) Jobbers –manage service collaboration for `PUSH` signatures;
c) Spacers – manage service collaboration for `PULL` signatures using space-based computing [7];
d) Contexters – provide data contexts for `APPEND` signatures;
e) FileStorers – provide access to federated file system providers [2, 27];
f) Catalogers – Servicer registries, provide management for QoS-based federations;
g) SlaMonitors - provide monitoring of SLAs [18];
h) Provisioners - provide on-demand provisioning of services by SERVME [17, 18];
i) Persisters – persist data contexts, tasks, and jobs to be reused for interactive EO programming;
j) Relayers – gateway providers; transform exertions to native representation, for example integration with Web services and JXTA;
k) Authenticators, Authorizers, Policers, KeyStorers – provide support for service security;
l) Auditors, Reporters, Loggers – support for accountability, reporting, and logging
m) Griders, Callers, Methoders – support for a conventional compute grid;
n) Notifiers - use third party services for collecting provider notifications for time consuming programs and disconnected requestors.

Both sos-providers and app-providers do not have mutual associations prior to the execution of an exertion; they come together dynamically (federate) for all nested tasks and jobs in the exertion.

Domain specific servicers within the federation, or *task peers* (*taskers*), execute task exertions. Rendezvous peers (jobbers, spacers, and catalogers) manage service collaborations. Providers of the `Tasker`, `Jobber`, `Spacer`, and `Cataloger` type are basic SOS service management providers; see Fig. 2. In the view of the P2P architecture [21] defined by the `Servicer` interface, a job can be sent to any servicer. A peer that is not a `Jobber` type is responsible for forwarding the job to one of available rendezvous peers in the SORCER environment and returning results to the requestor. Thus implicitly, any peer can handle any exertion type. Once the exertion execution is complete, the federation dissolves and the providers in the federation disperse to seek other exertions to join.

3.4   Federated Method Invocation

An exertion is executed by invoking its exert operation. The SORCER Federated Method Invocation (FMI) defines the following three related operations:

1. `Exertion#exert(Transaction):Exertion`
   join the sos-federation; the invoked exertion is bound to the available provider specified by the exertion's PROCESS signature (a rendezvous provider if a job, otherwise a matching tasker);
2. `Servicer#service(Exertion, Transaction):Exertion`
   SOS request for a service by the bound provider in 1); and if the argument exertion object accepted by the bound provider, then the provider calls 3)
3. `Exerter#exert(Exertion,          Transaction):Exertion`
   execute the argument exertion object by the service object of the provider accepting the service request in 2). Any component exertion of the parent exertion is then processed recursively by 1).

This above *triple command design pattern* [22, 9] defines various implementations of these three interfaces: `Exertion` (metaprogram), `Servicer` (service provider—peer), and `Exerter` (service object processing the data context of exertion). This approach allows for the P2P environment [21] via the `Servicer` interface, extensive modularization of `Exertions` and `Exerters`, and extensibility from the triple command design pattern so requestors can submit onto the network any EO program they want with or without transactional semantics. The triple command pattern is used by SOS as follows:

1. An exertion is activated by calling `Exertion#exert()`. The exert operation implemented in `ServiceExertion` uses `ServiceAccessor` to locate in runtime the provider matching the exertion's PROCESS signature.
2. If the matching provider is found, then on its access proxy the `Service#service()` method is invoked.
3. When the requestor is authenticated and authorized by the provider to invoke the method defined by the exertion's PROCESS signature, then the provider calls its own exert operation: `Exerter#exert()`.
4. `Exerter#exert()` operation is implemented accordingly by `ServiceTasker`, `ServiceJobber`, and `ServiceSpacer`. A `ServiceTasker` peer calls by reflection the operation specified in the PROCESS signature of the task object. All application-specific methods of an application interface have the same signature: a single `Context` type parameter and a `Context` type return value.

The exertion activated by a requestor can be submitted by SOS directly or indirectly to the corresponding service provider. In the direct approach, when signature's access type is PUSH, SOS finds the matching service provider against the service type and attributes of the PROCESS signature and submits the exertion object to the matching provider. The execution order of multiple signatures is defined by signature priorities, if the exertion's flow type is SEQUENTIAL; otherwise they are dispatched in parallel. EO programming has a branch exertion (`IfExertion`) and loop exertions (`WhileEx-ertion`, `ForExertion`) as well as two mechanisms for nonlinear flow control (`BreakExertion`, `ContinueExertion`). An exertion can reflect a process with branching and looping by applying control flow exertions [20].

Alternatively, when signature's access type is PULL, SOS uses a `Spacer` provider and simply drops the exertion into the shared exertion space to be pulled from by a matching provider. Spacers provide efficient load balancing for processing exertions from the shared space and are efficient for lengthy processes that might require services not present at all times during the process execution. The fastest available servicer gets an exertion from the space before other overloaded or slower servicers can do so. When an exertion consists of component jobs with different access and flow types, then we have the *hybrid* process execution when the collaboration potentially executes concurrently with multiple *pull* and *push* subcollaborations at the same time.

3.5 How to Create an Application Service?

To complete the example given in the Introduction, let's implement one of the arithmetic services, for example `Adder` that can be used by SOS.

A plain old Java object (POJO) becomes a SORCER service bean, injected into a `Tasker`, by implementing a Java interface (does not have to be `Remote`), which has the following characteristics:

1. Defines the service operations you'd like to call remotely
2. The single parameter and returned value of each operation is of the type `sorcer.service.Context`
3. Each method must declare `java.rmi.RemoteException` in its throws clause. The method can also declare application-specific exceptions
4. The class implementing the interface and local objects must be serializable

The interface for the `Adder` bean can be defined as follows:

```
interface Adder {
  Context add(Context context) throwsRemoteException;
}
```
The interface implementation:
```
public class AdderImpl implements Adder {
  public Context add(Context context) throws
    RemoteException {
      double result = 0;
      List<Double> inputs = context.getInValues();
        for (Object value : inputs)
          result += value;
    context.putValue(context.getOutPath(), result);
    return context;
  }
}
```

Finally start the `Tasker` with the following configuration file:

```
sorcer.core.provider.ServiceProvider {
  name = "SORCER Adder";
  beans = new String[]{"sorcer.arithmetic.AdderImpl"};
}
```

The same way you can implement and deploy `Multiplier` and `Subtractor` and you are ready to run the SO program given in the Introduction.

4 Conclusions

A distributed system is not just a collection of distributed objects—it is the unreliable network of objects that come and go. EO programming introduces the new abstractions of *service objects* and *exertions* for unreliable networks instead of *objects* and *messages* in object-oriented programming. Exertions encapsulate the triplet of *operations*, *data*, and *control strategy*. From the SORCER platform point of view, an *exertion* is the expression of service composition at the programming level, the *management federation* of service objects at the operating system level, and the *application federation* of service objects at the application service processor level. The exertions are programs that define reliable network collaborations in unreliable service networks. The SORCER operating system manages service collaborations on its virtual processor—the dynamically created federations that use FMI.

SORCER identifies a service with its service type. Applying the inversion principle, SOS looks up service objects by implemented interface types with optional search attributes, for example a provider name. SOS utilizes Jini-based service management that provides for dynamic services, mobile code shared over the network, and network security. Federations are aggregated from independent service-objects that do not require heavyweight containers like application servers.

The presented FMI framework allows P2P computing via the `Servicer` interface, extensive modularization of `Exertions` and `Exerters`, and extensibility from the triple command design pattern [20]. The SORCER platform uses a dynamic service discovery mechanism allowing new services to enter the network and disabled services to leave the network gracefully with no need for reconfiguration. This allows the exertion collaboration to be distributed without sacrificing the robustness of the service-oriented process. This architecture also improves the utilization of the network resources by distributing the execution load over multiple nodes of the network. The exertion's federation shows resilience to service failures on the network as it can search for alternate services and maintain continuity of operations even during periods when there is no service available.

The SORCER platform with EO programming has been successfully deployed and tested in multiple concurrent engineering and large-scale distributed applications [8, 12, 29]. It is believed that incremental improvements of SPOA will not suffice, so we plan to continue the development of *Service-Object Oriented Optimization Toolkit for Distributed High Fidelity Engineering Design Optimization* at the Multidisciplinary Science and Technology Center, AFRL with three layers of programming: *model-driven programming* (transdisciplinary complex processes), *var-oriented programming* (for var multifidelity evaluations and var compositions), and *exertion-oriented programming* (for network collaborations). We will investigate how *model-driven programming* can be used to address several fundamental challenges posed by the new value-filter-evaluator paradigm for real world complex optimization problems

I began my Introduction with Edsger Dijkstra's credo:

"Computing's core challenge is how not to make a mess of it."

The presented confrontation of computing and metacomputing, and the SORCER platform described in this paper implies that reducing both programming and metaprogramming to the same level of middleware programming and within the same computing platform (currently common practice for building SOA), introduces intolerable complexity for building large-scale adaptive and dynamic enterprise systems. SORCER defines clearly its separate metacomputing architectural layers: SO programming, management, and execution layers integrated via FMI. That introduces simplicity to the expression of SO processes at the application level using VO modeldriven with var-oriented and exertion-oriented programming. Flexible enterprise interoperability is achieved via SORCER three neutralities (service protocol, implementation, and location [22]) and architectural means (Fig. 4), not by neutral data exchange formats, e.g., XML, when overused introduce unintended complexity and degraded performance.

Acknowledgments

This work was partially supported by Air Force Research Lab, Air Vehicles Directorate, Multidisciplinary Science and Technology Center, the contract number F33615-03-D-3307, Algorithms for Federated High Fidelity Engineering Design Optimization. I would like to express my gratitude to all those who helped me in my SORCER research at AFRL, GE Global Research Center, and my students at the SORCER Lab, TTU. Especially I would like to express my gratitude to Dr. Ray Kolonay, my technical advisor at AFRL/RBSD for his support, encouragement, and advice.

References

1. Apache River, http://incubator.apache.org/river/RIVER/index.html (accessed on: August 10, 2010)
2. Berger, M., Sobolewski, M.: Lessons Learned from the SILENUS Federated File System. In: Loureiro, G., Curran, R. (eds.) Complex Systems Concurrent Engineering, pp. 431–440. Springer, Heidelberg (2007a)
3. Edwards, W.K.: Core Jini, 2nd edn. Prentice Hall, Englewood Cliffs (2000)
4. Fallacies of Distributed Computing (accessed on: August 10, 2010) http://en.wikipedia.org/wiki/Fallacies_of_Distributed_Computing
5. Fant, K.M.: A Critical Review of the Notion of Algorithm in Computer Science. In: Proceedings of the 21st Annual Computer Science Conference, pp. 1–6 (February 1993)
6. Foster, I., Kesselman, C., Tuecke, S.: The Anatomy of the Grid: Enabling Scalable Virtual Organizations. International J. Supercomputer Applications 15(3) (2001)
7. Freeman, E., Hupfer, S., Arnold, K.: JavaSpaces^{TM} Principles, Patterns, and Practice. Addison-Wesley, Reading ISBN: 0-201-30955-6

8. Goel, S., Talya, S.S., Sobolewski, M.: Mapping Engineering Design Processes onto a Service-Grid: Turbine Design Optimization. International Journal of Concurrent Engineering: Research & Applications, Concurrent Engineering 16, 139–147 (2008)
9. Grand, M.: Patterns in Java, vol. 1. Wiley, Chichester (1999) ISBN: 0-471-25841-5
10. Jini Architecture Specification (accessed on: August 10, 2010),
    http://www.jini.org/wiki/Jini_Architecture_Specification
11. Juric, M., Benny Mathew, B., Sarang, P.: Business Process Execution Language for Web Services BPEL and BPEL4WS, 2nd edn. Packt Publishing (2006) ISBN: 978-1904811817
12. Kolonay, R.M., Thompson, E.D., Camberos, J.A., Eastep, F.: Active Control of Transpiration Boundary Conditions for Drag Minimization with an Euler CFD Solver. In: 48th AIAA/ASME/ASCE/AHS/ASC Structures, Structural Dynamics, and Materials Conference on AIAA 2007-1891, Honolulu, Hawaii (2007)
13. Linthicum, D.S.: Cloud Computing and SOA Convergence in Your Enterprise: A Step-by-Step Guide. Addison-Wesley Professional, Reading (2009) ISBN-10 0136009220
14. Lynch, D., Rose, M.T. (eds.): Internet System handbook. Addison-Wesley, Reading (1992)
15. Markov, A.A.: Theory of Algorithms, trans. by Schorr-Kon, J.J. Keter Press (1971)
16. Metacomputing: Past to Present (August 10, 2010),
    http://archive.ncsa.uiuc.edu/Cyberia/MetaComp/MetaHistory.html
17. Rio Project, http://www.rio-project.org/ (accessed on: August 10, 2010)
18. Rubach, P., Sobolewski, M.: Autonomic SLA Management in Federated Computing Environments. In: International Conference on Parallel Processing Workshops, Vienna, Austria, pp. 314–321 (2009)
19. Sobolewski, M.: Multi-Agent Knowledge-Based Environment for Concurrent Engineering Applications. Concurrent Engineering: Research and Applications (CERA), Technomic (1996), http://cer.sagepub.com/cgi/content/abstract/4/1/89
20. Sobolewski, M.: Exertion Oriented Programming. IADIS 3(1), 86–109 (2008) ISBN: ISSN: 1646-3692
21. Sobolewski, M.: Federated Collaborations with Exertions. In: 17th IEEE International Workshop on Enabling Technologies: Infrastructures for Collaborative Enterprises (WETICE), pp. 127–132 (2008)
22. Sobolewski, M.: Metacomputing with Federated Method Invocation. In: Akbar Hussain, M. (ed.) Advances in Computer Science and IT, pp. s337–s363 (2009) In-Tech, intechweb.org, ISBN 978-953-7619-51-0,
    http://sciyo.com/articles/show/title/metacomputing-with-federated-method-invocation (accessed on: August 10, 2010)
23. Sobolewski, M.: Object-Oriented Metacomputing with Exertions. In: Gunasekaran, A., Sandhu, M. (eds.) Handbook On Business Information Systems. World Scientific, Singapore (2010) ISBN: 978-981-283-605-2
24. SORCERsoft, http://sorcersoft.org (accessed on: August 10, 2010)
25. Sotomayor, B., Childers, L.: Globus® Toolkit 4: Programming Java Services. Morgan Kaufmann, San Francisco (2005)
26. Thain, D., Tannenbaum, T., Livny, M.: Condor and the Grid. In: Berman, F., Hey, A.J.G., Fox, G. (eds.) Grid Computing: Making The Global Infrastructure a Reality. John Wiley, Chichester (2003)
27. Turner, A., Sobolewski, M.: FICUS—A Federated Service-Oriented File Transfer Framework. In: Loureiro, G., Curran, L.,, R. (eds.) Complex Systems Concurrent Engineering, pp. 421–430. Springer, Heidelberg (2007) ISBN: 978-1-84628-975-0
28. Waldo, J.: The End of Protocols (accessed on: August 10, 2010),
    http://java.sun.com/developer/technicalArticles/jini/protocols.html
29. Xu, W., Cha, J., Sobolewski, M.: A Service-Oriented Collaborative Design Platform for Concurrent Engineering. Advanced Materials Research 44-46, 717–724 (2008)

Towards a Support Framework for Enterprise Integration

Ovidiu Noran

Griffith University Australia, School of ICT
O.Noran@griffith.edu.au

Abstract. Knowing 'what to do next' and what artefacts to use so as to achieve the desired future state of an enterprise is a recurring management conundrum. This paper describes a framework (and a possible application) aimed to support the efforts to achieve and maintain enterprises (or networks thereof) in a state where the flows of material and information are seamlessly integrated so as to achieve the internal and external synergy and agility required to survive but also to *thrive* in today's fast-evolving business environment. The framework is based on the integration of a structured repository containing architecture framework elements and a set of steps guiding the creation of specific enterprise engineering tasks. An outline of the theoretical foundation is followed by a high-level description of the requirements and architectural design descriptions of the proposed support framework and its potential application as a decision support system.

1 Introduction

Typically, the Enterprise Engineering (EE) tasks involved in reaching and maintaining Enterprise Integration (EI) are on-going, complex, and often involve partially- and / or ill-defined constraints. This is also because EI is indeed a multi-faceted concept involving consistency of data, dynamic allocation of resources and consistency in decision-making so as to address a coherent set of local and/or distributed objectives [1].

Thus, EE project managers are expected to constantly evaluate and understand the current situation, clarify and choose an optimal future state, grasp the scope and content of the change process required, gather knowledge of useful artefacts, and then select, model and communicate the 'way forward' to the organisation(s) involved.

Enterprise Architecture (EA) holds the promise to help stakeholders manage the on-going EE effort in a consistent and coherent fashion, both within and between organisations, so as to achieve and maintain EI. However, EA itself is currently a rather new field and as such lacking agreed-upon consistent definitions. As a result, stakeholders and EE project managers are still rather confused as to a) 'what needs to be done next' to achieve / maintain integration and b) what artefacts (e.g. models, methods, frameworks, or combinations thereof) to use to model, evaluate, choose and communicate a).

Current systems such as Executive Dashboards, based on Executive Information Systems principles as described by Volonino and Watson [2], focus more on presenting existing data rather than on actively assisting the decisional effort. This paper describes

R. Meersman et al. (Eds.): OTM 2010 Workshops, LNCS 6428, pp. 202–210, 2010.

interim results of the on-going research efforts aiming define a framework to support decision-making in EE projects by using the analysis of the interactions between project participants in the context of their lifecycles. The framework assists in the EE effort by eliciting the domain know-how of the project stakeholders and using it to discover and describe the relevant aspects of the EE project at hand - such as processes and their associated data, relations between participating entities, decisional aspects, etc. Mainstream Architecture Framework (AF) elements and supporting tools are employed by the system in order to model the new knowledge thus created and help the participant organisation(s) understand and internalize it.

Note that due to scope and space limitations, the main aim of this paper is to explain the concepts and high-level structure of the proposed framework, rather than provide a full description. The interested reader can find such details in [3].

2 Requirements for the Proposed Framework

There are notable challenges in achieving EI (and implicitly, interoperability and compatibility as described in [4]). Panetto and Molina [5] summarize a substantial set of current issues in EI and interoperability featuring among others the need for design and engineering methodologies, reference model repositories (encapsulating reusable enterprise engineering (EE) models) and tools required to integrate business and manufacturing models. Currently, a considerable number of AFs offer artefacts aiming to satisfy the above-mentioned requirements; however, their terminology and coverage typically displays gaps and overlaps that make them confusing to intended users [6]. Most AFs also offer proprietary approaches and supporting tools - thus triggering the 'vendor lock-in' risk.

In addition, according to Molina, Panetto et al. [9], new 'killer'-type ICT-based applications and systems likely to become ubiquitous must support and satisfy several fundamental requirements, notably including EI and interoperability, human - software / hardware integration, cooperation and agility.

Past and current research of the author has tried to define the guidelines for an approach tackling the above-mentioned needs in an integrated manner by providing a framework integrating a repository of AF artefacts supporting EI / EE / EA and a method to create specific EE tasks based on a set steps and the selection of artefacts from the above-mentioned repository. It is hoped that this approach will help address the methodology, modelling and reusability aspects of the above-mentioned challenges identified in the EI domain.

3 Theoretical Base and Components of the Support Framework

The foundation of the proposed support system originates in research attempting to assess the feasibility and define the principles of a method to create methods ('meta-methodology') guiding specific projects in the Collaborative Network (CN) and Virtual Organisation (VO) area [8, 10]. As the name implies, the main result of the meta-methodology application to a specific project is a method typically expressed in one of more activity models depicting tasks necessary to accomplish that project. The research has defined several steps required to achieve the above-mentioned outcome:

thus, the project stakeholders must first understand the problems of the current state, then reason about possible ways to solve them and subsequently select the optimal solution for the project at hand. This involves modelling various viewpoints using appropriate views, formalisms, reference models (RMs) possibly grouped in modelling frameworks (MFs). The meta-methodology assists stakeholders in using their (often tacit) domain knowledge (Fig. 1 left) to infer new facts by following a guided process of business modelling. The newly created knowledge is explicit (expressed in the models created) and used primarily to accomplish the project. However, it will typically be also internalised by other stakeholders and reflected in future decision-making [11], thus enriching and completing the corporate knowledge lifecycle. The meta-methodology has been tested in several case studies [10, 12].

3.1 A Step-by-Step Method to Construct Methods

As can be seen from Fig. 1, currently the meta-methodology comprises three major stages and a set of sub-steps. In the first stage, the user is prompted to create a list containing entities of interest to the project in question, making sure to include project participants, target entities (organisations, other projects being built / managed by the project at hand) and importantly, the EE project itself. The second stage comprises the creation of business models showing the relations between the previously listed entities in the context of their lifecycles, i.e. illustrating how entities influence each other within each life cycle phase. The third stage assists the user in inferring the set of project activities by reading and interpreting the previously represented relations for each life cycle phase of the target entities. The activities must be detailed to a level deemed as comprehensible (and thus usable) by the intended audience. This task is assisted by other models and artefacts built and adopted during the second stage.

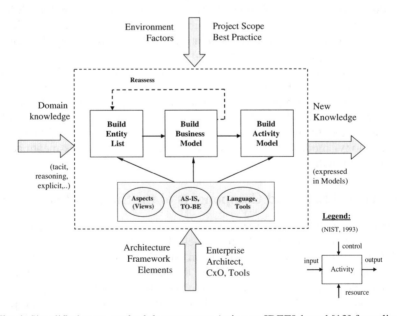

Fig. 1. Simplified meta-methodology concept (using an IDEF0-based [13] formalism)

The first meta-methodology sub-step calls for the selection of suitable aspects, or viewpoints reflecting stakeholder concerns [14, 15] to be modelled in each stage (note that the life cycle viewpoint representation is mandatory and essential to the meta-methodology). The selection of a MF is also recommended, as MFs typically feature structured collections of views that can be used as checklists of candidate aspects and their intended coverage. This sub-step also requires the identification and resolution of any aspect dependencies. The second sub-step asks the user to determine if the present (AS-IS) state of the previously adopted views needs to be shown and whether the AS-IS and TO-BE (future) states should be represented in separate, or in combined models. The third sub-step requires the selection of suitable modelling formalisms and modelling tools for the chosen aspects.

Importantly, research and testing has determined that although originating in the CN / VO area, the meta-methodology in fact applicable to any EE project type, due to its open character and neutral approach towards all major AFs and enterprise modelling approaches [3].

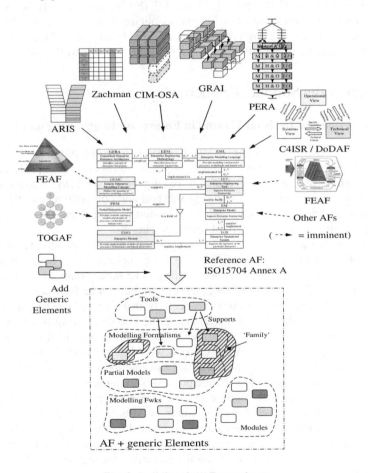

Fig. 2. Building the AF repository

3.2 A Structured Repository of AF Elements

The meta-methodology concept relies on creating and interpreting models depicting various aspects of the EE project participants. This modelling effort requires the selection of methods, languages, tools, MFs and RMs according to specific project requirements and best practice. Since such artefacts are typically structured in AFs, the question is how to find suitable sets of AF components for specific projects.

A possible answer is to construct ranked lists of suitable AF elements and ask the stakeholders to pick the most appropriate ones based on their domain knowledge. For this to be possible, AFs must first be decomposed in elements assessed on their scope, integration, dependencies, etc and organised in a coherent collection using a set of consistent criteria. Mainstream AFs have been (and still are) assessed and decomposed in respect to ISO15704 Annex A (GERAM , see [14] for details).

PERA [16], GRAI-GIM [17, 18], CIM-OSA [19], ARIS [20], Zachman [21] and DoDAF [22] have been decomposed using GERAM [7, 23] (see Fig. 2., top). Other AFs, such as TOGAF [24], TEAF [25] and FEAF [26] are currently being added to the repository. The collection of AF elements obtained in this way (see Fig. 2., bottom) has been structured using criteria such as type, family, etc. The result of this arrangement is referred to hereafter in this paper as the 'Structured Repository' (SR).

4 Design of the Support Framework

4.1 Knowledge and Decision Making in Enterprise Engineering and Integration

Knowledge is present in all organisations in various forms (explicit, tacit, descriptive, procedural, reasoning) but also continuously produced (or converted [27]) as a consequence of knowledge-intensive decision-making processes [28]. Knowledge is an enabler of organisational agility, ensuring survival and competitiveness; thus, its capturing, representation, processing and the selection of supporting technology and infrastructure [29] is a major concern of management.

EI tasks present as part of the EE effort often display a semi-structured character due to insufficient information and the inherent complexity of organisational change processes. This may require EE project managers to make 'semi-programmed' decisions [30] that are difficult to encode in a program, but can be facilitated by a decision support system (DSS) [30]. This obvious need for decision-making guidance and support in EE has led to the idea of materialising the knowledge acquisition, structuring and transformation capabilities of the meta-methodology presented in section 2.1 in the form of a support framework for EE that would help stakeholders such as enterprise architects, project managers and Chief Information Officers identify problems, find suitable solutions and define change processes to implement them.

EE mandates a cooperative and interactive support framework, allowing the users to address the part of the problem that cannot be structured and to use their own insights to modify and/or refine the solutions proposed by the system [31]. Interactivity and cooperation promote acceptance of the approach proposed by the framework; equally important, they put to use natural knowledge management skills and talents that cannot be programmed into a machine [28].

4.2 The Architectural Design of the Proposed Framework

The close connection between EE decision-making and knowledge management has suggested a rule-oriented knowledge-based paradigm [28] for the proposed framework and its practical application as a DSS. The adopted structure of the system builds on previous mainstream research in this area. Thus, essential elements of knowledge-based DSS described by Sprague and Carlson [32, 33] and Marakas [34] are present in this design – such as a rule-based knowledge base, a model base (populated by AFs' RMs and from previous projects) and a dialog generation mechanism.

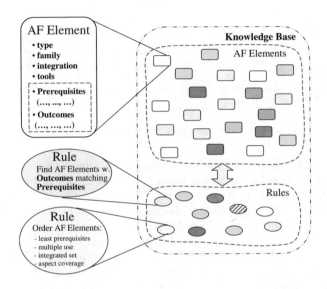

Fig. 3. Structured Repository in Knowledge Base format

Hence, the DSS based on the proposed framework will seek to apply best practice using rules / ranking facts and to consider user insights using run-time asserted facts. This will construct a set of solutions ordered by suitability and presented in a form that will assist the decision-making effort [35].

Figure 3 presents the knowledge base approach adopted for the SR described in section 2.2, containing rules for element selection (e.g. via pattern matching) and ordering (for ranked lists), fixed facts (e.g. AF element representations) and other rules containing the logic necessary for system operation. Typically, rules take the form of IF / THEN statements (their implementation depending on the specific inference engine used). For example, the rule to decide whether to model the present state (AS-IS) in an EE project could take the following form:

$$\text{IF ((TO-BE\_obtained\_from\_AS-IS) OR (AS-IS\_not\_understood))}$$
$$\text{THEN (model\_AS-IS)} \tag{1}$$

Thus, the 'model the present state' (model_AS-IS) rule will fire if the user asserts the fact that the AS-IS is not understood or the fact that the TO-BE will be obtained from the AS-IS.

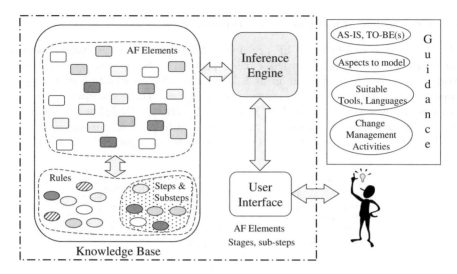

Fig. 4. Decision support framework architecture and possible outcomes

The stages and sub-steps of the underlying meta-methodology (see Fig. 1) have been incorporated as rules in the knowledge base, as shown in Fig. 4 bottom-left. Thus, the meta-methodology stages, sub-steps and logic required for their proper operation are modelled by rules, the AF elements are represented by fixed facts while the user motivations / decisions (accept / override system recommendations) and other inputs are modelled via run-time asserted facts. As expected, the solutions are to be built by a) rules implementing stage and sub-step logic, firing according to run-time asserted facts and b) pattern-matching routines, ensuring that all dependencies of the fixed facts representing recommended and/or selected AF elements are satisfied.

5   Conclusions and Further Work

The EE effort aiming to achieve and maintain EI is a complex, on-going, and often ill-defined undertaking. The stakeholders need all the help they can get in order to understand the present state of affairs and turn the rather generic 'need for integration and continuous improvement' into concrete change steps towards achieving and upholding these aims. The proposed support framework and its practical DSS application attempt to address these issues by offering guidance towards the creation of an enterprise modelling method specific to the EE project at hand. They also provide for model reuse and identification of gaps and overlaps between the various mainstream AFs currently available.

Future work will aim to incorporate elements of other AFs into the SR, refine the logic of the meta-methodology steps contained in the knowledge base facts and rules, evolve and mature the structure of the proposed decision framework and continue to test it in further case studies.

References

1. Vernadat, F.: Enterprise Modeling and Integration (EMI): Current Status and Research Perspectives. Annual Reviews in Control 26(1), 15–25 (2002)
2. Volonino, L., Watson, H.J.: The strategic business objectives method for guiding executive information systems development. Journal of Management IS 7(3), 27–39 (1990-1991)
3. Noran, O.: Discovering and Modelling Enterprise Engineering Project Processes. In: Saha, P. (ed.) Enterprise Systems Architecture in Practice, pp. 39–61. IDEA Group, Hershey (2007)
4. Panetto, H.: Towards a Classification Framework for Interoperability of Enterprise Applications. International Journal of CIM 20(8), 727–740 (2007)
5. Panetto, H., Molina, A.: Enterprise Integration and Interoperability in Manufacturing Systems: trends and issues. Special issue on Enterprise Integration and Interoperability in Manufacturing Systems 59(5) (2008)
6. Chen, D., Doumeingts, G., Vernadat, F.: Architectures for Enterprise Integration and Interoperability: Past, Present and Future. Special issue on Enterprise Integration and Interoperability in Manufacturing Systems 59(5) (2008)
7. Noran, O.: A Mapping of Individual Architecture Frameworks (GRAI, PERA, C4ISR, CIMOSA, Zachman, ARIS) onto GERAM. In: Bernus, P., Nemes, L., Schmidt, G. (eds.) Handbook of Enterprise Architecture, pp. 65–210. Springer, Heidelberg (2003)
8. Noran, O.: A Meta-methodology for Collaborative Networked Organisations: Creating Directly Applicable Methods for Enterprise Engineering projects. VDM Verlag Dr. Müller, Saarbrücken (2008)
9. Molina, A., et al.: Enterprise Integration and Networking: Challenges and Trends. Studies in Informatics and Control 16(4), 353–368 (2007)
10. Noran, O.: A Decision Support Framework for Collaborative Networks. International Journal of Production Research 47(17), 4813–4832 (2009)
11. Kalpic, B., Bernus, P.: Business process modeling through the knowledge management perspective. Journal of Knowledge Management 10(3) (2006)
12. Noran, O.: A Meta-methodology for Collaborative Networked Organisations: A Case Study and Reflections. In: Bernus, P., Fox, M., Goossenaerts, J.B.M. (eds.) Knowledge Sharing in the Integrated Enterprise: Interoperability Strategies for the Enterprise Architect, pp. 117–130. Kluwer Academic Publishers, Toronto (2004)
13. NIST, Integration Definition for Function Modelling (IDEF0), Computer Systems Laboratory, National Institute of Standards and Technology (1993)
14. ISO/IEC, Annex A: GERAM, in ISO/IS 15704:2000/Amd1:2005: Industrial automation systems - Requirements for enterprise-reference architectures and methodologies (2005)
15. ISO/IEC, ISO/IEC 42010:2007: Recommended Practice for Architecture Description of Software-Intensive Systems (2007)
16. Williams, T.J.: The Purdue Enterprise Reference Architecture. Computers in Industry 24(2-3), 141–158 (1994)
17. Doumeingts, G.: La Methode GRAI. University of Bordeaux, Bordeaux (1984)
18. Doumeingts, G.: GIM, Grai Integrated Methodology. In: Molina, A., Kusiaka, A., Sanchez, J. (eds.) Handbook of Life Cycle Engineering - Concepts, Models and Methodologies, pp. 227–288. Kluwer Academic Publishers, Dordrecht (1998)
19. CIMOSA Association, CIMOSA - Open System Architecture for CIM. Technical Baseline, ver 3.2. Private Publication (1996)
20. Scheer, A.-W.: Architecture for Integrated Information Systems. Springer, Berlin (1992)

21. Zachman, J.A.: A Framework for Information Systems Architecture. IBM Systems Journal 26(3), 276–292 (1987)
22. DoD Architecture Framework Working Group. DoD Architecture Framework Version 1.0 (2004), http://www.dod.mil/cio-nii/docs/DoDAF_v1_Volume_I.pdf, http://www.dod.mil/cionii/docs/DoDAF_v1_Volume_II.pdf   [cited 2007 February 2007]
23. Noran, O.: An Analytical Mapping of the C4ISR Architecture Framework onto ISO15704 Annex A (GERAM). Computers in Industry 56(5), 407–427 (2005)
24. The Open Group, The Open Group Architecture Framework (TOGAF 8.1.1 'The Book') v8.1.1 (2006)
25. Treasury CIO Council. Treasury Enterprise Architecture Framework v.1 (2000), http://www.eaframeworks.com/TEAF/teaf.doc [cited 2007 February 2007]
26. The CIO Council. Federal Enterprise Architecture Framework (v1.1) (1999), https://secure.cio.noaa.gov/hpcc/docita/files/federal_enterprise_arch_framework.pdf [cited 2007 February 2007]
27. Nonaka, I., Takeuchi, H.: The Knowledge-Creating Company. How Japanese companies create the dynamics of innovation. Oxford University Press, Oxford (1995)
28. Holsapple, C.W., Whinston, A.B.: Decision Support Systems: A Knowledge-Based Approach. West Publishing, Minneapolis (1996)
29. Davenport, T., Prusak, L.: Working Knowledge. Harvard Bus. Schl Press, Boston (1998)
30. Keen, P.G.W., Scott_Morton, M.S.: Decision Support Systems: An Organizational Perspective. Addison-Wesley, Inc., Reading (1978)
31. Turban, E.: Decision support and expert systems: management support systems. Prentice Hall, Englewood Cliffs (1995)
32. Sprague, R.H.: A Framework for the Development of Decision Support Systems. Management Information Systems Quarterly 4(4), 1–26 (1980)
33. Sprague, R.H., Carlson, E.D.: Building Effective Decision Support Systems. Prentice-Hall, Inc., Englewood Cliffs (1982)
34. Marakas, G.M.: Decision support systems in the twenty-first century. Prentice Hall, Upper Saddle River (1999)
35. Mallach, E.G.: Understanding Decision Support and Expert Systems. Richard D. Irwin, Inc., Illinois (1994)

Application-Services Integration among Multi-clouds for Small and Middle Scale Enterprises

Qing Li, Cheng Wang, Jing Wu, Jun Li, and Ze-Yuan Wang

Department of Automation, Tsinghua University, Beijing 100084, P.R. China
liqing@tsinghua.edu.cn

Abstract. With the development of application services providing and cloud computing, more and more small or middle scale enterprises do not invest on their own information systems any more, and use software services and even platform services provided by professional information service companies. These information service companies provide management information system services as public resources to support business process operation of their customers. However, for transformation from inter enterprise information systems to extra enterprise clouds, no application service provider can satisfy the full functional requirements of information systems of an enterprise. Therefore, enterprises have to use systems distributed in different clouds. This paper presents a framework to integrate applications deployed in different clouds. An operation platform across different clouds for an enterprise is developed later. A business process oriented technique is also developed to improve the feasibility of information systems under cloud computing environment.

Keywords: Application service providing, Cloud computing, Service oriented architecture (SOA), Web service, System integration.

1 Introduction

With the development of information techniques, computing and storage cost is reducing quickly and continuously. Some new business patterns are emerged [3,4,5].

Nicholas G. Carr compares the technical and business environments of Edison's age and current age, and concludes that information systems will be provided as services. Cloud computing is internet-based computing, with which shared hardware, software, and information are provided to computers and other devices on demand, like the electricity grid. According to Nicholas Carr, the strategic importance of information technology is reducing as it becomes standardized and less expensive. He points out that the cloud computing paradigm shift is similar to the displacement of electricity generators by electricity grids early in the 20th century [1].

Currently, cloud computing is a hot topic in IT researching and business field. As well as the Internet of Things, they are forming the infrastructure of future computing environment.

However, data security is the key barrier for cloud computing implementation. Data or information is the key competency for large scale companies. They will not use public data storage service to store their core data. At the same time, because

R. Meersman et al. (Eds.): OTM 2010 Workshops, LNCS 6428, pp. 211–218, 2010.

these companies have invested huge money on their information systems for a long history, they tend to construct a private cloud instead of using a public cloud.

Data security is also a key issue for middle and small scale companies. However, comparing with the grand investment on information techniques, introducing into public clouds is reasonable. As foreseen by Nicholas G. Carr, there are more and more public cloud computing providers which can satisfy requirements of the business operation of an enterprise. For example, cloud provided by Google.com is used by companies to treat their documents, search information, and explore geographic data; taobao.com is an e-business platform for small companies in China; and sales-force.com provides the customer relationship management tools.

However, a single service provider always focuses on limited business domains and cannot provide full functionality as an integrated enterprise information system. Therefore, an enterprise has to use functions supported by different clouds. How to integrate these functions distributed on different clouds becomes a big challenge. Therefore, it is necessary to develop a integrated operating platform for companies to integrate functionalities provided by outside clouds with inter enterprise information systems as show in Fig.1.

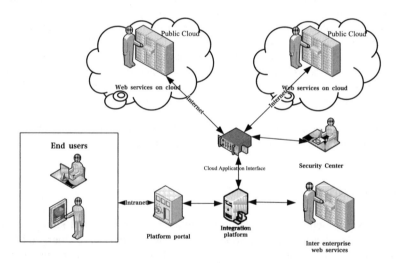

Fig. 1. System integration among multi clouds

This paper presents a framework to integrate applications deployed in different clouds. An operating platform across different clouds for an enterprise is developed. A business process oriented technique is also developed to improve the feasibility of information systems under cloud computing environment.

2 Application Services Integration Framework among Multi Clouds

In order to achieve low cost and high efficiency, middle and small scale companies tend to use internet resources to fulfill their own operating requirements. The cloud, as an emerging technique, provides a cheap but effective method. It is not supervising that in the future many vendors will offer plenty of diversified services through different clouds. On the other hand, a single company may adopt several cloud systems to support its business operation, which however brings a new problem of the integration among multi clouds.

Intuitively, the communication between different clouds could be accomplished by manpower. But when it comes to a large scale, human being will be no longer qualified to complete the job punctually and precisely. Therefore, a certain platform, or mechanism, is necessary to offer a unique interface for end users to access different clouds, and to organize cloud services to support business processes.

Based on the understanding of business demand and the cloud technique, a platform for the integration among multi clouds is supposed to complete following tasks.

1. Cloud services are able to be access through platform interface.
2. A certain mechanism should be built up to support the intercommunication among clouds.
3. The cloud services could be organized to support a company's business processes and the process could be accessed through platform interface.
4. The cloud services, business processes and others applications shall be well managed and under monitoring. They could be dynamically enabled or disenabled.
5. Users are free of multi login, which means the platform shall automatically deal with the cloud service authorization.

Taking all these targets into account, an integrated operating platform framework is proposed in Fig.2. There are six major functions in this platform, namely Runtime Environment, Cloud Application Interface, Business Execution Component, Platform Data Storage, User Interface and Business Integration Tools.

Runtime Environment only contains an Application Service Bus. It is the foundation of the whole platform. It completes data exchange and routing.

Cloud Application Interface consists of different cloud APIs. The API is designed to connect the cloud and the platform. It has a mapping mechanism to realize bidirectional message exchange so that the platform could invoke cloud services and get its result. Meanwhile, it maintains the information of company's accounts at cloud service vendor. When necessary, it will login (or logout) specific cloud before (or after) cloud service invocation.

Business Execution Components are set to complete platform operation. Application Execution receives request from user interface and completes application or process running. It will search operating database to determine the location of a specific cloud service and transfer the request to corresponding API. Application Management is supposed to manage all applications on the platform. It allows platform administrator to introduce new applications, maintain their status and eliminate some of them if necessary. Security component is responsible for keeping the whole platform from illegal access and violation.

The platform provides a portal as user interface. It should be based on Browser/Server structure. User Access Management authorizes the rights of invoking different cloud service, business flow and other applications to certain groups of users based on their roles in the company. When a user login portal, the web page will be structured to show the applications the user is authorized to access.

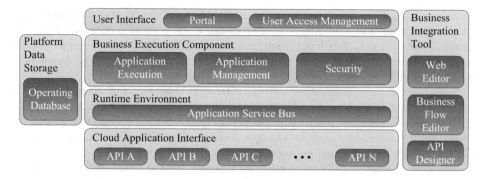

Fig. 2. Application services integration platform among multi clouds

Platform data is stored in operating database, including local data, cloud service information, business flow information and user access authorization.

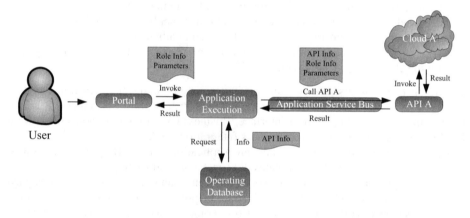

Fig. 3. Cloud service invocation mechanism

Business Integration Tools are offered as application development kit. It contains API Designer and Business Flow Editor. New API could be built up and existing API could be edited in API Designer. Business Flow Editor enables people to organize cloud services into business processes so that complex business logic could be completed without human's participation. Web Editor aims to offer an IDE for developer to build up web pages for application invocation.

As show in Fig.3, if a user wants to invoke a cloud service, he or she will login the portal and submit a request through a web page in portal. Portal would forward this request which includes the parameters and user role to Application Execution module. Application Execution (AEM) Module will then access Operating Database to get the information of the API with which the cloud service is connected (In this case, it's API A). With the API A's information, AEM send what it receives to API A. API A firstly determines the cloud login account according to one's role and sets up a connection. It will then converse the parameters into the format that the cloud could accept and invoke the cloud service. After the result is summarized by the cloud, the response will be sent all along the way back to the web page the user is surfing.

3   Key Enabling Techniques for Multi Clouds Integrating Platform

The authors' research team has developed a Business Process Oriented Platform for heterogeneous systems integration named BPO-P [2]. It is a good base to be extended for the new requirements.

In order to construct the integrated operating platform for multi clouds, some enabling techniques shall be achieved.

1. Cloud Application Interface
Cloud application interface (CAI) provide an interface for the platform to use services deployed in target clouds.

If applications deployed in a cloud provide standardized API for outside accessing, CAI will encapsulate these APIs as web services so as to encapsulate these applications as web services and then deploy them on the platform.

If these applications is already realized as web services, CAI will re-encapsulate them into inter web services on the platform.

If these applications can only be accessed with browser without any API, CAI shall provide additional web page capturing and interacting tools.

2. Business Logic / Flow Editor
Similar to the service orchestration, the business logic/flow editor can link services encapsulated from different applications in different clouds to form a complete automation flow for a business process.

3. Operating Database within Enterprises
In order to protect private data, original data created by the enterprise and presented to a cloud will be backuped in the operating database within the enterprise.

The operating database presents a mechanism for private data protection. If the cloud service is crashed, the database will restore the application quickly.

The database also presents a mechanism for cloud transformation. If the enterprise wants to use services provided by another cloud, it can increase the data initiation process greatly.

4   Case Study

AAA is one of the telecommunication carriers of China. Its call centre provides majority of information services for customers. However, the original information services are limited to telephone number inquiry or simple services through voice navigation.

AAA expects to expand and rebuild its call centre into a brand-new provider of integrated city information and services. AAA will build an expandable integrated city information services platform, which can provide dynamic and interactive, all-sided, convenient, timing and customized city information services for tourists and local residents.

To realize these objectives, the key point is how to acquire more abundant information and services resources, and how to integrate and manage them. Therefore, the platform is supposed to support cooperative operation modes effectively, and to realize the separation of information services provision and information services release. The telecommunication carrier will cooperate with SP/CP (Service Provider/Content Provider) to fulfil their operation. Thus all kinds of external information and services from different systems and different sources with different clouds (including different information providers, different service providers of mature operation) can be accessed. They can be integrated and managed, if necessary, with the internal information and services from AAA to provide more comprehensive and integrated services.

Founded on the former discussion on cloud computing, it is a feasible solution to construct the open and integrated city information services platform based on cloud computing and multi clouds integrating platform.

The open integrated city information services platform is based on SOA among multi cloud computing environment. It has the architecture shown in Fig. 1 and Fig. 2. Since the integrated services platform would be constructed between platform owner and multi service providers deployed in different clouds, Internet would be the media of connection between the platform and application clouds.

An application scenario is built to compare the constructed platform with multi application clouds and the original call centre on information and services provision.

Recently, a visitor is invited to attend an important conference in the Great Hall of the People in Beijing. With a limited budget, the visitor is planning to find the cheapest airline ticket, a hotel room less than $100 a night. He also wants to taste Chinese food with specialties, especially spicy food. For the hotel, he wants to find one that is near the Great Hall of the People that has a bar and a swimming pool. As for the restaurants, he hopes they are located near the hotel.

The above application scenario involves three kinds of separate services deployed in different clouds:

1. Airline ticket finder service: This service searches for flights between two cities in a certain timeframe, lists all available flights and their prices, and provides the capability to make flight reservations.
2. Hotel finder service: This service provides the ability to search for a hotel in a given city, list room rates, check room availability, list hotel amenities, and make room reservations.
3. Restaurant finder service: This service provides the ability to search for a restaurant in a given city, list restaurant speciality and average expense, and make reservations.

For the original call centre of AAA, call centre operators may handle what the visitor request. However, call centre operators may not have the corresponding resources and provide corresponding services for the visitor's requirements. It needs to check every operation service provider cloud and helps him through reservation respectively, like searching the website www.airchina.com.cn and booking flight ticket, searching the website www.ctrip.com and making hotel reservation, searching the website www.fantong.com and making restaurant reservation. During the inquiry and reservation process, call centre operators may need to confirm with the visitor many times about his every requirement, which makes the whole process a burden to both sides.

Moreover, it is hard to synthesize all the visitor's requirements, and due to the lack of information and service resources, the final result cannot be assured to be optimal.

For the integrated city information services platform of AAA, CAIs is developed to access and integrate application clouds, like AirChina.com, Ctrip.com and Fantong.com, and so forth. First, Customer Interface Service (it is an integrated system service) finds the right existing Web services based on the visitor's request, and orchestrate all these services according to his needs. Then it provides an integrated Web service which can satisfy his requirements. All the visitor need to do is just to login the website of AAA integrated city information services platform, fill in the required information for his trip and answer a few questions online. After he is prompted to make a few basic selections, all of his travel plans are confirmed.

1. The Customer Interface Service receives the visitor's requirements and then sends a message to the hotel finder Web service in Ctrip.com cloud, looking for the name, address, and the rates of hotels (with a bar and swimming pool, and rates below $100 a night) available in the Beijing and near the Great Hall of the people. At the same time, the Customer Interface Service sends a message to the airline ticket finder Web service in Airchina.com cloud, requesting the cheapest ticket to Beijing.
2. After getting the available hotels list, the Customer Interface Service requests the visitor to make a choice for hotel. After receiving the confirmation on the flight, the Customer Interface Service books this flight reservation and then makes a room reservation at the desired hotel by sending messages respectively to the airline ticket finder Web service and the hotel finder Web service. If the flight confirmed or the hotel selected is no longer available, the visitor is requested to make other choices.
3. The Customer Interface Service sends a message to the restaurant finder Web service, looking for the name, address, and average expense of restaurants which are famous for local speciality in Beijing (such as spicy food) and near the hotel selected.
4. After getting the available restaurants list, the Customer Interface Service requests the visitor to select desired restaurants and then makes a reservation in each restaurant selected. If a restaurant selected is not available anymore, you are requested to make another choice.
5. Finally, all of the visitor's travel plans are confirmed and the Customer Interface Service sends the visitor all the related information for his requirements.

5 Summary and Conclusion

Cloud computing and public service providing are the trend of business and technical development. More and more middle and small companies will transfer their business to these public application clouds, so as to reduce investments on information techniques.

However, no application service provider can satisfy the full functional requirements of information systems of an enterprise. Therefore, enterprises have to use systems distributed in different clouds.

Integrating techniques can integrate applications in multi clouds together and then provide a suitable solution to satisfy companies' requirements. Related platform will accelerate the usage of public cloud computing and public cloud services.

Acknowledgements

This work was sponsored by the China High-Tech 863 Program, No. 2001AA415340 and No. 2007AA04Z1A6, the Beijing Natural Science Foundation, No. 9072007, China / Ireland Cooperation Foundation, and Tsinghua Asian Research Centre 2010 Youth Project C1.

References

[1] Carr, N.G.: The Big Switch: Rewiring the World, from Edison to Google. W. W. Norton, New York (2008)
[2] Li, Q., Zhou, J., et al.: Business processes oriented heterogeneous systems integration platform for networked enterprises. Computers in Industry 61, 127–144 (2010)
[3] Rittinghouse, J., Ransome, J.: Cloud computing – implementation, management, and security. CRC Press, Boca Raton (2009)
[4] Miller, M.: Cloud computing – web-based applications that change the way you work and collaborate online. QUE
[5] Stanoevska-Slabeva, K., et al. (eds.): Grid and cloud computing – a business perspective on technology and applications. Springer, Heidelberg (2010)

Semantic Annotation of XML-Schema for Document Transformations

Julius Köpke and Johann Eder

Department of Informatics-Systems, University of Klagenfurt, Austria
firstname.lastname@uni-klu.ac.at
http://isys.uni-klu.ac.at

Abstract. The W3C recommendation Semantic Annotations for WSDL and XML-Schema (SAWSDL [7]) has the primary goal of annotating web service descriptions with a semantic model. In addition to the annotation of WSDL documents it can also be used to annotate arbitrary XML-Schemas. In this paper we will discuss the application of SAWSDL to create declarative annotations of XML-Schema. We will show problems that arise and present a solution that creates SAWSDL compliant annotations with the required expressiveness. Such an annotation method can then be used to assist automatic document transformations between different schemas. The transformations can act as an enabler for interoperable applications that exchange XML-documents.

1 Introduction

Semantic annotation is proposed to be a good solution to enable interoperable applications [11]. Semantic annotations represent the relationships between an annotated artifact (web page, XML document, schema, web service, etc.) and a reference ontology. Semantic annotation at the instance level (web pages, XML-documents, ...) received a lot of attention [11], however annotation at the XML-Schema level [7] is used in a much lesser degree. Semantic annotations of XML-Schema can be used to lift data from XML documents to some semantic representation such as RDF [8] or OWL [3]. A transformation of a document from a source XML-Schema to a document that complies with the target XML-Schema can therefore be created by lifting the data from the source document to it's semantic representation, (e.g. ontology instances) make some computations on the ontology-level and lower it back to the XML representation of the target schema. Such an approach is very flexible but requires the computation of every single instance document on the ontology level. Preliminary tests have shown that even with a very small ontology the speed of a direct XSLT transformation is significantly faster compared to the loading of the instance data, reasoning over the ontology and lowering the data back to the target XML representation. To achieve industry-scale performance we therefore propose to generate XSLT transformation scripts with the knowledge from the ontology. This requires the annotation of the source and the target schema in a declarative way. Such an annotation allows the matching of the source and the target schema at build

R. Meersman et al. (Eds.): OTM 2010 Workshops, LNCS 6428, pp. 219–228, 2010.

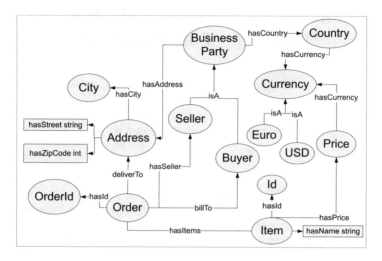

Fig. 1. Example reference ontology

time. This matching can then be used to create transformation scripts [4] (e.g. XSLT) that directly operate on the XML documents without the need to lift instance data to the ontology.

Both approaches are addressed in the W3C recommendation SAWSDL. The lifting and lowering approach is realized by the specification of references to arbitrary scripts that perform the lifting or lowering of instance data. The declarative annotations can be realized by so called *model-references*. A model-reference forms a reference between a schema element (XML-Element, XML-Type or XML-Property declaration) and a concept of some semantic model. In this paper we will investigate the applicability of SAWSDL model-references for the declarative annotation of XML-Schemas with a reference ontology. We discuss shortcomings and present an annotation method that solves these problems while being compatible with SAWSDL. Such an annotation can then be used as a basis for a system that transforms instance documents from an annotated source schema to an annotated target schema.

2   Motivating Example

In order to show shortcomings of model-references we will first introduce an example. We will try to use model-references for the direct annotation of a simple XML-Schema of a business document (see figure 2) with a small reference ontology (see figure 1). The domain of a SAWSDL model-reference is an XML-Element, XML-Type or XML-Attribute declaration of an XML-Schema. The range is a list of URIs that point to concepts of a semantic model. If multiple URIs are specified every URI applies to the annotated element. No further relationships between the different URIs can be specified.

```
<xs:schema xmlns:xs="http://www.w3.org/2001/XMLSchema" xmlns:sawsdl="http://www.w3.org/
  <xs:element name="order" sawsdl:modelReference="/order">
    <xs:complexType>
      <xs:sequence>
        <xs:element name="BuyerZipcode"/>
        <xs:element name="BuyerStreet"/>
        <xs:element name="BuyerCity" sawsdl:modelReference="City"/>
        <xs:element name="BuyerCountry" sawsdl:modelReference="Country"/>
        <xs:element name="SellerCountry" sawsdl:modelReference="Country"/>
        <xs:element name="Item" maxOccurs="unbounded" sawsdl:modelReference="Item">
          <xs:complexType>
            <xs:attribute name="ID" use="required" sawsdl:modelReference="Id"/>
            <xs:attribute name="Name" use="required"/>
            <xs:attribute name="Price" use="required" sawsdl:modelReference="Price"/>
          </xs:complexType>
        </xs:element>
      </xs:sequence>
    </xs:complexType>
  </xs:element>
</xs:schema>
```

Fig. 2. Sample XML-Schema with model-references

In figure 2 an example order document is shown. It is directly annotated with the reference ontology (see figure 1). We will now investigate whether the correct meaning of each element can be defined.

- The element *BuyerZipcode* could not be annotated at all because the zip-code is modeled in form of a data-type property and not by a concept in the ontology. The same problem exists for the *BuyerStreet* element and for the name of an item.
- The *BuyerCountry* element is annotated with the concept country. This does not fully express the semantics because we do not know that the element should contain the country of the buying-party. In addition the *Seller-Country* element has exactly the same annotation and can therefore not be distinguished.
- The attribute *Price* is annotated with the concept *Price*. Unfortunately this does not capture the semantics. We do not know the subject of the price (an item) and we do not know the currency.

In the examples above we assumed that we have only annotated data-carrying elements. If we would in addition also annotate the parent elements in this case the *order* element we could add a bit more semantic information. It would be clear that the annotations of the child-elements of the order-element can be seen in the context of an order. Unfortunately this would not help for the ambiguities between the *BuyerCountry*- and the *SellerCountry* element. In general it would require a very strong structural relatedness between the ontology and the annotated XML-Schema which we cannot guarantee when many different schemas are annotated with a single reference ontology. In addition SAWSDL does not define that there are any relations between the annotations of parent and child

```
<xs:schema xmlns:xs="http://www.w3.org/2001/XMLSchema" xmlns:sawsdl="http://www.w3.org/ns/sawsdl" elementFormDefault="qualified" attri
  <xs:element name="order" sawsdl:modelReference="/Order">
    <xs:complexType>
      <xs:sequence>
        <xs:element name="BuyerZipcode" sawsdl:modelReference="/Order/deliverTo/Address/hasZipCode"/>
        <xs:element name="BuyerStreet" sawsdl:modelReference="/Order/deliverTo/Address/hasStreet"/>
        <xs:element name="BuyerCity" sawsdl:modelReference="/Order/deliverTo/Address/hasCity/City"/>
        <xs:element name="BuyerCountry" sawsdl:modelReference="/Order/billTo/Buyer/hasCountry/Country"/>
        <xs:element name="SellerCountry" sawsdl:modelReference="/Order/hasSeller/Seller/hasCountry/Country"/>
        <xs:element name="Item" maxOccurs="unbounded" sawsdl:modelReference="/order/hasItems/Item">
          <xs:complexType>
            <xs:attribute name="ID" use="required" sawsdl:modelReference="/Order/hasItems/Item/hasId/Id"/>
            <xs:attribute name="Name" use="required" sawsdl:modelReference="/Order/hasItems/Item/hasName"/>
            <xs:attribute name="Price" use="required" sawsdl:modelReference="/Order/hasItems/Item/hasPrice/Price[hasCurrency/Euro]"/>
          </xs:complexType>
        </xs:element>
      </xs:sequence>
    </xs:complexType>
  </xs:element>
</xs:schema>
```

Fig. 3. Sample XML-Schema document with proposed annotation method

elements. Nevertheless such annotations could help to give additional knowledge to structural XML-matching methods such as [10]. Another solution would be the usage of a more specific reference ontology, which contains concepts that fully match the semantics of each annotated element. For example it would need to contain the concept *InvoiceBuyerCountry* and *InvoiceBuyerZipCode*. Enhancing a general reference ontology with all possible combinations of concepts leads to a combinatorial explosion. This is definitely not suitable for the annotation with a general reference ontology but can nevertheless be used if very specific ontologies are used for the annotation.

3   Annotation Method

As shown in the introduction the direct usage of model-references is not suitable for the direct annotation of an XML-Schema with a reference ontology. To overcome this shortcoming we propose to create the required more specific ontology concepts out of well defined path expressions at runtime of the schema-matching engine. We will first introduce the path expressions with some examples and provide the formal definitions in section 3.1. The example schema document in figure 3 is annotated with the proposed path expressions. We will discuss some examples: The element *BuyerZipcode* is annotated with */Order/deliverTo/Address /hasZipCode*. The annotation of the *BuyerCountry* element is */Order/billTo/ Buyer/hasCountry/Country*. The steps that are marked bold refer to concepts. The other steps refer to object-properties or data-type properties of the reference ontology. Now the *BuyerCountry* element can be clearly distinguished from the *SellerCountry* element and the elements *BuyerZipcode* and *BuyerStreet* can be annotated. The shown paths refer to concepts, object properties and data-type properties. Another requirement could be to address instances of the ontology. For example the path */Order/billTo/Buyer[Mr_Smith]/hasCountry/Country* defines that the Buyer is restricted to one specific buyer with the URI *Mr_Simth*.

In most cases we assume that a simple annotation path as shown in the examples above is sufficient for an annotation. Nevertheless there can be cases where additional restrictions are required: When using a simple path expressions as shown above the *Price* attribute of the example schema could be annotated with */**Order**/hasitems/**Item**/hasPrice/**Price***. Unfortunately this does not express the currency of the price. Since the example ontology has no specialized price-concept for each currency we need to define the price within the annotation. The correct currency of a price can be defined by a restriction of the price concept. This restriction is denoted in square brackets and expresses that the price must have a *hasCurrency* property that points to the concept *Euro*. This leads to the full annotation of the *Price* attribute: */**Order**/hasitems/**Item**/hasPrice/ **Price**[hasCurrency/**Euro**]*.

3.1   Formal Definition of the Annotation Method

In order to define the annotation method we will first introduce definitions for the reference ontology and an annotated schema.

Definition 1. *Ontology:*

An ontology O is a tuple $O = (C, DP, OP, I, R)$, where C is a set of concepts (also often referred as classes), DP as set of data-type-properties, OP a set of object-properties, I a set of individuals and R a set of restrictions. Each element in C, DP and OP is a tuple $(uri, definition)$. All URIs of concepts can be obtained by $C.uri$, $URIs$ of properties by $DP.uri$ and $OP.uri$ and URIs of instances by $I.uri$ respectively.

Definition 2. *Annotated XML-Schema:*

An annotated XML-Schema S is a tuple $S = (T, E, A)$, where T is a set of types, E a set of elements, and A is a set of semantic annotations. An XML-Schema forms a tree structure. Each $t \in T$ has a type $e.type = \{simple \mid complex\}$, an optional name $t.name$ and an optional SAWSDL mode reference $t.annotation$ $\in A$. An element $e \in E$ can have an optional type $e.type \in T$, an optional SAWSDL model-reference $e.annotation \in A$ and a set of attributes $e.attribute$. Each attribute $a \in e.attribute$ can have a simple type $a.type \in T$ and an optional model-reference $a.annotation \in A$. Each annotation must be a valid annotation path according to definition 3 and 4.

Definition 3. *Annotation Path:*

The set of all annotation path expressions is P. An annotation path $p \in P$ is a sequence of steps. Each step is a tuple s=(*uri, type, res*). The value $s.uri$ of a step is some URI of an element of the reference ontology O. The type $s.type$ can be *cs* for a concept-step, *op* for an object-property step or *dp* for a data-type-property step. The URI $s.uri$ determines the type of the step: $s.uri \in C.uri \Rightarrow s.type = cs$; $s.uri \in OP.uri \Rightarrow s.type = op$; $s.uri \in DP.uri \Rightarrow s.type = dp$.

Only concept-steps may have a set of restrictions $s.res$. Each restriction $\in s.res$ can either be an individual $\in I.uri$ or a restricting path expression. Such a path expression adds a restriction to the corresponding step s. If $s.res$ contains multiple restrictions they all apply to the corresponding step s (logical and). The succeeding step of s in p can be obtained by $s.succ$, the previous step by $s.prev$. The first step of p is denoted f_s and the last step l_s.

Definition 4. *An annotation path is structurally valid iff:*

- $f_s.type = cs$ - The first step must refer to a concept.
- $l_s.type = \{dp|cs\}$ - The last step must refer to a concept or a data-type property.
- $\forall s \in p|s.type = cs \land s \neq l_s \Rightarrow s.succ.type = \{dp|op\}$ The successor of a concept-step must be an object-property or data-type-property step.
- $\forall s \in p|s.type = op \Rightarrow s.succ.type = \{cs\}$ An object-property step must be followed by a concept-step.
- $\forall s \in p|s.type = cs \land s \neq f_s \Rightarrow s.prev.type = op$ The previous step of a concept-step must be an object-property step (except the fist step).
- $\forall s \in p|s.type = op \Rightarrow s.prev.type = cs$ The previous step of an object-property step must be a concept-step.
- $\forall s \in p|s.type = dp \Rightarrow s = l_s$ Only the last step can refer to a data-type property.

3.2   Reuse of Global Types or Elements

If the annotated XML-Schema reuses types or elements (via type or ref properties) and both the element and the referenced element or type are annotated then the semantics need to be constructed based on the annotation of the element and the annotation of the referenced element. Due to the hierarchical structure of XML this needs to be applied recursively.

Let e be an element with the annotation $e.annotation$ and the XML-Type $e.type$. Let s be an annotated sub-element of the XML-Type $e.type$. Then the complete path of s needs to be constructed by combining the annotation $e.annotation$ and $s.annotation$. In particular the combination is achieved by removing the last step of $e.annotation$ and concatenating it with $s.annotation$.

As an example we may have an XML-element called *DeliveryAddress*. It is itself annotated with the annotation path */**Order**/deliverTo/**Address***. It has a type definition *address*. The address type itself contains various elements. One of them is *street* which is annotated with */**Address**/hasStreet*. In order to construct the complete semantics of the *street* element that has the parent element *DeliveryAddress* we need to build the path */**Order**/deliverTo/**Address**/hasStreet*. This path combination needs to be performed by the schema matching engine. It must be noted that this path combination adds structural dependencies between the schema and the reference ontology. Therefore one XML-Type should only be reused for semantically related entities. This approach is a specialization of the SAWSDL model reference propagation.

4   Transformation of an Annotation Path to an Ontology Concept

In the last section we have defined an annotation path expression as a sequence of steps. In order to specify the semantics of such a path expression it has to be represented as an ontology concept. This allows concept-level reasoning over the annotated elements in order to assist the matching of schema elements. The name/URI of such a concept is the corresponding path expression and can therefore directly be used as a SAWSDL model-reference. OWL defines concepts with logical expressions in form of restrictions over it's individuals. We will illustrate the generation of concepts with an example.

```
1  Class:  Order/billTo/Buyer[Mr_Smith]/hasCountry/Country
2  EquivalentClasses(
3        Country and inv
4           (hasCountry) some
5              (Buyer and {Mr_Smith} and inv (billTo) some (Order)
6           ))
```

Listing 1. Representation of an annotation path in OWL

In listing 1 the OWL representation of the path */Order/billTo/Buyer [Mr_Smith]/hasCountry/Country* is depicted. It creates a specialization of a *country* concept. In particular a *country* that has an inverse *hasCountry* object-property to a *Buyer*. This buyer must be an individual of the enumerated class {Mr_Smith} and must have an inverse *billTo* relation to an *Order*.

Obviously such a translation can be achieved fully automatically by iterating over the steps of the path. The generation of the concepts can be realized by the schema-matching engine. The generated concepts are only required as long as a matching is created.

In general a standard annotation path as shown in the example always creates a sub-concept of the last concept-step. Therefore the inverse of the object properties must be used. Annotation paths p that are used in restrictions $p \in s.res$ of some concept-step s always create sub-concepts of the corresponding concept with the URI $s.uri$. Thus the object-properties can directly be used.

5   Validation of Annotations

In the last sections we have defined the structure of an annotation path and have shown how an annotation path can be transformed to an OWL concept. This does not guarantee that the generated concepts do not introduce contradictions to the ontology. As an example we may have a path:

/Order/deliverTo/PoBox and the ontology defines that the *deliverTo* may never point to a post office box. When this path is represented as an OWL concept it can never contain individuals and thus introduces contradictions to the ontology.

In addition the ontology may contain data-type restrictions that restrict values of data-types to specific types such as string or integer. If such restrictions exist in the ontology they must also exist in the schema. The constraints in the schema must be at least as restrictive as in the ontology. Another type of restriction that may occur in the ontology are cardinality restrictions. For example the ontology may define that an invoice must have a maximum of one order address *hasAddress*. The schema must then also restrict the max-occurs value of the corresponding element. Due to the Open World Assumption of OWL it is not needed to check if an element occurs often enough but it must be ensured that an element can not occur too often in the schema.

The considerations above lead to the definition of the consistency of an annotated schema:

Definition 5. *A schema S and a set of annotation paths P are consistent with an ontology O iff:*

1. Every annotation path $p \in$ P is structurally valid (see definition 4).
2. Every annotation path $p \in$ P can be expressed as an OWL-concept in O that is a sub-concept of OWL-Thing.
3. All annotated elements in S are more ore equally constraining the values as the corresponding data-type properties in O do.
4. No cardinality restrictions in O are violated by S.

Obviously these requirements can be checked fully-automatically: The first check can be realized on the structural level. Each referenced concept and property must be a concept or property of the reference ontology and the restrictions from definition 4 must not be violated. The second check is a typical reasoning task that can be done by any OWL reasoner. Checks 3 and 4 can be realized by traversing the schema and querying the restrictions from the ontology.

6   Related Work

In contrast to the annotation of web resources there is only a small number of related work in the field of XML-Schema annotation. To the best of our knowledge there is no comparable approach for a concrete and formal definition of declarative semantic annotations for XML-Schema that allows class-level reasoning over the annotated elements. We see the application of the annotations in the possibility to create more precise schema matchings than traditional structure based approaches [10]. As soon as a matching can be found transformations can be created that transform the actual documents on the XML-level [4]. In [2] an annotation method for RDFS-Schemata is presented. The annotation method is similar to our's as it also expresses the annotations as simple paths that are transformed to ontology concepts. In contrast to our approach it directly supports the definition of operators like split or join in order to allow the annotation of elements which carry data that needs to be transformed before they can be linked to the ontology, which we plan to realize in an additional ontology layer.

In contrast to our approach it is not formally described, it does not directly address XML-Schema and it does not allow direct document transformations on the XML-layer. In [1] another approach for the annotation of models is proposed. At first a meta-model that is expressed in OWL is created for every type of model (Relational database, XML-Schema, ...) which should be annotated. Afterwards an individual for a specific schema is created. This means there is a representation of the concrete schema as an instance in the ontology. Annotations are just mappings between the reference ontology and the individuals of the schema. This solution is therefore not based on direct XML-level annotations as proposed by SAWSDL.

In [12] an approach is presented that automatically discovers mappings between XML-Schemas and ontologies with the help of a given set of simple correspondences between the schema and the ontology. It assumes a structural relatedness and the discovered mappings are expressed in form of rules. Since first order logic rules can only modify instances this approach is well suited for a lifting approach that transforms XML-Data to ontology instances. In contrast our method creates ontology concepts that form declarative descriptions which are a basis to build XML-level transformations without the need of lifting instance data to the ontology at runtime. In [5] the differences between ontologies and XML-Schemas are discussed. The authors propose to model the domain via an ontology and transform this specification to an XML-Schema or database schema. In [6] a system is proposed that automatically creates annotations for Web Service descriptions. It can use a reference ontology but does not need one. If no reference ontology is provided the ontology is created during the approach. The provided annotations are basically enhancements of the schema-elements with vocabulary of the ontology. They do not provide a complete declarative description. Nevertheless approaches that automatically generate annotations like [12] or [6] can possibly be a basis to semi-automatically create annotations for our annotation method.

7   Conclusion

In this paper we have proposed a method for the declarative semantic annotation of XML-Schema that enhances the semantic expressiveness of SAWSDL-model-references. The annotation method has two representations. On the XML-level there are well-defined annotation paths that can be added to XML-Schemas by schema designers without deep ontology engineering skills. These annotation paths can automatically be transformed to ontology concepts. These concepts provide a declarative description of the annotated elements and can be used for class-level reasoning over schema elements in order to create mappings between XML-schemas. These mappings can then be used for the generation of scripts that transform instance-data from one schema to another. We are currently working on a prototype that realizes these transformations. It must be noted that our annotation method does not directly resolve all possible conflicts [9] between the schema and the reference ontology. For example if the attribute granularity of the ontology and the schema differs no direct annotation is possible. We plan to solve such heterogeneities with an additional ontology layer that also adds knowledge for explicitly defined transformations. In our scenario the actual transformation of instance documents takes place on the XML-level without the need to interact with the ontology and is therefore well-suited for applications with a huge amount of instance documents. In addition to our annotation method we have provided mechanisms to check whether the annotations are valid with regard to the ontology.

References

1. Beneventano, D., El Haoum, S., Montanari, D.: Mapping of heterogeneous schemata, business structures, and terminologies. In: DEXA 2007: Proceedings of the 18th International Conference on Database and Expert Systems Applications, Washington, DC, USA, pp. 412–418. IEEE Computer Society, Los Alamitos (2007)
2. Callegari, G., Missikoff, M., Osimi, M., Taglino, F.: Semantic annotation language and tool for information and business processes - appendix f: User manual, athena deliverable d.a3.3 available at the leks (laboratory for enterprise knoweldge and systems), http://leks-pub.iasi.cnr.it/astar/ Technical report
3. Dean, M., Schreiber, G.: OWL web ontology language reference. W3C recommendation, W3C (February 2004), http://www.w3.org/TR/2004/REC-owl-ref-20040210/
4. Jiang, H., Ho, H., Popa, L., Han, W.-S.: Mapping-driven xml transformation. In: WWW 2007: Proceedings of the 16th international conference on World Wide Web, pp. 1063–1072. ACM, New York (2007)
5. Klein, M., Fensel, D., van Frank, H., Horrocks, I.: The relation between ontologies and xml schemata. In: Workshop on Applications of Ontologies and Problem-Solving Methods (August 2000)
6. Küngas, P., Dumas, M.: Cost-effective semantic annotation of xml schemas and web service interfaces. In: IEEE International Conference on Services Computing, pp. 372–379 (2009)
7. Kopecký, J., Vitvar, T., Bournez, C., Farrell, J.: Sawsdl: Semantic annotations for wsdl and xml schema. IEEE Internet Computing 11(6), 60–67 (2007)
8. Miller, E., Manola, F.: RDF primer. W3C recommendation, W3C (February 2004), http://www.w3.org/TR/2004/REC-rdf-primer-20040210/
9. Missikoff, M., Taglino, F.: Semantic mismatches hampering data exchange between heterogeneous web services. In: W3C Workshop on Frameworks for Semantics in Web Services (2005)
10. Rahm, E., Bernstein, P.A.: A survey of approaches to automatic schema matching. The VLDB Journal 10(4), 334–350 (2001)
11. Uren, V., Cimiano, P., Iria, J., Handschuh, S., Vargas-Vera, M., Motta, E., Ciravegnac, F.: Semantic annotation for knowledge management: Requirements and a survey of the state of the art. Web Semantics: Science, Services and Agents on the World Wide Web 4(1), 14–28 (2006)
12. Yuan, A., Borgida, A., Mylopoulos, J.: Discovering and Maintatining Semantic Mappings between XML Schemas and Ontologies. Journal of Computer Science and Engeneering 5, 1–29 (2007)

Ontology Approach for the Interoperability of Networked Enterprises in Supply Chain Environment

Yan Lu[1], Hervé Panetto[1], and Xinjian Gu[2]

[1] CRAN UMR 7039, Nancy-Université, CNRS, France
[2] Institute of Manufacturing Engineering, Zhejiang University, P.R. China
{Yan.lu,Herve.Panetto}@cran.uhp-nancy.fr, xjgu@zju.edu.cn

Abstract. The *System-of-Systems* (*SoS*) paradigm is widely recognized and has become quite studied since a decade, as it has potentially practical applicability in systems engineering. SoS-organized systems could make efficient use of resources from a variety of domains. In this paper, we are studying one of the typical forms of networked enterprises: the supply chain. We will apply the *SoS* paradigm to this kind of "so-called" system-of-networked enterprises and we will then explore and analyze the interoperation problem in heterogeneous networked enterprises systems. Focusing on information flows in supply chain, we are proposing an approach for developing a supply chain ontology for networked enterprises interoperability, based on an extension of the ONTO-PDM product ontology.

Keywords: product ontology, supply chain, interoperability, SCOR, ONTO-PDM.

1 Introduction

With the development of global manufacturing, systems should not be seen isolated; enterprises collaboration is no longer just between each other, and is evolving to enterprise networks, in the form of supply chain, extended enterprise and virtual enterprise and so on [1]. This new paradigm has increasing demands for information or knowledge exchange among enterprises. Meanwhile mass information or knowledge spread out in various formats among different enterprise systems, which leads to semantic interoperability issues between the existing enterprises applications systems. The heterogeneity of these systems and the knowledge disunity of expression methods are becoming barriers for the knowledge acquisition by stakeholders. While the collaboration is going on, there would be excessive knowledge accumulated, unorganized and decentralized, which could lead to a considerably low efficiency and inconsistency in their treatments. All these issues will definitely affect the comprehension of everyone's intelligence when enterprises collaborate in the context of networked enterprises.

In this paper, we give an insight into interoperability in networked enterprises, by analysing the *System-of-Systems (SoS)* paradigm and studying its characteristics in the context of networked enterprises. Considering that enterprises collaborating for a certain purpose may be considered as a kind of system-of-networked enterprises (SoNE), we then contribute to the "connectivity" (interoperability) property of supply

R. Meersman et al. (Eds.): OTM 2010 Workshops, LNCS 6428, pp. 229–238, 2010.

chain networked enterprises by extending the ONTO-PDM Product Ontology developed by [2] with the SCOR model. The main perspective of this ongoing work is then the definition of a product-centric supply chain ontology for facilitating the interoperation between all enterprise applications involved in an extended supply chain.

2 Background and Problem Analysis

2.1 System-of-Systems (SoS) Paradigm

The term *System-of-Systems (SoS)* is widely recognized and has become quite studied since a decade. Its application area spans from original military to other domains, especially system engineering. Researchers tried to formalise this new paradigm in the field of information system, complex system in military and enterprise since many years [3][4][5][6]. Further, various efforts have been made to give a common definition to specify the characteristics or principles of the paradigm. Widely cited definitions are for example *Systems-of-Systems (SoS)* are large-scale concurrent and distributed systems, the components of which are complex systems themselves." [3], as well as [5]. Whichever definition is used, there are several principles that distinguish *SoS* from monolithic systems. The classical five principles are known as Maier's criteria [7]: operational independence of the constituent systems, managerial independence of the constituent systems, geographical distribution of the constituent systems, evolutionary development, and emergent behaviour. Based on the characteristics mentioned by Boardman [8] and DeLaurentis [9], Auzelle [10] summarized and extracted six characteristics of *SoS*, as shown in Fig. 1.

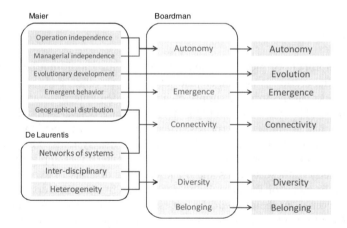

Fig. 1. Characteristics of *SoS*, based on the works of [7][8][9], adapted by [10]

Each characteristic means respectively:

- Autonomy: exercised by constituent systems in order to fulfil the purpose of the *SoS*
- Evolution: The *SoS* adapts to fulfil its (possibly evolving) mission as a whole as the underlying technologies evolve with time

- Emergence: Enhanced by deliberately not being foreseen, though its crucial importance. It creates an emergence capability climate that will support early detection and elimination of bad behaviours.
- Connectivity: Dynamically supplied by constituent systems with every possibility of myriad connections between constituent systems, possibly via a net-centric architecture, or by interoperability processes, to enhance *SoS* capability.
- Diversity: Increased diversity in *SoS* capability achieved by released autonomy, committed belonging, and open connectivity
- Belonging: Constituent systems choose to belong on a cost/benefits basis; also in order to cause greater fulfilment of their own purposes, and because of belief in the *SoS* supra purpose.

These characteristics represent the main distinguishes of fundamental components of a *SoS*. Thus, we could recognize a *SoS* by identifying whether the components are qualified with these characteristics or have capability to achieve these. A *SoS* is a concept at the core of research and development works to study the structure and dynamics of large scale collaboration between enterprise systems. The *SoS* approach does not advocate particular tools, methods, or practices; instead, it promotes a new way of thinking for solving grand challenges through the interactions of technology, business, even enterprises.

2.2 Interoperability of Networked Enterprises

Enterprises architecture could be classified in 5 types: sub-enterprise, single enterprise, multi-sites enterprise, extended enterprise and virtual enterprise. Table 1 shows an analysis of these different enterprise architecture crossed with the previously mentioned six *SoS* characteristics. At the sub-enterprise level and single-enterprise level, systems or applications are naturally belonging to a relatively homogeneous area, and normally systems do not have so much freedom to develop by themselves separately, they are usually bind together to execute a process for an enterprise. Meanwhile, multi-sites enterprises are generally an issue faced by large companies (e.g., Boeing, IBM, General Motors, and EADS), in integrating heterogeneous systems throughout their facilities [11]. A multi-sites enterprise has more autonomy, but its systems remain not fully independent. At a higher level, extended enterprises are loosely coupled and considered as a self-organizing network of firms that combine their economic output to provide products and services offerings to the market. Finally, virtual enterprises are a temporary alliance of enterprises that come together to share skills or core competencies and resources in order to better respond to business opportunities, and whose cooperation is supported by computer networks. So extended and virtual are not limited in one single enterprise, but span from enterprise to enterprise. They form a loosely or temporary network. Enterprises operate independently, share resources, skills, information, to achieve common goal or benefit. Related to these two kind of networked enterprises, autonomy, connectivity, and diversity *SoS* characteristics are obvious, while evolution and emergence characteristics appear as a result of each constituent. Based on the analysis of these *SoS* characteristics, we can conclude that extended and virtual enterprises fall into the paradigm of a SoS-like system, that we can call Systems-of-Networked Enterprises (SoNE).

Table 1. Differentiating *SoS* characteristics for each kind of enterprise architecture

Level of integration	Autonomy	Evolution	Emergence	Connectivity	Diversity	Belonging
Sub-enterprise	none	By itself	Depends on itself	Processed by sub-systems or none	None	nature
Single-enterprise	none	By itself	Depends on itself	Processed by sub-systems	None	nature
Multi-site enterprise	limited	By itself	Depends on itself	Processed by sites	None or exists among sites	nature
Extended enterprise	complete	Result of constituent enterprises	Achieved by constituent enterprises	Processed by constituent enterprises	Exists among constituent enterprises	Can Choose
Virtual enterprise	complete	Result of constituent enterprises	Achieved by constituent enterprises	Processed by constituent enterprises	Exists among constituent enterprises	Can Choose

Our work contributes mainly to the "connectivity" characteristic, falling in the domain of networked enterprises interoperability. The IEEE defines interoperability as: the ability of two or more systems or components to exchange information and to use the information that has been exchanged [12].

Camarinha-Matos L.M et al, provides a high level classification of collaborative network, which use ICT for supporting the development of collaborative business.Supply chain was defined as a category of collaborative networks, and in the example of Supply Network Shannon, currently it have no common ICT infrastructure in place[13]. As it is frequent to find information often scattered within enterprises: say in the applications used to manage technical data (e.g.: Product Data Management systems (PDM)), in the applications that manage business information (e.g.: Enterprise Resource Planning (ERP)) and, finally, in the applications that manage manufacturing information (e.g.: Manufacturing Execution Systems (MES)). Related work [2][13][14][15][16] demonstrated that, while product is the centred value of enterprises processes, its information-based model may act as a common pivotal information system to make all enterprise systems interoperating. It is even more; the Product Ontology proposed by [2] is then a component element of *SoS*, embedded with the technical information related to product life cycle. However, in a networked supply chain, it must also contain information about business processes applied to such product [17].

3   SCOR and Product Ontology in Networked Enterprises

Supply-Chain Operations Reference-model (SCOR) is a process reference model developed and endorsed by the Supply-Chain Council[1] (SCC). The SCOR model provides a unique framework that links business processes, metrics, best practices and

---

[1] http://www.supply-chain.org

technology features into a unified structure to support communication among supply chain partners and to improve the effectiveness of supply chain management and related supply chain improvement activities. Several researches have already been done for decision making based on the SCOR model. Through building an ontology based on the core concept of the SCOR model, and inference rules, a coordination model was developed for supplier selection [19]. Another ontology was built for supply chain simulation modelling using SCOR as a core, which integrated several supply chain views and captured the required distributed knowledge [20].

In a complementary way, Tursi et al. [2] have worked on the product-centric information system interoperability in networked manufacturing enterprises, and proposed a Product Ontology, the ONTO-PDM, for Product Data Management and interoperability. This integrated and common model formalizes the knowledge related to product data management at the business and the manufacturing levels of enterprises (B2M, Business to Manufacturing), in order to achieve the interoperability between systems. Fig. 2 shows an extract of the ONTO-PDM ontology concepts [2]. It adopts two standards: the IEC 62264 [21] and the ISO 10303 STEP-PDM [22], and it concentrates technical data span during the whole product lifecycle, from its development to its manufacturing.

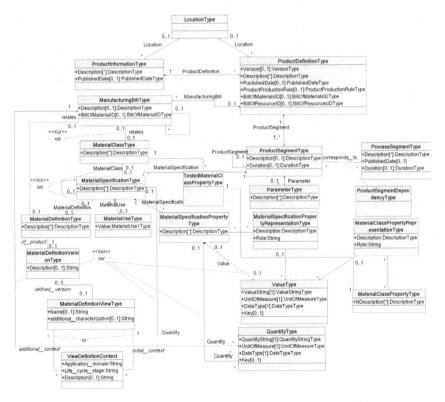

Fig. 2. An extract of the ONTO-PDM Product Ontology [2]

4   Towards a Product-Centric Supply Chain Ontology

4.1   Instanciation of SCOR Process from ONTO-PDM

In the context of networked enterprises, and mainly in supply chain environment, product data emphasize more about inter-enterprise relationships, which are not concerning only products but also processes related to customers, market and so on. Its focus is moving from integrated intra-enterprise application packages to internet-based and inter-enterprise application software. Improving Supply Chain Management (SCM) and Customer Relationships Management (CRM) are key processes to enable enterprise value chain [23]. Thus in order to reach maximum comprehension between enterprises, more knowledge is needed other than product data. As mentioned above, ONTP-PDM consists of the IEC 62246 and the ISO 10303 STEP-PDM. Meanwhile, IEC 62246 can be used to integrate business system such as ERP, supply chain management, with manufacturing system. The process segment schema of IEC 62246 is defined to present the process segment definitions that may be exchanged between business systems and manufacturing operations systems. Thus, ONTP-PDM has the promising capability to describe the information concerning supply chain processes. Then we try to formulise a detailed SCOR process by describing it as an instance of process segment model of ONTO-PDM. Fig.3 shows a detailed process element of SCOR level 2, M1 (Make-to-Stock). It describes the process of manufacturing in a make-to-stock environment which adds value to products through mixing, separating, forming, machining, and chemical processes. Make to stock products are intended to be shipped from finished goods or "off the shelf," are completed prior to receipt of a customer order, and are generally produced in accordance with a sales forecast. Each process of M1 is seemed as an instance of *ProcessSegmentType* of ONTO-PDM. And *ProcessSegmentDependencyType* is used to differentiate the sequence of the whole process, as showing in Fig.4. Besides, the inputs and outputs of each process are also presented by a most approximate instance of ONTO-PDM models, such as, *Equipment Plan* is presented by *EquipmentSegmentSpecificationType* as an input of M1.1, and *Product Schedule* is presented by *ProductionScheduleType* as an output of M1.1. However, there are still some inputs and outputs information could not be presented by models of ONTO-PDM appropriately. For example, the inputs of M1.2 *WIP Handling Rules*, *WIP Location Rule*, and also the outputs *Replenishment Signal*, *Sourced Product Location Information*. Therefore, although ONTO-PDM is a promising candidate for enabling interoperability of supply chain environment, a more specific ontology is needed to fully support information expression.

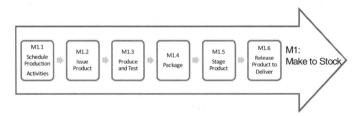

Fig. 3. A detailed process element of SCOR level 2 M1 (Make-to-Stock)

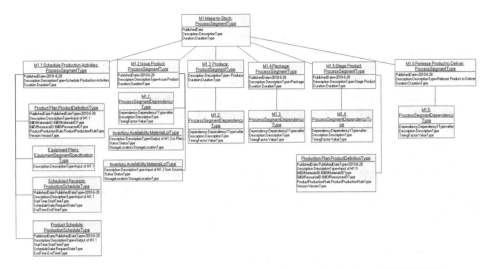

Fig. 4. An instance of SCOR process M1 (Make-to-Stock) based on ONTO-PDM

4.2 Architecture of Supply Chain Ontology

Then, focusing on information flows in supply chain, we are proposing a supply chain ontology architecture for networked enterprises interoperability, in which the knowledge concerns not only the whole product life cycle, but also products sales, marketing, purchasing and dismissing, related to customers activities, marketing processes, human and organization structure, as summarized in Fig. 5.

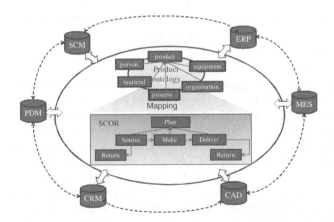

Fig. 5. Architecture of Supply Chain ontology for networked enterprises interoperability

As it shows in Fig.5, the Supply Chain ontology extends the ONTO-PDM, considered as an upper ontology, and links it with SCOR ontology. The ONTO-PDM defines entities related to product engineering and manufacturing, for example product, equipment, material, person, process and so on. And it also has the definitions about process, which could be used for expressing information linked business systems with manufacturing systems. From a supply chain process perspective, products can also be considered as main objects with all the corresponding properties related to ordering, producing, delivering, and returning. So is the other objects related to product. Therefore, ONTO-PDM could act as an upper ontology to support specific supply chain expression in the architecture. As a complement, we are defining a SCOR ontology [24] [25] with more specific expression about supply chain processes. The SCOR ontology defines not only interacted activities between suppliers, customers and market, but also metrics used to better formalize supply chain process with close relation to SCM. It could be considered as a specific domain ontology in our architecture. The ONTO-PDM and SCOR ontology is linked through concept mapping. We compared the entities of ONTO-PDM with the inputs and outputs concept, and processes concepts of SCOR, then Table 2 illustrates the concept mapping segment between them with semantic relationships such as inclusion ($\subset$, $\supset$) or equivalence ($\equiv$).

Table 2. Fragment of mapping relations between ONTO-PDM and SCOR

Entity of ONTO-PDM	Relationship	Concept of SCOR
EquipmenType	$\supset$	equipment
PersonType	$\supset$	customer
MaintenanceInformationType	$\subset$	maintenance
ProductInformationType	$\supset$	product
ProductionCapabilityType	$\equiv$	production-capability
ProductionPerformanceType	$\subset$	performance-plan
ProductionScheduleType	$\subset$	production-schedule

5   Conclusions

The main objective of this paper is to present a proposed research methodology to develop a Supply Chain Ontology for networked enterprises interoperability. We are only at the starting point of this work but our previous development of the ONTO-PDM ontology allows us to be effective in the next step to define a product-centric supply chain ontology by taking the ONTO-PDM one as upper ontology, and defining a more specific domain ontology--SCOR ontology, with core concepts coming from the SCOR model. Ontology is adopted to unify the metadata model to express knowledge resources which are diverse in types and disunite in forms. The current step of our research work concerns the formalization of ontological patterns for expressing semantics mapping between product concepts and enterprise processes inputs and outputs in order to facilitate the interoperation of enterprise software application in a supply chain context. A prototype, taking advantage of Web 2.0 techniques, will be developed to demonstrate the usability of such common ontology in a semi-industrial perspective.

References

1. Jagdev, H.S., Thoben, K.D.: Anatomy of enterprise collaborations. Production Planning and Control 12/5, 437–451 (2001)
2. Tursi, A., Panetto, H., Morel, G., Dassisti, M.: Ontological approach for Products-Centric Information System Interoperability in Networked Manufacturing Enterprises. IFAC Annual Reviews in Control 33/2, 238–245 (2009) ISSN: 1367-5788
3. Kotov, V.: Systems-of-Systems as Communicating Structures. Hewlett Packard Computer Systems Laboratory, Paper HPL-97-124, 1–15 (1997)
4. Pei, R.S.: Systems-of-Systems Integration (SoSI) – A Smart Way of Acquiring Army C4I2WS Systems. In: 2000 Summer Computer Simulation Conference on Society for Computer Simulation, Vancouver, B.C., pp. 574–579 (2000)
5. Sage, A.P., Cuppan, C.D.: On the Systems Engineering and Management of Systems of Systems and Federations of Systems. Information, Knowledge, Systems Management 2/4, 325–345 (2001)
6. Carlock, P.G., Fenton, R.E.: System-of-Systems (SoS) Enterprise Systems for Information-Intensive Organizations. Systems Engineering 4, 242–261 (2001)
7. Maier, M.W.: Architecting principles for systems-of-system. Journal of Systems Engineering 1/4, 267–284 (1998)
8. Boardman, J., Sauser, B.: System of Systems–the meaning of. In: 1st IEEE/SMC International Conference on System of Systems Engineering, pp. 4–10 (2006)
9. DeLaurentis, D., Callaway, R.: A System-of-Systems Perspective for Public Policy Decisions. Review of Policy Research 21/6, 829–837 (2004)
10. Auzelle, J.-P.: Proposal a product-centred multi-level model for information system in enterprise. PhD Thesis, University of Nancy, France (2009) (in French)
11. Panetto, H., Molina, A.: Enterprise Integration and Interoperability in Manufacturing Systems: trends and issues. Special issue on Enterprise Integration and Interoperability in Manufacturing Systems. Computers In Industry 59/7, 641–646 (2008)
12. Institute of Electrical and Electronics Engineers: IEEE Standard Computer Dictionary: A Compilation of IEEE Standard Computer Glossaries. New York, NY (1990)
13. Camarinha-Matos, L.M., Afsarmanesh, H., Galeano, N., Molina, A.: Collaborative Networked Organizations - Concepts and practice in Manufacturing Enterprises. Journal of Computers & Industrial Engineering 57, 46–60 (2009)
14. Terzi, S., Panetto, H., Morel, G., Garetti, M.: A holonic metamodel for product lifecycle management. International Journal of Product Lifecycle Management 2/3, 253–289 (2007)
15. Vegetti, M., Henning, G.P., Leone, H.P.: Product ontology: definition of an ontology for the complex product modelling domain. In: 4th Mercosur Congress On Process Systems Engineering (2005)
16. Tursi, A., Panetto, H., Morel, G., Dassisti, M.: Ontological approach for Products-Centric Information System Interoperability in Networked Manufacturing Enterprises. IFAC Annual Reviews in Control 33/2, 238–245 (2009)
17. Zdravković, M., Trajanović, M.: Integrated Product Ontologies for Inter-Organizational Networks. Computer Science and Information Systems 6/2, 29–46 (2009)
18. Zdravković, M., Panetto, H., Trajanović, M.: Concept of semantic information pool for manufacturing supply networks. International Journal of Total Quality Management and Excellence 37/3, 69–74 (2010)
19. Stewart, G.: Supply-chain operations reference model (SCOR): the first cross-industry framework for integrated supply-chain management. Logistics Information Management 10/2, 62–67 (1997)

20. Yiqing, L., Lu, L., Chen, L.: Decision-Making for Supplier Selection Based on Ontology and Rules. In: 2nd International Conference on Intelligent Computation Technology and Automation, pp. 176–179. IEEE Press, Washington (2009)
21. Fayez, M., Rabelo, L., Mollaghasemi, M.: Ontologies for supply chain simulation modeling. In: 37th Conference on Winter Simulation Conference, Orlando, pp. 2364–2370 (2005)
22. Enterprise-control system integration. Part 1. Models and terminology. Part 2: Model object attributes: ISO/IEC FDIS Standard, IEC and ISO, Geneva, Switzerland (2002)
23. ISO/TS 10303 STEP modules related to Product Data Management: Industrial automation systems and integration - Product data representation and exchange, Geneva (2004)
24. Kirchmer, M.: E-business process networks – successful value chains through standards. Journal of Enterprise Information Management 17/1, 2–30 (2004)
25. Zdravković, M., Panetto, H., Trajanović, M.: Concept of semantic information pool for manufacturing supply networks. International Journal of Total Quality Management and Excellence 37(3), 69–74 (2010)
26. Zdravković, M., Panetto, H., Trajanović, M.: Towards an Approach for Formalizing the Supply Chain Operations. In: 6th International Conference on Semantic Systems, ACM ICP, Graz, Austria (2010)

Towards Semantic Performance Measurement Systems for Supply Chain Management

Artturi Nurmi, Thierry Moyaux, and Valérie Botta-Genoulaz

Université de Lyon
INSA-Lyon, LIESP, 69621 Villeurbanne Cedex, France
{artturi.nurmi,thierry.moyaux,valerie.botta}@insa-lyon.fr

Abstract. The literature on Supply Chain Management (SCM) supports the integration of key business processes, including the performance management process, in order to increase the performance within and between the organisations. Nevertheless, the lack of proper shared performance metrics, frameworks and technology in order to design, implement and manage Performance Measurement Systems (PMSs), have been identified as problems for achieving integration. Semantics-based technologies, especially ontologies, have been suggested to address such problems. The purpose of this paper is to discuss how ontologies may be used to raise interoperability and shared understanding in inter-organisational PMSs from syntactic to semantic level by introducing the concept of Semantic PMS. We also suggest future research issues for approaching collaborative performance management problems.

Keywords: Performance Measurement Systems, Supply Chain Management, Ontology Engineering, SCOR, Business Process Management.

1 Motivation

A Supply Chain (SC) is "a set of three or more entities (organisations or individuals) directly involved in the upstream and downstream flows of products, services, finances, and/or information from a source to a customer" [1]. The goal of Supply Chain Management (SCM) is to increase the long-term performance of the individual entities and the SC as a whole via strategic collaboration, profit sharing, and by integrating and managing the flows of products, services, finances, and/or information between and within the SC entities [1-4]. Many problems exist in SCM due to the fact that the performance of any entity depends on the decisions of the others, and increasing the performance of the SC hence depends on the willingness and abilities of the individual entities [5]. Today, successful SCM requires the integration of demand- and supply-focused market knowledge and activities, and is based on high performing collaborative knowledge management processes, which provide aid in decision-making for the entities involved in the management of the SC [6].

One of the main problems for the goal of increasing the performance of an SC is the lack of proper SC performance measures/metrics which may result in decreased customer satisfaction, suboptimal performance, lost competitive advantage and conflicts within the SC [7]. Performance Measurement Systems (PMSs) also tend to stay

R. Meersman et al. (Eds.): OTM 2010 Workshops, LNCS 6428, pp. 239–248, 2010.

static although the need to keep measures aligned with strategy [8]. The integration of PMSs with other systems or management practices has also been identified as a problem [8]. Different frameworks for the measurement of performance have been proposed from which the Supply-Chain Operations Reference model (SCOR) is the most well-known. However, tools based on SCOR or other models that provide aid in decision making are scarce [9]. Problems also arise because of inconsistent terminologies and semantics caused by differences in business backgrounds, cultures and information systems [10]. For instance, an organisation may use "price" while its supplier prefers "value" to designate the same thing. Ontologies seem to have promising applications to address such issues. An ontology is a kind of formal model - "an engineering product consisting of a specific vocabulary used to describe a part of reality, plus a set of explicit assumptions regarding the intended meaning of that vocabulary" [11]. Few papers studying the applications of ontologies to SCM or BPM can be found, but the area is still relatively new and fragmented. Performance Management (PMgt) and PMSs have been almost completely neglected.

In this paper, we discuss the applications of ontologies from the point of view of Performance Management (PMgt) of SCs. For this purpose, a literature review is conducted on SCM, BPM, PMgt, Ontology Engineering, and Knowledge Management. Key articles are selected, analysed and synthesised in order to identify the state-of-the-art of PMgt and PMSs in a SC environment. The concept of semantic PMS is being discussed.

The main contribution of this paper is to present the idea of using ontology-based semantic technologies in the PMgt of SCs, particularly in the collaborative design, implementation and management of PMSs, which has not been discussed before. As another contribution, we shed light on some relevant problems related to current inter-organisational PMgt and PMS research, which allows us to provide direction for future research on semantic PMSs.

The paper is organized as follows. We first introduce the basics of SC PMgt and SCOR in Section 2. Section 3 summarises ontology engineering, Semantic Business Process Management (SBPM) and ontologies in SCM. In Section 4, we introduce our view for Performance Measurement Systems in SC environment. We conclude in the Section 5.

2 Supply Chain Performance Management

Performance measurement can be defined as "the process of quantifying the efficiency and effectiveness of action" where "action leads to performance" [12]. In an SC, efficiency can be explained as "how economically the SC can produce the product and/or service to match the demand" [13-15]. Effectiveness means "how well the SC is meeting the customer requirements on deliverables and customer service" [13-15]. From the point of view of Business Process Management (BPM), increasing the performance of SCs can be approached by "integration of key business processes" [16]. SCM is thus interested in the financial and non-financial aspects of Performance Management (PMgt), but proper performance measures and programs that address the individual organisations as well as the SC as a whole are needed [17]. In addition, frameworks for developing and designing such measures, and a shared understanding between the SC members has to be reached in order to efficiently work together [18]. Interoperable information systems are also needed for effective information sharing [19].

Performance Measurement Systems

A Performance Measurement System (PMS) is the core of a general management process often described as the *Performance Management (PMgt) process*, which defines how an organisation uses various systems to manage its performance [20]. According to a recent literature review, a PMS has only two necessary features: 1) to have *performance measures* and 2) to provide *supporting infrastructure* such as the information system facilitating the performance measures or also the personnel required to manage the PMS [21]. The only necessary role of the PMS is to measure performance and other roles might include strategy management, internal and external communication, influence behaviour, and learning and improvement [21]. Fig. 1 clarifies the role of collaborative performance measurement of SC partners. Collaborative performance measurement is the process that produces valuable information from the financial, non-financial, internal and external activities. Its' purpose is to aid the partner organisations in their decision making and taking actions aiming to increase the performance of the individual organisation and the performance of the SC as a whole. Performance measurement provides the feedback from day-to-day activities which form the data for monitoring the progress of operational, tactical and strategic decisions and to take corrective actions when needed. These corrective actions may be managerial actions, directed at changing the organisation such as: changing business processes, information systems, policies, instructions, personnel or other systems. Or these corrective actions might be organisational actions such as: producing products and services according to received orders, communicating with suppliers, customers and other parties by using the systems and tools provided by the managers. Collaborative measurement should be as efficient and effective as possible, but current internal PMSs are not capable for delivering the needed support. Many papers concerning performance measurement, and PMS design and implementation for SCs can be found, e.g., by Beamon [22], Lambert and Pohlen [7], Gunasekaran *et al.* [17], Gunasekaran and Ngai [19], Folan and Browne [23], Shepherd and Günter [8], and

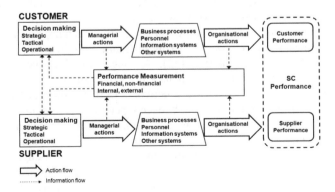

Fig. 1. Relationships Between Collaborative Performance Measurement and SC Performance

Jeschonowski *et al.* [24]. The common message of these papers is that SCM is still lacking proper frameworks, tools and technology in order to design, implement, and manage SC-wide PMSs. In fact, organisations are still struggling with implementing internal PMSs [25].

Findings from the literature support the need to integrate the PMgt process between SC members [9]. Different frameworks have been proposed, from which the Supply-Chain Operations Reference model (SCOR) is the most famous and may be considered as a standard [26].

SCOR

The SCOR model has been produced and maintained by the Supply Chain Council since 1996 and its purpose is to be used as a cross-functional business process reference model for SCM [27] . This model can be used for the modelling, re-design, and performance metrics design of SC processes. SCOR combines Business Process Reengineering (BPR), benchmarking, and best practices, and provides a cross-industry exhaustive hierarchical list of performance metrics with formal definitions. In SCOR, SCM is considered as the management of generic processes of Plan, Source, Make, Deliver and Return, and is intended to be used by all the members of the SC, from the suppliers' suppliers to the customers' customers. SCOR provides a common SC framework with standard terminology, and can also be used as a common model for evaluating, positioning, and implementing SC application softwares [28].

To get the best ouf of SCOR, like any other framework, it should be put into practice. Therefore, it has to be implemented in a manner that aids decision making aiming to solve business problems. Some papers describing tools using SCOR have been published, such as a computer-aided SC design tool [28] and IBM SmartSCOR [29], but in general, the lack of operational tools for SC PMgt has been acknowledged [9].

3   Ontology Engineering in SCM

Lately, ontologies have been proposed to approach these kinds of problems, since one of the advantages of ontologies is to capture complex relationships in order to define an SC [30]. An ontology is a kind of formal model, commonly referred to as "an explicit specification of a conceptualization", where conceptualization is "an abstract, simplified view of the world that we wish to represent for some purpose" [31]. An ontology is an engineering artefact built upon a specific vocabulary used to describe a certain reality, in addition to a set of explicit assumptions regarding the intended meaning of words in the vocabulary [32]. A long-term objective of research in ontologies is to produce libraries of reusable knowledge components and knowledge-based services that can be invoked over networks [33]. Ontologies have been suggested to benefit in 1) communication between people and organisations because ontologies enable shared understanding and communication between people with different viewpoints, 2) inter-operability between systems since ontologies can be used as inter-lingua between software components and 3) system engineering due to the fact that ontologies fulfil the requirements for specification, reliability and reusability for efficient knowledge management and transfer [34]. Ontologies form the basis for the Semantic Web technology, which is mostly composed of ontology languages, repositories, reasoners and query languages providing scalable methods and tools for machine-readable representation and knowledge management [35]. Semantic Web services are based on semantic web technologies allowing the representation, reasoning, discovery and composition of Web services in order to achieve a more complex service taking into account business rules and preconditions [36]. Because of the similarity of Web services/processes and business processes, semantic Web services can be used to form complex sequences of business activities allowing support for BPM. This area is referred to as Semantic Business Process Management (SBPM).

Semantic Business Process Management (SBPM)

BPM can be defined as "supporting business processes using methods, techniques and software to design, enact, control and analyze operational processes involving humans, organisations, applications, documents and other sources of information" [37]. The problem with current BPM approaches (without ontologies) is that it relies on human labour, which in turn is time-consuming, costly and erroneous [38]. Semantic Web services have been applied to the automation of BPM by adding semantic-based technologies to BPM in order to obtain SBPM [35]. The objective is to semantically enrich BPM with ontologies such that the manual work required in various steps, between putting the business perspective into the actual implementation of the information system, can be mechanized. This enables the process implementation to be more efficient and effective and, in addition, information sourcing from the semantically enriched space of processes becomes more effective as intelligent queries can be performed without the need for human intervention [35]. SBPM has been developed for some years now and resulted in promising theory and practice. From the point of view of PMgt, SBPM can also be used for performance monitoring based on machine reasoning [39]. However, problems are still to be solved such as how to harness the business people in the organisations to have the skills to manipulate ontologies because such people are not educated in this field yet.

Ontologies for SCM

Little research can be found on semantic SCM although SCM can be considered to be based on the integration of key business processes and thus is based on BPM. Chandra [40-43] has been quite active. First steps towards semantic SCM were probably taken in a paper introducing the idea of collaborative knowledge management based on ontology engineering to aid decision-making and SC integration [43]. From the point of view of PMgt, ontologies have also been suggested for developing inter-organisational information systems at the semantic level [44] and for automatic order monitoring [45]. An approach of using ontology engineering to capture distributed knowledge in the SC for building reusable and shareable simulation models based on SCOR have also been discussed [46], a tool for SC modelling and simulation based on an ontology and SCOR has been developed [47], and it has been applied in a real case for SC configuration and performance evaluation [48]. In general, approaching SC integration with ontologies could be beneficial, because there is evidence that collaborative ontology development and management can be used to support knowledge management [31, 35, 43], enterprise and SC modelling [34, 40, 41, 49], systems engineering [34, 42, 49] and BPM [35, 39, 50], which are all key a spects of successful SCM today and in the future. Efforts for combining SCOR with ontologies in the SC environment have been published, but we have not found any article discussing how ontologies might be used for the design, implementation and management of PMSs enabling better integration of SC-wide PMgt processes.

4   Semantic Performance Measurement Systems for SCM

Traditional approaches are not efficient or effective enough in providing support for the continuous management of knowledge, processes and systems for achieving optimal SC performance. Designing, implementing and managing a PMS is a challenge for an individual organisation for many reasons. In addition to the technical challenges, the sociocultural factors such as how the employees will accept changes in their rewarding system or does the management of the organisation actually use the PMS as it was intended to be used may cause problems [25]. A PMS project has a wide impact on the organisation and concerns all personnel – project failures are not unusual [25]. Even if an organisation has successfully implemented an internal PMS, developing and maintaining a functional PMS amongst several organisations is an even more complex issue, because intra-organisational PMSs are usually not designed to be connected together [23].

A supplier and a customer have to agree on how they will measure the performance of their shared inter-organisational processes, because "shared understanding results in integration, and integration leads in turn to organisational performance" [18]. For example, a supplier and a customer agree to measure the performance of the suppliers' "order-to-delivery process" which is responsible for delivering the products or services according to the order. The equivalent process of the customer is the "purchasing process" which is responsible for timing the purchases so that products or services are available according to the purchase order. For measuring the "order-to-delivery process", the supplier and the customer will use a measure "delivered on time", but this can mean different things. The supplier might understand that "delivered on time" means "shipped on time" while the customer might consider it as meaning "received on time". This would of course lead to a situation where the transportation time is not calculated and possible availability problems. After realising the miscomprehension, the supplier and customer would agree that the measure is as the customer has defined "received on time". This would not completely solve the problem as the supplier might understand that it means "first delivery received on time" while the customer would actually mean "delivered completely on time" if the delivery is carried out in several batches. Change is continuous, but having proper up-to-date performance measures that are defined and understood at the semantic level is a prerequisite for a high performing PMS. A flexible infrastructure for the PMS, capable of making fast and accurate changes at the semantic level, is needed.

Detecting semantic mismatches (such as described in the "order-to-delivery" and "purchasing process" example above) would aid the organisations in their PMS design, implementation and management. Ontology engineering can provide solutions for such modelling, communication and systems interoperability issues at the semantic level. Reference models such as SCOR could provide needed common framework, and definitions for processes and performance measures to support intra- and inter-organisational semantic PMS development efforts. Ontology-based semantic technologies could enable higher collaboration and integration within and between organisations, thus allowing seamless information flows and higher automation between organisations leading to increased overall performance. Based on the evidence discussed in this paper, we believe that ontology-based semantic technologies could provide solutions for the continuous management of knowledge, business processes, and various systems that are needed to be up-to-date in order to achieve a high performing PMS, thus leading to SC wide PMgt process integration.

5 Conclusion

In this article, we have identified some key problems for improving the performance of SCs. These problems are related to the design, implementation, and management of the Performance Management System (PMS), which is needed for the integration of the Performance Management (PMgt) process within and between the organisations. Problems arise from 1) the lack of proper shared performance metrics, frameworks and understanding, which are needed in the development of inter-organisational PMSs, 2) the lack of operational tools for the integration of the PMgt process, 3) the lack of efficiency and effectiveness of the traditional BPM approach to tackle the continuous need to transform business objectives into IT supported business processes, and 4) the need for a technology capable of approaching these problems at the semantic level.

We have discussed the applications of ontology-based technologies for BPM and SCM from the PMgt point of view. Our main contribution is presenting the idea of using ontologies for the benefit of the collaborative development of PMS – presenting the concept of semantic PMS - which has not been discussed before.

This research has also some limitations. Not all of the literature has been reviewed in this paper, but, instead, we have selected some key publications since the purpose of this paper is to provide an overview of the state-of-the-art of PMgt and PMSs in SC environment, and what kind of applications can be found based on ontologies.

Future research should be conducted on testing and validating the feasibility of using ontology-based semantic technologies for 1) reaching shared understanding in collaborative development of performance measures, and automatically detecting semantic mismatches, and 2) collaborative design, implementation and management of inter-organisational semantic PMSs, compared to traditional non-semantic approaches.

References

1. Mentzer, J.T., DeWitt, W., Keebler, J.S., Min, S., Nix, N.W., Smith, C.D., Zacharia, Z.G.: Defining supply chain management. Journal of Business Logistics 22, 1–25 (2001)
2. Childerhouse, P., Towill, D.R.: Simplified material flow holds the key to supply chain integration. Omega 31, 17–27 (2003)
3. Fugate, B., Sahin F., Mentzer J.T.: Supply chain management coordination mechanisms. Journal of Business Logistics. 27. 129–161 (2006)
4. Towill, D.R.: The seamless supply chain - the predators strategic advantage. International Journal of the Techniques of Manufacturing 13, 37–56 (1997)

5. Swaminathan, J., Smith, S., Sadeh, N.: Modeling supply chain dynamics: a multiagent approach. Decision Sciences 29, 607–632 (1998)
6. Esper, T., Ellinger, A., Stank, T., Flint, D., Moon, M.: Demand and supply integration: a conceptual framework of value creation through knowledge management. Journal of the Academy of Marketing Science, 5–18 (2009)
7. Lambert, D.M., Pohlen, T.L.: Supply Chain Metrics. The International Journal of Logistics Management 12, 1–19 (2001)
8. Shepherd, C., Günter, H.: Measuring supply chain performance: current research and future directions. International Journal of Productivity and Performance Management 55, 242–258 (2006)
9. Forslund, H., Jonsson, P.: Obstacles to supply chain integration of the performance management process in buyer-supplier dyads. International Journal of Operations and Production Management 29, 77–95 (2009)
10. Ye, Y., Yang, D., Jiang, Z., Tong, L.: Ontology-based semantic models for supply chain management. The International Journal of Advanced Manufacturing Technology 37, 1250–1260 (2008)
11. Daconta, M.C., Smith, K.T.X., Obrst, L.J.: The Semantic Web: A Guide to the Future of XML, Web Services, and Knowledge Management. John Wiley & Sons Inc., Chichester (2003)
12. Neely, A., Gregory, M., Platts, K.: Performance measurement system design: A literature review and research agenda. International Journal of Operations & Production Management 25, 1228–1263 (1995)
13. Agarwal, A., Shankar, R., Tiwari, M.K.: Modeling the metrics of lean, agile and leagile supply chain: An ANP-based approach. European Journal of Operational Research 173, 211–225 (2006)
14. Jüttner, U., Christopher, M., Baker, S.: Demand chain management-integrating marketing and supply chain management. Industrial Marketing Management 36, 377–392 (2007)
15. Min, S., Mentzer, J., Ladd, R.: A market orientation in supply chain management. Journal of the Academy of Marketing Science 35, 507–522 (2007)
16. Lambert, D.M., Cooper, M.C.: Issues in Supply Chain Management. Industrial Marketing Management 29, 65–83 (2000)
17. Gunasekaran, A., Patel, C., McGaughey, R.E.: A framework for supply chain performance measurement. International Journal of Production Economics 87, 333–347 (2004)
18. Neely, A.: Business performance measurement: Unifying Theory and Integrating Practice. Cambridge University Press, Cambridge (2008)
19. Gunasekaran, A., Ngai, E.W.T.: Information systems in supply chain integration and management. European Journal of Operational Research 159, 269–295 (2004)
20. Bititci, U.S., Carrie, A.S., McDevitt, L.: Integrated performance measurement systems: a development guide. International Journal of Operations & Production Management 17, 522–534 (1997)
21. Franco-Santos, M., Kennerley, M., Micheli, P., Martinez, V., Mason, S., Marr, B., Gray, D., Neely, A.: Towards a definition of a business performance measurement system. International Journal of Operations & Production Management 27, 784–801 (2007)
22. Beamon, B.: Measuring supply chain performance. International Journal of Operations & Production Management 19, 275–292 (1999)
23. Folan, P., Browne, J.: A review of performance measurement: Towards performance management. Computers in Industry 56, 663–680 (2005)

24. Jeschonowski, D., Schmitz, J., Wallenburg, C., Weber, J.: Management control systems in logistics and supply chain management: a literature review. Logistics Research 1, 113–127 (2009)
25. Bititci, U., Mendibil, K., Nudurupati, S.S., Garengo, P.: Dynamics of performance measurement and organizational culture. International Journal of Operations and Production Management 26, 1325–1350 (2007)
26. Leukel, J., Kirn, S.: A Supply Chain Management Approach to Logistics Ontologies in Information Systems. In: Proceedings of the 11th International Conference on Business Information Systems (BIS 2008), pp. 95–105. Springer LNBIP, Innsbruck (2008)
27. Supply-Chain Council: Supply Chain Operations Reference Model. Version 9.0 (2008)
28. Huang, S.H., Sheoran, S.K., Keskar, H.: Computer-assisted supply chain configuration based on supply chain operations reference (SCOR) model. Computers & Industrial Engineering 48, 377–394 (2005)
29. Dong, J., Ding, H., Ren, C., Wang, W.: IBM SmartSCOR - a SCOR based supply chain transformation platform through simulation and optimization techniques. In: Proceedings of the 2006 Winter Simulation Conference, Winter Simulation Conference, Monterey, pp. 650–659 (2006)
30. Fayez, M.: An Automated Methodology for a Comprehensive Definition of the Supply Chain Using Generic Ontological Components. The Department of Industrial Engineering and Management Systems. University of Central Florida Orlando. p. 230 (2005)
31. Gruber, T.R.: Toward principles for the design of ontologies used for knowledge sharing. International Journal of Human-Computer Studies 43, 907–928 (1995)
32. Guarino, N.: Formal Ontology and Information systems. In: Proceedings of FOIS 1998, pp. 3–15. IOS Press, Amsterdam (1998)
33. Gruber, T.R.: A translation approach to portable ontology specifications. Knowledge Acquisition 5, 199–220 (1993)
34. Uschold, M., Gruninger, M.: Ontologies: principles, methods and applications. The Knowledge Engineering Review 11, 93–136 (1996)
35. Hepp, M., Leymann, F., Domingue, J., Wahler, A., Fensel, D.: Semantic Business Process Management: A Vision Towards Using Semantic Web Services for Business Process Management. In: Proceedings of the IEEE International Conference on e-Business Engineering, pp. 535–540. IEEE Computer Society, Washington (2005)
36. Sycara, K., Paolucci, M., Ankolekar, A., Srinivasan, N.: Automated discovery, interaction and composition of Semantic Web services. Web Semantics: Science, Services and Agents on the World Wide Web 1, 27–46 (2003)
37. van der Aalst, W., ter Hofstede, A., Weske, M.: Business Process Management: A Survey. In: van der Aalst, W.M.P., ter Hofstede, A.H.M., Weske, M. (eds.) BPM 2003. LNCS, vol. 2678, pp. 1–12. Springer, Heidelberg (2003)
38. Pedrinaci, C., Domingue, J., Brelage, C., van Lessen, T., Karastoyanova, D., Leymann, F.: Semantic Business Process Management: Scaling up the Management of Business Processes. In: Proceedings of the 2008 IEEE International Conference on Semantic Computing, pp. 546–553. IEEE Computer Society, Santa Clara (2008)
39. Wetzstein, B., Ma, Z., Leymann, F.: Towards Measuring Key Performance Indicators of Semantic Business Processes, In: Business Information Systems, pp. 227–238 (2008)
40. Chandra, C.: Supply Chain Workflow Modeling Using Ontologies. In: Collaborative Engineering, pp. 61–87. Springer, Boston (2008)
41. Chandra, C., Tumanyan, A.: Ontology Driven Knowledge Design and Development for Supply Chain Management. In: Proceedings 13th Annual Industrial Engineering Research Conference, Houston (2004)

42. Chandra, C., Tumanyan, A.: Organization and problem ontology for supply chain information support system. Data & Knowledge Engineering 61, 263–280 (2007)
43. Smirnov, A.V., Chandra, C.: Ontology-Based Knowledge Management for Cooperative Supply Chain Configuration. In: Proceedings of the American Association of Artificial Intelligence Spring Symposium, pp. 85–92. AAAI Press, Menlo Park (2000)
44. Hellingrath, B., Witthaut, M., Böhle, C., Brügger, S.: An Organizational Knowledge Ontology for Automotive Supply Chains. In: Holonic and Multi-Agent Systems for Manufacturing, pp. 37–46 (2009)
45. Zimmermann, R., Käs, S., Butscher, R., Bodendorf, F.: An Ontology for Agent-Based Monitoring of Fulfillment Processes. In: Ontologies for Agents: Theory and Experiences, pp. 323–345 (2005)
46. Fayez, M., Rabelo, L., Mollaghasemi, M.: Ontologies for supply chain simulation modeling. In: Proceedings of the 37th Conference on Winter Simulation, Winter Simulation, Conference, Orlando, pp. 2364–2370 (2005)
47. Cope, D., Fayez, M., Mollaghasemi, M., Kaylani, A.: Supply chain simulation modeling made easy: an innovative approach. In: Proceedings of the 39th conference on Winter simulation: 40 years! The best is yet to come, pp. 1887–1896. IEEE Press, Washington (2007)
48. Cope, D.: Automatic Generation of Supply Chain Simultion Models from SCOR Based Ontologies. Department of Industrial Engineering and Management Systems. University of Central Florida Florida (2008)
49. Uschold, M., Gruninger, M.: Ontologies and semantics for seamless connectivity. SIGMOD Rec. 33, 58–64 (2004)
50. Hepp, M., Roman, D.: An Ontology Framework for Semantic Business Process Management. In: Proceedings of Wirtschaftsinformatik, pp. 423–440. Universitätsverlag, Karlsruhe (2007)

A Semantic Framework for Distributed Nano Assembly and Engineering

Joe Cecil[1], Gobinath Narayanasamy[2], and Joshua Long[1]

[1] Center for Information based Bioengineering and Manufacturing (CINBM),
School of Industrial Engineering and Management,
Oklahoma State University,
Stillwater, Oklahoma 74078, USA
{j.cecil,joshdl}@okstate.edu
[2] Information Technology Specialist,
Madras, India
gobinath@gmail.com

Abstract. In this paper, the creation of a semantic framework to support a Virtual Enterprise (VE) oriented approach for the assembly of nano devices is described. The domain of Nano Assembly provides an interesting and new context of developing products in an emerging domain of importance. Nano assembly is a complex domain and there is a need to collaboratively address a given nano assembly problem using diverse expertise and resources. By adopting a VE oriented approach within a Semantic Web based framework, a group of engineering organizations can collaborate and respond to specific customer requirements. In this paper, the design of such a semantic web based framework to support nano assembly activities is outlined.

Keywords: nano assembly, virtual enterprise, distributed collaboration, agent based systems, semantic frameworks.

1 Introduction

In today's distributed engineering environment, a VE oriented holds the potential of responding quickly to an emerging customer need (or product). In a VE, a temporary partnership is formed involving various organizations who usually posses a diverse expertise and resources. When a customer need for a specific product or service is identified, then such a VE can be formed by a group of partners interested in collaborating in such an enterprise. However, there are many hurdles in realizing the notion of a VE in today's IT intensive work environments. One of these problems relates to semantic interoperability and the seamless flow of information exchange among the partners in a virtual enterprise. This issue is addressed as part of the overall semantic web based framework discussed in this paper.

Nano Assembly refers to the assembly and manipulation of nano sized devices or particles using contact or non contact methods. It is an emerging domain of importance with a substantial global market. Nano manipulation and assembly are considered key areas of engineering where technological breakthroughs are expected to have

R. Meersman et al. (Eds.): OTM 2010 Workshops, LNCS 6428, pp. 249–256, 2010.

a substantial impact on producing new devices in biotechnology, semiconductor manufacturing, surveillance devices and other areas. However, a major problem is that in nano assembly no single engineering or manufacturing organization can respond independently (without collaboration) to changing customer requests. As these nano engineering resources are expensive and nano engineering enterprises possess a different core expertise (ranging from assembly planning, simulation, assembly, etc.), the adoption of a VE based approach is useful as it enables collaborative partnership that support for sharing of heterogeneous and diverse resources.

This paper is organized into several sections. In Section 2, a review of relevant literature is provided. Section 3 discusses the design of the semantic web based framework. An overview of various nano assembly life cycle agents is provided in section 4. An example scenario of this framework is described in section 5 followed by the conclusion in section 6.

2   Related Literature Review

In this section, a limited review of papers related to virtual enterprise design and web based collaborations is provided. In [9], Co-operative or Concurrent Engineering (CE) techniques are cited as one of the key reasons for forming collaborative working environment at enterprise levels. Camarinha-Matos et al [2] described a Virtual Enterprise (VE) as a consortium which allowed the development of a common working environment to manage diverse resources towards achieving a common goal. In [5], the concept of forming Virtual Enterprises using Agent based systems is discussed.

In [6], the role and usefulness of web services markup is emphasized; they enable agent technologies to efficiently capture the 'meta' data associated with the services and reason about them. OWL-S is an ontology of services that will allow users and software agents to discover, invoke, compose, and monitor Web resources offering particular services and having particular properties [7]. OWL-S is an acronym Web Ontology Language; S is for services within the OWL-based framework for describing Semantic Web Services.

Several papers including [1] have emphasized the importance of using ontology in manufacturing domains. In [14], the model of ontology with social dimensions is extended with a tripartite representation of actors, concepts and instances. In [11], Farooq et al have described a web ontology model for Semantic Web applications. In [13], the use of Semantic Web services technology in the domain of supplier chain management. In [12], criteria for evaluation of semantic classification are proposed to enable the design of class hierarchies with reduced inconsistency errors.

Nanotechnology has been the research of numerous research efforts in recent years [8, 10]; the development of new fabrication methods has contributed to this growing importance of this domain. However, many of these advances have yet to be realized because of problems and limitations associated with nano manipulation . The field of nano manipulation is in its infancy and there is a need for resources to be used collaboratively to respond to target nano manipulation requirements given by customers; in this context, there is a need to develop innovative methods and frameworks which allow an array of distribute software and analysis modules to work together to address engineering requirements in the domain of nano manipulation and assembly.

An example of a nano-manipulation process is the assembly of nano particles using an Atomic Force Microscope probe as a gripper.

3 Design of the Semantic Framework

In the proposed framework, an agent termed the Nano Assembly Enterprise Manager (NAEM) oversees the life cycle activities to be accomplished. The NAEM interacts with the customer and coordinates the various lifecycle activities of the Virtual Enterprise. The life cycle of this VE focuses on meta planning, planning, analysis, virtual prototyping / simulation and assembly/manipulation of target nano particles.

For a given customer input, the NAEM first interprets the level of information provided and then creates a top level meta plan which is needed to satisfy the customer requirements. The customer can provide a target nano particle manipulation or assembly to be completed or a potential way to complete the nano manipulation activity (as well as other information belonging to the various aspects of the nano life cycle mentioned earlier. By using a life cycle ontology developed for the nano assembly domain, the NAEM can inquire and reason about the information inputs provided by the customer and then formulates an adequate plan to complete the needed life cycle services for nano assembly. In our view of the VE model of the future, when a customer requirement is presented to the NAEM, it assumes a leadership and coordinating role in forming a VE. The key steps involved include understanding what the customer wants, identifying partners who will help satisfy the customer requirements, establishing a temporary partnership with the heterogeneous partners, requesting these partners to complete their services in an integrated manner and finally providing the end product to the customer. This 'end' product could be an information outcome (e.g. an assembly plan, analysis, etc.) or a physical product (a product as an outcome of a nano assembly process.

The first phase involves identifying potential partners who can perform each of the various life cycle activities to satisfy the needs of the customer in a given nano assembly / manipulation context. The capabilities of potential partners can be represented as software modules or agents which act as virtual partners interested in being part of the Nano VE. These software agents can possess three major attributes (autonomy, reactivity, and pro activity). These agents can be created using software languages such 3APL (which is based on the Java programming language). For the nano level planning, a variety of nano manipulation planning strategies can be encapsulated in various software modules. In a similar manner, analysis of the nano manipulation alternatives can be studied. Subsequently, using virtual prototyping environments, the potential outcome of a given manipulation /assembly scenario can be studied. Finally, a specific nano assembly or manipulation approach is selected based on the preceding analysis and virtual prototyping activities.

As the VE for nano assembly is viewed as a collection of agents, the issue of semantics needs to be resolved between the various agents involved in the life cycle. This is achieved by developing an Ontology for Nano Assembly domain. The agents or software modules including the various managers in this framework can be implemented with cognitive abilities. Such agents possess an understanding of (a) their own beliefs in their context of application or environment, (b) own intentions to perform needed modifications about such environments and (c) potential plans to initiate and complete those modifications. For the nano assembly framework, the 3APL platform is a viable choice for implementation. 3APL stands for An Abstract Agent Programming Language [4]. A 3APL agent developed using this language is a four tuple comprising of a Belief base, a set of practical reasoning rules, an action base and a Goal base. The Goal Base defines the collection of goals that an agent has to satisfy. These agent can manipulate their goals by using a set of practical reasoning rules. These reasoning rules specify a plan of action for an agent to execute its goals. The collection of primitive basic actions that an agent can execute is specified in the Action base.

Figure 1 provides an overview of the Semantic framework for Nano Assembly and Manipulation. A Customer Coordinating Agents provides the user inputs to the NAEM. As mentioned earlier, the NAEM interacts with various software and hardware resources and is responsible for the completion of all necessary activities to satisfy the customer requirements. The NAEM generates a top level plan based on the customer requirements and then requests the Nano Assembly Services Manager to discover, compare, identify and select appropriate organizations or software agents / modules who can accomplish identified services as part of the overall nano assembly life cycle or plan.

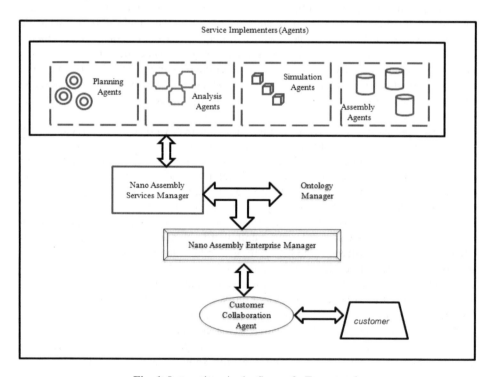

Fig. 1. Interactions in the Semantic Framework

The Nano Assembly Services Manager is responsible for 'discovering' the resources which are available to meet the functions identified in the nano assembly plan. This life cycle plan can include: (a) performing planning (for nano assembly tasks, which is accomplished by planning modules or agents which represent distributed organizations or partners who possess these tools or accomplish them as part of the nano assembly service), (b) performing analysis (related to nano assembly e.g. analyzing interactive forces coming into play for a given manipulation strategy) (c) performing simulation or virtual prototyping (e.g. organizations can create physics based virtual prototypes to gain a better understanding of manipulation approaches) (d) performing the target nano particle manipulation or assembly using physical resources (e.g.: using an AFM to manipulate nano particles or use a dielectrophoresis approach to assemble a given set of nano particles, etc.

4 Agents in the Nano Assembly Framework

The Customer Coordination Agent receives the customer inputs and interacts with the NAEM. Queries to the customer or other software modules which act on behalf of the customer are handled through this agent. The Nano Assembly Enterprise Manager can be viewed as a Enterprise level agent which coordinates the information exchange between the various entities in the overall nano assembly life cycle. Its activities include receiving customer and other inputs (from the customer coordination agent), interacting with the ontology agent and obtaining meta information about the customer inputs as well as coordinating various activities with the Nano Assembly Services Manager.

The Nano Assembly Services Manager is responsible for maintaining a nano services directory relevant for the nano assembly life cycle. It can be viewed as an yellow pages from which potential partners who provide specific nano services can be identified. It also is responsible for facilitating access to potential partners (or agents) after they are identified to be part of the nano assembly enterprise. A service directory can be maintained using Oracle UDDI registry where a description of relevant services can be stored. Such descriptions are stored using OWL-S.

The Ontology Manager is an agent which enables the NAEM gain a better understanding of the customer inputs provided; it essentially provides the meta information with the help of ontology. Various editors are available for such tasks. The Protégé editor can be used for this task. The various services for the nano assembly domain are provided by the service implementer agents. These include life cycle planning, assembly planning, analysis, simulation and physical assembly services. These service implementer agents can be viewed as representatives of nano technology and engineering enterprises that come together and form a virtual enterprise.

5 Collaborative Nano Assembly Example Scenario

In this section, an example scenario is provided from the Nano Assembly domain to highlight the functioning of this semantic framework. As explained in previous sections, Nano assembly is completely a new area of product development where engineering partners have limited number of sophisticated tools and resources to accomplish a full life cycle of nano assembly based product development. With this assumption in hand, suppose that there exists an interaction agent with the following goal: study and determine the alternate ways to manipulate and assemble a set of nano sized devices from one position to another. With these inputs, the goal of the interaction agent is to (a) initially find nano engineering partners who will be capable of helping address the customer requirements (b) interact with various distributed resources or service implementer agents and complete the needed activities to satisfy the customer requirements.

The collaborative activities using the discussed framework begin with input requirements provided by to the NAEM by the customer coordination agent. The NAEM then interacts with the ontology agent and obtains the needed meta information with the help of the developed ontology (which was deployed on a Tomcat server). The nano assembly services required are formulated which include those who can perform assembly planning, manipulation design, force analysis and simulation. Using the meta information and the customer requirements, the NAEM works with the Nano Assembly Services Manager to identify agents for implementing various services. These agents are the services implementers.

For a given nano assembly life cycle function (e.g.: analysis of interactive forces), there is a possibility that more than one organization can provide these services. In a real world context, many factors have to be taken into consideration including reliability of the potential partner (based on their history of services), cost of their service and software implementation details (language, platform, etc). There is also a possibility that none of the service implementers available in the directory of services are capable of meeting the customer requirements. In such situations, the Nano Assembly Services Manager passes this information to the NAEM, which in turn communicates to the customer the inability of the VE to satisfy the customer requirements.

A brief discussion of two service implementer (or agents) related to analysis and virtual prototyping based simulation is provided. Among the capabilities needed in the nano assembly life cycle are partners who can perform analysis of the various forces coming into play during a given nano manipulation context. For example, let us assume that one of the possible nano particle approaches involved use of dielectrophoresis to manipulate nano particles from one point to another on a substrate. One of the analysis tasks that a software agent implementer needs to accomplish is determining the van der Waals force interactions (in a contact manipulation approach) between the probe-tip, nano particle and substrate. Other service implementer agents include those that are capable of performing virtual reality based simulations using the force analysis information and integrating it to generate a system state in real-time. Such software agents can be viewed as virtual prototypes. A brief discussion of this virtual prototyping service agent follows. A view of the virtual environment provided by this agent is shown in figure 2.

Using the capabilities of such a service implementer, van der Waals force interactions to model forces between the probe-tip, nano particle and substrate can be studied. Other service implementers can analyze the impact of other force components which may come into play at the nano scale. The probe-tip and nano-particle interaction (for the scenario shown in figure 2) resembles a typical probe based nano-manipulation scenario where a probe attempts to manipulate a target nano particle

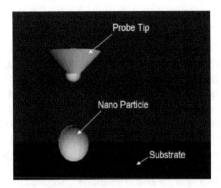

Fig. 2. A virtual prototyping environment which is one of the service implementer agents in the nano assembly life cycle. Such an implementer can be one of the services provided by a potential partner in the nano assembly virtual enterprise.

which is at rest on a substrate below. With the help of dielectrophoresis, the nano particle can be manipulated by the probe. The net force on the nano particle in this scenario can be represented as

$$F_{net} = F_{vdw\text{-}tip} - F_{vdw\text{-}subs} - F_{grav} + F_{dielect} . \tag{1}$$

where $F_{vdw\text{-}tip}$ is the van der Waals force between the probe tip and nano particle shown (in figure 2), $F_{vdw\text{-}subs}$ is the van der Waals force between the nano particle and substrate and F_{grav} is the force of gravity on the particle (which is negligible at the nano scale). $F_{dielect}$ is the dielectrophoretic force that can be used by the probe to manipulate the nano particle [9].

Once a given agent has been identified by the NAEM to perform a specific service, the various nano assembly life cycle services (based on the top level plan) can be executed. This can be achieved by using the access point URLs of these service implementers on the web enterprise.

6 Conclusion

In this paper, the design of a semantic framework to support the creation of a Virtual Enterprise for nano assembly is outlined. The domain of nano assembly is an emerging area of importance. Today and in the future, there is a great need to develop Internet based frameworks which will enable a group of nano engineering organizations (with diverse expertise and resources) to collaborate and respond to customer requirements. The outlined framework provides a basis to develop and implement a VE oriented approach which also addresses semantic interoperability issues.

Acknowledgments. Funding for research activities which resulted in this publication was obtained from the National Science Foundation (NSF) through NSF grant number 0965153. Some of the agents were created as part of an earlier NSF grant (number 0304269) funded through the Nanotechnology in Undergraduate Education (NUE) program.

References

1. Borgo, S., Leitão, P.: The Role of Foundational Ontologies in Manufacturing Domain Applications. In: Meersman, R., Tari, Z., et al. (eds.) OTM 2004. LNCS, vol. 3290, pp. 670–688. Springer, Heidelberg (2004)
2. Camarinha-Matos, L.M., Asfarmanesh, H.: Virtual Enterprise Modeling and Support Infrastructures: Applying Multi-Agent System Approaches. In: Luck, M., Mařík, V., Štěpánková, O., Trappl, R. (eds.) ACAI 2001 and EASSS 2001. LNCS (LNAI), vol. 2086, p. 335. Springer, Heidelberg (2001)
3. Hardwick, M., Spooner, D.L., Rando, T., Morris, K.C.: Sharing manufacturing information in virtual enterprises. Communications of ACM 39(2), 46–54 (1996)
4. Hindriks, K.V., De Boer, F.S., Van Der Hoek, W., Meyer, J.-J.C.: Agent Programming in 3APL. Autonomous Agents and Multi-Agent Systems 2(4), 357–401 (1999)
5. Petersen, S.A., Gruninger, M.: An Agent-based Model to Support the Formation of Virtual Enterprises. In: International Symposium on Mobile Agents and Multi-Agent in Virtual Organizations and E-Commerce, Australia (2000)
6. McIlraith, S., Son, T.C., Zeng, H.: Semantic Web Services. IEEE Intelligent Systems 16(2), 46–53 (2001)
7. The OWL Services Coalition, http://www.daml.org/services/owl-s/1.0/owl-s.html
8. Sitti, M.: Survey of Nanomanipulation Systems. In: IEEE-Nanotechnology Conference, Maui, USA, pp. 75–80 (November 2001)
9. Wilbur, S.: Computer Support for Co-operative Teams: Applications in Concurrent Engineering. In: IEEE Colloqium on Current Development in Concurrent Engineering Methodologies and Tools (June 1994)
10. Cecil, J.: A Semantic Web based Test Bed for the Assembly of Micro Devices. Technical Report, Center for Information based Bioengineering and Manufacturing, Oklahoma State University (November 2009)
11. Farooq, A., Shah, A., Asif, K.H.: Design of ontology in Semantic Web engineering process. In: High Capacity Optical Networks and Enabling Technologies HONET 2007, vol. 1(6), pp. 18–20 (November 2007)
12. Fahad, M., Qadir, M.A., Noshairwan, M.W.: Semantic Inconsistency Errors in Ontology. In: IEEE International Conference on Granular Computing, GRC 2007, vol. 2(4), pp. 283–283 (November 2007)
13. Preist, C.: Automated Business-to-Business Integration of a Logistics Supply Chain using Semantic Web Services Technology. In: Proceedings of Fourth International Semantic Web Conference (2005)
14. Mika, P.: Ontologies Are Us: A Unified Model of Social Networks and Semantics. In: Gil, Y., Motta, E., Benjamins, V.R., Musen, M.A. (eds.) ISWC 2005. LNCS, vol. 3729, pp. 522–536. Springer, Heidelberg (2005)

ISDE'10 - PC Co-chairs Message

Information System in Distributed Environment (ISDE) is rapidly becoming a popular paradigm in this globalization era due to advancement in information and communication technologies. The distributed development of information systems as well as their deployment and operation in distributed environments impose new challenges for software organizations and can lead to business advantages. In distributed environments, business units collaborate across time zones, organizational boundaries, work cultures and geographical distances, something that ultimately has led to an increasing diversification and growing complexity of cooperation among units.

Increased popularity of ISDE due to various factors has resulted in quite a number of research and industrial studies. Since information system development and implementation in distributed environments is still evolving and presents novel challenges. Therefore, it is crucial to understand current research and practices in this regard and share with researchers and practitioners in these areas. This year we are pleased to include the first international workshop on Adaptation in Service Ecosystems and Architectures (AVYTAT) 2010 as a special track with our workshop. AVYTAT explores relevant topics to the development of open service-oriented systems as a particular case of information systems in distributed, highly dynamic environments where adaptation is pivotal.

Following selected papers of ISDE 2010 international workshop in conjunction with OTM conferences present recent advances and novel proposals in this direction.

Luis Iribarne, Nicolas Padilla, Javier Criado, and Cristina Vicente-Chicot in their paper "An interaction meta-model for cooperative component-based user interfaces" presented a proposal for an interaction meta-model, as a part of a model-evolution methodology for cooperative Graphical User Interfaces (GUI) through Component-Based Development (CBD) approaches along with case study based on an Environmental Management Information Systems (EMIS). "Early Validation of Requirements in Distributed Product Development - An Industrial Case Study" by Samuli Heinonen and Hannu Tanner reported a potential solution for assistance in the selection of requirements validation practices in distributed product development environment.

Hendrick Decker and Francesc Muñoz-Escoí "Revisiting and Improving a Result on Integrity Preservation by Concurrent Transactions" revisited a well-known result on the preservation of integrity by concurrent transactions. It has improved in two ways the serializability of integrity-preserving transactions yields integrity-preserving histories.

Experimental Evaluation of "On-Site Customer' XP Practice on Quality of Software and Team Effectiveness" by Adam Wojciechowski, Maciej Wesolowski, Wojciech Complak provided a description of experiment based on extended version of educational game eXtreme89 as well as results collected in experiment

R. Meersman et al. (Eds.): OTM 2010 Workshops, LNCS 6428, pp. 257–258, 2010.
© Springer-Verlag Berlin Heidelberg 2010

and analysis of quality of software produced by teams working according to different software creation paradigms.

Mayu Mtsubara and Masato Oguchi in their paper "Evaluation of Meta-verse Server in a Widely-Distributed Environment" have focused on a server side of metaverse system, analyzed its behavior, and clarified the cause of its long response time. In their paper "A Software Inspection Process for Globally Distributed Teams" Deepti Mishra and Alok Mishra have extended a software inspection process in the distributed software development towards quality assurance and management.

We would like to thank the authors for their submissions, and the OTM chairs and organizers for their kind support in facilitating this workshop.

August 2010   Alok Mishra
                                                    Jürgen Münch
                                                    Deepti Mishra
                                                    ISDE'10

An Interaction Meta-model for Cooperative Component-Based User Interfaces

Luis Iribarne[1], Nicolas Padilla[1], Javier Criado[1], and Cristina Vicente-Chicote[2]

[1] Applied Computing Group
University of Almeria, 04120 Almeria, Spain
{luis.iribarne,npadilla,javi.criado}@ual.es
[2] Department of Information Technology and Communications,
Technical University of Cartagena, Spain
cristina.vicente@upct.es

Abstract. *Model Driven Engineering* (MDE) aims to help software developers to abstract the system implementations by means of models and meta-models. In *Web-based Collaborative Information Systems* (WCIS) modelling plays an important role, especially in the user-interface field. In this kind of systems, where groups of users (with different roles) cooperate through distributed user interfaces, and the complexity of interaction between different elements involved in the system (e.g., actors, roles, tasks, interaction rules, etc.) is usually high, MDE could represent a good solution to model evolvable user interfaces. This paper describes a proposal for an interaction meta-model, as a part of a model-evolution methodology for cooperative *Graphical User Interfaces* (GUI) through *Component-Based Development* (CBD) approaches. The paper also presents a case study based on an *Environmental Management Information Systems* (EMIS), where three actors (a politician, a GIS expert, and a technician) cooperate for assessing natural disasters.

Keywords: MDE, collaborative systems, user interfaces, interaction.

1 Introduction

Globalization of the information and of the knowledge society implies the use of a varied (and sometimes complicated) social interaction which requires more collaborative Information Systems. *Environmental Management Information Systems* (EMIS) [1] [2] are a good example of social interaction. A wide range of final users and actors (such as politicians, technicians or administrators) cooperate with each other and interact with the system for decision-making, problems resolution, etc. In this kind of systems, groups of users (who often have different roles) cooperate through distributed user interfaces, where the complexity of interaction between different elements involved in the system (e.g., actors, roles, tasks, interaction rules, etc.) is usually high. Due to the variety of social interaction, interfaces must adapt themselves to the needs of users and/or groups of

R. Meersman et al. (Eds.): OTM 2010 Workshops, LNCS 6428, pp. 259–268, 2010.

users who cooperate. Cooperative user interfaces must be able to be dynamically regenerated at runtime depending on the type of interaction (individual or collective) and the purpose of interaction (management, technical purpose, etc.).

In this scenario, our research interest lies in giving a solution to cooperative user interfaces that operate in Web-based collaborative information systems. There are many different reasons. Firstly, Web-based information systems are the most widespread and used systems in distributed social interaction (for instance, social networks). Secondly, they allow us to have non-compiled Web user interfaces, easily interchangeable at runtime. Thirdly, and particularly, our methodological proposal gives a *Component-Based Development* (CBD) solution to cooperative component-based user interfaces of gadgets/widgets-type. iGoogle[1] gadgets are a good example of interface-component.

Furthermore, our methodology pursues evolutive user interfaces: changeable and adaptable to the user needs at runtime. Such evolution is caused by the cooperative interaction between users (and/or groups) and the user interface (UI). As a solution to this approach (i.e., cooperative, evolutive Web component-based user interfaces), our proposal is inspired on principles of *Model-Driven Engineering* (MDE) [3], especially runtime models, model evolution and model transformation issues. Therefore, it uses models and metamodels to abstract the dynamic behaviour of user-interfaces and the interaction of users. *Interaction* is one of the metamodels used by methodology, where the elements of the cooperative user interface are defined at high level (i.e., mainly groups, actors, roles, choreographies, tasks and interface-components). This article is focussed on the definition of cooperative interaction meta-model for evolutive user interfaces.

The remainder of the article is organised as follows. Section 2 describes some related work. Section 3 defines model evolution for runtime interfaces. Section 4 shows a cooperative interaction metamodel. Section 5 describes a case study of cooperative interaction for assessing natural disasters as an instance of the metamodel. Finally, some conclusions and future work are presented.

2   Related Work

In **Collaborative** Information Systems (CIS) **models** play an important role, especially in the UI field. In this kind of systems, where groups of users (with different roles) cooperate through distributed **user interfaces**, and the complexity of interaction between different elements involved in the system (e.g., actors, roles, tasks, interaction rules, etc.) is usually high, Collaborative Software Engineering (CSE) [4] and **MDE** could represent a good solution to model (evolvable) user interfaces [5] and cooperative interaction [6].

In the literature there are many model-based proposals for modelling user-interfaces (e.g., IDEAS, OVID, WISDOM, UMLi, etc.); see [7] for a survey. Some of them use an MDE perspective for Web-based user interfaces, as in [10] and [11], though they do not consider cooperative interaction models. Other proposals as in [8] present a metamodel for designing the various user-interfaces

---

[1] http://code.google.com/apis/gadgets/

of a workflow information system, which integrates some different interaction elements, such as process, task, domain, job, among others. This proposal does not define an interaction metamodel for cooperative Web user interfaces either.

From the point of view of collaborative systems, MDE plays an important role too. In [9] authors propose an awareness meta-model that conceptualizes collaborative systems to carry out modeling activities. The proposal distinguishes between five meta-model views: (a) work group view, (b) actions view, (c) workspace view, (d) domain view, and (e) awareness mechanisms view. Cooperation between users is carried out through the "workspace" view, which represents the user interface. In [12] authors present a model-driven approach to construction of web-based collaborative environments. In [13] they propose a collaborative metamodel to define collaborative work practices. Nevertheless, none of the aforesaid proposals considers an interaction model for cooperative interfaces or choreographies among groups of users. In our case, we model them through state machines defined in the metamodel itself.

3   User-Interface Model-Evolution

As previously advanced, the interaction metamodel is a part of a methodology based on MDE model evolution to regenerate user interfaces at runtime. Some features of such methodology[2] will be explained here to provide the reader with a context, before describing the interaction meta-model in the following section.

This methodology is appropriate only for certain types of UI: (a) **Component-**based interfaces. We consider UI as a collection of interface-components with dependences (functional, interaction, visual or temporal dependences, among others). An example of component interface is the iGoogle interface, made up of interface portions (or "gadgets") that together form the UI; (b) **COTS** (*Commercial Of-the-Shelf*) **UI components**: commercial UI components developed by third-parties, available in public repositories and accessible by *traders* [14] [15] for UI architecture configuration. Here, the UI is considered as a component architecture. We called components as "cotsgets" (COTS and gadgets/widgets); (c) Interfaces should be **self-reconfigurable**. The UI should be able to adapt itself to the user. For this purpose we do not aim to work with complex UI or interface-components ("cotsgets"). We just take into account WIMP interfaces, simple UI made up of graphical elements such as *Windows, Icons, Menus and Pointers* (WIMP) [16]; (d) Finally, our methodology is suitable for **WIS interfaces**, Web-based information system interfaces. WIS user interfaces do not need to be compiled environments, which justifies even more specifically the suitability of this solution to these (Web) interfaces.

As a solution to the interface evolution process, our methodology is based on an MDE approach of model evolution [17] by considering the interface architecture as models capable of evolving at runtime [18]. We solve the model evolution in two phases: (a) *model transformation* and (b) regeneration (by means of *trading*). We consider a starting UI as a set of models. A model is an instance of a

---

[2] http://www.ual.es/acg/soleres/jism

meta-model, which establishes the rules and elements that describe our system through a model. Our system is built on the basis of two meta-models (Figure 1): the architecture metamodel (AMM), and the runtime component metamodel ($RTCMM$). AMM defines the component architecture by describing the structure and behaviour of components. This metamodel is divided into three subsets: the structural metamodel (SM), the visual metamodel (VM) and the interaction metamodel (IM). The first one models composition dependences between components through connection ports (i.e., provided and required interfaces). The visual metamodel models the components behaviour from a visual point of view (open, close, show, hide components, etc.) by means of a state machine. The interaction metamodel models the user-interaction behaviour and describes the structure of interaction tasks that users may fulfil in the system (roles, tasks associated with those roles, choreography, etc.). The architecture model is used as an input of transformation process. The transformer implements the evolution. As an input, it uses a set of rules that define the transformer behaviour, the current architecture model (AM_i), including the interaction model (IM_i).

As an output, the transformer creates a new architecture model (AM_j) with its corresponding interaction models. The transformation process is invoked ("operates") when certain events occur in the system. Such events inform us that some changes have been made (for instance, interaction between user interfaces, time interval fulfilment, etc.), affecting the component architecture. Therefore, our transformer executes a model-to-model transformation (M2M) of MISO type (*Multiple Input and Single Output*). Finally, a trading service (trader) [14][15] calculates the best configuration to satisfy the architecture requirements, starting from abstract component requirements and a set of concrete components in repositories linked to the trader; as a result, we get a runtime component model ($RTCM$) that will be shown to the user.

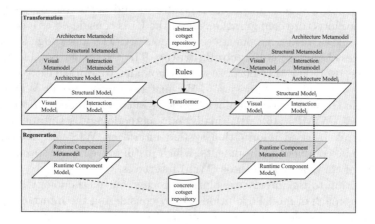

Fig. 1. A MISO model transformation for user interface evolution

4   Interaction Meta-model

Here we present the cooperative interaction meta-model. Figure 2 shows the
architecture metamodel subset that describes the interaction (i.e., interaction
meta-model). It conceptually describes the structure of the cooperative system,
based on roles (`Role`) and groups (`Group`) of actors. Each actor has at least one
role associated. Each role is made up of a set of *tasks* and thus we can identify the
activities carried out by actors who belong to the same system role. Any task can
be interrupted by another one at a specific time. We can distinguish between two
types of tasks: `CooperativeTask` and `NonCooperativeTask`. Both are modelled
similarly, taking into account that cooperative tasks have some conceptual and
implementation restrictions such as the fact that at least two actors may take
part (with the same or different role). In turn, each task is made up of task units
(`TaskUnit`). A task unit can be a subtask or an action. A `SubTask` is a set of
task units (actions or new subtasks). The `Action` is the atomic unit of a task,
so, it cannot be decomposed into different actions. All these actions are related
to the actors who use such actions and to the artefacts which the actors interact
with. The artefacts used in our system are the "cotsgets" components.

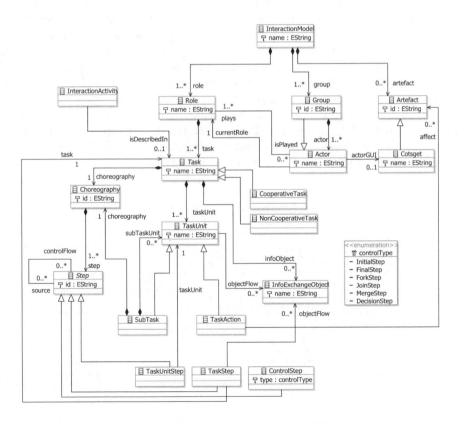

Fig. 2. The interaction meta-model

Each task and subtask always has a choreography associated. A choreography models the steps necessary for task or subtask execution. There are three different steps. Firstly, `TaskUnitStep` is used to model the invocation of a task unit, and consequently, it relates subtasks or actions within the same task or different tasks. Secondly, `TaskStep` is used to model the invocation of a new task. Lastly, `ControlStep` is used to add control flow capacities. There are different control capacities. On the one hand, `DecisionStep` is used to implement a selection of steps among a group of possible steps. On the other hand, `MergeStep` joins control flows (equivalent to a logic OR). `ForkStep` creates several concurrent control flows starting from only one control flow. `JoinStep` joins the control flows that are dependent on each other (equivalent to a logic AND). Finally, there are `InitialStep` and `FinalStep` that delimit the sequence of steps to be followed in a choreography. Both `TaskUnitStep` and `TaskStep` can use the `InformationExchangeObject` concept. This object contains the information exchanged from an activity to another one. Lastly, `InteractionActivity` (on the top left of the figure) and Cotsget (on the top right) represent joinpoints with the other two subsets of the architecture metamodel (*AM*) (i.e., Visual Metamodel and Structural Metamodel).

We've also established a set of OCL constraints in order to improve the interaction model construction. Table 1 shows a sublist of four constraints which specifically refer to the definition of choreography steps and their relationships through `ControlFlow` and `Source` roles of the reflexive association of the `Step` concept. Constraints of Table 1 mean the following. A step cannot be connected by itself (constraint #1). An initial step can only be connected to `ForkStep`, `TaskStep` or `TaskUnitStep` (constraint #2). A `ForkStep` has one incoming connection and two or more outgoing connections (constraint #3). A non cooperative task doesn't have any `TaskStep` either `TaskUnitStep` connected with a task or task unit from a different actor (constraint #4). It implies the task choreography and all subtask choreographies of the task.

Table 1. Some OCL restrictions on the interaction meta-model

Context	OCL Expression
Step	inv: self.controlFlow->forAll(c | c.id <> self.id)

Control Step	inv: self.type = controlType::InitialStep implies(
	     self.controlFlow->forAll(c | c.oclAsType(ControlStep).type = controlType::ForkStep
	     or c.oclIsTypeOf(TaskStep) or c.oclIsTypeOf(TaskUnitStep)))

Control Step	inv: self.type = controlType::ForkStep implies((self.source->size()=1) and (self.controlFlow->size() >=2))

Task	inv: self.oclIsTypeOf(NonCooperativeTask) implies(
	     (self.choreography.step->forAll(s|s.oclIsTypeOf(TaskStep)).
	     oclAsType(TaskStep).task.parent.isPlayed.name = self.parent.isPlayed.name)
	   and (self.choreography.step->forAll(s|s.oclIsTypeOf(TaskUnitStep)).
	     oclAsType(TaskUnitStep).taskUnit.parent.parent.isPlayed.name = self.parent.isPlayed.name)
	   and (self.taskUnit->forAll(st|st.oclIsTypeOf(SubTask)).oclAsType(SubTask).choreography.
	     step->forAll(s|s.oclIsTypeOf(TaskStep)).oclAsType(TaskStep).task.parent.isPlayed.name =
	     self.parent.isPlayed.name)
	   and (self.taskUnit -> forAll(st|st.oclIsTypeOf(SubTask)).oclAsType(SubTask).choreography.
	     step->forAll(s|s.oclIsTypeOf(TaskUnitStep)).oclAsType(TaskUnitStep).taskUnit.parent.
	     parent.isPlayed.name = self.parent.isPlayed.name))

5   A Case Study

In this section we will examine a case study for a better understanding of the metamodel described above. We will identify the actions that users should carry out in a cooperative task. The case study is related to a typical cooperative task in EMIS for decision-making when assessing natural disasters. This cooperative task allows us to assess damages caused by a catastrophe in a particular area of land (for instance, a flooded area). Three users with three different roles take part in such a task. Firstly, there is a politician (`PoliticianRole`) who is interested in conducting a damage assessment and, therefore, he is the only user who can initiate the cooperative task as he is responsible for it. Secondly, there is a GIS technician (`ExpertGISRole`) who is in charge of analysing the affected areas in order to classify the types of soil, damaged infraestructure, extensions of each affected area and so on. Thirdly, there is an administrator (`EvaluatorRole`) who carries out an economic estimate of the affected soils, damaged infraestructure, etc. starting from the information provided by the GIS expert.

Figure 3 shows a diagram describing the relationships between users as well as their activities for cooperative task execution. The activity starts as soon as the politician starts the task `DamageEvaluationTask`. As indicated above, all tasks and subtasks have a choreography and begin with the control-flow `InitialStep` and finish with the `FinalStep`.

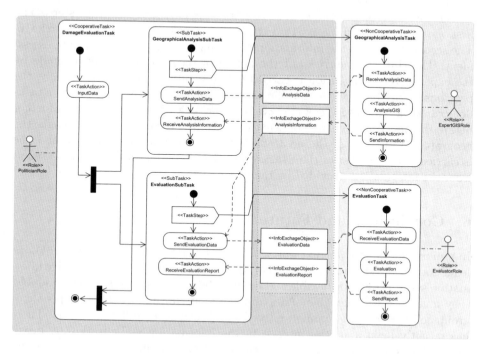

Fig. 3. A cooperative interaction scenario as an instance of the metamodel

The `DamageEvaluationTask` choreography includes three steps (regardless of `InitialStep` and `FinalStep`). On the one hand, there is a `TaskUnitStep` used so that the politician can carry out an action to introduce basic data necessary for assessment, providing some information about the study area, infraestructure, etc. Then, a `ForkStep` is carried out. This step allows us to initiate two sub-tasks: `GeographicalAnalysisSubtask`, which identifies the appropriate actions for the geographical analysis of the study area, and the `EvaluationSubtask`, which identifies actions for damage assessment. Initiating both subtasks makes the two affected users are informed in a cooperative task. Both have their own choreography which will be described next. Finally, there is the `JoinStep`, which allows to synchronize the two subtasks initiated in the previous step; as long as both subtasks are not executed, it is not possible to carry out the following step in the choreography, which will finish with the cooperative task in our exam-ple. The choreography of the `GeographicalAnalysisSubtask` carries out three steps (regardless of `InitialStep` and `FinalStep` again). The first is the exe-cution of the `GeographicalAnalysisTask`, which will be fulfilled by a user of the `GISExpert` role. This user has cotgets components (not described here) that allow him to manipulate or visualize maps in order to carry out his activity. The second step enables to send data (`AnalysisData`) so that the expert can initiate his activity. Finally, the subtask choreography ends by executing the `ReceiveAnalysisInformation` action allowing the user to receive the analysis made by the GIS expert. As we will describe next, this information is necessary for the `EvaluationSubtask`.

The choreography of the `EvaluationSubtask` also provides three steps. The first one is used to fulfil the `EvaluationTask` that belongs to the `EvaluatorRole`. The second one sends the information necessary to make the appropriate assess-ment. The third one carries out the action of receiving the analysis made by the expert. Once this action is carried out, the subtask will finish. Finally, the previous Figure 3 shows the specific choreographies of the non-cooperative tasks `GeographicalAnalysisTask` and `EvaluationTask`. Without going into further detail, the first task is carried out by the user of the `ExpertGISRole` to make the geographical analysis of the area affected by the catastrophe. The second one is carried out by a user of the `EvaluatorRole` to conduct a damage assessment from the information provided by the GIS expert.

6   Conclusions and Future Work

In a more open and changing world, where information globalization and know-ledge society are spreading in Internet, the modern Web-based cooperative infor-mation systems must be flexible and ready to be easily adaptable and extendable; they must also be accessible and manipulable at runtime by different people or groups of people with common interests and located at different places. There has recently been a special interest in the information globalization by provi-ding the systems with a common vocabulary through ontologies and semantics for the Web. There has also been much attention focussed on the standardized way in which the information is retrieved in the Web using powerful search engines based on ontologies and intelligent software agents. Nevertheless, WCIS user interfaces are still being built based on traditional software development paradigms without taking into account (as well as the knowledge they manage) the main criterion of the globalization: they have to be distributed, open and changeable. This implies that UIs of a WCIS can self-generate themselves at runtime depending on the type of cooperative interaction and its purpose (political, management, technical purpose, etc.). Due to the inherent complexity of user interfaces (from a functional, visual and interactive point of view), our research is determined by the following premises: (a) User interfaces are simple and made up of WIMP-type elements (Windows, Icons, Menus and Pointers), (b) User interfaces are used for Web-based collaborative information systems, (c) User interfaces are formed on the basis of the composition of interface portions (widgets/gadgets-type). The interaction of user (groups) with the interface portions in their user interfaces makes them change at runtime. This viewpoint allows us to consider evolutive user interfaces that are somehow dependent on the interaction between the groups of users who are involved and collaborate in the system (WCIS).

In this article we present an interaction metamodel that is used as part of an evolutive model methodology for cooperative user interfaces. This proposal is inspired in basic principles of *Model-Driven Engineering* (MDE), particularly runtime models, model evolution and model transformation issues. The proposed interaction metamodel basically uses six concepts: groups, actors, rules, choreographies, tasks and cotsgets. *Cotsgets* are widget/gadget-type interface-components that together form the user interface. We also present an interaction scenario for decision-making in environmental impact assessment, usual in GIS (*Geographical Information Systems*). The example scenario models the interaction of a cooperative task between three users with three different rules (a politician, an expert and an evaluator). The interaction metamodel and the example described in this paper are a part of the SOLERES system, an *Environmental Management Information System* (EMIS) [2].

As future work we'd like to develop a graphical tool using the *Eclipse Graphical Modeling Framework* (GMF[3]) in order to easily draw new scenarios such as instances (models) of the interaction metamodel. Nowadays, models are directly written in XMI and manually drawn as activity and object diagrams by using Visual Paradigm for Eclipse. We are also interested in to study possible change detection in the interaction metamodel by means of automated co-evolution mechanisms and metamodel adaptation [19] [20].

Acknowledgment. This work has been supported by the EU (FEDER) and the Spanish Ministry MICINN under grant of the TIN2007-61497, TIN2010-15588, and TRA2009-0309 projects, http://www.ual.es/acg/soleres.

---

[3] www.eclipse.org/gmf/

References

1. El-Gayar, O., Fritz, B.D.: Environmental Management Information Systems (EMIS) for Sustainable Development: A Conceptual Overview. Comm. of the Assoc. for Inf. Syst. 17(1), 34 (2006)
2. SOLERES project: A spatio-temporal Information System for the Enviromental Management based on Neural-Networks, Agents and Software Components. University of Almeria, http://www.ual.es/acg/soleres
3. Schmidt, D.C.: Model-Driven Engineering. Computer 39(2), 25–31 (2006)
4. Mistrik, I., Grundy, J., Hoek, A., Whitehead, J.: Collaborative Software Engineering. Springer book, Heidelberg (2010) ISBN: 978-3-642-10293-6
5. Obrenovic, Z., Starcevic, D.: Model-driven development of user interfaces: Promises and challenges. In: EUROCON 2005, vol. 1(2), pp. 1259–1262 (2005)
6. Bourguin, G., Derycke, J.C., Tarby, J.C.: Beyond the interfaces, Co-evolution inside Interactive Systems: A proposal founded on the Activity Theory. In: Proc. of the Human Computer Interaction 2001, Springer, Berlin (2001)
7. Pérez-Medina, J.L., Dupuy-Chessa, S., Front, A.: A Survey of Model Driven Engineering Tools for User Interface Design. In: Winckler, M., Johnson, H., Palanque, P. (eds.) TAMODIA 2007. LNCS, vol. 4849, pp. 84–97. Springer, Heidelberg (2007)
8. Guerrero, J., Lemaigre, C., Gonzalez, J.M., Vanderdonckt, J.: Model-Driven Approach to Design User Interfaces for Workflow Information Systems. Journal of Universal Computer Science 14(19), 3160–3173 (2008)
9. Gallardo, J., Crescencio, B., Redondo, M.A.: Developing Collaborative Modeling Systems Following a Model-Driven Engineering Approach. In: Meersman, R., Tari, Z., Herrero, P. (eds.) OTM-WS 2008. LNCS, vol. 5333, pp. 442–451. Springer, Heidelberg (2008)
10. Chavarriaga, E., Macia, J.A.: A model-driven approach to building modern Semantic Web-Based User Interfaces. Advan. Eng. Soft. 40, 1329–1334 (2009)
11. Angelaccio, M., Krek, A., D'Ambrogio, A.: A Model-Driven Approach for Designing Adaptive Web GIS Interfaces. LNGC, pp. 137–148. Springer, Heidelberg (2009)
12. Levytskyy, A., Vangheluwe, H., Rothkrantz, L., Koppelaar, H.: MDE and customization of modeling and simulation web applications. Simulation Modelling Practice and Theory 17, 408–429 (2009)
13. Hawryszkiewycz, I.T.: A metamodel for modeling collaborative systems. Journal of Computer Information Systems 5(3), 63–72 (2005)
14. I.S.O,Information Technology — Open Distributed Processing — Trading Function: Specification. ISO/IEC 13235-1, ITU-T X.950
15. Iribarne, L., Troya, J.M., Vallecillo, A.: A Trading Service for COTS Components. The Computer Journal 4(3), 342–357 (2004)
16. Almendros, J., Iribarne, L.: An Extension of UML for the modeling of WIMP user interfaces. J. of Visual Lang. and Computing 19(6), 695–720 (2008)
17. Mens, T.: Introduction and Roadmap: History and Challenges of Software Evolution, pp. 1–11. Springer, Heidelberg (2008)
18. Blair, G., Bencomo, N., France, R.B. (eds.): Models@Run.Time. Special Issue, Computer. IEEE Computer Society, Los Alamitos (2009)
19. Cicchetti, A., Di Ruscio, D., Eramo, R., Pierantonio, A.: Automating Co-evolution in Model-Driven Engineering. In: 12th Int. IEEE EDOC, pp. 222–231 (2008)
20. Wachsmuth, G.: Metamodel Adaptation and Model Co-adaptation. In: Ernst, E. (ed.) ECOOP 2007. LNCS, vol. 4609, pp. 600–624. Springer, Heidelberg (2007)

Experimental Evaluation of 'On-Site Customer' XP Practice on Quality of Software and Team Effectiveness[*]

Adam Wojciechowski, Maciej Wesolowski, and Wojciech Complak

Poznan University of Technology, Institute of Computing Science
ul. Piotrowo 2, 60-965 Poznan, Poland
{Adam.Wojciechowski,Wojciech.Complak}@cs.put.poznan.pl,
Wesolowski.Maciej@gmail.com

Abstract. Extreme Programming (XP) is an agile software production methodology based on organizational foundations collected in so-called practices. One of them: *On-site Customer* is focused on frequent and intensive involvement of customer representative in software creation process. It is said that no one knows customer's business and its specific needs better than the customer himself. However, it is hard to argue whether *On-site Customer* practice brings positive results on quality of software and effort effectiveness without experimental evaluation of the procedure. In order to provide assessment of the influence how *On-site Customer* affects quality of produced software and effectiveness of software team we performed an experiment where six software teams worked in parallel having an on-site customer while the other seven teams could only contact their customer representative by telephone or email. Results collected in the paper provide a description of experiment based on extended version of educational game *eXtreme89* as well as results collected in experiment and analysis of quality of software produced by teams working according to different software creation paradigms. Data gained during the experiment confirmed that *On-site Customer* practice has substantial positive influence on quality of communication and speed of software production. Experimental results gave us quantitative assessment in discussion on effectiveness of this software production XP practice.

Keywords: eXtreme Programming, On-Site Customer, experimental validation.

1 Introduction

Extreme Programming[1] is an agile software development methodology based on organizational foundations collected in so-called practices. One of them: *On-site Customer* is focused on frequent and intensive involvement of customer representative in software creation process. Customer plays an important role in defining software requirements as well as in assessment of software features importance observed from business point of view. It is said that no one knows customer's business and its specific needs better than the customer himself. However, the customers are often skeptical when it comes to delegate an important business person to frequent and intensive

[*] This research was partially supported by the grant 91-439/10-BW.

R. Meersman et al. (Eds.): OTM 2010 Workshops, LNCS 6428, pp. 269–278, 2010.
© Springer-Verlag Berlin Heidelberg 2010

co-operation with software team. One should notice that XP practices are considered controversial and a good way for statistical assessment is experimental evaluation on programming tasks big enough to observe real influence of chosen methodology on software teams, e.g.[4].

A market researcher DataMonitor estimates that global software industry was worth US\$ 303.8 billion in 2008. DataMonitor's forecasts informs that in 2013 the figure will be US\$ 457 billion. According to British Computer Society's research 40% of IT projects fail to meet the original objectives. These overwhelming values prove the importance of attempts to improve the software creation process.

It is hard to argue whether *On-site Customer* practice brings positive results on software creation process and effort effectiveness unless we have experimental evaluation of the procedure. Literature study show that some research was done in the field by J.Koskela and P.Abrahamsson [2] but their research was rather focused on assessment whether constant presence of customer representative with software team is effectively utilized. Experiments reported in [2] revealed that *'On-site Customer' may create a false sense of confidence in to the system under development.* Partial realization of *On-site Customer* is discussed in [6] and Wake in [7] argues that high bandwidth communication overheads for team communication are justified by the benefits of flexibility and responsiveness. In order to provide assessment of the influence and measure how *On-site Customer* affects quality of produced software and effectiveness of team work we performed an experiment. Six software teams worked having an on-site customer while the other seven software teams could only contact their customer representative by telephone or email. Experiments were conducted in controlled environment at Poznan University of Technology, Poland. Software teams were staffed by 4th year students of Computer Science faculty. All of them were good, experienced programmers, however, the fact that teams were not composed of professional programmers working or long-term project might be considered a limitation.

Results collected in this research work provide a description of experiment based on extended version of educational game eXtreme89[3], experiment results and analysis of quality of software produced by teams working with and without direct face to face contact with on-site customer.

2   On-Site Customer: A Real Case

The motivation for our experimental research in *On-site Customer* assessment came from our observations collected during co-operation of Poznan University of Technology and our business partners – external software firms. Several software projects were conducted in cooperation of customers – firms and students who developed and managed the projects, under Software Development Studio – a part of Software Engineering curricula at PUT. Another source of real life experience on cooperation between software developers and customers were expert panels and working meetings organized by XPrince Consortium[5].

In several reported cases customers who passed software requirements specification to developers had a feeling that their role in the process was *sleeping* until assessment of final stage of the system. The programmers suffered from missing informal contact with customer representative. Doubts and not precise specification of requirement of software features were often solved by programmer's intuition. Such a sequence might lead not only to sad surprise and disappointment but also to late delivery of software system and financial loose.

A better comfort of cooperation and progress in software system development was reported in cases where customer representative was involved in frequent visits and talks with developers. For both sides – customer and developers – those meetings were occasions for instant reaction for encountered problem or clarifying doubts. However, in none of the projects where we participated or they were reported to us, a customer representative was all the working time available for developers. A real case, in our assessment close to model, was frequent planned meetings – at least once a week – and possibility to contact customer representative by phone, videoconferencing tools like *Skype* or email. In such realization an *On-site Cutomer* is better defined by term *On-line Customer*.

Customer's cost of *On-site Customer* is not only the time of a single employee delegated to assist developers in their everyday work. A person playing the role of *On-site Customer* needs to have knowledge in expected functionality of particular modules of produced software and he must be a person able to make important business decisions, whose availability may be difficult to achieve[8]. In this light, in practice, the role of *On-site Customer* often requires several persons to be involved in representing customer's interest in the project. A single role of Customer Representative may be played by changing persons.

3 Experiment Methodology

3.1 Main Assumptions

Software teams might earn points for delivering proper solutions of given problems. Number of tasks and their complexity was chosen in such a way that it was practically impossible to solve all the problems in given time. Points initially assigned to particular tasks were proportional to problem complexity. In order to gain points solution presented by a team had to be accepted by moderator who had a set of quick but deep test cases which practically eliminated possibility of accepting a solution with errors. Value of bonus (number of points to earn) for delivering proper solution of particular problem was changing (decreasing) whenever a team delivered correct result. Time of experiment was 3h and 20min. Computer science students participating in experiment were randomly assigned to particular teams.

3.2 Team Work Efficiency Measure

A simple definition of work efficiency is a proportion of gained profit related to effort. In our experiment all the teams had equal time for work: 200 minutes and teams were built of equal number of members (2 programmers and 1 customer). In this context effort devoted to produce solutions was estimated to be equal. Bare numbers of earned points were our measure to compare efficiency of team work.

3.3 Software Quality

It is more complex to measure software quality than team efficiency. Initially we tried to follow Garvin definition of eight dimensions of quality: performance, features, reliability, conformance, durability, serviceability, aesthetics and perceived quality[9]. But soon it appeared that assessment of software produced during experiment lasting no more than 3h and 20min. would be very difficult or even impossible. For example measures like durability or serviceability require long term assessment. Having the above in mind we decided to follow another quality definition by Crosby[10], who says that quality is *conformance to the requirements*. In our experiment, requirements were specified precisely and clearly, and proper, expected solution was known. We chose such a binary quality assessment because of its simplicity and objective nature.

We also defined the following acceptance criteria:

1. Teams obtain problem description and all the knowledge required to solve it, definition of input data format and specification of result format.
2. Task can be accepted (considered as solved) if delivered program produces correct result for all moderator's test cases.

3.4 Software Development Teams

The main aim of the experiment was to confront working with an on-site customer available for programmers for instant face to face consulting versus team working with customer available via email and telephone (distant customer). A common condition for all the teams was that knowledge required to solve problems and earn points was divided into parts for programmers and customers. Communications between programmers and customer was a necessary condition to learn how to solve given problem.

3.4.1 On-Site Customer

Programmers and customers sit in the same laboratory. Programmers have one computer for their work and another computer is available for customer. Customers and programmers may freely communicate and pass their knowledge to each other in any form, except they are not allowed to show each other sheets with problem description provided by moderator (it was allowed to re-write the contents). Free communication was a chance for entire team not only to communicate but also the customer might observe progress in work on programmers' screen, they might define new test cases working together over one sheet of paper (it could not be the sheet of paper with customers' or programmers' knowledge given by moderator).

3.4.2 Distant Customer

Customers and programmers work in separated laboratories. Programmers have one computer and the other one is in customer's location. Both computers are equipped with microphones and speakers to allow oral communication between programmers and customer. As a communication media teams could use *Skype* for oral talks and email for text and graphics delivery. Team members are allowed to pass all their knowledge, including reading or re-writing their knowledge sheets given by moderator. In particular the teams could exchange documents, data files and their interpretation how they understand the problem. However, programmers and customer could not send or exchange original problem definition sheets in form of a scan or a photo made by mobile phone camera.

Experiment participants worked in controlled environment – in each of locations (programmers' lab. and customers' lab.) there was a moderator who watched if the teams obeyed the rules.

3.5 Knowledge Flow

An important feature of eXtreme89 game is knowledge separation. Knowledge given to programmers and customer is different but supplementary. Having just one piece of information it is impossible to solve the problem. While programmers get more technical specification the customer has knowledge related to business case of given problem. Communication is obligatory to disseminate knowledge and have a possibility to solve the problem, see fig. 1.

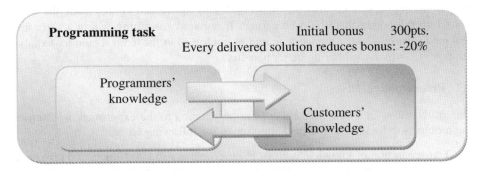

Fig. 1. Knowledge flow and dissemination as a consequence of team communication

3.6 Conditions that Make the Game Close to Real Programming Work

We paid much of our efforts to assure that experiment, although played in form of a game, would simulate real business conditions and collected results would provide evidence on whether *On-site Customer* XP practice is worth to be implemented in real projects or not. The first element that makes the experiment close to real software development is separation of customer's knowledge from knowledge given to programmers. In real business conditions development team has technical skills and experience in programming but particular business cases and priorities must be presented by the customer at the stage of Planning Game – a phase when software requirements are collected and prioritized and programmers estimate effort required for realization.

It is customer's job in XP development team to make business decisions and decide about priorities of particular functionalities of produced software. In eXtreme89 customer knows current value of task to be solved – how much a team can earn for delivering proper solution. Programmers, who know technical difficulty of implementation, estimate required effort and time. Good communication on very early stage of development (effort estimation and planning game) and right decisions made by the customer are crucial for success, especially when bonus for good solution is shrinking after each successful acceptance of solution provided by a team.

In real life it often happens that a customer representative playing the role of distant customer in XP team is delegated to support developers but also has his everyday routines and tasks to do. In practice such a customer representative is not available for programmers in every moment. In experimental conditions we simulated customer temporal unavailability. In parallel to supporting programmers, distant customers got a psychological test (300 quick questions) to answer. Filling entire questionnaire by the customer during the experiment was an obligatory condition for a team to earn points for delivered solutions of programming tasks.

Extreme programming methodology is said to be flexible solution for software development in conditions of changes being introduced to software requirements. In our experiment teams had to deal with two sorts of changes: minor modification or extensions in problem description (planned and provided by moderator) and dynamic shrinking of bonus value that teams could earn for delivering proper solution. It might happen during experiment that business conditions (decreased bonus) made the work not worth the points that could be earned. It required consulting within a team and making decision whether the work should be continued or the team should try to solve another task which could bring better benefits.

3.7 Programming Tasks

One of the most important elements of our preparation to the experiment was selecting problems to be solved. We paid attention to the following criteria:

- Clear separation of knowledge given to programmers and customers and providing the knowledge in such a way that bidirectional communication was necessary to understand the problem.
- Programming task could not be too difficult. Time for experiment was limited to 200 minutes and it should be enough to solve at least some out of five given task.
- Nature of problems (tasks) makes them easy to solve in any programming language or even in spreadsheet program. Skills in particular programming language were not a barrier for participants.
- And finally, we paid special care to make the tasks interesting. Participation in experiment was a chance to learn and rose discussion after the game among participating students. List of selected problems included:

    - Elections to European Parliament
    - Selecting locations for EURO2012 football arenas
    - Global economic crisis
    - Cryptogramme
    - Pig flu disease

Complete body of problems used in the experiment is available at [11].

4   Experiment

The experiment was conducted at Poznan University of Technology. We built thirteen 3-person teams (2 programmers and 1 customer):

- 7 teams working with distant customer
- 6 teams working with on-site customer

The teams had 5 programming task:

- Task 1. Initial bonus 200pts., shrinking by 20% after each successful delivery
- Task 2. Initial bonus 150pts., shrinking by 10% after each successful delivery
- Task 3. Initial bonus 300pts., shrinking by 30% after each successful delivery
- Task 4. Initial bonus 150pts., shrinking by 10% after each successful delivery
- Task 5. Initial bonus 200pts., shrinking by 20% after each successful delivery

The teams had equal time of 200 minutes for solving problems. Whenever a solution was accepted by the moderator adjusted bonus value was communicated to customer representatives. We did not experienced any technical or organizational problems during the game and students were pretty enthusiastic about competition. Winning teams (teams which earn the most of bonus points) were promised to have increased mark on semestral exam.

During the game we observed some slow-down in work after ca. 1.5h of work. But last 60 minutes of experiment warmed up the atmosphere. All teams wanted to win.

5   Comparison of Results Observed in Teams with On-Site Customer and Distant Customer

Teams working with On-site Customer had visibly less questions addressed to moderator. We observed that teams working with On-site Customer discussed within the team issues that were hard to understand for teams which had only a possibility to talk by phone with the customer.

On fig. 2. it is presented when the teams tried to submit their solution (accepted by the moderator or rejected due to encountered errors).

Between 96 and 154 minute of the experiment none of submitted solutions was accepted by the moderator. Decreased activity observed after 96th minute may be attributed to tiredness and lassitude.

Comparison of bare points collected during experiment required small scaling. Because we had 13 teams: 7 working with distant customer and only 6 teams working with on-site customer, we decided to multiply summarized results of on-site customer teams by 7/6 to make results comparable.

Points earned by the teams during experiment and their comparison are collected in table 1.

The main aim of the experiment was to assess how *On-site Customer* XP programming practice affects effectiveness of work and software quality. Collected results gave evidence that instant availability of customer representative for face to face

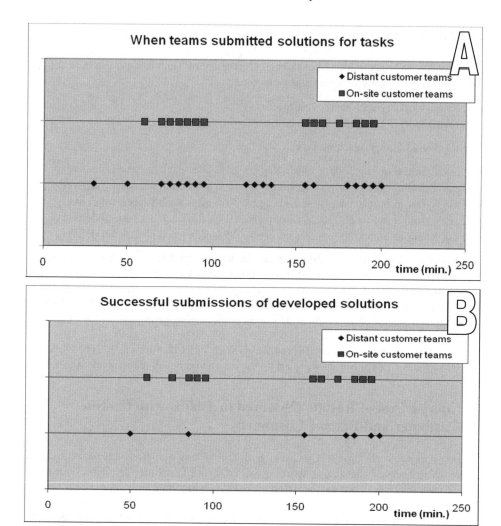

Fig. 2. Submission approaches (A) and successful submissions (B) of produced software

consulting with programmers has substantial and positive influence of software development. Facts are the following:

- On-site customer teams earned 2080 points (after scaling 2426,7pts.) while teams working with distant customer earned only 1265,5 points. Strict following *On-site Customer* practice outperformed results obtained in distant telephone or email access to customer. Earning of *On-site Customer* teams are 165% (193% after scaling) when compared to earnings of teams following distant customer paradigm (100%).
- Teams working with on-site customer solved 11 (12,8 after scaling) programming tasks versus 7 task solved by the teams supported by distant customer. Bare – solved problems – results of on-site customer teams are equal to 157% (183% after scaling) of distant customer teams achievement.

- On-site customer teams were visibly more effective: 11 out of 14 approaches to acceptance of delivered products was successful. Teams working with distant customer had only 7 accepted task out of 19 approaches to acceptance. The customers in all teams got some acceptance tests (test cases) from moderator. However the internal assessment went better in case when the customer could manually check program prepared by programmers.

In analysis of experiment results it is worth to mention that initial bonus (number of points a team can get for delivering proper solution) was based on our intuition and our assessment of relative difficulty of particular tasks. Minor difference in observed ratio of collected points in both groups and ratio of solved problem numbers in both groups confirms that our assessment of difficulty was rational and chosen approach worked well.

Table 1. Number of successful and failed submissions or designed solutions

	Distant customer 7 teams (A)	On-site customer 6 teams (B)	On-site customer x7/6 (C)	B/A	C/A
Solved problems	7	11	12,83	1,57	1,83
Number of submissions	19	14	-	0,74	-
Effectiveness: solved/submissions	0,37	0,79	-	2,14	-
Earned points	1256,5	2080,0	2426,7	1,65	1,93

6 Conclusions

Data and experience gained during the experiment confirmed that *On-site Customer* XP practice had substantial positive influence on quality of communication and speed of software production. Experimental results gave us quantitative assessment in discussion on effectiveness of this particular software production practice. Considering number of solved programming tasks teams working with on-site customer outperformed teams supported by distant customer by 83%. In dimension of points earned in the game simulating changing market conditions, where the first provider of a solution gets the highest income, on-site customer teams appeared better by 93% than teams with possibility of telephone and email consulting with the customer. One may also notice that work instantly controlled by the customer representative who had ability to test software on very early stages by his own test cases made the creation process more predictable. On-site customer teams had only 3 failures out of 14 acceptance approaches, while distant customer teams had 12 failures out of 19 acceptance tests.

Direct face to face contact and possibility to exchange knowledge on a sheet of paper (making notes, drawings etc.) as well as instant customer control over software produced by programmers appeared to be a key to success in experimental assessment of influence how *On-site Customer* affects speed of work and quality of produced software.

References

[1] Beck, K.: Extreme programming explained: Embrace change. Addison Wesley Longman, Inc., Reading (2000)
[2] Koskela, J., Abrahamsson, P.: On-Site Customer in an XP Project: Empirical Results from a Case Study. In: Dingsøyr, T. (ed.) EuroSPI 2004. LNCS, vol. 3281, pp. 1–11. Springer, Heidelberg (2004)
[3] Nawrocki, J., Wojciechowski, A.: Extreme89: An XP War Game. In: Guelfi, N., Savidis, A. (eds.) RISE 2005. LNCS, vol. 3943, pp. 278–287. Springer, Heidelberg (2006)
[4] Nawrocki, J., Wojciechowski, A.: Experimental evaluation of Pair Programming. In: Maxwell, K., et al. (eds.) Proceedings of the 12th European Software Control and Metrics Conference ESCOM 2001 Project Control: Satisfying the Customer, pp. 269–276. Shaker Publishing, Maastricht (2001)
[5] Consortium XPrince (April 2010), http://www.xprince.net
[6] Farell, C., Narang, R., Kapitan, S., Webber, H.: Towards an Effective Onsite Customer-Practice. In: XP 2002, Sardinia, Italy (2002)
[7] Wake, W.C.: Extreme Programming Explored. Addison-Wesley, Reading (2002)
[8] Yourdon, E.: Death March: The Complete Software Developer's Guide to Surviving 'Mission Impossible' Projects. Prentice-Hall, Englewood Cliffs (1999)
[9] Garvin, D.A.: What Does 'Product Quality' Really Mean? Slogan Management Review (26), 25–31 (1984)
[10] Crosby, P.B.: Quality is free: The art of making quality certain. McGraw Hill Custom Publishing, New York (1979)
[11] Programming tasks (April 2010),
http://www.cs.put.poznan.pl/awojciechowski/research/eXtreme89

Early Validation of Requirements in Distributed Product Development – An Industrial Case Study

Samuli Heinonen and Hannu Tanner

VTT Technical Research Centre of Finland, P.O. BOX 1100,
90571 Oulu, Finland
{Samuli.Heinonen,Hannu.Tanner}@vtt.fi

Abstract. An inevitable aspect of product development is that the developer needs to be sure what customers and other stakeholders want from the system under development. Plenty of best practices for requirements engineering have been introduced in the scientific literature, as well as studies about the related pitfalls, but requirements engineering still remains a problematic area in product development. Operating in distributed development environment not only emphasizes these problems, but also creates new ones. Typically the biggest challenges for industrial practitioners are the lack of awareness about the existing solutions as well as the difficulty of selecting the right methods for certain kind of situations during the development. In this article, one potential solution for assistance in the selection of requirements validation practices in distributed product development environment is presented. Based on interviews made within the company and solutions found from literature, a proposal for potential improvement actions is presented.

Keywords: Requirements engineering; requirement validation, distributed development.

1 Introduction

Developing high quality products is a key factor of success and an integral part of the strategy of global high-tech companies. However, the quality of products is irrelevant, if the products do not meet the needs and expectations of end-users and other stakeholders. A number of studies ([1], [2], [3], and [4]) have stressed the importance of correct and unambiguous requirements, as many serious failures can be traced back to problems in the requirements engineering (RE) process.

It can be argued that the most important issue in requirements definition process is to validate that requirements are correct, unambiguous and complete, and that they meet the needs of customers. Requirements validation means actions to confirm that the behavior of a developed system meets user needs, whereas requirements verification means actions to confirm that the product of a system development process meets its specification, e.g. the design must meet the system requirements. [4]

Globally distributed development poses many challenges for requirements engineers, like problems in communication and cultural differences between the ways of working in distributed teams [5]. Thus, RE process in distributed development should

R. Meersman et al. (Eds.): OTM 2010 Workshops, LNCS 6428, pp. 279–288, 2010.
© Springer-Verlag Berlin Heidelberg 2010

allow validating requirements in different ways, while still ensuring that local processes do not cause problems with higher level processes [6].

2 State-of-the-Art in RE Area

It has been reported over several decades in various empirical research studies and surveys that project success depends on good requirements management. Ensuring that system stakeholders' expectations are met accurately is a complex task, because multiple stakeholders with different needs and perspectives are involved in requirements gathering process [7]. According to the latest Standish Group report, only 32% of the real world IT projects were successful, 44% were finished late, over budget, and/or with less than the required features and functions and 24% of features in all products were never used or failed the completion [8].

In practice industry often uses quite simple and approved software engineering methods and tools. One reason for not adopting more of the available methods or tools is that industry is not necessarily aware what is available and when the methods are applicable. Selecting and introducing a new technology in real-life projects is typically considered to be too laborious and risky. Moreover, new technologies are often not mature enough, or they are too complex to be applied in real-life applications. Other claim is that there is a gap between research and practice, so companies need guidelines on how to use the existing research results effectively. [9]

In this context, a method is understood as a larger thematic entity, which may include concise, more rigorous actions. The amount of methods introduced in literature is vast and they often look at the problem from different viewpoints, emphasizing different aspects. Certain methods, like inspections, reviews and workshops, are very generic in nature, as the same approach can be utilized not only with requirements, but also with other artifacts. For example, source code inspections/reviews and design workshops are generally used during the development lifecycle, whereas requirements checklists, "good enough" technique and ambiguity recognizing are practices that are meant to be used only for requirements validation. In addition, many kinds of formal methods for describing and validating requirements have been proposed. The advantage of using formal method is that they offer an exact description about a requirement and they can be used to automate the validation work. Drawbacks are that formal methods are often quite laborious to set up and teach for the practitioners, and that they are not suitable for all kinds of situations.

The main problem of requirements validation is that there is very little against which the requirements can be validated. The validation process can only increase the confidence that the specification represents a system which will meet the real needs of the system stakeholders. [4]

Moreover, one of the major problems with requirements validation in industry is the lack of validation practices. Companies practice validation on ad-hoc basis due to lack of requirements validation experts. More attention is typically given to testing phase which is usually carried out when all modules of a product are integrated. [9]

3   Industrial Case Study

In order to study the early validation of requirements, an industrial case study was car-ried out within a large, globally distributed telecommunications company. The company has over 50000 employees working in more than 100 countries, in all continents of the world. The main objectives of the case study was to analyze the existing RE process, collect improvement ideas and, based on case data and literature study, propose an im-proved solution for requirements validation to be adopted into existing RE process. This case study was part of a broader effort for improving the current RE process in the case organization. The proposed solution mainly focuses on the validation of requirements, and it is defined as a plug-in, so that it could be easily adopted in the existing process.

   The data of the case study has been collected primarily in interview sessions with members of the RE process improvement workgroup of the case organization. In addition, a detailed process description about the current RE process was available for analysis. The proposed solution for early validation process was defined based on these data and complemented with results from a literature study.

3.1   Current RE Process

The case organization's current RE process is a gateway-based, funnel-type process, to which all the requirements are fed. The purpose of the RE process is to check the business value of a requirement for the customer and the business potential for the company itself. The goal is to handle all requirements that might concern any changes to upcoming releases. Figure 1 illustrates the process in high level.

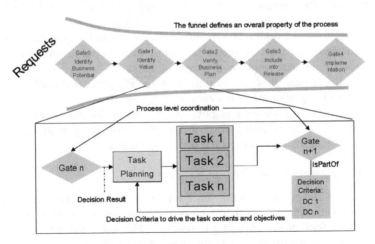

Fig. 1. Current RE process in the case organization

   The emphasis in the RE process is on filtering stakeholders' requirements from business point of view. This means that only those requirements which seem to have potential business value should be entered into development in the right time, whereas non-valuable requirements should be rejected as early as possible in order to avoid unnecessary work. Every gate has decision criteria, which is used to help in making the decision about whether the requirement in question should qualify to the next phase or not. Because the process is like a funnel, every gate should eliminate some of the proposed requirements. Every requirement that is handled by the RE process have a nominated person in charge, who is responsible for managing and developing the requirement through the entire RE process.

Parviainen et al [7] have drawn up a list of project and product characteristics that affect the RE process. These characteristics were tailored and analyzed against the existing RE process in the case organization and the analysis results are used to describe the current operational environment of the case organization, as follows.

Characteristics of the development projects:

1. Total number of requirements is high, making the classification and prioritization of requirements very important. Likewise, analyzing and maintaining the relations between requirements becomes challenging.
2. Number of developers and stakeholders involved in projects is huge, stressing the need for documentation. Prioritizing and agreeing on requirements becomes more complicated as there is a higher chance of conflicting interests.
3. The case organization operates in a distributed working environment, leading to increased need for requirements documentation and traceability policies.
4. Some of the requirements are sent to subcontractors for implementation. This forces the requirements to be described as rigorously and clearly as possible, so that that they can be managed in co-operation with the subcontractor.

Characteristics of the product being developed:

1. Safety criticality of the product is not especially high, but requirements for system reliability require suitable traceability policies to enable analyzing the impact of possible changes in requirements in detail.
2. There are tight real-time requirements and constraints for systems, which means that requirements analysis methods should provide means for modeling state behavior, timing, and response time requirements.
3. Because the product lifecycle is quite long, the RE process should concentrate on comprehensive requirements traceability policies.
4. The amount of legacy data is huge, so requirements analysis should provide mechanisms for combining new design elements easily with legacy data or engineering legacy data to meet the new requirements.

3.2 Main Challenges in the Current RE Process

Even though the current RE process was quite thoroughly documented, a set of interview sessions with members of the case organization was arranged in order to gather the main challenges in the current RE process. The main findings based on these information sources regarding the existing RE process were as follows:

1. Requirements lead-time from elicitation to implementation is currently too long
2. The real requirements from customers and other stakeholders are not passed on as such to the implementation phase
3. Requirements validation processes are not sufficient enough
4. Customers complaint that the company does not understand their needs
5. Acceptance criteria for requirements are not specified with stakeholder during the requirements elicitation process

4   Proposed Solution for Improved RE Process

The scientific literature emphasizes having interaction with the customer as much as possible to ensure that a consensus and clear understanding of real customer requirements can be acquired. The organization structure in the case organization prevents requirements engineers to communicate with customers directly. This forces the requirement engineers to do their work utilizing quite much documentation in their work. However, this increases the lead-time from requirements elicitation to requirements validation, causing the loss of the "nearness in time" factor. When validation activities are performed as shortly as possible after the elicitation, it provides the benefit of the clarity of information in the stakeholders' minds. [3]

Considering all the aforementioned boundary conditions, it was decided that the improved RE process should include two validation points. Performing the early validation of requirements right after Gate0 brings clear benefits. At that time, the real understanding of stakeholder needs should be gathered and ensured through appropriate validation practices. Another validation round should take place before the Gate2 decision, just before a requirement is to be included in release plans. At that point, the used term changes, as the requirement has evolved into an implementable feature. A single requirement may even be split in several features. Before the feature is included into a release plan, it must be ensured that the feature is valid for stakeholders and that the feature is technically feasible. In this article only the first round of the validation process is presented in detail. The requirements for the second round validation are introduced, but the detailed description about it is not included.

The most often used methods in validation and verification of requirements are *formal requirements inspections*, *requirements testing*, and *requirements checklists* [10]. Other widely used validation methods are *reviews*, *prototyping* and *scenarios*. The proposed solution is described from the requirements engineers' point of view, and it is strongly based on methods and practices that are widely used and approved.

4.1   Proposal for First Round Validation

This section describes the first part of Validation Plug-in process task-by-task starting from the task Practice Selection. The following sections explain the process model, which is illustrated in the Figure 2. All rectangles inside the validation plug-in in the Figure 2 represent separate tasks which are described in the following sections.

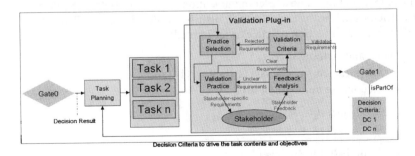

Fig. 2. An improved RE process with validation plug-in

4.1.1 Practice Selection

Practice selection is the task where the availability of effort for validation is analyzed and proper validation practices are selected. It is important not to over-validate the requirements and features at this point, because performing thorough validation in distributed environment requires time, effort and money. For example, if the organization has previously implemented a similar feature, it is not meaningful to re-perform thorough validation. On the other hand, if the requirement's priority is high and new technology may be needed to implement the requirement, it is sensible to validate those requirements rigorously in order to minimize the risks.

Different kinds of validation practices are needed for requirements of different type. For example, functional requirements may be validated by utilizing scenarios or use cases, while it might be wise to validate critical requirements through inspections or prototypes in collaboration with the stakeholders. Moreover, certain validation practices, like checklists, might be practical for requirements derived from standards and regulations. In difficult situations it is also possible to utilize multiple validation practices at the same time. It should also be noticed that using common high-level processes and allowing local processes is a good practice [6]. Thus, analyzing the effort needed for validation is strongly dependent on the following characteristics:

- What is the *familiarity* of the requirement for developers? Do they have experience on developing similar requirements?
- What are the *risk factors* of the requirement?
- What is the *value* of the requirement for customer and for organization?
- What is the *time window* for making the go/no-go decision?
- Which *requirement class* does this requirement belong to? (E.g., Mandatory, Contract-based, Non-functional, Standard-based, etc.)

Lobo et al. [3] present a set of criteria to be used in the selection of practices: Time, Cost, Personnel and Completeness. For the case study, the criteria were simplified so that Time and Cost form one combined factor, while availability of dedicated personnel is included in to Completeness-factor. Thus, early validation practices have two criteria, as follows:

- Time and Cost - Selection based on how quickly the practice needs to be performed, and how much can be invested in conducting the practice.
- Completeness - Selection based on the coverage of the validation practice

Practices that require intensive communication, e.g., workshops and inspections, are more difficult and costly to perform in distributed development. Thus, the following classification for validation practices was defined:

- Quick and Affordable
  - Requirements checklists [12], [13], [14],
  - Recognize ambiguity [14]
- Moderate effort
  - Audits [13]
  - Round-Robin Review [13]

- Extensive and Costly
  - Workshops [12], [13]
  - Inspections [13], [14]
  - Scenarios [4], [13], [12]

The following figure (Figure 3) depicts a proposal of how the requirement character-istics can be used to support the selection of the most suitable validation practices. The figure suggests that if we are familiar with a certain kind of requirement, there are no high-level risks involved. On the other hand, if the requirement is not known beforehand, the risk factor is at least moderate. Same kind of 'rule out' method is used in other decision branches, so that the decisions tree can be used to support decision making and yet be kept simple enough.

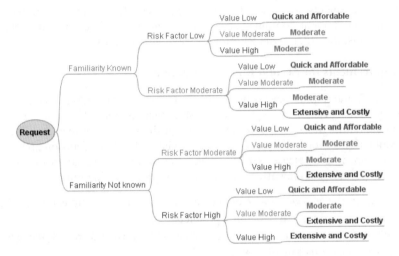

Fig. 3. Decision tree for selecting the proper validation practices

4.1.2 Validation Practice and Feedback Analysis

Depending on the validation practice, it is possible to start the Validation Criteria analysis right after validation without communication with stakeholder. For example, performing activities such as recognize ambiguity, checklists and audits does not necessarily require communication with certain stakeholders at all.

Feedback analysis may vary a little depending on what validation practice is used. The main goal is deciding if a requirement is clear enough after the feedback from stakeholder. If it is not, another validation round with the stakeholder should be per-formed, so that the requirement is ready for the Validation Criteria analysis.

4.1.3 Validation Criteria

After the first round validation, every requirement has to fulfill the quality attributes set for requirements and any open or unresolved issues should be closed. In addition, consensus must be achieved that all stakeholders' needs have now been recorded. These issues constitute the high-level exit criteria for early validation phase, which are common for all requirements regardless of which validation method is used. Validation criteria are as follows [13]:

- Acceptability – each requirement should be acceptable with responsible stakeholder
- Ambiguity – each requirement has only one possible interpretation and it is presented at the right level of precision
- Completeness – agreement that all stakeholder requirements are gathered and every requirement is necessary
- Verifiability – each requirement should include the acceptance criteria so that the implementation can be verified against it
- Understandability – each requirement should be comprehensible by all readers (users, customers, developers, etc.)

Rejected requirements are returned to the practice selection action, where the validation of the requirement continues accordingly. Otherwise, if the requirement is acceptable against the criteria, the RE process can continue normally.

4.2 Requirements for Second Round Validation

Before Gate2, the requirement is turned into a feature, so the second round validation handles features instead of requirements. Moreover, in this phase the stress is put more on validating the technical feasibility and business value of features. The second round validation is very important, because in Gate2, the final decision about including the feature into a release is made. Thus, the following characteristics and questions are important and they affect the selection of proper validation practices:

1. What is the *market model* of the feature? What is the time frame when the feature is valid in the upcoming products?
2. What is the *priority* of a feature? What is the business model and which are business case factors of a feature?
3. What is the *technical feasibility* of a feature? What kind of dependencies are there to existing features?

5   Discussion

Distributed development environment sets challenges for the RE solution. In this case the solution is to use common high-level processes and allow local modifications to the processes. Välimäki et al. [6] have defined best practices as process patterns for distributed project management. Common high-level practices have been judged as a good practice for distributed development. It is also important that local adaptations are allowed. However, the local adaptations should not cause problems with the high-level process that sets the constraints for the operation. Therefore, the high-level validation criteria are always the same, but the validation practices can vary. This gives adequate flexibility for requirements engineers to utilize the best-fit practices in distributed development. The solution proposal is developed to be used mainly in distributed development but it can also be applied in non-distributed development.

The challenges perceived in the case organization were introduced in the section 3.4 and the solution for solving the problems was presented in chapter 4. The reasoning for the proposed solution with respect to the challenges can be demonstrated as follows:

1. Requirements lead-time from elicitation to implementation is currently too long. Streamlining the RE process by merging Gate1 and Gate2 and utilizing more rigorous requirements elicitation process should help to shorten the requirements lead-time.

2. The real requirements from customers and other stakeholders are not passed on as such to the implementation phase. Validation criteria are provided in requirements elicitation phase so that practitioners are conscious about what is needed from the requirements. This forces the elicitation of requirement to be more precise, which should help the practitioners to gather the real requirements of stakeholders.

3. Requirements validation processes are not sufficient enough. The proposed solution includes support for quick selection of proper validation practices in various situations, while it is simple and light-weight enough to be utilized in practice.

4. Customers complaint that the company does not understand their needs. The proposed requirement elicitation process includes validation criteria for early validation of requirements. It should improve communication with the customer, ensure that all raw requirements are gathered from customers and provide practical tools for validated them.

5. Acceptance criteria for requirements are not specified with stakeholder during the requirements elicitation process. Acceptance criteria are now required for passing the Gate0, and requirements without that criteria can't be approved to the next phase.

6   Conclusions and Future Work

As stated earlier, the main problem of requirements validation is that there is very little against which the requirements can be validated. The validation process can only increase the confidence that the specification represents the real needs of the system stakeholders. Other major challenge is the adaptation of proper methods for requirements validation. According to the studies, companies often practice validation on ad-hoc basis due to lack of requirements validation experts.

This article introduced one potential solution for selecting and utilizing the proper validation practices in distributed environment from the requirement engineers' point of view. Certain characteristics of requirements may affect the requirements validation selection: familiarity, risk factors, value, class, and time window. Based on these characteristics and effort available for validation, the following two criteria were selected to support the selection: Time and Cost, and Completeness. By utilizing the proposed decision tree, requirements validation can be easily performed by selecting the most suitable validation practice for use in different situations. Distributed development environment affected the process description so that clear high-level criteria for validation was required, but also enough flexibility to operate according to the specific needs of local sites. The proposed solution has been reviewed and preliminary accepted for a pilot project by the case organization.

Before the proposal can be included in the common process, the first round validation process plug-in — including practice selection and validation practices — should be tested in a pilot project to ensure its capacity. In the time of the writing this text, arrangements for the pilot project are ongoing. After the pilot project, the results and experiences should be gathered and analyzed thoroughly, and proposals for process improvement should be made. The second round validation practice selection should be also further developed based on user comments and feedback from the pilot project. The second round validation process is going to be similar to the first round validation process, but it has to be more extensive and rigorous, because after the second round validation, the decision about implementation is made.

If pilot project runs successfully, the new practices can be taken into real use in the case organization. However, improvement work should not stop even at that point, but all comments and improvement ideas from users should be gathered and analyzed, in order to fine-tune the validation process.

References

1. Sukumaran, S., Sreenivas, A., Venkatesh, R.: A rigorous approach to requirements validation. In: Proceedings of the fourth IEEE International Conference on Software Engineering and formal Methods, SEFM 2006 (2006)
2. Stevens, R., Brook, P., Jackson, K., Arnold, S.: Systems engineering – Coping with Complexity. Prentice-Hall, Englewood Cliffs (1998)
3. Lobo, O.L., Arthur, J.D.: Effective Requirements Generation: Synchronizing Early Verification and Validation, Methods and Method Selection Criteria, Virginia Tech. (2005)
4. Sommerville, I., Sawyer, P.: Requirements Engineering, A good practice quide. John Wiley & Sons, Chichester (2004)
5. Hanisch, J., Corbitt, B.: Impediments to requirements engineering during global software development. European Journal of Information Systems (2007)
6. Välimäki, A., Kääriäinen, J., Koskimies, K.: Global Software Development Patterns for Project Management. In: EuroSPI (2009)
7. Parviainen, P., Tihinen, M.: A Survey of Existing Requirements Engineering Technologies and Their Coverage. International Journal of Software Engineering and Knowledge Engineering (6), 827–850 (2007)
8. The Standish Group report CHAOS Summary (2009), http://www.standishgroup.com/newsroom/chaos_2009.php
9. Jiang, L., Eberlein, A., Far, B.H.: A case study validation of a knowledge-based approach for the selection of requirements engineering techniques. RE Journal (2008)
10. Jiang, L.: A Framework for the Requirements Engineering Process Development, Doctoral Thesis of Philosophy, University of Calgary (2005)
11. IEEE Standard 1012-2004 for Software Verification and Validation (2004)
12. Raja, U.: Empirical Studies of Requirements Validation Techniques, Blekinge Tekniska Högskole, Ronneby, Sweden. In: 2nd International Conference on Computer, Control and Communication (2009)
13. Lobo, O.L.: Analysis and Evaluation of Methods for Actibities in the Expanded Requirements Generation Model, Master's Thesis in Virginia State University (2004)
14. Requirements Tool Box, http://www.construx.com/Page.aspx?nid=204
15. Grady, J.O.: System validation and verification. CRC Press LLC, Boca Raton (1998)
16. Sutcliffe, A.: Scenario-based Requirements Engineering. RE Mini tutorial (2003)

A Software Inspection Process for Globally Distributed Teams

Deepti Mishra and Alok Mishra

Department of Computer Engineering, Atilim University,
Incek, 06836, Ankara, Turkey
deepti@atilim.edu.tr, alok@atilim.edu.tr

Abstract. Globally distributed software development is an accepted trend towards delivering high-quality software to global users at lower costs. Globally distributed software development teams particularly face communication and coordination problems due to spatial, temporal and cultural separation between team members. Ensuring quality issues in such projects is an important issue. This paper presents a software inspection process in the distributed software development towards quality assurance and management.

Keywords: Global Software Development, Distributed Software Development, Software Inspection, Tool.

1 Introduction

Software inspection is structured, collaborative and established method of ensuring quality in software engineering. Traditional inspection processes cannot be simply adapted for being included into offshore or distributed software development where, large permanent companies are replaced by temporary group of developers collaborating on projects over the internet and in this context the inspection process must be supported by web based environment [2]. The web based system facilitates support for distributed inspection in virtual environment among global software development teams. Distributed software development is a complex venture and distributed tasks have been proven to take up to 2.5 times more effort to complete than if the tasks were to have been done by co-located personnel [8].

According to Porter and Johnson [15], face-to-face meetings do not make the defect detection process significantly less effective and also supported by [9, 10] that there should be no substantial differences in efficiency between traditional and computer-supported inspections. Virtual software inspection is a process that conforms to a defined workflow and is performed in a distributed manner with the aid of an inspection tool. Tool support for software inspection evolved in 1990s and during this evolution the principles of distributed and asynchronous inspections were outlined [5]. Instead of a fixed process model, virtual inspection tools should provide capabilities for customizing the process for an individual organization or project [6]. Virtual software inspection process can include asynchronous and synchronous phases through a network but conventional face to face meetings can be included if required. The synchronous activities of inspection include discussion of correlated

R. Meersman et al. (Eds.): OTM 2010 Workshops, LNCS 6428, pp. 289–296, 2010.

faults, reaching a consensus on the faults, recording the action items, and determining the inspection's status [11]. Teleconferencing and video-conferencing tools can be used for discussion purpose among participants. Traditional face-to-face discussions suffer from a number of process losses such as air-time fragmentation, blocking, evaluation apprehension, domination and free-riding [14]. Asynchronous computer-mediated communication systems tend to promote richer discussions than face-to-face exchanges but present additional coordination challenges to team members working in this environment [1]. Although asynchronous communication could be more efficient in promoting more carefully worded comments or more balanced participation, it could be less desirable due to the difficulty of conceptually integrating divergent contributions in order to produce the expected outcome [14]. The two main asynchronous activities of software inspection are the individual reviews and the producer's (authors of documents and codes) correlation of faults [11].

An inspection tool is a software package particularly designed for inspection collaboration, and it should be capable of at least managing and delivering the inspection documentation on-line, enabling the effortless recording of defects and automatic gathering of defects [6]. The objective of inspection is to locate potential defects (faults), not correct them. On-line inspection related material reduces paperwork, makes the latest material available to participants and thus facilitates in meeting. Material used in inspection includes the target material, the inspection-criteria list (check list), individual fault lists, the merged fault list, the action-item list, and the status report [11]. The inspection information can be used for review and metrics collection to monitor the quality assurance. An inspection tool should support metrics and automate the collection, storage and analysis of the necessary data [7]. Hedberg and Lappalainen [7] further argued that to encourage process improvement, it must be possible to calculate the derived metrics automatically, and the set of metrics must be flexible enough to focus on the most important aspects of a given situation.

There are three significant aspects to be taken care of in virtual software inspection [6]:

a. **Tools that** enable efficient running of the process. Independence of time and place, on-line recording of issues and data management can be achieved through network tools.
b. **Flexibility** of the process and supporting tools to ensure tolerable adoption effort and acceptance of the method.
c. **Interoperability** of the processes and tools, to enable convenient everyday use of the method and improves the effectiveness of inspections.

The remainder of the paper is organized as follows: Section 2 presents related works of distributed software inspection tools. Section 3 describes global software inspection process. Section 4 provides details of global software inspection tool. Section 5 presents advantages and limitations of the proposed process and tool. Section 6 concludes with conclusion and future work.

2   Literature Review

In distributed software development, effective inspection process lead to increased correctness of analysis of results which is critical for success of the project. Stein et al. [16] found that distributed, asynchronous software inspection is feasible, cost effective means of collaboration for geographically distributed software development teams and suggested web-based tool Asynchronous Inspector of Software Artifacts (AISA) for such purpose. AISA was one of the first web-based software inspection tools. This is also supported by Mashayekhi et al. [11] that cost-effectiveness of inspection would be improved further by a distributed collaborative meeting environment that eliminates the need for face to face meetings. They reported Collaborative Software Inspection (CSI) project to work from separate locations. Caivano et al. [2] proposed Internet-Based Inspection System (IBIS) to support scalable and distributed software inspections. Tervonen et al. [17] introduced WiT (Web inspection Tool) towards virtual meetings and on-line recording of artefacts, checklists and other related documents. Based on the analysis of 16 tools and their experience Hedberg and Harjumaa [6] concluded that flexibility and integration are two most significant features for implementing the next generation of inspection tools. According to Harjumaa et al. [4], there are two reasons for the full utilization of inspection software being extremely challenging: the variety of the inspection material qualities, and interfaces with other development tools and procedures. In most distributed inspection tools which are based on web, web services and servers are usually very limited and kept isolated from production system for security reasons along with great deal of manual work towards control of an inspection tool [4]. Computerized software tools are the essence of the distributed software inspection process. Hedberg and Harjumaa [6] discussed the concept and features of virtual software inspections for distributed software projects and observed that document management for interoperability and mechanism for workflow control should be integral part of distributed software inspection tool. Recently, Calefato and Lanubile [3] reported about EConference - a distributed conferencing system which can be used as collaboration tool for distributed meetings.

Although this area has been studied intensively and numerous implementations exist, no tool has achieved a break-through. As distributed aspect has become more and more relevant in software development, therefore, the need for tools is now greater than ever [5]. Here, we have extended our previous work [12, 13] by including global software inspection process to provide effective means for geographically distributed work groups.

3   Global Software Inspection Process

Currently an updated and improved version of global software inspection process is used by automating the inspection and meeting processes. Various stages of global software inspection process are shown in figure 1.

The inspection process begins when entry criteria are satisfied. The main entry criterion is that the product to be inspected is complete and mature enough to be used after the defects will be removed. The author informs the software quality team leader about the completion of the product that will be inspected.

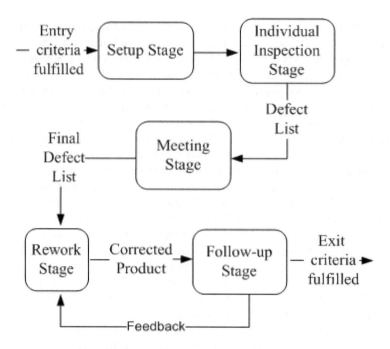

Fig. 1. Stages in Global Software Inspection Process

Setup Stage: In the setup stage, the inspection team leader selects the members of the inspection team and generates an inspection plan. Then, the document to be inspected as well as other necessary documents i.e. checklists, are uploaded on the tool by the leader. The leader can also send an email to the members regarding the details of the planned inspection that also includes their responsibility, deadlines etc., via the tool. The leader can also put an announcement consisting these details on the tool itself.

Individual Inspection Stage: Inspectors inspect the product independently with the help of checklists provided in the tool and store their comments on the web-based tool. Inspection is done according to the checklists appropriate for the inspected product, like the code review checklist, requirements inspection checklist or design review checklist. These checklists are available to inspectors in the tool. Inspectors cannot see each others comments because it may influence them. The inspection team leader can see all comments entered by every inspector.

Meeting Stage: In this stage, all inspectors, including the leader, get together to have online inspection meeting via the tool. The timing of the meeting is intimated to the team by the leader either by via e-mail or by posting an announcement. They discuss defects they have found during the individual inspection stage. These discussions help in identifying the true defects and eliminating the false defects from the defect list. Then a final defect list is made by the leader which is then emailed to the author.

Rework Stage: In this stage, the author of the product performs a rework over the materials to correct them. The author updates the product according to the final defect list and takes notes next to every defect explaining what changes have been done along with their locations.

Follow-up Stage: The inspection team leader or one of the inspectors performs a follow-up to ensure that every issue is addressed and every defect is corrected. If all defects are not removed, the product is given back to the author to correct them, so the product goes back to Rework Stage.

4 Global Software Inspection Tool

The global software inspection process was automated by developing a tool as shown in figure 2. This tool is developed with PHP, MySQL, and Apache Server. The primary elements are termed as "actors", and the processes are termed as "use cases". There are three types of actors: admin, inspection team leader, and inspectors.

Admin is an actor and the use cases of the actor are:

- Start a new inspection project
- Assign permissions for a specific project
- Revoke permissions

Leader is an actor and leader can also play the role of inspector at the same time. The use cases of the leader are:

- Assign inspectors to a new inspection project
- Upload documents for inspection including checklists etc.
- Download documents for inspection
- Add announcements for the inspection team
- Delete announcements
- The leader adds a comment for a document
- The leader deletes a comment made by him/her.
- The leader updates a comment made by him/her.
- List comments made by inspectors
- Start meeting
- Approve a comment
- Disapprove a comment
- Finish meeting
- Create log of meetings
- Create logs of approved comments
- Delete inspectors from the project
- Finish project

Inspector is an actor and the use cases of this actor are:

- Inspector downloads documents for inspection
- Inspector adds a comment for a document
- Inspector deletes a comment made by him/her.
- Inspector updates a comment made by him/her.

- Inspector enters an inspection meeting
- Create log of meetings
- Create logs of approved comments

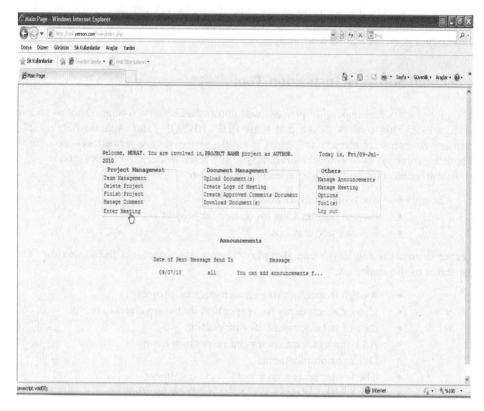

Fig. 2. global Software Inspection Tool

5 Advantages and Limitations of the Proposed Process

Some of the advantages are:

- This model is asynchronous. Inspectors inspect the product or part of the product independently without coming together at one place and send their comments via a web-based tool.
- Inspection meeting is done online through the tool without coming together physically. If an inspector can not login during the meeting time, He/she can still download the log of the meeting to know the details about the meeting.
- This inspection method is automated by developing a web-based tool so it eliminates lots of labor-intensive paperwork. Total inspection and meeting time is reduced, people resource is saved. Paper usage is reduced towards green computing.

- Due to the usage of tool in this inspection method, getting the inspection data from the past projects is easier. This data can be helpful for the estimation of time, cost and resource for inspection in future projects. Also it can be used to further improve the inspection process.
- All the checklists are available in the tool which helps inspectors in terms of efficiency and productivity.
- This inspection process includes early life cycle artifacts (for example, requirements) along with inspection of code.

The Limitations are:

- Many studies suggest that face-to-face meeting is best to find defects in complex software development problems. In the proposed process, although meeting is done online with the help of tool but, if required, face-to-face meeting can be organized.

6 Conclusion

Due to the proliferation of distributed software development, the role of virtual software inspection will be more significant in the future. Distributed software development projects can not make use of traditional methods although their communication and quality assurance needs are the same. Integration with data repositories, project and version management system will enhance the importance of software inspection. Web technology facilitates the collaborative aspects of inspection. Apart from the flexibility of the inspection meetings it also enables easy, manageable distribution of the artifacts for inspection, including the checklists and other related documents. The proposed global software inspection process with tool support has been implemented in a software organization. As a future work it is planned to compare this process and tool support with existing distributed inspection process towards further improvement.

References

1. Benbunan-Fich, R., Hiltz, S.R., Turoff, M.: A comparative content analysis of face-to-face vs. asynchronous group decision making. Decision Support Systems 34, 457–469 (2002)
2. Caivano, D., Lanubile, F., Visaggio, G.: Scaling up Distributed Software Inspection. In: Proceedings of the ICSE Workshop on Software Engineering over the Internet (2001), http://sern.ucalgary.ca/~maurer/icse2001ws/submiss
3. Calefato, F., Lanubile, F.: Using frameworks to develop a distributed conferencing system: an experience report. Softw. Pract. Exper. 39(15), 1293–1311 (2009), http://dx.doi.org/10.1002/spe.v39:15
4. Harjumaa, L., Hedberg, H., Tervonen, I.: A Path to Virtual Software Inspection. In: Proceedings of the Second Asia-Pacific Conference on Quality Software, December 10-11, p. 283. APAQS. IEEE Computer Society, Washington (2001)
5. Hedberg, H.: Introducing the Next Generation of Software Inspection Tools. In: Bomarius, F., Iida, H. (eds.) PROFES 2004. LNCS, vol. 3009, pp. 234–247. Springer, Heidelberg (2004)

6. Hedberg, H., Harjumma, L.: Virtual Software Inspections for Distributed Software Engineering Projects. In: Proceedings of ICSE International Workshop on Global Software Development (2002),
http://www.tol.oulu.fi/i3/2002/hedberg_icse_2002.pdf
7. Hedberg, H., Lappalainen, J.: A Preliminary Evaluation of Software Inspection Tools, with the DESMET Method. In: Proceedings of the Fifth International Conference on Quality Software (QSIC 2005), pp. 45–54. IEEE Computer Society, Los Alamitos (2005)
8. Herbsleb, J.D., Mockus, A.: An Empirical Study of Speed and Communication in Globally Distributed Software Development. IEEE Trans. Softw. Eng. 29(6), 481–494 (2003),
http://dx.doi.org/10.1109/TSE.2003.1205177
9. Johnson, P.M., Tjahjono, D.: Does Every Inspection Really Need a Meeting? Empirical Softw. Engg. 3(1), 9–35 (1998),
http://dx.doi.org/10.1023/A:1009787822215
10. Laitenberger, O., Dreyer, H.M.: Evaluating the Usefulness and the Ease of Use of a Web-based Inspection Data Collection Tool. In: Proceedings of the 5th international Symposium on Software Metrics, March 20-21. METRICS, p. 122. IEEE Computer Society, Washington (1998)
11. Mashayekhi, V., Drake, J.M., Tsai, W., Riedl, J.: Distributed, Collaborative Software Inspection. IEEE Softw. 10(5), 66–75 (1993),
http://dx.doi.org/10.1109/52.232404
12. Mishra, D., Mishra, A.: Simplified software inspection process in compliance with international standards. Computer Standards and Interfaces 31(4), 763–771 (2009),
http://dx.doi.org/10.1016/j.csi.2008.09.018
13. Mishra, D., Mishra, A.: An efficient software review process for small and medium enterprises. IET Software 1(4), 132–142 (2007)
14. Nunamaker, J., Dennis, A., Valacich, J., Vogel, D., George, J.: Electronic meeting systems to support group work. Communications of the ACM 34(7), 41–61 (1991)
15. Porter, A.A., Johnson, P.M.: Assessing Software Review Meetings: Results of a Comparative Analysis of Two Experimental Studies. IEEE Trans. Softw. Eng. 23(3), 129–145 (1997), http://dx.doi.org/10.1109/32.585501
16. Stein, M., Riedl, J., Harner, S.J., Mashayekhi, V.: A case study of distributed, asynchronous software inspection. In: Proceedings of the 19th international Conference on Software Engineering, ICSE 1997, Boston, Massachusetts, United States, May 17-23, pp. 107–117. ACM, New York (1997), http://doi.acm.org/10.1145/253228.253250
17. Tervonen, I., Iisakka, J., Harjumma, L.: Software Inspection- a blend of discipline and flexibility. In: Proceedings of ESCOM-ENCRESS conference, pp. 157–166 (1998)

Revisiting and Improving a Result on Integrity Preservation by Concurrent Transactions

Hendrik Decker and Francesc D. Muñoz-Escoí[*]

Instituto Tecnológico de Informática, UPV, Valencia, Spain

Abstract. We revisit a well-known result on the preservation of integrity by concurrent transactions. It says that the serializability of integrity-preserving transactions yields integrity-preserving histories. We improve it in two ways. First, we discuss divergent interpretations and restate them more precisely. Second, we make it applicable in the presence of inconsistency.

1 Introduction

Transactions in distributed information systems are bound to happen concurrently. Each transaction that involves updates may violate the integrity of stored information. We assume that integrity conditions are expressed by declarative constraints in the database schema of the information system.

Concurrent transactions usually are required to be serializable, in order to prevent anomalies that may lead to violations of integrity. The requirement of serializability is based on the well-known result that, if transactions preserve integrity when executed in isolation, then also each serializable concurrent execution of such transactions preserves integrity [8,2]. Thus, concurrency seems to be harmless, as long as each transaction is ensured to preserve integrity in isolation. However, there are two big problems with this result.

First, there are essentially two different interpretations in the literature, and it is not always clear which is meant. Both are correct, but one of them turns out to be unfair, and both are unfeasible for long histories and ad-hoc transactions.

Second, the result outsources the responsibility of ensuring the integrity preservation of a single transaction T to all preceding and concurrent transactions: If any of them doesn't make sure to preserve integrity on their part, then no guarantees for T are made. Thus, the result is not robust and in fact inapplicable if integrity violations are caused by preceding or concurrent transactions. That intolerance is unrealistic, since most information systems in practice tend to suffer from some (mostly slight) amount of inconsistency, while behaving reasonably well. As it stands, the result is unable to predict such behavior.

---

[*] Both authors are supported by ERDF and the Spanish grants TIN2009-14460-C03 and TIN2010-17193.

R. Meersman et al. (Eds.): OTM 2010 Workshops, LNCS 6428, pp. 297–306, 2010.

In section 2, we formally revisit standard notions and results of concurrency and integrity. In section 3, we propose solutions for the two problems identified above. In section 4, we address related work. In section 5, we conclude. We assume a basic familiarity with concurrency [2] and integrity [18].

2   Revisiting Concurrency and Integrity

In 2.1 and 2.2, we synthesize notions and formalizations traditionally used in the literature on transaction concurrency and data integrity. In 2.3, we recapitulate the mentioned result about the integrity preservation by concurrent transactions.

2.1   Concurrency

Drawing from [8,2,17], we introduce, in 2.1.1 - 2.1.3, our notions of 'resource' (a.k.a. 'data item'), 'fixed-time' and 'dynamic' database state, 'action' (a.k.a. 'operation'), 'transaction', 'history' (a.k.a. 'schedule') and 'serializability'. Our concurrency model does not recur on physical data items nor on fixed-time states, but on truth values of relational tuples in dynamic states of information systems.

2.1.1 Resources, States, Transactions

Throughout, we assume that a well-defined schema of the database that underlies a considered information system is always tacitly given. Also, we assume a universal language $\mathcal{L}$ by which the contents of the relational tables and the integrity constraints of a schema are described.

A *resource* (sometimes also called 'data item') is a unit of storable information accessed by transactions. As in [17], the only resources considered in this paper are the elements of the Herbrand base of $\mathcal{L}$, i.e. all facts expressible in $\mathcal{L}$.

A *state* of an information system is a mapping from the set of all resources to {*true, false*}. A state is *partial* if the mapping is partial. For a state S and a resource r, we say that the value of r is *known* in S if it is known to be either *true* or *false* in S, for which we also write $S(r) = true$ or, resp., $S(r) = false$. Otherwise, r is said to be *unknown* in S.

In [2], "the values of the data items at any one time comprise the state". We call such states *fixed-time states* ('dynamic' states are defined in 2.1.2). For convenience, we sometimes identify a fixed-time state with the point of time at which it is fixed. States are changed over time by actions.

An *action* is an atomic operation on precisely one resource, except *begin* and *end*, as defined below: *begin* acts on no resource, *end* may act on many resources.

Each action takes place at precisely one point of *system time*, which we assume to be an unbounded, linear sequence of discrete *time points*.

A *transaction* is an atomically executed, finite set of actions. (We may speak elliptically of a transaction T when in fact we mean an execution of T.) Each transaction T consists of precisely one *begin*, precisely one *end* of the form *commit* or *abort*, and a finite set of *accesses*, each of the form *read(r)* or *write(r)*, where r is a resource. The *begin* (*end*) of T is earlier (resp., later) than each access of T. The *commit* of T means that the last write to each resource written by T is confirmed. The *abort* of T means that all writes of T are undone. Two actions are said to be *conflictive* if both access the same resource and at least one of them is a *write*. Conflictive actions in T are never executed at the same time.

Distinguished fixed-time states are the states at the time a transaction T begins and, resp., ends, which we denote by S_T^b and, resp., S_T^e.

To *read* a resource r means to query if r is *true* or *false* of a given state. So, queries correspond to transactions that read the resources needed to return answers. To *write* r means to either *insert* or *delete* r, i.e., effect a state change such that r becomes *true* or, resp., *false*. For actions $read(r)$ and $write(r)$ of a transaction T, we also say that T *accesses* (*reads* or, resp., *writes*) r.

For a transaction T, let $\mathbb{C}_T$ denote the set of transactions that are concurrent with T, i.e., that execute at least one action in the interval between the begin and the end of T. In particular, $T \in \mathbb{C}_T$.

Transactions that abort are supposed to leave the database unchanged. Thus, they cannot cause a violation of integrity. So, for each transaction, we can assume that it does not abort unless its commitment would violate integrity. Other aborts, due to hardware failure, wrong input, deadlock, etc., are not considered.

2.1.2 Histories, I/O States

Informally, a history is a possibly concurrent execution of transactions, i.e., actions of several transactions may be executed at the same or interleaved points of time. Formally, a *history H* of a set of transactions $\mathbb{T}$ is a partial order of the union of all actions of all $T \in \mathbb{T}$, such that, for each $T \in \mathbb{T}$ and each pair of actions (A, A') in T such that A is before A' in T, A also is before A' in H, and conflicting actions in H are never executed at the same time. Two actions in H *conflict* if they access the same resource r and at least one of them writes r.

We may say 'T *in H*' if H is a history of a set of transactions $\mathbb{T}$ and $T \in \mathbb{T}$. For each T in H, we assume that also each $T' \in \mathbb{C}_T$ is in H, since, otherwise, scheduling may not be able to take all possible conflicts into account. Thus, histories may be arbitrarily long, particularly in systems with 24/7 services that may always be busy. Distinguished fixed-time states at which no access takes place are the states at the time of the earliest *begin* and the latest *end* in H, denoted by S_H^b and, resp., S_H^e. S_H^e is also called the *final state* of H.

For a resource r and a point of time t, the *committed value of r at t in H* is defined as the value of r as committed most recently by some T in H. Thus, for the commit time t_c of T, $t_c \leq t$ holds, and no transaction in H other than T commits r at any time in the interval $[t_c, t]$.

There are *dynamic* states that are not necessarily fixed-time, e.g., 'states seen by transactions' [8], or 'global states' [9,4]. Dynamic states consist of values of resources committed at different but related points of time in some history H.

For example, *committed states*, defined by the committed value of each resource at some time t in H, are dynamic. In general, the committed state at time t is different from the fixed-time state at t.

The dynamic states defined next, collectively called *I/O states*, are partial, since transactions usually 'see' (access) only part of the database. In 2.1.3, we use I/O states for characterizing serializability, and in 3.1 for stating precisely which state transition is meant when we discuss the integrity preservation of T.

For a transaction T and a resource r, the value of r in the *input state* S_T^i of T is the committed value of r immediately before T accesses r first. The value of r in the *output state* S_T^o of T is the value of r immediately after T accessed r last. If a resource is not accessed by T, its values in S_T^i and S_T^o remain unknown.

Clearly, $S_T^i = S_T^b$ and $S_T^o = S_T^e$ if T is executed in isolation. I/O states are dynamic, since they may not exist at any fixed point of time. In particular, S_T^i and S_T^o may be different from S_T^b or, resp., S_T^e.

For instance, a resource may be committed after the begin of T but before T accesses it first. Or, a resource, after having been accessed last by a read operation of T, may be written by some T' in $\mathbb{C}_T$ before T ends. Also, S_T^i and S_T^o are not necessarily identical to any committed state at any point of time.

For example, consider distinct resources r, r' and a history H of transactions $T0$, $T1$, $T2$ which begin at a time, then $T0$ inserts r and r' at a time and commits, then $T1$ reads r, then $T2$ deletes r and r' at a time and commits, then $T1$ reads r' and commits. Clearly, r is *true* and r' is *false* in $S_{T1}^i = S_{T1}^o$, which is not a committed state at any time of H. Yet, in general, S_T^i and S_T^o are the first and, resp., the last state 'seen by' T.

I/O states facilitate the modeling of long histories, e.g., for 24/7 applications, where the initial or terminal committed states at the time of the begin or the end of histories may be forgotten or out of sight, respectively. Also the modeling of histories with relaxed isolation requirements is easier with I/O states, since they do not necessarily coincide with committed states.

2.1.3 Serializability

The serializability of a history H (usually taken care of transparently by a module called *scheduler*) prevents anomalies (lost updates, dirty reads, unrepeatable reads) that may be caused by concurrent transactions in H [2].

A history H is *serial* if, for each pair of distinct transactions T, T' in H, the begin of T is before or after each action of T', i.e., transactions do not interleave. Intuitively, a serializable history H "has the same effect as some serial execution" of H, where the "effects of a history are the values produced by the Write operations of unaborted transactions", thus preventing that actions of concurrent transactions would "interfere, thereby leading to an inconsistent" state [2]. Anomalies are not the only possible cause of integrity violation. Thus, serializability helps to avoid some, but not all possible integrity violations.

There are several definitions of serializability in the literature [21]. The following one generalizes view serializability [2], but still ensures that, for each serializable history H, the same effects are obtained by some serial execution of H. A history H is called *serializable* if the output state of each transaction in H is the same as in some serial history H' of the transactions in H such that $S_{H'}^b = S_H^b$. For example, the history of $T0$, $T1$, $T2$ in 2.1.2 is not serializable.

In practice, less permissive but more easily computable definitions of serializability are used. Locking, time stamping or other transaction management measures may be used for implementing various forms of serializability [8,2].

2.2   Integrity

In 2.2.1 - 2.2.2, we revisit the notions of 'update', 'integrity constraint' and 'case'. The latter is fundamental for inconsistency-tolerant integrity preservation by concurrent transactions, as addressed in 3.2.2. Inconsistency tolerance guarantees that all constraints that are satisfied before a transaction remain satisfied afterward, even if some constraints are violated before.

2.2.1 Updates, Constraints, Cases

Integrity is endangered whenever an update U to be committed changes a state S to an *updated* state, which we denote by S^U.

An *update* of a state S is a bipartite set (Del, Ins) of resources such that the *deletes* in Del and the *inserts* in Ins are disjoint. S^U is defined by mapping each delete in Del to *false*, each insert in Ins to *true*, and the value of each other resource is as in S. The *writeset* W_T of a transaction T is the set of all writes w in T of the form $delete(r)$ or $insert(r)$ such that any other write of r in T is earlier than w. Let U_T denote the update corresponding to W_T.

An *integrity constraint* I (in short, *constraint*) is a sentence in L_S which states a condition that is expected to hold in each I/O state. W.l.o.g., we assume that each constraint is represented in *prenex form*, i.e., all quantifiers precede all predicates and connectors. That includes constraints in denial form [14] and prenex normal form [19]. An *integrity theory* is a set of integrity constraints.

A $\forall$-quantified variable in a constraint is called *global* if its quantifier is not preceded by any $\exists$ quantifier. For a substitution ζ of the global variables of a constraint I, a constraint of the form $I\zeta$ is called a *case* of I. Clearly, each constraint subsumes each of its cases, and each constraint is a case of itself.

If a constraint I is violated by some transaction, then often only a single case of I is violated, while all other cases of I remain satisfied. As we shall see in 3.2, cases are very useful for obtaining an inconsistency-tolerant generalization of the results in 3.1 and 3.2. It does not insist on the total integrity satisfaction of all constraints in all committed states, as opposed to traditional results.

2.2.2   Integrity Satisfaction, Violation and Preservation

For an integrity theory IC, a state S *satisfies* IC if each constraint I in IC is satisfied in S. Let $S(I) = sat$ denote that S satisfies I, and $S(I) = vio$ that S violates I. Further, let $S(IC) = sat$ denote that S satisfies IC, and $S(IC) = vio$ that S violates IC. Common synonyms for 'integrity satisfaction' and 'violation' are 'consistency' and, resp., 'inconsistency'. There are several non-equivalent definitions of integrity satisfaction and violation in the literature. A natural one, which we adopt, is to logically evaluate each constraint according to the truth values of resources in S. Thus, $S(I) = sat$ $(S(I) = vio)$ if I evaluates to *true* (resp., *false*) in D, and $S(IC) = sat$ if $S(I) = sat$ for each $I \in IC$, else $S(IC) = vio$.

For a constraint I, a transaction T is said to *preserve I in isolation* if, for each state S such that $S(I) = sat$, also $S^{U_T}(I) = sat$ holds. For an integrity theory IC, T is said to *preserve IC in isolation* if T preserves each constraint in IC

in isolation. The phrase 'in isolation' can be omitted whenever it is understood. We may also say that T *preserves integrity* when I or IC is understood.

2.3   A Well-Known Result

As already indicated, a well-known result of concurrency theory seems to provide an immediate solution to the problem stated in the introduction. We cite this result from [2]: "If each transaction preserves consistency, then every serial execution of transactions preserves consistency. This follows from the fact that each transaction leaves the information system in a consistent state for the next transaction. Since every serializable execution has the same effect as some serial execution, serializable executions preserve consistency too." In other words: if each of several transactions preserves integrity in isolation, then integrity is preserved also when these transactions are executed concurrently in a serializable history. Let us represent this by the following schematic rule:

$$isolated\ integrity\ +\ serializability\ \Rightarrow\ concurrent\ integrity \quad (*)$$

3   Improving the Predictions of (*)

We are going to assess the shortcomings of (*) as mentioned in section 1 and improve its predictions. In 3.1, we observe that the more common of two divergent interpretations of (*) unfairly ignores the committed states of transactions whose commit is not the last one in a given history. In 3.2, we argue that both interpretations of (*) are questionable for long histories and ad-hoc transactions. We then state refinements of (*) that are applicable for long histories, ad-hoc transactions, and extant integrity violations.

3.1   Divergent Interpretations

For a serializable history H the transactions of which preserve integrity in isolation, there are two valid interpretations of the conclusion of (*). One is that integrity is satisfied in S_H^e if it is satisfied in S_H^b. We call that *final-state integrity* (many authors speak of 'final state consistency', e.g., [16]). The other interpretation is that, for each transaction T in H, the transition from S_T^i to S_T^o preserves integrity. A premise of both is that S_H^b satisfies integrity. However, note that this premise may not be applicable in long histories, the beginning or end of which may be unknown or out of sight.

Final-state integrity has been investigated, e.g., in [20,15,12]. That interpretation unfairly ignores output states of transactions that commit before the last commit of H. The final-state interpretation makes no integrity guarantees for such states, although they should be trustable for applications that 'see' them.

The second meaning of (*), as identified above, is what we are after in this paper. But, which state transition is meant by asking whether a transaction T preserves or violates integrity when executed concurrently? It cannot be the transition between S_T^b and S_T^e, since each fixed-time state may be inconsistent, due to possible intermediate integrity violations by concurrent transactions. Rather, T transfers its input state S_T^i to its output state S_T^o. But, can it be said that the transition between partial states S_T^i, S_T^o preserves or violates integrity? Indeed, it can, if the values of all resources to be read for determining if integrity is preserved or violated are known. That, however, we can simply assume, since each of these resources would need to be read by, and thus known to T if T would have to cater by itself for preserving integrity in isolation. Hence, we can re-state both interpretations of (*) as follows.

Theorem 1. Let IC be an integrity theory, H a serializable history such that $S_H^b(IC) = sat$, and T a transaction in H. Further, let each transaction in H preserve IC in isolation. Then, the following holds.

a) $S_H^e(IC) = sat$, i.e., integrity is satisfied in the final state of H.

b) $S_T^o(IC) = sat$, i.e., integrity is satisfied in the output state of T. $\square$

Clearly, theorem 1a) corresponds to the first, 1b) to the second of the mentioned interpretations of (*). Note that the premises of theorem 1 also entail that each committed state at any time in H satisfies integrity, by the same argument as cited in 2.3 from [2]. Similarly, the premises of theorem 1 entail that also S_T^i satisfies integrity, since, for each resource r accessed by T, $S_T^i(r)$ is the committed value of r at the time it is accessed first by T.

3.2   Robust Integrity Guarantees for Concurrent Transactions

The preconditions of Theorem 1 are quite strong. They demand that IC be totally satisfied from the beginning of the history, and that all transactions make sure that all of IC remains satisfied. However, for obtaining desirable consistency guarantees for T, much less needs to be required.

In 3.2, Theorem 2 shows that it is not necessary, as in Theorem 1, to require integrity guarantees from any transaction that commits before T begins nor from any transaction that is concurrent with T. In 3.2.2, Theorem 3 improves Theorem 2 by abandoning the unnecessarily strict requirement that integrity be satisfied without exception at the beginning of T. Theorem 3 states that all cases of constraints in IC that are satisfied in the input state of T will remain satisfied in its output state if T preserves integrity if it were executed in isolation. Again, note that no such requirement is made for any transaction that precedes T or is concurrent with it. Thus, Theorem 3 is an unprecedented result about inconsistency-tolerant integrity preservation through concurrent transactions.

3.2.1   Independence of Preceding and Concurrent Transactions

Theorem 1 requires that integrity be satisfied in the initial state S_H^b of H. However, for a long history H, S_H^b may be out of reach, i.e., the values and hence the integrity status of S_H^b may be unknown. Moreover, 1b) requires that each transaction in H preserves integrity in isolation. That is scary, particularly in multi-user databases where different agents may issue transactions independently of each other. Hence, the guarantees of integrity preservation made for T in 1b) are betting on something that may be beyond their control. In fact, having to trust on the integrity preservation of preceding or concurrent transactions issued by other, possibly unknown agents is unacceptable.

Hence, is is desirable to relax the related premises of theorem 1, as done in the following result. Its validity is justified by the argument in [2] as cited in 2.3. It also applies to long histories in 24/7 systems. Moreover, it is independent of the preservation of integrity in isolation by transactions other than T in H.

Theorem 2. Let IC be an integrity theory, H a serializable history, and T a transaction in H such that $S_T^i(IC) = sat$ and T preserves IC in isolation. Then, $S_T^o(IC) = sat$. $\square$

The essential differences between theorems 1b) and 2 are as follows. The premise in theorem 1 that $S_H^b(IC) = sat$ is replaced by the premise in theorem 2 that $S_T^i(IC) = sat$. Thus, the initial state of H, which may be out of reach, does no longer have to be considered. Further, the premise in theorem 1 that each transaction in H preserves IC in isolation is abandoned in theorem 2. It is needed in theorem 1 in order to ensure that integrity remains satisfied from the beginning to the end of H. Theorem 2 predicts that integrity remains satisfied from the input to the output state of an arbitrary transaction T in H, and therefore does not need the abandoned premise. The conclusions are the same, but in theorem 1b), the conclusion holds for each transaction in H, in theorem 2 just for T. Thus, theorem 2 only considers the state transition effected by T. It does not depend on the integrity satisfaction in states at any time before T begins, nor on the integrity preservation by any other transaction.

3.2.2 Inconsistency-Tolerant Integrity Preservation

The premise $S_T^i(IC) = sat$ of theorem 2 effectively requires that each case in IC be satisfied in S_T^i. However, the prediction of a successful integrity preservation by T should not depend on cases that are irrelevant to U_T. Such cases may be violated by transactions that precede or are concurrent with T. More generally, it is desirable to tolerate any extant violations, even of relevant cases (e.g., of 'soft' constraints). The following result relaxes the overly exigent premise $S_T^i(IC) = sat$. Theorem 3 focuses on cases that are satisfied in S_T^i, without requiring that all of them be satisfied, as opposed to theorem 2.

Theorem 3. Let IC be an integrity theory, H a serializable history and T a transaction in H that preserves integrity in isolation. Then, for each case C in IC such that $S_T^i(C) = sat$, it follows that $S_T^o(C) = sat$.

Proof. The set of cases such that $S_T^i(C) = sat$ is an integrity theory that is satisfied in S_T^i. Hence, theorem 3 follows from theorem 2. $\square$

Theorem 3 is an *inconsistency-tolerant* result, in that it makes predictions of integrity preservation by a concurrently executed transaction T, while admitting integrity violations in S_T^i and S_T^o, even of relevant cases. In contrast to theorem 1b), already theorem 2 is inconsistency-tolerant, in a sense: as long as

$S_T^i(IC) = sat$ holds, any integrity violation in any state of H before S_T^i is immaterial. Theorem 3 goes beyond the inconsistency tolerance of theorem 2 since the former also tolerates any amount of extant violations of constraints in S_T^i.

4   Related Work

In early work [11,7,13,8,1,10], a distinction is made between integrity violations caused either by anomalies of concurrency or semantic errors. In [7,13], concurrency is not dealt with any further. In [11,8,1,10], integrity is not looked at in detail. Also in later related work, either concurrency or integrity is largely passed by, except papers that address final-state integrity (cf. 3.1), and [3,17].

In [17], it is described how to automatically augment concurrent write transactions with additional read actions for simplified integrity checking, and with locks to protect those actions, so that integrity preservation can be guaranteed for serializable executions. However, neither long histories nor ad-hoc transactions are not considered in [17].

The author of [3] observes that integrity checks are read-only actions without effect on other operations, possibly except abortions due to integrity violation. Some scheduling optimizations made possible by the unobtrusive nature of read actions for integrity checking are discussed in [3].

In none of the cited papers, inconsistency tolerance is an issue.

5   Conclusion

We have defined states 'seen by' concurrent transactions as dynamic partial states called I/O states. They typically contain unknown values than may violate integrity. Thus, an inconsistency-tolerant approach is needed. Based on I/O states, we have scrutinized, restated and generalized the classic result that integrity preserved in isolation is sufficient for preserving integrity concurrently.

The classic result is always stated informally, while our versions are more formal and lucid. Our versions also are more practical because they allow for ad-hoc transactions, long histories and the toleration of extant inconsistency.

We have only considered flat transactions. Yet, it should be interesting to study the preservation of integrity when there are read-only subtransactions. That has been already done in [6], but without much attention to concurrency. Alternatively, a concurrent, history-wide or perpetual built-in transaction could be conceived, for checking if user transactions preserve integrity. We intend to study these issues in future work. Also, we intend to take recovery issues into account, which are important for distributed systems but have not been addressed in this paper.

References

1. Bayer, R.: Integrity, Concurrency, and Recovery in Databases. In: Samelson, K. (ed.) ECI 1976. LNCS, vol. 44, pp. 79–106. Springer, Heidelberg (1976)
2. Bernstein, P., Hadzilacos, V., Goodman, N.: Concurrency Control and Recovery in Database Systems. Addison-Wesley, Reading (1987)

3. Böttcher, S.: Improving the Concurrency of Integrity Checks and Write Operations. In: Kanellakis, P.C., Abiteboul, S. (eds.) ICDT 1990. LNCS, vol. 470, pp. 259–273. Springer, Heidelberg (1990)
4. Chandy, M., Lamport, L.: Distributed Snapshots: Determining Global States of Distributed Systems. ACM TOCS 3(1), 63–75 (1985)
5. Decker, H., Martinenghi, D.: Inconsistency-tolerant Integrity Checking. To appear in Transactions of Knowledge and Data Engineering. Abstract and preprints at http://www.computer.org/portal/web/csdl/doi/10.1109/TKDE.2010.87
6. Doucet, A., Gançarski, S., León, C.: Checking Integrity Constraints in Multidatabase Systems with Nested Transactions. In: Batini, C., Giunchiglia, F., Giorgini, P., Mecella, M. (eds.) CoopIS 2001. LNCS, vol. 2172, pp. 316–328. Springer, Heidelberg (2001)
7. Eswaran, K., Chamberlin, D.: Functional Specfication of a Subsystem for Data Base Integrity. In: Proc. 1st VLDB, pp. 48–68. ACM Press, New York (1975)
8. Eswaran, K., Gray, J., Lorie, R., Traiger, I.: The Notions of Consistency and Predicate Locks in a Database System. CACM 19(11), 624–633 (1976)
9. Fischer, M., Griffeth, N., Lynch, N.: Global States of a Distributed System. IEEE-Trans. Software Eng. 8(3), 198–202 (1982)
10. Gardarin, G.: Integrity, Consistency, Concurrency, Reliability in Distributed Database Management Systems. In: Delobel, C., Litwin, W. (eds.) Distributed Databases, pp. 335–351. North-Holland, Amsterdam (1980)
11. Gray, J., Lorie, R., Putzolu, G.: Granularity of Locks in a Shared Data Base. In: Proc. 1st VLDB, pp. 428–451. ACM Press, New York (1975)
12. Grefen, P.: Combining Theory and Practice in Integrity Control: A Declarative Approach to the Specfication of a Transaction Modfication Subsystem. In: Proc. 19th VLDB, pp. 581–591. Morgan Kaufmann, San Francisco (1993)
13. Hammer, M., McLeod, D.: Semantic Integrity in a Relational Data Base System. In: Proc. 1st VLDB, pp. 25–47. ACM Press, New York (1975)
14. Kowalski, R.: Logic for Problem Solving. North-Holland, Amsterdam (1979)
15. Lilien, L., Bhargava, B.: A Scheme for Batch Verification of Integrity Assertions in a Database System. IEEE Trans. Software Eng. 10(6), 664–680 (1984)
16. Lindsay, B.: Jim Gray at IBM -The Transaction Processing Revolution. SIGMOD Record 37(2), 38–40 (2008)
17. Martinenghi, D., Christiansen, H.: Transaction Management with Integrity Checking. In: Andersen, K.V., Debenham, J., Wagner, R. (eds.) DEXA 2005. LNCS, vol. 3588, pp. 606–615. Springer, Heidelberg (2005)
18. Martinenghi, D., Christiansen, H., Decker, H.: Integrity checking and maintenance in relational and deductive databases and beyond. In: Ma, Z. (ed.) Intelligent Databases: Technologies and Applications, pp. 238–285. Idea Group, USA (2006)
19. Nicolas, J.-M.: Logic for improving integrity checking in relational data bases. Acta Informatica 18, 227–253 (1982)
20. 20. A. Silberschatz, Z. Kedem. Consistency in Hierarchical Database Systems. JACM 27(1):72-80, 1980.
21. Vidyasankar, K.: Serializability. In: Liu, L., Özu, T. (eds.) Encyclopedia of Database Systems, pp. 2626–2632. Springer, Heidelberg (2009)

Evaluation of Metaverse Server in a Widely-Distributed Environment

Mayu Matsubara and Masato Oguchi

Ochanomizu University, 2-1-1, Otsuka, Bunkyo-ku, Tokyo 112-8610, Japan

Abstract. "Metaverse" is a new service that connects users to three dimensional virtual space constructed as electronic data through the Internet, which is expected to be popular in the future. Although Metaverse is expected as a promising platform for information exchange and communication among Internet users, it has several shortcomings such as a requirement of relatively high-performance client terminals and its long response time in some cases. We have analyzed the problem of the response time from a viewpoint of load of the server in order to construct an efficient and high-performance server.

OpenSim server that provides the metaverse service as open source software has been constructed and evaluated. In this paper, we have made OpenSim server in grid mode to analyze distributed Metaverse service. We have evaluated Metaverse server performance during the phase of user login to Metaverse service and teleport from one region to another. That is to say, we have focused on a server side of Metaverse system, analyzed its behavior, and clarified the cause of its long response time.

1 Introduction

Recent years, the Internet culture led by user is pervading because broadband networks at home are spread and standard PC performance is improved. Thus, it has been strongly desired to evolve a communication and information service among users over a network. "Metaverse" discussed in this study is three dimensional space like real world constructed as electronic data through the Internet. By connecting to the space, we can enjoy more real and more easier communication.

Users are not passive but becoming active creator to information service. Therefore Metaverse service has been attracting a lot of attention. One of the most famous Metaverse service is Second Life provided by LINDEN RESERCH laboratory in US[1]. In Japan, CyberAgent has started to provide "Ameba pigg" that is becoming popular Metaverse service[2]. Other Metaverse services are also known such as IMVU[3], Moshi Monsters[4], and Meet-Me[5].

On the other hand, it needs a high spec client PC, especially high-performance graphics, in using Metaverse service[1]. Until now, although they are not spread

---

[1] Recommended hardware requirements for Second Life client viewer is that CPU is 1.5GHz or more, Main Memory is 1GB or more, and as Graphic card, Nvidia is 6700 or more and ATI is X800 or more.

R. Meersman et al. (Eds.): OTM 2010 Workshops, LNCS 6428, pp. 307–316, 2010.

more than expected in this world, According to a LINDEN RESEARCH report in March 2010, one million users login Second Life in the past one month. Region scale in Second Life and the amount of original currency in circulation are increasing. In addition, we expect that the problem of low spec of client PC will be solved before long because performance of PC is advancing rapidly.

2 Metaverse

2.1 An Overview of Metaverse

Metaverse means virtual world of three dimensional space in the Internet. Users can communicate with others by operating another human being that is called "avatar" in this space. It also provides a number of services to users by using original money available within Metaverse. For example, we can purchase or sell items(clothes, vehicle, and house), communicate within the company, and so on. Metaverse is similar to online game, although prepared goal (bring down enemies, for example) is not provided by the service, and users play according to their own purpose.

Second Life. Second Life is one of the largest Metaverse service. As the name suggests, it provides the space to enjoy "Second Life". It provides visually beautiful graphics, it is possible to make objects with smooth interface, we can purchase and sell objects we made, and change LINDEN dollar which is valid in Second Life to US dollar. However, there are differences between real world and virtual world: There is no physical constraint. Avatar can fly the sky freely, and access region around the world in a moment. LINDEN RESEARCH laboratory which provides Second Life has not opened the source code of Server Software of Second Life. However, they started to open the code of client viewer.

OpenSim. OpenSim is open-software of Metaverse server. In other words, this is platform for constructing a virtual world[6]D Since OpenSim Server is based on the client viewer of Second Life, it is possible to access from the client viewer of Second Life to OpenSim Server. That is to say, compatibility is guaranteed with Second Life Server. We can construct our own server and customize it easily, because this is open source software.

In addition, OpenSim Server can be operated at two kinds of mode; standalone mode and grid mode. With standalone mode, it is possible to construct virtual world easily. OpenSim uses common data format with Second Life. Therefore, when a lot of designers create a region of virtual space, they preview its preproduction in OpenSim operated at standalone mode. By utilizing the characteristics of standalone mode, it can be used as three dimensional presentation tool, guide at hospital and amusement park. Although standalone mode is easy for configuration, it does not have scalability.

On the other hand, grid mode is operation mode to create virtual world such as Second Life. At grid mode, by making distributed OpenSim Servers interconnect, it is possible to construct a large seamless virtual world which consists of some regions. We can move to neighbor region and teleport to distant region at this mode.

2.2   Related Research

An evaluation of client viewer in Second Life is performed in reference[7]. It reports that client has much load while Second Life is running. On the other hand, it also shows a result of simulation and numerical analysis on server side. In this research, we analyze server utilization on the basis of observation and measured results on server side while Metaverse is running.

3   Evaluation of Centralized and Distributed Metaverse Server

3.1   Experimental Environment of Centralized Metaverse Server

Metaverse is a type of client-server system. Centralized Server is a system in which servers who receive a lot of requests from clients are connected at one place. Users access to one server because data is gathered on it. Centralized Server of OpenSim is able to construct with both standalone mode and grid mode. We have constructed a server with installing OpenSim.

3.2   Experimental Environment of Distributed Metaverse Server

Distributed Server is a system in which information is connected among distributed servers. Web Server is typical example of distributed server. Distributed Server in Metaverse such as OpenSim is linked among servers. Client accesses somewhere in OpenSim Server. That is, the data client wants is somewhere in OpenSim Server. When Metaverse Server is constructed at grid mode using OpenSim0.6.8, it consists of four server modules, User Server, ROBUST Server, Messaging Server, and Region Server. These Server modules are able to run either on a single machine or multiple machines. User Server is a server which manages user(avatar). ROBUST Server is a server which manages objects, inventory of avatar, position of grid, and so on. Messaging Server is a server which handles message. Region Server is a server which manages region (meaning land, size of 256m x 256m).

Figure 1 and 2 show experimental environment of this reserach work. Figure 1 uses two server machines, one machine is constructed with User Server, ROBUST Server, Messaging Server, and Region Server. The other is constructed with only Region Server which links to other server. Servers have spec as follows; CPU is Intel Xeon 3.6GHz and 2.4GHz, Main Memory is 4GB and 512MB, OS is Fedora 12(Linux2.6.31.5), and OpenSim0.6.8. On the other hand, Figure 2 shows the case in which each server module is set on five server machines.

We have used a relatively high spec client PC. The details are CPU is Intel Pentium 4 3.0GHzCMain Memory is 2.5GB, OS is Windows XPCand graphic is Intel 82945G Express Chipset Family.

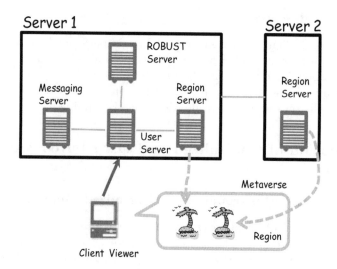

Fig. 1. 2 Distributed Metaverse Servers with 2 Server Machines

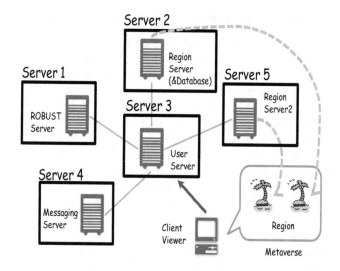

Fig. 2. 5 Distributed Metaverse Servers

4   Login Time on Centralized and Distributed Server

4.1   An Overview of Experiment

In this research work, we have measured user login time after constructing Open-Sim Server with Centralized and Distributed Server. Login time means from the time user pushes login button until OpenSim fully operates.

4.2   Result of a Measurement and Discussion

Figure 3 shows a result of a measurement. Login time of servers with different ways of construction shows that it takes about 16 seconds at standalone mode, about 18 seconds at grid mode, about 32 seconds at two distributed servers, about 31 seconds at five distributed servers.

Comparing a case of standalone mode with that of grid mode, grid mode takes a little longer time to login than standalone mode. There is not much difference between the cases of two distributed servers and the case of five distributed servers. However comparing the former two (centralized servers) with the latter two (distributed servers), they have a feature that the difference of login time is about double. These experimental results indicate that there is a difference of login time between centralized server and distributed server. However it takes too long login time in each case comparing to the case of Web. In order to make Metaverse popular, the improvement of response time is necessary. Therefore, we have analyzed the response of Metaverse server in the rest of this paper.

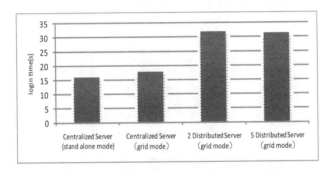

Fig. 3. Login Time of Servers with Different Construction Ways

5   Log Analysis at User Login on Distributed Server

5.1   An Overview of Experiment

In this paper, we have analyzed server log in distributed Metaverse Server when user login Metaverse, because we expect Metaverse becomes popular like Web system. That is to say, we have profiled server at user login after constructing distributed server by using OpenSim Server with grid mode. The details of the experiment is, when users login OpenSim, processing time of each server is calculated by getting logs from each server. Next, execution of all servers is sorted by time to analyze what kind of execution and how long it takes by color cording.

5.2   Process of Each Server Module

Figure 4 shows a process for accessing to server in five distributed servers (grid mode). This analysis is led by color cording of server logs after getting the logs

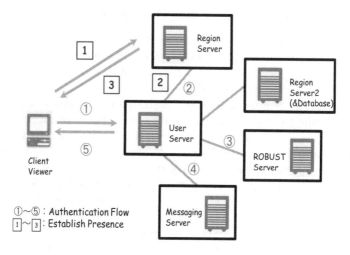

Fig. 4. Login Process in Distributed Servers

server	time	process
User1	16:55:35	16:55:35 - [LOGIN BEGIN]: XMLRPC Received login request message from user 'TEST' 'AVATAR'
User2	16:55:35	16:55:35 - [LOGIN]: XMLRPC Client is Second Life Developer 2.0.0.203055, start location is last
User3	16:55:35	16:55:35 - [LOGIN]: Telling TEST_SIM2 @ 1000,1010 (http://192.168.10.248:9000/) to prepare for client connection
ROBUST1	16:55:35	16:55:35 - [INVENTORY SERVICE]: Getting inventory skeleton for 38f6d23a-a8fe-4c9a-8532-1b5331943b40
messaging1	16:55:36	16:55:36 - [LOGIN]: User TEST AVATAR logged into region 1099511628034560 as root agent, building indexes for user
messaging2	16:55:36	16:55:36 - [MESSAGE SERVICE]: Requesting friends list for 38f6d23a-a8fe-4c9a-8532-1b5331943b40 from http://192.16
User4	16:55:36	16:55:36 - [LOGIN]: Found appearance for TEST AVATAR
User5	16:55:36	16:55:36 - [USER AUTH]: Verifying session a0eaf9a0-7834-b4d5-b067-44e58472d89b for 38f6d23a-a8fe-4c9a-8532-1b5:
User6	16:55:36	16:55:36 - [UserManager]: CheckAuthSession TRUE for user 38f6d23a-a8fe-4c9a-8532-1b5331943b40
User7	16:55:36	16:55:36 - [MSGCONNECTOR]: Sending login notice to registered message servers
User8	16:55:36	16:55:36 - [USER SERVER FRIENDS MODULE]: BEGIN XmlRpcResponseXmlRPCGetUserFriendList from 192.168.10.250:3
User9	16:55:36	16:55:36 - [USER SERVER FRIENDS MODULE]: END XmlRpcResponseXmlRPCGetUserFriendList from 192.168.10.250:382
User10	16:55:36	16:55:36 - [LOGIN]: Notified : http://192.168.10.250:8006 about user login
User11	16:55:36	16:55:36 - [LOGIN END]: XMLRPC Authentication of user TEST AVATAR successful. Sending response to client.
region1	16:55:36	16:55:36 - [CLIENT]: Told by user service to prepare for a connection from TEST AVATAR 38f6d23a-a8fe-4c9a-8532-1b5
region2	16:55:36	16:55:36 - [CONNECTION BEGIN]: Region TEST_SIM2 told of incoming root agent TEST AVATAR 38f6d23a-a8fe-4c9a-85
region3	16:55:36	16:55:36 - [OGS1 USER SERVICES]: Verifying user session for 38f6d23a-a8fe-4c9a-8532-1b5331943b40
region4	16:55:36	16:55:36 - [CONNECTION BEGIN]: User authentication returned True

Fig. 5. Log of All Servers at Grid Mode

from each server and sorting the log by time as shown in Figure 5, in reference to [8].

First, OpenSim Server executes the following procedure to authenticate an avatar.

1. Access from client to User Server (sending user name and password).
2. Access from User Server to Region Server (sending user ID to connect)
3. Access from User Server to ROBUST Server (request appearance and inventry information).
4. Access from User Server to Messaging Server (telling user login).
5. Access from User Server to Client (affirimation of session again)

With this procedure, client is authenticated and login process finishes. 22 steps are executed at this time, and it takes about 7 seconds.

Next, initialization of avatar is executed.

1. Access from client to Region Server (addind avatar to Region Server).
2. Access from Region Server to User Server (Getting friend list).
3. Access to Region Server to Client (update of avatar appearance)

28 steps are executed at this time, and it takes about 23 seconds.

Dividing these measurements into each server, execution time of each server is shown in Figure 6 and 7.

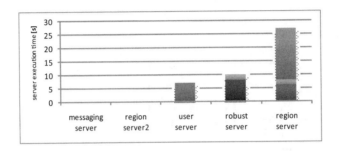

Fig. 6. Execution Time of Each Server Module at Login in 2 Distributed Metaverse Servers

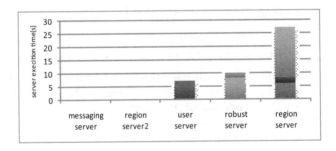

Fig. 7. Execution Time of Each Server Module at Login in 5 Distributed Metaverse Servers

5.3 Result of a Measurement and Discussion

From Figure 5, 6 and 7, the difference of login time and server process are little between the cases of 2 distributed servers and 5 distributed servers.

In order to reveal specific processes, we have analyzed the log and found that most steps take under a second and some steps take a few seconds. The step which takes long time is as follows: In specific, it takes about 6 seconds to add new queue to Region and about 19 seconds to update user appearance on Region Server. It takes about 8 seconds to get user inventory on ROBUST Server and about 7 seconds to send response for authentication to Client. That is to say, it is possible to shorten login time drastically by improving performance of these steps.

6   Evaluation of User Login on Widely Distributed Server

6.1   An Overview of Experiment

In general, distributed servers communicates in a widely distributed environment. Therefore, in this paper, Metaverse Server is not only distributed to each server module but also it is measured in a widely-distributed environment. Figure 8 shows our experiment in a widely-distributed environment. It is possible to construct by inserting a Dummynet between client or one of servers, and one way delay time changes from 0ms to 100ms.

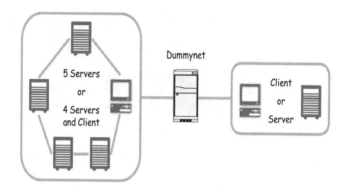

Fig. 8. Widely-Distributed Environment

6.2   Result of a Measurement and Discussion

Figure 9 shows the result of a measurement. Figure 9 indicates that it shows little change in widely-distributed environment for client and Region Server. However, User Server shows a difference about 10 seconds comparing the case of 0ms to 100ms delay. As shown by the Figure 4, it is possible to consider the reason is that User Server executes much processes.

7   Evaluation of Teleport Time in a Widely-Distributed Environment with Distributed Metaverse Server

When Metaverse is distributed like web, a large Metaverse space should be constructed in the world. In such a case, it should happen that teleport will be increased among physically distributed servers. Therefore we have evaluated the teleport time on distributed Metaverse Server.

7.1   An Overview of Experiment

As shown by the Figure 8, Dummynet is inserted between teleported region. One way delay time is changed from 0ms to 100ms, and teleport time is measured. In this measurement, we prepared three scenarios. Teleport1 is a teleport to neighbor region in Metaverse. Teleport2 is a teleport to three distant region in Metaverse. Teleport3 is a teleport to 10 distant region in Metaverse.

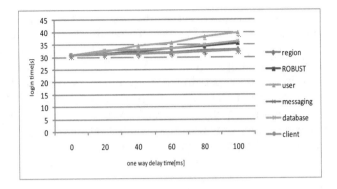

Fig. 9. Login Time in Widely-Distributed Environment in Distributed Metaverse Server

7.2   Result of a Measurement and Discussion

Figure 10 shows the result of measurement.Figure 10 shows that it has a difference of teleport time according to teleported region by comparing Teleport1 with Tereport2 and Teleport3. However, by comparing Teleport2 with Teleport3, it does not take longer teleport time when it teleports to distant region in Metaverse. Moreover, it is clarified that teleport time is affected by physical position of server machine.

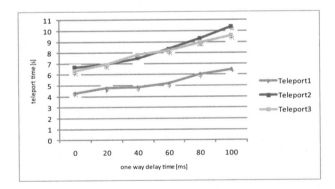

Fig. 10. Teleport Time in a Widely-Distributed Environment with Distributed Metaverse Server

8   Conclusion and Future Works

In this paper, we have constructed centralized server and distributed server using OpenSim, measured user login time to login Metaverse Service and profiled log of Metaverse Server. Moreover, we have measured login time and teleport time in a widely-distributed environment.

From these results, distributed server discussed in this paper takes about double login time than centralized server. Therefore, the construction way of distributed server is changed in the experiment, and improvement of server procedure is verified by profiling server logs. After that, by measuring login time and teleport time in a widely-distributed environment, several problems are revealed. For example, we must consider the problem of position of User Server, the problem of a region position at teleport in Metaverse, and so on. In the future, to improve each server process, we will construct more larger virtual world by increasing region, and make an experiment on it.

References

1. SecondLife, `http://jp.secondlife.com/`
2. Ameba Pigg, `http://pigg.ameba.jp/`
3. IMVU, `http://www.imvu.com/`
4. Moshi Monsters, `http://www.moshimonsters.com/`
5. Meet-Me, `http://www.meet-me.jp/`
6. OpenSimulator, `http://opensimulator.org/`
7. Kumar, S., et al.: Second Life and the New Generation of Virtual Worlds. IEEE Computer 41(9), 46–53 (2008)
8. `http://wiki.secondlife.com/wiki/Currentloginprotocols`

MONET'10 and P2PCDVE'10 – PC Co-chairs Message

The research areas of mobile technologies, social networking and mobile services applications are receiving wide interest from private and public companies as well as from academic and research institutions.

The mobile and networking technologies, the new generation of wireless local area networks and ad hoc networks are devoted to playing an important role in many areas of social activities, predominantly in those areas where having the right data at the right time is a mission-critical issue. Mobile and networking technologies for social applications serve groups of people "on the move", sharing activities and/or interests; in particular these technologies involve geographically distributed groups who are collaborating on some task in a shared context or independently from their location. By their real nature, mobile technologies can be considered multidisciplinary technologies involving social aspects; indeed, they often involve personal, group and ubiquitous issues, supporting inter-personal connections and involving human-technology interaction in different, and dispersed, contexts. Mobile technologies also play an essential role in personalizing working and interaction contexts, while supporting experimentation and innovation, and the advancement of the field is fundamental for developing social networking. Moreover, mobile technologies are the base for Collaborative Distributed Virtual Environments (CDVE) enabling geographically distant users to exchange information, communicate and collaborate. A special session of the workshop was organized on them. Social networking technologies bring friends, family members, co-workers and other social communities together. These technologies are convergent, emerging from a variety of applications such as search engines and employee evaluation routines, while running on equally diverse platforms from server clusters to wireless phone networks.

Social networking and its connection with the use of mobile devices represents one of the most relevant phenomena related to the networking technologies and their emerging problems of use, robustness, vulnerabilities to reliability and performance due to malicious attack.

The fifth International Workshop on Mobile and Networking Technologies for social applications (MONET 2010) was held in October 2010 in Hersonissou, Crete, Greece. The workshop allowed researchers, experts from academia and industry, and practitioners to discuss new mobile and networking technologies, social networking and mobile applications; this debate has represented a stimulus to identify challenging problems in the social applications of those technologies and to show results and experiences connected with social networking, business applications and, mobile applications and services. This year, after a rigorous review process, seven papers were accepted for inclusion in the conference proceedings related with the following issues:'

R. Meersman et al. (Eds.): OTM 2010 Workshops, LNCS 6428, pp. 317–318, 2010.

- Improving Social Networking: service-oriented architectures, location-based services, and multimodality;
- P2P- Collaborative Distributed Virtual Environments (CDVE);
- Applicative Issues and Solutions in Networking and Mobile Applications.

The success of the MONET 2010 workshop would not have been possible without the contribution of the OTM 2010 workshops organizers, PC members and authors of papers, all of whom we would like to sincerely thank.

August 2010

Fernando Ferri
Patrizia Grifoni
Irina Kondratova
Arianna D'Ulizia
Laura Ricci
MONET'10

Service-Oriented Communities: Visions and Contributions towards Social Organizations

Vincenzo De Florio and Chris Blondia

University of Antwerp,
Department of Mathematics and Computer Science,
Performance Analysis of Telecommunication Systems group,
1 Middelheimlaan, 2020 Antwerp, Belgium
Interdisciplinary Institute for Broadband Technology,
8 Gaston Crommenlaan, 9050 Ghent-Ledeberg, Belgium

Abstract. With the increase of the populations, resources are becoming scarcer, and a smarter way to make use of them becomes a vital necessity of our societies. On the other hand, resource management is traditionally carried out through well established organizations, policies, and regulations that are often considered as impossible to restructure. Our position is that merely expanding the traditional approaches might not be enough. Systems must be radically rethought in order to achieve a truly effective and rational use of the available resources. Classical concepts such as demand and supply need to be rethought as well, as they operate artificial classifications that limit the true potential of systems and organizations. Here we propose our vision to future, "smarter" systems able to overcome the limitations of the status quo. An example of such systems is the social organization that we call Service-oriented Community, which we briefly describe. We believe that such organizations—in heterarchical coexistence with traditional systems—provide the features necessary to prevent societal lock-ins like the ones we are experiencing in assisting our elderly ones.

1 Introduction

With the increase of the human population, resources are becoming scarcer, and a smarter way to make use of them becomes a vital necessity if we want to get rid of or at least postpone unmanageability and chaotic behaviours. Assistance of the elderly population is a typical example: The share of the total population older than 65 is constantly increasing worldwide [1,2], while the current organizations still provide assistance in a non-efficient, inflexible way. Though effective when the context was different and a large amount of resources was available to treat a smaller demand, this approach is now becoming too expensive and thus unacceptable. Merely expanding the current organizations without properly restructuring them is simply not working anymore.

R. Meersman et al. (Eds.): OTM 2010 Workshops, LNCS 6428, pp. 319–328, 2010.

As remarked already in [3], another case of this "syndrome" can be found in other domains as well, e.g. in network software engineering. Let us consider the software principle of layered design—dealing with the problem of an ever growing design complexity by decomposing functionality into specialized layers. This strategy proved very effective in the infancy of the Internet, when hosts where limited in number and static in nature. The current scenario of a predominantly mobile Internet pervading all aspects of human society including goods and environments brought about new unprecedented requirements that are hardly compatible with the current needs for flexibility, adaptability, and personalized behavior. The extra performance granted by technology improvements is often wasted or under-utilized if we do not restructure the software architectures they are embedded into.

Business entities and even societies are no exception to this trend. Indeed, often such systems were built under similar "relaxed" conditions—market and demographic contexts that were much less stringent than the current ones. It is then no surprise that, even though ever increasing amounts of resources are being pumped up into these organizations, still they experience congestion and at times fail to meet their expected quality of service.

A thorough analysis of the reasons behind these inefficient organizations is beyond the scope of this text; what we would like to remark here is that one of the factors that most likely play an important role here is that of the so-called "lock-in", defined by Stark as "the process whereby early successes can pave the path for further investments of new resources that eventually lock in to suboptimal outcomes" [4]. When applied to society and its organizational structures, lock-ins represent the loss of the ability to rethink or at least revise well established services such as health-care. Interestingly enough, Stark refers to this ability as *adaptability*. A system (be it e.g. a computer system, or a business entity, or a societal service) is called by Stark adaptable when it is able to actuate "ongoing reconfigurations of organizational assets". Lock-ins are the result of a loss of adaptability, that is the loss of the ability to *innovate* (evolve, best-fit etc.) *through recombination* [5].

In what follows we propose our vision to future, "smarter" systems able to overcome the limitations of the status quo. Our position is that such systems require what Boulding called "gestalts" [6], namely concepts able to "directing research towards the gaps which they reveal". In this paper we elaborate on this and show how such gestalts can pave the way towards novel reformulations of traditional services able to reach a better and more sensible management of the available resources and cope with their scarcity. A way to achieve this is also briefly sketched as a generalization of our concept of a "mutual assistance community" [7], which we called Service-oriented Community.

The structure of this paper is as follows: First in Sect. 2 we briefly recall the design of our first mutual assistance community. Section 3 discusses guidelines, conceptual tools, and hypotheses of such socio-technical systems. Next, in Sect. 4, we briefly introduce our Service-oriented Community and show how this may be

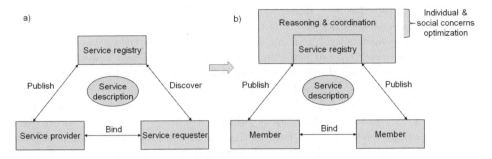

Fig. 1. In a), the classical service-oriented model is recalled. In b), a simplified representation of the MAC model is displayed.

considered as an example of what Boulding calls a social organization [6]. Finally in Sect. 5 we draw our conclusions.

2 An Exercise in Innovation Through Recombination: The Mutual Assistance Community

What we call the mutual assistance community (MAC) is a service-oriented architecture [8] coupling services provided by smart devices with services supplied by human beings into an alternative organization for AAL services. Semantically annotated services and requests for services are published into a service registry (the coordination center) and trigger semantic discoveries of optimal responses. Such responses are constructed making use of the available resources and of the available context knowledge so as to optimize both individual and social concerns. Figure 1 summarizes the peculiar differences between the classical service-oriented model and that of our MAC. A detailed description of the MAC may be found in [7].

The key idea behind MAC is that, in order to find an effective and also cost-effective solution to big societal problems such as those addressed by AAL, the whole of society must be included in the picture. When considering most of the available approaches to AAL (as surveyed e.g. in [9]), one may observe that a common aspect is often that people are divided into classes, e.g. primary users (the elderly people themselves), secondary users (carers) and tertiary users (society at large). This artificial classification limits the effectiveness of optimally recombining the available assets into an effective and timely response to requests for assistance. Furthermore, this classification into an active part of society, able to contribute with worthy services, and a "passive" part only on the receiving side is already a source of discomfort for people that are thus brought to feel they were *once* part of a society that now confines them to a lesser state and dignity. Trying to reach emerging behaviours such as so-called e-Inclusion [10] starting from assumptions such as these is probably not the best course of action. When designing the MAC we started from a different, more peer-to-peer approach in which people—be them elderly or otherwise—are just members of a community—for instance the citizens of a small village or the people who subscribed to a gym course. Members are *diverse*, and this translates into a rich variety of services. Diversity of course implies here different know-hows (e.g. those of a general practitioner, or of a gardener, or of a retired professor of biology), different policies in providing their services (e.g. well defined time schedule and associated costs, or dynamically varying availability to provide free-of-charge services as occasional informal carers), different value systems, and so on. Another important characteristic here is that members are not "stationary" but *mobile*: They would "wander around" getting dynamically closer to or farther from other members. When a request for assistance is issued, a response can be orchestrated by considering the available members, their competence, their availability, and their location with respect to the requester. A key aspect here is the ability to reason in an intelligent way about the nature of the requests and that of the available assets. Unravelling analogies through semantic reasoning [11] promotes both a higher level of resource utilization and a stronger degree of e-Inclusion [12].

In a nutshell, our MAC is a socio-technical system in which AAL services (human or otherwise) can be queried, located and dynamically orchestrated. In a MAC, elderly people would not always be passive receivers of care and assistance, but occasionally they could play active roles. As an example, if member A feels lonely and wants to have a walk with someone, while member B feels like having some physical exercise with someone, then the MAC is able to capture the semantic similarities of those requests and realize that B could be the care giver of A and vice-versa—through the so-called "participant" model [12] of our system. Societal resources can then be spared, at the same time also preserving human dignity. Simulation [13] indicates that systems such as this— able that is to intelligently exploit the dynamically available resources—have the potential to reduce significantly societal costs at the same time increasing

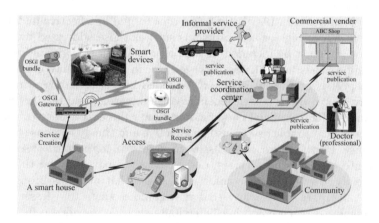

Fig. 2. Representation of our prototypic OSGi-based implementation of a Mutual Assistance Community [7]

efficiency, manageability, and e-Inclusion. Evidence of the widespread of such ideas can be found also in the text of the third call of the European AAL Joint Programme [14], whose main focus is on "solutions for advancement of older persons' independence and participation in the *self-serve society*".

Figure 2 sketches our prototypic implementation of the MAC based on the OSGi middleware.

3   On Reflection

In what follows we provide our reflections on two issues: What guidelines and tools are most needed when trying to devise adaptable organizations? And what are the necessary underlying hypotheses of organizations such as our MAC?

3.1   Conceptual Tools and Design Guidelines

As already stated, we refer to our MAC as an exercise in the above mentioned "innovation through recombination": No new assets are on purpose devised in our community; instead, a new organization of already existing assets is proposed where the inherent potentials of our societies (mobility, diversity, density, etc.) are exploited in a different way to the benefit of society itself.

What are the main lessons we can derive from our exercise? How can we generalize it and use it as a model to tackle the problem of other societal lock-ins? We found an insightful guideline to answer these questions in the work of Kenneth Boulding and especially in his classical paper [6]. In such a relatively short text we found a number of important concepts that reverberate throughout our overall research experience. In particular, Boulding provides his interpretation of General Systems Theory as a unitary conceptual framework in which "to point out similarities in the theoretical constructions of different disciplines, where these exist, and to develop theoretical models having applicability to at least two different fields of study". Being able to capture the similarities in the theoretical construction of two or more disciplines allows the theorist (or the designer) to identify what Boulding calls a "gestalt": Concepts that are devised in the framework of a specific discipline but can find a direct application or a direct analogue in another discipline. Gestalts are greatly important: As disciplines in general evolve at different paces, identifying gestalts in related disciplines permits to direct research towards gaps or local minimums. In our experience, gestalts also allow *lock-ins* to be identified and provide practical guidelines to treat them.

As an example, the concept of *feedback loop* is a gestalt that can be identified in as different a discipline as cybernetics, biology, control theory, computer architectures, and social science [15]. Organizations that are based on or make use of feedback loops are able e.g. to structure their function in accordance with a subset of the current endogenous and exogenous conditions—that is, a subset of the current *context*[1]. Such subset represents a choice of context variables that

---

[1] Context is defined in [16] as "any information that characterizes a situation related to the interaction between humans, applications and the surrounding environment."

are deemed as "sensible enough" to steer optimally the function of the system. Another important aspect in these context-aware organizations is the type and quality of the response they can provide.

It is again Boulding's cited paper that provides us with a detailed analysis of classes of context-aware organizations. The bottom level of Boulding's classification is given by so-called "frameworks" and "clockworks". Such systems have a "predetermined, necessary motion" [6] that is they are quasi context-agnostic. Next level is the one of "thermostats," or systems that "move to the maintenance of any given equilibrium, *within limits*" [6]. Such systems focus on a very limited set of context variables and ignore all the rest, exactly as a thermostat does with any variable other than monitored temperature. The only response they can exhibit is also intended to affect that same variable only. Continuing his classification, Boulding proposes other organizations ("cells", "plants", and "animals"), each of which is characterized by a more sophisticated degree of feedback loops, with a larger amount and quality of sensory and actuation apparatuses. It is only with the level of "human beings" and especially with that of "*social organizations*" that systems are able to introspect, analyze and locate their limiting factors—that is, their **lock-ins**—and to some extent can learn how to reconfigure and reshape themselves so as to face a dynamically varying set of environmental conditions. In other words, at this level Boulding introduces Stark's adaptability. Our conjecture is that this is the feature we need to seed or steer in our organizations in order to let them face unprecedented harsh conditions such as the ones our society are experiencing today. Thanks to the generality of this gestalt, we have been able to apply successfully this concept to two different contexts: The mutual assistance community described in Sect. 2 and a software framework called ACCADA [17]. In the former, the subset of context variables and actuation actions was extended so as to include both technological and social aspects and services. The latter case is an attempt to encode the reconfiguration capability into the feedback loop process itself so as to create truly adaptable component-based software architectures.

3.2   Underlying Hypotheses

A key aspect in the effectiveness of our scheme is that members of our communities must be successfully motivated to use the service and to offer their own services—our studies show that the more this happens, the more the general welfare of the system increases [12]. From this we derive two main "lessons": First, that systems such as these must be designed so as to adaptively restructure themselves according to each and every user. This adaptive personalization would allow to overcome "usability barriers" such as the so-called "grey digital divide" [18] and foster the participation of the greater part of society. Secondly, we observe how another important key to a successful spread of a heterarchical system such as our MAC calls for an overturn of social negative values. Unfortunately, often a clash exists between this need and those social techniques and trends that favor personal profit over the public interest [19,20,21]. This model's indiscriminate use of negative values to manufacture consent is often used even in politics (stir social division, draw fake enemies, fight diversity etc.) and results in the widespread loss, embezzlement, or misuse of a sort of "Social Energy"—*viz.*, the self-serve, self-organization, and self-adaptability potentials of our societies.

4 Extending the Concept: Service-Oriented Communities

As already remarked, effective adaptable organizations are characterized by an "ongoing reconfiguration of organizational assets". When trying to design socio-technical systems such as our MAC an important requirement is then the ability to reorganize dynamically a set of computer-based and human-based services. Service orientation [22] becomes *the* privileged choice to designing complex adaptive systems, its main characteristic being a set of well-defined, standard-regulated policies to recombine loosely coupled atomic functionality. In recent years such functionality were extended so as to include human-based services [23,24,25].

It does not come as a surprise, then, how such *gestalt* is being successfully applied to several and seemingly unrelated domains. The organization presented in Sect. 2 is indeed just another example of service-oriented architecture, in this case applied to AAL. A similar example is given by openAAL [26]—an open source service-oriented middleware also addressing ambient-assisted living.

Our question here is: Would it be possible to extend an organization such as our MAC to other socio-technical domains? Would it make sense? What would be the societal returns in so doing?

To provide our answer to such questions let us begin by introducing a real-life case, given by the Belgian enterprise Cambio (www.cambio.be). Cambio (and possibly other similar enterprises) provide simple car renting services to their clients. Unlike other big players in car renting, Cambio allows cars to be rented with shorter notice and for reduced durations and rates, thus fine-tuning the traditional concept of renting a car. Obviously this concept could be further extended with e.g. intelligent car sharing policies: Instead of just renting one car to one person, the system could reason about incoming requests such as "user u needs to leave from source S and reach destination D within time t" and try to build up an optimal schedule that match several criteria. Meaningful explicit criteria could include cost, number of hops, speed, reliability, and so on. Implicitly, such system would also have an effect on important social matters, such as pollution from fuel combustion, traffic congestion, road dimensioning requirements, intermediate consumption [27], et caetera. Note that no new resource would be especially required to provide such services—which actually were already common at the beginning of last century when people used to advertise for a traveling companion to share expenses [28]. A novel organization based on service orientation, custom semantic reasoning, and proper human computer interaction devices, could provide the necessary socio-technical foundation for such a service.

It is our conviction that an organization such as our MAC could be easily tailored towards such new service context. Moreover we believe that several other classes of services could be supplied by tailored MAC's. Should our conjecture prove true, then it would be possible to conceive a sort of multi-purpose system where devices and human beings with different capabilities, competence, and information could be optimally orchestrated to devise intelligent responses to situations ranging from a stroke to a earthquake or a fire, or to needs such as connecting people together to share knowledge or collaboratively achieve a common goal. Such "service-oriented community" would make use of a higher level feedback loop to reorganize itself and its services to better match the current context—from both a personal and a general, societal perspective. Our ACCADA middleware [17] could be used to set up such "meta-adaptive" loop.

5   Conclusions

Currently resource management is mostly carried out through traditional, well established organizations, policies, and regulations that are often regarded as immutable to the point that any restructuring is considered as unthinkable or even dangerous. The current trend to deal with this problem is to complement the existing systems with other "compatible" approaches based e.g. on information and communication technology. One such approach is given by the use of smart devices and houses for elderly people. Our position in this paper is that merely *complementing* the traditional approaches be not enough. We believe that systems and their ecosystems must be radically *rethought* if we want them to achieve a truly effective and rational use of the available resources. Concepts such as demand and supply, as well as roles such as producer and consumer, need to be thoroughly revised too, as their artificial classifications prevent systems and organization to achieve their true potential. The peer-to-peer "participant" model [12] of our model provides a concrete example of this, removing when possible the unnecessary distinction between care-givers and patients.

In this paper we have proposed our vision to future, "smarter" systems able to overcome the limitations of the status quo. Such systems require what Boulding called *gestalt*, namely concepts able to "directing research towards the gaps which they reveal". In this text we elaborated on this and showed how such gestalts can pave the way towards novel reformulations of traditional services that are able to exhibit a better and more sensible management of the available resources and to cope with their scarcity. Our vision of a Service-oriented Community was also introduced as a generalization of our concept of a Mutual Assistance Community. We believe that such communities—in heterarchical coexistence with traditional systems—provide the necessary diversity and innovation orientation to prevent societal lock-ins such as the ones we are experiencing today in assisting our elderly ones.

Our position is that the traditional, hierarchical model of governmental- or enterprise-driven and -regulated services could be replaced by a more "heterarchical" view [4,29] of concurrent providers based on different approaches and possibly different values and missions. Such a new model would allow our societies to function as Boulding's social organizations, in which "the unit [...] is not perhaps the person but the *role*—that part of the person which is concerned with the organization or situation in question. Social organizations might be defined as a set of roles tied together with channels of communication" [6]. A dynamic management of such roles—as foreseen in our vision of a service-oriented community and promised by recent trends and emerging concepts such as Web 3.0 and the Internet of Services—is possibly a necessary condition towards turning our societies into effective social organizations.

Finally, we would like to highlight how preliminary experiments and common sense suggest that another important prerequisite to truly reaching this highly ambitious goal is learning how to channel the potential of our "Social Energy" to the true benefit of society itself.

Acknowledgments

We like to acknowledge how several of the key ideas discussed in here are the result of many discussions with M. Tiziana Bianco. Also our gratitude goes to Hong Sun and Ning Gui, with whom we carried out several of the research activities discussed in this paper [7,9,12,13,17,30], as well as to our reviewers for their useful suggestions.

References

1. Eurostat: ECHP UDB manual. European Community Household Panel Longitudinal Users' Database. Technical report, Eurostat, Luxembourg (July 2004)
2. Goulding, M.R.: Public health and aging: Trends in aging — United States and worldwide (morbidity and mortality weekly report). Technical report, Centers for Disease Control and Prevention (2003)
3. De Florio, V., Blondia, C.: On the requirements of new software development. International Journal of Business Intelligence and Data Mining 3(3) (2008)
4. Stark, D.C.: Heterarchy: Distributing Authority and Organizing Diversity. In: Clippinger III, J.H. (ed.) The Biology of Business: Decoding the Natural Laws of Enterprise, pp. 153–179. Jossey-Bass, San Francisco (1999)
5. Holland, J.H.: Hidden Order: How Adaptation Builds Complexity. Addison-Wesley, Reading (1995)
6. Boulding, K.: General systems theory—the skeleton of science. Management Science 2(3) (April 1956)
7. Sun, H., De Florio, V., Gui, N., Blondia, C.: The missing ones: Key ingredients towards effective ambient assisted living systems. Journal of Ambient Intelligence and Smart Environments 2(2) (Apri 2010)
8. Erl, T.: Service-oriented Architecture: Concepts, Technology, and Design. Prentice Hall, Upper Saddle River (2005)
9. Sun, H., De Florio, V., Gui, N., Blondia, C.: Promises and challenges of ambient assisted living systems. In: Proc. of the 6th International Conference on Information Technology: New Generations, ITNG 2009 (April 2009)
10. Wikipedia: E-inclusion, http://en.wikipedia.org/wiki/EInclusion
11. Blanco-Fernandez, Y., et al.: Semantic reasoning: a path to new possibilities of personalization. In: Bechhofer, S., Hauswirth, M., Hoffmann, J., Koubarakis, M. (eds.) ESWC 2008. LNCS, vol. 5021, pp. 720–735. Springer, Heidelberg (2008)

12. Sun, H., et al.: Participant: A new concept for optimally assisting the elder people. In: Proc. of the 20th IEEE International Symposium on Computer-Based Medical Systems (CBMS-2007), Maribor, Slovenia (June 2007)
13. Sun, H., De Florio, V., Blondia, C.: A design tool to reason about ambient assisted living systems. In: Jinan, P.R. (ed.) Proceedings of the International Conference on Intelligent Systems Design and Applications (ISDA 2006), China (October 2006)
14. Anonymous: Call 3 for proposals to the ambient assisted living joint programme (April 2010), http://www.aal-europe.eu/calls/aal-call-3-2010/call-3-full-text-with-eligibilty-criteria-5-ed-10-vi.2010
15. Van Roy, P.: Self management and the future of software design. Electronic Notes in Theoretical Computer Science 182 (June 2007)
16. Dey, A.K., Abowd, G.D., Salber, D.: A conceptual framework and a toolkit for supporting the rapid prototyping of context-aware applications. Human-Computer Interaction 16(2), 97–166 (2001)
17. Gui, N., De Florio, V., Sun, H., Blondia, C.: ACCADA: A framework for continuous context-aware deployment and adaptation. In: Guerraoui, R., Petit, F. (eds.) SSS 2009. LNCS, vol. 5873, pp. 325–340. Springer, Heidelberg (2009)
18. Millward, P.: The "grey digital divide": Perception, exclusion and barrier of access to the internet for older people. First Monday 8(7) (July 2003)
19. Herman, E.S., Chomsky, N.: Manufacturing Consent: The Political Economy of the Mass Media. Pantheon Books, New York (1988)
20. Chomsky, N.: Media Control, The Spectacular Achievements of Propaganda. Seven Stories Press (2002)
21. Mullen, A., Herman, E.S., Chomsky, N.: The propaganda model after 20 years: Interview with Edward S. Herman and Noam Chomsky. Westminster Papers in Communication and Culture 6(2) (2009)
22. Allen, P.: Service orientation, winning strategies and best practices. Cambridge University Press, Cambridge (2006)
23. Agrawal, A., et al.: WS-BPEL Extension for People (BPEL4People) v1.0 (2007)
24. Agrawal, A., et al.: Web Services Human Task (WS-HumanTask), v1.0 (2007)
25. Schall, D., Truong, H.L., Dustdar, S.: On unifying human and software services for ad-hoc and process-centric collaboration. IEEE Internet Computing 12(3) (2008)
26. Wolf, P. et al.: OpenAAL — the open source middleware for ambient-assisted living. In: AALIANCE Conference, Malaga, Spain, March 11-12 (2010)
27. United Nations Statistics Division: SNA table of contents — vi. the production account (1993), http://unstats.un.org/unsd/sna1993/tocLev8.asp?L1=6\&L2=8
28. The Internet Movie Database: Going Bye-bye! http://www.imdb.com/title/tt0025185
29. Rocha, L.M.: Adaptive webs for heterarchies with diverse communities of users. In: Proc. of the Workshop From Intelligent Networks to the Global Brain: Evolutionary Social Organization through Knowledge Technology, Brussels (July 2001)
30. Gui, N., et al.: A service-oriented infrastructure approach for mutual assistance communities. In: Proc. of the First IEEE WoWMoM Workshop on Adaptive and DependAble Mission- and bUsiness-critical mobile Systems (ADAMUS 2007), Helsinki, Finland (June 2007)

SpotAFriendNow:
Social Interaction through
Location-Based Social Networks

Bibi van den Berg and Martin Pekarek

Tilburg University,
Tilburg Institute for Law, Technology and Society
P.O. Box 90153, 5000 LE Tilburg, The Netherlands
http://www.tilburguniversity.nl/faculties/law/research/tilt/

Abstract. Location-based social networks – or 'SpotAFriendNow applications', as we call them – are currently undergoing tremendous growth. These mobile Internet applications combine geographic or locational data with social network functionalities. To date, researchers have extensively discussed two trends in network and mobile technologies over the last decades: (1) the virtualization of our social interactions in everyday life; (2) the ongoing individualization and the anti-social nature of mobile communication. We argue that SpotAFriendNow applications can be understood as an interesting response to these two trends. First, since these applications base their behaviors on the user's bodily location in the real world, the physical is returned to the equation in technologically mediated social interactions. Second, SpotAFriendNow applications enable individuals to connect with (unknown) others in their physical proximity, thereby facilitating what we call '*ad hoc intimacy*', and thus countering the ongoing trend of hyper-individualization enabled by (mobile) technologies.

Keywords: location-based services, social network sites, SpotAFriendNow, virtualization, sociality, mobile technologies.

1 Introduction

In recent years millions of computer users worldwide have turned to the blossoming realm of *social network sites* on the Internet – domains such as Facebook, Friendster and LinkedIn, in which users create a personal profile to present themselves to others, and engage in contact with those they mark as their connections, i.e. friends, colleagues, family members, old schoolmates and so on and so forth [1]. Many social network sites have also started offering their functionality for mobile Internet use. Facebook and LinkedIn are examples in case. These mobile social network applications enable users to communicate their whereabouts and activities to their network in real time using their mobile phones or PDAs, thereby greatly increasing the dynamics of the platform.

R. Meersman et al. (Eds.): OTM 2010 Workshops, LNCS 6428, pp. 329–338, 2010.

One of the interesting phenomena that have emerged in recent years is what we label '*SpotAFriendNow applications*': mobile Internet applications that combine geographic or locational data with social network functionalities. These applications use a map as their main interface, on which the user's location is visualized. The map also shows where other members of the same service are located – ranging from one's direct physical proximity to entire continents, depending on how far one chooses to zoom in or out. By clicking on the icon of other people on the map the user can make contact with them, for instance through instant messaging or a voice connection. All SpotAFriendNow applications offer the possibility of marking other users as 'friends', a functionality similar to that of social network sites.

The emergence of SpotAFriendNow applications raises a variety of interesting questions regarding the changes brought about by mobile technology in social interaction and the construction and maintenance of social networks. In this article we will start with a brief overview of SpotAFriendNow applications, and describe their key characteristics and functionalities. After that we will analyze what is new in these applications when compared to other location-based services and to regular social network sites.

2   SpotAFriendNow Applications: An Overview

In recent years a new kind of application has started to appear for mobile phones and PDAs, which we call *SpotAFriendNow applications*. In these applications social network site facilities are mixed with real-world location information. Generally, individuals may use these kinds of applications for one of two goals: (1) finding members of the same network (possibly but not necessarily existing contacts) within the user's physical vicinity, to connect with or even to meet; or (2) finding out where existing contacts find themselves on the entire globe. While the former focuses on the physical *nearness* of existing and possible new contacts, the latter provides information regarding the '*whereness*' of existing contacts. Note that both of these goals are captured in the term 'SpotAFriendNow': one can use these applications to 'spot' other members of the same service in one's physical proximity, contact them and perhaps even add them to one's list of contacts as a new friend, but one can also use it to find out in which 'spot' existing contacts are physically located. The 'now' in SpotAFriendNow points towards its real-time character.

SpotAFriendNow applications have recently truly started blossoming, or even mushrooming indeed. ABI Research, a research company specializing in investigating emerging technologies, reports that in 2008 the number of subscribers to handset-hosted location-based services (LBS) increased to more than 18 million. In terms of total subscribers, mobile-based navigation services are still the most popular, but two other application areas – enterprise and community (including social networking) – posted the highest year-to-year growth rates [2]. In a more recent study, Gartner Inc., another information technology research company, forecasts a growth of subscribers to location-based services from 41 million US dollar in 2008 to 95.7 million US dollar in 2009, while revenue is anticipated to increase from 998.3 million US dollar in 2008 to 2.2 billion US dollar in 2009 [3]. Although the figures of these studies vary by a sizable margin, they both indicate a large uptake of mobile location-based services. In yet another research report, ABI Research focuses specifically on SpotAFriendNow applications, thus concentrating on a specific area of the mobile location-based services industry. It forecasts that the use of location-based mobile social networking applications, or what we have called SpotAFriendNow applications in this article, will continue to expand worldwide and calculates that in all likelihood there will be more than 82 million subscriptions by 2013 [4].

One of the most obvious questions to ask is why these location-based social network services have suddenly gained such popularity. In the rest of this article we attempt to provide some answers to this question. The easiest and most obvious answer would be, of course, that the *technological requirements* for the widespread use of SpotAFriendNow applications have been met to such an extent that a tipping point for their dissemination on a grand scale seems straightforward. An increasing percentage of mobile phones has access to mobile (3G) Internet, and the speed of mobile Internet is steadily increasing. More and more users include mobile Internet use in their subscription. Moreover, mobile phones are increasingly equipped with GPS or other 'locative technologies', which, as we have argued above, is an enabling backbone for SpotAFriendNow applications. But there is more to the rising popularity of SpotAFriendNow applications than merely having the technical infrastructure in place. After all, users must want to use these applications, and use them quite extensively, for the phenomenon to actually take flight. In the rest of this article we will discuss two key characteristics of SpotAFriendNow applications, and show in which ways they contribute to the rising popularity of these new applications.

3   Hybrid Space and the Return of the Physical

Over the past decade various social scientists and philosophers studying the impact of modern information and communication technologies on social interactions and behavior patterns in everyday life have pointed towards the fact that *place* and *time* have become less relevant as categories of experience because of the characteristics of these technologies [5,6,7,8,9,10,11]. Information travels across the world almost instantaneously, thereby obliterating the relevance of place/space, time and time differences. Geographer David Harvey has labeled this phenomenon *time-space compression* [12]. Since more and more people spend an increasing part of their lives using information and communication technologies, one could argue that our lives have become progressively more 'virtualized'. Some would even argue that a larger part of our (social) lives now takes place in virtual worlds than in the physical world that we still inhabit with our bodies, if not with our networked, forever-in-contact minds. The advent of mobile technologies has further increased this 'migration to cyberspace'. Nowadays, it literally does not matter anymore where you are, because mobile phones and laptop computers enable you to surf the web, look up information, use entertainment services and be in touch with whomever you choose wherever you are – as long as the others are plugged into the network as well. Barry Wellman has famously argued that with the rise of network and especially of mobile technologies '[t]*he person has become the portal*' [13]. He writes:

> ...mobile phones afford a fundamental liberation from place... [...] Their use shifts community ties from linking people-in-places to linking people wherever they are. Because the connection is to the person and not to the place, it shifts the dynamics of connectivity from places [...] to individuals [13].

Now, we do not aim to contest the validity of this claim per se – mobile technology use does, in fact, remove the relevance of one's physical place as a key parameter in many of the kinds of interactions these technologies afford. Think, for instance, of making a phone call, sending text messages, or using one's browser to read the latest news. However, mobile technologies increasingly use one's physical location as a source of adjusting the information and services they provide so that these will be relevant for the specific place in which the individual finds himself. For example, users can retrieve location-specific weather forecasts, public transport timetables and information on restaurants or shops of their liking in their vicinity. SpotAFriendNow applications, as a specific kind of location-based service, also fall in this category, of course. We argue that what such applications do, first and foremost, is *to re-introduce the physical world into the equation through the emphasis they place on individuals' physical location*, which forms the 'raw material' for providing services, information, and, most importantly, for engaging in contact with others. Whereas, as Wellman rightly noted, mobile technologies originally shifted '*the dynamics of connectivity from places* [...] *to individuals*' we argue that location-based services, and particularly SpotAFriendNow applications, with their emphasis on social interaction with others in one's physical vicinity, can be viewed as a *response* to this trend by re-introducing places as one of the main ingredients for establishing connectivity. SpotAFriendNow applications, thus, can be understood as an interesting counterweight against the processes of 'virtualization' and the ongoing 'migration to cyberspace' that many researchers have pointed to in the last decade.

This does not entail that the process of 'virtualization' comes to a halt entirely, but rather that it is continued by different means. Our social interactions and connections are still *mediated* by the virtual world, but now come in a new guise with the regained importance of the physical. Moreover, it means that the process of virtualization is now *accompanied* by one of *place-centering*: physical places in the real world are taken as both the starting point and the end point of individuals' actions in the virtual worlds of their mobile technologies. The physical environment in which the user finds himself is now *augmented* with virtual information, or, to phrase it differently, SpotAFriendNow applications function as '*portholes into information spaces*' that are directly and relevantly related to the user's physical environment [14]. Thus, the balance between the virtual and the physical is restored, at least to some degree, in and through

SpotAFriendNow applications and other location-based services. What's more, because SpotAFriendNow applications add physical location to the existing infrastructure of mobile technology use, they redefine and alter what it means for users to be *accessible*. Whereas mobile technologies traditionally focused on *availability* – that is, on being reachable and able to reach others from anywhere at any time – adding the parameter of physical location shifts the focus to *presence* instead. With these applications, as we have said before, *where* the user is has regained relevance, or rather, it has become a key element for his interactional accessibility. SpotAFriendNow applications show which members of the same network are in his direct physical environment, and who is open to interaction. Simultaneously, of course, they make the individual's whereabouts visible to others as well, so that they may contact him. Presence in the real world, rather than availability in the virtual world, becomes a central factor through the use of SpotAFriendNow applications. Here, too, we see a counterweight to the 'migration to cyberspace' so often associated with mobile and other information and communication technologies.

It is important to note that we do not claim that SpotAFriendNow applications lead to a return to the 'days before virtualization', when physical place was still the main parameter in catalyzing social interaction. Such a claim would obviously be false. SpotAFriendNow applications are not enablers for a restoration of the nostalgic dynamics of social interaction of old – as the analysis below will show in more detail. The advent of modern technology, and of mobile technologies in particular, has changed both the face and the content of our everyday lives for good and such changes could not be (wholly) undone. But, as De Souza e Silva notes, what location-based mobile technologies do is *combine* physical places and virtual worlds:

> Unlike [in] traditional social public places, such as bars, squares, and automobiles, [. . .] users are simultaneously moving through physical space while connected in real time to other users via digital technology depending on their relative positions in physical space [15].

Thus, SpotAFriendNow, and other location-based services, generate so-called 'hybrid spaces': '*Hybrid spaces are mobile spaces, created by the constant movement of users who carry portable devices continuously connected to the Internet and to other users*' [15]. In hybrid spaces there is a mixture of the physical space as-is and virtual information that is superimposed on that physical space, thereby enriching the experience of everyday life and creating what has been termed '*augmented reality*' [14,16].

Interestingly, Wellman's famous phrase, 'the person is the portal', is still as true in a world of SpotAFriendNow applications as it was in the high days of virtualization, but it has gained a new meaning. After all, what such applications do is precisely to literally place the individual in the center of his own world, that is, on the map that forms the key element of their interfaces. The map, moreover, reaches outwards from the user's physical location and visualizes the members of the same network available in his vicinity. Being in *this* physical location rather than *that* one, affects whom one may interact with, and while the person is still the portal in one respect, viz. in the fact that he is taken to be the center of his own (virtual and physical!) universe, what is central *about* him is no longer his position as a node in his virtual networks, but rather his *bodily location in the real world*. He is a portal in an extended meaning of the phrase. The shift from availability to presence as a key parameter in engaging in social interaction, which we described above, will further enhance the user's awareness of his actual physical surroundings. SpotAFriendNow applications thus contribute to a rebalancing of the virtual and the physical in several ways. That this may lead to new forms of sociality is the subject of the next paragraph.

4   Ad Hoc Intimacy and New Forms of Sociality

One of the oft-heard complaints in a world of mobile technology is the claim that the use of such technologies, particularly in public or semi-public spaces, leads to the undermining of interactional norms and values that existed in the social realm before their advent. Mobile technologies, it is said, call forth anti-social behavior in the public realm. They enable us to engage in contact with others who are not present in the same physical location, thereby making the caller unavailable for social interaction with those he is sharing the same space with, and causing inconvenience to those people who are present in that same space. This, it is often argued in more or less disapproving wordings, undermines codes of behavior, rules of etiquette, and senses of social involvement in public spaces [17,18,19,20,21,22], and contributes to already ongoing processes of increasing individualism[1] and the rise of ego-cultures. For instance, Rosen argues that mobile phones are technologies '...*used as a means to refuse to be in the social space; they are the technological cold shoulders*' [23], and Gergen speaks of '*the erosion of face-to-face community, a coherent and centered sense of self, moral bearings, depth of relationship, and the uprooting of meaning from material context*' (Kenneth Gergen, quoted in [23]). Chambers is more nuanced about the effects of mobile phone use and says:

> The mobile phone offers the remarkable flexibility of both binding and avoiding face-to-face interaction. On the one hand, this communication device can *cement* face-to-face relationships, not only through regular contact with friends and loved ones, but also through mobile phone sharing, a custom practiced by young people [...]. On the other hand, the mobile phone can be used to *fragment* face-to-face contact by allowing individuals to withdraw from engagement with physically present others by concentrating on the virtual moment. [...] ...the

---

[1] The rise of individualism, of course, is not the simple result of technological developments alone. Rather, it is a development that stems from a wide variety of processes, ranging from (but not limited to) globalization, the decline of religious observance in many Western countries, the massive displacement of both people and goods across the globe, the resulting loss of senses of (local) rootedness and social collectivity, and various other factors.

disembedding quality of the mobile phone lends itself not only to *social intimacy* but also to *social distancing* [24] (emphasis in the original).

The aim of SpotAFriendNow applications is twofold. On the one hand, using such applications enables users to engage in contact with others in their network who do *not* share the same physical location – chat functionality, posting messages, texting, making calls, and exchanging pictures are all modes of communication enabled by these applications to facilitate *virtual communication*. In this sense they are no different from other mobile phone functionalities, and hence do not contribute to more social involvement with those directly surrounding the user in his physical environment. However, using a map adds an interesting new element to virtual sociality. In research on mobile phone use it has been argued that using a mobile phone allows people to go back to forms of communication that are labeled '*pre-modern*', that is, communication within small, close-knit communities of people that know each other well and are constantly in close touch with one another [25]. Mobile phone users, the argument goes, incessantly 'tap in' with a very small group of close connections to (re)affirm social ties and confirm where the others in the network find themselves. All of this, of course, is at the expense of engaging in larger, looser networks, which are labeled 'modern'. Now, whether or not a characterization of mobile phone use as 'pre-modern' is valid or helpful is not the point we wish to discuss here – what is important here is the fact that research shows that mobile phone users do, in fact, often predominantly engage with only a small, tight-knit group of close friends, and that they engage with this group with a high frequency. What we want to point out is that SpotAFriendNow applications support and may even strengthen users' 'pre-modern' desire to know where everyone else in their small community is spending their time, by literally *visualizing* it on a map. If (one of) the mobile phone's key functionalities is to facilitate small-group, close-knit sociality, then SpotAFriendNow applications may function as one more vehicle for this kind of sociality.

However, that is not the only type of sociality, and perhaps not even the most important one, that SpotAFriendNow applications support. We propose that SpotAFriendNow applications for mobile technologies are an interesting new development, in that they appear to provide a remedy against the alleged instigation of anti-social behavior in public or shared spaces caused by mobile technology use. As we have argued above, SpotAFriendNow applications reintroduce the user's physical location into the equation and turn this location into the starting point for engaging in social interaction. These applications are designed to enable users to engage in face-to-face interaction with others in the same physical environment, rather than those absent from it, and while they also facilitate the latter, we suspect that it is the former that will attract users to them. This means that SpotAFriendNow applications can be understood as an answer to the 'absent presence' caused by mobile phone use (or reading a book, or daydreaming in the presence of others for that matter). The map displaying who else is present in the same location is the central feature for this goal. We label the new form of sociality that arises through the use of SpotAFriendNow applications '*ad hoc intimacy*'.

There are two reasons why users would want to turn to SpotAFriendNow applications to meet new people. First, users may be interested in finding new contacts in their direct vicinity based on *shared interests* or *goals* by consulting personal interests specified in the publicly available profile or through tags in the SpotAFriendNow application. Uncovering this unexpected overlap may move the individual to engage in face-to-face interaction with this hitherto unknown person. Similarly, an uncomfortable social occasion, such as a party at which one knows no one, could be turned into a slightly less uncomfortable one with the help of a SpotAFriendNow application on one's mobile phone, because the application enables individuals to 'scan the venue' and see if any like-minded souls (in whatever guise or form, and relating to whatever interest) are available. The second reason why it may be interesting for users to turn to SpotAFriendNow applications is to find *shared friends*, that is, to engage in social interaction with strangers based on the fact that both people share a contact. For instance, sitting on the train I may discover that the person opposite me is my colleague's sister. Had I not accessed my SpotAFriendNow application, I would probably never have known, and hence would not have had any reason to talk to this person. Using the application reveals that we share a social circle and may therefore instigate a face-to-face interaction. What is interesting about SpotAFriendNow applications, then, is the fact that they may bring together strangers in the same (public) space, who would probably not have engaged in social interaction had they not known, through the use of their mobile technologies of the *interests* (goals, characteristics) or the *relations* (connections, contacts) that they shared.

We argue, then, that SpotAFriendNow applications instigate *new forms of sociality* – by coupling social networking capabilities to real world (and real time) settings they facilitate face-to-face interactions with formerly unknown others, leading to what we call 'ad hoc intimacy'. The social networking environments that users have so enthusiastically turned to in the virtual world over the last few years now find a new expression in the physical world, bringing together people who, in all likelihood, would not have found one another if it hadn't been for the SpotAFriendNow application's mediating role. This means that through such applications the social is returned into the equation by allowing users to 'befriend' unknown strangers merely on the basis of their being in the same physical surroundings. Therefore, SpotAFriendNow applications can be viewed as a vehicle to *re-establish* social interaction and lead to new forms of sociality.

5   In Conclusion

As we have seen at the beginning of this article, SpotAFriendNow applications have seriously started blossoming in the last few years. Partially, we have argued, their rising popularity can be explained with reference to the widespread maturation of the technological infrastructure needed for their broad dissemination. SpotAFriendNow applications can also be viewed as an exponent of a rising culture of social networking and self-presentation via the Internet on the one hand, and a regained need for social engagement in the physical world on the other. These applications provide a new, medium-specific means of engaging in social contact, and therefore contribute to changes in our conception of the public sphere and our engagements with others in that sphere. Critics might argue that SpotAFriendNow applications symbolize one more step in the erosion of the public sphere, since, apparently, nowadays we need a mobile device to help us instigate a social interaction with someone sitting opposite us on the train – we have become such cowards that we can only engage in interaction with others after we've 'screened' them with our mobile phones. While this critique has a point, it misses the central thrust of SpotAFriendNow applications. These applications facilitate users' search for new senses of belonging and social participation. Reengaging in social interactions in the public sphere, and reestablishing means of engagement in that sphere are crucial steps in response to a widely shared sense of discontent with respect to what many perceive to be excessive individualism. The critics are correct in the sense that perhaps we have lost the ability to engage socially in the public sphere, but at least SpotAFriendNow applications enable us to regain some of that capacity. In their contribution to countering the trend of virtualization and providing new forms of sociality the emergence of SpotAFriendNow applications is worthy of our attention not only in social-scientific research but also, more generally, in understanding the societal developments facilitated by and through technology.

Acknowledgments. The research for this paper is part of PrimeLife, a European project funded by the European Commissions 7th Framework Programme, which aims to create sustainable privacy and identity management to future networks and services.

References

1. boyd, d., Ellison, N.B.: Social network sites. Definition, history, and scholarship. Journal of Computer-Mediated Communication 13, 210–230 (2008)
2. ABI Research (2009), http://www.abiresearch.com/press/1423
3. Gartner Research, http://www.gartner.com/it/page.jsp?id=1059812
4. ABI Research, http://www.abiresearch.com/research/1003335
5. Castells, M.: The rise of the network society. Blackwell Publishers, Oxford (2000)
6. Castells, M.: Informationalism networks and the network society. A theoretical blueprint. In: The network society: A cross-cultural perspective, pp. 3–47. Edward Elgar Publishers, Cheltenham (2004)
7. Gergen, K.J.: The saturated self: Dilemmas of identity in contemporary life. Basic Books, New York (1991)
8. Hofflich, J.R.: A certain sense of place: Mobile communication and local orientation. In: Nyiri, K. (ed.) A sense of place: The global and the local in mobile communication, pp. 159–168. Passagen Verlag, Vienna (2005)
9. Meyrowitz, J.: No sense of place: The impact of electronic media on social behavior. Oxford University Press, New York (1985)
10. Meyrowitz, J.: The generalized elsewhere. Critical studies in mass communication 6, 326–335 (1989)

11. Meyrowitz, J.: The rise of glocality: New senses of place and identity in the global village. In: Nyiri, K. (ed.) A sense of place: The global and the local in mobile communication, pp. 21–30. Passagen Verlag, Vienna (2005)
12. Harvey, D.: The condition of postmodernity: An enquiry into the origins of cultural change. Blackwell Publishers, Oxford (1989)
13. Wellman, B.: Physical place and cyberplace. The rise of personalized networking. Int. Journ. of Urban and Regional Research 25, 227–252 (2001)
14. Spohrer, J.C.: Information in places. IBM Systems Journal 38, 602–629 (1999)
15. De Souza e Silva, A.: Mobile technologies as interfaces of hybrid spaces. Space and Culture 9, 261–278 (2006)
16. O'Hara, K., Shadbolt, N.: The spy in the coffee machine. Oneworld Publications, Oxford (2008)
17. Gergen, K.J.: The challenge of absent presence. In: Katz, J.E., Aakhus, M.A. (eds.) Perpetual contact: Mobile communication, private talk, public performance, pp. 227–241. Cambridge University Press, Cambridge (2002)
18. Ling, R.: One can talk about common manners!: The use of mobile telephones in inappropriate situations. In: Themes in mobile telephony. Final report of the COST 248 Home and Work group. Telia, Stockholm (1997)
19. Ling, R.: Mobile telephones and the disturbance of the public sphere, http://www.richardling.com/papers/2004_disturbance_of_social_sphere.pdf
20. Ling, R.: New tech, new ties: How mobile communication is reshaping social cohesion. MIT Press, Cambridge (2008)
21. Love, S., Perry, M.: Dealing with mobile conversations in public places: Some implications for the design of socially intrusive technologies. In: Computer-Human Interaction (CHI) 2004, Vienna (2004)
22. Meyrowitz, J.: Global nomads in the digital veldt. In: Nyiri, K. (ed.) Mobile democracy: Essays on society self and politics, pp. 91–102. Passagen Verlag, Vienna (2003)
23. Rosen, C.: Our cell phones ourselves. The New Atlantis 6, 26–45 (2004)
24. Chambers, D.: New social ties: Contemporary connections in a fragmented society. Palgrave Macmillan, New York (2006)
25. Geser, H.: Is the cell phone undermining the social order?: Understanding mobile technology from a sociological perspective. Knowledge Technology and Policy 19, 8–18 (2006)

An Advanced Multimodal Platform for Educational Social Networks

Maria Chiara Caschera, Arianna D'Ulizia, Fernando Ferri, and Patrizia Grifoni

Institute of Research on Population and Social Policies (IRPPS)
National Research Council (CNR)
00185, Rome, Italy
{mc.caschera,arianna.dulizia,fernando.ferri,
patrizia.grifoni}@irpps.cnr.it

Abstract. Multimediality and multimodality have demonstrated significant potential supporting students in learning activities; providing them with multimodal interaction can be a crucial issue for improving accessibility to the multimedia contents in learning environments. In fact, involving multiple input and output modalities enables a broader spectrum of users with different ages, skill levels and abilities to access these contents. In this paper, we present AMPLE, an advanced multimodal platform for e-learning that provides users with a multimodal access to an educational social network. The platform is based on a distributed architecture that integrates social networking technologies and multimodal facilities, enabling a collaborative learning experience to learners.

Keywords: Learning environment, Multimodal interaction, Web 2.0 networking technologies, Social networks.

1 Introduction

The use of Web 2.0 social networking technologies, such as chatting, blogging and text messaging, enables users to share personal information, connect themselves with other users, edit and upload multimedia contents including video, audio and even 3D data. These technologies have the great potential to support formal learning contexts, as they provide a new form of engagement that is participatory and collaborative. They can be used to facilitate collaborative problem solving, to share course materials, to follow interactive lessons, and to promote peer-to-peer interaction. A series of experiments [1] [2] demonstrated the usefulness of multimediality in supporting students in their learning activities. Multimedia learning contents are more easily and intuitively accessed if available over several channels, and offered in a multimodal fashion.

This paper describes our effort in improving the access to multimedia learning contents through an Advanced Multimodal Platform for e-LEarning (AMPLE). The platform supports multimodal access to a multimedia repository, enabling the retrieval, editing and sharing of multimedia contents in an educational social network.

The remainder of the paper is structured in four main sections. Section 2 summarizes related works on social networking technologies, learning and multimodality.

R. Meersman et al. (Eds.): OTM 2010 Workshops, LNCS 6428, pp. 339–348, 2010.
© Springer-Verlag Berlin Heidelberg 2010

The third section provides details of the proposed advanced multimodal learning environment. In Section 4, a case study is described, which explains the functioning of the system. Section 5 concludes the paper.

2 Related Work

The social networking technologies in educational environments can support learning and exchanging ideas, knowledge, skills, experience, and competencies. The communication and the collaboration are efficiently supported by the use of technology results and the development of more efficient forms of education. The use of technological media and tools provides learning environment where teachers and learners are separated by time and/or space. In this environment education takes place in a virtual learning environment that can be viewed as a software system designed to support teaching and learning by tools, such as discussion forums, blogs and whiteboards.

Several works in the literature investigate the use of social networking technologies in educational environments [3] [4] [5] [6], proving the growing interest in this research area. As Zane Berge [7, p.28] argued, "the trend in online education is toward a Web-based, desktop, virtual classroom - the result of text-based e-mail, mailing lists, conferencing and chat functions as well as the video, graphics, and audio channels that deliver interactive multimedia over the Internet". An example of educational environment, offering several learning tools to the community members, such as synchronous chat rooms, threaded discussion boards, whiteboards, file and public link sharing, is Educational MUVES [8]. Another example is the educational social network proposed by Varlamis and Apostolakis [9], which provides a knowledge base for the educational material, a profile base for the storage of learners' history and a collaboration environment for the communication and participation in synchronous activities.

In the attempt to improve accessibility to multimedia learning contents, multimodal interfaces are a powerful tool that facilitates the access to the different contents. Many research studies [10] [11] [12] emphasize the advantages of multimodal interfaces, compared to traditional graphical user interfaces, since they make human-computer communication more intuitive, natural and efficient, enabling a broader spectrum of users with different ages, skill levels and abilities to access to computational systems, and increasing the level of freedom offered to users. In the literature, various multimodal learning environments have been proposed [13] [14] [15]. MultiLezi [13] allows users to access to teaching materials across various channels, devices (the Web, the telephone, and hand-held devices) and contexts and with different modalities (speech, mouse and keyboard). It provides, indeed, a multimodal interface for accessing learning contents using a standard point-and-click interaction paradigm integrated with vocal commands. AmbiLearn [14] is another example of multimodal learning environment devoted to provide educational contents to children by using a combination of speech and pen input. Client server architecture has been used in AmbiLearn for supporting multiple users within the learning environment. Differently from AmbiLearn, the multimodal learning environment, called LEMMA [15], provides also an authoring system that enables teachers to develop and evolve multimodal learning content, in addition to an interactive environment that enables students to access these contents by speech, written text, and 2D/3D imagery.

The examined multimodal learning environments have a set of advantages and drawbacks, which are summarized in Table 1. In MultiLezi, a personalization of the multimodal interaction occurs, since multimedia content can be navigated and accessed, according to the characteristics of the user detailed in the user profile. However, it cannot be exploited in a social networking environment since it does not support multiple users. Moreover, it is addressed mainly to learners, since it does not provide an authoring environment that allows teachers to edit learning material, but only an interactive learning environment that enables students to access to learning contents. This drawback can also be found in AmbiLearn. Moreover, this system relies on the kind of supported modalities, which are only speech and pen-based gesture, without the possibility to visually interact with the system. However, AmbiLearn is the only examined system that provides a client server architecture that enables multiple users to access and collaborate within the learning environment. LEMMA, indeed, is the only examined environment that provides an authoring environment, which allows teachers to edit learning material. Moreover, similarly to MultiLezi, it enables a personalization of the multimodal interaction allowing users to adjust presentations according to their preferences. The main disadvantage of LEMMA relies on its inability to support multiple users and, consequently, collaborative learning tasks.

Table 1. Advantages and drawbacks of the examined multimodal learning environments

	MULTIMODAL LEARNING ENVIRONMENTS		
	MultiLezi	**AmbiLearn**	**LEMMA**
ADVANTAGES	• It allows to personalize the multimodal interaction to the features of the user	•It supports collaborative learning tasks	• It provides an authoring environment for editing multimedia contents • It allows to personalize the multimodal interaction to the features of the user
DRAWBACKS	• It does not support collaborative learning tasks • It does not provide an authoring environment for editing multimedia contents	•It does not provide an authoring environment for editing multimedia contents • It does not support the visual input modality, but only speech and touch	• It does not support collaborative learning tasks

The learning environment proposed in this paper joins together the advantages of the examined multimodal learning environments, trying to overcome most of their drawbacks. In particular, the proposed environment, similarly to AmbiLearn, follows a distributed architecture where learners and teachers can access the server from their own devices (laptops, as well as mobile devices), supporting collaborative learning tasks. Moreover, analogously to MultiLezi, our environment provides authoring functionalities and the possibility to personalize the multimodal interaction to the features of the user. A detailed description of the proposed learning environment and its functionalities are given in the following sections.

3   The Advanced Multimodal Platform for e-LEarning

The investigation of existing learning environments, provided in the previous section, leads us to believe that a distributed architecture, networking technologies, and multimodal facilities have to be integrated to enable a collaborative learning experience to learners. Therefore, in this paper an Advanced Multimodal Platform for e-LEarning (AMPLE) is presented, which enables the retrieval, editing and sharing of multimedia contents in an educational social network through a multimodal interface. This platform allows efficiently managing multimodal communication between people, participating in an educational social network.

In the following sections, the architecture of the proposed platform and its functionalities are described.

3.1   AMPLE Architecture

AMPLE is based on client-server architecture as depicted in Figure 1. A similar architecture has been proposed in our previous work [16], more focused on supporting the interaction in a gamed-based learning environment.

Each person (i.e. learner and teacher) can access to AMPLE from its own device that is equipped with a *multimodal interface*. Therefore, an AMPLE client includes specific I/O devices, such as, for example, display, cameras, microphone, and loudspeakers, as well as the components for extracting features from the received signals. The feature extraction occurs on the client side, since it requires limited amount of memory and computational power, whilst the recognition processes, which consist in matching the extracted features with a predefined set of patterns, are executed on the server. The *multimodal interaction management* and the *educational social network* are provided on the server side.

The *multimodal interaction management*, whose architecture has been proposed in our previous work [17], is responsible for recognizing unimodal input coming from the features extractors of each modality, appropriately interpreting these inputs, integrating these different interpretations into a semantic interpretation, and understanding which is the better way to react to the interpreted multimodal request by activating the most appropriate output devices. This component includes:

- the unimodal input recognizers, such as, for example the Automatic Speech Recognizer and the gesture recognizer, and the output generators, such as the Speech Synthesizer;
- the multimodal interpreter that integrates the recognized inputs, and applies the production rules stored in the Multimodal Grammar Repository, to parse the multimodal input;
- the modeling components, that are aimed at capturing some information used during the interpretation phase for leading up to the most probable interpretation of the user input (e.g. user, content and context modeling components);
- the multimodal output manager for generating appropriate output information, through the available output modalities (multimodal fission).

A user can interact with AMPLE for retrieving, editing and sharing multimedia contents within the educational social network. For instance, the user can ask information about the topic of a multimedia document by using speech in combination with sketch, handwriting, or pointing gesture that complete the meaning of the speech sentence. When the multimodal message is interpreted, it is sent to the educational social network in order to accordingly activate the AMPLE learning functionalities. Analogously, the multimedia information required by the user is sent to the multimodal output manager that allows visualizing it by using the appropriate output devices.

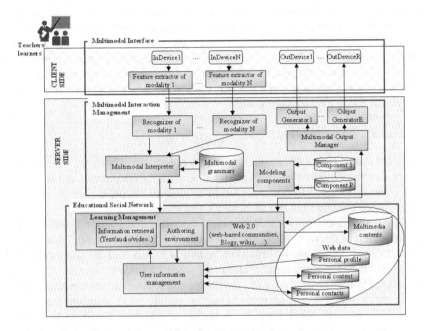

Fig. 1. Architecture of the Advanced Multimodal Platform for e-LEarning

The *educational social network* consists of two main components: the learning management system and the user information management. The learning management system has three components:

- Information retrieval Module that supports advanced indexing, search and retrieval methodologies for all content types based on semantic tagging. The multimedia learning contents are stored in a networked repository and are accessible by the multimodal interface. This networked repository provides facilities to store the following types of multimedia content: text, images, different formats of audio content, different forms of video content, Macromedia flash movies, Power-point presentations and others.
- Authoring environment that supports multimedia data management, including multimedia content editing, integration, and synchronization. The contents are edited, uploaded and managed by the multimodal interface. Once created or edited, multimedia contents are stored into the networked repository.
- Web 2.0 Module that provides social networking services, such as blogs, wikis, and web-based communities, for supporting students in the learning activities.

In particular, these services can be used for stimulating social real time interaction among students but also between teachers and students. For instance, blogs and wikis are useful tools for online discussions and forums, while video-sharing web-sites provide the possibility to upload video-based tutorials that can be shared with other students.

The user information management is another module of the educational social network, devoted to store and manage personal data of network members. In particular, it provides controlled access to the network and to user information, such as personal profile (user's interaction behaviors), contents and contacts. These data are contained in three networked repositories. The user information management cooperates with the learning management system, particularly, when new multimedia learning contents have to be edited from personal contents, as well as the user searches for information contained in the personal profile.

3.2 AMPLE Functionalities

AMPLE combines the features of the multimodal systems with the e-learning environments functionalities. The multimodal interaction environment allows easily accessing contents using different interaction modalities according to the contexts and user knowledge contained in the *Modeling components.*

The client side consists of the *Multimodal Interface* that was designed for allowing the use of different interaction channels in order to edit and retrieve educational materials and to post messages. Information, which are extracted by the modal features extractor of the client, are captured and recognized by the *Recognizers of modalities,* and combined using the *Multimodal interpreter* employing the *multimodal grammar.*

In the server side, the *multimodal interaction management*, combined with the *education social network* (see Figure 1), provides several functionalities to support the learning process. The retrieval of multimedia contents is enabled by the *information retrieval* module and it can be performed using different modal inputs thanks to the functionalities of the modules that compose the *multimodal interaction management.* This process is supported by information about personal profile and contents obtained by the *user information management* module. Moreover, comments and messages can be posted using different interaction modalities and the *Web 2.0* module. The interaction process is customized adapting interaction to the user profile, context and available modalities, which are information contained in the *modeling components.* The *authoring environment* manages data formats and low-level representations, and it ensures consistency of the learning contents. Moreover, it enables the author of learning content to easily write and modify contents through a multimodal user interface, and the learner cannot use contents before the author has given permission. The fruition and the visualization of information are provided by the *multimodal output manager* that supports several views of the contents, as described in Section 4.

4   A Scenario to Access Multimedia Learning Contents

AMPLE can be usefully applied to support the fruition of multimedia learning materials by multimodal interaction, and it is based on the visualization system proposed in

[18]. In AMPLE, the multimedia contents are collected in order to offer and integrate different visualization views by using the *multimodal output manager* according to the user's purpose. In particular, it provides the possibility: to cluster multimedia contents, depending on media types in which they are available, through the *authoring environment*; to visualize them on a map according to the landscape metaphor, and to provide a visual representation of the temporal evolution of the media types of the multimedia contents through the *multimodal output manager*. In particular, let us suppose that risk management materials concern: *forests fire, extreme floods events in large river basins, earthquake, governance for hospital* and *health due to e-commerce*. Those materials are available in different media types: *text, image, sound* and *video*. The user accesses the AMPLE system by using the functionalities of the *multimodal interface*.

Let us suppose that the user says by speech:

"Show me information about this topic"

and she/he selects the icon connected with the risk management materials by gesture. The *multimodal interaction management* recognizes unimodal inputs, which come from the modality *features extractors*, and it reacts to the interpreted input (by the *multimodal interpreter*) providing the visualization of the multimodal learning contents considering media types by which they are provided according to the landscape metaphor (see Figure 2.a). In the example shown in Figure 2.a, material about *forest fire* risk management is available by *video, image* and *sound*, while learning contents about *earthquake* risk management is available by *video, text* and *sound*.

In order to analyze the accessibility levels of the multimedia learning contents, the visualization focuses on class of media types showing them as 3D half-ovoid solids having circular horizontal sections. The visualization allows displaying colored areas that represent classes of media types and a specific learning content is placed in the landscape. The width of each area of class of media types is proportional to the number of multimedia learning contents that are provided by the specific media type. The height of the position, associated with each multimedia content on the ovoid, reflects the *media access* level of the multimedia content according to the media types. Therefore, isolines in the landscape identify levels of media access of multimedia contents in the classes of media types. The multimedia content that has the higher value of media access level according to media type is located in the higher position on the solid visualizing the specified class of media types. Moreover, each multimedia content can be provided by more than one class of media type. For example, Figure 2.a shows three multimedia contents (*Forest fire, Hospital,* and *Health due to e-commerce*) that can be provided by *image* (yellow ovoid). In this figure, the multimedia content *Forest fire* is also provided by *video* and *sound* (visualized using black edges). This visualization of the educational learning contents considering media types can support the analysis of available learning contents about risk management materials in an educational social network. It enables users to detect which contents are available through specific media types in order to evaluate which channels can be used to access to the document. This functionality is originated from the fact that, frequently, the needed contents are not available by different media types and only specific channels can be used to access them.

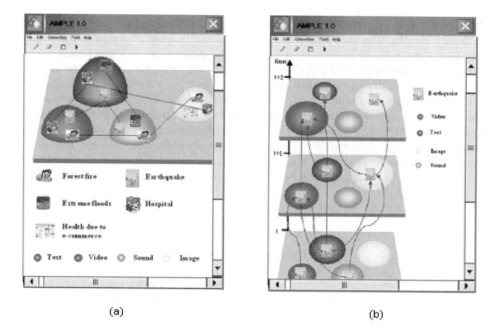

(a)   (b)

Fig. 2. Possible visualizations offered by the AMPLE system: (a) Multimedia contents, visualized according to the media types, and their access level; (b) Visualization of the evolution of the *earthquake* contents according to the media types at time t, t+1, t+2

The presented visualization can be also usefully applied to find out which are the people who have edited the multimedia learning contents, and to establish a direct connections with them creating shared awareness by the *Web 2.0* module of the AMPLE system. In this case, the dimensions are: 1) the 3D virtual representation of colored ovoids that represents the available multimedia learning contents; 2) people who have edited content, which are positioned in different points of the ovoid according to the number of multimedia learning contents they have edited in the network. The person who has inserted the higher number of multimedia learning contents is positioned in the higher position on the ovoid.

Moreover, AMPLE offers the possibility to visualize the evolution of the media types of the multimedia contents during the time (see Figure 2.b). In fact, a further dimension, which can be visualized alternatively to the media access level, is the *time*. For example, let us suppose that a user says by speech:

"Visualize the temporal evolution of the kinds of media by which I can access this material"

and she/he simultaneously points the icon of the content about *earthquake* on the touch screen display. The *multimodal interaction manager* interprets and recognizes the input, and the *educational social network* retrieves the information requested by the user. This information is presented by the *multimodal interface,* displaying the evolution over time of *earthquake* content according to the media types by which it has been provided. Figure 2.b presents the transformations of the media types at time t, t+1, t+2. This figure shows the evolution of multimedia *earthquake* contents, which at the time *t* are provided by *video*, *text* and *sound*, and at the time *t+1* by *video*, *text* and *image* due to the fact that *sound* contents have been changed into *video* and *image* contents, and some *text* contents have been also changed into *video* contents. Considering time *t+2*, the figure shows that the *video* contents increase because both *text* and *image* contents have changed into *video*.

Information obtained from the sequence of temporal layers allows analyzing how the media types of the learning contents are evolving during time. The evolution of the media types of learning contents is due to the feedback from users' interactions, and it points at fitting the users' needs [19]. Therefore, analyzing the changing of media types allows understanding the transformation of the user interaction behaviors in the fruition of learning contents.

5 Conclusion and Future Work

The spreading of the Web 2.0 social networking technologies has offered great support to formal learning contexts improving the processes of knowledge building, working together, information sharing and problem solving. In this paper, social networking technologies for learning environments have been combined with multimodal interaction functionalities in order to access multimedia learning contents. Starting from an overview of the main features of social networking technologies and an analysis about how multimodal interaction supports the access to multimedia learning contents, the AMPLE has been designed in order to efficiently support multimodal communications among people in a community and the participation in educational social networks. The client-server architecture of the AMPLE system has been depicted describing the client side composed of the *multimodal interface*, and the server side made up of the *multimodal interaction manager* and the *educational social network*. Examples of the functionalities provided by this system have been described focusing on the visualizations offered by this system.

The presented system has been tested and evaluated in the scenario of scientific seminars participation, organization and management involving 77 people, with ages from 25 to 65. All the participants answered to a questionnaire to investigate the users' satisfaction on the proposed system in order to express a qualitative evaluation. It consisted of a short interview that involved all the participants. The evaluation of the proposed system has produced very satisfactory results both, in term of stimulating social networking and in term of users' satisfaction. An interesting task for future work is the evaluation of the system by comparing the usability of AMPLE with other existing learning environments. Such a comparison will provide possible improvements on the system.

References

1. Mayer, R.E., Anderson, R.B.: The instructive animation: Helping students build connections between words and pictures in multimedia learning. Journal of Educational Psychology 84, 444–452 (1992)
2. Mayer, R.E., Sims, V.K.: For whom is a picture worth a thousand words? Extensions of a dual-coding theory of multimedia learning. Journal of Educational Psychology 86, 389–401 (1994)

3. De Wever, B., Mechant, P., Hauttekeete, L., Veevaete, P.: E-learning 2.0: social software for educational use. In: Proceedings of Ninth IEEE International Symposium on Multimedia Workshops (ISMW 2007), pp. 511–516 (2007)
4. Lockyer, L., Patterson, J.: Integrating Social Networking Technologies in Education: A Case Study of a formal learning environment. In: Proceedings of 8th IEEE International Conference on Advanced Learning Technologies, Santander, Spain, July 1-5, pp. 529–533 (2008)
5. Collins, D., Schwarte, A.R., Alkire, K., Adkinson, P., Rosichelli, M., Kallish, A.: Social Networking for Learning Communities: Using e-portfolios, blogs, wikis, pod casts, and other Internet based tools in the foundation art studio. FATE in Review 29, 4–9 (2008)
6. Jin, L., Wen, Z.: An Augmented Social Interactive Learning Approach through Web2.0. In: Proceedings of 33rd Annual IEEE international Computer Software and Applications Conference (COMPSAC 2009), Seattle, Washington, pp. 607–611 (2009)
7. Berge, Z.: Components of the online classroom. In: Weiss, R., Knowlton, D., Speck, B. (eds.) Principles of effective teaching in the online classroom, San Francisco, Jossey Bass, pp. 23–28 (2000)
8. Cooper, J.: Educational MUVES: Virtual Learning Communities. Journal of Education, Community and Values (2003),
http://bcis.pacificu.edu/journal/2003/09/cooper/cooper.php
(accessed Septmeber 2009)
9. Varlamis, I., Apostolakis, I.: A Framework for Building Virtual Communities for Education. In: EC-TEL 2006, pp. 165–172 (2006)
10. Oviatt, S.L., DeAngeli, A., Kuhn, K.: Integration and synchronization of input modes during multimodal human-computer interaction. In: Proceedings of Conference on Human Factors in Computing Systems, pp. 415–422
11. Oviatt, S.L., Cohen, P.R.: Multimodal interfaces that process what comes naturally. Communications of the ACM 43(3), 45–53 (2000)
12. Oviatt, S.L., Cohen, P.R., Wu, L., Vergo, J., Duncan, L., et al.: Designing the user interface for multimodal speech and pen-based gesture applications: State-of-the-art systems and future research directions. Human-Computer Interaction 15, 263–322 (2000)
13. Sbattella, L., Mainetti, L., Barbieri, T., Bianchi, A., Bruna, S., Pernici, B.: MAIS MultiLezi: an adaptable multichannel and multimodal environment for e-learning. Rivista del Politecnico di Milano 10, 42–47 (2006)
14. Hyndman, J., Lunney, T., Mc Kevitt, P.: AmbiLearn: Ambient Intelligent Multimodal Learning Environment for Children. In: Proceedings of the 10th Annual PostGraduate Symposium On The Convergence of Telecommunications Networking & Broadcasting PG Net, June 22 – 23, pp. 277–282. John Moores University, Liverpool (2009)
15. Breisinger, M., Höllerer, T., Ford, J., Folsom, D.: Implementation and Evaluation of a 3D Multi Modal Learning Environment. In: Kommers, P., Richards, G. (eds.) Proceedings of World Conference on Educational Multimedia, Hypermedia and Telecommunications, pp. 2282–2289 (2006)
16. Caschera, M.C., D'Ulizia, A., Ferri, F., Grifoni, P.: Multimodality in Game-based Learning Environments. IEEE Learning Technology Newsletter 12(1), 20–22 (2010)
17. D'Ulizia, A., Ferri, F., Grifoni, P.: Toward the Development of an Integrative Framework for Multimodal Dialogue Processing. In: Meersman, R., Tari, Z., Herrero, P. (eds.) OTM-WS 2008. LNCS, vol. 5333, pp. 509–518. Springer, Heidelberg (2008)
18. Caschera, M.C., Ferri, F., Grifoni, P.: SIM: A dynamic multidimensional visualization method for social networks. PsychNology Journal 6(3), 291–320 (2008)
19. Leung, C.H.C., Chan, W.S., Liu, J.: Collective Evolutionary Indexing of Multimedia Objects. In: Gervasi, O., Taniar, D., Murgante, B., Laganà, A., Mun, Y., Gavrilova, M.L. (eds.) ICCSA 2009. LNCS, vol. 5592, pp. 937–948. Springer, Heidelberg (2009)

Towards Optimal Multi-item Shopping Basket Management: Heuristic Approach[*]

Adam Wojciechowski and Jedrzej Musial

Poznan University of Technology, Institute of Computing Science
ul. Piotrowo 2, 60-965 Poznan, Poland
{Adam.Wojciechowski,Jedrzej.Musial}@cs.put.poznan.pl

Abstract. Shopping as a social activity may be a source of pleasure even if the shopping is very expensive. However, in many real-life situations customers are interested to buy products at possibly low prices. A shopping paradigm based on price comparison may be applied for both: buying in traditional shops and internet shopping. Unfortunately, price comparison applications available nowadays are focused on supporting customers in single product selection. Because of computational complexity, there is no support for managing multiple-item shopping basket optimization. Problem of optimal realization of multiple-item customer basket in Internet shops was proved to be NP-hard in computational sense. In the paper we propose a heuristic approach to optimizing shopping basket and report results of computational experiment. An application based on proposed algorithm provides an instant support for a customer while he builds his basket of products to be purchased.

Keywords: shopping basket optimization, heuristic algorithm.

1 Introduction

High availability and strong competition among Internet shops bring both: price wars and growing difficulty to compare numerous offers. While the price competition leads to customers' savings the complexity of offers comparison rise serious difficulty and rarely can be entirely performed manually. Partial solution to the problem comes from software agents [3, 5], so called price comparators. However their current functionality is limited to building a price rank for a single product among registered offers that fit to customer's query (search phrase). Another shopping support comes from recommender systems (RS) [8, 9]. Depending on design of particular recommender systems they may provide a customer with suggestion *what to buy* and *where to buy* the product. In order to suggest products or services RS needs to know the customer – his preferences, location and history of purchase. The more the RS knows about a user the better recommendation may be proposed. The wisdom of RSs lies in collecting behavioral information on many users, and clustering them into groups that share interests, fashion preferences etc. It is worth to notice that recommender systems not necessarily tend to minimize shopping cost. They are more oriented on customer

---

[*] This research was partially supported by the grant 91-439/10-BW.

R. Meersman et al. (Eds.): OTM 2010 Workshops, LNCS 6428, pp. 349–357, 2010.

satisfaction in domain of product/service selection. RS and its suggestion algorithm can be designed to maximize sells regardless of real customers' needs.

The benefit of shopping on-line, when compared to buying products in traditional shops, comes from lower prices[10] (wider competition) and possibility of purchase in distant locations. However, cheaper shopping over the Internet carries an extra cost of product delivery and has a hidden cost of searching effort. This extra work is time consuming and requires manual human interaction with price comparison computer systems where products are not defined in identical manner and it happens that only a human can finally decide if compared offers relate to identical products. Searching for a bargain – a single product – is pretty well supported by so called price comparison applications. In research conducted among American Internet users *42% of music buyers said online information helped them save money on music purchases, 41% of cell buyers said they spend less as a result of information they got online and 29% of those who used the internet in researching a new place to live said it helped get them a better price*[2].

Making purchase decisions after comparing prices in several shops is effective for a customer if savings are worth the effort of additional work. *68% of internet users either agree (47%) or agree strongly (21%) with the notion that online shopping saves them time*[3]. One should notice that individuals who practice comparison shopping in their mass enforce competitive pressure on prices[6, p.33]. As a consequence, in case of Internet shopping, retailers tend to offer products in low prices and shift a part of their operational costs to postage and packing fee. The effect of strong pressure on sellers to provide products in low prices is stronger if search and price comparison becomes less costly and easily available, e.g. on mobile devices[7].

Searching problem becomes more complex when the consumer basket consists of many products which could be bought in various shops. Problem of optimal realization of multiple-item customer basket in Internet shops, named *Internet shopping optimization problem* (ISOP), was proved to be NP-hard in computational sense[1]. In this research we propose a heuristic approach to optimize multiple-item shopping basket (shopping list). Results (prices of purchase) provided by proposed algorithm are validated and compared to total cost of buying entire shopping list by selecting the cheapest provider for each product in the basket. Selection of the best (the cheapest) offer is gathered from price comparators.

In Section 2 price comparison sites are shortly presented with stress on their weaknesses. Multiple-Item Basket Optimization Problem (MIBOP) is defined in Section 3. Section 4 contains description of environment for computational experiments. Heuristic approach to MIBOP is proposed in Section 5 and in Section 6 we present results of computational experiment. The paper concludes with a summary.

2   Price Comparison Sites

Price comparison sites belong to the most popular and frequently visited web pages. Price rank of available offers produced on request for a specified product is usually used by customers to select the cheapest provider of required product. Price comparators may also be used to increase customer's confidence when a product and its provider is already selected but the customer wants to make sure that price he is to pay is competitive. According to Alexa Rank the most popular price comparators belong to top 1000 mostly visited websites worldwide:

- nextag.com: 498's place,
- shopping.com: 635's place,
- bizrate.com: 767's place.

(site popularity results registered in February 2010, www.alexa.com).

Price comparison applications cooperate very well with web search services. Queries related to product names addressed to web search engines usually give references to price comparators among first ten matching results related to the product. It comes partly from the fact that price comparators always produce an answer (a document) for request on every product they are asked (even when no provider can be found) – the outcome of price comparison sites is designed to be search engine optimization (SEO) friendly. But popularity of search engines comes mainly from their common use in shopping decision making. There are two main customer's savings coming from use of price comparators: possibility of quick selection the best available offer known to the price comparator and good penetration of the market. The range of prices of the same product reported by price comparators may reach as high as 50% or even more. Manual visits in dozens of virtual shops, checking product availability and its price might cost hours of work. Quality metrics for price comparators were proposed and discussed in [11].

An evident weakness of currently available price comparison applications is a lack of support for managing multiple-item basket optimization. The reason why such a service is not available is computational complexity of the optimization process and missing same identification of identical products offered by various shops. Aside from technical drawbacks we may also consider organizational issues that keep many merchandisers away from price comparators. It is a rule that price comparator operators charge some fee from the sellers, either for submitting their shop offer to the system or for redirecting customers from the price comparator to particular on-line shop. The fee is worth to be paid by a seller if his price offer is reported to customers on top positions in price rank generated by price comparator. Then it is likely that potential customers choose the offer and are redirected to a particular shop. If an offer is not on top positions in price rank it is very unlikely that customers would be interested in such offer. Price ranking based on single criterion – the lower price, the better offer –force sellers to reduce their margins to a one-digit percent to be on the top of the rank. The simple method of comparing offers leaves no space for information about quality of service provided by the sellers. The problem has been noticed in some price comparators and it is currently becoming a common practice that customers may feed the database with their assessment and impressions of on-line shop presented by the system. The low-margin problem is important issue for merchandisers, because, according to research, reported in 2007 by Mediarun.pl, even 85% of on-line shops may be not indexed by price comparators.

Although the current state of price comparators is rather primitive those systems are considered to be among the most promising web applications.

3 Multiple-Item Basket Optimization Problem

Optimization problem is defined according to ISOP[1]. Let's assume that:

n   number of products

m   number of shops

N_i multiset of products available in shop i

C_{ij} cost of product j in Ni

d_i delivery cost for shop i, i = 1; ...; m

$X = (X_1; ...; X_\square)$ sequence of selections of products in shops 1; ...; m
$F(X)$ sum of product and delivery costs

$\delta(X_i)$: $\begin{cases} 0 - \text{if none of the products is bought in shop } i \\ 1 - \text{if any of the product is bought in shop } i \end{cases}$, for i = 1; ...; m

X^* optimal sequence of selections of products
F^* optimal (minimum) total cost

Formally we can define optimization problem as follows. A single buyer is looking for a multiset of products N = {1;...; n} to buy in m shops. A multiset of available products Ni, a cost cij of each product j ∈ Ni, and a delivery cost di of any subset of the products from the shop to the buyer are associated with each shop i, i = 1; ... ;m. It is assumed that cij = ∞ if j ∉ Ni. The problem is to find a sequence of disjoint selections (or carts) of products X = (X1;...; Xm), which we call a cart sequence, such that Xi ⊆ Ni, i = 1;...;m, ∪mi=1=Xi = N, and the total product and delivery cost, denoted as F(X):= Σ mi=1 (δ|Xi|)|di+Σj∈ XiCij, is minimized. Here Σ mi=1 (δ|Xi|)|di denotes sum of all shipping costs for every shop i, and $\Sigma_{j\in X_i}C_{ij}$ is the total cost of products we have in the basket. Optimal solution of the problem is X*, and its optimal solution value is F*.

The problem was proved to be NP-hard[1]. In this context computational complexity justifies considering heuristic approaches as compromise solution balancing computational time and results close to optimum.

4   Model Definition

A challenging step in experimental research was to create a model as close to real internet shopping conditions as possible. We studied relationship between competitive structure, advertising, price and price dispersion over the Internet stores. Considering a group of representative products to be taken into account in computational experiment we chose books, because of their wide choice over the virtual (Internet) stores and popularity to buy over that kind of shopping channel.

Creating model we took some information and computational results from Clay et al. [4]. It mainly focus on electronic bookstores model definition, prices, acceptances factor, retailer brand [5] and, what is important for optimization problem model definition, price dispersion. One should also notice that Consumers may choose among a large number of Internet bookstores. Yahoo.com reports more than one hundred online bookstores on its list. Data were collected from thirty-two stores in our sample cover the largest United States-based stores, including Amazon, BarnesandNoble.com, Borders.com, Buy.com, and Booksamillion. Afterwards, top sellers among internet bookstores in Poland like: empik.com and merlin.pl.

Environment for computational experiments is built on the assumptions derived from [4]:

- Book can belong to one of the five categories, which has different median prices: 5, 10, 15, 20, 25,
- Shipping costs vary between 0 and 30,
- Prices for products are computed randomly according to formula (minimum=median*0.69) and (maximum=median*1.47) for product P [4],
- Price range is divided into 9 intervals as follows, percent values in brackets describe density data allocation – percent of all products assigned to the specified interval – numbers are presented by the lower bound:

  o [32%] minimum price,
  o [9%] minimum + (median - minimum)/4,
  o [9%] minimum + (median - minimum)/2,
  o [8%] minimum + (median - minimum)/1.25,
  o [13%] median,
  o [6%] median + (maximum - median)/4,
  o [11%] median + (maximum - median)/2,
  o [8%] median + (maximum - median)/1.25
  o [4%] maximum price.

Price dispersion histogram is presented in Figure 1.

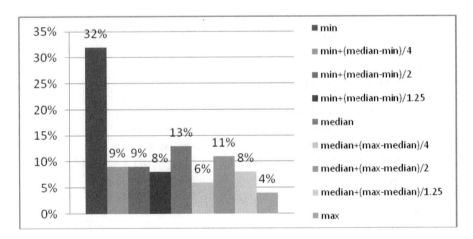

Fig. 1. Product price dispersion histogram used in experiments

5 Heuristic Approach

Due to NP-hardness of the optimization problem a heuristic solution is proposed and evaluated for customer basket optimization problem to make it applicable for solving complex shopping cart optimization in on-line applications. The algorithm named *2-way basket optimization* (2WBO) is given below.

5.1 2-Way Basket Optimization Algorithm

Starting conditions

$N = \{1, \dots, n\}$ – products to buy

$M = \{1, \dots, m\}$ – shops

$C_{ij}; j = 1, \dots, n; i = 1, \dots, m$ – price of product j in shop i

$D_i; i = 1, \dots, m$ – delivery costs for each shop i

$RP_j; j = 1, \dots, n$ – retailer recommended price (acquired from the model) for each product j

$S = 0$ – summary value of shopping, including products price and shipping costs

$\forall_{j \in N} R_j = 0$ – choosing indicator (realization list), for each product j

Heuristic optimization algorithm

1. Sort all products by RP_j ascending. N – sorted list.
2. Select first product $j = 1$ from the sorted list N.
3. Select the shop l for product j where $(C_{ij} + D_i) == min(C_{ij} + D_i); i = 1, \dots, m$.
4. $R_j = i$.
5. $S = S+(C_{ij} + D_i)$.
6. $D_i = 0$;
7. *If* $(j == n)$ go to 9.
8. Select next product from the list $N; j{:=}j{+}1$.
9. $S_{min} := S$.
10. $R_{min} := R$.
    end of one way optimization.
    - - - - - - - - - - - - - - - - - - -
11. Set starting conditions.
12. Sort all products by RP_j descending. N – sorted list.
13. Select first product $j = 1$ from the sorted list N.
14. Select the shop l for product j where $(C_{ij} + D_i) == min(C_{ij} + D_i); i = 1, \dots, m$.
15. $R_j = i$.
16. $S = S+(C_{ij} + D_i)$.
17. $D_i = 0$;
18. *If* $(j == n)$ go to 22.
19. Select next product from the list $N; j := j + 1$.
20. $S_{max} := S$.
21. $R_{max} := R$.
    end of second way optimization.
22. $S := min(S_{min}, S_{max})$. - final results.
23. $R := min(R_{min}, R_{max})$. - final results.

6 Computational Experiment

Proposed 2WBO algorithm was tested in close to real on-line market conditions. We built a model (including price of the products, shipping costs, etc.) according to live data available on the Internet. Algorithm optimization processing for all set of data (every of the set includes price range and flat shipping cost for every shop) were repeated many times to provide overall statistical results without outbound failures. Cumulatively 800 measurements were made. Each of the test was repeated 50 times, and average result is presented in the following table 1. In our experiment prices were rounded to integer numbers. There were few additional sets of values (more products in the basket). Results (after aggregation) were compared with price comparison sites ranking lists results. One approach where price comparators did not count shipping costs, and the other with shipping cost included to the bill. In every case (every of 800 runs) 2WBO gave better results than price comparison site (PCS) engines. Solutions provided by Price Comparison Sites without taking delivery prices into account was denoted as PCS. Solutions provided by the upgraded algorithms of Price Comparison Sites which count delivery prices was denoted as PCS+.

Selected results are presented in Table 1. Results for different number of books in the basket offered by 20 shops, and few options of shipping costs are presented in

Table 1. Experimental result comparison of PCS, PCS+ and 2WBO algorithms

# prod	shipping cost	PCS	PCS+	2WBO	2WBO >PCS	2WBO <PCS+
3	15-30	541	508	387	1,40	1,31
3	20-25	650	474	387	1,68	1,22
3	20-30	512	465	353	1,45	1,32
3	15-15	425	425	294	1,45	1,45
5	15-30	809	666	537	1,51	1,24
5	20-25	819	654	509	1,61	1,28
5	20-30	602	496	412	1,46	1,20
5	15-15	693	693	508	1,36	1,36
8	15-30	1134	848	758	1,50	1,12
8	20-25	1099	808	634	1,73	1,27
8	20-30	838	740	624	1,34	1,19
8	15-15	780	780	601	1,30	1,30
10	15-30	1134	1083	802	1,41	1,35
10	20-25	1187	1106	825	1,44	1,34
10	20-30	967	977	857	1,13	1,14
10	15-15	983	983	752	1,31	1,31

356   A. Wojciechowski and J. Musial

table 1. Each row represents 10 shopping baskets. In columns *2WBO>PCS* and *2WBO>PCS+* it is shown how far 2WBO algorithm appeared better than PCS and PCS+ algorithms, $(\frac{PCS}{2WBO}, \frac{PCS+}{2WBO})$.

Concerning all results collected in computational experiment 2WBO algorithm gives an average of 44,25% better result (lower basket cost including shipping) than price comparison site without shipping costs, and 27,5% better result than price comparison site with shipping costs declared beside each product price. There was not even one computation (among all 800 tests) where 2WBO algorithm gave worse result than price comparison with or without shipping cost. Solving time for all sets of data was on acceptable level (less that 2 seconds) that it can easily works as an on-line application.

Amount of money needed for buying all products in customer basket for all of experiment instances is presented on fig. 2.

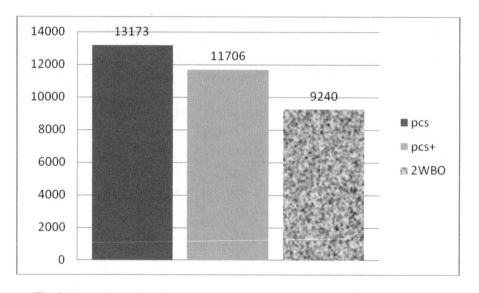

Fig. 2. Comparison of total shopping costs summarized in all experimental instances

7 Conclusions

Internet shopping becomes more and more popular with every upcoming year. Products available in on-line stores are often cheaper than ones offered by regular local retailers and wide choice of offers is available just a click away from the customer. Very important aspect of online shopping is time spent on comparing offers and comfortable way of shopping regardless of shop location. Another strong advantage of the on-line purchase is a wide choice of alternative retailers which, in general, remain at the same distance from the customer – at least one day for shopping delivery. Shipping cost are usually non zero, so that is a good idea to group purchased products into sets and buy them from small number of retailers to minimize delivery cost. Making such decisions requires three elements: information where required products are available, access to price lists in considered shops and finally specialized analytical tool that could find the minimal subset of shops where all the products from customers shopping list could be bought at the lowest price.

2-Way Basket Optimization (2WBO) algorithm proposed in the paper for optimizing multiple-item shopping basket gave satisfying result in computational experiment. In a series of experimental shopping optimization processes heuristic algorithm 2WBO outperformed shopping based on single-product price rankings by almost 30%. It is also worth to mention that optimization process in 2WBO is performed quickly (below 2 seconds in our experiments), while computing optimal solution may cost hours.

References

[1] Blazewicz, J., Kovalyov, M.Y., Musial, J., Urbanski, A., Wojciechowski, A.: Internet Shopping Optimization Problem. International Journal of Applied Mathematics and Computer Science 20(2) (2010)

[2] Horrigan, J.: The Internet and Consumer Choice (May 2008),
http://www.pewinternet.org/~/media//Files/Reports/2008/
PIP_Consumer.Decisions.pdf.pdf

[3] Horrigan, J.: On-line Shopping (February 2008),
http://www.pewinternet.org/pdfs/PIPOn-lineShopping.pdf

[4] Clay, K., Krishnan, R., Wolff, E.: Prices and Price Dispersion on the Web: Evidence from the Online Book Industry. In: National Bureau of Economic Research, Inc, vol. 8271 (2001)

[5] Chu, W., Choi, B., Song, M.R.: The Role of On-line Retailer Brand and Infomediary Reputation in Increasing Consumer Purchase Intention. International Journal of Electronic Commerce 9(3), 115–127 (2005)

[6] Vulkan, N.: The Economics of e-Commerce. Princeton University Press, Princeton (2003)

[7] Wojciechowski, A.: Supporting Social Networks by Event Driven Mobile Notification Services. In: Meersman, R., et al. (eds.) OTM-WS 2007, Part I. LNCS, vol. 4805, pp. 398–406. Springer, Heidelberg (2007)

[8] Holsapple, C., et al.: Decision Support Applications in Electronic Commerce. In: Shaw, M., et al. (eds.) Handbook on Electronic Commerce, Springer, Heidelberg (2000)

[9] Santangelo, A., Augello, A., Sorce, S., Pilato, G., Gentile, A., Genco, A., Gaglio, S.: A Virtual Shopper Customer Assistant in Pervasive Environments. In: Meersman, R., Tari, Z., Herrero, P. (eds.) OTM-WS 2007, Part I. LNCS, vol. 4805, pp. 447–456. Springer, Heidelberg (2007)

[10] Lee, H.G.: o Electronic Marketplaces Lower the Prices of Goods? Communications of the ACM 41(1), 73–80 (1998)

[11] Wojciechowski, A., Musial, J.: A Customer Assistance System. Optimizing Basket Cost, Foundations of Computing and Decision Sciences 34(1), 59–69 (2009)

Gossiping for Autonomic Estimation of Network-Based Parameters in Dynamic Environments

Panagiotis Gouvas[1], Anastasios Zafeiropoulos[1,2], and Athanassios Liakopoulos[2]

[1] National Technical University of Athens, Heroon Polytechneiou, 15773 Zografou, Greece
[2] Greek Research & Technology Network, Mesogion 56, 11527 Athens, Greece
pgouvas@mail.ntua.gr,{tzafeir,aliako}@grnet.gr

Abstract. Future networks are becoming larger in scale, more dynamic and heterogeneous. In such environments, adaptation of algorithms in the current networking conditions is necessary in order to increase the efficiency and performance of the deployed mechanisms. Knowledge of network based parameters may facilitate the decision making processes in a dynamic environment. Self-awareness will help the network to diagnose faults and realize the current status and, thus, proceed to self-optimization actions. In this paper, a neighbour to neighbour gossiping mechanism is proposed for autonomic estimation of network based parameters. The described mechanism is evaluated in terms of message exchanges and convergence time until accurate parameters' estimation.

Keywords: autonomic networks, gossiping techniques, NEURON, self-optimization, self-awareness.

1 Introduction

In next generation networks, there is a paradigm shift to networks that present dynamic characteristics and are always aware of the current conditions. Mobile ad-hoc networks, peer-to-peer networks and wireless sensor networks for advertising, multimedia content exchange and environmental monitoring purposes, are widely deployed. Context and situation awareness is crucial in these networks since the increasing size and complexity of the network combined with continuous topology changes make traditional monitoring systems inadequate to be effectively adjusted to the network conditions. A complete, accurate and updated knowledge of the network status is required since it facilitates the decision making process aiming at the optimization of the existing mechanisms and the efficient management and operation of the network.

The support of autonomic functionalities by the network nodes, such as self-awareness and self-healing, enables the adaptation of nodes to unpredictable conditions in a dynamic environment [1]. Self-awareness facilitates the network to efficiently sense current network conditions and quality of services provision and proceed to corrective actions (self-healing) in case of identified problems. Therefore, the monitoring components within an autonomic network may be continuously adapted, in a flexible manner, to an ever changing network infrastructure without ignoring the goals and the constraints that the administrator has set for the network as a whole.

R. Meersman et al. (Eds.): OTM 2010 Workshops, LNCS 6428, pp. 358–366, 2010.

Self-awareness may be succeeded through the interaction and exchange of information among the existing entities in the network. Knowledge is shared among the network entities, changes in the network are disseminated, consensus is achieved when required by the supported mechanisms and decisions are taken autonomously.

Several techniques have been proposed for information sharing in dynamic environments, varying from overlay networking distributed approaches [14,15] to gossip-based dissemination protocols [2,16]. In this paper, focus is given on the evaluation of neighbour to neighbour gossiping based techniques for the autonomic estimation of network based parameters. Existing algorithms have been enhanced in our previous work in order gossiping to be implemented in an autonomous manner [3]. However, the trade off between the precision and the convergence period for the autonomic estimation of parameters with the overhead imposed in the network has not been studied in detail.

The paper is organized as follows; Section 2 briefly presents the current work in the field of existing algorithms for estimation of network-based parameters. Section 3 describes the design principles of the evaluated algorithm and details specific implementation issues while Section 4 presents the emulation results regarding the proposed algorithm. Finally, Section 5 concludes the paper with a short summary of our work and identifies open issues for future work.

2   Related Work

Algorithms for estimation of network-based parameters, such as the network density, are very important in dynamic environments since they allow the observation of the changing conditions in a network. These algorithms are based on dissemination of information through broadcasting or gossiping techniques. In the case of ad-hoc or wireless sensor networks where the connections are dynamically established or torn down, the use of gossip-based dissemination protocols is preferable than the use of flooding mechanisms, as they consume significantly less network resources [2, 4]. Gossiping protocols are able to exploit local information available in the node and, through a series of interactions with peering nodes, to estimate network based parameters. Furthermore, they support the design and implementation of autonomic functionalities since these protocols are fully decentralized and particularly adapted for implementing self-organizing behaviours in dynamic networks [2,4].

The main use of gossip-based dissemination protocols is the estimation of aggregated values, such as average, minimum or maximum values for specific parameters. Aggregated values for the network size, density, the average utilization and packet loss may help the administrator to proceed to corrective actions, e.g. failure detection [6] or group management [7]. Since each node holds only a local state of the under estimation parameters and exchanges messages with a small set of peering nodes, gossip-based protocols are usually scalable [2, 5]. However, since they are applied to resource limited environments, network friendliness is a major concern. Gossip-based dissemination may be based in a "push" or "push-pull" manner [2]. In the first case, each node that receives a gossiping message, exchange its view with its peers until information is spread to all the nodes in the network. In the latter case a periodic request is sent by an active thread in a node and handled by a passive thread in another node. The "push" model is more suitable for dissemination of information within the network, while the "push-pull" model is more suitable for estimation of parameter values in the network (e.g. average network density).

Several gossip-based protocols have been proposed in the literature [16] where dissemination of information is realised through exchange of views between neighbours. In [5] a gossip-based protocol for computing aggregate values over network components in a fully decentralized fashion is proposed. The approach is based on the principles of neighbour-based gossiping and specifically using averaging techniques based on neighbour-based gossiping. The class of aggregate functions is very broad and includes many useful cases such as counting, averages, sums, products, and external values. The protocol is considered suitable for extremely large and highly dynamic systems due to its proactive structure. In [8], sensor nodes gossip with their neighbours about their sensing coverage region in order to decide locally whether to forward or to disregard packets. Energy consumption is spread to different sensor nodes, maximum sensing coverage is achieved and the network lifetime is prolonged.

Furthermore, gossiping mechanisms are also proposed in cases where dissemination of information is realised through exchange of views between nodes (not necessarily neighbouring ones). The routing protocol GOSSIP [9] is proposed for ad hoc networks and chooses some sets of nodes to gossip with a probability p. In [10], a gossip-based technique is proposed that allows each node in a system to estimate the distribution of values held by other nodes. This approach allows any node in the network to estimate the entire distribution in a decentralized and efficient manner. T-MAN [11] is also a gossip-based approach for the creation of an overlay network, where each node refines its view about its relative position in an overlay network based on the 'knowledge' of the 'closest' nodes that exist in a buffer. Each node that participates in a network uses a ranking function to evaluate its distance from another node. T-MAN allows communications with any node in the overlay network contrary to other gossiping protocols that permit communications with only the one-hop-away neighbours.

One of the challenges of gossiping protocols is the issue of synchronization among the participant nodes in order to be able to converge to estimated values at each time period [5,13,14]. In a real environment, the clocks among nodes are not synchronized and, thus, special adaptations have to be proposed. The insertion or leave of new nodes in the network has also to be handled. In [14], a loosely synchronized algorithm, aiming to compute global statistic averages based on a random event triggering mechanism, is proposed, in order to eliminate the requirement for global round synchronization.

In our previous work, we have updated the approach proposed in [5] by applying probabilistic techniques in order to support the autonomic estimation of network-based parameters. The NEURON [12] protocol has been proposed for energy efficient deployment, clustering and routing in WSNs that focuses on the incorporation of autonomic functionalities in the existing approaches. Its operation is based on the knowledge of network based parameters within the WSN that could be estimated in an autonomous manner by using an Autonomic Estimation Algorithm. In this paper, we further extend this algorithm so as to handle synchronization and performance issues. Our objective is the reduction of the bandwidth overhead while achieving satisfying performance.

3 Proposed Algorithm

In the proposed algorithm, an estimation of the network-wide parameters is autonomously generated and updated regularly without imposing significant network
overhead in terms of message exchanges. The algorithm is activated in each node
when the network bootstraps or after a topology change. The mechanism is designed in order to converge in a short time period and be also applicable to large
scale networks.

The proposed algorithm follows a "push-pull" model since it is applied for estimation of network based parameters. Two parallel threads, an active and a passive
one, are initiated in each node for neighbour to neighbour gossiping (see Table 1).
Each node maintains a list with its active neighbours and sets an initial (local) value
for the parameter under estimation across the network. In the active thread, a mutual exchange of values is conducted with one of the node's neighbours that is randomly selected. The neighbouring node is marked as been served in the local list
maintained by the initiator node. In the next mutual exchange of values (between
neighbours), the initiator node selects one of the neighbouring nodes that are not yet
served. When all the node's neighbours are served, the process is re-initiated. In the
passive thread, the node waits for messages from neighbouring nodes. Upon receipt
of a message, it exchanges values with the requesting node. After an exchange of
values is completed, each node revises the parameter value using a weighting average. It is important to note that in the active thread, the node firstly updates its estimation and then replies with the updated value. On the contrary, in the passive
thread the node firstly sends the current value to the other node and afterwards updates its estimation.

If the updated value after the completion of a mutual exchange differs less than a
specified threshold, the parameter is considered as *locally converged*. In this case, the
node sends its converged value in the next mutual exchange along with a flag that
indicates that it considers the estimation as precise. If a node that is considered locally
converged for a parameter, receives messages with the convergence flag from all its
neighbours for the same parameter, it considers the estimated value as *final* and terminates the gossiping mechanism. Gossiping is re-initiated by any node in the network after a topology change or after a significant change in an estimated parameter.

The proposed algorithm may be successfully applied in static and dynamic environments. Since gossiping is performed in a decentralized manner, scalability should
be achievable. In static environments, upon convergence, the proposed algorithm does
not require periodically exchanges of messages among the nodes. In dynamic environments, the algorithm may achieve superior (if topology changes are seldom) or
inferior (if topology frequently changes) performance (in terms of the total number of
messages) compared to other approaches. In any case, though, the proposed algorithm
is able to handle synchronization issues by maintaining the list of nodes that have
been already served in previous cycles and exchanging values with the rest nodes until convergence is succeeded. On the contrary, most of the already proposed algorithms pre-assume time synchronisation among the nodes in the network, which is
difficult to achieve in real networking environments.

Table 1. Parameter Estimation through neighbour to neighbour gossiping

```
parameter_value;                                  do forever{
local_converged=false;                                     while(!incoming_packet){}
global_converged=false;                           else {
handshake_id=0;
neighbours_coverged_map;                          send_packet_to_target(target,
                                                      parameter_value,function,
do forever{                                           incoming_packet.handshake_id,
                                                      local_converged);
    if(!global_converged) {                                      parame-
        target=select_from_neighbours_not_served(); ter_value=UPDATE(sent_parameter_val
        handshake_id++;                           ue, current_parameter_value);
        send_packet_to_target(target,parameter_value,            lo-
function,handshake_id,local_converged);           cal_converged=check_convergence
        timeout=false;                            (sent_parameter_value,
        while(no_response){ //containing handshake_id current_parameter_value);
          sleep(x);                                       }
          if(x>timeout) {timeout=true; break;}    }
        }

    if(!timeout){ //i have a sender
        parameter_value=UPDATE(sent_parameter_value,
current_parameter_value);
        local_converged=check_convergence
    (sent_parameter_value, current_parameter_value);
        neighbours_coverged_map.put
    (sender,senderpacket.local_converged);
        if(local_converged) {
        global_converged=CheckNeighborsConvergence
    (neighbours_coverged_map);
        }
        else {
         continue;
        }
    }

  }

}
```

active thread	passive thread

4 Experimental Results

In this section the performance of the proposed algorithm is evaluated for a wide set of topologies. The prototype implementation is developed in Java and supports the bootstrapping of a (multi-hop) ad-hoc network and the communication among the participant nodes. In the bootstrapped network, the autonomic estimation algorithm is applied for the estimation of various parameters. It is important to note that multiple instances of the prototype implementation may run to the same node for experimental purposes.

A topology editor is also implemented that permits the creation of an experimental topology and the emulation of the algorithm in the specified topology. The following topologies that are representative of global characteristics of real networks are supported: *Hypercube, Star, Rotated* Tree, *RingLattice* and *Barabasi-Albert*. These topologies are helpful for understanding the behaviour of the gossiping mechanism in various graphs models. An indicative screenshot with the form of each topology is shown in Figure 1.

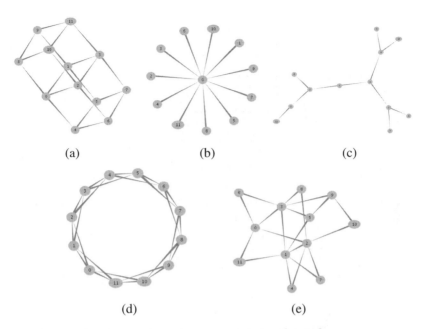

(a)   (b)   (c)

(d)   (e)

Fig. 1. Various Topologies; (a) Hypercube, (b) Star, (c) Rotated Tree, (d) RingLattice and (e) Barabasi-Albert

According to each experiment, multiple nodes are simultaneously activated without any preconfigured state information. In Figure 2, the total number of messages that are exchanged -until convergence of the estimated value is succeeded in the emulated network with threshold set to 10%- is depicted for various network sizes. The threshold refers to the difference in the estimated value between two consecutive cycles.

In topologies where the density is almost stable for all the nodes (i.e. the Tree and Circular topologies) the total messages required are less than those for topologies that present non uniform distribution of the network density (i.e. Barabasi – Albert, Hyper-Cube and Star). Especially in the Star topology, the total messages required were more than double from the other topologies (Circular and Tree topologies), since the centralized structure is not suitable for neighbour to neighbour gossiping (inconsistency is present due to many mutual exchanges of messages with the central node). The proposed algorithm is claimed to be scalable since there is almost linear behaviour in all the types of topologies. However, further study is necessary in larger networks in order to validate that the number of messages is proportional to the size of the network.

In Figure 3, the emulation time -until convergence of the estimated value is succeeded in the emulated network- is depicted for various network size. In all types of topologies, the emulation time is increasing linearly with the increase in the network size. The smallest time is needed in case of Tree topologies.

In Figure 4, the number of messages required for convergence is depicted in case of threshold 1% and 10% for difference between two consecutive values. The emulation is performed in case of Tree topology. It is clear that an increase in the accuracy of the estimated value necessitates more messages for convergence.

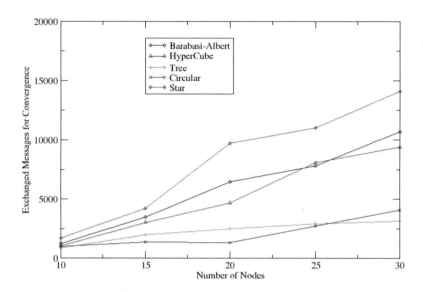

Fig. 2. Number of messages for convergence

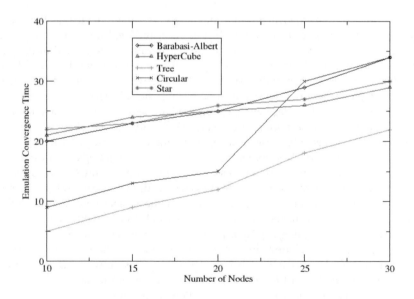

Fig. 3. Emulation time for convergence

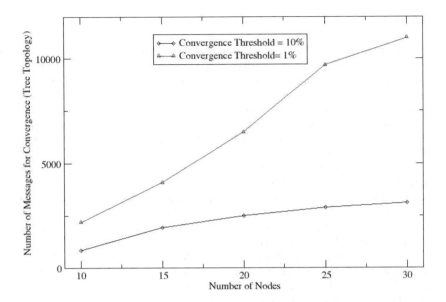

Fig. 4. Emulation time for convergence

5   Conclusions – Future Work

The knowledge of network-based parameters is crucial for achieving high efficiency and optimising mechanisms in a dynamic network. The estimation of such parameters is challenging in autonomic environments, especially when there is no global view available. Gossiping mechanisms combined with probabilistic techniques for autonomic estimation of network based parameters may be proven really useful towards this direction.

In this paper, the performance of a proposed algorithm for neighbour to neighbour gossiping is evaluated in an emulation environment. The algorithm handles synchronization issues and may be applied in static and dynamic environments. According to the experimental results, it is shown that the algorithm may be applied in a diverse set of topologies and convergence may be succeeded in reasonable time period.

In our future work, we plan to evaluate the performance of the proposed algorithm in cases where the network topology changes dynamically and to provide a comparative evaluation with other related algorithms in the literature. A dynamic model will be incorporated to the prototype for this reason. Scalability and convergence issues will be also studied in case of large networks (up to 1000 nodes). Finally, self-optimisation mechanisms for the exploitation of the acquired gossiping information for the dynamic adaptation of the existing mechanisms in the network will be developed.

Acknowledgments. This publication is based on work partially performed in the framework of the European Commission ICT/FP7 project EFIPSANS (www.efipsans.org).

References

1. Liberal, F., Fajardo, J., Koumaras, H.: QoE and *-awareness in the Future Internet. To-wards the Future Internet - A European Research Perspective. IOS Press Books, Amsterdam (2009), doi:10.3233/978-1-60750-007-0-293 ISBN 978-1-60750-007-0
2. Serbu, S., Rivière, É., Felber, P.: Network-Friendly Gossiping. In: Guerraoui, R., Petit, F. (eds.) SSS 2009. LNCS, vol. 5873, pp. 655–669. Springer, Heidelberg (2009)
3. Zafeiropoulos, A., Gouvas, P., Liakopoulos, A., Mentzas, G., Mitrou, N.: NEURON: Enabling Autonomicity in Wireless Sensor Networks. Sensors 10(5), 5233–5262 (2010)
4. Shah, D.: Network gossip algorithms. In: Proceedings of the 2009 IEEE international Conference on Acoustics Speech and Signal Processing. ICASSP, pp. 3673–3676. IEEE Computer Society, Washington (2009)
5. Jelasity, M., Montresor, A., Babaoglu, O.: Gossip-based aggregation in large dynamic networks. ACM Trans. Comput. Syst. 23(3), 219–252 (2005)
6. Van Renesse, R., Minsky, Y., Hayden, M.: A Gossip-Style Failure Detection Service. Technical Report. UMI Order Number: TR98-1687., Cornell University (1998)
7. Jelasity, M., Kermarrec, A.: Ordered Slicing of Very Large-Scale Overlay Networks. In: Proceedings of the Sixth IEEE international Conference on Peer-To-Peer Computing P2P, pp. 117–124. IEEE Computer Society, Washington (2006)
8. Tran-Quang, V., Miyoshi, T.: A novel gossip-based sensing coverage algorithm for dense wireless sensor networks. Comput. Netw. 53(13), 2275–2287 (2009)
9. Haas, Z.J., Halpern, J.Y., Li, L.: Gossip-based ad hoc routing. IEEE/ACM Trans. Netw. 14(3), 479–491 (2006)
10. Haridasan, M., Van Renesse, R.: Gossip-based Distribution Estimation in Peer-to-Peer Networks. In: International Workshop on Peer-to-Peer Systems, IPTPS 2008 (2008)
11. Jelasity, M., Babaoglu, O.: T-Man: Gossip-Based Overlay Topology Management. In: Brueckner, S.A., Di Marzo Serugendo, G., Hales, D., Zambonelli, F. (eds.) ESOA 2005. LNCS (LNAI), vol. 3910, pp. 1–15. Springer, Heidelberg (2006) ISBN: 978-3-540-33342-5
12. Iwanicki, K., Van Steen, M., Voulgaris, S.: Gossip-based clock synchronization for large decentralized systems. In: Keller, A., Martin-Flatin, J.-P. (eds.) SelfMan 2006. LNCS, vol. 3996, pp. 28–42. Springer, Heidelberg (2006)
13. Dongsheng, P., Weidong, L., Chuang, L., Zhen, C., jiaxing, S.: A loosely synchronized gossip-based algorithm for aggregate information computation. In: 33rd IEEE Conference on Local Computer Networks LCN, pp. 451–455 (2008)
14. Zuo, K., Hu, D.M., Wu, Q.W.: A Bandwidth Efficient Overlay for Information Exchange in Pervasive Computing Environment. International Conference on Computer Science and Software Engineering 3, 524–527 (2008)
15. Gouvas, P., Zafeiropoulos, A., Liakopoulos, A., Mentzas, G., Mitrou, N.: Integrating Overlay Protocols for Providing Autonomic Services in Mobile Ad-hoc Networks. In: IEICE Communications, Special Issue on: Implementation, Experiments, and Practice for Ad Hoc and Mesh Networks, vol. E93-B(8) (August 2010)
16. Makhloufi, R., Bonnet, G., Doyen, G., Gaïti, D.: Decentralized Aggregation Protocols in Peer-to-Peer Networks: A Survey. In: Gonzalez, A., Pfeifer, T. (eds.) MACE 2009. LNCS, vol. 5844, pp. 111–116. Springer, Heidelberg (2009)

OnToContent'10 - PC Co-chairs Message

We are this year at the sixth edition of the International Workshop on Ontology Content (OnToContent 2010), held in conjunction with the On The Move Federated Conferences and Workshops. But first signs of old age are fare to be perceived. Actually, the different trends that marked the evolution of information systems did not affected the topical interest on quality ontology (i.e. good quality conceptualizations, encoded in portable and extensible format) that is orthogonal to technical and procedural aspects.

This workshop focuses on content issues, such as methodologies and tools concerned with modeling good ontologies. Each year the workshop also aims at investigating some topical issue. This year our attention was focused on "Ontology in Social Enterprise".

The workshop counts on a very active Program Committee, composed of world-wide recognized experts from academy and industry, as well as young and emerging researchers, comprising 26 members of 11 nationalities. After the review process we accepted 50% of the submissions, which ultimately included 65% of those submitted as full papers. We are grateful to the referees for their dedication and effort in reviewing the submitted abstracts. We also thank the Committee members for their invaluable help.

The program of the workshop is structured in two sessions. First session gives room to contributions related to ontology engineering and includes papers contributing on the evolution of methodological aspects as well as reporting on specific case studies. Second session is dedicated to "Ontology in Social Enterprise" i.e. approaches that relate conceptualizations of social dynamics and business process.

The paper by Yalemisew Abgaz, and Claus Pahl proposes an "Empirical Analysis of Impacts of Instance-Driven Changes in Ontologies". Riccardo Albertoni and Monica De Martino describe their results in evaluating "Semantic Similarity and Selection of Resources Published According to Linked Data Best Practice". Emanuele Caputo, Angelo Corallo, Ernesto Damiani, and Giuseppina Passiante discuss "KPI modeling in MDA perspective". Carlos Sá, Carla Pereira, and António Lucas Soares propose their results and discuss the different implications of "Supporting collaborative conceptualization tasks through a semantic wiki based platform". Lina Bountouri, Christos Papatheodorou, and Manolis Gergatsoulis deals with "Modelling the Public Sector Information through CIDOC Conceptual Reference Model". Carneiro Luis, Sousa Cristivao, Soares Antonio discuss the "Integration of domain and social ontologies in a CMS based collaborative platform".

To conclude, let us remember that we are indebted to all authors for their submissions, and the OTM organizers for their excellent support in setting up and finalizing this workshop.

August 2010

Mustafa Jarrar
Paolo Ceravolo
OnToContent'10

R. Meersman et al. (Eds.): OTM 2010 Workshops, LNCS 6428, p. 367, 2010.
© Springer-Verlag Berlin Heidelberg 2010

Empirical Analysis of Impacts of Instance-Driven Changes in Ontologies

Yalemisew M. Abgaz, Muhammad Javed, and Claus Pahl

Centre for Next Generation Localization (CNGL),
School of Computing, Dublin City University, Dublin 9, Ireland
{yabgaz,mjaved,cpahl}@computing.dcu.ie

Abstract. Changes in the characterization of instances in digital content are one of the rationales to evolve ontologies that support a domain. These changes can have impacts on one or more of interrelated ontologies. Before implementing changes, their impact on the target ontology, other dependent ontologies or dependent systems should be analysed. We investigate three concerns for the determination of impacts of changes in ontologies: representation of changes to ensure minimum impact, impact determination and integrity determination. Key elements of our solution are the operationalization of changes to minimize impacts, a parameterization approach for the determination of impacts, a categorization scheme for identified impacts, and prioritization technique for change operations based on the severity of impacts.

Keywords: ontology evolution, impact determination, instance-driven change.

1 Introduction

Ontology evolution is a continuous process. Whenever there is a change in the domain, its conceptualization or specification, the ontology needs to be changed [1,2,3]. Ontologies, built to give support for specific content within a domain, change as content and embedded ontology instances change and need to be updated synchronously with changes in the domain [4,5,6].

When new concepts are added or existing ones are deleted or modified in the content, the respective ontology needs to be updated. Implementing the changes requires understanding them correctly and representing them accurately using ontology change operations. However, this only solves few of the problems associated. These changes can trigger further cascaded changes and affect one or more interrelated ontologies. The effects of the change may propagate back to the domain instances in the content leaving the process in a circle. An ontology engineer who detects a change of an instance in a content document and trying to maintain the ontology accordingly may end up with so many unseen impacts. In large and interrelated ontologies, the process of determining impacts of change operators will become time consuming and error prone. Thus, the determination of change impact is crucial.

R. Meersman et al. (Eds.): OTM 2010 Workshops, LNCS 6428, pp. 368–377, 2010.

In this research, some of the key features we investigate are:

- a case-based real-world requirement analysis.
- an analysis to determine the impacts of instance-driven changes in ontologies:
  - Operationalization: how to operationalize changes to ensure minimum impact? We measure minimum impact in terms of consistency, validity, number of operations, cascaded effect, ontologies affected etc
  - Parameterization and Categorization: how to determine different impact categories and parameters to determine impact?
  - Integrity: how to determine the integrity (consistency within and among dependent ontologies and validity within instances and ontologies) of the ontology due to the changes?
  - Prioritization: how to choose the best options with minimum impacts in different situations?

While a significant number of approaches [7,8,9,10] focus on addressing consistency and validity of the ontology at the time of change, we focus on analysis and determination of impacts of change operations to minimize their impact on not yet evolved ontologies. We operationalize changes to ensure minimum impact, define parameters to identify and determine impacts, categorize impacts to deal with them at different levels of expertise and prioritize impacts to enable us to choose the options with minimum impacts in different situations.

This paper is organized as follows: Section 2 describes the empirical study and Section 3 focuses on the selection of schemes for impact analysis and identification of parameters. Section 4 presents our proposed framework for the impact determination process. The actual categorization of impacts using different criteria is discussed in Section 5. Evaluation of the results and related work is given in Section 6. We give conclusions in Section 7.

2   Empirical Study

We conducted an empirical study on a repository of help files of a content management software system with the aim of supporting our proposed theoretical solution with an empirical experiment. The case study is selected because it has a wide coverage of domains from the application domain to software systems, which are interdependent on another. Moreover concepts and instances are distributed throughout the content of the help files and create a strong link between the instances in the content and the concepts in the ontologies. This makes it of great interest to investigate instance-driven change impacts because the changes made in the content of the help files will have a direct impact on the ontology and vice versa. We use the term elements to refer to ontology elements such as classes, individuals, attributes, relations, axioms etc [11].

There are four primary ontologies identified for supporting software systems help files. A high-level description of these ontologies and their dependencies are depicted in Fig. 1. The DocBook ontology gives structure to and defines how elements in the help ontology are organized. The help ontology guides the

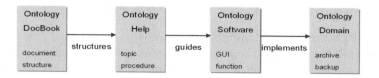

Fig. 1. Ontology Interrelation

software ontology in a way that explains how the software ontology makes use of the topics, procedures etc. The software ontology allows us implement the ontology domain which is specific to the components in each application. Using the help files, we identified representative scenarios that explain possible changes that may occur when there is a new software release, technology change and/or software structure adjustment. The scenarios further represent frequent changes that occur on the instances of the help files. The scenarios are extracted from the real world changes in the software industry - specifically changes between an old and a new version of the software help content. Our focus is on content changes that trigger a change in an ontology and the scenarios are selected based on the impact of changes in instances. Initially, 15 scenarios were identified that cover all the four ontologies. Based on the frequency of the change, their cascaded impacts, the operations involved and the number of ontologies affected, we selected scenarios that are most representative of the evolution process. Two scenarios are discussed below.

Scenario 1: The new version of the software resulted in a change of component "X" which contains other two sub components "Y" and "Z". The component "X" and its subcomponent "Y " are removed but the subcomponent "Z" is moved up. Here, all the previous instances of "X" and "Y" are preserved as instances of "Z". The desired output is an updated ontology which reflects the change requested. The primary ontology affected is the domain ontology(Fig. 1). The change operations are:

- Move up ("Z")
  • Add instance of ("instance of X", "Z")...
  • Add instance of ("instance of Y", "Z")...
- Delete concept ("Y")
- Delete concept ("X")

Scenario 2: The software engineers introduced a new software component "NC". The new component has new associated help files. The desired output is a software application ontology that has a description of the new component and its properties. The primary ontology affected are the domain and help ontologies (Fig. 1). The change operations are:

- Add Concept ("NC")
- Add sub concept ("NC", "software application")
- Add instance ("help file")...
- Add instance of ("help file", "NC")

3   Schemes for Impact Analysis

In situations where interrelated ontologies are used, the change of one element in one ontology may have an impact on other elements within the same ontology or elements among the interrelated ontologies. The dependency between ontologies, especially when they are used in a specialized domain is often high. Thus, the impact determination process focuses on identifying impacts of change operations on one or more interrelated ontologies.

3.1   Types of Ontology Change Impact

The term impact refers to a consequential change of elements in the ontology due to the application of a change operation on one or more of the elements in the ontology [8,1,12]. The impact can be structural or semantic. Structural impact is an impact that occurs on the structural relationship between the elements of the ontology. Semantic impact is an impact that occurs on the interpretation of the ontology and its elements.

Structural impacts are possible consequences on the structure of the ontology due to a structural change.

- Broken Structure:
  - Orphan concept: the change operator may introduce an orphan concept in the ontology
  - Orphan Properties: the change operator may introduce an orphan property in the ontology (properties without domain or without parents)
  - Orphan instance: the change operator may introduce an orphan instance in the ontology
- Cyclic structure: the change operator may introduce a cyclic structure

Semantic impacts are possible inconsistencies and invalidities that arise from the interpretation of the ontology due to structural changes [8].

- Generalization/ specialization: elements (concepts, instances, domains/ranges of properties) move up or down in the hierarchy
- More/less description: a data type property or instance level object property is added to or deleted from a concept
- More/less restrictive: a change to the restriction further restricts or extends its semantics
- More/less extended: a change to its axioms further extends or restricts its semantics

To determine the impact of change operations, we identified the following parameters that determine the nature of impact of a change operation on the elements of an ontology, see Table 1. An example shall explain the approach. All instances of the concept "Assign Role", from the help ontology, in one version of a help file have been changed to either "Assign AdministrativeRole" or "Assign UserRole" in the newer software version. This change can be represented by a

Table 1. Sample parameters for impact determination

General Parameters	Concept Parameters	Property Parameters	Axiom Parameters
Operation	Target concept	Target property	Target axiom
Ontology element type	Has sub/super class	Has sub/super property	Has domain
Ontology target element	Has domain/range	Has data/object property	Has range

composite operation SplitConcept ("Role", "AdministrativeRole", "UserRole"). To determine the impact of the change on the ontology, we need to know what the target entity is (the concept "Role"), whether it has subclasses and/or super class, whether it has a data property or object property, and if it is a domain or a range of a property. These parameters about the target concept provide us with information about what potential impacts are associated with a change.

3.2 Change Operations

The following is a list of possible changes that may occur on the structure and the semantics of ontology. Changes can be atomic, composite or domain specific. Higher levels of changes (composite and domain-specific) are created by combining atomic changes in a certain order [13]. Renaming can be done by a series of addition and deletion operations; thus, is not discussed here. Addition and deletion are applied to concepts, properties, restrictions, axioms and instances as target elements. Thus, we have change operations like Add concept, Delete concept, Add property, and Delete axiom.

4 Framework for Change Impact and Integrity Analysis

The empirical study further clarifies that impact determination is a step-by-step process, see Fig. 2. These steps fit into the semantics of change phases of the general ontology evolution process [1].

4.1 Change Request Capturing and Representation

In this first step, the objective is to represent detected changes using suitable change operators that ensure the efficient implementation of the required change. The execution depends on how the change is represented [14,15] and relies on two factors. First, the selection of the appropriate operator and, second, the order of execution of the operations focusing on efficient ordering of atomic change operations into composite and higher-level granularity to minimize impact [12,13].

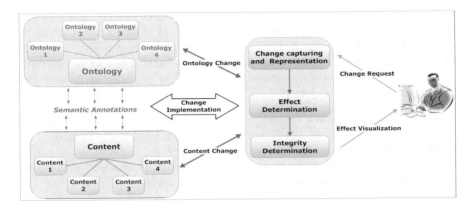

Fig. 2. Instance-driven change and impact determination process

4.2 Impact Determination

This step mainly focuses on determining the impacts of the captured change operations on the elements of the ontology. Impact determination process focuses on analyzing the nature of the operations and the target ontology elements using different parameters. Based on these parameters, this phase enables the categorization of change operations into different category of impacts. This phase further identifies the part of the ontology that is affected by the change. This process is crucial to deal with those identified parts.

4.3 Integrity Determination

Consistency. Once the scope of the impact of the change operations is identified, the next step is to analyze how the consistency of the ontology is affected by these changes. Consistency is analyzed based on consistency rules that are defined for the ontology. Since these rules are defined prior to the implementation of the change operations, it is possible to determine which consistency rules will be violated if a change is made on the ontology [16]. Defining consistency rules is important for consistency analysis. We focus here only on the following widely used rules for an ontology [14]:

1. *Identity invariant:* no two elements should have the same id (URI)
2. *Rootedness invariant:* there should be a single root in the ontology
3. *Concept hierarchy invariant:* no element should have a cyclic graph
4. *Closure invariant:* every concept should have at least one parent concept except the root concept
5. *Cardinality invariant:* the cardinality of a constraint should be a non-negative integer greater than or equal to the minimum cardinality and less than or equal to the maximum cardinality
6. *User-defined constraints:* these constraints are user-defined and needs to be stated in the way they can be implemented like the other invariants.

Validity. Instances in content centric systems are linked to the ontology using semantic annotation [5]. Thus determining the impact of change operations with regard to the instances is crucial. The determination of the validity of instances and instance properties is also based on the validity rules. Theses rules determine how instances/ instance properties should exist in the ontology structurally and how they should be interpreted:

1. *Invalid instance:* given a consistent ontology, if there is an instance that does not correspond to any of the concepts, then that instance is invalid.
2. *Invalid interpretation:* given a consistent ontology, if there is an instance whose interpretation contradicts any interpretation denoted by the consistent ontology, that instance has an invalid interpretation.

5   Categorization of Impact

The categorization of impact is important to systematically handle changes and prioritise crucial impacts to save much time.

5.1   Impact Based on Severity

Severity is the degree of impact of a change operation on ontology. The impact is measured qualitatively using consistency and validity, or quantitatively using number of change operations required, ontology elements affected and cascaded effect on dependent ontologies. The impact can be on the structure or semantic, consistency or validity of the existing ontology. Using the selected scenarios to determine the severity of impact of change operations, we analyze how different change operations impact the ontologies. This gives us a better understanding of which operations under what condition have a more severe impact than the others. Defined categories and identified properties are needed as input for automatic categorization at a later stage.

1. *Less or no impact:* changes with no effect on the consistency or the validity of the ontology, e.g. addition of a concept at the bottom of a hierarchy.
2. *Medium impact:* changes with medium impact that can be solved using predefined operations, e.g. addition of concepts in the middle of a hierarchy.
3. *High impact:* changes that create structural inconsistency and require little or no human involvement, usually restricted to a single ontology, e.g. deletion of concepts with subclasses and annotation links.
4. *Crucial impact:* changes that significantly affect the consistency of the ontology, affecting dependent ontologies and instances and their interpretations. They require expert involvement, e.g. deletion of concepts or addition of axioms which create invalid or inconsistent interpretation of elements.

5.2   Impacts Based on Type of Operation and Target Elements

Based on the parameters identified in Table 1; Table 2 summarizes the severity of impacts of atomic change operations. The table indicates the severity of the

Table 2. Severity of change operations and type of elements

Operation Type	Element Type
Deletion	Concept, Property [object property, then data property]
	Axioms, Restrictions
	Instances, then instance properties
Addition	Axioms, Restrictions
	Properties, concepts
	Instances, instance properties

change operations when they are applied to the target elements in the ontology. The severity of impacts of composite change operations can be determined using the atomic change operations involved. The severity within the operations is given in decreasing order. However the severity among the operations is highly tied to the element types and other parameters, for example, addition of an axiom has a more severe effect than deletion of an instance.

5.3 Impacts Based on Constraints Violated

The constraints that are violated by the change operation have different levels of impact on the ontology. This idea is backed by the empirical study and is described below.

1. the strength of the consistency and validity rules being violated, e.g. invariant constraints, soft constraints and user defined constraints.
2. the level of human involvement required, e.g. can the system carry out the operations autonomously or does it need a human intervention?

The severity of the constraints violated is listed below in descending order.

- Invalid interpretation, Closure invariant
- Concept hierarchy invariant, Invalid instances, Cardinality invariant
- Identity invariant, Rootedness invariant, Soft constraints
- User defined invariants, maybe severe based on the requirements of the user

6   Discussion and Related Work

Our approach has been evaluated based on its practical and operational applicability in the real world. From the case study, we found out that the proposed solution is effective in allowing to reduce the number of change operations, and consequently the number of cascaded impacts, significantly. We found that it enables us classify impacts into the appropriate categories.

To put our findings into context, we give a brief summary of current practice in the area of ontology evolution, specifically in handling instance-driven change. An interesting research [8] looks at determining the validity of instances in evolving ontologies. The authors evaluated the validity of data instances against changing ontologies and came up with a formal model. They presented a formal notion of structural and semantic validity of data instances. Compared to our work, their work focuses on determination of validity of data instances after a change takes place, but do not address the problem of determining impact. In [3], the effects of domain changes on the performance and validity of the knowledge-based systems are discussed. They analyzed the problems using non-evolved ontologies and present a solution for enabling consistent description of knowledge sources. However, their work emphasizes problems related with metadata evolution and annotation and does not focus on impact determination. The work in[16] discusses consistent evolution of OWL ontologies with the aim of guaranteeing consistency whenever the ontology evolves. Their focus is on structural, logical and user-defined consistency, but does not formally focus on analysis, parametrization and categorization of change impact.

7   Conclusion and Future Work

In this paper, we empirically analyzed and determined the impact of instance-driven change in ontologies. Based on results of the empirical study, we can operationalize, categorize, parameterize and prioritize changes and can analyze their impacts. Based on the severity of the impact, the changes are further analyzed. The case study has highlighted details of problems associated with instance-driven ontology changes and the difficulty of the problem solutions.

The major contribution of our work is the determination of the impact of change operations that are carried out on content-oriented ontologies. The research further contributes to identifying and categorizing change operations based on their impacts, identifying parameters that play significant role in determination of impacts and categorization of the change operations based on the severity of the impacts. We identified parameters for determining severity of the impacts like the cascaded effect, the time required (number of operations) and the human involvement to resolve complex choices.

Our future work will focus on content-oriented ontology change impact determination in a web-based multilingual environment. Specifically, we will focus on sliced Web content annotated using the domain ontologies[17]. Another complexity to be investigated is multilingual content and ontology infrastructures. We will also investigate how we can translate the empirical result into ontology languages such as Web Ontology Language (OWL).

Acknowledgment. This material is based upon works supported by the Science Foundation Ireland under Grant No. 07/CE/I1142 as part of the Centre for Next Generation Localisation (www.cngl.ie) at Dublin City University (DCU).

References

1. Stojanovic, L.: Methods and tools for ontology evolution. PhD thesis, University of Karlsruhe (2004)
2. Maedche, A., Motik, B., Stojanovic, L., Studer, R., Volz, R.: Ontologies for enterprise knowledge management. IEEE Intelligent Systems 18 (2), 22–33 (2003)

3. Stojanovic, N., Stojanovic, L., Handschuh, S.: Evolution in the ontology-based knowledge management systems. In: Proceedings of the European Conference on Information Systems - ECIS 2002, Gdańsk, Poland (2002)
4. Benjamins, V., Contreras, J., Corcho, O., Gomez-perez, A.: six challenges for the semantic web. In: Cristani, Med: KR2002 Workshop on the Semantic Web, Toulouse, France (2002)
5. Uren, V., Cimiano, P., Iria, J., Handschuh, S., Vargas-Vera, M., Motta, E., Ciravegna, F.: Semantic annotation for knowledge management:requirements and survey of the state of the art. In: Web Semantics: Science, Services and Agents on World Wide Web, vol. 4 (1), pp. 14–28 (2006)
6. Boyce, S., Pahl, C.: The development of subject domain ontologies for educational technology systems. IEEE Journal of Educational Technology and Society (ETS) 10(3), 275–288 (2007)
7. Stojanovic, L., Maedche, A., Motik, B., Stojanovic, N.: User-driven ontology evolution management. Matrix Eigensystem Routines - EISPACK Guide 6(4), 285–300 (2002)
8. Qin, L., Atluri, V.: Evaluating the validity of data instances against ontology evolution over the semantic web. Information and Software Technology. 51 (1), 83–97 (2009)
9. Liang, Y., Alani, H., Shadbolt, N.: Ontology change management in protégé. In: Proceedings AKT DTA Colloquium (2005)
10. Gruhn, V., Pahl, C., Wever, M.: Data model evolution as a basis of business process management, pp. 270–281. Springer, Heidelberg (1995)
11. W3C: Owl web ontology language guide, w3c recommendation (February 10, 2004), http://www.w3.org/TR/owl-guide
12. Plessers, P., De Troyer, O., Casteleyn, S.: Understanding ontology evolution: A change detection approach. Web Semantics: Science, Services and Agents on the World Wide Web. 5 (1), 39–49 (2007)
13. Javed, M., Abgaz, Y., Pahl, C.: A pattern-based framework of change operators for ontology evolution. In: Meersman, R., Herrero, P., Dillon, T. (eds.) On the Move to Meaningful Internet Systems OTM 2009 Workshops. LNCS, vol. 5872, pp. 544–553. Springer, Heidelberg (2009)
14. Stojanovic, L., Maedche, A., Stojanovic, N., Studer, R.: Ontology evolution as reconfiguration-design problem solving. In: Proceedings of the 2nd international conference on Knowledge capture (2003)
15. Oliver, D.E., Shahar, Y., Shortliffe, E.H., Musen, M.: Representation of change in controlled medical terminologies. Artificial Intelligence in Medicine 15 (1), 53–76 (1999)
16. Haase, P., Stojanovic, L.: Consistent evolution of owl ontologies. In: Gómez-Pérez, A., Euzenat, J. (eds.) ESWC 2005. LNCS, vol. 3532, pp. 182–197. Springer, Heidelberg (2005)
17. Holohan, E., McMullen, D., Melia, M., Pahl, C.: Adaptive courseware generation based on semantic web technologies. In: Proceeding of the International Workshop on Applications of Semantic Web Technologies for E-Learning (SW-EL2005) at the Twelveth International Conference on Artificial Intelligence in Education (AIED2005). IOS Press (2005)

Semantic Similarity and Selection of Resources Published According to Linked Data Best Practice

Riccardo Albertoni and Monica De Martino

CNR-IMATI,
Via De Marini, 6 – Torre di Francia – 16149 Genova, Italy
{albertoni,demartino}@ge.imati.cnr.it

Abstract. The position paper aims at discussing the potential of exploiting linked data best practice to provide metadata documenting domain specific resources created through verbose acquisition-processing pipelines. It argues that resource selection, namely the process engaged to choose a set of resources suitable for a given analysis/design purpose, must be supported by a deep comparison of their metadata. The semantic similarity proposed in our previous works is discussed for this purpose and the main issues to make it scale up to the web of data are introduced. Discussed issues contribute beyond the re-engineering of our similarity since they largely apply to every tool which is going to exploit information made available as linked data. A research plan and an exploratory phase facing the presented issues are described remarking the lessons we have learnt so far.

1 Selecting Complex Resources

Effective sharing and reuse of data are still desiderata of many scientific and industrial domains, e.g., environmental monitoring and analysis, medicine and bioinformatics, CAD/CAE virtual product modelling and professional multimedia, where the selection of tailored and high-quality data is a necessary condition to provide successful and competitive services. For example, in the domain of environmental data, many data resources are usually obtained through complex acquisition-processing pipelines, which typically involve distinct specialized fields of competency. Oceanographers, biologists, geologists may provide heterogeneous data resources, which are encoded differently in text, tables, images, 2D and 3D digital terrain models.

Semantic web and in particular the emerging linked data best practice [1] provide a promising framework to encode, publish and share complex metadata of resources in these scientific and industrial domains. Enabling factors for establishing the web of data as preferred selling point for complex resources are: (i) linked data best practice relies on light-weighed ontologies encoded in Resource Description Framework (RDF) which can be exploited to provide ontology driven metadata. Such a kind of metadata takes advantage from the Open Word Assumption, enabling the adoption of complex, domain specialized and independently developed metadata vocabularies, which are pivotal to document resources produced in complex and loosely coupled pipelines; (ii) linked data best practice relies on content negotiation exploiting the standard HTTP protocol, it is not proposing a brand new platform replacing the existing technologies.

R. Meersman et al. (Eds.): OTM 2010 Workshops, LNCS 6428, pp. 378–383, 2010.

Rather, it can be placed side by side to domain specific protocol and standards (e.g., Open Geospatial Consortium specification for the geographic domain) making metadata available in human and machine consumable format; (iii) technological headways have brought to mature prototypes in order to expose resource as linked data (e.g., D2R and Pubby), to query them by appropriate query language (i.e., SPARQL), to retrieve their pertaining RDF fragments published around the web (e.g., Sindice), to reason, store and manipulate these fragments once there are retrieved (e.g., JENA API).

However, even supposing the linked data was massively adopted to share the metadata of complex resources, the **selection** of the most suitable datasets for complex domains like environmental analysis would still be an enervating task. A huge amount of resource features and their complex relations must be considered during the selection process.

Especially for assisting in this process, semantic similarity algorithms supporting a deep comparison of resource features are pivotal. The term "semantic similarity" has been used with different meanings in the literature. It sometimes refers to *ontology alignment,* where it enables the matching of distinct ontologies by comparing the names of the classes, attributes, relations, and instances [2]. Semantic similarity can also refer to *concept similarity* where it assesses the similarity among terms by considering their distinguishing features [3, 4]; their encoding in lexicographic databases [5,6,7,8]; their encoding in conceptual spaces [9].

In this position paper, however, semantic similarity is meant as *instance similarity* since this similarity is fundamental to support detailed **comparison, ranking** and **selection** of multidimensional data through its ontology driven metadata.

Different methods to assess instance similarity have been proposed. Some rely on description logics [10]; some have been applied in the context of web services [11]; some others have been applied to cluster ontology driven metadata [12, 13].

Surprisingly, none of these methods supports recognition in the case of those instances, albeit different, have effectively the same informative content: they lack of an explicit formalization of the role of *context* in the entity comparison, and they fail identifying and measuring if the informative content of one overlaps or is contained in the other. Thus, the similarity results are not easily interpretable in terms of gain and loss the users get adopting a resource in place of another. To address these problems, we have recently proposed an asymmetric and context dependent semantic similarity among ontology instances, which meets the aforementioned requirements. The results are shown to be very promising for fine-grained resource selection when operating on a local repository of resources [14]. Unfortunately, there are still many issues that have to be addressed to scale the instance similarity up to the web of data. In this position paper, we are going to discuss these issues.

2 Identified Issues

As more and more data resources are exposed on the web, semantic similarity should locate data on the fly on the web of data, considering multiple and possibly unknown sources. Extending instance similarity at such a scale forces to redesign the similarity addressing its invariance with respect to metadata varieties, which arise when independent stakeholders provide resources. In particular we have to deal with

(i) *non-authoritative metadata*, namely metadata published by actors who are nei-
     ther the resource producers nor the owners, as it happens for metadata docu-
     menting resources that have been re-elaborated or reviewed by third parties;
(ii) *heterogeneous metadata,* i.e., metadata provided according to different, some-
     times interlinked, more often overlapping metadata vocabularies, as it happens
     when the metadata for a resource are provided by stakeholders with different
     fields of competency;
(iii) *non-consistently identified metadata*, namely metadata occurring when the same
     resource has different identifiers in distinct metadata sets.
(iv) *efficiency and computational issue:* in a longer perspective an accurate similarity
     assessment might result computationally prohibitive as soon as the number of
     resources discovered and features considered increase.

3   Research Plan and Exploratory Phase

We propose a quite challenging research plan to fit the similarity into the web of data:

(i)   *non-authoritative metadata* can be investigated considering how synergies with
        semantic web indexes (e.g., Sindice [15]) can be used to retrieve non authorita-
        tive features;
(ii) *heterogeneous metadata* can be addressed deploying schema and entity level
        consolidation using both explicit metadata statements and mining implicit
        equivalences through co-occurring resources annotations;
(iii) *non-consistently identified metadata* could be eased deploying reasoning tech-
        niques to be applied to web datasets, e.g., to smush fragments of distributed
        metadata, or developing specific scripts to interlink resources relying on a-priori
        knowledge about how datasets have been originated;
(iv) *efficiency and computational problems* can deploy strategies to speed up the
        assessment of semantic similarity, in particular, solutions based on the cashing
        of intermediate comparisons and techniques to prune the comparisons according
        to a specified application context might resolve the less severe cases. Moreover,
        algorithms for efficient parallelization can be studied, e.g., using the Map Re-
        duce cluster-computing paradigm.

Before engaging in this challenging research plan, we have undertaken an exploratory
phase analyzing real web data. The goal is to get a first-hand experience in varieties
introduced by data providers publishing metadata. Although publishing metadata
according linked data best practice has a huge potential for documenting resources
produced in complex pipelines, it is not yet a common practice in the specialized
domains we have mentioned. For this reason, we have been forced to move on a
simpler domain considering the scientific publications exposed as linked data by Semantic Web Dog Food-SWDF (http://data.semanticweb.org/) and DBLP in RDF
(http://dblp.l3s.de/d2r). We aim at comparing a limited set of researchers considering
the number of publications they wrote.

   We have set up a first linked data enabled instance similarity redesigning the prototype developed in [14] in order to have a live test bed for experimenting and deepen the
aforementioned issues. In particular, we have extended the notion of context making

explicit to which namespaces properties belong to, so it is possible to build context considering properties from different RDF schemas. We have also updated the ontology model, which was previously based on Protégé-API, to a more linked data oriented module querying RDF models by SPARQL. Then we have started experimenting the new prototype to assess the semantic similarity among researchers whose metadata are available as linked data.

According to the linked data best practice, researchers are identified by URI, then our similarity prototype compares two researchers considering their URIs (i.e., http://dblp.l3s.de/d2r/resource/authors/giovanni_tummarello and http://dblp.l3s.de/d2r/resource/authors/Renaud_Delbru). The following context is provided to parameterize our instance similarity assessment:

```
PREFIX foaf: <http://xmlns.com/foaf/0.1/>

[foaf:Person]->{{},{(foaf:made, Count)}}
```

According to this context the more two researchers are related through the foaf:made property to a similar number of entities, the more the researchers are considered similar. This is just a simple example of context, more complex cases can be easily considered as discussed in [14].

During the similarity assessment, researchers' URIs are dereferenced in order to get their authoritative RDF fragments. Researcher publications are either provided by DBLP or semantic web dog food, but dereferencing the DBLP researchers' URIs we get the publications from DBLP and not from semantic web dog food, which is in this case a non-authoritative info w.r.t. DBLP.

A first attempt to face with *Non-authoritative metadata* is then done considering Sindice. Given an URI, Sindice returns a ranked list of RDF fragments published all over the web and containing such a URI. Unfortunately, if you ask for http://dblp.l3s.de/d2r/resource/authors/giovanni_tummarello, Sindice returns just the fragments from DBLP, namely the authoritative fragment that corresponds to such an URI, and all the fragments that can be obtained dereferencing URIs contained in that authoritative fragment. We know SWDF RDF fragment pertaining to Tummarello provides metadata about his publications, but unfortunately it refers to other Tummarello's URIs. So these non authoritative info cannot be exploited during our similarity assessment. **First lesson: *Non-authoritative metadata* and *Non-consistently identified metadata* are tightly inter-related in the real practice. To effectively deal with the former issue often we have to care about the latter issue.**

Considering that we know a priori, semantic web dog food provides researcher's URI in the form http://data.semanticweb.org/person/name-[midlename]-[familyname], we can add for each SWDF researcher the following owl:sameAs triples on the web to overcame the previous problem at least in this specific example.

```
<http://data.semanticweb.org/person/name-[midlename]-
[familyname]>  owl:sameAs
<http://dblp.l3s.de/d2r/resource/authors/name_[middle-
name]_familyname>
```

Assuming that each URI in the retrieved RDF fragments is dereferenced, we are then able to retrieve the non-authoritative RDF fragments from SWDF. The reasoner of JENA is exploited in the linked data enabled instance similarity to induce the symmetry

382   R. Albertoni and M. De Martino

and the transitivity of owl:sameAs and to exploit coherently the entities that have been already consolidated. In this simple case, the *heterogeneous metadata issue* does not appear, in fact both DBLP and SWDF use FOAF schema. We would have experienced this issue if one of the two datasets had used Dublin Core instead of FOAF. However, we experienced another sort of heterogeneous metadata: triples provided by DBLP relate publications to researchers by foaf:maker and not by its inverse property foaf:made specified in the context. The similarity ignores foaf:made is the inverse of foaf:maker unless that is specified by an ontology schema or a specific rule added a priori. **Second lesson: ontology/schema must be dereferenced as much as entity's URIs to make the semantics of properties exploitable.**

On the other hand, we must be careful dereferencing ontologies\schemas and adding rules otherwise we end up with huge RDF graph making even worst the efficiency and computational problems. Dereferencing schemata and URIs is extremely slow, and it adds to RDF graph plenty of info that is not exploited during the semantic similarity assessment (i.e., info not pertaining to specified context). Some kind of context driven crawling and local caching supporting by persistent RDF models has to be considered. **Third lesson: specific and context driven policies to dereference the URI and retrieve RDF fragments should be deployed in order to ease efficiency and computational problems.**

As soon as fragments are dereferenced, we can compare the researchers' publications. Some publications are provided twice, both by DBLP and SWDF, and of course they are provided with distinct URIs. If similarity considered them as distinct publications it would count twice some of the researchers' publications returning wrong results. **Fourth lesson: *Non-consistently identified metadata* is a recursive problem. Consolidating researcher without consolidating papers brings to wrong similarity results. We must be sure entities and properties in the similarity context have been properly consolidated before applying instance similarity.**

4 Conclusion

In this position paper, we discuss linked data best practice to make available metadata of resources produced throughout a complex pipeline. We claim our asymmetric and context dependent instance similarity as a tool for comparing complex metadata but some issues have to be faced. A research programme dealing with these issues is drafted and an exploratory phase shows how some new sub-problems came up exploiting linked data even in very simple scenarios. We think relying on real data provided by third parties is pivotal in order to learn more about the metadata varieties. That time consuming practice is inspiring to make linked data consuming tools work effectively and to fully demonstrate the linked data potential in everyday business practices.

Acknowledgement. Part of the activity described in the paper has been carried out within the CNR Short Mobility programme granted to Riccardo Albertoni in 2009. We thank Dr. Bianca Falcidieno and Dr. Giovanni Tummarello for their precious suggestions, Dr. Renaud Delbru and Dr. Michael Hausenblas for their support during the short visit at DERI.

References

1. Bizer, C., Heath, T., Berners-Lee, T.: Linked Data - The Story So Far. Int. J. Semantic Web Inf. Syst. 5(3), 1–22 (2009)
2. Euzenat, J., Shvaiko, P.: Ontology Matching. Springer, Heidelberg (2007)
3. Rodríguez, M.A., Egenhofer, M.J.: Comparing geospatial entity classes: an asymmetric and context-dependent similarity measure. IJGIS 18(3), 229–256 (2004)
4. Janowicz, K., Keßler, C., Schwarz, M., Wilkes, M., Panov, I., Espeter, M., Bäumer, B.: Algorithm, Implementation and Application of the SIM-DL Similarity Server. In: Fonseca, F., Rodríguez, M.A., Levashkin, S. (eds.) GeoS 2007. LNCS, vol. 4853, pp. 128–145. Springer, Heidelberg (2007)
5. Rada, R., Mili, H., Bicknell, E., Blettner, M.: Development and Application of a Metric on Semantic Nets. IEEE Trans. on Systems Man and Cybernetics 19(1), 17–30 (1989)
6. Resnik, P.: Using Information Content to Evaluate Semantic Similarity in a Taxonomy. In: Proceedings of the 14th Int. Joint Conf. on Artificial Intelligence, IJCAI (1995)
7. Lin, D.: An Information-Theoretic Definition of Similarity. In: Proc. of the Fifteenth In-Conference on Machine Learning, pp. 296–304. Morgan Kaufmann, San Francisco (1998)
8. Pirrò, G.: A semantic similarity metric combining features and intrinsic information content. Data Knowl. Eng. 68(11), 1289–1308 (2009)
9. Schwering, A.: Hybrid Model for Semantic Similarity Measurement. In: Meersman, R., Tari, Z. (eds.) OTM 2005. LNCS, vol. 3761, pp. 1449–1465. Springer, Heidelberg (2005)
10. D'Amato, C., Fanizzi, N., Esposito, F.: A dissimilarity measure for ALC concept descriptions. In: SAC 2006, pp. 1695–1699 (2006)
11. Hau, J., Lee, W., Darlington, J.: A Semantic Similarity Measure for Semantic Web Services. In: Web Service Semantics: Towards Dynamic Business Integration workshop at WWW 2005 (2005)
12. Maedche, A., Zacharias, V.: Clustering Ontology Based Metadata in the Semantic Web. In: Elomaa, T., Mannila, H., Toivonen, H. (eds.) PKDD 2002. LNCS (LNAI), vol. 2431, pp. 348–360. Springer, Heidelberg (2002)
13. Grimnes, G.A., Edwards, P., Preece, A.D.: Instance Based Clustering of Semantic Web Resources. In: Bechhofer, S., Hauswirth, M., Hoffmann, J., Koubarakis, M. (eds.) ESWC 2008. LNCS, vol. 5021, pp. 303–317. Springer, Heidelberg (2008)
14. Albertoni, R., De Martino, M.: Asymmetric and Context-Dependent Semantic Similarity among Ontology Instances. In: Spaccapietra, S. (ed.) Journal on Data Semantics X. LNCS, vol. 4900, pp. 1–30. Springer, Heidelberg (2008)
15. Oren, E., Delbru, R., Catasta, M., Cyganiak, R., Stenzhorn, H., Tummarello, G.: Sindice. com: A document-oriented lookup index for open linked data. International Journal of Metadata Semantics and Ontologies Inderscience 3(1), 37–52 (2008)

KPI Modeling in MDA Perspective

Emanuele Caputo[1], Angelo Corallo[1], Ernesto Damiani[2], and Giuseppina Passiante[1]

[1] CCII – ISUFI, University of Salento, Lecce, Italy
{emanuele.caputo,angelo.corallo,
giuseppina.passiante}@ebms.unile.it
[2] Dept. of Computer Technology, University of Milan, Italy
ernesto.damiani@unimi.it

Abstract. Enhancing competitiveness, shortening the response time to environmental changes, increasing profits and so forth are all goals that refer to the same concept: 'improvement'. Yet, these elements are bounded to the same necessity: 'measurement'. On such bases, this work intends to provide an operative framework which, using many heterogeneous typologies of tools and technologies, would enable enterprises to define, formalize and model key performance indicators (KPIs) according to Model Driven Architecture (MDA) vision. The tools required for achieving this goal belong to different categories, according to the particular step of the framework: the theories for identification of KPIs are the balanced scorecard (BSc) and the goal question metric (GQM); process modeling is realized trough BPMN (Business Process Modeling Notation); KPIs were modeled using semantics of business vocabulary and business rules (SBVR), so as to enable automatic parsing, according to MDA vision. Finally, the mathematical formulas were represented in machine readable format through MathML.

Keywords: KPI, metric, measure, probe, MDA.

1 Introduction

The present work starts from two fundamental aspects. The first is the need to monitor different aspects of the operative life of an enterprise. Such monitoring can be aimed to verify the achievement of firm's goals[1]; the alignment between organizational required infrastructure and available infrastructure [1]; and the performances, at different levels, in comparison with the best practices of the same industrial sector. For all the previous aims, the same approaches and techniques are required: business modeling; detection of aims to achieve and identification of Key Performance Indicators (KPIs) needed for their monitoring; creation of the probes for capturing metric values, and usage of a system for management of the collected information for supporting the decision making process. The second aspect refers to the Model Driven Architecture (MDA), which aims to the automatic development of code starting from the model of the required system. In this scenario, the problem can be decomposed in three different steps: KPI identification

---

[1] In the last three decades, several theories have been formulated for this aim. In this work, two major theories were used: Balanced Scorecard (BSc) and Goal Question Metric (GQM).

R. Meersman et al. (Eds.): OTM 2010 Workshops, LNCS 6428, pp. 384–393, 2010.

(which requires methodological approach), KPI definition (which provides the machine readable format of KPIs and of their rules), and formula definition (which provides the mathematical formula of each KPI filling a gap of previous step).

The present paper is structured as follows. First, a characterization of KPIs is provided; subsequently, two different theories for KPIs identification are applied. Finally, the definition of KPI and KPI's formulas in MDA perspective are described.

2   KPI Taxonomy

Before starting with the identification and definition of KPIs, it is necessary to understand and verify if some specific categories can be identified, in order to determine an ad hoc way for their construction and their management.

A possible approach for KPI's taxonomy identification relies on the decomposition of the enterprise in three levels: strategic, tactical, and operational. This perspective [2] adopts a categorization according to a hierarchic model (in which KPIs in the top level refer to the enterprise), strategic level (KPIs focused on process) and operational level (KPIs that manage a superior level of details and refer to sub-processes). Other similar approaches use four levels [3][4], introducing an executive level and using four different perspectives as shown in Table 1:

Table 1. Process-Based Performance Measurement Framework

Level	Perspective
Strategic	Strategy-driven
Business	Business Type-driven
Implementation	Business Activity-driven
Executive	Data-driven

In Strategic Monitoring Framework (SMF) [4], similarly to Process-Based Performance Measurement Framework[2] (PPMF), three levels are used: strategic, tactical, operative. The three-level approach allows the monitoring of different hierarchic levels inside the enterprise, from strategic to operative aspects according to the chosen perspective that drives the monitoring activity (Table 1).

Other possible classifications of KPI can be based at the moment when the measurement is being performed. The evaluation of a process can be realized in different times in the life cycle of the business itself. The first step is to accurately design the process, thus enabling the process itself to achieve high performance. The proposed solution may not be the perfect solution; therefore, it has to be monitored during the execution time and, if necessary, a redesign should be applied.

The previous consideration suggests a second possible characterization of KPIs: KPIs that can be used at the design time of the process (ex-ante KPI), KPIs that are used at runtime (runtime KPI) and, finally, KPIs used after the execution of a process (ex-post KPI). In this classification, for example, process complexity evaluation is an

---

[2] Process-based performance measurement frame work [2].

ex-ante KPI, as it estimates the complexity of the process at the design time before its implementation.

Another important aspect in KPIs definition is the nature of KPI itself. In the past, the focus was on financial aspect; nevertheless, this approach proved belated in showing problems in the business. Although the Financial KPIs can be useful for business monitoring, they require the adoption of operational KPI which enables the real-time monitoring for the performance improvement and for preventing possible problems. Starting from this idea, a decomposition of the problem can applied in financial KPIs and operative KPIs.

The last characteristic provided in this work distinguishes between the indicators are directly measured during the process execution and those that are not directly measured but are calculated using other KPI's values.

Other related works make the same distinction:

- *"A 'Performance Measure' is a description of something that can be directly measured (e.g. number of reworks per day).*
- *A 'Performance Indicator' is a description of something that is calculated from performance measures (e.g. percentage reworks per day per direct employee)."* [5].

The same assumption with different names can be read in [6]:

"...indicators can be classified in two categories:
- *Primary indicators: indicators directly obtained from the observation in a real empirical system;*
- *Derived indicators: obtained by the combination or the synthesis of other primary or derived indicators."*

It seems to be a natural classification for indicators and can be very useful in the operative step, since it creates a distinction between performance measure (or direct indicators), which does not require a mathematical formula for its calculation (it is directly measured), and performance indicator (or derived indicator), which needs the definition of a formula.

3 KPI Identification

At the state of the art, several theories were proposed with the aim to identify which parameters can allow the evaluation of the performance, the verification of the alignment between two different aspects of the same business, or simply the comparison of the performance of the enterprise with the best practice in the same sector. Although these theories often were not specifically intended for business process evaluation, the adopted approach is useful and suitable also for this application. There are two generic types of approach to Process Improvement:

Analytic model and Perspective model [7][8].

Analytic models are characterized to be goal-oriented, measurement-based and bottom-up driven. This type of approach uses quantitative evidence in determining where an improvement is needed and, later, whether or not the improvement initiative has been successful. The Plan-Do-Check-Act Cycle, by Shewhart & Deming, and the Goal Question Metric (GQM) technique [9] can be considered as analytic models.

On the other hand, prescriptive models are described to be closed, staged, assessment-based and top-down-vision driven. This type of approach uses a formal and prescriptive improvement model that includes a structured set of practices.

The theories used in this work are Balanced Scorecard (BSc) [10] and GQM [11]: the former was originally developed as an instrument for supporting strategic management of the enterprise; the latter is designed for software metric but defines an approach that can be applied in business context.

The BSc approach is a perspective model developed by Kaplan and Norton in 1992. This model provides a framework for studying a causal link analysis based on internal performance measurement through a set of goals, drivers and indicators grouped into four different perspectives: Financial Customer; Internal business process; and Learning and Growth. BSc represents a milestone in performance measurement. BSc emphasises not only financial indicators, but also suggests to identify KPI starting from strategic mission of the enterprise. The idea to realise the identification of KPIs starting from different points of view provides management with an instrument that helps to focus the attention on each particular aspects of the enterprise without disregarding the mentioned perspectives. However, there is some problem concerning its appropriateness for the new paradigm of organizational structure: the Internetworked Enterprise [19] (IE). An IE has two types of processes: internal processes and processes tightly shared with its partners. This last type of process is not considered in BSc.

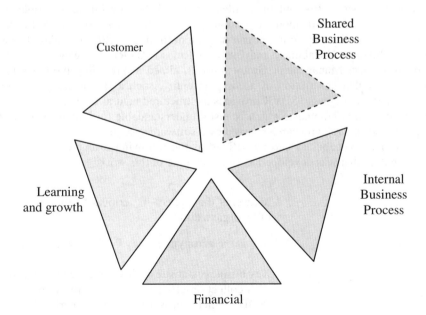

Fig. 1. A new perspective for enabling BSc in IE performance evaluation

The utilization of BSc, in IE scenario, requires a fifth perspective for allowing the performance evaluation of shared business process, i.e. processes that Enterprise has in common with its partners.

In the set of analytic models, GQM was chosen. It provides a top-down methodological approach for identifying the metrics aimed to evaluate achievement of pre-fixed goals; therefore, according to the previous definition, GQM is an analytical approach [9]. Within the paradigm of an IE, it could be useful to identify and monitor goals without focusing the attention exclusively on firm's goals, but also managing network's goals, creating the specific KPI coming down form conceptual level to quantitative level, finding the required metric which could be measured inside the firm or inside the network are key elements. This approach seems to be more flexible and adaptable to several types of organizational structure.

The shortcoming of this methodology is its inadequacy in terms of providing a global vision of a firm or of a network. Indeed, it enables the management to identify a generic goal without being related to a specific area or theme or group. This methodology can be essentially used for identifying KPI after the identification of an area, of a perspective of interest.

According to [12], GQM can be complementary to BSc, rather than alternative. On such bases, GQM could be used in each specific area previously identified by BSc.

4   KPI Definition

After the identification of the sets of KPIs for each perspectives of BSc, a formal definition is required. To satisfy MDA requirement, a machine readable format is necessary. However, KPIs and their rules are established by business people who often are not familiar with modelling languages. It is necessary to provide business people with a user friendly tool that can help them to model KPIs and rules. The Semantics of Business Vocabulary and Business Rules (SBVR)[3] is a widespread standard of the Object Management Group (OMG), aimed at providing the basis for a formal and detailed description of a complex entity, such as a business, through a structured natural language. SBVR provides a 'structured natural language' (English), a sub part of natural language, which is easily understandable for humans and, at the same time, is structured and can be parsed by a software system.

A term of the vocabulary can be defined as the following example derived from KPI Vocabulary that was developed as final outcome of this work:

KPI

Definition:	Measures that reflect the critical factors of success of an organization.
Definition:	KPI is the acronym ok Key Performance Indicator.
Definition:	Key business statistic such as number of new orders, cash collection efficiency, and return on investment (ROI), which measures a firm's performance in critical areas.

---

[3] http://www.omg.org/spec/SBVR

Concept type:	role
Necessity:	It is obligatory that a <u>KPI</u> *is* quantifiable
Note:	KPIs help to measure progress toward organizational goals and to verify the alignment between strategy and Information System

performance-measure

Definition:	It is a <u>KPI</u> directly measured from the activity or process
Definition:	specific measure of an **organization performance** in some area of its business
Concept_type:	<u>String</u>

performance-indicator

Definition:	<u>KPI</u> achieved through a formula that *links* one or more <u>performance-measures</u>

Previous definition uses standard notation of SBVR (colour, underline, etc.).

5   Formula Definition

It is important to observe that SBVR is inappropriate for formula definition and, however, formulas are necessary for KPI calculation. One of the aim of this work was to integrate the definition of KPIs into the Business Model. In fact, the KPI Vocabulary needs to be machine readable and, at the same time, the used language has to be user friendly for people who don't belong to IT sphere. SBVR solves the second part of the previous requirement because, although it is a structured language, it uses a set of contractions that are a sub-part of a natural language and can be understood and written by non-IT experts. According to its characteristic to be structured, SBVR is also machine readable but it is very difficult to realize a formula using SBVR. After some attempts to define all the aspects regarding KPI, including its formula, it was clear and evident the inadequacy of SBVR for formula definition. Starting from this ascertainment (several attempts were made with different formulas), it was necessary to individuate a language for formula definition which could have the same characteristics required for SBVR:

- Machine readable;
- User friendly.

This tool was chosen between two candidates: MathML[4] and openMath[5]. Both are XML base languages that allow user to write a formula in XML without requiring the

---

[4] http://www.w3.org/Math/
[5] http://www.openmath.org/software/index.html

knowledge of XML by user. In fact, several tools are available for writing formula in a simple math editor and obtaining its openMath or MathML format.

During the definition[6] of Formula Vocabulary, tools were not available for open-Math. In fact, webpage[7] for openMath editors contained only deadlinks except one: Sentido[8]. Conversely, the, MathML has numerous tools[9] for writing formula and obtain its XML format and, tools for reverse operation i.e. obtain formula starting from XML format.

Formula Vocabulary was realized using "MathML Editor"[10] available also for reverse operation[11].

Table 2. MathML formula for defined KPI, derived from KPI Vocabulary

```
<m:math y='30' x='0'
 xmlns:m='http://www.w3.org/1998/Math/MathML' >
   <mrow color='#000000' fontsize='12' fontfamily='_serif' >
      <mtext>PETime</mtext>
      <mo>&equals;</mo>
      <mfrac linethickness='2' >
        <mrow>
           <mtext>SetupTime</mtext>
           <mo>+</mo>
           <mtext>ProductionTime</mtext>
           <mo>+</mo>
           <mtext>TearDownTime</mtext>
        </mrow>
        <mtext>TotalNumbOfOrders</mtext>
      </mfrac>
   </mrow>
</m:math>
```

Example of complete KPI definition composed by the following items:

- SBVR KPI definition;
- MathML formula;
- XML relation for linking the KPI definition to its formula (the two object are stored in different files);

---

[6] February, 2009

[7] ://www.openmath.org/software/index.html

[8] http://www.matracas.org/sentido/

[9] http://www.w3.org/Math/Software/mathml_software_cat_editors.html#Iintegre_mathml_equation_editor

[10] http://www.learn-math.info/mathml.htm?action=editor

[11] http://www.learn-math.info/mathml/formula/displayML.html

<u>**Production-Execution-Time**</u>[12]

Definition:	It is the <u>**Average time**</u> a **product** spends on a <u>**resource**</u> or on a machine.
Concept_type:	<u>role</u>
Note:	<u>Calculation</u>: (Setup Time + Production Time + Tear Down Time) / Total number of orders
General_Concept:	<u>**Key-performance-indicator**</u>

MathML formula:
In a complete and integrated system, it could be possible to have a unique editor which allows the creation, in one single step, of all the elements needed for KPI design: SBVR definition and MathML formula. Unfortunately, such a tool is not available and a third file is required for guaranteeing the correct correlation between SBVR KPI and MathML formula. In this file, each item has the following format:

Table 3. relation between KPI definition and its mathematical formula, derived from KPI Vocabulary

```
<Relation>
     <KPI>Production-Execution-Time</KPI>
     <Variable>PETime</Variable>
</Relation>
```

6   Conclusion and Future Research

After studying several theories on Performance Measurement System focused on traditional organizational structures or supply chains, no theory for Internetworked Enterprise was found. The 'traditional' theories about Supply Chain Performance Evaluation are not able to consider partners integration and, in some cases, do not consider all the aspects of the Supply Chain itself [13]. The most adaptable theory seems to be the Balanced Scorecard [14][15] with the addition of a fifth, new perspective: Partners perspective. After the definition of the aims in these five perspectives, another theory (GQM) can be used to improve the operative validity of BSc.

GQM is not suitable as affirmed by Basili et al.("...*Although GQM has served the software industry well for several decades, it never provided explicit support for integrating its software measurement model with elements of the larger organization, such as higher-level business goals, strategies, and assumptions.*" [16], 2007), but it can improve BSc because they are complementary and interchangeable.

In the second step, a taxonomy of metric was realized. Using different theoretical approaches, the following types of metrics were identified:

- ex-ante, ex-post, run-time;
- financial, operative;
- strategic, tactical, operational [2][4];
- performance measure and performance indicator [17][5]

---

[12] Derived from KPI Vocabulary developed for this work.

Finally, the modeling aspects were discussed. MDA [18] vision requires the use of a machine readable format for all the modelled components. For software modeling there are several languages (like UML) that all satisfy this request, while for business rules this aspect is an open research topic, because although logical languages are structured and formal, they are not user-friendly and suitable for business people. Conversely, natural languages are user-friendly but very hard to be managed, being unstructured. SBVR is a good solution because it offers a Structured Natural Language that can be simply understood and used by business people and automatically parsed by a software.

SBVR solves the problem of formal definition and description of KPI, but it does not solve the definition of its mathematical formula. The choice of a second language for formula definition is a direct practical consequence of this problem. Using an XML based language, it is possible to write the formula in a user-friendly interface and automatically define the XML format. MathML is the language identified and chosen for this aim. The system needs to preserve the relation between SBVR definition of a KPI and its mathematical formula. Actually, there is not a unique system that allows to realise the two aspects together; as a consequence, it is necessary to define and store the two objects in two different files, using a third file to track the relation between them in a similar way to m-n relation in database definition.

The final outcome of this work was a KPI Vocabulary developed using SBVR, which is a structured language for automatic parsing. According to SBVR characteristics, KPI Vocabulary is extensible, i.e. starting from a basic vocabulary it is possible to design an *ad hoc* vocabulary for a specific enterprise. This vocabulary can be automatically parsed in order to enable automatic translation following MDA stack and, finally, to enable automatic development of code.

Finally, it is worth mentioning that another important aspect that was not explored in this work is the probe. In a general context a probe is an instrument that can capture the value of a measurement. Each performance measure requires a specific probe for its evaluation and the design of the probes has an impact on the feasibility of a Performance Measurement System (sub part of a Performance Management System) and on its cost. The probes, their definition and their modeling are the open questions and future researches derived from this work.

References

1. Damiani, E., et al.: SAF: Strategic Alignment Framework for monitoring Organization (2008)
2. Han, K.H., Kang, J.G., Song, M.: Two-stage process analysis using the process-based performance measurement framework and business process simulation (2008)
3. Junginger, K., Bayer, K.: Workflow-based Business Monitoring. In: Fischer, L. (ed.) Workflow Management Coalition: Workflow Handbook, pp. 65–80 (2004)
4. Lichka, C.: Strategic Monitoring and Alignment to Achieve Business Process Best Practices DEXXA (2005)
5. Browne, J., Devlin, J., Rolstadas, A., Andersen, B.: Performance Measurement: The ENAPS Approach
6. Franceschini, F., Galetto, M., Maisano, D.: Indicatori e misure di prestazione per la gestione dei processi Ed. Il sole24ore

7. Thomas, M., McGarry, F.: Top-down vs. Bottom-up Process Improvement. IEEE Software 11(7), 12–13 (1994)
8. Pfleeger, S.L., Rombach, H.D.: Measurement-based process improvement. IEEE Software 11(7), 8–11 (1994)
9. Basili, V.B., Caldiera, G., Rombach, H.D.: Experience Factory, Encyclopædia of Software Engineering, pp. 469–476. Wiley, Chichester (1994)
10. Kaplan, R., Norton, D.: The Balanced scorecard – Measures that drive Performance (1992)
11. Basili, V.R., Caldiera, G., Rombach, H.D.: The Goal Question Metric Approach (1994)
12. Buglione, L., Abran, A.: Balanced Scorecards And GQM: What Are The Differences? (2000)
13. Lambert, D.M., Pholen, T.L.: Supply Chain Metrics. International Journal of Logistics Management (2001)
14. Essiga, M., Dorobekb, S.: Adapting the Balanced Scorecard to Public Supply Chain Management (2001)
15. Brewer, C., Speh, W.: Using the balanced scorecard to measure supply chain performance. Journal of Business Logistics 21(1), 75–93 (2000)
16. Basili, V., Heidrich, J., Lindvall, M., Munch, J., Regardie, M., Trendowicz, A.: Gqm+ strategies – aligning business strategies with software measurement. In: First International Symposium, Empirical Software Engineering and Measurement, ESEM September 20-21, pp. 488–490 (2007)
17. Franceschini, F., Galetto, M., Maisano, D.: Indicatori e misure di prestazione per la gestione dei processi sole24ore, 2nd edn.
18. OMG, MDA Guide, version 1.0 (2003)
19. Corallo, A., Passiante, G.,, P.: The Digital Business Ecosystem. In: Edward Elgar Publishing, Edward Elgar Publishing (2007)

Supporting Collaborative Conceptualization Tasks through a Semantic Wiki Based Platform

Carlos Sá[1,3], Carla Pereira[1,2], and António Lucas Soares[1,3]

[1] INESC Porto, Campus da FEUP, Rua Dr. Roberto Frias, 378, 4200 - 465 Porto, Portugal
[2] Escola Superior de Tecnologia e Gestão de Felgueiras – Instituto Politécnico do Porto,
Rua do Curral, Casa do Curral, Margaride, 4610-156, Felgueiras, Portugal
[3] Dep. Engenharia Informática - Faculdade de Engenharia - Universidade do Porto,
Rua Dr. Roberto Frias, 4200-465, Porto, Portugal
cmsa@inescporto.pt, csp@inescporto.pt, als@fe.up.pt

Abstract. The process of collective development of conceptual models has not been satisfactorily addressed in the knowledge representation research literature. Nevertheless, a shared conceptualization of a given reality is the cornerstone to build semantic artifacts such as ontologies. This paper presents a new platform that implements the ColBlend method, designed to support a collaborative conceptualization process. The platform is based on semantic technologies and proposes a set of functionalities for importing, creating, manipulating, discussing and documenting conceptual models that can act e.g., as the specification of a formal ontology. The platform is being tested and used in two research projects[1].

Keywords: Shared conceptualization, social construction of meaning, socio-semantics.

1 Introduction

The use of semantic artifacts, such as taxonomies or ontologies, in organizations is becoming more and more frequent and important. If we consider organizational networks, particularly the ones where relationships are materialized mainly in collaborative processes (collaborative networks), these artifacts become even more important and this is reflected, for instance, in the support provided to discussion and negotiation activities during the initial stages of common projects, or in the implementation of processes for information classification, structuring and retrieval. Focusing on ontologies (as a computational semantic artifact), it is widely accepted that, since they are the "specification of a conceptualization", the construction of a shared conceptualization is a fundamental process. Nevertheless, this process has not been sufficiently studied and there are no suitable and effective tools to support it, particularly if considered within a collaborative network of organizations. We described in other papers

---

[1] This paper describes results obtained in the pmColNet and the cogniNet projects funded by the Fundação para a Ciência e Tecnologia under the contracts PTDC/GES/71482/2006 and PTDC/EIA-EIA/103779/2008.

R. Meersman et al. (Eds.): OTM 2010 Workshops, LNCS 6428, pp. 394–403, 2010.

[4][5] a method (and its theoretical foundations) aiming at being operationalised in the initial phases of the development of semantic artifacts, specifically for the guidance and support to collaborative conceptualization tasks. Such a method can only be operationalised through the use of a collaborative platform featuring, between others, collaborative editing of conceptual models, free textual discussions indexed to the model components (concepts and relationships), and management of models (snapshots, tree offsprings, versioning, etc.). Being the conceptualization process the main focus point of this research work, this paper presents a new system named "*Semantic System for Continuous Construction of Meaning*" (*SemSys4CCM*) which supports the method proposed in [4][5] along the lines described above. The specification of the *SemSys4CCM* was accomplished in an iterative and incremental mode, considering the knowledge obtained mainly during two action-research based projects [10]. The first part of this paper gives an overview of the *ColBlend* method, while the second describes the main features of a collaborative platform that integrates concept maps and a semantic wiki supporting the aforementioned method.

2   The *ColBlend* Method

Even though the most used definition of ontology [11] "*An ontology is a formal, explicit specification of a shared conceptualization*" presupposes the collaborative construction of conceptualizations, [12] refers that "*While different degrees of formalizations have been well investigated and are now found in various ontology-based technologies, the notion of a shared conceptualization is neither well-explored, nor well-understood, nor well-supported by most ontology engineering tools*". Agreeing with [3], the ontology research, therefore, should focus more on developing the ontological meaning negotiation process. With meaning negotiation, such as [3], we are pointing to developing ontology-guided, community-oriented processes for agreeing upon and reaching the appropriate amount of consensus on terminology and concept definitions. Such processes are necessary in order to allow for the development of effective collaborative services in stakeholder communities with multiple meanings and interests. Sharing the view of Hayes mentioned in [15], the need to focus in knowledge content, not only on knowledge form as common practice in academic AI, is a reality. Accordingly [15], insisted on the importance of *a priori*, task-independent conceptual analysis in order to avoid to *"get caught into conceptual traps"* due to a lack of breadth and depth in the analysis of a domain. Hayes reinforces the importance of the conceptualization process in the ontology development process. The ColBlend method [4][5] is a method to support the collaborative conceptualization process and it rests upon the Conceptual Blending Theory (CBT) from [20]. CBT accounts for the emergence of meanings by adopting the view that meaning construction involves emergent structure, i.e., conceptual integration is more than the sum of its component parts. An integration network is thus a mechanism for modeling how emergent meaning might come about, accounting for the dynamic aspects of meaning construction. CBT representation gives rise to complex networks by linking two (or more) input spaces by means of a generic space. The generic space provides information that is abstract enough to be common to all the input spaces. Elements in the generic space are mapped onto counterparts in each of the input spaces, which motivate the identification of cross-space counterparts in the input spaces. A further space in this model of integration network is the blended space or blend. This is the space that contains new or emergent structure: information that is not contained in either of the inputs. The blend takes elements from both inputs, but goes further on providing additional structure that distinguishes the blend from either of its inputs. In other words, the blend derives a structure that is contained in neither input. The so called input spaces (I) are considered as "conceptualization proposal spaces" where each organization participant in the network presents its proposals. The generic space known as "shared space" works as a space where only information and knowledge consensually accepted by all is shared. We call the blend space as the "Negotiation and decision-making Space" and is used during the negotiation process. CBT and the socio-semantic framework (named *2S framework*) form what was called the *ColBlend* method. In the *2S framework* each organization with their conceptualizations constitutes a socio-semantic network. The conceptualization of each organization (partner in the collaborative network) is represented as an "input space". This means that there will be (at least) as many input spaces as partners in the network, each partner representing its conceptualization proposal in an input space (figure 4). These input spaces are parts of their semantic networks. The final semantic network will be the shared conceptualization presented in the "generic space". The generic space works as "shared space", where the preliminary conceptualization proposal and the several shared conceptualizations, resulting of the various iterations of the method, are presented. The final socio-semantic network represents the relationship between all organizations that compose the network and the collective conceptualization. The blend space, although not having an explicit representation in the *2S framework*, is viewed as the "negotiation and decision-making space" where different proposals are presented for discussion during the process. These proposals are generated automatically, but the participants may also present proposals. The proposals for which consensus exist are "copied" into the "generic space", i.e., at the end of the process the "generic space" contains the collective conceptualization.

3   The *SemSys4CCM* Platform

The "Semantic System for Continuous Construction of Meaning" (*SemSys4CCM*) is a collaborative platform built to integrate and support the *ColBlend* method described in the previous section. In this section we give an overview of the system, as well as an example of its use. Finally the required functionalities and the *SemSys4CCM* logical architecture are presented.

3.1   *SemSys4CCM* Overview

The *SemSys4CCM* is based on the Semantic Media Wiki (SMW) and its extensions, thereby exploiting the semantic and collaborative capabilities inherent in those. Due to the collaborative nature of the platform, it is necessary that it provides a high level of availability and accessibility, ease of use, have graphical representations of the working models and semantic properties. Thus, the platform's users can access the conceptual models, manipulate them, sharing their knowledge and ideas while discussing, rating and commenting their points of view with other users. *SemSys4CCM* is intended to be intuitive and easy to use, supporting users to build shared conceptualizations. It contains mechanisms for discussion, feedback, evaluation and supervision in order to support the negotiation process and reach agreements about a conceptualization. The system includes functionalities to manage user authentication and permissions that can be applied to name spaces or conceptualization spaces. Aiming to increase the usability of the platform and reduce inconsistency in the interpretation of conceptual models, the application provides a graphical representation of these models, allowing users to view its elements and navigate between them. Conceptual models are presented as a concept maps due to its simplicity and ease of use. Finally, *SemSys4CCM* is able to import or export the results from/to standard formats, enabling interoperability with other applications. Besides the above features, the system is capable of providing advanced editing and manipulation operations of conceptual models, as well as management functionalities, i.e., review the change history, performing backups and snapshots or generate relevant statistical information.

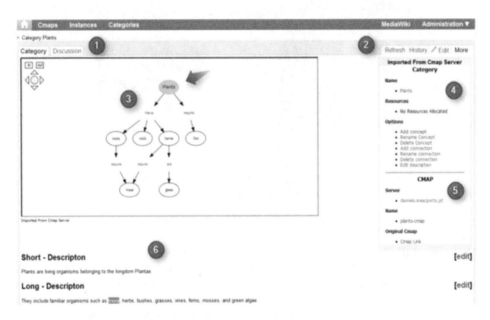

Fig. 1. Using SemSys4CCM to visualize and manipulate conceptual models

In Fig. 1 the Web user interface of *SemSys4CCM* is presented, more specifically an imported conceptual model. After importing the conceptual model "Plants-Cmap", the system creates the wiki pages by mapping its elements (i.e. Concepts to Categories, Connections to Properties) and a simple representation (3) similar to a Concept Map. In the case of Fig. 1, the user is currently viewing the Category "plants" (1), as well as all information about the current element, and information about the conceptual model it belongs (5). While viewing it, users can participate in discussions, commenting and rating (1) or edit its structure (4) (2), like editing the concept, add new connections, edit resources, etc. When adding or editing an element, is possible to add a description (6) to better specify its meaning, and then providing better understanding of the conceptual model.

3.2 *SemSys4CCM* Functionalities

The functional view of the platform is depicted in Fig. 2. Below there is an overview of its main functionalities.

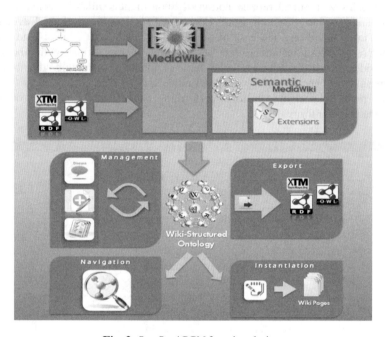

Fig. 2. *SemSys4CCM* functional view

Web user interface: The user interface is one of our main concerns in the development of *SemSys4CCM*. The system is based on *Semantic MediaWiki* (SMW), thus web-based. The user can modify the conceptual model, view and navigate between its elements in an understandable graphical representation. On the other hand users can easily exploit the semantic features of SMW using its semantic extensions.

Visualization Generator: This is the component responsible for the generation of the graphical representation of the conceptual model. As previously said we choose to represent conceptual models in a graphical and easily understandable way, enabling users to rapidly understand it, and navigate between its elements interactively. Its representation follows a concept map structure and is updated with every change detected, triggering the re-generation of the diagram.

System Management: The System Management component is used for administrative management. Administrators can create and manage groups, assign users to groups, change permissions to the conceptual models and spaces. On the other hand, administrators may protect wiki pages from editing, manage the status of the working conceptual models and moderate the negotiation process.

Conceptual model Interoperability: This component is responsible for importing and exporting conceptual models from and to the *SemSys4CCM*. The required import/export formats are CXL[2], RDF[3], OWL[4] and XTM[5]. When importing a conceptual model, specified in any format, its structure is created in wiki pages in accordance with the wiki meta model. The export process consists in converting the structure of an accepted conceptual model to a standard format.

Conceptual model Manipulation: As the name implies, this component provides functionalities for manipulation and edition of conceptual models. These operations consist in adding, renaming and removing concepts or links. It also allows users to attach or remove resources to concepts and finally add descriptions. This component is responsible for managing changes of the conceptual models, making the necessary updates to the wiki pages.

Conceptual model Management: The conceptual model management module has a considerable weight on the platform usability. The main responsibilities of this component are to provide functionalities for managing the changes history in the conceptual model and navigation between versions, allowing users to rollback to a previous state of the conceptual model. It also allows users to create snapshots, i.e. selecting a subset of elements of the conceptual model, and from there create a separated one from it. The conceptual models pass through several states [5] that are translated as conceptualization spaces in the system. This module also allows managing the life cycle of the conceptualization process, enabling to change between phases and executing the operations proposed in the ColBlend method presented in [2] [5].

Conceptual model Negotiation: Communication in the development of conceptual models by communities or groups is a fundamental aspect, as well as achieving consensus when conflicts arise. Thus, in *SemSys4CCM* is possible to discuss via forum, negotiate, comment and rate each element of the conceptual model, allowing users to collaborate while enriching it. Users have the option to "watch" a particular element of the conceptual model, in the wiki, and thus be notified whenever changes are made.

SMW Meta model: The SMW Meta model is used to construct the structure of the conceptual model, thus enabling users to navigate between its elements. This component allows transposing the structure of the imported conceptual model into a wiki pages structure, i.e., concepts are represented by Categories and Connections by Properties. In SMW, categories can have sub-categories, thus creating a kind of hier-

---

archy. Articles or pages can be categorized and can be created using semantic forms or templates.

Triple Store Connector: The existing conceptual model in *SemSys4CCM* is stored into a Triple store allowing to build advanced queries in SMW. The Triple Store connected to *SemSys4CCM* can be an alternative way to access the conceptual models data and to retrieve large amounts of information, also as for advanced reasoning and querying functionalities. The persisted data in the triple store can also be accessed by third-party applications.

3.3 *SemSys4CCM* Architecture

In the implementation of *SemSys4CCM*, it has been defined to use SMW as base platform, as users are familiarized with MediaWiki and there is a huge community of developers as well as many open source extensions.   The access to CmapServer is made through a Web Service provided by IHMC [7] responsible for CmapTools, which provides the possibility to share information with other applications using a specific API developed for this effect.

Due to the complexity of the *SemSys4CCM*, is needed to contextualize it with the several platforms with which it interacts. In this sense, Figure 3 shows an high level architectural view.

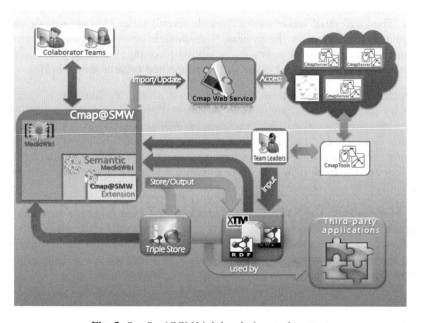

Fig. 3. *SemSys4CCM* high level view and context

4 Related Work

Tools and methodologies for the collaborative development of ontologies have been emerging in the last years, but only a few focuses in the first stages of the ontologies development process, more specifically in the conceptualization process. The *OntoShare* platform, described in [8], is closely related to the On-To-Knowledge methodology. This tool is a Java based client where users can share their knowledge in a virtual community, contributing for the grow of the shared ontology. According [8], OntoShare has the capability to summarize and extract keywords from the Web, thus allowing users to automatically share information and create RDF-annotated information resources. The conceptualization process is carried out during the kickoff stage, where the requirements specification of the ontology are developed. In the conceptualization process, users can send requests through OntoShare, creating annotations in the system, then the system may suggest a set of concepts which are related to the new annotation. Others methodologies like Two-layered approach to knowledge representation [1], opt to use graphical representations to allow users to share their ideas in the collaborative conceptualization process. According to [7], concept maps are an effective way of representing a person understanding of a domain of knowledge. Based on our experience, we also agree that concept maps are a simple and effective way to represent and knowledge. HCOME [9] supports the ontologies development and evaluation in the context of communities. Users have access to different spaces where ontologies can be stored. These are personal spaces, where users can work on their conceptualization before sharing it, where users can collaborate and share their ideas. When the ontologies are accepted they are moved to the Agreed space. In the context of this methodology a prototype was developed, HCONE [13], but unfortunately it has not been updated and currently there is no support. This system was developed in java and provides tools for the management of ontologies in an integrated environment, supports communication between users, provides reasoning services for consistency, coherency and disambiguation checking. One interesting aspect in HCONE is the strong participation by the users in the conceptualization process, heavily focusing in the participation and discussions or sharing their knowledge by suggesting other ways of achieving the same goal. The NeOn Toolkit[6] is a free, open source ontology editor, developed under the NeOn Project. It provides an extensive set of plug-ins covering a variety of ontology engineering activities, including annotation and documentation, development, interaction and several others. Although these systems suggest interesting approaches, currently there is none that provide a rich set of functionalities to collaboratively develop a shared conceptual model, within a semantic enabled platform.

5 Conclusions and Future Work

In this paper an approach to support the development of shared conceptualizations was presented. This was achieved by developing a platform based on Semantic MediaWiki

---

[6] http://neon-toolkit.org/wiki/Main_Page

and an extension to support the required functionalities. Visual knowledge representation and consensus building are the main areas of the collaborative conceptualization process supported by the *SemSys4CCM* platform. The experiments carried out through an action-research approach in two multi-national projects revealed an high receptiveness regarding the use of the approach. We can conclude that this approach is a good way to overcome the problem that untrained users cannot be expected to conform to the constraints of a formal semantics. Nevertheless, a more rigorous approach to the evaluation of the tool is needed. As intended future work, it is necessary to further develop the implementation of the management and interoperability features, as well as merging the visualization technique with manipulation functionalities, to improve the usability of the platform.

References

1. Gómez-Gauchía, H., Díaz-Agudo, B., González-Calero, P.: Two-layered approach to knowledge representation using conceptual maps and description logics. In: Cañas, A.J., Novak, J.D., González, F.M. (eds.) Proc. of the First Int. Conference on Concept Mapping (2004)
2. Pereira, C.: A organização da informação e conhecimento em redes colaborativas como um processo de construção social do significado: uma teoria e um método prático. PhD Thesis. Faculdade de Engenharia da Universidade do Porto (2010)
3. Moor, A.: Ontology-Guided Meaning Negotiation in Communities of Practice. In: Proc. of the Workshop on the Design for Large-Scale Digital Communities at the 2nd International Conference on Communities and Technologies, Milano, Italy (June 2005)
4. Pereira, C., Sousa, C., Soares, A.: Short-Term Semantic Consensus: Towards Agile Ontology Specification for Collaborative Networks. Leveraging Knowledge for Innovation in Collaborative Networks. In: IFIP Advances in Information and Communication Technology. Springer, Boston (2009)
5. Pereira, C., Sousa, C., Soares, A.: A socio-semantic approach to collaborative domain conceptualization. In: Meersman, R., Herrero, P., Dillon, T. (eds.) On the Move to Meaningful Internet Systems: OTM 2009 Workshops. LNCS, vol. 5872, pp. 524–533. Springer, Heidelberg (2009)
6. Siorpaes, K., Hepp, M.: myOntology: The marriage of ontology engineering and collective intelligence. Bridging the Gep between Semantic Web and Web (2007)
7. Cañas, A.J., et al.: Cmaptools: A Knowledge Modeling And Sharing Environment - Concept Maps: Theory, Methodology, Technology (2004)
8. Davies, J., Duke, A., Sure, Y.: ntoshare: a knowledge management. environment for virtual communities of practice. In: K-CAP (2003) of the international conference on Knowledge capture, ACM Press, New York (2003)
9. Kotis, K., Vouro, G.: Human-centered ontology engineering: The HCOME methodology. In: Knowledge and Information Systems. Springer, Heidelberg (2006)
10. Kotis, K., Vouro, G.A.: The HCONE approach to ontology merging. In: Bussler, C.J., Davies, J., Fensel, D., Studer, R. (eds.) ESWS 2004. LNCS, vol. 3053, pp. 137–151. Springer, Heidelberg (2004)
11. Kremer, R.: Concept Mapping: Informal to Formal. Appeared in Proceedings of the International Conference on Conceptual Structures, University of Maryland (994)

12. Eskridge, T., Hayes, P., Hoffman, R., Warren, M. "Formalizing the informal: a confluence of concept mapping and the semantic web". Concept Maps: Theory, Methodology, Technology. Proc. of the Second Int. Conference on Concept Mapping, A. J. Cañas, J. D. Novak, Eds., Costa Rica (2006)

13. Pereira, C., Sousa, C., Soares, A.: Building an informal ontology to support collaborative network operation: a case study. Accepted in the 11th IFIP Working Conference on VIRTUAL ENTERPRISES, SaintEtienne, France (October 2010)

14. Gruber, T.: A Translation Approach to Portable Ontology Specifications. Knowledge Acquisition 5(2), 199–221 (1993)

15. Staab, S.: On understanding the collaborative construction of conceptualisations. In: International and Interdisciplinary Conference Processing Text-Technological Resources at the Center for Interdisciplinary Research (ZiF - Zentrum für interdisziplinäre Forschung), Bielefeld University pp. 13–15. (March 2008)

16. Beers, P., Bots, P.: Eliciting conceptual models to support interdisciplinary research. Journal of Information Science (March 2009)

17. Pereira, C., Soares, A.: Ontology development in collaborative networks as a process of social construction of meaning. In: Meersman, R., Tari, Z., Herrero, P. (eds.) OTM-WS 2008. LNCS, vol. 5333, pp. 605–614. Springer, Heidelberg (2008)

18. Guarino, N., Poli, R.: Formal Ontology in Conceptual Analysis and Knowledge Representation. Special issue of the International Journal of Human and Computer Studies 43(5/6) (1995)

19. Cahier, J.-P., Zaher, L.H., Leboeuf, J.-P., Guittard, C.: Experimentation of a socially constructed, In: Proceedings of the IJCAI 2005 workshop on KMOM "Topic Map"by the OSS community, Edimbourg (2005)

20. Fauconnier, G., Turner, M.: The way we think: Conceptual blending and the mind's hidden complexities. Basic Books, New York (2003)

Modelling the Public Sector Information through CIDOC Conceptual Reference Model

Lina Bountouri[1], Christos Papatheodorou[1,2], and Manolis Gergatsoulis[1]

[1] Database & Information Systems Group (DBIS),
Laboratory on Digital Libraries and Electronic Publishing,
Department of Archive and Library Sciences, Ionian University, Corfu, Greece
[2] Digital Curation Unit,
Institute for the Management of Information Systems (IMIS),
Athena R.C., Athens, Greece
{boudouri,papatheodor,manolis}@ionio.gr

Abstract. Nowadays, due to the growing development of eGovernment information systems, there is an increasing need to handle Public Sector Information (PSI) in a homogeneous way. Ontologies are currently a powerful tool to act as semantic reference models for the development of information systems and as semantic mediators for achieving interoperability. In this paper, we analyze the procedures that lead to the PSI's production and management and we present all the concepts and agents that relate to it. Based on this analysis and given that CIDOC CRM ontology is able to define the rich semantics of the historical records' production and management, we propose the CIDOC CRM to represent the public records' conceptualization and to act as a reference model for PSI.

Keywords: Public Sector Information, eGovernment, Ontologies.

1 Introduction

The *Public Sector Information* (*PSI*) or *Government Information* is the information created, collected and freely disseminated in the form of public records by the *Public Administration* (*PA*). Indicative examples of PSI are financial and business information, legal and administrative information, scientific and cultural information etc. The management of PSI deals mainly with the facilitation of the transactions with PA, the access to PSI and its use and reuse so as to act as the basis for the provision of added value services within PA and/or to external users (citizens and business).

Public sector is considered as the largest information provider in almost every country and various PSI systems have been developed aiming to satisfy the augmented needs. An important part of such systems is the adoption of standards for the documentation, organization and dissemination of information, for the administrative terminology as well as standards/protocols for their communication and interoperability.

The public records carry significant information and have their own characteristics. They are documented through standards, usually depending on the

R. Meersman et al. (Eds.): OTM 2010 Workshops, LNCS 6428, pp. 404–413, 2010.

country it produces them, such as eGMS in the UK [13] and AGLS in Australia [12]. Furthermore, they may be penetrated by different documentation logics and records management policies, for example differences have been observed in their philosophy, since some of them are more oriented to the management of PSI, while others are oriented to facilitate the citizens to access PSI.

As a consequence, interoperability issues related to the Government Information are not only technological, but they also cover a wide range of aspects, such as the adopted policies, the lack of agreement on common standards and vocabularies etc [10]. The dimensions of interoperability needed to be addressed between the PSI information systems are the organizational view (i.e. by making the services widely available), the technical view (i.e. by achieving data integration) and the semantic view (i.e. by achieving the PSI's semantic conformance). Besides, even if various conceptual models have been proposed to semantically define the wider PSI domain or parts of it, most of them are oriented: a) to define concepts needed specifically for the provision of eGovernment services [7], or b) to represent the Public Administration views [2], or c) strictly to deal with records management and not related to the basic notions of PSI [8]. It is important to notice that even if these efforts serve their goals in a specific context, they cannot deal in parallel with the important building blocks of the PSI's production and management: a) the events and functions in the citizen's, business' and government's life on which the production of PSI is based, b) the archives and records management policies, and c) the need to provide added value services to the internal and external users.

In our research, we deal with the semantic interoperability issues, which could also promote the PSI's semantic integration. Our purpose is not to represent all the existing concepts related to PSI systems, but to a) bring out the main PSI's semantics and b) propose the use of a tool that can act as the basis for the semantic alignment of the PSI metadata and the provision of interoperable services, always based on the fundamental archives and records management practices and, at the same time, without leaving unexplored the role of the eGovernment services. In order to achieve these goals, we propose the use of the ontology CIDOC Conceptual Reference Model [4] as a reference model of the PSI domain, since *ontologies* provide rich constructs to express the meaning of data, promote reasoning and are widely used as mediators between heterogeneous sources. CIDOC CRM, specifically, is an event-based ontology and this characteristic, as it will be analyzed in the following sections, enables the representation of functions that generate the PSI. Hence, the added value feature of this work is that it associates the public records not only with their producers, but also with the PA's functions which generate, modify and use the records.

Notice that we already have explored the role of the CIDOC CRM for the archival information in [15] and since the *public archives* are *records* of continuing value selected for permanent preservation, while the *public records* refer to the documents that are still in current use, their strong relationship is obvious. Given that both the public archives and records provide evidence for the daily functions of the PA, the objective of this work is to integrate the concepts penetrating the management of the two types of documents and to promote interoperability between information and service providers. Reusing CIDOC CRM for PSI's conceptualization and alignment promotes the PSI's incorporation to the wider archival semantic environment.

In this paper, we firstly derive the domain specific requirements for the PSI, analyze its conceptualization, based on the study of the international standards and practices, and present all the involved agents and ideas related to its management. Secondly, we introduce the CIDOC CRM to represent the semantic structure of the involved knowledge, by demonstrating how its conceptualizations can be used to document PSI, by assigning the main PSI's notions to specific CIDOC CRM paths. Finally, related efforts and conclusion are presented.

2   The Production and Management of the PSI

The delivery of PSI's services typically involves the interaction between the citizens, the business and the PA in a complex scenario, not only in terms of technology, but also of how the relationships and the processes are organized and how the necessary data are structured and handled. In this section we analyze these PSI's concepts and relations. A more extended analysis can be found in [3].

PSI refers to the operation of the *Public Administration*, having the form of the public *records*. In particular, the PSI is produced either during the *PA*'s internal procedures or during its communication to external users, such as *citizens* and *business*. In both cases, specific *functions* are executed and *records* are produced to accomplish the tasks to be completed. The *PA* consists of government's agencies that control and supervise public programmes and have executive, legislative, or judicial authority over other institutions within a specified area. These agencies also set the strategies, recommend the creation of *laws* and generate the *mandates*. The various agencies in the public sector are typically engaged in the organization and the production of *services* [17].

A *function* is any high-level purpose, responsibility or task, assigned to the accountability agenda of a corporate body by *legislation, policy* or *mandate* [14]. *Functions* are decomposed into a related set of *activities*, which are the tasks performed by a corporate body to accomplish each of its *functions*. *Activities* encompass *transactions*, which in turn produce *records*. The importance of the notion of *function* in PSI is proved through the archives' and records' management practice, which strongly connects the creation of *records* to *functions*. *Functions* are considered as a more stable point of reference than administrative structures, because administrative structures are often merged or devolved when restructuring takes place [5]. Moreover, they are strongly related with the *citizens* and *business* through specific *business situations* and *life-events*. Due to that fact, records management and business classification schemes document or are based on *functions*, such as eGMS [13], AGIFT [11] and ISDF [14].

A *record* is in line with [9], information in any form or medium, created or received and maintained by an organization or person in the transaction of business or the conduct of affairs. *Records* are essential parts for the accountability of the governments to maintain the democracy and to provide the access to the public. The public *records* provide authentic and reliable evidence of the past and current *functions* and of the *transactions* that result from them. Public *records* have their own characteristics that enable their identification and management. According to [13,11,19], some if these are: (a) the *language* of the *record*, which is of crucial importance, especially in multi-lingual environments (i.e. the E.U.), (b) the unambiguous *identifier* of the *record* within a specific context, (c) the *place* where the *record* can be reached or found, and (d) the *title* given to it.

What is more, *citizens* and *business* are an important part of the PSI's documentation, since they have daily communication with the *PA* and the right to require *services*. The *citizens* participate in the *life-events*, which are everyday life situations in which a citizen uses *PA services* to confront them. Some of the most common *life-events* are: moving home, bereavement etc. *Business* participate in *business situations*, which are situations where they trigger the public services or interactions with the public authorities, such as founding a company, (re-)constructing factory premises etc. *Life-events* and *business situations* are highly important eGovernment concepts participating in the PSI's management and this is proved by the fact that specific ontologies have been created for these concepts [7].

Furthermore, the actions taken by the *PA* are based on *laws* and *mandates* recommended by the *PA*. In the PSI's context *laws* and *mandates* are specific warrants that require the resource to be created or provided [12] and they introduce and clarify the *function/activity* to produce the public *records* [14]. Another important notion for the PSI's creation and management is the notion of *policy*, which is a plan of action adopted by the *PA* aiming to achieve particular targets. In the PSI context, *policy* comprises, among others, activities related to *records*'s management and dissemination, such as accessibility and reproduction.

A concept of crucial importance in the PSI's production and management is the *time*, which is usually formed as a date associated with a specific event in the life cycle of the PSI (i.e. production, copyright, modification) [13]. The *Public Administration* is also related to other concepts, such as *place*, defining for example where the *PA* units are located or where the *records* can be found. Various *names* are used to identify individuals of the *PA*, such as the *businesses*, the *citizens*, the *places* etc.

A PSI reference model, in order to act as the basis for the creation of metadata, to improve the communication between interest parties and to be a mediator for the alignment of PSI sources, must be able to describe all the mentioned conceptualizations, their complexity and interrelations.

3   Using the CIDOC CRM for the PSI's Modelling

3.1   The Followed Methodology

The *CIDOC Conceptual Reference Model (CIDOC CRM, ISO 21127:2006)* is a core ontology, which consists of a hierarchy of 86 *entities* (or *classes*) and

137 *properties*. Its main target is to promote a shared understanding by providing a common and extensible semantic framework to which information can be mapped, to facilitate the information integration for cultural heritage information sources and to help the implementers to formulate the requirements for information systems, serving as a guide for conceptual modelling [4]. CIDOC CRM expresses semantics as a sequence of path(s) of the form entity-property-entity. It is an event-based model and its main notions are the temporal entities. As a consequence, the presence of CIDOC CRM entities, such as actors, dates, places and objects, implies their participation to an event or an activity.

The methodology followed was based on the identification of specific CIDOC CRM classes and properties and their between paths to represent the main PSI's concepts and relations presented in Section 2. More tools, such as standards [12] and ontologies [16] can be used to further specialize the CIDOC CRM's semantics for PSI, however, it is out of the scope of this paper to deal with more custom PSI's aspects. Given that CIDOC CRM is a semantically rich model, further classes and properties can be used to represent additional, but of secondary importance, PSI's notions not presented in this paper due to space reasons.

As part of our methodology, we studied in depth the Government Information metadata to explore their "hidden" semantics and their interrelationships. We did not restrict our study to Government Information, but we also studied the records management policies (i.e.[6]) and the archival description standards (i.e. [14,9]). This action was taken given that the PSI is encapsulated in the public records and archives; hence, ensuring the effective documentation and management of the records and archives by applying the relevant standards and policies results over time in the efficient management and exploitation of the PSI. Duranti [18] emphasizes the importance of records for the PSI, stating that they play a crucial role in most human activities and they are essential to all business and social exchanges, being the basis of the legal system.

The PSI model is partially presented in Figure 1 and analyzed in the two following sections. In Figure 1, the entities of CIDOC CRM are presented in the upper part of the circles and in the lower part their corresponding PSI semantics are presented. The relations between the entities are indicated through arrows.

3.2   The PSI Model: The Entities

The CIDOC CRM classes that represent the three main concepts of PSI (*PA*, *function* and *record*) are respectively instances of the classes E40 Legal Body, E7 Activity and E22 Man-Made Object. E40 Legal Body includes instances that represent the institutions or groups of people that have obtained a legal form as a group, can act collectively and can be held collectively responsible for their actions. The instances of E7 Activity are actions intentionally carried out by instances of E39 Actor and its subclasses (such as E40 Legal Body) that result in changes of state in the cultural, social, or physical systems. Hence, its instances can be used to represent the *functions* carried out by the *PA* for the creation and modification of PSI. Notice that the *functions* include *activities* and *activities* include *transactions*, which are also represented as instances of E7 Activity.

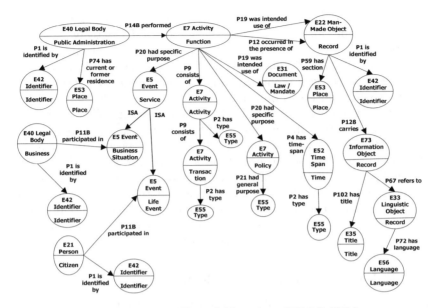

Fig. 1. The PSI model based on CIDOC CRM

The *records* are represented through E22 Man-Made Object that defines the physical objects purposely created by human activity. A *record*, apart from being an object created on purpose, it is also an information carrier. The informational view of the *record* can be represented as an instance of E73 Information Object. In case the *record* includes text, it is also an instance of E33 Linguistic Object.

Citizens and *business* are denoted as instances of E21 Person, which includes the instances of real persons who live or are assumed to have lived, and E40 Legal Body. In addition, the *services* provided by the *PA* to the society are modelled as instances of E5 Event, which comprises the changes of states in cultural, social or physical systems. *Life-events* and *business situations* are depended on the *services*, hence can be also modelled as instances of E5 Event, being in an ISA relationship with the class E5 Event representing the *PA*'s *services*.

Identifiers are represented as instances of E42 Identifier that includes the strings or codes assigned to instances of almost every CIDOC CRM class, in order to identify them uniquely and permanently within the context of one or more organizations. For example, a *citizen* may have a unique identifier as an employee in the public or private sector, as a member of an insurance/health system or as a tax payer. Moreover, the *titles* of the public *records* are instances of E35 Title because this class includes the names assigned to works.

As mentioned in Section 2, *laws* and *mandates* recommend and control the creation of public *records*. To represent this notion, E31 Document is used, since its instances are information objects that comprise the immaterial items making propositions about reality. The *policy* adopted by the *PA* can be modelled as instances of E7 Activity, given that it is a set of actions intentionally carried out by instances of E39 Actor, which result in changes. To further specialize the type of the *policy*, i.e. to define that a *policy* is targeted to the PSI's preservation, instances of E55 Type can be associated to instances of E7 Activity.

E53 Place covers the *places* where *PA*'s bodies are located and where the public *records* can be found. These places could be organized in a taxonomic hierarchy indicating the geographic divisions. Another important PSI's notion is the dates that surround the various activities (such as creation dates, deletion dates etc). *Time* is represented in CIDOC CRM via the E52 Time-Span.

It is worthy of note that the instances of E55 Type can be associated to almost every CIDOC CRM class used in this model, to further specify its meaning. For example, it can be used to specialize the type of the *time*, by associating instances of E52 Time-Span to instances of E55 Type. An additional example is its use to further specify the type of *functions*, *activities* and *transactions* (instances of the class E7 Activity). The same applies to instances of E41 Appellation, which are used in order to provide names to instances of a large number of CIDOC CRM classes, such as E21 Person, E40 Legal Body etc.

3.3   The PSI Model: The Semantic Relations

The classes described in Section 3.2, form a rich semantic network through the use of the CIDOC CRM properties that relate their instances. In order to express the main concepts of the PSI's generation and management (*PA*, *function* and *record*) and their interrelations, instances of E40 Legal Body are related to instances of E7 Activity via the property P14B performed and instances of the E7 Activity are related to instances of E22 Man-Made Object via the property P12 occurred in the presence of, with the purpose of representing that the *PA* (E40 Legal Body) performs *functions* (E7 Activity) in an environment which produces/manages *records* (E22 Man-Made Object). To define that the public *records*, created by the *PA*'s *functions*, are evidence of these *functions*, the property P19 was intended use of is introduced between instances of the class E7 Activity (representing the *functions*) and instances of the class E22 Man-Made Object (representing the *records*) to express that specific objects are created for use in the *functions*. Besides, instances of E22 Man-Made Object are related to instances of E73 Information Object via the property P128 carries to express that the produced *record* carries information. Additionally, instances of E73 Information Object are related via the property P67 refers to with instances of E33 Linguistic Object to denote that sometimes the produced *record* can be expressed in natural language(s), independently of the medium that carries it.

The class E40 Legal Body representing the *PA* is also related to instances of the classes E42 Identifier and E53 Place through the properties P1 is identified by and P74 has current or former residence respectively, to define specific *identifiers* that the *PA* may have, i.e. identifiers for the ministries, their departments etc, and specific *places* where the offices, departments etc of the *PA* are located.

Furthermore, the decomposition of the *functions* to the *activities* and then to the *transactions* is declared through the property P9 consists of that relates instances of E7 Activity, representing *functions*, to instances of E7 Activity, representing the *activities*, to instances of E7 Activity, representing the *transactions*.

At this point, notice that instances of E7 Activity, representing the *functions*, are also related to instances of E5 Event via P20 had specific purpose to define that some of the *functions* are intended to serve *life-events* and *business situations*. E40 Legal Body (representing the *business*) and E21 Person (representing the *citizens*) are both related to instances of E5 Event representing the *life-event* and *business situation* respectively. Both are related to these instances by the use of the relationship P11B participated in. Besides, instances of E40 Legal Body and E21 Person are related to instances of E42 Identifier, through P1 is identified by, to denote the relationship between them and the identifiers assigned to them.

Aiming to express that the *functions* are based on *laws* and *mandates*, the property P19 was intended use of is used between instances of the class E31 Document (representing the *functions*) and instances of the class E7 Activity (representing the *laws* and the *mandates*). E7 Activity (representing the *PA*'s *policy*) is related to E7 Activity (representing the *PA*'s *functions*) through the relationship P20 had specific purpose, stating the relation between the *policies* and the every day operation of the *PA*. In particular, through this CIDOC CRM path it is expressed that some of the *PA*'s *functions* usually affect the generation of *policies*. With the purpose of specifying the type of the *policy* followed (e.g. in the PSI context, preservation, appraisal, disposal, rights, accessibility and reproduction policies could be applied) the instances of the class E7 Activity (representing the *policy*) are related to instances of the class E55 Type through the property P21 had general purpose, since this property involves activities intended as preparation for some type of event.

For the expression of the *time* of the *functions*, the P4 has time-span is used to relate instances of E7 Activity to instances of E52 Time-Span. Notice also that the instances of E41 Appellation are reached through almost every class via P1 is identified by and can express names which refer to and identify specific instances [4], i.e. the names of the *citizens*. E55 Type can also be reached through almost every CIDOC CRM class through P2 has type. In the PSI context, this class can be used to express sophisticated semantic needs.

The CIDOC CRM classes and properties used to model PSI can be further analyzed to a taxonomy of classes and subclasses. For instance, the *PA* can be analyzed to Central and Regional Administration and then the Central Administration to be analyzed to the classes Ministries and Supervised Public Organizations, and the Regional Administration to the hierarchy Regions, Prefectures, Municipalities. Nevertheless, this analysis is not of interest for this paper, which focuses on the representation of the main concepts of the PSI' s production and management processes and not on the provision of analytic conceptualizations, which usually form part of thesauri, vocabularies etc.

4   Related Work and Discussion

Lately, the PA is facing many challenges like improving its services and reducing costs. Due to that fact, many related efforts are currently running to facilitate the PA's tasks in a national and international level.

In [1] a PSI framework for data sharing and reuse to support interoperability is proposed. This framework includes a cross-application reference model, which provides instructions for modelling the processes in the PA's context and can be customized with domain specific metadata and ontologies. In [8] a conceptual metadata schema model for records management is defined, based on the ISO 15489 and ISO 23081 guidelines. This schema's target is to maintain the international compatibility and standard management procedures. It is a record-centered model consisting of three basic elements: "Records", "Business" and "Mandate". The first model proposed is oriented to cover mostly eGovernment needs, without taking into consideration records management policies. The second model is orientated to records management and due to that fact, even if it can deal with parts of PSI, it is not related to the basic notions of eGovernment, such as services offered by the PA (life-events and business situations).

It is important to notice that the existing conceptual models for PSI do not explicitly associate the notion of the public records' production with the PA's functions as well as with the citizens or business operations, but they consider independently either the PA's characteristics and their relation with the business situations and life-events, or the public records with their producers. In [2] a PA ontology is proposed representing some of the PA's views (legal, organizational, business, IT, end-user). Nevertheless, this ontology is adapted as a part of a mechanism inside a life-event portal, it includes very broad concepts and, since it is not based on records and archival policies, it is inadequate for use as an interoperability tool between the PSI's documentation.

In our research, CIDOC CRM does not intend to replace metadata schemas that describe the PSI, but to define a conceptual view of it, which could complement the wider aspect of PSI's management, describing the most important concepts and their relations. Our main target is to bring out the main semantics related to the PSI's production and management.

To conclude, this emergence is promoting the use of CIDOC CRM as a semantic reference point for the PSI metadata in various applications, such as government portals, reasoning systems and integration architectures. In regard to the integration, the CIDOC CRM could be adopted act as the mediator between diverse PSI sources in a metadata interoperability scenario. An indicative example is its use in governmental portals which offer one-stop services to citizens and for this purpose integrate information form different PSI sources (municipalities, ministries, etc.) having possibly different metadata schemas, all of them mapped to the ontology. The satisfaction of a citizen's application might require the integration of information form several distributed sources. In a such case particular queries translated to suitable forms for each source should be promoted by the mediator, using the appropriate mappings, and then the answers should be integrated before returned to the user.

References

1. Baralis, E., Cerquitelli, T., Raffa, S.: A Cross-Application Reference Model to support Interoperability. In: 2nd Eur. Summit on Interoperability in the iGovernment, Rome (2008)

2. Bercic, B., Vintar, M.: Ontologies, Web Services, and Intelligent Agents: Ideas for Further Development of Life-Event Portals. In: Traunmüller, R. (ed.) EGOV 2003. LNCS, vol. 2739, pp. 329–334. Springer, Heidelberg (2003)
3. Bountouri, L., Papatheodorou, C., Soulikias, V., Stratis, M.: Metadata Interoperability in Public Sector Information. Journal of Information Science 35(2), 204–231 (2009)
4. CIDOC CRM SIG. Definition of the CIDOC CRM. Technical report (January 2010)
5. Shepherd, E., Yeo, G.: Managing records: a handbook of principles and practice, ch. 3, p. 74. Facet Publishing (2003)
6. International Organization for Standardization. ISO 15489 1:2001, Information and Documentation: Records Management Part 1: General. ISO, Geneva (2001)
7. Kavadias, G., Tambouris, E.: GovML: A Markup Language for Describing Public Services and Life Events. In: Wimmer, M.A. (ed.) KMGov 2003. LNCS (LNAI), vol. 2645, pp. 106–115. Springer, Heidelberg (2003)
8. Han, S.-K., Lee, H.-S., Jeong, Y.-S.: Conceptual model of metadata schema for records management. In: Proc. of 2nd Int. Symp. on Know. Processing and Service for China, Japan and Korea, Metadata and Ontology, Beijing, pp. 21–31 (2006)
9. International Council on Archives. Committee on Descriptive Standards. ISAD(G): General International Standard Archival Description. ICA, 2nd edn. (2000)
10. Interoperability Solutions for European Public Administrations. European Interoperability Strategy (EIS): Document for public consultation (February 2010), http://ec.europa.eu/idabc/servlets/Doc?id=32595
11. National Archives of Australia. AFIGT (2005), http://www.naa.gov.au/records-management/create-capture-describe/describe/AGIFT/index.aspx
12. National Archives of Australia. AGLS Metadata Standard Reference (2008), http://www.agls.gov.au/documents/aglsterms/
13. Cabinet Office. e-GMS v.3.1 (August 2006), http://www.cabinetoffice.gov.uk/media/273711/egmsv3-1.pdf
14. International Council on Archives. Committee on Best Practices and Standards. ISDF: International Standard for Describing Functions (2007), http://www.ica.org/sites/default/files/ISDF ENG.pdf
15. Stasinopoulou, T., Bountouri, L., Kakali, C., Lourdi, I., Papatheodorou, C., Doerr, M., Gergatsoulis, M.: Ontology-Based Metadata Integration in the Cultural Heritage Domain. In: Goh, D.H.-L., Cao, T.H., Sølvberg, I.T., Rasmussen, E. (eds.) ICADL 2007. LNCS, vol. 4822, pp. 165–175. Springer, Heidelberg (2007)
16. Stojanovic, L., Kavadias, G.,Apostolou, D., Probst, F., Hinkelmann, K.: Ontology-enabled e-Gov Service Configuration (June 2004), http://ec.europa.eu/information_society/activities/egovernment/docs/pdf/ont ogov.pdf
17. US Census Bureau. North American Industry Classification System (2002), http://www.census.gov/epcd/naics02/
18. Wilson, G.: Keeping the Records Straight: Pr. L. Duranti put 17th-century monks to work for the Pentagon (1998), http://www.publicaffairs.ubc.ca/ubcreports/1998/98mar05/98mar5pro.html
19. Archives New Zealand. NZGLS Metadata Element Set Version 2.1. (2004), http://www.e.govt.nz/standards/nzgls/standard

Integration of Domain and Social Ontologies in a CMS Based Collaborative Platform

Luís Carlos Carneiro[1,2], Cristovão Sousa[1,3], and António Lucas Soares[1,2]

[1] INESC Porto, Campus da FEUP, Rua Dr. Roberto Frias, 378, 4200-465 Porto, Portugal
[2] Dep. Engenharia Informática - Faculdade de Engenharia - Universidade do Porto,
Rua Dr. Roberto Frias, 4200-465, Porto, Portugal
[3] Escola Superior de Tecnologia e Gestão de Felgueiras { Instituto Politecnico do
Porto, Rua do Curral, Casa do Curral, Margaride, 4610-156, Felgueiras, Portugal}
luis.c.carneiro@inescporto.pt, cpsousa@inescporto.pt,
asoares@inescporto.pt

Abstract. This paper describes an approach and an implementation for the semantic integration of social and domain ontologies in a collaborative platform. The platform, built based on the Drupal CMS framework, aims to offer SMEs possibilities to access specific knowledge by means of a collaborative community. A model to semantically express the socio-collaborative activities of the platform connected with the domain knowledge related to the project is presented. The model is based on existing W3C ontologies such as FOAF, SIOC and SIOC-types for the socio-collaborative semantics and SKOS to describe the domain knowledge. An architecture to support the model and related applications of the semantic metadata generated in the platform are also described.

Keywords: Ontology integration, collaboration and domain ontologies, collaborative networks of organizations.

1 Introduction

Collaborative networks of organisations (CNO) are organisational forms increasingly adopted both in the business and non-business sectors. Between other benefits, they enable small organisations to compete or to handle challenges that could not be addressed while standing alone. Collaborative networks are distinct from a common network in that their relational processes are mainly collaborative processes. The IT support to such networks is continuously being developed in the form of several flavours of collaborative platforms, but there is a clear focus on the semantic aspects as these are a structural for collaboration, information and knowledge management.

The work described in this paper addresses the problem of integrating collaboration ontologies with domain ontologies in a way that is adequate to be used in collaborative platforms supporting CNOs. Although this may sound as a trivial knowledge engineering problem, the fact is that there aren't any attempts in the research literature to handle this problem at a general level. Our goal is thus to develop a general approach to integrate social related ontologies with specific domain ontologies, dependent on the area of intervention of the CNO. To achieve this, we began by

R. Meersman et al. (Eds.): OTM 2010 Workshops, LNCS 6428, pp. 414–423, 2010.

studying the problem at a specific and concrete level, using as case study the european RTD project H-Know[1] (Heritage Knowledge) (2009-2011) in the domain of rehabilitation, restoring and maintenance of cultural heritage and general purpose buildings.

H-Know aims to develop a socio-collaborative platform where SMEs can share knowledge about restoration and maintenance activities, inducing learning and training of partners and collaboration amongst partners. The H-Know platform is built according to a perspective of collaboration enabled by a social network approach. Users have a personal profile with their personal and professional information so as the Entities and Collaborative Spaces (ColSpaces) they are connected with as well as their partners. Collaborative places have a inter-organizational collaboration perspective while Entities are used for intro organizational collaboration. The main objective of the ColSpace is to provide a mean where different experts can share information about the activities they are undertaking together. Both ColSpaces and Entities have a set of tools for collaboration such as an Event Manager, a Gallery Manager, Pages, a Blog, Forums or a File Repository. We can see this tools as "Content Containers".

The H-Know platform is built over the Drupal CMS[2]. Drupal provides a wide number of extensions and customizations, mostly of them implemented as Modules. Some Modules were crucial for the H-Know implementation, such as CCK to define the different types of content in the platform or Organic Groups to create the groups and some specific modules in the area of web semantics, that will be described later on this paper. In this platform content is produced which deals with a specific area of knowledge, represented in a knowledge structure. Most of the concepts of the knowledge structure are based on the CIK (Construction Industry Knowledge) ontology from the project Know Construct(2005-2007)[3]. For H-Know, some modules were eliminated, others were revised and some other were created, specific for the area of old building restoration and cultural heritage. In figure 1 we see the first level of concepts of our domain.

Fig. 1. H-Know knowledge domain, first level concepts

Basically, we can say that in the Construction Industry we apply Construction Resources to Construction Processes that will lead to Construction Results. Construction Resources are constrained by Technical Topics. This basic structure is based on ISO 12006-2 [8]. Each one of the concepts presented is extended in several sub-concepts

---

[1] H-Know (Heritage Knowledge) http://www.h-know.eu/
[2] http://drupal.org/about
[3] http://www.know-construct.com/

which are not presented here. In a platform with the characteristics described and with such a kind of knowledge structure, we want to be able to answer "Competency Questions" such as: "Which projects exist about the legal systems of a construction?" or "Who is publishing more about the rehabilitation process of a bridge?". From the context described above we have a goal which is improving the knowledge organization and inference of the content produced in the platform, by semantically expressing the socio-collaborative activities held there connected with the domain knowledge of the H-Know project.

2   Design and Integration of Social and Domain Ontologies in the Platform

2.1   An Approach for the Integration of Semantics in a Socio-collaborative Platform

To build the integration of semantics in a already developed and published socio-collaborative platform, an approach with several steps is presented in the diagram 2.

The approach is organized in 3 different sets of steps, represented with different colours, with the labels of the relations in the diagram representing the order of the steps in the approach.

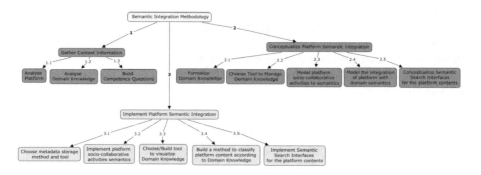

Fig. 2. Semantic integration approach

To integrate semantics in a socio-collaborative platform, first of all we need to understand the context of the problem. This means analysing the platform structure, purposes and background (**1.1**) and having a global vision about thedomain knowledge managed in the platform (**1.2**).

These two steps allow us to build competency questions (**1.3**), essential to define the importance and the objectives of the semantics for the platform and to understand what kind of questions the semantic enhancing of the platform can answer that traditional ways of searching cant.

The conceptualization of the semantics in the platform can start after these base tasks are finished. We should start by defining an approach to formalize the Domain Knowledge (**2.1**) and a tool to build and manage that knowledge (**2.2**). Then, picking up the structure of the platform, its actors and activities, a model to semantically describe the platform socio-collaborative activities should be designed (**2.3**). To relate the domain knowledge of the problem with the socio-collaborative activities, we need to build another model to integrate both semantics (**2.4**). The last step of this conceptualization process should focus on the designing of searching interfaces enhancing the semantic generated metadata of the platform (**2.5**), taking into account the "Competency Questions" previously formulated.

The last group of steps are intended to implement the conceptualizations previously done. First, the method and tool for the semantic metadata storage must be defined (**3.1**). Then, from the semantic model defined to describe the socio-collaborative activities, we should implement it in the platform (**3.2**), so it can generate and store semantic metadata. Since the platform has a specific domain knowledge managed there, a tool to visualize that domain must be chosen or built (**3.3**) together with a method to allow platform users to classify the content produced (**3.4**). The last step of all the process is making use of the semantic metadata generated, implementing the semantic interfaces (3.5) that were previously defined.

2.2   Formalization of the Platform Domain Knowledge

To describe the domain knowledge previously presented in a formal way, **SKOS** data model, which is intended to represent Knowledge Organisation Systems (KOS) like thesauri, term lists and controlled vocabularies, was the chosen solution. Using the SKOS data model to translate the domain knowledge, we can define each concept as an individual of the **skos:Concept** class and the **skos:narrower** and **skos:broader** properties, to construct the knowledge structure. For non-hierarchic linking we can use the property **skos:related**. When we have hierarchical transitive relations between the concepts we use the relational properties **skos:narrowerTransitive** and **skos:broaderTransitive**. Using lexical labels of SKOS (**skos:prefLabel**, **skos:altLabel** and **skos:definition**) we give the exact meaning we want to each one of the concepts of the domain knowledge. Language tags are used to describe each concept in different languages, an important requirement of the H-Know project.

In the cases we need to define different properties than the ones offered in the core of SKOS, to express extra information, we specialize the SKOS model. Following the recommendations of SKOS primer documentation [4], SKOS allows an application designer to create new properties. For example:

```
hknow:employs rdfs:subPropertyOf skos:narrowerTransitive
```

An example of a concept described using SKOS data model can be:

```
hknow:Space rdf:type skos:Concept;
skos:prefLabel "Space"@en;
skos:prefLabel "Espaço"@pt;
skos:definition "A material construction result contained within or associated
with a building or other construction entity"@en;
skos:definition "Um resultado de contrução material, contido ou associado
a um edifício ou outra entidade de construção"@pt.
```

2.3   Semantic Description of Platform Socio-collaborative Activities and Their Connection with the Domain Knowledge

Picking up the main elements of the platform, a model was built to semantically describe the platform socio-collaborative activities.

The first important thing to do in order to model the platform structure to ontologies is to focus on the very essential of Drupal's pages: a **node**. Everything from a user profile to a content item is a node.

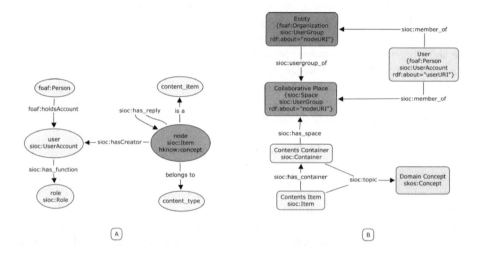

Fig. 3. A) Drupal node structure mapped into ontologies (based on [2]) **B)** Integration of SIOC + FOAF + SKOS into the H-Know platform

In the schema 3 A), every Drupal node is considered a **sioc:Item**. A sioc:Item is a class that describes something that can be in a container [6]. It has subclasses that can specify different types of Items such as **sioc:Post** to describe a Forum post. With the SIOC Types Module, we can create new types of sioc:Item to describe other types of content.

Platform users are represented with the class **sioc:UserAccount**. A user, apart from the platform, is classified as a **foaf:Person**, with his own set of characteristics and interests, independent from the platform. A User is connected to the Person he represents by the property **foaf:holdsAccount**. To connect the node with the user that created it, we use the property **sioc:has creator**.

Coming one level upper in abstraction, we built another model (3 B)) to describe the specific elements of the platform and the relations between them. From it we can discuss many of the options took to classify the platform. In this diagram we specify for the main elements, their **rdf:about** property, to define the subject of the triple statements.

First of all, it was decided to define a ColPlace with two different SIOC classes: **sioc:Space** and **sioc:UserGroup**, using as resource identifier the URI of the node that is the index page of that ColPlace. This approach was followed because of the multiple behaviour of a ColPlace. It is both a place to aggregate information and platform agents (users and entities). So, since a sioc:Space "is defined as being a place where data resides" [6], we use it as the location for a set of containers. Any data that resides in a sioc:Space, can be linked to it using the property **sioc:has space**.

In a ColPlace, we have different types of content containers with their content items associated. The content containers of a ColPlace are classified using SIOC and SIOC Types. Each content Item is linked to its container using the property **sioc:has container**.

An entity, in its individual identity, is defined as a **foaf:Organization**, "a kind of Agent corresponding to social institutions such as companies, societies".

In the context of the H-Know platform, an Entity can also be seen as a **sioc:Usergroup**,"a set of UserAccounts whose owners have a common purpose or interest" [6].

To classify the group behaviour of a ColPlace the **sioc:UserGroup** structure is used. To link the H-Know users to the ColPlaces they are part of, we use the **sioc:member** of property. The association entities have with a ColPlace is expressed by the property **sioc:usergroup of**.

To describe the relationships between platform users, we use the RELATIONSHIP ontology[2], which extends the **foaf:knows** core property, providing extra types of relationships between users such as: **Employed_By**, **Employer_Of** or **Works_With**, enriching the description of the platform interactions.

To connect platform content items with the domain knowledge, it's used as a bridge the property **sioc:topic** to a **skos:Concept**. This property can be applied to most of the classes defined in the SIOC ontology. So, we can for example assign a set of concepts to a container and then propagate those topics to its items.

Each content item may have a set of Domain Concepts related to it. So, we will have triples where the **subject** is the URI of a content item, classified with the SIOC vocabulary, the **predicate** is the sioc:topic property, making the bridge between a content item and a concept and the **object** is a skos:Concept class representing a concept in the domain knowledge. This way we can specify the concepts which relate to each content item of the platform.

2.4 Conceptualizing a Semantic Search Interface for the Platform

After having the information produced in the H-Know platform semantically classified, users should be able to make searches taking advantage of that classification.

One possible approach is to build facet-browsing search interfaces, where users can, by the means of filters, continuously redefine their searching criteria. Starting from a non-filtered set of web references, users can use pre-defined filters to decrease the set of results, getting just what they were trying to find.

The idea is, using all the metadata generated in the platform, to get results relating domain knowledge concepts with the socio-collaborative activities.

We define 2 sets of facets filters: one for the socio-collaborative characteristics of the content item, such as the author of a content, the type of content or the type of collaboration place where it is produced and another set of filters related to the topics defined in the domain ontology.

[2] http://vocab.org/relationship/.html

This way we can get an answer for a question like: "Which blog-entries Manuel created about churches?", filtering creator for "Manuel", type for "blogentry" and Construction Result Space for "Church".

3   A Technological Architecture for the Platform Semantics Integration

From the conceptualizations presented before in this paper, the diagram 4 describes the technological architecture implemented in the H-Know platform.

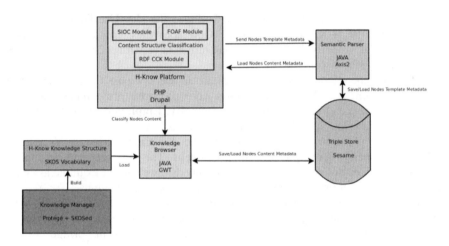

Fig. 4. H-Know platform Semantic module architecture

So, starting from the bottom layer of the architecture, to store the metadata triples, **Sesame** framework was chosen. Sesame was chosen as the triple store because it provides a fast and reliable native triples store, with a comprehensive back-end managing interface (Workbench) and a very complete and easy to use Java API with functions to interact with it.

Changing the focus to the Drupal platform, for the node's template semantic classification, a conjunction of three different customized Drupal modules (**RDF CCK Module**, **FOAF Module** and **SIOC Module**) was the solution. RDF CCK is an "out-of the-box" module, that provides an extension to the content types manager (CCK), to map each content type (node template) and its fields to ontology vocabularies. This module, exports the semantic metadata of each node template in different ways, such as RDFa or to a file with the semantic information of a node. In addition to this module the FOAF and SIOC modules were used, with some modifications, to describe the platform socio-collaborative characteristics which are not expressed by RDF CCK. These modules act the same way as RDF CCK, exporting FOAF and SIOC information of the nodes to RDF/XML files.

To establish a connection between Drupal and Sesame, since Drupal is built over Php language and Sesame API is Java, a **"Semantic Parser"** was built to work as an intermediate between Drupal and Sesame, using a Web Service. This application is used both to save Drupal metadata in Sesame and to load metadata from Sesame into Drupal. This application then uses the API of Sesame to perform the required actions (saving or loading of metadata). The **"Knowledge Domain"** is managed using **Protégé** with a plugin for the construction of SKOS vocabularies (**SKOSed**).

To implement the semantic classification of the nodes content, it was developed from scratch a Java GWT application,**"Knowledge Browser"**, to load the domain knowledge structure of the platform and give users the chance of choosing concepts which relate with the content they are producing. This browser loads the knowledge structure using a Java API called **SKOS API** and interacts with the Sesame triple store using its API.

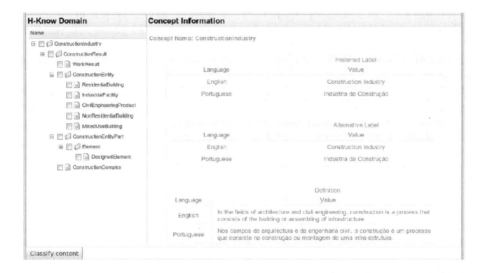

Fig. 5. Ontology Browser interface

Users select the concepts and then click the "Classify content" button which presents a report of the selected concepts performs the classification. The browser is integrated inside Drupal. In every node edition, a user can use it to classify the content he is publishing.

4   Related Work

Research on semantically enhanced systems is growing although only few of the projects focus on CMSs. Good examples of that are [10] or [11] which describe architectures to integrate semantics in CMSs from scratch. In [9] is presented a generic architecture for the integration of semantic annotation and usage in a CMS. We have a different approach since we use a already available CMS (Drupal).

The closest studies to our work are presented on [2]. We use a module presented on this paper (RDF CCK) which automatically generates semantics from the ontologies defined in CCK (Content Construction Kit). In this paper, they suggest a solution which stores the metadata on the Drupal installation database (a non native triple store), providing a SPARQL endpoint for the generated metadata. Our approach is different since we store the metadata outside Drupal in a native triple store (Sesame).

There was no "out-of the-box" solution to classify content items according to a domain ontology, so it was developed from scratch, a browser for it which loads SKOS vocabularies. That browser was integrated in the Drupal framework.

In the other hand, making use of the technological architecture suggested, this paper presents a ontology model using existing W3C ontologies: FOAF, SIOC and SKOS. Drupal is structured and organized in a way where the integration of SIOC and FOAF to describe the socio-collaborative activities can be naturally integrated. In [5] is presented a model to analyse the social relations between users through the content that they create and an exporter for that model. Another project in the area of socio-semantics is Flink [13], a system for the extraction, aggregation and visualization of online social networks. In this paper we present a model which intends to semantically describe the social network of the H-Know platform, the collaborations held there and the connection of these with Domain Knowledge, described using SKOS data model. One of the most interesting SKOS projects is PoolParty [14] a web application to create and maintain thesauri with a easy to use user-interface. The solution presented aims to integrate both socio-collaborative and knowledge semantics, a kind of approach we haven't seen so far in other research projects.

5   Conclusions and Further Work

The work presented in this paper is part of a more general research project aiming at integrating collaboration and domain ontologies to be used in IT platforms supporting collaborative networks of organisations. The approach followed was action-research like, meaning that we addressed firstly a practical problem posed by the H-Know platform requirements and we will follow on deriving general knowledge from this first case-study.

Summarising, a model to express the socio-collaborative activities managed in the platform integrated with the Domain Knowledge was thus described. Existing W3C standard ontologies were used. A technological architecture to implement the model was also described. All the generated metadata is stored outside of the platform in a native triple store application, Sesame. In a sum, we have the content created in the H-Know platform semantically described, ready to be consumed by any application that wants to take advantage of the information available in the H-Know platform.

References

1. Bojars, U., Breslin, J.G., Finn, A., Decker, S.: Using the Semantic Web for linking and reusing data across Web 2.0 communities. In: Web Semantics: Science, Services and Agents on the World Wide Web (2008)

2. Corlosquet, S., Delbru, R., Clark, T., Polleres, A., Decker, S., Haller, A., Marmolowski, M., Gaaloul, W., Oren, E., Sapkota, B., others: Produce and Consume Linked Data with Drupal! In: International Semantic Web Conference (2009)
3. Stephane Corlosquet: Drupal RDF Schema proposal | groups.drupal.org, http://groups.drupal.org/node/9311 (visited on April of 2010)
4. Antoine Isaac, Ed Summers.: SKOS simple knowledge organization system primer, http://www.w3.org/TR/skos-primer/ (visited on March of 2010)
5. Bojars, U., Heitmann, B., Oren, E.: A Prototype to Explore Content and Context on Social Community Sites. In: SABRE Conference on Social Semantic Web, CSSW (2007)
6. D. Brickley, L. Miller.: FOAF Vocabulary Specification, http://xmlns.com/foaf/spec/ (visited on May of 2010)
7. Bojars, U., Breslin, J.: SIOC core ontology specification, http://rdfs.org/sioc/spec/ (visited on May of 2010)
8. ISO 12006-2 Building construction | Organization of information about construction works - Framework for classification of information DIS Version (2001)
9. Laleci, G.B., Aluc, G., Dogac, A., Sinaci, A., Kilic, O., Tuncer, F.: A Semantic Backend for Content Management Systems. Knowledge-Based Systems (2010)
10. Garcia, R., Gimeno, J.M., Perdrix, F., Gil, R., Oliva, M.: The Rhizomer Semantic Content Management System. In: Lytras, M.D., Carroll, J.M., Damiani, E., Tennyson, R.D. (eds.) WSKS 2008. LNCS (LNAI), vol. 5288, pp. 385–394. Springer, Heidelberg (2008)
11. Le, D.M., Lau, L.: An Open Architecture for Ontology-Enabled Content Management Systems: A Case Study in Managing Learning Objects. On the Move to Meaningful Internet Systems 2006, France, October 29 - November 3 (2006)
12. Aumueller, D., Rahm, E.: Caravela: Semantic Content Management with Automatic Information Integration and Categorization. In: Franconi, E., Kifer, M., May, W. (eds.) ESWC 2007. LNCS, vol. 4519, pp. 729–738. Springer, Heidelberg (2007)
13. Mika, P.: Flink: Semantic Web technology for the extraction and analysis of social networks. Journal of Web Semantics (2005)
14. Schandl, T., Blumauer, A.: PoolParty: SKOS Thesaurus Management utilizing Linked Data. In: The Semantic Web: Research and Applications (2010)

ORM'10 - PC Co-chairs Message

Following successful workshops held in Cyprus (2005), France (2006), Portugal (2007), Mexico (2008) and Portugal (2009), this is the sixth fact-oriented modeling workshop run in conjunction with the OTM conferences. Fact-oriented modeling is a conceptual approach to model and query the semantics of business domains in terms of the underlying facts of interest, where all facts and rules may be verbalized in language readily understandable by users working in those domains. Unlike Entity-Relationship (ER) modeling and UML class diagrams, fact-oriented modeling treats all facts as relationships (unary, binary, ternary etc.). How facts are grouped into structures (e.g. attribute-based entity types, classes, relation schemes, XML schemas) is considered a design level, implementation issue irrelevant to capturing the essential business semantics. Avoiding attributes in the base model en-hances semantic stability and populatability, and facilitates natural verbalization and thus more productive communication with all stakeholders. For information modeling, fact-oriented graphical notations are typically far more expressive than those provided by other notations. Fact-oriented modeling includes procedures for mapping to attribute-based structures, so may also be used to front-end those approaches.

Though less well known than ER and object-oriented approaches, fact-oriented modeling has been used successfully in industry for over 30 years, and is taught in universities around the world. The fact-oriented modeling approach comprises a family of closely related "dialects", including Object-Role Modeling (ORM), Cognition enhanced Natural language Information Analysis Method (CogNIAM) and Fully-Communication Oriented Information Modeling (FCO-IM). Though adopting a different graphical notation, the Object-oriented Systems Model (OSM) is a close relative, with its attribute-free philosophy. The Semantics of Business Vocabulary and Business Rules (SBVR) proposal adopted by the Object Management Group in 2007 is a recent addition to the family of fact-oriented approaches.

Software tools supporting the fact-oriented approach include the ORM tools NORMA (Natural ORM Architect), ActiveFacts, InfoModeler and ORM-Lite, the CogNIAM tool Doctool, and the FCO-IM tool CaseTalk. The Collibra ontology tool suite and DogmaStudio are fact-based tools for specifying ontologies. Richmond is another ORM tool under development. General information about fact-orientation may be found at www.ORMFoundation.org.

This year we had 27 abstracts and 22 full submissions for workshop papers. After an extensive review process by a distinguished international program committee, with each paper receiving three or more reviews, we accepted the 12 papers that appear in these proceedings. Congratulations to the successful authors! We gratefully acknowledge the generous contribution of time and effort by

R. Meersman et al. (Eds.): OTM 2010 Workshops, LNCS 6428, pp. 424–425, 2010.
© Springer-Verlag Berlin Heidelberg 2010

the program committee, and the OTM organizing committee, especially Robert Meersman and Tharam Dillon (OTM General Co-chairs), and Pilar Herrero (OTM General Co-chair and OTM Workshops General Chair).

August 2010   Terry Halpin
                                                                 Herman Balsters
                                                                 ORM'10

Using Object Role Modeling in a Service-Oriented Data Integration Project

Ilkka Melleri

Aalto University School of Science and Technology,
P.O. Box 19210, FI-000760 Aalto, Finland
`ilkka.melleri@tkk.fi`

Abstract. Communication between business and IT experts is challenging, because business requirements are often specified in subjective and
vague terms compared to the formality needed for technical implementation. In the service-oriented architectures (SOA) context this issue is
especially important, because the value proposition of SOA is based on
a business awareness of the systems. In this paper we address this challenge by using the Object Role Modeling (ORM) method in a case study
focusing on a service-oriented data integration project. The results of
this study indicate that the automatic verbalizations combined with the
automatic XML Schema generation of the ORM models could be useful
in SOA integration projects to support the collaboration between the
business and IT experts. The main concerns that were identified relate
to the change management of the ORM models, managing the high level
of detail in the models and the workload if no adequate automation is
provided.

1 Introduction

1.1 Background

Service-oriented architecture (SOA) is an architectural style that aims to support
the design and implementation of business aware IT systems [1]. This means
that SOA systems should be flexible and scalable to meet changing business
requirements effectively and efficiently [2].

However, business requirements are often specified in vague and subjective
form using natural language, with sentences such as "we need to exchange the
customer data between these systems". In order to be able to implement this
kind of requirement in an IT system, there needs to be specific and formal details
about, for example, what is meant by *a customer*, and what data is *customer
data* in this context.

A common approach to address this communication challenge is conceptual
modeling [3]. Conceptual models describe the business domain using business
concepts that are familiar to the domain experts [4]. However, the conceptual
models should also provide an unambiguous, formal, representation in order to
support the technical experts implementation tasks. If the conceptual models

R. Meersman et al. (Eds.): OTM 2010 Workshops, LNCS 6428, pp. 426–435, 2010.
© Springer-Verlag Berlin Heidelberg 2010

lack a formal foundation, the models still need to be interpreted by the technical expert before implementation, which might affect the intended business meaning. Therefore, the most useful conceptual models are those that can transform the business concepts and their relationships to formal representations that can be implemented in a system.

In the context of data modeling, one such approach is the Object Role Modeling (ORM) method [4]. ORM supports the business experts understanding by enabling the models to be presented with natural language sentences. On the other hand, the foundation of ORM is rooted in first order predicate logic, which supports the formalism needed by the technical expert.

Based on the above, ORM seems to fit well with the SOA objectives of enabling increased business support with information systems. However, the reported use of ORM in the SOA context has been limited. Other approaches, such as the Unified Modeling Language (UML) and Business Process Modeling Notation (BPMN) are commonly used in modeling SOA solutions [3,5].

To address this issue, this study explores the use of the ORM method in a service-oriented systems integration project.

1.2 Case Description

This study was done in co-operation with an international industrial company located in Finland. The company has annual sales of nearly 2 billion Euros and operates with personnel of 10,000 people worldwide.

The company has recently started to streamline its operations through a global master data management (MDM) system. The MDM system can be characterized as an advanced "phone book" because it holds all general customer and supplier information, such as company identification numbers, addresses and phone numbers. The MDM system acts as a central repository for the information that has previously been spread out in multiple systems.

Introducing the MDM system means that the number of integration projects has increased dramatically, because all other systems are required to query the MDM system for customer and supplier information. Moreover, because of the strategic importance of the MDM system, there is an increasing emphasis put on the business awareness of designing and implementing the integration solutions. Figure 1 illustrates the integration landscape in the company with regard to the MDM system. The focus in this paper is on one of the needed integrations, namely between the MDM system and a sales configuration system (system 2).

For modeling, the company has recently started to utilize Aris software, especially for business process design. However, most modeling is still done in ad-hoc fashion with different people using different tools such as PowerPoint, StarUML and MS Visio.

For implementing integrations, the company is increasingly using a service-oriented approach by utilizing Web Service technologies such as WSDL and SOAP along with message broker technologies. The business data that is transferred in the SOAP messages is specified with XML Schema. However, Excel

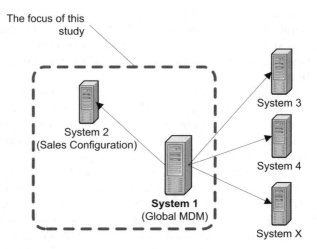

Fig. 1. The MDM integration landscape in the case company

files are commonly used for communicating with the business experts about the integration data.

The main challenge in the integration projects is the lack of systematic documentation in a way that would be accessible to both technical experts and business experts. As described above, different modeling approaches have been used in an ad-hoc fashion, which has lead to the situation where documentation is spread across Word documents, Excel files and in implementation details.

Moreover, using Excel files and PowerPoint drawings to communicate integration issues is not considered optimal. Rather, the company is looking for techniques and methods that would bring more structure and formalism into the design and implementation processes, while at the same time enabling a closer participation of the business experts in order to ensure the business validity of the solutions.

1.3   Research Objective and Research Question

The objective of this study is to explore how the Object Role Modeling method can be utilized to enhance the communication and collaboration between business and IT experts in a service-oriented systems integration project. The context of the integration project is master data management, and the focus is especially on data integration of customer data.

The research question formulated from this objective is:

– *How does the Object Role Modeling method support the communication between business and IT experts in a service-oriented data integration project?*

1.4   Structure of the Paper

In section 2 the research methodology and the research process of the study are described in detail. Section 3 covers related work from the literature, and in section 4 the findings of the study are presented and discussed. Finally, in section 5 the study is concluded along with suggestions for further study.

2   Research Methodology and Research Process

The research for this paper was conducted using the action research methodology described in [6]. The methodology is characterized by a focus on problems with practical relevance and a close collaboration between the researchers and the study's subjects.

In this study, focusing on an ongoing systems integration project highlighted the practical relevance, and the collaborative nature of the study was achieved by conducting the research through collaborative workshops with the integration project participants.

The research process in action research follows an iterative model with four main phases: 1) identifying primary problems, 2) specifying actions to deal with problems, 3) implementing the specified actions and 4) evaluating the outcomes [6]. How these phases were implemented in this study is presented in the following subsections.

2.1   Identifying Primary Problems

Two primary problems were identified in the integration project, namely specifying the business data and implementing technical interoperability between the systems.

Specifying the business data between the systems means that both systems need to agree on the business semantics of the data to be exchanged. The business data in this case is basic customer and supplier data. However, both system 1 and system 2 have different definitions of what data constitute a customer and a supplier. These differences need to be solved in order to integrate the systems.

The mapping of the data types addresses the technical interoperability aspect of the integration problem. As mentioned earlier, the company is utilizing XML technologies and a message broker for implementation. Therefore, the technical challenge in the integration case was to specify the XML Schema structures of the integration data, and to implement the mappings between the XML Schemas into the message broker.

2.2   Specifying Actions to Deal with Problems

To address the identified problems, three actions were specified: 1) creating the ORM models of both systems' data models, 2) validating the ORM models with the participants and 3) interviewing the participants. Figure 2 illustrates the general approach of using the ORM method in the integration between systems 1 and 2.

The actions were specified to address the identified problems by supporting the specification of the business data through generating the ORM verbalizations, and by supporting the technical implementation through generating the XML Schemas.

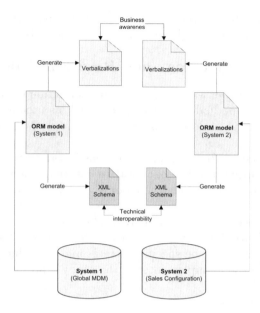

Fig. 2. Applying ORM in data integration between system 1 and system 2

2.3   Implementing the Specified Actions

The actions were implemented through three collaborative workshops that were held together with the participants. The study involved four participants from the case organization, namely one business expert and one IT expert for both system 1 and system 2. The profiles of the participants are presented in table 1.

Table 1. Profiles of the participants

	Role	Title	Modeling Experience
Person 1	IT Expert of System 1	Configuration owner	ER
Person 2	Business Expert of System 1	Concept owner	PowerPoint
Person 3	IT Expert of System 2	Systems architect	UML, ER
Person 4	Business Expert of System 2	Project manager	PowerPoint

None of the participants had prior experience with ORM. The IT experts had used UML and ER, while the business experts relied on PowerPoint drawings.

Before the first workshop, initial ORM models were created based on existing documentation from the two systems. This documentation consisted of Power-Point presentations and screenshots of the main functionalities, along with Excel files that specified the XML document structures of the both systems ingoing and outgoing data.

The ORM models were created with the Natural ORM Architect (NORMA)[1] tool. In addition to the ORM model diagrams also automatic verbalizations and XML Schema documents were created with NORMA. Moreover, in order to create compact lists of the verbalizations, the ActiveFacts[2] tool was utilized.

Figure 3 illustrates a part of the ORM diagram for System 1, namely the system distribution functionality.

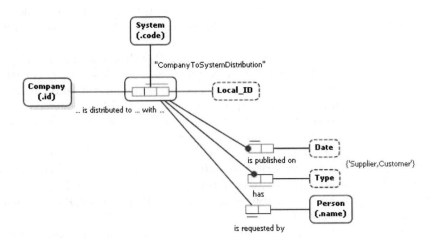

Fig. 3. ORM model of the distribution functionality in system 1

As system 1 is the global MDM system, it includes integrations to many other systems. The system distribution functionality keeps track of the different local identifiers (*Local_ID* value type) a specific customer or supplier (*Company(.id)* entity type) has in the different systems.

2.4   Evaluating the Outcomes

All participants were individually interviewed after the modeling workshops were completed. Each interview lasted between 32 and 51 minutes and the interviews followed a semi-structured format, where the discussion for each interviewee was allowed to develop individually. However, the general theme for all interviews was the same, namely the benefits and challenges of using the ORM method.

The objective of the interviews was to support the analysis of the study, as suggested in [7].

---

[1] http://sourceforge.net/projects/orm/
[2] http://dataconstellation.com/ActiveFacts/index.shtml

3   Related Work

In [8,9] ORM is studied in the context of data federations. The setting in both papers is an information systems landscape with multiple, autonomous, local systems that need to be interoperable. The lack of shared semantics is acknowledged as a central challenge in these kinds of data integrations [9]. In other words, a shared understanding of the local data models is needed, before a common global model can be created. The ORM method is argued as a suitable approach for addressing the problem of common semantics, because it provides a linguistic basis that helps non-technical domain experts understand the information models.

The context of this paper is similar as in [8] and [9], and similar challenges were identified relating to explicating business semantics of the technical implementations.

In [10] a method for using ORM to design XML Schema documents is presented and motivated. The main idea in the paper is to enable a more conceptual design of XML documents in order to specify and communicate data requirements for human audiences. As mentioned also in [11] XML schema is seen too technical and complex to support efficient communication between humans, especially non-technical business domain experts [10].

This paper takes a similar approach as [10], by using ORM in conceptual modeling of data that is transferred in XML format. However, the focus in this study is not on the mapping between ORM models and XML Schema per se, but rather to gain experiences from practice when utilizing the ORM approach to conceptual data modeling.

Furthermore, in [12] ORM is used to model an application domain ontology. The paper addresses semantic definitions of business processes in the SOA context.

Finally, [11] argues that XML is becoming more important at the higher-layers of software architectures and can no more be seen merely as a transport layer syntax. This shift is highlighted by an increasing number of applications that use XML as a native data format, and that more sophisticated XML technologies such as XML Query Language (XQuery) have been developed [11].

This study fits within the context of [11], because there was an identified need to explicate the business semantics of the XML-based implementations, and thus, XML was regarded important at a higher level of abstraction as argued in [11].

All in all, this paper can be seen as a complementary study to those presented above, by providing experiences from practice. The main premise of this study is similar, namely conceptual data modeling with focus on XML, along with enhancing the understanding of common business semantics with the help of the ORM method.

4   Findings

4.1   Introduction

The findings are categorized into ORM strengths and ORM challenges. With this categorization, the aim is to explicate the main issues raised by participants after their experience with ORM. Table 2 summarizes the results, which are further discussed in the following subsections.

Table 2. Summary of the findings

ORM Strengths	ORM Challenges
Clear diagrams	Change management
Verbalizations	Automation and tool support
XML Schema generation	Communication with different stakeholders
Detailed and formal modeling process	Complexity due to high level of detail

4.2 ORM Strengths

Generally, the ORM model diagrams were considered visual and easy to understand. One of the more technical participants viewed ORM to be *"a nifty way to model things"*, whereas the business participants considered the diagrams to be understandable for also non-technical people.

The diagrams and verbalizations were considered the most interesting, because they could potentially be used in collaboration with non-technical people. As one participant put it: *"[the verbalizations] allow us to talk about issues in natural language and not just in bytes and code"*.

XML Schema generation from the ORM models was also considered useful and important, because XML Schema files are increasingly being used in the company. Moreover, as the company does not have a standardized method to create XML schema files, ORM was seen as a potential candidate for addressing this issue.

Additionally, the detailed modeling process was considered a strength in ORM. The participants viewed that the ORM modeling process directs the modeling towards precise definitions of business facts and constraints, which supports the IT experts' implementation work. The participants considered, for example, that it was easier to describe and discuss the business data of the systems with the help of the ORM models compared to existing PowerPoint drawings and Excel files.

4.3 ORM Challenges

The primary challenges identified by the participants were change management of the ORM models, automation and tool support, communication with different stakeholders and complexity of the ORM models.

Regarding change management and tool support, concerns were raised about whether the models could be created and updated without too much effort compared to the benefits. Even though tools such as NORMA are available, there were concerns regarding how well the ORM tools could be utilized in synchronization with other integration tools, such as message broker software or database management tools. As one participant questioned, *"If we need to implement the changes to the current tools, and additionally to the ORM tools, will the efforts in updating the ORM models be justified with the benefits of using the models?"*.

The level of detail in the ORM models raised questions regarding the communication with different stakeholders. One of the participants summarized the findings by commenting: *"The enterprise architects don't care about the details of the data structures, and the sales people want pretty pictures. But using ORM for explaining the XML structures to the project manager, or validating the business constraints with the domain experts? Absolutely."*

Finally, even though the ORM modeling process was seen as a strength, it also raised concerns relating to the complexity of the models. Some participants were worried that due to the detailed modeling process, the models could eventually become too complex to understand and manage. Thus, the participants stressed the importance of abstraction and modularity features in the ORM tools.

5   Conclusions

In this paper, a case study was conducted to explore the use of the Object Role Modeling method in a service-oriented data integration project. The research question for the study was: *"How does the Object Role Modeling method support the communication between business and IT experts in a service-oriented data integration project?"* The research question was addressed by identifying potential strengths and challenges with the ORM method in this context.

Based on this study, ORM seems to be a useful modeling method for service-oriented data integration solutions. The verbalizations provide access for business experts to validate the models in order to ensure business interoperability, whereas the XML Schema generation supports the technical interoperability of the XML-based integration solutions.

However, change management, tool support and complexity of the models are among the challenges of applying ORM in this context. The high level of detail in the ORM models creates challenges in managing the changes in the models along with dealing with the evolving complexity as the solutions and businesses evolve. Additionally, adequate tools are necessary not just for creating the models, but also for managing the models and integrating the models with other tools and technologies. Otherwise, the workload required might be too high for making a business case for the adoption of the ORM method.

It should be noted that as the scope of this study was on using ORM as a tool for documentation and modeling, implementation issues were addressed only partially. For example, the generated ORM to XML Schema transforms should be investigated more carefully before using them in actual implementations.

For future research, we plan to extend this study by utilizing the created models in upcoming integration projects in the company. The goal is to enhance the analysis of the actual effects of using the ORM method in practice.

Acknowledgements

The author would like to thank the SOLEA[3] project for supporting this work. Additionally, this work benefitted from discussions with Hannu Virkanen.

References

1. Erl, T.: SOA Principles of Service Design. Prentice Hall International, Reading (2007)
2. Papazoglou, M.P., Heuvel, W.J.: Service oriented architectures: approaches, technologies and research issues. The VLDB Journal 16(3), 389–415 (2007)
3. Roussopoulos, N., Karagiannis, D.: Conceptual Modeling: Past, Present and the Continuum of the Future. In: Borgida, A.T., Chaudhri, V.K., Giorgini, P., Yu, E.S. (eds.) Conceptual Modeling: Foundations and Applications. LNCS, vol. 5600, pp. 139–152. Springer, Heidelberg (2009)
4. Halpin, T.: Information Modeling and Relational Databases, 2nd edn. Morgan Kaufmann, San Francisco (2008)
5. Vemulapalli, A., Subramanian, N.: Transforming Functional Requirements from UML into BPEL to Efficiently Develop SOA-Based Systems. In: Meersman, R., Herrero, P., Dillon, T. (eds.) OTM 2009 Workshops. LNCS, vol. 5872, pp. 337–349. Springer, Heidelberg (2009)
6. Baskerville, R.L.: Investigating information systems with action research. Communications of the AIS 2(3) (1999)
7. Myers, M.D.: Qualitative research in information systems. MIS Quarterly 21(2), 241–242 (1997)
8. Balsters, H., Halpin, T.: Modeling Data Federations in ORM. In: Meersman, R., Tari, Z., Herrero, P. (eds.) OTM-WS 2007, Part I. LNCS, vol. 4805, pp. 657–666. Springer, Heidelberg (2007)
9. Balsters, H., Haarsma, B.: An ORM-Driven Implementation Framework for Database Federations. In: Meersman, R., Herrero, P., Dillon, T. (eds.) OTM 2009 Workshops. LNCS, vol. 5872, pp. 659–670. Springer, Heidelberg (2009)
10. Bird, L., Goodchild, A., Halpin, T.: Object Role Modelling and XML-Schema. In: Laender, A.H.F., Liddle, S.W., Storey, V.C. (eds.) ER 2000. LNCS, vol. 1920, pp. 661–705. Springer, Heidelberg (2000)
11. Wilde, E.: Towards Conceptual Modeling for XML. In: Proceedings of Berliner XML Tage 2005, pp. 213–224 (2005)
12. Bollen, P.: Service-oriented conceptual modeling. In: Meersman, R., Tari, Z., Herrero, P. (eds.) OTM-WS 2008. LNCS, vol. 5333, pp. 678–687. Springer, Heidelberg (2008)

[3] http://www.uku.fi/solea/english.html

Real-Time Integration of Geo-data in ORM

Herman Balsters[1], Chris Klaver[1], and George B. Huitema[1,2]

[1] University of Groningen, The Netherlands
h.balsters@rug.nl, c.klaver@student.rug.nl , g.b.huitema@rug.nl
[2] TNO, The Netherlands
george.huitema@tno.nl

Abstract. Geographic information (geo-data; i.e., data with a spatial component.) is being used for civil, political, and commercial applications. Modeling
geo-data can be involved due to its often very complex structure, hence placing
high demands on the modeling language employed. Many geo-applications
would greatly benefit from the possibility of integrating existing geo-databases.
Data integration is a notoriously hard problem, and integrating geo-databases in
practice often adds the extra requirement that the integration should result in a
real-time system. This paper provides a case study and a design method for
real-time integration of geo-databases based on the ORM modeling language.
We will show that the use of ORM is superior to competing approaches, and
that the so-called ORM federation procedure will yield correct design of integrated geo-databases.

1 Introduction

Geographic information is being used for civil, political, and commercial applications.
This information is based on geographical information (geo-data); i.e., data with some
spatial component. Geo-data is gathered by numerous applications and by sensors
placed in our environment. Geo-data can directly concern physical objects like buildings, streets, waterways, but it can also concern such objects indirectly, e.g. a billing
address. The use of geo-data is overwhelming: 70-80% of information collected by
government is spatial in nature [27].

We distinguish two important user groups: the government and the commercial
world of the mobile content providers. For government, geo-data is crucial for using
space in an intelligent and sustainable manner. For commercial parties, geo-data can
be a valuable strategic asset. Mobile providers, handset manufactures, apps developers, and media companies continuously seek new and innovative ways to create differentiation. Using geo-data, users can be provided with value-added information,
e.g., *Location Based Services (LBS)* [22], such as points-of-interest (POI), emergency
services, and tracking.

Usually, geo-data is stored in databases together with means for manipulating and
querying; such databases are called *Geographic Information Systems (GIS)* [1,8]. A
major problem is the *open accessibility* of these systems and databases (geo-portals).
Similar problems on accessibility are found when dealing with geo-data in operational
web-mapping services and cloud services [15,16], where security and privacy are

R. Meersman et al. (Eds.): OTM 2010 Workshops, LNCS 6428, pp. 436–446, 2010.

main concerns. We also mention the *Global Spatial Data Infrastructure (SDI)* wishing to ensure a wide availability of accurate and exchangeable geo-data. Examples in this direction are the INSPIRE guidelines (aiming to stimulate new standards and uniformity in order to obtain an European SDI) and the Open Geospatial Consortium (aiming at geo-data interoperability) [21,26]. Another major problem is the lack of advanced technologies for *integration of multi-resources* of geo-data, and the *real-time* acquisition and accessibility of integrated data.

Common approaches in integrating geo-data are mainly based on UML [25] for modeling purposes, and on Service Oriented Architecture (SOA, [12]) for implementation. Both approaches have important shortcomings when dealing with the integration of geo-data. (ER modeling [9] is hardly applicable to data integration, due to its severe lack of expressiveness.)

Drawbacks of UML in data modeling have been extensively described in [20]. We can safely say that UML was never intended as a specific modeling language for databases. UML does not have, for example, a facility for directly specifying keys in class models, and also it has no facility for directly specifying a large class of constraints specific to roles inside a particular fact type (such as set-comparison constraints, join path constraints, and ring constraints). One could, of course, resort to the Object Constraint Language (OCL, [29]), but OCL is very hard to read and write for non-technical experts, and OCL has only limited tool support. UML class models are also difficult to validate, because UML class models are not based on fact-based modeling principles [5,13,14,18,19,20]), and are also incomplete (due to lack of ability to express typical database constraints).

SOA is currently a very popular technique for architecting software, allowing for quick development of software, tailor-made for end users requiring a certain set of services. Also in data-integration projects, SOA has succeeded in gaining a permanent place. However, the same reason that explains SOA's success as an implementation platform in data-integration projects, also explains its weakness: each query on the integrated database resulting from a SOA-based solution, requires programming of a specific service. End users not requiring a specific set of queries (all known beforehand), but rather an *ad hoc* query facility, will experience the SOA-solution as fundamentally non-sustainable.

ORM, on the other hand, overcomes the insufficiencies of the UML and SOA approach, and has as additional value that it has a completely formal basis [17], offers semantic stability of its models, and is equipped with a very powerful modeling tool [10]. In papers [2,3], we have also introduced a step-by-step procedure for integrating a collection of databases based on the principle of ORM federation. The ORM federation procedure results in a virtual, and real-time integration of data, and has the added benefit of a complete *ad hoc* query facility.

We will show how to use the ORM federation method, together with a principle developed in this paper, called the *Global Bounding Box principle*, to model and construct real-time integrations in the specific case of geo-databases. Starting from a case study we will explain the basic problems in integrating geo-databases. From the particular cases, we will move on to an abstraction, explaining how to integrate geo-databases in general. We will also discuss implementation issues pertaining to geo-data; it turns out that –due to the particular nature of geo-data – that measures have to be taken in order to arrive at industrial-strength and real-time solutions. This paper uses basic ORM notations, cf. [18,19,20].

2   Case Study

In order to explain the basic integration problems, we refer to a case study taken from
the Applied Computing Science Department of TNO. This case study involves the so-
called CityObject geo-database, initially created by the University of Berlin [11], and
the so-called AnySense geo-database, developed at TNO for storage of sensor
data [23].

The CityObject geo-database stores, represents, and manages virtual 3D city models by using special programs on top of a standard spatial-relational database. In this
paper, we mainly restrict ourselves to city objects that are buildings. A building model
specifies the geometry of a building, together with additional semantics of a building.
In the CityObject model, the geometry of buildings is represented by a list of coordinates representing vertices that can be used to render a concave three-dimensional
polygon depicting the building. Below, we offer a (re-engineered) ORM model of the
original CityObject database.

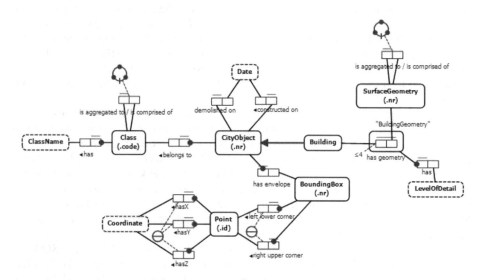

Fig. 1. CityObject Model

The fact type "Type is comprised of Type" indicates that types, e.g. *BuildingType,*
can be the root of a tree of other types. In the fact types "Building has SurfaceGeometry", and "SurfaceGeometry is comprised of SurfaceGeometry", We distinguish consecutive Levels of Detail (LOD), where objects become more detailed with increasing
LOD regarding both geometry and thematic differentiation.

In the figure 2 below, we depict some population samples of building geometries
and LOD's. Figure 3 illustrates a typical tree hierarchy (no cycles) associated to a
particular surface geometry.

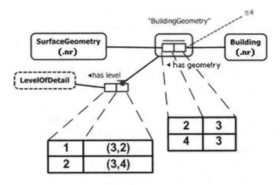

Fig. 2. Levels of detail

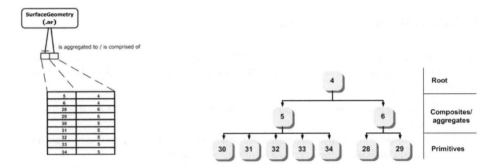

Fig. 3. Tree hierarchy of surface geometries

AnySense database

The second database in our case study is called AnySense; this database is supplied by TNO, and has been developed to provide for real-time and permanent storage of sensor data [23]. Below, we offer a (re-engineered) ORM model of the original AnySense database.

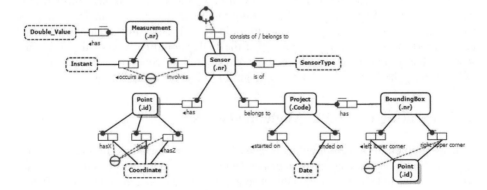

Fig. 4. The AnySense Model

Each Sensor has exactly one Coordinate, used to geometrically represent the Sensor as a three-dimensional point in space. Moreover, a Sensor belongs to exactly one so-called Project, associated to a geometry in the form of a bounding box. We furthermore have a constraint that require Sensors -belonging to a particular Project- to lie within the boundaries specified by the bounding box of that Project. Note that multiple distinct Project entities can have an identical bounding box. This means that the fact that a coordinate lies within a bounding box is a necessary, but not sufficient, condition to determine whether a Sensor belongs to a Project. The type of a Sensor is used to distinguish between, for instance, a smoke measuring sensor or a humidity measuring sensor. Sensor entities can form a hierarchy, as seen from the *consists of/ belongs to* predicate, in the form of an acyclic graph. Furthermore, we have the constraint that measurements performed by a Sensor, can only take place between start- and end date of the Project that the Sensor belongs to.

3   Integrating Geo-data: Criteria

As mentioned in the introduction, the integration result of two geo-databases must satisfy the following criteria for this result to be considered successful. The integration result must be

1.   *virtual*: source databases remain autonomously intact, hence no migration of data
2.   *real-time*: sensor measurements are reflected immediately in the global, integrated database, hence no datawarehouse solution
3.   able to *support ad hoc queries*: sustainable query facility, hence no SOA-based solution, where each query has to be programmed as a separate service
4.   the result of a *general design procedure*: design procedure must be applicable to any set of given geo-databases
5.   *realizable*: theory should lead to the design of a working system, prototype as proof of concept

These criteria support our choice to use a federated database approach [2,3,4] to realize the integrated geo-database. Federated databases (FDB) offer a virtual integrated database, where the source databases remain completely autonomous. Furthermore, when the federated database is realized using relational database technology, then we can use *materialized views* as a means to build virtual tables in the global FDB that also conform to the extra requirement that the FDB should be in sync in a real-time mode with any changes in a participating source database. Since we can then also use SQL to query the FDB, one automatically gets a full ad hoc query facility.

4   Integrating Geo-data: Modeling Issues

A major problem in integrating data is caused by lack of semantics. In order to understand the combined collection of all of the data available in the participating local systems, there has to be consensus on the meaning of the data. Naming conflicts, different formats in data, as well as global identification of local data objects, can make life very difficult for the designer of an integrated information system. Ideally, the data sources should be combined automatically into a so-called federation. Such an automatically generated federation can then provide the desired real-time overview, outlining the business data needs. Federations exist with a wide range of approaches. A number of papers [3,4,7,14,24,28] have been devoted to offering a conceptual framework for the integration of a collection of heterogeneous data sources into one coherent federation. A major feature common to many of these approaches is the use of the concept of *Global as View* [24,28]. The federation is said to be *virtual* as the federation constitutes a view on a collection of existing local databases.

5   Construction of the Federated Database

In papers [2,3], a federation procedure has been described, based on an ORM modelling and implementation framework. This procedure contains the following three elements:

1. *global identification* (the necessity of creating global identifiers and making explicit their connection to local identifiers)
2. *renaming* (homonyms and synonyms)
3. *conversion* (different data types and/or derivations for related attributes)

In the case of our two CityObject (figure 1) and AnySense (figure 4) databases, together with a so-called *Global Bounding Box principle* (introduced later in this section), we will illustrate how to systematically use these three steps in order to arrive at the desired federation of the two geo-databases.

Global identification

Global identification refers to the case where one single object in reality can be defined by two (or more) local objects. These corresponding object types often partially share a common structure. In interest of our integration, this shared common structure should be integrated into a global object:

1. Introduction of the global object. This global object contains the shared common structure, as found in the local objects.
2. Sub/supertyping is applied to the global (supertype) and local (subtype) objects.
3. The global object is assigned a global identifier. Introducing a new identifier allows local objects to be identified by their local identifier.
4. Introduce a discriminating role value on the global level. Not all global objects are defined by all their subtypes. Therefore a discriminating role is introduced to define all the roles the global object plays.
5. Show the correspondence between local and global identifiers.

We refer to the two ORM schemas as depicted in figures 1 and 4. The criterion to decide which entity types in the two schemas are candidates for integration on the global, federated level, is as follows: only when two entity populations have (or are expected to have) an overlap in physical reality, will the two entity types be candidates for integration. The only two candidate local entity types to form a global entity type are the Building entity type from the CityObject schema and the Project entity type from the AnySense schema, since their associated populations could contain entities that refer to the same object in physical reality (viz. some building). In order to construct a global entity, called Global-Building, to capture the integration result, various renaming and conversion problems will also have to be identified and resolved. Below, we will present a schema of the federated schema.

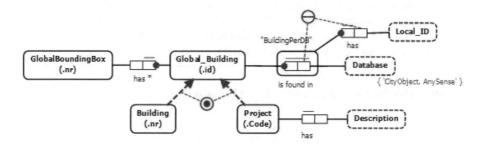

Fig. 5. Federated schema

In the schema above, a global object is introduced called Global_Building, of which the local Building and Project entities are subtypes. We see that the Global_Building can be uniquely identified if we take the combination of data source (AnySense or CityObject) and their respective Local_ID (.nr or .Code). This will indeed result in a unique id, if we take into account that the local id's are already unique in the local databases. Figure 5 still needs to be augmented with definitions of the subtypes in terms of the global entity:

> **Each** Building **is a** Global_Building **that** is found in Database `CityObject'
> **Each** Project **that** has Description 'Building' **is a** Global_Building **that** is found in Database `AnySense'

The question arises of how to populate the Global_Building entity type: which object in the population of Building corresponds to another object in the population of Project? Unless the objects share some global identifier, it is impossible to decide on this matter by looking at the data alone. The business/organization will have to provide these data, also called external data, since such data has to be provided from some external source, i.e., outside the specified source databases. Such external data consists of a simple extra base table, called a data-reference table.

From this table, we see that Building-17 and Project-X37 refer to the same building object in reality, and are, therefore, given the same global identifier value (in this case 2). Populating such a data-reference table is subject to a procedure called *data resolution* (cf. [2]), offering semi-automated support, but is beyond the scope of this paper.

Table 1. Local objects sharing a global identifier

Global_entity_identifier	Source_name	Local_identifier
1	Building	13
2	Building	17
2	Project	X37
3	Project	Y31

We will assume that the two schemas have already been subjected to proper renaming in order to rule out any naming conflicts. In practice, however, renaming issues (homonyms, synonyms) can be the subject of heated debate.

Another potential role for the Global_Building entity lies within the fact that both a Building and a Project store geometry. For the CityObject we have the *has envelope* role played by a CityObject entity and a BoundingBox entity, and the *has geometry* role played by a Building entity and a SurfaceGeometry entity, which –in turn- plays the role *has* with a Geometry value. In BoundingBox, two three-dimensional points are stored; one point to denote the left lower corner point of the box, the other to denote right upper corner point. In Geometry, a set of three dimensional points is stored which constitute the vertices of a three dimensional surface. As explained earlier, a tree-like hierarchy of SurfaceGeometry entities is formed per Building entity, where the entire tree describes a concave three-dimensional polygon belonging to that particular building.

For the AnySense database, we see that a Project plays the role *has* with a BoundingBox, with the same data structure as BoundingBox in the CityObject schema. Since each Building entity and each Project entity has exactly one bounding box, this implies that we can have at most two different bounding boxes associated to one 'real life building'. Now we have a problem, since if the two boxes are not identical, then which one belongs to the Global_Building? After consultation (with the owners of the two databases), it was decided that the bounding box of the Global_Building would be constructed in such a way that it contains both the local bounding boxes, and has the smallest volume as possible. We coin this approach as the *global bounding box principle*.

The global bounding box can easily be achieved if we realize the following. Given four three-dimensional points, the left lower corner point of the Building bounding box $l_{Building} = (x_{11}, y_{11}, z_{11})$, the left lower corner point of the Project bounding box $l_{Project} = (x_{21}, y_{21}, z_{21})$, the right upper corner points $r_{Building} = (x_{12}, y_{12}, z_{12})$ and $r_{Project} = (x_{22}, y_{22}, z_{22})$; then for the Global_Building we can **derive** the following values for the global bounding box

$$l_{Global\text{-}Building} = (\min(x_{11}, x_{21}), \min(y_{11}, y_{21}), \min(z_{11}, z_{21}))$$
$$r_{Global\text{-}Building} = (\max(x_{12}, x_{22}), \max(y_{12}, y_{22}), \max(z_{12}, z_{22}))$$

We note that, in practice, one problem still had to be overcome: both bounding boxes turned out to be defined in different coordinate systems. Calculating the global bounding box of the Global_Building without properly *converting* the coordinates first would yield nonsensical results. We will assume here that these conversions have indeed been carried out beforehand

6 Generalization of the Integration Procedure

The federation procedure that we used in the previous section, is –in principle- applicable to *any* situation involving a collection of (relational) databases [2,3]. Geo-databases have as a common feature that they always contain information pertaining to coordinates, geometry, hierarchies of data-structures, temporal aspects, etc. The CityObject and Anysense databases could be considered typical (albeit simplified versions of) geo-databases encountered in practice. As illustrated in our case study, ORM can be used to model the typical complexities of such geo-data. Furthermore, the ORM federation procedure, together with a principle developed in this paper, called the *Global Bounding Box principle* (cf. section 5 above), can be used to integrate a collection of geo-database schemas into a global schema. We note that once we know how to integrate two (geo-)databases, it easily generalizes to the federation of any number of source databases, by pairwise iteration of the federation procedure ([4]).

7 Implementation Issues: Prototyping and Beyond

Paper [2] dealt with offering an implementation framework exploiting ideas taken from [3,4] and used to offer a conceptual design procedure of a database federation. This design procedure is used in combination with the IBM Infosphere Federated Server (IBM-IFS, [6]). The IBM-IFS techniques of nicknaming and wrapping, and the reverse- and forward-engineering techniques of the ORM tools, combined with the methodological framework of [2,3], results in an effective implementation platform for development of semantically consistent and high-performance database federations. The complete framework is built upon six processes, as seen in the table below.

Table 2. Processes of the Framework

Process	Input	Output
Source Definition	Existing databases	Selection of tables from the existing databases
Nicknaming	Selected tables	Nicknames
Reverse Engineering	Nicknames	Local ORM schemas
Schema Integration	Local ORM schemas	Global ORM schema
Relational Model Generation	Global ORM schema	Relational model
View Generation	Nicknames Global ORM schema Relational model	DBMS specific DDL with view definitions and table definitions for external data

The processes are executed in succession, starting with the top, and ending at the bottom. The output of each process is the input for subsequent processes. The final step in the framework is the transformation from the integrated ORM model to the actual integrated sources. This final step is split into two processes within the framework. The first process is to generate a relational model from the integrated model; the second process is to create views on this relational model. This procedure, in our case, eventually results in a collection of (materialized) views on top of the two original CityObject and AnySense databases.

8 Conclusions and Future Research

Geographic information, also known as geo-data, refers to data with some spatial component. Modeling geo-data can be involved, due to its often very complex structure, hence placing high demands on the modeling language employed. It turns out that ORM is capable of modeling many of the typical geo-constructs found in practice. Many geo-applications would benefit from the possibility of integrating existing geo-databases. Data integration is a notoriously hard problem, and integrating geo-databases in practice often adds the extra requirement that the integration should result in a real-time system. This paper has provides a case study and a design method for real-time integration of geo-databases based on the ORM modeling language. The global identification problem turned out to be a non-trivial issue, tackled by introducing the concept of a global bounding box. We have demonstrated that the use of ORM modeling language and tools are superior to competing approaches (for example UML and SOA), and that the so-called *ORM federation procedure*, together with a newly introduced *Global Bounding Box principle*, will yield correct design of integrated geo-data bases.

References

1. Ahonen-Rainio, P.: User needs for metadata services. In: The 18th Nordic GIS Conference, Helsinki (2006)
2. Balsters, H., Haarsma, B.: An ORM-driven Implementation Framework for Database Federations. In: Meersman, R., Herrero, P., Dillon, T. (eds.) OTM 2009 Workshops. LNCS, vol. 5872, pp. 659–670. Springer, Heidelberg (2009)
3. Balsters, H., Halpin, T.: Data Integration with ORM. In: Meersman, R., Tari, Z., Herrero, P. (eds.) OTM-WS 2007, Part I. LNCS, vol. 4805, Springer, Heidelberg (2007)
4. Balsters, H., de Brock, E.O.: Integration of integrity constraints in federated schemata based on tight constraining. In: Meersman, R., Tari, Z. (eds.) OTM 2004. LNCS, vol. 3290, pp. 748–767. Springer, Heidelberg (2004)
5. Bakema, G., Zwart, J., van der Lek, H.: Fully Communication Oriented Information Modelling, Ten Hagen Stam, The Netherlands (2000)
6. Betawadkar-Norwood, A., Lin, E., Ursu, I.: Using data federation technology in IBM WebSphere Information Integrator, IBM developerWorks (2005),
   http://www.ibm.com/developerworks
7. Cali, A., Calvanese, D., De Giacomo, G., Lenzerini, M.: Data integration under integrity constraints. In: Pidduck, A.B., Mylopoulos, J., Woo, C.C., Ozsu, M.T. (eds.) CAiSE 2002. LNCS, vol. 2348, p. 262. Springer, Heidelberg (2002)
8. Carver, S.: Participation and Geographical Information. In: Position paper for the ESF-NSF Workshop on Access to Geographic Information and Participatory Approaches Using Geographic Information, Spoleto (2001)
9. Chen, P.P.: The entity-relationship model—towards a unified view of data. ACM Transactions on Database Systems 1(1), 9–36 (1976)
10. Curland, M., Halpin, T.: Model Driven Development with NORMA. In: Proc. 40th Int. Conf. on System Sciences (HICSS-40), IEEE Computer SocietyX, Los Alamitos (2007)
11. Döllner, J., Kolbe, T.H., Liecke, F., Sgouros, T., Tiechmann, K.: The Virtual 3D City Model of Berlin- Managing, integrating and communicating complex urban information. In: Proceedings of the 25th International Symposium on Urban Data Management, UDMS 2006, Aalborg (2006)
12. Dreibelbis, A.: Enterprise Master Data Management, A SOA Approach. IBM Press (2008)
13. Embley, D.W.: Object Database Development. Addison-Wesley, Reading (1997)
14. Embley, D.W., Xiu, L.: A composite approach to automating direct and indirect schema mappings. Inf. Syst. 31(8), 673–697 (2006)

446   H. Balsters, C. Klaver, and G.B. Huitema

15. ESRI1, Commercial Development of Cloud GIS, Software developments of ESRI (Environmental Systems Research Institute),
http://www.esri.com/technology-topics/cloud-gis
16. ESRI2, The New Age of Cloud Computing and GIS, white paper by Victoria Kouyoumjian, ESRI IT Strategy Architect
17. Halpin, T.: A Logical Analysis of Information Systems: static aspects of the data-oriented perspective, doctoral dissertation, University of Queensland (1989),
http://www.orm.net/Halpin_PhDthesis.pdf
18. Halpin, T.: ORM 2. In: Meersman, R., Tari, Z., Herrero, P. (eds.) OTM-WS 2005. LNCS, vol. 3762, pp. 676–687. Springer, Heidelberg (2005)
19. Halpin, T.: ORM/NIAM Object-Role Modeling. In: Bernus, P., Mertins, K., Schmidt, G. (eds.) Handbook on Information Systems Architectures, 2nd edn., pp. 81–103. Springer, Heidelberg (2006)
20. Halpin, T., Morgan, T.: Information Modeling and Relational Databases, 2nd edn. Morgan Kaufmann, San Francisco (2008)
21. Directive 2007/2/EC of the European Parliament and of the Council of establishing an Infrastructure for Spatial Information in the European Community (March 14, 2007),
http://www.inspire-geoportal.eu
22. Küpper, A.: Location-based Services - Fundamentals and Operation. Wiley, Chichester (2005)
23. Langius, E., Helmholt, K.: AnySense Technology for real world monitoring and control, TNO white paper (to appear, 2010)
24. Lenzerini, M.: Data integration: a theoretical perspective. In: ACM PODS 2002. ACM Press, New York (2002)
25. Object Management Group UML 2.0 Superstructure Specification (2003),
http://www.omg.org/uml
26. The Open Geospatial Consortium, http://www.opengeospatial.org
27. The Open Knowledge Foundation, http://okfn.org/geo
28. Ullman, D.: Information Integration Using Logical Views. In: Afrati, F.N., Kolaitis, P.G. (eds.) ICDT 1997. LNCS, vol. 1186, pp. 19–40. Springer, Heidelberg (1996)
29. Warmer, J., Kleppe, A.: The Object Comnstraint Language. Addison Wesley, Reading (2003)

A Metamodel for Master Data

Baba Piprani[1] and Suneil Dham[2]

[1] MetaGlobal Systems, Canada
[2] Office of the Superintendent of Financial Institutions, Canada
babap@metaglobalsystems.com, SDHAM@osfi-bsif.gc.ca

Abstract. The term 'Master Data' brings up different interpretations and connotations, especially with vendors espousing the "single version of the truth". Is there a single version of the truth? Practical realities suggest that we need to continue to live with existing versions – at least until the "single version" is reached. So how do we handle the co-existence of "multiple versions" of the truth? This paper examines a metamodel that defines what master data is, the types of master data, and criteria for determining master data. The metamodel visits master data administration, privileges and master data services including change management, metadata migration and data migration for master data is also reviewed. The impact of changes to an enterprise going the master data route, along with the emphasis to influence future management direction is also examined. Several administration aspects make use of established ISO standards in metadata IS:11179-3 and IS:19763.

Keywords: Master Data, metamodel, ORM, metadata, ISO 19763, ISO 11179, Metadata Registry, MDM.

1 Why Metadata First?

Data Processing, Web Services and Electronic Data Interchange rely heavily on accurate, reliable, controllable and verifiable data recorded in databases or in some persistent state. A prerequisite for correct and proper use and interpretation of data is that both users and owners of data have a common understanding of the meaning and representation of the data as per the Helsinki Principle [1]. To facilitate this common understanding, a number of characteristics, or attributes, of the data have to be agreed upon and defined. These characteristics of data are known as "metadata", that is, "data that describes data". The ISO/IEC 11179-3 Metadata Registry standard [2] provides for the attributes of data elements and associated metadata to be specified and registered as metadata items in a Metadata Registry.

Metadata, or data about data, provides administrators and business users with descriptions of the data or informational objects that they can access.

There are two types of metadata; technical metadata and business metadata. Both types of metadata are important in application software deployment, construction, maintenance, and the use of a data warehouse or data mart.

Technical metadata is used by administrators and software tools, and provides the technical descriptions of data and operations. Technical metadata includes information about source data, target data, and the rules that are used to extract, filter, enhance,

R. Meersman et al. (Eds.): OTM 2010 Workshops, LNCS 6428, pp. 447–456, 2010.

cleanse, and transform source data to target data. Technical metadata could be created by a relational database management system, by data warehouse and transformation tools, or by the data warehouse operations personnel. Examples of these include database statistics, descriptions of transformations, scheduling, etc.

Business metadata is used by business analysts and end users, and provides a business description of informational objects. It assists end users in locating, understanding, and accessing information in the data mart, data warehouse, or other informational sources. Business metadata might include the calculation used to create a particular value, the data and time a report was created, or a description of the approval status of the projected forecast.

In other words, metadata is a general term for data that describes information. The information so described may be information represented in a computer system; e.g. in the form of files, databases, running program instances and so on. Alternatively the information may be embodied in some system, with the metadata being a description of some aspect of the system such as a part of its design. This metadata may describe any aspect of a system and the information it contains, and may describe it to any detail and rigour depending on the metadata requirements of the organization.

2 So Let's Get to Data, and Master Data...

All businesses use data. While we discussed metadata in the paragraphs above, the business is more concerned with the 'truth' value of the data it operates with. Agreed, we need both metadata and data as a type-instance pair to operate in a sane and normal environment. This is where several problems arise. Data is assumed to be sacrosanct since our friendly and reliable computer system is giving it to us, right? Not so! The truth of the matter is that in more than 50% of the cases, data quality and data integrity of the business data is questionable, see Gartner [4].

Data duplication and data integrity are major issues confronting IT applications today. It is not uncommon to come across multiple sets of redundant data on customers and other items of primary focus in an organization. A good average figure that is the norm is that there is about 30 to 60 percent redundant data or duplicated data on clients or customers in a typical organization. The search goes on...for the 'single version' of the truth.

Enter Master Data Management...which basically refers to data relevant to the conduct of the business on which transactions or analyses are based. Creating and maintaining good quality master data has become a necessity, and actually is critical today---considering the recent emphasis on regulatory compliance, Service Oriented Architecture (SOA) thrusts, enterprise integration, mergers and acquisitions. In a nutshell, master data is non-transactional data about people, things, places, and concepts [3], typically held in what used to be 'master file' data in legacy systems, circa 1970's. This basically means master data is the organization's non-transactional data, and the supporting reference data. In other words there are basically two kinds of master data – the common reference data like types and categories pertaining to the properties or characteristics of data (e.g. Country code, Address Type), and the other being 'master file' type data like, customers, clients, vendors, products, etc...essentially data that the organization uses for tracking through transactions.

What this means is that every application or service in an organization is concerned with the sanctity of Master Data and transactional data. So let us ask ourselves...what then is the scope of Master Data? Is it just separating out the Customer records, or

Product records etc…namely, business common data on which transactions are based, and the reference tables, or, is it yet another little item to attend to and move along, or, is there something more to it?

This paper establishes a model for Master data, defining its scope via a Process Model Decomposition, then defines ORM [6] schemas as applicable for managing Master Data. This will help analysts and business managers in establishing project resources or scoping the efforts involved in managing Master Data in an enterprise.

3   The Master Data Business Process Model Decomposition

Figure 1 defines a Master Data process model decomposition that highlights typical business processes involved with going the Master Data route. This model is borrowed from current user experience involved in establishing and stabilizing master data hub and associated master data hub services to address Service Oriented Architecture (SOA) requirements.

We feel it is important that this paper discusses in detail the Business Processes P1, P2 and P3 in Figure 1, for which ORM/NIAM [7] metamodels are provided below. The processes P4, P5 and P6 will need to be addressed during Master Data deployment.

Note that the notation used in the ORM/NIAM schema for Fact Types is using Fact Type Identifiers and omits role names for the purpose of making the diagrams less crowded due to space limitations in this publication. Thanks to Ooriane Corp. for the use of Ooriane Designer and Ooriane Semantic Analyzer for ORM/NIAM graphics.

3.1   Manage Master Data Definition (P1.1) - Define Master Data

It is best at this stage to get our mindset to think both "type" and "instance" for Master Data as a 'married pair'. In other words, when we talk about Master Data, it means both the metadata and the data associated with it.

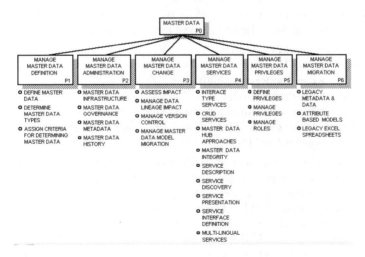

Fig. 1. Master Data Process Model Decomposition (IDEF0 notation, BPWin)

Firstly, we need to define data relevant to the conduct of the business on which transactions or analyses are based, e.g. the basic business tombstone data.

Then we need to identify common data and data roles that are shared across business functions, e.g. Country code used at head office and also used at branch location.

Next is common metadata shared across business functions. E.g. common semantics like customer definition, client definition. It is here there is a major ROI return and payoff in establishing a metadata registry concerning the essential semantics of the data relevant to the business model of the enterprise. A data definition template was designed for use to collect metadata about master data artifacts, called 'Form 19'. An example metamodel of an extract of a "Form 19" used at the Office of the Superintendent of Financial Institutions (OSFI) in Canada is depicted in Figure 2. This Form 19 is based on the ISO 11179-3 Metadata Registry Standard.

3.2 Manage Master Data Definition (P1.2) - Types of Master Data

As mentioned previously, Master Data pertains to Reference Data e.g. country code, address type etc., and, Non-Transactional Data, e.g. employee position, contact information, client information etc.

3.3 Manage Master Data Definition (P1.3) - Criteria for Determining Master Data

Some of the essential requirements or criteria for determining master data are:

- Data or data roles that are shared over multiple functional areas
- Need a single consistent version with standard terminology, definitions and business rules (NOTE: there may be multiple versions to begin with…plan for migration to a single version and strategy to co-exist and transition in the interim)
- Willingness to collaborate on centralized governance of the selected data.

3.4 Manage Master Data Administration (P2)

It is important to establish accountability and responsibility for managing master data administration---much like there is a role in the organization for data base administrators and data administrators. Items involved in this category are:

- Infrastructure administration
- Stewardship and Trustee
  - ➤ Roles and Responsibilities
  - ➤ Governance Model
  - ➤ Master Data Administration (Models and Data)
- Metadata Management (OSFI Form 19, a subset of ISO 11179-3 Metadata Registry Standard and ISO 19763 Metamodel for Interoperability Standard)

See Figure 2 for a model for metadata definition, as a subset of ISO11179-3.

Figure 2 depicts a Metamodel subset for Metadata Definition for Data Elements in a Metadata Registry for Master Data capture.

The following ORM/NIAM schemas depict the constituent formal schemas for each of the sub-registries referenced in Figure 2.

Figure 3 depicts an ORM/NIAM schema of the metadata artifacts being collected pertaining to business oriented definitions and semantic relationships that would facilitate drawing up a domain ontology for a Data Element (DE). The relevant definitions are provided in Table 1.

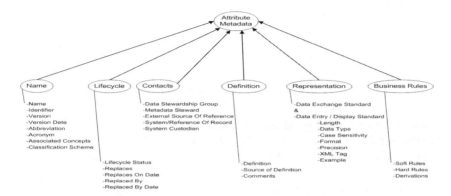

Fig. 2. Metamodel (subset) for Master Data Metadata Definition (Form 19)

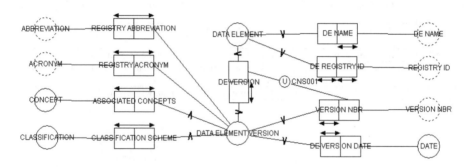

Fig. 3. Metadata Management - Name

Table 1. ORM/NIAM Schema Definitions for Metadata Management - Name

#	Object	Definition
1.1	Name	Business term name in its unabbreviated form.
1.2	Identifier	Any user defined data attribute identifier used for reference purposes
1.3	Version	Version number of metadata definition.
1.4	Version Date	Version date of the version number
1.5	Abbreviation	Recommended short form of the attribute name using standard abbreviations, if any.
1.6	Acronym	Recommended acronyms of the attribute name
1.7	Associated Concepts	Perspective, abstract idea or another attribute with which this data attribute is associated with, or is a property of, or can be mapped to.
1.8	Classification Scheme	Descriptive information for a generic level arrangement of objects into groups based on characteristics that the objects have in common.

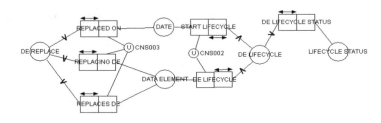

Fig. 4. Metadata Management – Lifecycle

Figure 4 depicts an ORM/NIAM schema of the metadata artifacts being collected pertaining to relevant lifecycle semantics that would facilitate on-going maintenance of metadata for a Data Element. The relevant definitions are provided in Table 2.

Table 2. ORM/NIAM Schema Definitions for Metadata Management - Lifecycle

#	Object	Definition
2.1	Life Cycle Status	Condition of the metadata in its lifecycle (draft, proposed, approved, retired).
2.2	Replaces	Name of attribute (old attribute), which is being replaced by this attribute.
2.3	Replaces on date	Date of replacement for the old attribute
2.4	Replaced by	Name of attribute (new attribute), which replaces this attribute.
2.5	Replaced by on date	Date on which this attribute was replaced.

Fig. 5. Metadata Management – Contacts

Table 3. ORM/NIAM Schema Definitions for Metadata Management - Contacts

#	Object	Definition
3.1	Data Stewardship Group	The organization(s) responsible for the accuracy of the attribute's definition.
3.2	Data Steward	The person(s) responsible for the attribute meta-data definition (name, contacts, definition, business rules).
3.3	Source of Reference	Reference number and/or title of an adopted data/metadata standard from an external source.
3.4	System or Reference of Record	The manual or automated system that serves as the authoritative source for accurate data values.
3.5	Custodian	The person(s) responsible for the maintenance and quality of the actual data in the system of record.

Figure 5 depicts an ORM/NIAM schema of the metadata artifacts being collected pertaining to Contact semantics that would facilitate on-going Data Governance requirements of metadata for a Data Element. The relevant definitions are provided in Table 3.

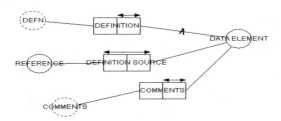

Fig. 6. Metadata Management – Definition

Figure 6 depicts an ORM/NIAM schema of the metadata artifacts being collected pertaining to Definition semantics as per ISO/IEC 11179-4 that would facilitate on-going Data Governance requirements of metadata for a Data Element. The relevant definitions are provided in Table 4.

Table 4. ORM/NIAM Schema Definitions for Metadata Management - Definition

#	Object	Definition
4.1	Definition	The textual description of the attribute as per ISO/IEC 11179-4, see [5]
4.2	Source of Definition	The publication, directive, standard, system, organization or person(s) responsible for developing the attribute definition.
4.3	Comments	Additional information to aid users in understanding the purpose and use of attribute.

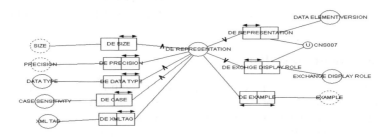

Fig. 7. Metadata Management – Representation

Figure 7 depicts an ORM/NIAM schema of the metadata artifacts being collected pertaining to Data Exchange semantics concerning representation and display of metadata for a Data Element. The relevant definitions are provided in Table 5.

Table 5. ORM/NIAM Schema Definitions for Metadata Management – Representation

#	Object	Definition
5.1	Exchange Display Role	The data element representation mode whether for data exchange or data entry/display formatting purposes
5.2	Size	The maximum & minimum allowable lengths for the raw data.
5.3	Data Type	The kind of data. Examples are: alphabetic, binary, numeric, alpha-numeric
5.4	Case Sensitivity	A specification of whether or not the data is to be upper, lower, or mixed case.
5.5	Format	A specification of the way the raw data should be arranged.
5.6	Scale and Precision (if numeric)	The total number of digits and positioning of the decimal point if applicable.
5.7	XML Tags	Specific XML (Extensible Markup Language) tags associated with attribute
5.7	Example	Provide example(s) of valid raw data and descriptor, if appropriate.

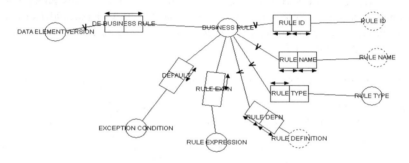

Fig. 8. Metadata Management – Business Rules

Figure 8 depicts an ORM/NIAM schema of the metadata artifacts being collected pertaining to Business Rule semantics for a Data Element. The relevant definitions are provided in Table 6.

3.5 Change Management (P3)

It is important to recognize that changes do occur to both metadata and data pertaining to master data in particular. We need to be able to conduct:

- Impact assessment (e.g. if the data model for master data is changed, what systems are affected)
- Lineage management (e.g. what systems (applications, databases, reports) are using the data)
- Version Control (e.g. versioning of the master data data model)
- Migration (e.g. migration of a new master data model version through deployment environments like Development/Test/User Acceptance/Production as well as data)

Table 6. ORM/NIAM Schema Definitions for Metadata Management – Business Rules

#	Object	Definition
6.1	Business Rules	Contains rules that are business subject area specific and are used to identify the business rule data violators to provide data quality and integrity. Integrity violations on the data will be reported on using this category classification. The corresponding error reports will be forwarded to the data stewards. The Business Rules for definition call for: - Cardinalities of relationships (one-to-zero/one/many, many-many, recursive, parent-child update/delete rules) - Value domains - Super/sub-type - Nullability - Derivations (computed values) - Unique constraints for business keys (not surrogate keys) - Other business rules The Business Rules for Execution call for: - Handling exception conditions - Notification - CRUD sequencing (e.g. can it recognize cardinality rules e.g. insert supertype first then subtype)

3.6 Master Data Services (P4)

The involvement and depth of adoption of Master Data Services depends on the degree of commitment of the organization towards SOA and transitions to the proposed infrastructure and technology. Important in this area are:

- Interface types (SQL, Web Services…)
- Create/Retrieve/Update/Delete/Search
- Federated or Consolidated master data hub approaches
- Managing Referential Integrity between master data and any referencing data
- Service description and discovery
- Service presentation
- Services interface definition
- International Language support

3.7 Privileges (P5)

Security and access are particularly important for when changes or inserts are taking place. However, depending on the nature of business involved, security for read access may become an important issue. Privileges may need to be involved with both at the model level and the data level. Attention needs to be given of privileges over the time continuum based on affects of temporality. Some of the basic functions involved are:

- Define Privileges
- Manage Privileges
- Manage Roles

3.8 Migration of Metadata and Data (P6)

Migration towards Master Data is often overlooked and can involved serious issues when it comes to how the metadata is going to be migrated. Not every vendor offers a smooth and complete metadata transfer. Also needing to be addressed is metadata quality and data quality issues. Some of the issues to be noted are migration of metadata and data from:

-   Existing schemas and data to new Master Data registry
-   Existing data models
-   Existing business rule declarations
-   Existing Excel or other spreadsheet ad hocs
-   Parallel versions of 'multiple versions of the truth' i.e. the master data version as the single version and, the local legacy version accompanied with mappings during transition, etc.

4 Conclusion

Migrating towards Master Data needs a lot of consideration and planning – in particular: data quality issues, establishing semantic equivalence, co-existence/transitioning. This paper has provided an insight on a model for migrating to a master data environment. Of particular concern, there is widespread confusion and mixed direction in terms of availability of decent migratory software that is of decent industrial strength quality that can be applied with real semantics towards establishing a strong foundation for corporate master data. It is not a simple exercise like purchasing a Master Data package and magic will happen! The encompassing of a SOA based environment will require an engineerable approach to adopting Master Data, including planned phases for the inevitable exercise in data harmonization and data cleansing. Caveat emptor…

References

1. van Griethuysen, J., ed.: Technical Report on Concepts and Terminology for the Conceptual Schema and the Information Base. ISO Technical Report ISO IEC TR9007:1987. International Standards Organization, Geneva (1987)
2. International Standard ISO IEC 11179-3:2003 Metadata Registries, International Standards Organization, Geneva
3. Wolter R., Haselden K.:The What, Why, and How of Master Data Management, http://msdn.microsoft.com/en-us/architecture/bb190163.aspx
4. Gartner Group Report: Gartner Press Release, Gartner Website – Media relations (2005), http://www.gartner.com/press_releases/pr2005.html
5. International Standard ISO IEC 11179-4 Rules and guidelines for the formulation of data definitions, International Standards Organization, Geneva
6. Halpin, T., Morgan, T.: Information Modeling and Relational Databases, 2nd edn. an imprint of Elsevier. Morgan Kaufmann Publishers, San Francisco (2008) ISBN: 978-0-12-373568-3
7. Nijssen, G.M., Halpin, T.A.: Conceptual Schema and Relational Database Design. Prentice Hall, Victoria (1989)

ORM and MDM/MMS:
Integration in an Enterprise Level Conceptual Data Model

Necito Dela Cruz, Patricia Schiefelbein, Kris Anderson, Patrick Hallock,
and Dick Barden

Boston Scientific Corporation

Abstract. The integration of a number of facets of reference data, metadata, data models, governance, and services continues to grow and become more important and pragmatic to businesses. Since 2004 a growing number of companies have heavily invested many resources into pulling together related components into more and more unified approaches that attempt to help solve the problem of managing data. More specifically, Master Data Management and closely related components to MDM such as metadata management systems (MMS) and business glossaries are critical to delivering a complete organically grown product with a single, clean architecture. This paper will describe a scenario of how Object Role Modeling could be leveraged to provide the enterprise with a fact based conceptual model that is integrated with an MDM's business glossary. The ultimate goal is to provide a common understanding of the business at a conceptual level and at the same time deliver on the capability of providing a comprehensive and deep 'where used' capability for the delivery of a variety of common functions desperately need by companies today. This scenario is based on the evaluation of three major MDM vendors during the past year by Boston Scientific Corporation.

Keywords: Master Data Management, Data lineage, Metadata Management, Business Glossary, Data Governance.

1   Introduction

In late 2009, a team of IS and BA (Business Analyst) personnel at Boston Scientific Corporation (BSC) were tasked with evaluating the need for a Master Data Management (MDM) solution. The team evaluated a number of critical systems within BSC. Based on our assessment of the need for an MDM the team submitted a request to management to proceed with a comprehensive Evaluation of Technology (EOT). Prior to the EOT, the team sent out a lengthy tool assessment to each of the vendors with whom we have interest. Based on the initial responses and preliminary vendor interviews we narrowed the final list of vendors to three:

- SAP
- IBM
- Informatica

R. Meersman et al. (Eds.): OTM 2010 Workshops, LNCS 6428, pp. 457–463, 2010.
© Springer-Verlag Berlin Heidelberg 2010

BSC, as it is today, is a merging of companies that have been acquired over the last 25 years, not unlike many other companies. Currently, there are a number of duplicate systems, the same information stored redundantly and without many controls; systems have evolved in a patchwork of connected systems that resist the concerted efforts of many business analysts to efficiently understand how they fit together. Information that is gathered is not easily maintainable. This has a significant impact on many aspects of quality of data, meaning of data, and the common understanding of business concepts across multiple organizations that are a part of BSC.

Additionally, for the past 8 years ORM has been used in a number of projects in BSC for gathering requirements and developing a variety of systems. In 2007, a proof of concept was completed to demonstrate the effectiveness of harvesting metadata from operational systems in order to relate it to the ORM of these various subject areas. A proceeding about this proof of concept was presented at the 2008 ORM Workshop in Portugal [1].

2   BSC Justification for MDM

Boston Scientific currently does not have a Master Data Management (MDM) and Data Governance (DG) processes or tools to manage enterprise-wide master data within multiple business and Information Systems. Only recently has BSC IS leadership team recognized that MDM has a strategic value and place in the suite of enterprise level solutions.

By implementing common MDM and DG processes and tools, the benefits that Boston Scientific may realize are:

- Efficiencies and reduced risk which currently exist in many systems as manual data reconciliations
- Consistent use of data across systems, departments, and external communications thereby unifying our applications
- Improved control and minimization of replicated master data that is deployed and used across the enterprise
- Improved accuracy and timeliness of BI and reporting thereby improving our responsiveness and effectiveness
- Cost savings due to reduced manual time spent on cross system reconciliation
- Reduced operational complexity thereby improving performance
- Enhance and reduce the cost of constructing 'Golden Records' for our Master Data domains
- Reduced and/or eliminated compliance risks
- Enhanced enterprise decision making
- Simplification of design and implementation of future projects
- Enhanced understanding of the lineage of data across multiple systems in the enterprise
- Improved efficiency for acquisitions and divestitures of businesses
- The impact of the potential problems and issues mentioned above will be quantified as part of the analysis
- The reliance on the reports generated from governed processes using master data lead to better and consistent reporting of data

3 Features for MDM

One of the critical goals of the MDM Team was to investigate the possibility of integrating ORM with MDM. Early on, before we had started to interview vendors, the team laid out a scenario where the interface could be accomplished by relating the ORM fact types to the metadata of the MDM. Exploring how that could be accomplished was always a topic that the team discussed with each vendor. It was realized that limiting the metadata to MDM objects would not be sufficient. Therefore, part of the EOT focused on a metadata solution that accounted for all the objects in all systems in the enterprise and not just objects within the MDM domains. The team identified these strategic features for the MDM Hub to achieve the benefits outlined in section 2:

- Hierarchy Management System
  - Manage different business points of views
    ▸ Business units have different and unique ways of analyzing data
  - Ability to create and manage different types of hierarchy structures, e.g. organizational, product, customer, etc.
    ▸ Keep historical data and provide "what if" impact analysis
  - Ability to represent complex relationships amongst MDM objects
- Metadata Management
  - Ability to track lineage; Upstream and downstream
    ▸ Impact analysis of changes
  - Create a common business glossary
    ▸ Ability to configure and/or customize an integration with ORM
  - Improve and maintain efficiency and productivity gains
    ▸ Automated code generation of rules
- Multi Domain Platform
  - Represent unified views of interactions and activities with: Customers, Providers, Products, Suppliers, Studies, etc and synchronize data with operational and analytical systems
  - Maintain enterprise-wide shareable reference data deemed as master data
    ▸ e.g. Alerts, Events, Corrective Actions, related reference data, etc.

It can be argued that some of these features are outside of the immediate scope of MDM, however they are closely related and should be considered when making the critical decision of vendor selection.

The remaining features are part of the common feature set of any well established MDM product:

- Common MDM Tactical Components
  - Cleanse → Match → Merge of master data
  - Web Services for MDM components
  - Synchronization of master data to subscribing systems

The team assembled a comprehensive EOT (Evaluation of Technology) and a set of use cases organized into the following work streams:

Workstream Item (WI) Title	Requirements
WI #1 - HCP Master - MDM Vendor Domain (HCP-Health Care Provider)	Demonstrate cleanse, match, merge, survivorship, etc of inbound data to target MDM domains
WI #2 - Lookup / Create MDM Vendor Domain	Cleanse, match, merge, survivorship, etc of bi- directional request for an MDM domain record
WI #3 - Mass Extract of MDM Vendor hub Records	Extract of changed records to an external system
WI #4 – Hierarchy Management	Construction and sending of hierarchy structures.
WI #5 – Metadata Management	Harvesting, manipulating, and integration of metadata
WI #6 - User Defined Domains; Models and Extensions	Extending Out-of-Box MDM Domains and creating new ones as well as relationships between them
WI #7 - Test various styles of interfaces, transfers, and data-base platforms	Demonstrate various style of transfer methods using the above WI tasks

Each Workstream Item (1 to 7) above is identified in the diagram below:

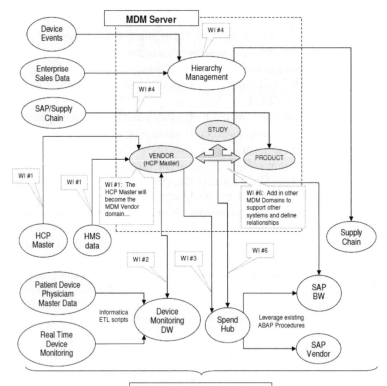

All the vendors were supplied with a subset of production data and a subset of the schemas of the production systems used in each of the use cases. The vendors were required to use the source data and demonstrate the various capabilities of the MDM tools such as matching, merging, data analysis and others as described in the EOT use cases.

3.1 Metadata in MDM

One of the key components of MDM is an integrated approach to Metadata Management that allows the metadata to be leveraged in a number of different ways. A process is required for identifying and clarifying data element names, definitions, and other relevant attribution is the discovery and documentation of enterprise-wide business metadata. In addition to collecting standard technical details regarding data elements, it is also important to determine business uses of each data element; which data element definitions refer to the same concept; the applications refer to the manifestations of that concept; how each data element and associated concepts are created, read, modified, or retired by different applications; the data quality characteristics; inspection and monitoring locations within the business process flow; and how uses are tied together. Therefore, a critical component of an MDM environment is an enterprise business metadata management system to facilitate the desired level of control and also supports the definition of master data objects themselves: which data objects are managed within the MDM environment, which application data sources contribute to their consolidation and resolution, the frequency of and processes used for consolidation – everything necessary to understand the complete picture of the distributed use of the master data objects across the enterprise [2].

The team envisions the use of ORM to capture the metadata properties through the use of the extended properties feature of the tool NORMA. The challenge that NORMA presents is how it can co-exist with the MDM metadata tool. Because of the semantic richness that is captured with ORM, we explored with the MDM vendors how to establish a link between ORM tools like NORMA. A specific area we wanted to integrate at least is associate ORM fact types to their Business Glossary.

3.2 Discussions with Vendors

All the vendors did not have a background in ORM, in fact the BSC team provided numerous papers to give each vendor enough information to be able to participate in recommending an approach. The integration of ORM was discussed as a part of Workstream Item #5 – Metadata Management.

All three vendors have a facet of the product set that is coined as a "Business Glossary". There is a wide ranging set of capabilities among the three vendors.

All vendors refer to the entries in their Business Glossary as a 'Business Term'. This actually fits somewhat nicely with the ideas that the team had in mind as a possible integration point with ORM.

3.3 Proposed Solution

One critical feature that sadly all of the vendors' products lacked was the ability to record information concerning how a 'Business Term' may be related to any other 'Business Term' in the Business Glossary. For example, here is a simple fact type from the device schema:

Device is implanted in Patient on Date

This fact type has three objects that can translate into three business terms:

- Device
- Patient
- Implant Date

Citing the above example, the metadata solution from all vendors does not have the facility to establish the semantic relationship between Device and Patient, between Patient and Implant Date, and between Device and Implant Date.

The team interviewed each of the vendors to determine how receptive they were to integrating their product with the metadata of ORM. Of course, each of them had an interest, however only one had the capability to actually extend their product in timely manner.

The integration that the MDM team recommended would require that the MDM vendor extend their Business Glossary to record a reference to the ORM fact type by facilitating the creation of relationships between the appropriate Business Terms in the Business Glossary. This extension would introduce additional schema structures to the vendor's product. The core part of this extension involves the following fact type:

Fact Type is source for Business Term

As an example, given the first BSC Fact Type above and a few others we can demonstrate a scenario for integration. BSC Fact Types:

- (FT1) Device is implanted in Patient on Date
    - o Nested as 'Implanted Device'
- (FT2) Implanted Device is implanted by Physician
- (FT3) Device is explanted on Date
- (FT4) Device is explanted from Patient

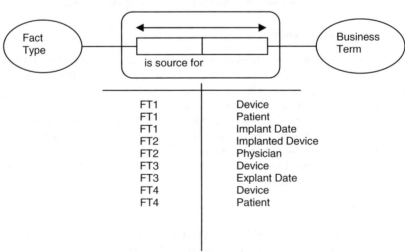

ORM Business Term Relationship

Fact Type	Business Term
FT1	Device
FT1	Patient
FT1	Implant Date
FT2	Implanted Device
FT2	Physician
FT3	Device
FT3	Explant Date
FT4	Device
FT4	Patient

The nested fact type, 'ORM Business Term Relationship' can be used to extend the properties of the vendors' business term. Some of these properties may be:

- derived from the ORM meta model
- derived from the vendor metadata package
- added to the schema and populated/maintained with an appropriate user interface

4 Conclusion

The relationship between ORM and the current business glossary products in these vendors is needed to give deeper meaning to the variety of roles that the business term plays in various information systems. Our short list of fact types illustrates that the object Device is used in more than one way. The products we reviewed at each vendor EOT session confirms that the information captured in their product does not sufficiently provide the deeper meaning of the businesses' understanding of their subject areas. This deeper meaning is captured very well with ORM. The relationship from ORM to the vendor Business Glossary gives ORM a portal into the other connections that are available via the Business Glossary, e.g.

- where the business term is used in lineage graphs
- how data for various usages of the term is transformed
- how data is moved through various systems, such as a Device being implanted and the subsequently explanted
- facilitates a direct connection to the ORM Object and the MDM Business Term and profiling the production data that is directly tied to these via a metadata manager

Choosing the best fit for integrating ORM to MDM has the potential to save time, effort, resources, and hence money by providing:

- Consistent use of semantics across systems, departments, and external communications thereby unifying our applications and simplify the design and implementation of future projects
- Enhanced understanding of the lineage of data across multiple systems in the enterprise
- Business people (BA's, SME's) the capability to collaborate and participate in the decision making process to incorporate their Business Terms using ORM and MDM

The ultimate goal is to use ORM to model the business at the enterprise level across all functional silos and provide the integration to MDM and metadata management for where-used functions as a starting point for new projects in their concept, requirements, and follow-on phases.

References

1. Shelstad, B., Hallock, P., dela Cruz, N., Barden, D.: Object Role Modeling Enabled Metadata Repository. In: OTM – ORM Conference, Portugal (2007)
2. Loshin, D.: Master Data Management. Morgan Kaufmann/OMG Press, Burlington, MA (2009)

A Fact-Based Meta Model for Standardization Documents

Peter Bollen

Department of Organization & Strategy
School of Business and Economics
Maastricht University,
The Netherlands
p.bollen@maastrichtuniversity.nl

Abstract. Recently, the OMG has been working on developing a new standard for a Business Process Model and Notation (BPMN). This standard development has resulted in documents that contain the latest approved version of a standard or a standard proposal that can be ammended. Such a standard document also serves as a specification for BPMN modeling tool. In this paper we show how a fact-based approach can improve the completeness and maintenance of such a specification.

Keywords: BPMN, ORM, Fact-Based Modeling.

1 Introduction

In recent years OMG has been working on a standard for a Business Process Model and Notation (BPMN), e.g. see [1, 2]. Although the development and standardization of a new business process modeling language of such a major standardization organization as OMG is welcomed by the scholars, tool developers and practitioners of business process modeling, the way in which such a standard is expressed could be improved. The current BPMN standard proposal [2] uses a blend of textual descriptions, UML state- and class diagrams and XML schemas. Furthermore, the description and explanation of the notational legend of the BPMN is intertwined with the semantics of the modeling constructs in the current standard document.

Practitioners, scholars and tool developers will benefit from a conceptual fact-based representation of the BPMN standard in which domain knowledge is represented conceptually as a list of concept definitions (including naming conventions), a set of fact types and the constraints or business rules that govern the actual instances of the fact types.

In this paper we will analyze the BPMN standard document [2] in combination with practitioner rules and guidelines on how to model in BPMN [3]. In this context BPMN serves as an example of a standard and we claim that the main findings in this article can be generalized to every (IT) modeling standard.

In section 2 we will apply the fact-based modeling methodology to the BPMN modeling constructs. In section 3 we will illustrate how we can derive additional business rules using the fact-based methodology. In section 4 we will give the BPMN

R. Meersman et al. (Eds.): OTM 2010 Workshops, LNCS 6428, pp. 464–473, 2010.
© Springer-Verlag Berlin Heidelberg 2010

meta-model for the level 1 palette of modeling constructs [3]. Finally, in section 5 conclusions will be drawn

1.1 Introduction to the Fact-Based Modeling Methodology

In the fact-based modeling methodology, the fact construct is used for encoding all semantic connections between entities. The 'role-based' notation makes it easy to define population constraints and derivation rules on the data structure and it enables the modeler to populate conceptual schemas with example sentence instances for constraint validation purposes. Over the years a number of dialects in fact-based modeling have evolved, i.e. ENALIM [4], (binary) NIAM [5], N-ary NIAM [6], Fully Communication Oriented Information Modeling (FCO-IM) [7], ORM (2) [8, 9] and CogNiam [10]. The OMG business rule standard SBVR can be considered the latest fact-based dialect [11]. The fact-based 'dialect' that we will use in this article is a combination of CogNIAM [12] and SBVR [13] for the list of concept definitions and naming conventions and the expression of concepts, fact instances, fact types and business rules in structured natural language [14]. As a graphical notation for the fact types and business rules we will use Object-Role Modeling's (ORM) notational convention [8].

2 The Fact-Based Modeling of BPMN's Level 1 Palette

In order to precisely show how a business information model is needed to create well-formed and well-integrated BPMN models we will start with the introduction of the BPMN modeling constructs that enable us to model the 'happy path', e.g. those sequences of activities that will be executed if everything goes as expected without exceptions [3]. We will restrict BPMN at this point to those 'happy-path' modeling constructs that comprise BPMN's level 1 palette [3]: Pool and Lane, User and Service Task, (collapsed and expanded) SubProcess, Start Event, End Event, Exclusive and Parallel Gateway, Sequence Flow and Message Flow, Data Object and Message Flow.

In this section we will give an overview of the 'Universe of Discourse' (UoD) that consists of the allowed BPMN expressions for 'level-1' BPMN models [3]. This will be the starting point for the derivation of a fact-based BPMN meta model by giving 'positive examples' that will lead the business analyst towards the object types and fact types in the meta model. Furthermore, the modeling rules and constraints and the 'non-allowed' examples in the defining and practitioner's literature [1, 3] will help the business analyst in defining the population constraints for the fact-based BPMN meta model. As a starting point for the fact-based analysis of BPMN example models we will use figure 5.7 on page 46 of [3]. For the complete fact-based BPMN meta model and explanation of the meta-modeling process we refer to [15].

In figure 1 we have given the 'example of communication' or 'data-use case' that we will use to in the derivation of the fact-based meta model for the BPMN palette 1 modeling constructs.

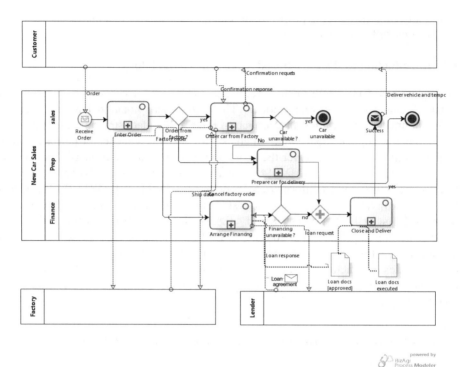

Fig. 1. Example BPMN model as in figure 5.7 of [3]

2.1 The List of Concept Definitions and Naming Conventions

In this section we will group and synthesize the definitions of the main modeling constructs in the BPMN in line with the definitions in the OMG standard document [1] and the modeling guidelines and naming conventions as they are recommended in [3]. The list of definitions is incrementally created in the process of analyzing the verbalizations of the example BPMN model in figure 1. For each non-trivial relevant concept that is encountered in such a verbalized sentence a definition will be constructed by scanning the standard and descriptive documents of BPMN for definitions and explanations. For the complete list of concept definitions for the BPMN level 1 palette modeling constructs we refer to [15]. An excerpt of this list can be found in figure 1.

In this paper we will use 'local domain-based' identifiers for domain concepts. This means that we have to give specific naming rules for domain concepts. These domain rules should be in line with the definition of the name classes in the list of concept definitions. E.g., an instance of the name class *event name* is defined as follows (see also table 1) :

'A name that designates a specific [Event] among the union of [Events]s within a given [Lane] of a given [Pool].'

This means that in verbalizing instances of a(n) (type of) event in a BPMN diagram, we should use a compound identifier as follows:

Table 1. Excerpt of list of definitions of terms (or concepts) for the BPMN 'palette 1' constructs in order of comprehension

Concept	Definition
Activity	An Activity is a generic term for work that company performs in Process [2, p.21]
Process	A Process is any [Activity] performed within or across companies or organization [1]
Process name	A name that designates a specific [Process] among the union of [Process]es
SubProcess	A SubProcess is a [Process] that is included within another [Process] [1]
Task	A Task is an atomic [Activity] that is included within a [Process] [2, p.24]
Task name	A name that designates a specific [Task] among the union of [task]s within a [SubProcess].
User Task	A User Task is a typical "workflow" [Task] where a human performer performs the [Task] with the assistance of a software application and is scheduled through a task list manager of some sort.[2, p.140]

' The **Terminate End Event** 'Success' within the **Lane** 'Sales' of the **White-Box Pool** 'New Car Sales'.

Another assumption for naming conventions that could have been chosen is to use 'abstract global unique' identifiers for instances of concepts (e.g. see [16]. In that case the former verbalization would be as follows:

'The **Terminate End Event** '140''.
'The **Terminate End Event** '140' has name 'Success''.

We note that on an application schema level the 'actual' naming convention will be determined by the communication structure of the application area.

2.2 Verbalization of Examples into Elementary Facts

Applying step 1 ('verbalization' or 'from examples to elementary facts') from the fact-based conceptual schema design procedure [6, 9, 17] will lead to the following fact verbalizations as fact instances:

The **Black-Box Pool** 'Customer' has an outgoing **MessageFlow** 'Order' to the **Message Start Event** 'Receive Order' within the **Lane** 'Sales' of the **White-Box Pool** 'New Car Sales'.

The **Black-Box Pool** 'Customer' has an outgoing **MessageFlow** 'confirmation response' to the **SubProcess** 'Order Car from Factory'.

Figure 5.7 in [3] provides the expressions in a top-level process diagram. In order to be able to derive all relevant semantic associations between the concepts in the list of concept definitions for the level 1 palette we will add a second real-life example of an 'expansion diagram' as is for example given in figure 6-4 of [3] (see for the integrated analysis and complete verbalizations of these examples [15]).

2.3 Abstracting Facts Instances into an Information Structure Diagram (ISD)

In this section we will show the results of grouping the fact instances and abstracting them into 'fixed parts' (or verbs) and 'variable parts' (or roles). The result of this transformation is a 'role-box' diagram that contains the abstraction of the fact instances and an example population in which 'variable names' in the fact instances are listed.

In figure 2 we have given an excerpt of the information structure diagram[1] with the abstracted domain fact types, sub-type fact types and the 'compound' naming convention fact types. We have introduced the naming convention for roles and fact types. In this way a domain information structure diagram (ISD) can be verbalized and analyzed, to see whether it complies to the meta model.

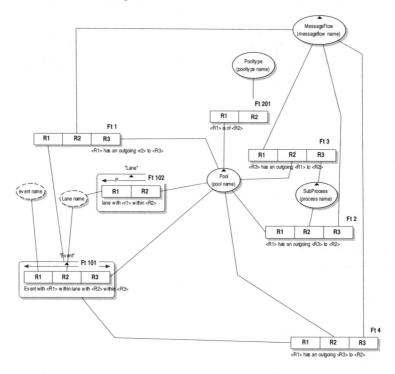

Fig. 2. Excerpt from Information Structure diagram for BPMN palette 1 modeling constructs

In figure 3 we have given an excerpt of our example ISD including the population of the fact types Ft3 and Ft201. using the ORM (1) notation in which explicit naming conventions for roles and fact types are added.

The content of the excerpt from figure 3 is equivalent to the following set of fact instances:

The **SubProcess** 'order Car from Factory' has an outgoing **MessageFlow** 'confirmation request' to the **Black-Box Pool** 'Customer'

The **SubProcess** 'Order Car from factory' has an outgoing **MessageFlow** 'Factory order' to the **Black-Box Pool** 'Factory'.

---

[1] For a complete fact-based information structure diagram we refer to [15, pp. 13-15].

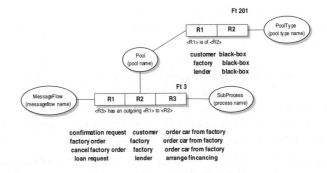

Fig. 3. Populated Information Structure Diagram for BPMN example excerpt

The **SubProcess** 'order Car from Factory' has an outgoing **MessageFlow** 'Cancel Factory order' to the **Black-Box Pool** 'Factory'.

The **SubProcess** 'Arrange Financing' has an outgoing **MessageFlow** 'Loan request' to the **Black-Box Pool** 'Lender'.

3 Adding Additional Business Rules to an Information Structure Diagram (ISD)

The next step in the fact-based modeling methodology consists of deriving and adding business rules to the information structure diagram. In this article we will apply the explicit derivation steps from the conceptual schema modeling procedure [9, 18]. We will call this way of deriving business rules the 'inside-out' approach. Another way of finding business rules is to interpret textual/diagrammatic descriptions. We will call that the 'outside-in' approach.

3.1 The Derivation of Constraints Using the CSDP (The Inside-Out Approach)

We will start to analyze the fact types in our ISD that originate in the verbalizations of the BPMN example. In our BPMN example, only one instance of fact type Ft1 is encountered. This means that we will have to create a significant example by adding different instances of outgoing message flows in a newly constructed example. The methodology works as follows. Take an allowed sentence which is normally a verbalized sentence from the example document:

The **Message End Event** 'Success' within the **Lane** 'Sales' of the **White-Box Pool** 'New Car Sales' has an outgoing **MessageFlow** 'Deliver vehicle and temporary registration' to the **Black-Box Pool** 'Customer'...(sentence 1)[2]

Then adapt this sentence into a second sentence as follows by changing the value of role R1:

---

[2] Using 'abstract globally unique' identifiers this verbalization would be equivalent to the following set of sentences: The **Message End Event** '121' has an outgoing **MessageFlow** '38' to the **Black-Box Pool** 'Customer'.The **Message End Event** '121' has the event name 'Success'. **The MessageFlow '38'** has the messageflowname 'Deliver vehicle and temporary registration'.

The **Message End Event** 'New buyer' within the **Lane** 'Sales' of the **White-Box Pool** 'New Car Sales' has an outgoing **MessageFlow** 'Deliver vehicle and temporary registration' to the **Black-Box Pool** 'Customer'..(sentence 2)

Transforming sentences 1 and 2 into a 'constructed excerpt' of a BPMN model will lead to a new 'constructed' process model example. Inspecting this newly constructed example (see [15]) will show that it is an allowed instance of a BPMN process model. We will therefore add the sentence to the significant set of sentence instances and we will create a third example sentence. This third example sentence can be created by taking the first sentence once again, now changing the value of role *R2*:

The **Message End Event** 'Success' within the **Lane** 'Sales' of the **White-Box Pool** 'New Car Sales' has an outgoing **MessageFlow** 'deliver brochure' to the **Black-Box Pool** ' Customer'...(sentence 3)

The BPMN analyst considers this as an example that is **not** allowed to exist because the message semantics between an end event and a white-box pool should be a pooled one. The fact that the third sentence is not allowed to co-exist with sentence 1, implies that we have found a uniqueness constraint *C17* that spans *all* roles except role *R2*. The last step in the analysis of uniqueness constraints for fact type Ft1 is the checking of the third adapted sentence with the first one (sentence 4). We will create this sentence by changing the value of role *R3* and check the coexistence of this sentence with sentence 1:

The **Message End Event** 'Success' within the **Lane** 'Sales' of the **White-Box Pool** 'New Car Sales' has an outgoing **MessageFlow** 'Deliver vehicle and temporary registration' to the **Black-Box** **Pool** 'Lender'...(sentence 4)

In the defining document of the BPMN standard we can not find any rule that forbids a creation of a BPMN process model as given in figure 11 in [15]. Therefore no uniqueness constraint defined over roles R2 and R3 of fact type Ft1 exists (see figure 4). This means that sentence 4 can coexist with sentence 1.

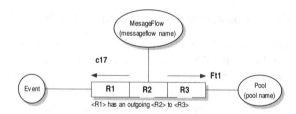

Fig. 4. Information Structure Diagram for fact type FT1 including uniqueness constraint

If we inspect an allowed example in figure 4-10 of [3] we see that it is allowed that two different sequence-flows coming out of two different sub-processes can enter the same gateway. This implies that the potential uniqueness constraint defined on role R2 of fact type *Ft8* does NOT exist (see figure 6).

To see whether a uniqueness constraint is defined on role R1 of fact type Ft8 we can create an example diagram based upon the following verbalization:

The **SubProcess** 'a1' has an outgoing SequenceFlow to **Gateway** 'b1'................(sentence 11)
The **SubProcess** 'a1' has an outgoing SequenceFlow to **Gateway** 'b2'................(sentence 12)

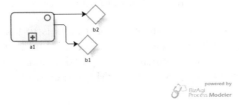

Fig. 5. Constructed Non-allowed BPMN model for checking the co-existence of sentences (11) and (12)

After carefully inspecting many examples of BPMN models in the OMG standard and other application text books we did not find a situation in which there are two different outgoing sequence flows from the same sub-process each to a different gateway as depicted in figure 5. Therefore, sentences 11 and 12 cannot exist at the same time, this implies the existence of uniqueness constraint *C3* on role *R1* of fact type *Ft8* in the BPMN meta model (see figure 6).

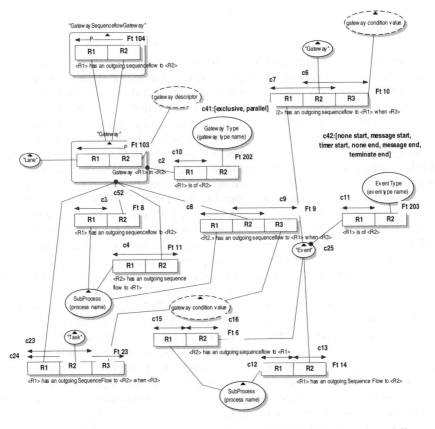

Fig. 6. Excerpt of ORM Information Structure diagram for BPMN palette 1 modeling constructs including population constraints

3.2   The Addition of Constraints Using the Outside-In Approach

A second way of 'discovering' uniqueness constraints is to take textual or diagrammatic documents, e.g. the BPMN standard document [1] or an explanatory text book, e.g. [3] and 'translate' a textual segment as a population constraint on a fact type from the ISD. For example on page 73 of the BPMN standard document [1] we find the following description:

'Each gate must have an associated outgoing sequence flow'.

This can be modeled as totality constraint *C52* for the object type gateway defined on role *R2* of fact type *Ft9* , role *R1* of fact type Ft11 and role *R1* of fact type *Ft23* (see figure 6).

4   The BPMN Meta Model Including Population Constraints

In figure 6 we have shown an excerpt of the the completed fact-based meta-model for the palette 1 modeling constructs in BPMN[3].

5   Conclusion

In this paper we have illustrated how fact-based modeling can help business analyst, standard developers, and tool-designers in capturing essential 'business rules' for applying (in this case) the BPMN process modeling standard. Although the standard document and a recent practitioner's text book were studied in detail we have shown that essential modeling constraints were derived from (the absence of) allowed BPMN model examples. Although we have limited ourselves in this paper to the palette 1 modeling constructs for BPMN the approach is fully scalable to cover the 'complete' BPMN standard or any other (IT) standard or knowledge domain. The advantage of using the fact-based modeling methodology lies amongst other things in the strengths of using examples. As we have illustrated in this article, it is the 'semantic richness' of tangible examples or 'data' use cases combined with the information structure diagram (ISD) that 'expose' the domain rules that govern the instances of the BPMN modeling standard in terms of uniqueness, mandatory role and other constraints that are not explicitly documented in the defining BPMN literature.

The main benefits for the business analyst and other business users that will apply BPMN in their day-to-day work of such a fact-based BPMN meta-model is in an accelerated learning curve for creating high-quality BPMN models. With respect to the tool-developers the benefits of using fact-based models as specifications for a model standard in general and for BPMN in particular will be significant because the fact-based models contain explicitly the modeling constraints that users will have to master and that need to be implemented in high-quality BPMN (or other) modeling tools.

Current tools that support fact-based modeling are DocTool [19] and NORMA [20]. These tools provide modeling support for large models and basically are fully scalable in terms of size and complexity.

---

[3] For a complete BPMN palette 1 meta model we refer to [15, pp. 25-27].

References

1. OMG, Business process modelling notation (BPMN) OMG available specification v 1.1. OMG (2008)
2. OMG, Business Process Model and Notation (BPMN). FTF Beta 1 for Version 2.0. (2009)
3. Silver, B.: BPMN Method & Style. Cody-Cassidy Press, Aptos (2009)
4. Nijssen, G.: On the gross architecture for the next generation database management systems. In: Information Processing, 1977, IFIP (1977)
5. Verheijen, G., van Bekkum, J.: NIAM: An Information Analysis method. In: IFIP TC-8 CRIS-I Conference, North-Holland, Amsterdam (1982)
6. Nijssen, G., Halpin, T.: Conceptual schema and relational database design: a fact oriented approach. Prentice Hall, NewYork (1989)
7. Bakema, G.P., Zwart, J.P., van der Lek, H.: Fully communication oriented NIAM. In: Nijssen, G., Sharp, J. (eds.) NIAM-ISDM 1994 Conference, Albuquerque NM, pp. 1–35 (1994)
8. Halpin, T.: Information Modeling and Relational Databases; from conceptual analysis to logical design. Morgan Kaufmann, San Francisco (2001)
9. Halpin, T., Morgan, T.: Information Modeling and Relational Databases; from conceptual analysis to logical design, 2nd edn. Morgan-Kaufman, San Francisco (2008)
10. Nijssen, G.: Kenniskunde, vol. 1A. PNA Publishing Heerlen (2001)
11. OMG, Semantics of Business Vocabulary and Business Rules (SBVR), v1.0 OMG Available Specification (2008)
12. Lemmens, I., Nijssen, M., Nijssen, G.: A NIAM 2007 conceptual analysis of the ISO and OMG MOF four layer metadata architectures. In: OTM 2007/ ORM 2007, Springer, Vilamoura (2007)
13. Nijssen, G., Hall, J.: SBVR diagram; a response to an invitation. Business Rules Journal 9(7) (2008)
14. Bollen, P.: SBVR: a fact oriented OMG standard. In: Meersman, R., Tari, Z., Herrero, P. (eds.) OTM-WS 2008. LNCS, vol. 5333, pp. 718–727. Springer, Heidelberg (2008)
15. Bollen, P.: BPMN: A Meta Model for the Happy Path, in Meteor research memo School of Business and Economics, Maastricht University (2010), http://edocs.ub.unimaas.nl/loader/file.asp?id=1472
16. Nijssen, G., Le Cat, A.: Kennis Gebaseerd Werken: de manier om kennis productief te maken 2009. PNA publishing b.v, Heerlen (2009)
17. Halpin, T., Orlowska, M.: Fact-oriented Modeling for Data Analysis. Journal of Information Systems 2, 97–118 (1992)
18. Nijssen, G.: Grondslagen van Bestuurlijke Informatiesystemen, Nijssen Adviesbureau voor Informatica Slenaken (1989)
19. Nijssen, M., Lemmens, I., Mak, R.: Fact-Orientation Applied to Develop a Flexible Employment Benefits System. In: ORM 2009, Springer, Vilamoura (2009)
20. Halpin, T.: Predicate Reference and Navigation in ORM. In: ORM 2009, Springer, Vilamoura (2009)

A Proposal for Folding in ORM Diagrams

Tony Morgan

INTI International University, Malaysia
goldbasilisk@live.com

Abstract. Object Role Modeling (ORM) can be used to produce conceptual models of any scale. Although small examples are often used to illustrate specific points, it is equally possible to produce large models covering extensive business domains. To help users navigate around a large model, the ORM diagram is typically split over several virtual pages. This gives a fairly coarse granularity and it is difficult for users to change the page structure to meet some temporary viewing need. This paper describes an alternative approach that allows objects of lesser interest to be temporarily 'folded' away and 'unfolded' when required. The folding and unfolding can be dynamically controlled by the user, but operates under the control of specific algorithms. Some possible algorithms are discussed and illustrated with examples, and a number of usability issues are raised.

1 Introduction

Modeling is an occupation that shares many features with programming. Amongst these is the need for the developer of the model (or program) to interact with a representation of the model constructs (or code) during modeling (or programming). In particular a modeler (or programmer) often needs to focus on different parts of the model (or code), depending on the need at hand and in a way that cannot really be predicted in advance.

A program listing can be visualized as a long strip of paper down which appears successive lines of code: older programmers will remember the physical manifestation of code in earlier times as a 'line printer listing'. This structure has a principal organization that is one-dimensional. Moving to a region of interest in the listing is accomplished by moving 'up' or 'down' the conceptual strip. Once the region is located, 'left' and 'right' scanning can be employed, but the 'horizontal' dimension is clearly subsidiary to the 'vertical' dimension.

Programmers often need to juxtapose segments of code that might be widely separated in the code listing. For example, some code may be defined in one place but used other places that are not immediately adjacent. During activities such as debugging it is convenient to see the definition and usage segments together whilst hiding other segments that are not immediately relevant. Given the linear structure of the code, this can be accomplished by conceptually folding a listing so that the regions of interest are brought together. This is illustrated in Figure 1, where the folding has brought the regions shown as A and B together, whilst hiding the intervening region which is assumed to be of no interest.

R. Meersman et al. (Eds.): OTM 2010 Workshops, LNCS 6428, pp. 474–483, 2010.

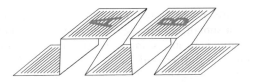

Fig. 1. Conceptual folding of a textual document

This type of operation is fairly easy to simulate in software, and 'folding editors' have been available to software developers for some time, even pre-dating graphical user interfaces. The basic idea is that blocks of code can be identified in some way and any block can be either shown or hidden through some simple user command. Modern development environments such as MS Visual Studio typically allow programmers to define regions which can be shown or hidden with a simple mouse click.

For graphical languages the situation is a little more complex. The need to juxtapose regions of interest is undiminished, but we are now dealing with a structure with a principal organization that is fully two-dimensional, and so moving 'left' and 'right' ranks equally with moving 'up' and 'down'. Implementing folding with a physical listing of a structure in a graphical language would be difficult: one could imagine some origami-like shape emerging, but this would hardly be practical. Fortunately, we can implement folding concepts in software without the constraints of the physical world. However, the challenge to present the user with some guiding concepts remains. Harel [1] discusses some issues involved in hierarchical graphical representations in the context of statecharts.

ORM is an example of a graphical language. An ORM diagram is essentially a bipartite graph with two kinds of nodes (object types and fact types) interconnected by links that define object-fact relationships. To date, ORM tools have tended to use a different metaphor to support navigation around large models. Current tools generally adopt a 'paged' organization, where different sections of the model are arranged on a series of virtual pages (and possibly printed out on separate physical pages). Although elements can be duplicated on multiple pages and users can switch between pages relatively easily, the two-dimensional nature of the structure makes it necessary to anticipate the required juxtapositions of elements at the time that the diagram is created, rather than when it is being viewed. A second disadvantage is that elements that are of no immediate interest to the user remain in view and may distract the user.

The assumption made in this paper is that folding should be applied algorithmically through some tool. The folding process should not rely on inspection and ad-hoc decisions by the user because the folded diagram may be used by someone other than the originator. We therefore need to identify algorithms that can be applied consistently to produce predictable results. The results of folding must also appear intuitive to the user: although detail will be suppressed, the result must maintain the key semantics of the model. It's possible to imagine a variety of algorithms that could meet these requirements. This paper presents some examples to illustrate the issues involved.

Section 2 of this paper illustrates the main principles using a simple algorithm which could be applied to models of low complexity. Section 3 discusses additional features that would be required to deal with more realistic cases. Section 4 provides a larger example that involves most types of ORM construct. Section 5 discusses some aspects of interactive user control over folding options. Section 6 describes an extended use of folding in supporting the import of packaged model fragments into larger ORM models. Finally, section 7 summarizes the main conclusions from the paper and suggests some areas for further work.

2   A Simple Folding Algorithm

We begin with a simple approach that avoids some of the complexities discussed later in the paper. This is based on a categorization of fact types into one-to-one, one-to-many and many-to-many. In order to provide a more compact explanation a shorthand notation is used here. The normal ORM role boxes replaced by arrowed lines, with an arrowhead indicating the 'one' end of the relationship — this effectively corresponds to 'functional dependency'. Internal mandatory constraints reference modes and the distinction between object and value types play no part in the folding algorithm, and are suppressed in this notation. Figure 2 shows an example of a simple model in ORM 2 notation [2] and the shorthand equivalent. The shorthand notation is not part of an ORM model: it is used here only for explanatory purposes.

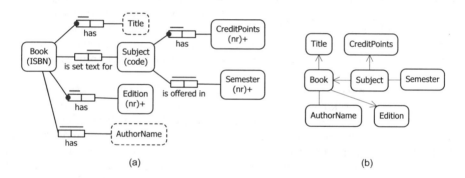

(a)   (b)

Fig. 2. A simple model (a) standard ORM2 notation, (b) shorthand notation

The association ends between object types are either a 'one end' or a 'many end', depending on the relationship. A leaf node is defined as a node connected to the remainder of the model by 'one end' connections only. In Figure 2(b), Title, Edition and CreditPoints are leaf nodes because they are at the 'one' end of a one-to-many relationship. Leaf nodes in a one-to-one relationship would also qualify, although there are none in this case. In this particular model each of the leaf nodes has only one parent, but it is possible for a leaf node to have multiple parents, particularly for common object types such as Date or MoneyAmount (which do not feature in Figure 2).

The simplest algorithm for full folding consists of only three steps:

1. Identify leaf nodes (as defined above)
2. Fold leaf nodes into parent(s)
3. Repeat steps 1 and 2 on the folded result.

The result of applying the algorithm to the model of Figure 2 is shown in Figure 3. The presentation to the user would be as shown in figure 3(b), where the doubled icons for Book and Subject indicate that these are folded nodes. It's important to remember that nothing in the underlying model has changed. The original object and fact types remain in the model, but some have been hidden by the folding process. Unfolding Figure 3 would reconstitute the full version shown in Figure 2. This paper assumes that some mechanism is available to provide automatic layout of diagram features in a reasonably compact and intuitive manner. Features appearing on a diagram through unfolding would be laid out automatically, and might therefore appear in a configuration that differs from the pre-folded layout.

Showing the reference mode of a folded node can become problematic, since this may have been a composite reference involving fact and object types that have now become folded inside the node. For simplicity, the approach taken here is that no reference mode is shown for folded nodes.

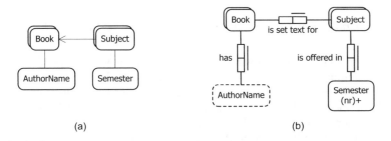

(a)   (b)

Fig. 3. Folded version of Figure 2 (a) Shorthand notation. (b) Modified ORM2 notation.

3   More Complex Relationships

3.1 N-ary and Objectified Fact Types

In the basic algorithm above, many-to-many relationships remained unchanged by folding. In more realistic diagrams such relationships can occur in forms other than the simple many-to-many case. Ternary and higher fact types will always involve many-to-many relationships, and binary many-to-many relationships may be objectified. In order to accommodate these, the simple algorithm must be modified to add an additional step that translates such relationships into an equivalent set of binary relationships and constraints that preserves the logic of the original model. Figure 4 shows examples of ternary and objectified fact types with the corresponding binary equivalent (higher-order relationships can be handled in a similar way but are not discussed here). The many-to-many relationship expressed or implied by the original construct is replaced by a pair of one-to-many relationships and an additional object type. An external uniqueness constraint maintains the properties implied by the original internal uniqueness constraint.

The additional object type, denoted by '*' in Figure 4(c), represents a relationship between a particular 'A' and a particular 'B'. There can be many such relationships, since each 'A' and each 'B' can be connected to many intermediate '*' nodes, each ' representing a unique 'A'-'B' relationship. Objects associated with an 'A'-'B' relationship, such as 'C' in Figures 4(a) and 4(b) become associated with the '*' node as shown in Figure 4(c). For N-ary relationships, such as the ternary fact type in Figure 4(a), the new intermediate node has no name in the model. If a name is required, a plausible option would be to use the concatenation of the names of the 'A' and 'B' nodes (an alternative is discussed later). For objectified relationships, such as the objectified binary fact type in Figure 4(b), the model already provides a suitable name ('D' in this case) which can replace the anonymous '*' as the name of the new intermediate node.

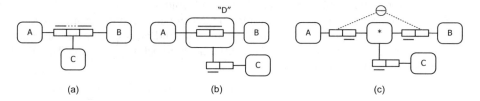

Fig. 4. (a) Ternary fact type. (b) Objectified fact type. (c) Binary equivalent.

It is clear that changing to binary fact types exposes new leaf candidates with the potential for folding as explained in the simple algorithm above. For example, Figure 4(c) could be folded to a single '*' node using the earlier rules, although in practice this would be modified by any other relationships that 'A', 'B', or 'C' might have. A later example shows how this works on a larger model.

An extra rule has to be added to the simple algorithm to avoid confusing external uniqueness constraints. Looking at Figure 4(c), if conditions allowed node 'A' to be folded into '*' but not node 'B' (because of other fact types relating to 'B'), we would have a situation in which one end of the external uniqueness constraint would be inside the fold and one end outside. One possibility would be to allow the fold of 'C' into '*' but not the fold of 'A' into '*' (because of the uniqueness constraint), as shown in Figure 5(a). A second possibility would be to fold 'A' and 'C' into '*' and change the internal uniqueness constraint between 'B' and '*' from one-to-many into many-to-many, as shown in Figure 5(b). This would be poor modeling practice in a base model, but preserves some of the intention of the original model while allowing a greater degree of folding. Further examples of this are provided later in the paper.

Fig. 5. (a) Uniqueness prohibits further folding. (b) Folded with modified uniqueness.

3.2 Subtypes

some care is required in folding subtypes to avoid results that are unintuitive because some semantically important features have been prematurely hidden. Figure 6 (adapted from [5]) shows a small model that includes subtyping.

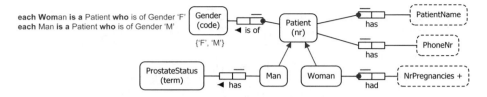

Fig. 6. Model with subtyping

The folding of subtypes can be considered as orthogonal to folding based on the characteristics of fact types. Figure 7 shows some options for folding the model of Figure 6. Figure 7(a) shows the result of folding the leaf nodes into their parents, but leaving subtypes unfolded. Figure 7(b) shows the subtypes folded but the fact types unfolded. Note that mandatory constraints become relevant when folding subtypes: the mandatory constraint on Woman had NrPregnancies becomes optional in Patient had NrPregnancies. Figure 7(c) shows the fully folded result, which is the same regardless of the path that is followed.

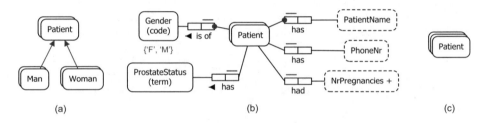

Fig. 7. Folding options (a) Fact types first. (b) Subtypes first. (c) Fully folded.

4   A Larger Example

The example shown in Figure 8 is based on a partial model of a hypothetical Internet bookstore specializing in anthologies of Science Fiction stories. This contains examples of most types of construct, except subtyping. Figure 9 shows the same model using this paper's shorthand notation, with the two ternary fact types and the objectified fact type converted to an equivalent binary form.

Applying the simple folding algorithm described earlier produces the result shown in Figure 10(a). Note that the Antology node contains three levels (Anthology → Publisher → Address). The anonymous intermediate node '*1' introduced by the conversion of the ternary fact type Reader gave Rating to Anthology to an equivalent binary form has been renamed as Rating. This differs from the earlier suggestion of concatenating the outer node names (which would give Reader-Anthology as the node name).

Testing with a number of models shows that concatenating the names of nodes folded into the anonymous node (just Rating in this case) produces node names that seem more intuitive. The other anonymous node '*2' is correspondingly named Movie. Figure 10(b) shows the result of further folding with modified uniqueness, in the style of Figure 5(b).

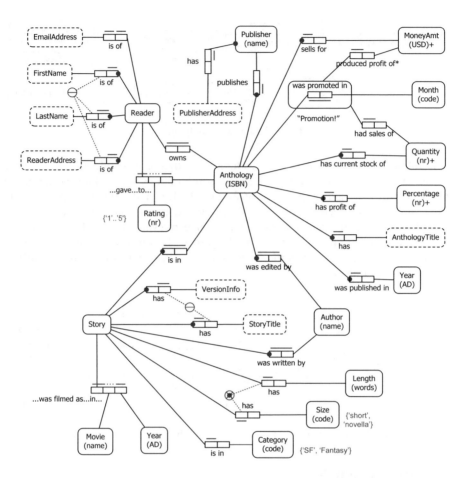

Fig. 8. Science Fiction anthologies in ORM2 notation

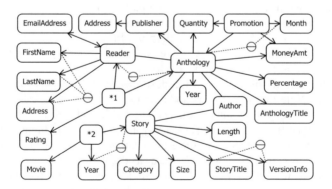

Fig. 9. The same model in shorthand notation

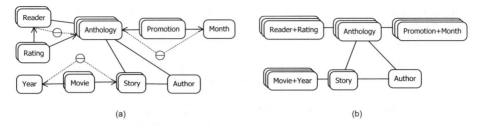

(a)   (b)

Fig. 10. (a) The model of Figure 9 after simple folding. (b) With modified uniqueness folding.

Expanding Figure 10(a) back to the more normal ORM notation could present the user with a layout similar to Figure 11. The only graphical extension required is visual indication of folding, shown here by replicating the relevant object shapes. Figure 10(b) could be expanded in a similar way.

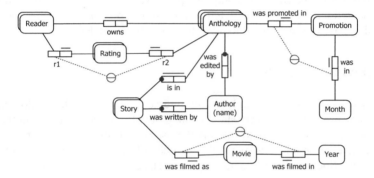

Fig. 11. The folded version of Figure 10(a) in modified ORM2 notation

Fact type readings between unfolded nodes are, of course, unchanged. Fact types involving folded nodes need some care to avoid confusing or misleading the user. If a fold is based around a defining object type (one that could be used to identify other nodes) then the folded name will be the same as the defining object type name. Readings involving such fact types related to the folded defining node can be preserved, as in Story was written by Author in Figure 11. In other cases this is not reliable, as in the fact types r1 and r2 in Figure 11. Readings for such fact types can still be constructed from an examination of the original model. For example, r1 and r2 could plausibly be replaced by reading such as ...gave..., and ...was for ... respectively, but the automated production of such interpretations would be difficult in the general case. To avoid undue complexity it may be adequate to define some simple policy, such as showing the fact reading if it relates to defining objects within a fold and omitting it otherwise.

5   User Controls

Although folding and unfolding is intended to be an algorithmic process, it should remain under user control. One can imagine that a user would be presented with folding options through, for example, pop-up or drop-down menus. Unfolding is essentially the same process in reverse, and so should have similar options.

Invoking a folding operation would have two main option areas.

(a) Specification of the scope of the folding operation. With no object type is currently selected, the folding operation would apply to the whole visible diagram In a large diagram split over several virtual pages this would be the current page. With one or more object types selected, folding would be limited to objects in those selections. Some configuration might be required to determine the details of this operation. For example, if just a leaf node is selected, should we fold only that leaf node, or all of the leaf nodes of its parent node?

(b) Specification of the level of folding. Once a fold has completed at one level, other nodes may become exposed as leaf nodes, making them candidates for a further level of folding. The main options for the user here would be to choose folding to the next level only, or to fold to the deepest level possible.

The diagram should be saved in a way that preserves the current state of folding. Like other presentational features, such as the positioning of objects on the drawing surface, folding has no effect on the logic of the underlying model.

6 Support for Packages

This paper has concentrated mainly on the interactive use of folding, allowing model developers or users to selectively show or hide detail in large models. Another potential use for this mechanism is to support the use of *packages* in modeling. Packages, as defined here, are model fragments that can be defined separately and imported into larger models. Such packages could be pre-constructed for common business scenarios to avoid continued re-invention. Correspondingly, model designers could rapidly create high-level models by leaving complex sub-parts simply represented as folded nodes, leaving the details to be completed at some later stage.

In effect, a folded node (or a set of folded nodes) can be used to define an interface through which additional concepts could be incorporated into a model. Packages could also be substitutable, so that several different packages could be defined to provide variants through which a model could be rapidly adapted to meet different needs.

As a simple example, a concept commonly encountered in modeling is PostalAddress. An address might be modeled simply as a value type, effectively indicating that the address is just treated as a string. Alternatively, the modeler may choose to define more structure by identifying object types for city, street, number, postal code, and so on. At an even finer level of detail the modeler may wish to reflect such things as possible differences in the order of presentation of address component. For instance "19 High Street" in England might correspond to "Hochstrasse 19" in Germany.

From a high level modeling perspective, the introduction of folded nodes (such as PostalAddress in the example above) can postpone the need to make a commitment to any particular address structure. It also facilitates the incorporation of external model fragments that may have been developed by third parties with special expertise in particular areas, who might be better qualified to create a sound model.

7 Conclusions and Future Work

The concept of folding, or hierarchical views, has been shown to be useful in many applications, and there seems no reason to suppose that it could not be applied in ORM as an alternative to the current 'paged' approach. The same concept could also be applied in other ways such as importing or exporting packaged concepts, although, as noted below, this would be likely to require stronger algorithms to give more precise control over the package semantics, as discussed in more detail in [3] and [4].

For interactive use, the preferred approach would be to fold/unfold using an algorithm, but to allow the user to select the area of the diagram to be folded or unfolded. Since the folding/unfolding process does not change the underlying model in any way, it appears to be possible to use quite simple algorithms and still get useful results. The main consideration here is to avoid the folded diagram from being misleading or confusing to the user. A particular challenge is the automation of verbalization for fact types relating folded nodes. Reasonable verbalizations can be found manually – 'by inspection' – but this would make the process more cumbersome and remove much of the attraction of the interactive approach.

Having a lightweight algorithm for interactive use is acceptable because no model transforms would be carried out on a folded view – transforms would always be based on the underlying full model. A folded view would be easy to undo by effectively applying the algorithm in reverse. However if any processing is to be carried out on a folded part of a model, a much stronger algorithm should be used with well-defined semantic properties.

The approach described in this paper has been tested on a variety of ORM models, and appears empirically to give acceptable results. More testing would be required on a range of ORM constructs and large models to validate its more general applicability. A useful adjunct to this would be the development of improved automatic layout algorithms capable of dealing with subsets of models as well as complete models.

References

1. Harel, D.: On Visual Formalisms. Communications of the ACM 31(5), 514–530
2. Halpin, T.: ORM 2. In: Meersman, R., Tari, Z., Herrero, P. (eds.) OTM-WS 2005. LNCS, vol. 3762, pp. 676–687. Springer, Heidelberg (2005)
3. Halpin, T., Campbell, L.: Automated Support for Conceptual to External Mapping, University of Queensland Technical Report
4. Campbell, L.J., Halpin, T.A., Proper, H.A.: Conceptual Schemas with Abstractions – Making flat conceptual schemas more comprehensible. Data & Knowledge Engineering 20(1), 39–85 (1996)
5. Halpin, T., Morgan, T.: Information Modeling and Relational Databases, 2nd edn. Morgan Kaufmann, San Francisco (2008)

A Basic Characterization of Relation Migration

C. Maria Keet and Alessandro Artale

KRDB Research Centre, Free University of Bozen-Bolzano, Italy
{keet,artale}@inf.unibz.it

Abstract. Representing and reasoning over evolving objects has been investigated widely. Less attention has been devoted to the similar notion of *relation
migration*, i.e., how tuples of a relation (ORM facts) can evolve along time. We
identify different ways how a relation can change over time and give a logic-
based semantics to the notion of relation migration to capture its behaviour. We
also introduce the notion of lifespan of a relation and clarify the interactions between object migration and relation migration. Its use in graphical conceptual
data modelling is illustrated with a minor extension to ORM2 so as to more easily communicate such constraints with domain experts.

1 Introduction

Object migration, where, say, John migrates from being an instance of Student to
one of Alumnus, has received ample attention in the temporal database and conceptual modelling communities [1,2,3,4,5,6]. But how do we migrate, say, the ORM fact
⟨John, CS2000⟩ ∈ EnrolledIn to ⟨John, CS2000⟩ ∈ GraduatedIn when John has completed the degree programme CS2000 successfully? Clearly, one can migrate John to
Alumnus and then manually add ⟨John, CS2000⟩ ∈ GraduatedIn in the GraduatedIn
table, but it is much more elegant from the conceptual point of view to declare such
business knowledge by imposing a temporal constraint on the possible evolution of EnrolledIn to GraduatedIn at the ORM fact type level so that a whole tuple (fact) migrates
at once.

In analogy to object migration, this paper claims the usefulness of a similar constraint for relations that we call *relation migration*. We are unable to find other accounts
—either formal or informal—for the notion of relation migration other than the notion
of *status relations* that were introduced for conceptual modelling in [7,8], which was
used for modelling essential and immutable part-whole relations. Tuple migration at the
physical schema level has received some attention in database integration scenarios and
in distributed databases, but in these scenarios a tuple "migrates" just to instantiate the
same relation that happens to be stored in different servers whereas here by "relation
migration" we intend the *change of membership* of a tuple from one relation to another.
Observe that modelling of relation migration is thus also distinct from state transition
diagrams that concern states of single objects, activity diagrams that concern processes
but do not explicitly consider the participating entities, and interaction diagrams for
modelling use cases. We focus explicitly on, in ORM terminology, the migration of
facts (called also *tuples* or *relation instances* in this paper) and the corresponding temporal behaviour of fact types (called also *relations* in this paper).

R. Meersman et al. (Eds.): OTM 2010 Workshops, LNCS 6428, pp. 484–493, 2010.
ⓒ Springer-Verlag Berlin Heidelberg 2010

The main purpose of this work is to fill this conceptual and formal gap by introducing the notion of *relation migration*. The natural questions we are trying to answer in this paper are about the different ways in which a relation migration can occur and how we can represent its behaviour such that it can be used in conceptual data models. We identify different ways how a relation can change over time and give it a logic-based semantics. With the formalization of relation migration, we can precisely define the notion of lifespan and its related notions for a relation, and show how interesting temporal properties of relations can be derived as logical implications from the provided formalization. In particular, we will show how interactions between object- and relation- migration can be captured in the proposed framework as logical implication. To achieve this, we build upon ideas from the framework for temporal conceptual modelling in $\mathcal{ER}_{VT}$ [1] with the ability to capture migration between relations in conceptual data models. Along these lines, we associate to the notion of relation migration a formalization in terms of a model-theoretic semantics and group migrations into *evolution* constraints, *persistence* constraints, and *quantitative* constraints. Using a formal foundation—be it the first order logic presented here or extending $\mathcal{ER}_{VT}$ that is based on the Description Logic $\mathcal{DLR}_{US}$—one will be able to check consistency of the constraints during conceptual data model development using an automated reasoner.

The remainder of the paper is structured as follows. Section 2 introduces examples of relation migration and identifies requirements that should be met for an adequate representation. The proposed formal characterisation of relation migration and lifespan for relations are described in Section 3. The properties that can be derived as logical implications from the proposed formalization are provided and illustrated in Section 4. We close with our final remarks in Section 5.

2   Requirements Analysis

In this section we demonstrate the relevance of the notion of relation migration in information systems and databases. We provide an informal idea of the characteristics that underpin the different ways of migration and describe the requirements that a temporal conceptual modelling language should be able to capture. The described behaviour can be extended to generic n-ary relations.

Example 1. Let us assume an airline company's passenger RDBMS and a passenger who books a flight, hence we have a relation $\langle$John, AZ123$\rangle \in$ Booking with John $\in$ Passenger and AZ123 $\in$ Flight, which are normally followed by the events that John also checks in and then boards the plane, $\langle$John, AZ123$\rangle \in$ CheckIn and $\langle$John, AZ123$\rangle \in$ Boarding. While the booking relation holds even after the tuple *extended* to the check-in relation, i.e., $\langle$John, AZ123$\rangle$ is a member of both Booking and CheckIn relations, this is not the case for the step from check-in to boarding which causes the tuple $\langle$John, AZ123$\rangle$ to be *moved* from one to the other relation in the operational database. In addition, for any tuple that is member of the Boarding relation, we know that it must have been a member of CheckIn relation sometime earlier. On the other hand, we cannot force a business rule where tuples of the CheckIn relation migrate sometime in the future to the Boarding relation since a flight can be cancelled after the check-in or the passenger may become ill and does not board the plane anymore.

One can construct a similar story line and type of behaviour for, say, census data with $\langle$John, Mary$\rangle \in$ Marriage, where John, Mary $\in$ Person and, as a consequence of a divorce event, we have that $\langle$John, Mary$\rangle \in$ Divorce. Since they can marry again, then we should allow for the same tuple $\langle$John, Mary$\rangle$ to become again member of the Marriage relation. On the other hand, in the event that either John or Mary dies, then $\langle$John, Mary$\rangle \in$ Widowhood, which, once it holds, it holds at all times in the future (i.e., being in Widowhood is a *persistent* relation).

One can also plan for specific time durations. For instance, it is expected that once $\langle$Professor1, DepartmentA$\rangle \in$ WorksFor, each professor also has to perform administrative duties, such as representing the department in the faculty council during some time of her employment (i.e., $\langle$Professor1, DepartmentA$\rangle \in$ Represents), and teach courses (i.e., $\langle$Professor1, DepartmentA$\rangle \in$ TeachesAt). The temporal behaviour of the Represents relation is different from that one of the TeachesAt. Indeed, assuming a scenario where professors do not change their departments, then all professors instantiate the TeachsAt relation which, in turn, can be modeled as a temporally persistent relation. On the other hand, professors do not always have to take part in faculty councils but there are scenarios where specific durations are enforced with business rules saying, for example, that *"each professor serving in a faculty council should have worked for the department since the previous year"*.

Example 2. Let us consider now part-whole relations [9]. A simple change in relation between two objects can be caused by the fact that (*i*) a is structurally a part of b but a gets loose so after that a becomes spatially contained in b, e.g., a component in a medical device breaks loose due to wear and tear. For part-whole relations that are not necessarily part-of in the mereological sense we introduce two examples. First (*ii*), the example of subquantity_of in [9] about a bottle of wine and pouring a subquantity of the wine into a wineglass so that this subquantity in the glass *used to be* a subquantity_of the wine in the bottle and one wants to maintain traceability of quantities over time, which is important especially in the food industry for food safety in the food processing chain. The second example is a case where object- and relation- migration interact. For instance, let's consider (*iii*), $\langle$John, ACompanyBoard$\rangle \in$ member_of with John $\in$ CEO and subsequently we have a migration of both the object and the relation such that John's role changes to John $\in$ Consultant and $\langle$John, ACompanyBoard$\rangle \in$ advisor_of.

We can add a further dimension regarding the behaviour of relation migration when we also consider rigidity of the objects and the relation that holds between the objects. In particular, to capture the temporal behaviour of part-whole relations, essential and immutable part-whole relations have been introduced [7,10]; e.g., the part-whole relation $\langle$wolfram-thread, candescent-light-bulb$\rangle \in$ structural_part, where the wolfram-thread is an immutable part of the candescent-light-bulb. When the light is broken, the tuple migrates *irreversibly* to $\langle$wolfram-thread, candescent-light-bulb$\rangle \in$ containment, unlike the medical device in example (*i*).

Types of behaviour for relation migration. Summarising and generalising from the examples, we have identified the following types of behaviour, which are in analogy to their object migration counterpart [1].

- *Evolution constraints* specify how elements of a relation can possibly migrate to another relation—e.g., the instance of Booking migrates (extends) to CheckIn.

- *Persistence constraints* specify persistent states for a relation—e.g., being in Widowhood is persistent for a couple.
- *Quantitative evolution constraints* specify the exact amount of time for the relation migration to happen—e.g., the case of professors who, to be members of the faculty council, should have been members of the faculty since one year.

3 Formalization of Relation Migration

In this section, we formalise the constraints for relation migration that were described informally in Section 2, and investigate the impact of relation migration on *lifespan* for relations. To keep the formal apparatus to a minimum, we avail of the notion of status relations—formalised in [7,8] and graphically depicted in Fig.2—that constrain the evolution of a tuple's membership in a relation along its lifespan and which apply only to temporal relations: R is the normal (active) relation, a relation is scheduled (Scheduled-R) if its instantiation is known but its membership will only become active some time later, a suspended relation (Suspended-R) is temporarily inactive, and disabled relations (Disabled-R) are expired relations that never can be used again. Based on the characterisation of relation migration (Section 3.1) and lifespan (Section 3.2), we can model the identified ways of relation migration precisely and explore the interactions between relation and object migration afterwards.

3.1 Basic Constraints for Relation Migration

We start by formalising the behavioural constraints without considering object migration. We distinguish between *evolution* constraints—specifying how elements of a relation can possibly migrate to another relation—*persistence* constraints—specifying persistent states for a relation—and *quantitative evolution* constraints—specifying the exact amount of time for the relation migration to happen. We present the textual syntax and the model-theoretic semantics considering, without loss of generality, binary relations. We use a *temporal interpretation* of the signature of a conceptual data model $\mathcal{L}$, which is a structure of the form: $\mathcal{I} = \left((\mathbb{Z}, <), \Delta^{\mathcal{I}}, \{ \cdot^{\mathcal{I}(t)} \mid t \in \mathbb{Z} \} \right)$, where $(\mathbb{Z}, <)$ is the set of integers denoting the intended *flow of time*, $\Delta^{\mathcal{I}} \neq \emptyset$ is the *interpretation domain*, and $\cdot^{\mathcal{I}(t)}$, for $t \in \mathbb{Z}$, is the *interpretation function* which assigns a set $C^{\mathcal{I}(t)} \subseteq \Delta^{\mathcal{I}}$ to each entity type $C \in \mathcal{C}$, and a set $R^{\mathcal{I}(t)}$ of tuples over $\Delta^{\mathcal{I}}$ to each relation $R \in \mathcal{R}$.

Evolution constraints. We distinguish between five different kinds of evolution constraints.

R RDEX R'. D*ynamic* EX*tension of a* R*elation.*

$$\langle o_1, o_2 \rangle \in \mathtt{R}^{\mathcal{I}(t)} \to \exists t' > t. \langle o_1, o_2 \rangle \in \mathtt{R'}^{\mathcal{I}(t')}$$

R RDEV R'. D*ynamic* EV*olution of a* R*elation.*

$$\langle o_1, o_2 \rangle \in \mathtt{R}^{\mathcal{I}(t)} \to \exists t' > t. \langle o_1, o_2 \rangle \in \mathtt{R'}^{\mathcal{I}(t')} \wedge \langle o_1, o_2 \rangle \notin \mathtt{R}^{\mathcal{I}(t')}$$

R SRDEX R'. S*trong* D*ynamic* EX*tension of a* R*elation.*

$$\langle o_1, o_2 \rangle \in \mathtt{R}^{\mathcal{I}(t)} \to \langle o_1, o_2 \rangle \in \mathtt{Scheduled\text{-}R'}^{\mathcal{I}(t)} \wedge \exists t' > t. \langle o_1, o_2 \rangle \in \mathtt{R'}^{\mathcal{I}(t')}$$

R RDEX⁻ R'. D*ynamic* EX*tension of a* R*elation in the past.*

$$\langle o_1, o_2 \rangle \in \mathtt{R}^{\mathcal{I}(t)} \to \exists t' < t. \langle o_1, o_2 \rangle \in \mathtt{R'}^{\mathcal{I}(t')}$$

C.M. Keet and A. Artale

R RDEV⁻ R′. D*ynamic* EV*olution of a* R*elation in the past.*

$$\langle o_1, o_2 \rangle \in R^{\mathcal{I}(t)} \rightarrow \exists t' < t. \langle o_1, o_2 \rangle \in R'^{\mathcal{I}(t')} \wedge \langle o_1, o_2 \rangle \notin R^{\mathcal{I}(t')}$$

Persistence constraints. We distinguish between five different kinds of persistence constraints.

R RPEX R′. P*ersistent* EX*tension of a* R*elation.*

$$\langle o_1, o_2 \rangle \in R^{\mathcal{I}(t)} \rightarrow \forall t' > t. \langle o_1, o_2 \rangle \in R'^{\mathcal{I}(t')}$$

R RPEV R′. P*ersistent* EV*olution of a* R*elation.*

$$\langle o_1, o_2 \rangle \in R^{\mathcal{I}(t)} \rightarrow \forall t' > t. \langle o_1, o_2 \rangle \in R'^{\mathcal{I}(t')} \wedge \langle o_1, o_2 \rangle \notin R^{\mathcal{I}(t')}$$

R SRPEX R′. S*trong* P*ersistent* EX*tension of a* R*elation.*

$$\langle o_1, o_2 \rangle \in R^{\mathcal{I}(t)} \rightarrow \langle o_1, o_2 \rangle \in \text{Scheduled-R}'^{\mathcal{I}(t)} \wedge \forall t' > t. \langle o_1, o_2 \rangle \in R'^{\mathcal{I}(t')}$$

R RPEX⁻ R′. P*ersistent* EX*tension of a* R*elation in the past.*

$$\langle o_1, o_2 \rangle \in R^{\mathcal{I}(t)} \rightarrow \forall t' < t. \langle o_1, o_2 \rangle \in R'^{\mathcal{I}(t')}$$

R RPEV⁻ R′. P*ersistent* EV*olution of a* R*elation in the past.*

$$\langle o_1, o_2 \rangle \in R^{\mathcal{I}(t)} \rightarrow \forall t' < t. \langle o_1, o_2 \rangle \in R'^{\mathcal{I}(t')} \wedge \langle o_1, o_2 \rangle \notin R^{\mathcal{I}(t')}$$

Quantitative constraints. We distinguish between five different kinds of quantitative constraints.

R RQEX R′. Q*uantitative* EX*tension of a* R*elation.*

$$\langle o_1, o_2 \rangle \in R^{\mathcal{I}(t)} \rightarrow \langle o_1, o_2 \rangle \in R'^{\mathcal{I}(t+1)}$$

R RQEV R′. Q*uantitative* EV*olution of a* R*elation.*

$$\langle o_1, o_2 \rangle \in R^{\mathcal{I}(t)} \rightarrow \langle o_1, o_2 \rangle \in R'^{\mathcal{I}(t+1)} \wedge \langle o_1, o_2 \rangle \notin R^{\mathcal{I}(t+1)}$$

R SRQEX R′. S*trong* Q*uantitative* EX*tension of a* R*elation.*

$$\langle o_1, o_2 \rangle \in R^{\mathcal{I}(t)} \rightarrow \langle o_1, o_2 \rangle \in \text{Scheduled-R}'^{\mathcal{I}(t)} \wedge \langle o_1, o_2 \rangle \in R'^{\mathcal{I}(t+1)}$$

R RQEX⁻ R′. Q*uantitative* EX*tension of a* R*elation in the past.*

$$\langle o_1, o_2 \rangle \in R^{\mathcal{I}(t)} \rightarrow \langle o_1, o_2 \rangle \in R'^{\mathcal{I}(t-1)}$$

R RQEV⁻ R′. Q*uantitative* EV*olution of a* R*elation in the past.*

$$\langle o_1, o_2 \rangle \in R^{\mathcal{I}(t)} \rightarrow \langle o_1, o_2 \rangle \in R'^{\mathcal{I}(t-1)} \wedge \langle o_1, o_2 \rangle \notin R^{\mathcal{I}(t-1)}$$

Concerning the specific examples metioned in Section 2, they can be modelled with the following migration constraints:

Booking	RDEX	CheckIn,	Widowhood	RPEX	Widowhood,
Boarding	RDEV⁻	CheckIn,	Represents	RQEX⁻	WorksFor,
Divorce	RDEV⁻	Marriage,	EssentialStructuralPart	RPEV	contained_in,
Marriage	SRDEX	Widowhood,	Disabled-SubQuantity	RDEV⁻	SubQuantity.

Thus, e.g., the penultimate constraint assumes that in the domain of interest and normal course of operation, it holds that for each working candescent light bulb, the wolfram thread always will break at some point in the future, and remain broken indefinitely, and the latter constraint can be used for, e.g., the amount of wine poured into the wineglass which used to be a subquantity of the wine in the bottle.

We leave it to Human-Computer Interaction experts to devise the optimal way to add relation migration to the ORM graphical and textual languages: the constraints can be added alike rules are added in pseudo-natural language analogous to [2] or, e.g., with named dashed lines that serve as syntactic sugar for the axioms. We use the latter option in the remainder of the paper thanks to its compactness; an example is shown in Fig. 1.

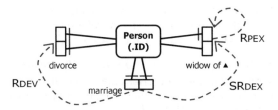

Fig. 1. Example of relation migration between various civil statuses (in ORM2 notation), where the dashed arrow denotes the direction of migration and its label the type of migration

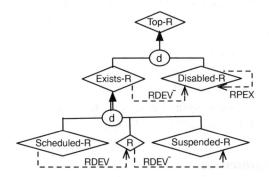

Fig. 2. Graphical depiction (in EER) of status relations (from [7]) extended with relation migration constraints between them, which are denoted with dashed lines and an arrow in the direction in which the relation migrates; e.g., a relation in Disabled-R was evolved dynamically (RDEV⁻) from Exists-R (i.e., used to be an instance of Exists-R). In ORM notation, the diamonds are replaced by rectangles, encircled d with double shafted arrow with disjoint exclusive notation.

3.2   Lifespan and Related Notions

The lifespan of an object with respect to a class describes the temporal instants where the object can be considered a member of that class [1]. In an analogous way, we introduce the lifespan and related notions for temporal relations. The lifespan of a particular relation instance (tuple, fact) $r = \langle o_i, o_j \rangle$ (for simplicity we consider binary relations) with respect to a relation R describes the temporal instants where the particular relation instance can be considered a member of the relation. With the notion of status relations, one can distinguish between the following aspects of lifespan: $\textsc{ExistenceSpan}_R$, $\textsc{LifeSpan}_R$, $\textsc{ActiveSpan}_R$, $\textsc{Begin}_R$, $\textsc{Birth}_R$ and $\textsc{Death}_R$, which are functions that depend on the relation's membership to the status relation associated to a temporal relation R.

The *existencespan* of a relation instance r describes the temporal instants where the relation is either a scheduled, active or suspended member of a relation (i.e., of Scheduled-R, R, or of Suspended-R). Recollecting the relational hierarchy in Fig. 2, where Exists-R subsumes the former three, then we have $\textsc{ExistenceSpan}_R : \Delta^{\mathcal{B}} \times \Delta^{\mathcal{B}} \to 2^{\mathcal{T}}$, such that:

$$\textsc{ExistenceSpan}_R(r) = \{t \in \mathcal{T} \mid \langle o_i, o_j \rangle \in \text{Exists-R}^{\mathcal{I}(t)}\}$$

The *lifespan* of a relation instance describes the temporal instants where the relation is an active or suspended member of a given relation (thus, $\text{LIFESPAN}_R(r) \subseteq \text{EXISTENCESPAN}_R(r)$). More formally, $\text{LIFESPAN}_R : \Delta^\mathcal{B} \times \Delta^\mathcal{B} \to 2^\mathcal{T}$, such that:

$$\text{LIFESPAN}_R(r) = \{t \in \mathcal{T} \mid \langle o_i, o_j \rangle \in \text{R}^{\mathcal{I}(t)} \cup \text{Suspended-R}^{\mathcal{I}(t)}\}$$

The *activespan* of a relation instance describes the temporal instants where the relation is an active member of a given relation (thus, $\text{ACTIVESPAN}_R(r) \subseteq \text{LIFESPAN}_R(r)$). More formally, $\text{ACTIVESPAN}_R : \Delta^\mathcal{B} \times \Delta^\mathcal{B} \to 2^\mathcal{T}$, such that:

$$\text{ACTIVESPAN}_R(r) = \{t \in \mathcal{T} \mid \langle o_i, o_j \rangle \in \text{R}^{\mathcal{I}(t)}\}$$

The functions BEGIN_R and DEATH_R associate to a relation instance the first and the last appearance, respectively, of the relation as a member of a given relation, while BIRTH_R denotes the first appearance of the relation as an active member of that relation. More formally, $\text{BEGIN}_R, \text{BIRTH}_R, \text{DEATH}_R : \Delta^\mathcal{B} \times \Delta^\mathcal{B} \to \mathcal{T}$, such that:

$$\text{BEGIN}_R(r) = \min(\text{EXISTENCESPAN}_R(r))$$
$$\text{BIRTH}_R(r) = \min(\text{ACTIVESPAN}_R(r)) \equiv \min(\text{LIFESPAN}_R(r))$$
$$\text{DEATH}_R(r) = \max(\text{LIFESPAN}_R(r)) \equiv \text{EXISTENCESPAN}_R(r)$$

We could still speak of existencespan, lifespan or activespan for snapshot relations, but in this case $\text{EXISTENCESPAN}_R(r) \equiv \text{LIFESPAN}_R(r) \equiv \text{ACTIVESPAN}_R(r) \equiv \mathcal{T}$.

4   Logical Consequences

In this section we show how further constraints can be derived as logical implications from the axiomatization proposed so far on relation migration (denoted with Σ_{st}) and the lifespan definitions. We will also study the interactions between object and relation migration.

The first result shows that mixing subtyping of entity types (ISA) with migration may result into inconsistent relations (see 'Case A' in Section 4.1 for an example).

Proposition 1 (ISA Vs. Relation Migration). *Let R, R' be two relations such that R' ISA R and R RMC R', with RMC $\in$ {SRDEX, SRPEX, SRQEX, RDEV, RPEV, RQEV, RDEV$^-$, RPEV$^-$, RQEV$^-$} then both R and R' are unsatisfiable, i.e., $\Sigma_{st} \cup \{R'$ ISA R, R RMC $R'\} \models \{R$ ISA $\bot, R'$ ISA $\bot\}$, with $\bot$ the empty set.*

Specifying constraints on relation migration can force new constraints on the lifespan of the related relations:

Proposition 2 (**Migration Vs. Relation Lifespan**). *Let R, R' be two relations, then:*
1. *If R RPEV R', then $\text{DEATH}_R(r) \le \text{DEATH}_{R'}(r)$.*
2. *If R RMC R', with RMC $\in$ {SRDEX, SRPEX, SRQEX}, then $\text{DEATH}_R(r) \le \text{BIRTH}_{R'}(r)$.*

To see why (2) holds, note that from the semantics of the relation migration involved in R RMC R' it immediately follows that (i) R and R' are two disjoint relations, and (ii) that R implies Scheduled-R'.

We now proceed to examine how the notion of lifespan for both classes and relations can interact with each other. Such interactions will be useful to understand how relation migration and object migration influence each other, which we address in the next subsection.

Proposition 3 (Objects Vs. Relations Lifespan). *Given the set of axioms Σ_{st} and the lifespan notions for both status classes and status relations, let R be an n-ary relation (where $n \geq 2$) to which object types $C_1, \ldots C_m$ participate (where $m \leq n$) and $r = \langle o_1, \ldots, o_n \rangle \in R$, then:*

1. ACTIVESPAN *of relations is shorter or equal to the* ACTIVESPAN *of objects participating in the relation.*
   ACTIVESPAN$_R(r) \subseteq$ ACTIVESPAN$_{C_i}(o_i)$, *for* $i = 1, \ldots, n$
2. BEGIN *of objects occurs at the same time or before the* BEGIN *of the relation they participate in.*
   BEGIN$_{C_i}(o_i) \leq$ BEGIN$_R(r)$, *for* $i = 1, \ldots, n$
3. DEATH *of relations occurs before or at the same time when one or more participating objects die.*
   DEATH$_R(r) \leq$ DEATH$_{C_i}(o_i)$, *for* $i = 1, \ldots, n$

The first property is a consequence of the "ACT" axiom ($\langle o_1, o_2 \rangle \in R^{\mathcal{I}(t)} \rightarrow o_i \in C_i^{\mathcal{I}(t)}$, $i = 1, 2$) of the formalization of status relations [7] saying that active relations involve only active classes. From this property follows that BIRTH$_{C_i}(o_i) \leq$ BIRTH$_R(r)$, for $i = 1, \ldots, n$. The second property is a consequence of the "RSUSP2" axiom ($\langle o_1, o_2 \rangle \in$ Suspended-$R^{\mathcal{I}(t)} \rightarrow o_i \in C_i^{\mathcal{I}(t)} \vee o_i \in$ Suspended-C$_i^{\mathcal{I}(t)}$, $i = 1, 2$) [7] saying that objects participating in a suspended relation have to be scheduled or active objects. The last property is a consequence of the "RDISAB4" axiom [7] saying that disabled classes can participate only in disabled relations. As an obvious consequence we have that LIFESPAN$_R(r) \subseteq$ LIFESPAN$_{C_i}(o_i)$ for $i = 1, \ldots, n$, similarly for EXISTENCESPAN.

4.1 Relation Migration Vs. Object Migration

We consider now how the migration of a relation and the migration of a participating object can influence the temporal behaviour of each other. We show that, in addition to explicitly asserting an object- or relation- migration constraint, the constraints already expressed in a temporal conceptual model can force such kind of migrations. We have found two cases, depicted in Fig. 3, where (case A) object migration implies a relation migration, and (case B) relation migration implies an object migration. Note that the object migration constraints have a semantics similar to the one for relation migration. We assume that the relations R, R' are generic n-ary relations with the same arity and that the entity types E_1, E_2 play the same role/position in R and R', respectively.

Case A: Object migration $\rightarrow$ relation migration. Given an object migration between two entity types, E_1, E_2, participating in two relations, R, R', respectively, then to derive an analogous migration between the relations, the constraint expressed in Fig. 3-A must hold, where the timestamp (not drawn in Fig. 3) forces R to be time-invariant, called also snapshot in the literature (i.e., $\langle o_1, o_2 \rangle \in R^{\mathcal{I}(t)}$, then $\langle o_1, o_2 \rangle \in R^{\mathcal{I}(t')}$ for all $t' \in \mathcal{T}$). Note that if the specified object migration constraints are one of DEV/PEV/QEV then the diagram in Fig. 3-A would be inconsistent (see Proposition 1).

Case B: Relation migration $\rightarrow$ object migration. Given a migration between two relations, R, R', bounded to entity types, E_1, E_2, respectively, then to derive an analogous migration between the corresponding participating entity types, the constraints

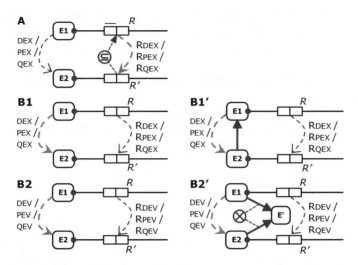

Fig. 3. Interaction between object- and relation migration; thin (pink) dashed line with open arrowhead = declared migration, thick (green) dashed line = implication for the relation or object. Observe that B1 includes cases like B1′. B2 vs. B2′ depends on the underlying formalism: E_1 and E_2 must be disjoint, which is either assumed to be so when the entity types are not in a hierarchy (B2, normally the case in conceptual models) or must added explicitly (when one principally uses an arbitrary suitable logic and uses an ORM diagram as 'syntactic sugar').

expressed in Fig. 3-B1/B1′ must hold; that is, E_1 and E_2 may, but do not need to be, disjoint. When the migration between the relations are one of RDEV/RPEV/RQEV, then to derive a similar object migration constraint, the entity types E_1, E_2 need to be disjoint in the conceptual diagram as shown in Fig. 3-B2 (if the underlying logic already takes care of disjointness of E_1 and E_2 by convention) or B2′ (declaring and communicating explicitly the disjointness of E_1 and E_2 in an ORM diagram). On the other hand, if the entity types E_1, E_2 are declared to be disjoint then, in its turn, the relation migration is forced to be one of RDEV/RPEV/RQEV.

We illustrate these two cases in the following example.

Example 3. For Case A, let us assume a company where, sooner or later, each employee—who works for exactly one department—will be promoted within the same department he or she works for and such that demotion does not occur. This means an object migration of type PEX between Employee and Manager; see Fig. 4-A. To maintain consistency of the model, this forces a relation migration of type RPEX between works for and manages.

For Case B, let us recollect the example of Section 2 about John as CEO and his membership in the CompanyBoard, which has a business rule that at some point he will cease to be a CEO and full member of the board but then must continue consulting the company board to foster continuation and smooth transition of the management, i.e., we have RDEV between member of and consultant of. In the ORM model depicted in Fig. 4-B, this forces John to dynamically evolve (DEV) from CEO to Consultant.

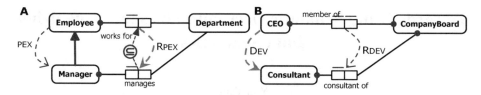

Fig. 4. Examples of interaction between object- and relation migration

5   Conclusions

We have identified different ways how a relation can change over time and given a logic-based semantics to the notion of *relation migration* to capture its behaviour precisely. Relation migration imposes constraints regarding the notions of lifespan of a relation, in a similar way as object migration does for lifespans of objects. In addition, we explored the interaction that exists between object- and relation migration. We presented two different cases showing how object migration influences relation migration and, vice-versa, how from a relation migration we can derive migration constraints for the classes participating in the relation.

Current and future work involves integrating aspects of rigidity, its effects on migrations between part-whole relations, and tractable reasoning with relation migration.

References

1. Artale, A., Parent, C., Spaccapietra, S.: Evolving objects in temporal information systems. Annals of Mathematics and Artificial Intelligence 50(1-2), 5–38 (2007)
2. Balsters, H., Carver, A., Halpin, T., Morgan, T.: Modeling dynamic rules in ORM. In: Meersman, R., Tari, Z., Herrero, P. (eds.) OTM 2006 Workshops. LNCS, vol. 4278, pp. 1201–1210. Springer, Heidelberg (2006)
3. Hall, G., Gupta, R.: Modeling transition. In: Proc. of ICDE 1991, pp. 540–549 (1991)
4. Etzion, O., Gal, A., Segev, A.: Extended update functionality in temporal databases. In: Etzion, O., Jajodia, S., Sripada, S. (eds.) Dagstuhl Seminar 1997. LNCS, vol. 1399, pp. 56–95. Springer, Heidelberg (1998)
5. Halpin, T.: Temporal modeling and ORM. In: Meersman, R., Tari, Z., Herrero, P. (eds.) OTM-WS 2008. LNCS, vol. 5333, pp. 688–698. Springer, Heidelberg (2008)
6. Parent, C., Spaccapietra, S., Zimányi, E.: Conceptual modeling for traditional and spatio-temporal applications—the MADS approach. Springer, Heidelberg (2006)
7. Artale, A., Guarino, N., Keet, C.M.: Formalising temporal constraints on part-whole relations. In: Brewka, G., Lang, J. (eds.) 11th International Conference on Principles of Knowledge Representation and Reasoning (KR 2008), pp. 673–683. AAAI Press, Menlo Park (2008)
8. Artale, A., Keet, C.M.: Essential, mandatory, and shared parts in conceptual data models. In: Halpin, T.A., Proper, H.A., Krogstie, J. (eds.) Innovations in Information Systems modeling: Methods and Best Practices, pp. 17–52. IGI Global (2008)
9. Keet, C.M., Artale, A.: Representing and reasoning over a taxonomy of part-whole relations. Applied Ontology 3(1-2), 91–110 (2008)
10. Guizzardi, G.: Ontological Foundations for Structural Conceptual Models. Phd thesis, University of Twente, The Netherlands. Telematica Instituut Fundamental Research Series No. 15 (2005)

Towards Using Semantic Decision Tables for Organizing Data Semantics

Yan Tang

VUB STARLab
10G731, Vrije Universiteit Brussel
Pleinlaan 2, 1050 Elesene
Brussels, Belgium
yan.tang@vub.ac.be

Abstract. In the ITEA2 Do-It-Yourself Smart Experiences project (DIY-SE), we are required to design an ontology-based ambient computing environment to support users to DIY their personalized solutions. In this paper, we illustrate how to manage data semantics using Semantic Decision Table (SDT). We use a simple rule writing language called Decision Commitment Language (DECOL) to store the SDT commitments. Semantic Decision Rule Language (SDRule-L), which is an extension to Object Role Modelling (ORM), is used to graphically represent DECOL. In this paper, we will demonstrate how SDT, together with SDRule-L and DECOL, are used by both technical and non-technical end users.

Keywords: Semantic Decision Table, Ontology, Do-It-Yourself.

1 Introduction and Motivation

The ITEA2 Do-It-Yourself Smart Experiences project (DIY-SE, http://dyse.org:8080) aims at allowing citizens to obtain highly personalized and social experiences of smart objects at home and in the public areas, by enabling them to easily DIY applications in their smart living environments.

The DIY aspect has been very important for decades. As Mark Frauenfelder points out, "DIY helped them take control of their lives, offering a path that was simple, direct, and clear. Working with their hands and minds helped them feel more engaged with the world around them" [3].

In the IT/ICT domain, the DIY culture has been adapted with the modern Internet technologies. For instance, YouTube (http://www.youtube.com) is a website that allows users to upload, publish and share their videos. Yahoo! Pipes (http://pipes.yahoo.com) is an application to help creating web-based applications through a graphical web interface. OpenChord (http://www.openchord.org) is an open source kit for interpreting the inputs from a regular or electronic guitar to computer commands.

We are required to design and implement an innovative DIY-enabled, ontology-based ambient computing environment. In particular, we use Semantic Decision Table (SDT) to manage evolving data semantics in a ubiquitous network.

R. Meersman et al. (Eds.): OTM 2010 Workshops, LNCS 6428, pp. 494–503, 2010.
© Springer-Verlag Berlin Heidelberg 2010

The paper is organized as follows. Section 2 is the paper background. Section 3 covers the discussions on how to use SDT and ORM in a DIY scenario for modeling data semantics. We represent the implementation in section 4. Section 5 contains the related work. In section 6, we conclude.

2 Background

The Developing Ontology Grounded Methodologies and Applications (DOGMA, [10]) applies the data modeling methods to ontology modeling. An ontology modeled in DOGMA has two layers: a lexon layer and a commitment layer.

A lexon is a simple binary fact type, which contains a context identifier, two terms and two roles. For instance, a lexon $\langle \gamma, teacher, teaches, is\ taught\ by, student \rangle$ presents a fact that "a teacher teaches a student, and a student is taught by a teacher", where "teacher" and "students" are two terms, "teaches" and "is taught by" are two roles. The context identifier γ points to a resource where "teacher" and "student" are originally defined and disambiguated.

A commitment (also called "ontological commitment") is an agreement made by a community (also called "group of interests"). It is a rule in a given syntax.

Table 1. An SDT on deciding whether a student studies or visits his friends

Condition				
Weather	Sunny	Sunny	Raining	Raining
Exam	Yes	No	Yes	No
Action				
Study	*		*	*
Visit friends		*		
SDT Commitments in DECOL				
1	P1=[Weather, has value, is value of, Value]: P1(Value)={Sunny, Raining}			
2	P2 = [Exam, has value, is value of, Value]: P2(Value) = {Yes, No}			
3	P3 = [Student, takes, is taken by, Exam]: MAND(P3)			
4	(P4 =[ENGINE, VERIFY, is verified by, Weather], P5 = [ENGINE, VERIFY, is verified by, Exam]): SEQ (P4(VERIFY, is verified by), P5(VERIFY, is verified by))			

Semantic Decision Table (SDT, [11]) is a decision table properly annotated with domain ontologies. It is modeled based on the DOGMA framework.

Table 1 is an SDT example. It contains a tabular presentation and an extra layer of commitments. We use a simple rule writing language called Decision Commitment Language (DECOL, [11]) to store the SDT commitments. It can be translated into a controlled natural language for the verbalization, and be published in an XML format.

A *graphical notation* for rule modeling is defined as a set of symbols for representing rule vocabulary and rules in concise and unambiguous manner [8]. Semantic Decision Rule Language (SDRule-L, [12]) is an extension to Object Role Modeling (ORM/ORM2, [5]). It contains a set of rich graphical notations for business rule modeling. We use it as the modeling means for DECOL. Note that the value range constraint and the mandatory constraint are reused from ORM/ORM2 (e.g., Commitments 1, 2 and 3 in Table 1). Its extensions to ORM/ORM are, for instance, cross-context subtyping and sequence.

The constraint of cross-context subtyping is used to populate the subtypes of a type when using SDT for ontology versioning. A detailed discussion can be found in [11].

The sequence is applied between conditions or between actions in an SDT, but not between a condition and an action. It tells the reasoner in which sequence it needs to validate the conditions or execute the actions. Fig. 1 shows an example.

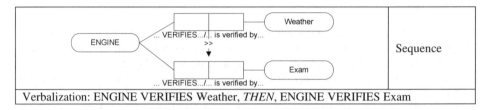

Verbalization: ENGINE VERIFIES Weather, *THEN*, ENGINE VERIFIES Exam

Fig. 1. Model Commitment 4 in Table 1 using SDRule-L

3   Use SDT to Manage Evolving Data Semantics

3.1   Design User-Friendly Decision Rules/Introduce New Concepts and Rules

The spreadsheet-style of decision tables is convenient for non-technical people to model procedural decision rules. An SDT, first of all, is a decision table. Therefore, it has the advantages of having a user-friendly presentation. As pointed out by Henry Bentz et al. [7], decision tables are an excellent tool as a medium of communication between technical and non-technical people. This is probably the biggest advantage.

In DIY-SE, there are three kinds of users – *professional* (e.g., technicians, engineers and experts), *semi-professional* (e.g., geeks and nerds) and *non-professional* (e.g., grandmothers and kids). A non-professional has the DIY needs. He/she knows the problem but probably does not know the solution. A professional has the technological abilities. He/she knows many solutions. A semi-professional has the abilities from both professional and non-professional. He/she probably does not know the problem or the technical solutions in depth. As he/she can play both roles, we will only discuss the roles of professional and non-professional in the rest of the paper.

Table 2. An SDT that decides whether to open the window or not

Condition	1	2	3	4	5	6
Weather	Sunny	Cloudy	Dark (night)	Sunny	Cloudy	Dark (night)
Air	Fresh	Fresh	Fresh	Dirty	Dirty	Dirty
Action						
Open window			*		*	*
Close window	*			*	*	
SDT commitment in DECOL						
1	P1 = [Weather, has, is of, Value]:P1(Value)={Sunny, Cloudy, Dark (night)}					
2	P2 = [Air, has, is of, Value]:P2(Value)={Fresh, Dirty}					

How we do is as follows: we first ask a non-professional to write down the problem. He/she has decision rules in mind, which are not in a tabular format, but in a natural language. For instance, he/she says "I want to sleep well, but I have a problem because I'm very sensitive to the lights. So if it is sunny, please close my window. I also want fresh air while sleeping, so if it is not sunny and the air in my room is not clean, then please open the window".

Then, a knowledge engineer (a professional) gets the requirements and designs an SDT as shown in Table 2. In order to design this SDT, he/she maybe need the graphical modeling support from SDRule-L. In the meanwhile, new lexons and concepts are collected at a local server. When some of the lexons/concepts appear several times, they will be uploaded to the ontology server for versioning.

At the end, the knowledge engineer passes the SDT to a technician (another professional), who installs the required ambient sets, e.g., a light sensor for the window and an automatic window handler, and implements the decision rules in the physical world. We will not discuss in detail as this process is out of the scope.

Note that SDRule-L and DECOL can also be translated into logical sentences. By doing so, readers can use many existing rule engines to reason the SDT commitments.

For instance, commitment 1 in Table 2 can be written in predicate logic as follows.

$$\forall x \forall y Value(x) \land Weather(y) \land has(y, x) \land isOf(x, y)$$
$$\rightarrow Sunny(x) \lor Cloudy(x) \lor DarkNight(x)$$

3.2 Cross Check Decision Rules/Audit Decision Rules

Suppose that we introduce a new SDT commitment to Table 2. The DECOL code is shown as below:

```
(P3 = [ENGINE, EXECUTE, is executed by, Open window],
P4 = [ENGINE, EXECUTE, is executed by, Close window]):
P_MAND_XOR (P3, P4).
```

This commitment written in predicate logic is illustrated as below.

$$\forall x \forall y \forall z ENGINE(x) \land OpenWindow(y) \land CloseWindow(z)$$
$$\rightarrow \neg \big(EXECUTES(x, y) \land EXECUTES(x, z)\big)$$

Or,

$$\forall x \forall y \forall z ENGINE(x) \land OpenWindow(y) \land CloseWindow(z)$$
$$\rightarrow EXECUTES(x, y) \lor EXECUTES(x, z)$$

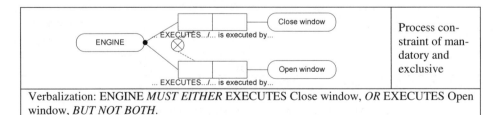

Verbalization: ENGINE *MUST EITHER* EXECUTES Close window, *OR* EXECUTES Open window, *BUT NOT BOTH.*

Fig. 2. Model Commitment 3 in Table 2 using SDRule-L

The graphical model and verbalization of this commitment is illustrated in Fig. 2.

The decision columns 2 and 5 in Table 2 are thus invalid because column 2 does not contain any actions and column 5 contains more than one action. The knowledge engineer then needs to modify Table 2. When more constraints are introduced, an SDT will contain more semantic information and we will have a more accurate implementation at the end.

Table 3. An SDT of deciding whether to study math or physics based on the previous exams

Condition	1	2	3	4	5	6	7	8
Previous exam – English	Y	Y	Y	Y	N	N	N	N
Previous exam – Chemistry	Y	Y	N	N	Y	Y	N	N
Previous exam – Math	Y	N	Y	N	Y	N	Y	N
Action								
Study math		*		*				
Study physics	*			*	*	*		
SDT commitment in DECOL								
1	(P1=[Person, has, is of, Previous exam], P2 = [Previous exam – English, is instance of, is, Previous exam], P3 = [Previous exam – Chemistry, is instance of, is, Previous exam], P4 = [Previous exam – Math, is instance of, is, Previous exam]): CARD (P1(has), <=2).							
2	P1=[Person, has, is of, Previous exam]: P1(Previous exam)={ Previous exam – English, Previous exam – Chemistry, Previous exam – Math}, CARD (P1(has), <=2).							

If conflicting rules are introduced by different knowledge engineers in the case one SDT had been designed by a group, then the group needs to have a formal agreement. This process is also called *ontological commitment process*.

Another example is to use the constraint of *occurrence frequency* to cross check the decision rules in an SDT. Suppose that we have an SDT shown in Table 3. There are two SDT commitments in Table 3. They are equivalent from the modeling perspective. The function CARD is taken from "cardinality". They can be graphically represented as in Fig. 3.

The SDT commitment 1 written in predicate logic is shown as follows.

$$\forall x \exists y \exists y' \exists y'' Person(x) \wedge PreviousExam(y) \wedge PreviousExam(y')$$
$$\wedge PreviousExam(y'')$$
$$\rightarrow \neg \left(Has\_exam(x,y) \wedge Has\_exam(x,y') \wedge Has\_exam(x,y'') \right)$$

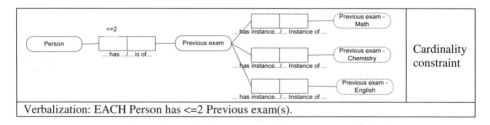

Verbalization: EACH Person has <=2 Previous exam(s).

Fig. 3. Model Commitment 1 or 2 in Table 3 Using SDRule-L

Note that the ontological commitment process results in a set of ontological commitments, which are uploaded to the ontology server for versioning.

Currently, we use the SDRule-L/DECOL constraints of uniqueness, mandatory, occurrence frequency, subset, equality, exclusion, value range, sequence, subtype, trans-context equality and trans-context subtyping for cross checking the rules.

3.3 Map Semantics to Data/Build a Component Network

In Ontology Engineering, instances are often stored together with an ontology. We separate instances from concepts for the following two reasons.

— We can achieve a higher level of *extensibility*. The ontology no longer needs to be updated when a new instance is introduced. We can save the efforts of ontology versioning.

— We can convert parts of the ontology into database schemas and use many existing powerful database engines to deal with the constraints. By doing so, the *performance* of the ontology-based system will be improved.

In DIY-SE, we have a data semantic server that deals with mapping and interpreting data from the heterogeneous databases. For example, the process information of a particular ambient environment is stored in such a database. When a new ambient object (also called an instance), i.e. a new window, is brought in, the server will have a problem of finding the proper map.

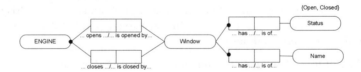

Fig. 4. An ORM-style SDRule-L model extended from Fig. 2

In order to solve this problem, we need to derive an ORM-style SDRule-L model from the previously designed SDRule-L model in order to deal with instances. Fig. 4 shows a model that is extended from Fig. 2. When a database engineer gets Fig. 4, he/she maps it into a database schema and implements it.

The database engineer (a professional) creates a database schema based on Fig. 4 as follows. He puts all the values of window in a table named "Window". As a window can be either open or closed, the data table contains a column of "Status", which contains NOT NULL values.

The data of a new window will be automatically inserted into the corresponding data table when we annotate it with the concept "Window" defined in the ontology.

When the knowledge engineers cannot find a type for an instance, they will need to first apply an ontology versioning method to introduce a new type.

3.4 Inspire New DIY Ideas/Regroup Decision Rules

In DIY-SE, the context of an SDT is specified with people, devices, events/tasks, time and location.

People are any group of human beings collectively. The group is specified with a common role that all the members play. A *device* is an instrument or equipment for a purpose. An event slightly differs from a task. An *event* is a set of circumstances or a phenomenon located at a single point in space-time. A *task* is defined as an execution path through spaces and time. A task in the field of management is often seen as a specific piece of work required to be done. Both task and event have the properties of space and time. *Time* is an identifiable instance or a period of a moment for some event. A *location* is a point or extent in space. It determines the place where an event that should happen or a task that needs to be executed.

Each context corresponds to a set of condition alternatives and action alternatives. New ideas can be inspired by merging several SDTs, or creating a new SDT based on the existing condition and the action alternatives in a same (or similar) context.

They can be created by the non-professional by simply selecting the decisional items from a context. The SDT engine takes the reasoning responsibly of checking the consistency. When they come up with some new rules that are not defined, the task of introducing new decision rules (section 0) will then be executed.

4   Prototype

We have been implementing a prototype in the existing SDT plug-in, which is a Java module integrated in the DOGMA Studio Workbench.

With regard to the decision table construction, we have developed a standalone module called Decision Table Constructor. It supports simple table editing functions.

Once a decision table is annotated with domain ontologies and the SDT commitments are properly built, we call it SDT. In order to support the paper idea, we have developed the following modules.

Module 1: Context Manager. The module is called DIBag (Decision Item Bag). A user uses it to specify a new context, introduce new condition and action candidates, and store the specification of a context in an XML file.

Module 2: Domain Ontology Manager. Users can browse/edit the concepts and lexon. The definitions of lexon terms can be visualized in TLex (graphs, [13]) or in SDT Term Dictionary (textual information). It contains a list of functions, including add lexons/definitions, set ontology/context, upload ontology to the remote DOGMA server, download ontology from the remote server, and, search dictionary/ontology. The lexons in the ontologies are grouped by their roles and visualized in a tree.

Module 3: Decision Item Annotator. With this module, users can annotate the decision items (such as the condition stubs and the action stubs and their sub items) with domain ontologies. For instance, we can annotate "People" from the condition stub "People move Ear" with the concept "Name" by creating a new lexon $\langle \gamma, People, has, is\,of, Name \rangle$. "OnProperty" is used to further explain this annotation. It means that "People" has a property of "Name".

Module 4: DECOL Editor. It supports users to write DECOL code without knowing their syntax. He/she can validate a combination of constraints, e.g., the mandatory constraint, by reading the automatically generated verbalization, e.g., "EACH Lamp has AT LEAST ONE Light".

We use *Decision Table Editor* to define user friendly decision rules (section 3.1). In order to cross check decision rules in SDTs (section 3.2), we use *DECOL Editor* and *SDT rule engine*. *Decision Item Annotator* is used to map semantics to data (section 3.3). The new DIY ideas are inspired with the assistance of *DIBag* and *Domain Ontology Manager* (section 3.4).

5 Related Work

ORM has been used as an ontology modeling tool right after the birth of DOGMA. NORMA tool [4] from Neumont University is a tool to support ORM2 notations.

Popular Ontology Engineering tools are Protégé from Stanford University [9], CoBrA from University of Edinburgh, CONE from VTT (Finland, [1]) and commercialized TopBraid composer[1]. Compared to them, ORM2 based T-Lex provides an excellent, easily controlled and community-based modeling feasibility.

Seeing that SDT is an extension to decision tables, the related work of SDT is second-order decision table [6] and fuzzy decision table [2, 14]. A second-order decision table uses second-order variables for condition entries. SDT does not specify whether the annotated decision table is a first order or a second order. A fuzzy decision table uses fuzzy logic to deal with the fuzziness of a condition entry. We do not deal with fuzzy logic, but specify the ambiguous condition entries by properly annotating them with domain ontologies.

In addition, SDT has the advantages of extensibility, formality, community-grounded, shareability and reasoning feasibility, which are brought forward by the modern Ontology Engineering technologies.

With regard to the related work of the SDT Editor, Corticon business rule modeler (http://www.corticon.com), IBM WebSphere Decision Table Editor (http://www-01.ibm.com/software/websphere/), JaretTable (http://www.jaret.de) and PROLOGA (http://www.econ.kuleuven.be/prologa/) are well known decision table editors. Corticon modeler supports users with online editing and browsing decision tables. IBM WebSphere DT Editor uses decision tables to generate program code. JaretTable is an open source editor written in Java SWT for managing projects and analyzing requirements. PROLOGA is a business rule modeling tool.

The approach to cross checking decision rules illustrated in this paper is to deal with the verification and validation (V&V) of the rules. The authors from [7] discuss how to how to deal with this issue based on a survey of the early papers on decision tables. Their V&V method is grounded on the semantics of basic mathematical operators. For instance, a decision table is considered inconsistent when it contains the conditions "X<=10" and "X<=20" at the same time, seeing that these two conditions are partly overlapped. In addition to the semantics of the basic mathematical operators, SDT takes one step further by using semantically rich ontological commitments.

6 Conclusion, Discussion and Future Work

In this paper, we have discussed how to use SDT to manage evolving data semantics in DIY environment. Our attempts of managing evolving data semantics are:

---

[1] http://www.topquadrant.com/products/TB_Composer.html (available on July 2, 2010)

- When we use SDTs to *design user friendly decision rules* based on the new requirements, the new lexons and concepts are collected and uploaded to the ontology server for versioning.
- When we *cross check decision rules* in (an) SDT(s), we often introducing some new meta-rules, which are considered as ontological commitments and are uploaded to the ontology versioning server.
- During the process of *mapping semantics to data*, new types will be introduced when the technicians cannot find a defined type of a smart component (an instance).
- When we *regroup decision rules*, new contexts are introduced. When the users have new inspired rules, they can introduce them as new SDTs. The new concepts will be formalized in the ontology of a newer version.

A decision rule is to formalize constraints and derivation rules in order to have a precise conclusion. SDT helps rule modelers to correctly capture the policies using their vocabulary. The purpose of using SDT can be further specified into 1) to control the updating of persistent stored decision rules and data; 2) to help implementing and updating the requirements in a tabular format; 3) to integrate the views from the non-professional and the professional by mapping the information between the requirement models and the desired computational models. These purposes are studied in this paper. We will continuously investigate on them in a broader context.

Acknowledgments. The work has been supported by the EU ITEA-2 Project 2008005 "Do-it-Yourself Smart Experiences", founded by IWT 459.

References

1. Aitken, S., Korf., R., Webber, B., Bard, J.: CoBrA: a Bio-Ontology Editor, PMID: 15513995 (2005), http://www.ncbi.nlm.nih.gov/pubmed/15513995
2. Chen, G., Vanthienen, J., Wets, G.: Using Fuzzy Decision Tables to build valid intelligent systems. In: Sixth International Fuzzy Systems Association World Congress (IFSA 1995), Sao Paulo, Brazil, July 22-28 (1995)
3. Frauenfelder, M.: Made by Hand: Searching for Meaning in a Throwaway World. Portfolio Hardcover (2010) ISBN-10: 1591843324, ISBN-13:978-1591843320
4. Curland, M., Halpin, T.: Model Driven Development with NORMA. In: Proc. 40th Int. Conf. on System Sciences (HICSS-40). CD-ROM, p. 10. IEEE Computer Society, Los Alamitos (2007)
5. Halpin, T.A.: Information Modelling and Relational Databases: From Conceptual Analysis to Logical Design. Morgan Kaufman Publishers, San Francisco (2001) ISBN-13: 978-1-55860-672-2, ISBN-10: 1-55860-672-6
6. Hewett, R., Leuchner, J.H.: The Power of Second-Order Decision Tables. In: Grossman, R.L., Han, J., Kumar, V., Mannila, H., Motwani(eds, R. (eds.) Proceedings of the Second SIAM International Conference on Data Mining (SDM 2002), Arlington, VA, USA, April 11-13. SIAM (2002) ISBN: 490-89871-517-2
7. Henry Beitz, E., Buck, N.H., Jorgensen, P.C., Larson, L., Maes, R., Marselos, N.L., Muntz, C., Rabin, J., Reinwald, L.T., Verhelst, M.: A modern appraisal of decision tables, a Codasyl report. ACM, New York (1982)

8. Lukichev, S., Jarrar, M.: Graphical Notations for Rule Modelling. In: Giurca, A., Gasevic, D., Taveter, K. (eds.) Handbook of Research on Emerging Rule-based Languages and Technologies: open solutions and approaches, vol. I, pp. 76–98. Information Science Reference,IGI Global (2009) ISBN978-1-60566-402-6
9. Noy, N.F., McGuinness, D.L.: Ontology development 101: A guide to creating your first ontology. Technical Report KSL-01-05, Knowledge Systems Laboratory, Stanford University, Stanford, CA, 94305, USA (2001)
10. Spyns, P., Tang, Y., Meersman, R.: An Ontology Engineering Methodology for DOGMA. In: Guizzardi, G., Halpin, T. (eds.) Journal of Applied Ontology, special issue on Ontological Foundations for Conceptual Modeling, vol. 3(1-2), pp. 13–39 (2008)
11. Tang, Y.: Semantic Decision Tables - A New, Promising and Practical Way of Organizing Your Business Semantics with Existing Decision Making Tools. LAP LAMBERT Academic Publishing AG & Co., Saarbrucken (2010) ISBN 978-3- 8383-3791-3
12. Tang, Y., Meersman, R.: SDRule Markup Language: Towards Modelling and Interchanging Ontological Commitments for Semantic Decision Making. In: Giurca, A., Gasevic, D., Taveter K. (eds.) Handbook of Research on Emerging Rule-based Languages and Technologies: Open Solutions and Approaches, vol. I, pp. 99–123. Information Science Reference, IGI Global (2009) ISBN978-1-60566-402-6
13. Trog, D., Vereecken, J., Christiaens, S., De Leenheer, P., Meersman, R.: T-Lex: a Role-based Ontology Engineering Tool. In: Meersman, R., Tari, Z., Herrero, P. (eds.) OTM 2006 Workshops. LNCS, vol. 4278, pp. 1191–1200. Springer, Heidelberg (2006)
14. Wets, G., Witlox, F., Timmermans, H., Vanthienen, J.: A Fuzzy Decision Table Approach for Business Site Selection. In: The Fifth IEEE International Conference on Fuzzy Systems, September 8-11, vol. 3, pp. 1605–1610 (1996) ISBN 0-7803-3645-3

Mapping ORM to Datalog: An Overview

Terry Halpin[1], Matthew Curland[2], Kurt Stirewalt[2], Navin Viswanath[2],
Matthew McGill[2], and Steven Beck[2]

[1] LogicBlox, Australia and INTI International University, Malaysia
[2] LogicBlox, USA
{terry.halpin,matt.curland,kurt.stirewalt,
navin.viswanath,matt.mcgill,steven.beck}@logicblox.com

Abstract. Optimization of modern businesses is becoming increasingly dependent on business intelligence and rule-based software to perform predictive
analytics over massive data sets and enforce complex business rules. This has
led to a resurgence of interest in datalog, because of its powerful capability for
processing complex rules, especially those involving recursion, and the exploitation of novel data structures that provide performance advantages over relational database systems. ORM 2 is a conceptual approach for fact oriented
modeling that provides a high level graphical and textual syntax to facilitate validation of data models and complex rules with nontechnical domain experts.
Datalog^{LB} is an extended form of typed datalog that exploits fact-oriented data
structures to provide deep and highly performant support for complex rules with
guaranteed decidability. This paper provides an overview of recent research and
development efforts to extend the Natural ORM Architect (NORMA) software
tool to map ORM models to Datalog^{LB}.

1 Introduction

In order to compete effectively in the information age, many businesses are exploiting
information technology as a way to promote efficiency and reduce costs. For example, business intelligence tools and rule-based software are being increasingly used to
perform predictive analytics over massive data sets and enforce complex business
rules. This has led to a resurgence of interest in *datalog*, because of its powerful capability for processing complex rules, especially those involving recursion. Moreover,
novel data structures such as column-oriented data stores are being exploited to provide performance advantages over relational database systems for complex analytics
and data warehousing tasks (http://en.wikipedia.org/wiki/Column-oriented_DBMS).

While datalog and related technologies are powerful, the effective use of them typically requires a considerable level of mathematical sophistication. This often results
in a communication gap when the business experts, who best understand the complex
business rules and queries needed for their business, attempt to validate that the
technical rules and queries used in the implementation actually conform to their requirements. This problem is best addressed by first formulating the models, rules and
queries at a conceptual level where they can be reliably validated with the business
domain experts, and then automatically transforming these high level constructs into
equivalent, lower level constructs (e.g. datalog code) for implementation.

R. Meersman et al. (Eds.): OTM 2010 Workshops, LNCS 6428, pp. 504–513, 2010.

This paper provides an overview of our recent research and development efforts to support such a model-driven engineering approach to business analytics. For the conceptual level, we use second generation *Object-Role Modeling* (*ORM 2*) [10]. Unlike attribute-based approaches such as Entity-Relationship (ER) modeling [5] and class diagramming within the Unified Modeling Language (UML) [22], ORM is *fact-oriented*, where all facts, constraints, and derivation rules may be verbalized naturally in sentences easily understood and validated by nontechnical business users using concrete examples. ORM's graphical notation for data modeling is far more expressive than that of industrial ER diagrams or UML class diagrams, and its attribute-free nature makes it more stable and adaptable to changing business requirements. Brief introductions to ORM may be found in [12, 15], a detailed introduction in [16], a thorough treatment in [18], and a comparison with UML in [14]. An overview of fact-oriented modeling approaches, including ORM and others such as RIDL [21], NIAM [23], and PSM [20], as well as history and research directions, may be found in [13].

For the datalog platform, we use $datalog^{LB}$, a vastly extended version of datalog developed by LogicBlox. Datalog^{LB} is a typed datalog [23] that employs fact-oriented data structures with performance benefits similar to those of column stores when processing very complex rules over vast data sets. For detailed coverage of traditional datalog, see [1, 6, 9]. Datalog^{LB} extends basic datalog with stratified negation, types, functions (including aggregate functions), transactions, modules (called "blocks"), constraints, default values, ordered predicates, metalevel support, and other features.

Early tool support for ORM introduced two textual languages. Formal ORM Language (FORML) was supported as an output verbalization language in InfoModeler and the ORM solution within Microsoft Visio for Enterprise Architects. Conceptual Query Language (ConQuer) enabled ORM models to be queried, and was implemented in the InfoAssistant and ActiveQuery tools [3, 4]. However, the ConQuer language was used only for formulating non-recursive ORM queries, not constraints or derivation rules, and tool support for it is no longer available.

Recently, ORM was extended to ORM 2, with tool support provided by Natural ORM Architect (*NORMA*) [8], including improved constraint verbalization in FORML 2 [17, 19] as well as further rule options such as semiderived types, deontic rules, and deep support for conceptual outer joins [18]. More recently, we developed a *role calculus* to formally capture derivation rules in ORM [7], and the VisualBlox team at LogicBlox has extended the NORMA tool to capture derivation rules and have also developed a VisualBlox tool to map ORM models to Datalog^{LB}.

Extensions to the NORMA tool allow ORM 2 derivation rules to be entered by clicking options in a Model Browser, and are then stored in a structure based on the role calculus, which offers a high level of semantic stability [7]. Compared to the ActiveQuery tool for ConQuer, NORMA's derivation support covers a wider range of rules (including recursion), has much better rule verbalization, and generates datalog code for implementation instead of SQL. While it is planned to add SQL generation for derivation rules at a later stage, our current efforts are focused on completing the datalog generation. NORMA's derivation language is designed to be relationally complete, and at the time of writing, about 90% of its constructs have been automatically transformed into Datalog^{LB}.

While the role calculus offers advantages such as compactness and semantic stability, its internal metamodel is technically challenging and its structures differ significantly from those of datalog or SQL. To simplify the task of transforming role calculus structures into target languages such as datalog and SQL, we first map the role calculus version of derivation rules to an intermediate structure based on the *domain relational calculus*, and then transform this second structure into the target code.

This paper provides a high level overview of some of this work, illustrating some of the mapping patterns by concrete examples. Discussion of the relevant metamodels and detailed transformation algorithms is beyond the scope of this paper, but portions of an early version of the role calculus metamodel may be found in [7].

The rest of this paper is structured as follows. Section 2 briefly illustrates how ORM object types, fact types, and constraints map to Datalog^{LB}. Section 3 discusses the basics of mapping ORM derivation rules map to Datalog^{LB}, including a rule for placing existential quantifiers. Section 4 considers some derivation rule examples involving use of scalar and aggregate functions. Section 5 summarizes the main results, outlines future research directions, and lists references.

2 Mapping ORM Object Types, Fact Types, and Constraints

In logic, an individual is a single thing of interest (e.g. a specific person, country, name, or number). An object in ORM corresponds to an individual in this sense. In first-order logic (FOL), predication is allowed only over individuals, not predicates, and quantification is allowed only over individual variables. First-order logic is undecidable, so there are some first-order formulas whose truth value can't be established by any algorithm. An algorithm to map ORM models into unsorted, first-order logic was provided by one of the authors in the late 1980s [10].

In the 1990s, the ConQuer query language for ORM was formalized in terms of sorted FOL, extended by a special operator for outer joins as well as set and bag comprehension [4]. Later, ORM 2 added modal operators to distinguish between alethic and deontic rules. Currently, deontic rules are ignored in mapping to datalog. While outer joins can be captured in NORMA derivation rules, their transformation to Datalog^{LB} awaits further work.

Datalog is designed for database work, and is a decidable fragment of first-order logic with powerful capabilities for storing, constraining, and deriving facts. As a logic programming language, datalog's support for recursive rules is more elegant and efficient than that provided by relational database systems. Unlike other logic programming languages such as Prolog, datalog programs are guaranteed to terminate.

Standard datalog uses prefix notation, with individual terms (individual variables or constants) listed in parentheses after the predicate name. In basic datalog, a *rule* is an expression of the form

$$q(\tau_1, ..., \tau_n) \leftarrow p_1(x_1, ...), ..., p_m(y_1, ...).$$

where the head predicate q has as argument an ordered list of individual terms $\tau_1, ... \tau_n$ ($n \geq 0$), each variable of which must occur in at least one argument of the body predicates $p_1 ... p_m$ ($m \geq 0$), the main propositional operator "$\leftarrow$" (read as "**if**") is the converse implication operator from logic, and a comma "," (read as "**and**") between predications is the logical conjunction operator. A predication (the application of a predicate to a list of variables or constants) is also known as an *atom* or *positive literal*. The head or the body may be empty (but not both). In classical datalog, a rule is treated as shorthand for a formula where the head variables are universally quantified at the top level, and any other variables introduced in the body are existentially quantified, with the existential quantifiers placed at the start of the body [1, p. 279]. For example, the following datalog rule

grandparentOf(x, y) $\leftarrow$ parentOf(x, z), parentOf(z, y).

is equivalent to the following FOL formula (using mixfix predicates)

$\forall x \forall y[x$ is a grandparent of $y \leftarrow \exists z(x$ is a parent of z & z is a parent of $y)]$.

Datalog adopts the closed world assumption (CWA), so if the same atom appears as the head of exactly n rules, the logical disjunction of the n rule bodies provides an if-and-only-if (iff) condition for the head. For example, the logical rule $\forall x \forall y[x$ is a parent of $y \leftarrow (x$ is a father of $y \lor x$ is a mother of $y)]$ may be set out in datalog as

parentOf(x, y) $\leftarrow$ fatherOf(x, y).
parentOf(x, y) $\leftarrow$ motherOf(x, y).

Datalog^{LB}, allows such *disjunctions* to be captured as a single rule, using a semicolon ";" for the inclusive-or operator. In Datalog^{LB}, "$\leftarrow$" is rendered as "<-" and no italics are used. So the above parenthood rule may be set out in Datalog^{LB} thus:

parentOf(x, y) <- fatherOf(x, y) ; motherOf(x, y).

Datalog extended with *negation* allows negated atoms (negative literals) in the body. Datalog^{LB} uses an exclamation mark "!" for the logical negation operator. An *anonymous variable* (denoted by an underscore "_" and read as "something") is used to existentially quantify a variable that is not referenced elsewhere in the formula (in which case the implicit existential quantifier has scope over only the atom in which the underscore occurs). For example, the derivation rule for living parents expressed as the FOL formula $\forall x[x$ is a living parent $\leftarrow (\exists y(x$ is a parent of $y)$ & ~ x died)] may be formulated thus:

livingParent(x) <- parentOf(x, _), !died(x).

Datalog^{LB} is a typed datalog, so each of its predicates is constrained to apply to a sequence of zero or more types. Object types are modeled in Datalog^{LB} as unary predicates. Entity types are directly supported, but value types are currently handled as implicit subtypes of the associated data type. Type declarations are specified as constraints, or "right-arrow" formulas, using "->" (read as "**implies**" or "**only if**") for the material implication operator. Entity types that are identified using reference modes are declared along with their reference modes, using a colon ":" in the variable list of the reference predicate. For example, Country(.code) maps to:

Country(x), country:code(x:y) -> string(y).

An ORM fact type corresponds to a set of one or more typed predicates. A Datalog^{LB} predicate represents exactly one ORM fact type, so qualified predicate names are often used to distinguish predicates that have the same predicate reading in ORM.

For example, the *m:n* predicates in Person runs Company and Horse runs Race may be declared respectively as follows:

```
person:company:runs(x, y) -> Person(x), Company(y).
horse:race:runs(x, y) -> Horse(x), Race(y).
```

If a fact type has a uniqueness constraint spanning *n*-1 roles, a square-bracket notation is used to indicate the functional nature of the predicate. For example:

```
person:birthcountry[p]=c -> Person(p), Country(c).
```

Additional uniqueness constraints need to be declared separately. Variable names may include letters and digits. For example, the ORM schema in Figure 1 may be declared in Datalog^{LB} as follows, using the functional predicate declaration style to capture the left-hand uniqueness constraint on the head of government predicate and a separate clause to capture the right-hand uniqueness constraint.

```
Politician(p), politician:name(p:n) -> Politician(p), string(n).
Country(c), country:code(c:cc) -> Country(c), string(cc).
politician:countryGoverned[p]=c -> Politician(p), Country(c).
politician:countryGoverned[p1]=c, politician:countryGoverned[p2]=c -> p1=p2.
```

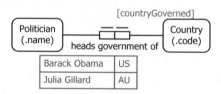

Fig. 1. A populated 1:1 ORM fact type

The above code is an example of a Datalog^{LB} program. Data files are declared separately using delta predicates. For example, the data population in Figure 1 may be declared using the following assertions, where the "+" indicates insertion (addition of a fact to a predicate's population). Facts may be retracted (using "−") or modified using other options.

```
+politician:countryGoverned["Barack Obama"] = "US".
+politician:countryGoverned["Julia Gillard"] = "AU".
```

To illustrate the benefits of Datalog^{LB} for capturing ORM constraints, consider the ORM schema shown in Figure 2(a), which is fragment of a larger schema discussed elsewhere [16]. Equivalent Datalog^{LB} code is shown in Figure 2(b). For discussion purposes, comments are inserted above the code for three constraints.

The mandatory role constraint that each book has a title is neatly expressed using an anonymous variable. The exclusion constraint that no book may be written and reviewed by the same person is also easily captured using negation. Finally, the acyclic constraint on the book translation predicate is enforced by introducing a recursively derived ancestor predicate and then declaring that to be irreflexive. This is much simpler than the equivalent SQL code, and also offers better performance.

(a)

(b)

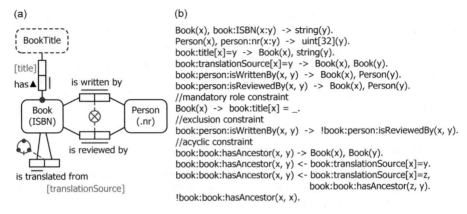

Book(x), book:ISBN(x:y) -> string(y).
Person(x), person:nr(x:y) -> uint[32](y).
book:title[x]=y -> Book(x), string(y).
book:translationSource[x]=y -> Book(x), Book(y).
book:person:isWrittenBy(x, y) -> Book(x), Person(y).
book:person:isReviewedBy(x, y) -> Book(x), Person(y).
//mandatory role constraint
Book(x) -> book:title[x] = _.
//exclusion constraint
book:person:isWrittenBy(x, y) -> !book:person:isReviewedBy(x, y).
//acyclic constraint
book:book:hasAncestor(x, y) -> Book(x), Book(y).
book:book:hasAncestor(x, y) <- book:translationSource[x]=y.
book:book:hasAncestor(x, y) <- book:translationSource[x]=z,
                                  book:book:hasAncestor(z, y).
!book:book:hasAncestor(x, x).

Fig. 2. (a) An ORM schema mapped to (b) Datalog^{LB}

3   Mapping Derivation Rules

The above acyclic constraint enforcement introduced a derived fact type under the covers. ORM users may also introduce derived fact types of their own, and have NORMA map these to Datalog^{LB}. For implementation, we first capture the derivation rules in a role-calculus based structure, and then transform this to an intermediate, domain relational calculus structure, from which the Datalog^{LB} code is generated.

Derivation rules may be used to derive either subtypes or fact types. The NORMA screenshot in Figure 3(a) includes two derived subtypes and one derived fact type. Figure 3(b) shows how the associated derivation rules are displayed in the Model Browser after being entered by selecting and clicking the relevant options.

(a)

(b)

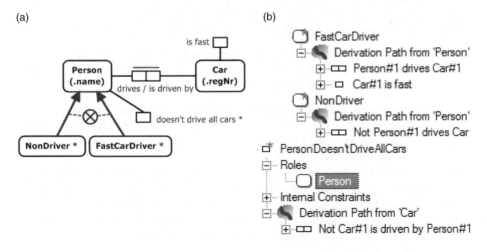

Fig. 3. NORMA screenshot of an ORM schema and its derivation rules

The derivation path for the subtype FastCarDriver starts with Person (the path root) and navigates via the drives predicate to Car and then onto the isFast predicate, performing a conceptual join on Car. NORMA generates the following verbalization for the derivation rule: ***Each** FastCarDriver **is some** Person **who** drives **some** Car **that** is fast. The role calculus form of the rule is translated to a named tree structure representing the following sorted, relational calculus formula $\{x{:}\text{Person} \mid \exists y{:}\text{Car}\ (x\ \text{drives}\ y\ \&\ y\ \text{is}\ \text{fast})\}$. This structure can be transformed into the following Datalog^{LB} rule by reducing sorted to unsorted logic and employing implicit quantification:

```
FastCarDriver(x) <- Person(x), Car(y), person:car:drives(x, y), car:isFast(y).
```

The derivation path for the NonDriver subtype starts with Person and then negates its entry into the drives predicate. This verbalizes as: ***Each** NonDriver **is some** Person **who** drives **no** Car. This maps to a named structure for the relational calculus formula $\{x{:}\text{Person} \mid \sim\exists y{:}\text{Car}\ (x\ \text{drives}\ y)\}$. VisualBlox generates the following Datalog^{LB} rule for this named structure: NonDriver(x) <- Person(x), !person:car:drives(x,_).

Figure 3 also includes the derived fact type in Person doesn't drive all cars. This is intended to return each person where there is at least one car not driven by that person. In this case, the derivation path starts with a car variable, and then uses negation to navigate to the person(s) who don't drive that car, and finally the derived role of Person is bound to that person variable. This verbalizes as: *Person doesn't drive all cars **if and only if for some** Car **it is not true that that** Person drives **that** Car.

A key aspect of generating the relational calculus version of the rule is knowing where to place existential quantifiers. Unprojected root variables are existentially quantified. Hence the derivation rule currently being discussed leads to the following relational calculus formula: $\{x{:}\text{Person} \mid \exists y{:}\text{Car} \sim x\ \text{drives}\ y\}$.

ORM is essentially a sugared, visual version of sorted logic, hence in ORM each variable that is projected is a typed variable. The act of projecting on a typed variable in the scope of a negation ensures that the type declaration for that variable is lifted outside the negation. As a more general approach that works also with unsorted relational calculus, we introduce the following *Existential Placement Rule (EP)*.

For each variable v that occurs only in the rule body, place $\exists v$ immediately before the minimal wff that contains all the v occurrences. Hence, if v occurs only inside a negation then place $\exists v$ immediately after the negation symbol.

For the current derivation rule, the unsorted relational calculus formula with implicit quantification is $\{x \mid \text{Person}\ x\ \&\ \text{Car}\ y\ \&\ \sim x\ \text{drives}\ y\}$. The only variable introduced in the rule body is y, and the minimal wff containing all its occurrences is Car y $\&\ \sim x$ drives y. Applying EP now yields $\{x \mid \text{Person}\ x\ \&\ \exists y(\text{Car}\ y\ \&\ \sim x\ \text{drives}\ y)\}$, which is equivalent to the sorted version given earlier. Using the Change of Scope rule $\exists v(p\ \&\ \Phi v).\equiv.\ p\ \&\ \exists v\Phi v$ where p is any wff in which v does not occur free, this now maps to the Datalog^{LB} code shown below. In contrast to our NORMA and VisualBlox implementation, the ActiveQuery tool [4], although dealing well with many tasks, fails to provide correct semantics for this rule when formulated as a query.

```
doesntDriveAllCars(x) <- Person(x), Car(y), !person:car:drives(x, y).
```

4 Functions

Figure 4 shows an ORM schema with two derived fact types. The FORML derivation rules involve a multiply operator and a sum function (both of these are treated as functions in NORMA). An earlier paper discussed how to capture these two rules in the role calculus [7]. We now discuss their transformation to Datalog^{LB}.

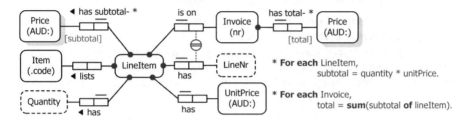

Fig. 4. Derivations involving a mathematical operator and aggregate function

The asserted fact types map in the usual way. Assuming a float32 data type for AUDValue, the subtotal derivation rule maps to a named version of the relational calculus expression: {*li*:LineItem, *st*:Float32 | $\exists q$:Quantity $\exists p$:AUDValue (*li* hasQuantity *q* & *li* hasUnitPrice *p* & *st* = *q* * *p*)}. This maps to the following predicate declaration and rule in Datalog^{LB}:

```
lineItem:subtotalValue[x]=y -> LineItem(x), float[32](y).
lineItem:subtotalValue[x]=y <- lineItem:quantity[x]=q, lineItem:unitPrice[x]=p, y=q*p.
```

The invoice total rule uses the subtotal rule, generating a named version of the following relational calculus expression: {*i*:Invoice, *t*:Float32 | *t* = sum{*st*:AUDValue | $\exists li$:LineItem (*li* is on *i* & *li* has subtotal value *st*)}}. Datalog^{LB} includes a function called "total" to sum over sets or bags of numeric values. This function may now be applied to the derived subtotal predicate to derive the invoice total predicate.

A special "agg" syntax is used for this as well as other aggregate functions (e.g. counts, minima and maxima). The type declaration and derivation rule for the invoice total is rendered by the following Datalog^{LB} code:

```
invoice:totalValue[x]=t -> Invoice(x), float[32](t).
invoice:totalValue[x]=t <- agg<< t=total(st) >> lineItem:invoice[li]=x, lineItem:subtotalValue[li]=st.
```

5 Conclusion

This paper provided a high level overview of our recent work to automatically transform ORM models, including derivation rules, to Datalog^{LB}, an extended version of datalog, using a sorted, relational calculus based structure as an intermediate format between the initial role calculus based source structure and the final Datalog^{LB} code. A general procedure was introduced for placement of existential quantifiers in the intermediate structure to ensure that the desired semantics are achieved. To assist

512   T. Halpin et al.

readers unversed in datalog, we have used simple, concrete examples to illustrate the main ideas. In practice, rules of far greater complexity are supported.

As future research, we plan to cater for Datalog^{LB} derivation rules that are not yet supported in NORMA and VisualBlox. For example, in Datalog^{LB} heights may be ordered using a meta-predicate and the top ranking function may then be used to return the top r height values via the following rule.

heightRank:heightVal[r]=hv <- agg<<hv = top[r](y)>> height:cmValue(_:y).

By adding high level support for such rules, we hope to empower nontechnical users to exploit the expressive power of Datalog^{LB}.

We also plan to extend our ORM-to-Datalog^{LB} conversion to 100% coverage, add support for dynamic rules [2], and extend both ORM and our mapping procedures to exploit new features being added to Datalog^{LB} (e.g. existential variables in rule heads).

Acknowledgment. The assistance of our LogicBlox colleague Martin Bravenboer in providing helpful feedback on related work is greatly appreciated.

References

1. Abiteboul, S., Hull, R., Vianu, V.: Foundations of Databases. Addison-Wesley, Reading (1995)
2. Balsters, H., Halpin, T.: Formal Semantics of Dynamic Rules in ORM. In: Meersman, R., Tari, Z., Herrero, P. (eds.) OTM-WS 2008. LNCS, vol. 5333, pp. 699–708. Springer, Heidelberg (2008)
3. Bloesch, A., Halpin, T.: ConQuer: a conceptual query language. In: Thalheim, B. (ed.) ER 1996. LNCS, vol. 1157, pp. 121–133. Springer, Heidelberg (1996)
4. Bloesch, A., Halpin, T.: Conceptual queries using ConQuer-II. In: Embley, D.W. (ed.) ER 1997. LNCS, vol. 1331, pp. 113–126. Springer, Heidelberg (1997)
5. Chen, P.P.: The entity-relationship model—towards a unified view of data. ACM Transactions on Database Systems 1(1), 9–36 (1976)
6. Colomb, R.: Deductive Databases and their Applications. Taylor & Francis Ltd., London (1998)
7. Curland, M., Halpin, T., Stirewalt, K.: A Role Calculus for ORM. In: Meersman, R., Herrero, P., Dillon, T. (eds.) On the Move to Meaningful Internet Systems: OTM 2009 Workshops. LNCS, vol. 5872, pp. 692–703. Springer, Heidelberg (2009)
8. Curland, M., Halpin, T.: The NORMA Tool for ORM 2. In: Pernici, B. (ed.) Advanced Information Systems Engineering. LNCS, vol. 6051, Springer, Heidelberg (2010)
9. Garcia-Molina, T., Ullman, J., Widom, J.: Database Systems: The Complete Book, 2nd edn. Pearson, London (2009)
10. Halpin, T.: A Logical Analysis of Information Systems: static aspects of the data-oriented perspective, doctoral dissertation, University of Queensland. Available as an 18 MB bitmap pdf file at (1989), http://www.orm.net/Halpin_PhDthesis.pdf
11. Halpin, T.: ORM 2 On the Move to Meaningful Internet Systems. In: Meersman, R., Tari, Z., Herrero, P. (eds.) OTM-WS 2005. LNCS, vol. 3762, pp. 676–687. Springer, Heidelberg (2005)

12. Halpin, T.: ORM/NIAM Object-Role Modeling. In: Bernus, P., Mertins, K., Schmidt, G. (eds.) Handbook on Information Systems Architectures, 2nd edn., pp. 81–103. Springer, Heidelberg (2006)
13. Halpin, T.: Fact-Oriented Modeling: Past, Present and Future. In: Krogstie, J., Opdahl, A., Brinkkemper, S. (eds.) Conceptual Modelling in Information Systems Engineering, pp. 19–38. Springer, Berlin (2007)
14. Halpin, T.: A Comparison of Data Modeling in UML and ORM. In: Khosrow-Pour, M. (ed.) Encyclopedia of Information Science and Technology, . Information Science Reference, Hershey PA, USA 2 edn. vol. II, pp. 613–618 (2008)
15. Halpin, T.: Object-Role Modeling. In: Liu, L., Tamer Ozsu, M. (eds.) Encyclopedia of Database Systems, Springer, Berlin (2009)
16. Halpin, T.: Object-Role Modeling: Principles and Benefits. International Journal of Information Systems Modeling and Design 1(1), 32–54 (2010)
17. Halpin, T., Curland, M.: Automated Verbalization for ORM 2. In: Meersman, R., Tari, Z., Herrero, P. (eds.)On the Move to Meaningful Internet Systems 2006 OTM 2006 Workshops. LNCS, vol. 4278, pp. 1181–1190. Springer, Heidelberg (2006)
18. Halpin, T., Morgan, T.: Information Modeling and Relational Databases, 2nd edn. Morgan Kaufmann, San Francisco (2008)
19. Halpin, T., Wijbenga, J.: FORML. In: Bider, I., et al. (eds.) Enterprise, Business-Process and Informa-tion Systems Modeling. LNBIP, vol. 50, pp. 247–260. Springer, Heidelberg (2010)
20. ter Hofstede, A., Proper, H., van der Weide, T.: Formal definition of a conceptual language for the description and manipulation of information models. Information Systems 18(7), 489–523 (1993)
21. Meersman, R.: The RIDL Conceptual Language, Int. Centre for Information Analysis Services, Control Data Belgium, Brussels (1982)
22. Object Management Group UML 2.0 Superstructure Specificatio (2003), http://www.omg.org/uml
23. Wintraecken, J.: The NIAM Information Analysis Method: Theory and Practice. Kluwer, The Netherlands (1990)
24. Zook, D., Pasalic, E., Sarna-Starosta, B.: Typed Datalog. In: Gill, A., Swift, T. (eds.) PADL 2009. LNCS, vol. 5418, pp. 168–182. Springer, Heidelberg (2009)

Subtyping and Derivation Rules in Fact-Based Modeling

Peter Bollen

School of Business and Economics
Maastricht University, the Netherlands
p.bollen@maastrichtuniversity.nl

Abstract. In this paper we will reflect on the derivation rule modeling concept and we will investigate how the definition of derivation rules is related to the subtypes and the subtype defining fact types in a conceptual schema. We propose the concept of 'derivation-logic induced' classifying fact types and what advantages this can have in terms of the creation and maintainability of conceptual schemas.

Keywords: Derivation rule, Subtyping, Classification fact type, ORM, Fact-based modeling.

1 Introduction

In fact-based- and other conceptual modeling languages, the modeling concept of derivation rule is used frequently to denote how attribute-, fact- or relationship instances can be 'derived' from 'base' or 'asserted' instances (e.g. see [1, 2]). The derivation logic that underlies a given derived fact type can range from a simple (attribute style) rule [1][1]:

For each Article
  Markup=retailPrice-wholesalePrice

To a more complex derivation in which (multiple) conditional clauses and branches of derivation logic might be contained:

For each Article
  If Productcategory= 'leisure'
  Then retailPrice = wholesalePrice * 1.4
  Else retailPrice= AVG(wholesaleprice) + 0.55

A fact-based information structure diagram contains all fact types that are of interest for a given subject domain together with population constraints and derivation rules defined on the roles of those fact types. The arithmetic derivations (step 3 in the conceptual schema design procedure (CSDP)) and logical derivations (step 5 in the CSDP) are added to the information structure diagram after the basic fact types are

---

[1] We refer to [3] for a role calculus notational convention to specify derivation rules.

R. Meersman et al. (Eds.): OTM 2010 Workshops, LNCS 6428, pp. 514–521, 2010.
© Springer-Verlag Berlin Heidelberg 2010

modeled (step 2 in the CSDP [1]). The derivation logic that governs the derivation of the instances of the derived fact types, therefore is phrased as a derivation rule that is defined on the asserted- and/or (other) derived fact types in the information structure diagram [1].

Subtyping [1, 4-6] is used in fact-based modeling: '..to declare that one or more roles are played only by a given sub-type.'[1, p.280]. In the ORM-CSDP the subtypes are derived in step 6 [1]. This means that subtypes are added after arithmetic derivations and logical derivations have been added to the information structure diagram.

In Halpin and Morgan [1] a specialization procedure is given as part of step 6 in the ORM CSDP. This procedure basically investigates each optional role in the information structure diagram and from there on tries to determine whether such an optional role is recorded only for a specific known subtype. This specialization procedure will lead to the possible detection of derived, asserted or semi-derived subtypes. In case subtypes are derived a (subtype) classifying fact type can be added to the information structure diagram and (a) subtype defining derivation rule(s) is (are) added to the conceptual schema.

In this paper we will show how the fundamental 'derivation logic' in an application domain can point at the existence of a 'derivation-logic induced classification', that might differ from the classification derived from 'regular' subtypes because this classification will not be recognized as such by the specialization procedure.

In section 2, we will introduce the running example for this paper. In sections 3 and 4, we will give two equivalent sets of derivation rules for the same application domain. In section 5 we will show how the derivation rules and a classifying fact type can be adapted whenever the derivation-logic changes. In section 6 we will introduce derivation rules that explicitly use classifying fact type(s). Finally in section 7 conclusions will be drawn and recommendations for future research will be given.

2 The Order, Freight and Transportation Example

The running example in this paper is a small example of business orders that contain freight and transportation costs of a fictitious ABC company. Consider the real-life examples (or 'data use cases') that make up the universe of discourse in figure 1.

The ABC company has two types of order documents. The document ad23 is the document that is used for domestic orders. The document ad26 is used for overseas customers. The difference is in the requirement of an explicit listing of freight and shipping cost on the ad26 document. Furthermore the ABC company has a VAT-tariff list (document ad24). The basic information model for this universe of discourse is given in figure 2. The interesting feature of this example UoD, lies in the distinction between *domestic* and *overseas orders* which follow from the application of the specialization procedure (SP) [1] The information model in figure 2 is a complete model for the static part of the UoD. However, the situation in which every instance of a derived fact type can be found by applying one derivation rule for all derived fact types at all times seems not to apply here.

ABC COMPANY ad23			
ORDER: *5678*			
ITEM	**PRICE**	**QUANTITY**	**TOTAL**
ab101	*12,50*	*8*	*100,--*
ab102	*5,00*	*7*	*35,--*
ab167	*8,00*	*3*	*24,--*
		VAT	*25,90*

	Order Total		*184,90*

ABC COMPANY ad26			
ORDER: *8912*			
ITEM	**PRICE**	**QUANTITY**	**TOTAL**
ab101	*12,50*	*4*	*50,--*
ab102	*5,00*	*7*	*35,--*
		VAT	*13,50*
Freight and Shipping cost			*7,50*

	Order Total		*106,00*

ABC COMPANY ad 24	
ITEM	**VAT-%**
ab101	*20*
ab102	*10*
ab167	*10*

Fig. 1. Order, Freight and Transportation example

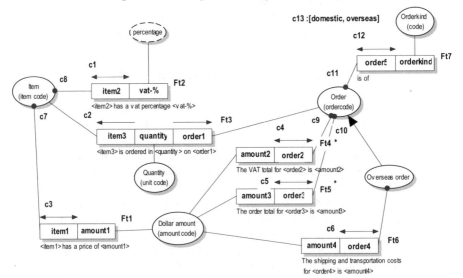

Fig. 2. ORM information structure diagram Freight and Transportation example using the overseas order subtype[2]

---

[2] We have chosen to include derived fact types in our information structure diagram or conceptual schema [7, p. 7].

In sections 3 and 4 we will give two examples of sets of derivation rules that can potentially be used in combination with the information structure diagram in figure 2 to arrive at a complete conceptual schema for the UoD.

3   The Definition of Derivation Rules

We will now give two sets of derivation rules referring to the derived fact types in the basic information model (denoted with * in figure 2). In the first set of derivation rules we need three different rules to capture the derivation process-semantics in our UoD.

3.1   Derivation Rule Set 1

It follows from mandatory role constraints $c9$ and $c10$ in the information structure diagram of figure 2, that at all times an *order total* fact instance and *vat amount* fact instances must be derived for an order. However, the derivation logic for the *order total* is dependent upon the specific type that an order instance has: domestic versus overseas.

Subtype defining derivation rule:
Each overseas order **is an** order that is of orderkind < > domestic

Derivation rule Dr1:

For each Order
    Order.amount2=SUM(Order.Item.quantity * Item.amount1 * Item.vat %)/100

Derivation rule Dr2:

For each Order
    Order.amount3=SUM(Order.Item.quantity * Item.amount1) + Order.amount2

Derivation rule Dr3:

For each Order
    Order.amount3=SUM(Order.Item.quantity * Item.amount1) + Order.amount2 +
               Order.amount4

In a conceptual schema for our example Universe of Discourse (UoD) the 'derivation semantics' in the UoD could be fully captured by incorporating all three derivation rules into the ORM conceptual schema. For any order instance exactly one of the following derivation rules sub-sets will be applicable: (DR1, DR2), (DR1, DR3). In the fact-based conceptual schema in figure 2 it is not possible to link this derivation logic precisely to the 2 derived fact types Ft4 and Ft5. The only way to model this until now was to create two distinct derived fact types for the order total: one for *domestic* orders (Ft5) and one for *overseas* orders (Ft8) (see figure 3).

In the ORM information structure diagram of figure 3 we now have a one-on-one mapping of the derivation rules Dr1 (onto fact type Ft4), Dr2 (onto fact type Ft5) and Dr3 (onto fact type Ft8). Conceptually, however the content of the information structure diagram in figure 3 is redundant because it contains 2 fact type representations for the 'order total' fact type.

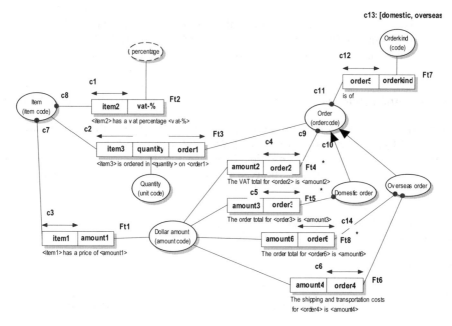

Fig. 3. ORM information structure diagram Freight and Transportation example using overseas order and domestic order subtypes

4   Derivation-Logic Induced Classification Fact Types

One of the modeling improvements that were made in fact-based modeling in the early eighties was the introduction of the sub-typing modeling concept [4]. By incorporating explicit sub-types in a conceptual schema it was possible to define additional typing constraints in the conceptual schema for roles played by instances of the specific sub-type [1]. This greatly improved the completeness of fact-based conceptual schemas.

So far, we have been considering derivation rules, merely as rules that specify *how* an instance of a derived fact type can be created when the instances of the ingredient fact types are known. In such a definition it is possible that multiple derivation rules can be defined for the same 'derived' fact type. The only limitation is that only one rule can be executed to derive one specific fact instance. The question then becomes '*under what condition*' a specific derivation rule among a set of derivation rules (e.g. (DR2, DR3)) will be executed.

If we inspect the ORM information structure diagram of our example application, there is only one derived subtype of *order* namely: *overseas order*. After we have 'discovered' this subtype, all other roles in which order play a role have mandatory role constraints attached to them. In order to establish a one-on-one mapping between derived fact types in the conceptual schema and the derivation logic we need to use classifying fact types in which not only traditional subtype classifications will be contained but also 'derivation-logic' induced classifications.

Having the classifying fact types of sub-types explicitly recorded in a fact-based conceptual schema might actually point at incorporating the relevant 'under what condition' knowledge into a derivation rule itself by using the sub-type classifying fact type as an 'ingredient' fact type for the derivation rule. By explicitly using the sub-type classifying fact-type Ft7 we could define the derivation rules *Dr21* and *Dr22* that could be mapped one-on-one to the derived fact types Ft4 and Ft5 (in figure 2) as follows:

Derivation rule Dr21:

For each Order
    Order.amount2=SUM(Order.Item.quantity * Item.amount1 * Item.vat %)/100

Derivation rule Dr22:
For each Order
    if Order.orderkind= 'domestic'
    then (Order.amount3=SUM(Order.Item.quantity*Item.amount1) + Order.amount2)
    else (Order.amount3=SUM(Order.Item.quantity*Item.amount1) + Order.amount2
      +Order.amount4)

We note that derivation rules Dr21, Dr22 are equivalent in terms of derivation logic to the derivation rules Dr1, Dr2 and Dr3 in section 3. The main advantage of derivation rules Dr21 and Dr22 is that they map one-on-one onto the derived fact types Ft4 and Ft5 in the information structure diagram in figure 2. In order to elegantly phrase the derivation rule Dr22 in terms of the underlying derivation logic we could use the 'sub-type' defining or (to put it more general) the classifying fact type Ft7 directly in the IF clause from derivation rule Dr22.

5   Adapting a Classification Fact Type Based upon an Adapted Derivation Logic

To illustrate the effect of the 'derivation-logic induced' classification we will adapt our running example with a change in regulations in which a third 'category' of orders is distinguished having a different 'derivation logic' for the order total.

A new business rule would state that overseas shipments that use air transportation would be billed with an additional surcharge per order item of 20 dollars. This rule would increase the number of different 'derivation logics' for the order total from 2 to three. However, the adapted classification of order into: *domestic, overseas air, overseas boat* allows us to maintain the conceptual clarity in the conceptual schema in which the derived subtype (overseas order) will stay. This would lead to the conceptual schema in figure 4.

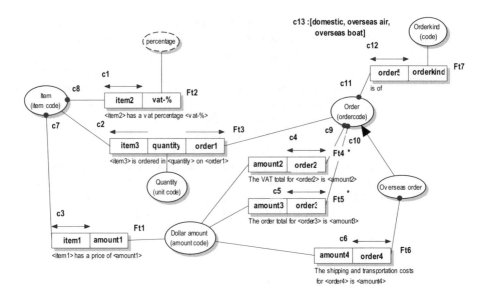

Fig. 4. ORM information structure diagram Freight and Transportation example having adapted values for classifying fact type Ft7

Each overseas order **is an** order that is of orderkind < > domestic

For each Order
　Order.amount2=SUM(Order.Item.quantity * Item.amount1 * Item.vat %)/100

For each Order
　if Order.orderkind= 'domestic'
　then (Order.amount3=SUM(Order.Item.quantity*Item.amount1) + Order.amount2)
　else if Order.orderkind = 'overseas air'
　　then (Order.amount3=SUM(Order.Item.quantity*Item.amount1) + Order.amount2
　　　+Order.amount4 + (SUM(Order.Item.quantity)* 20)
　　else (Order.amount3=SUM(Order.Item.quantity*Item.amount1) + Order.amount2
　　　+Order.amount4)

6   Conclusions and Recommendations

In this paper we have shown, that the application of classifying fact types within the context of subtyping should be extended to the context of derivation rules as well. This could be done by extending the specialization procedure [8] for a difference in derivation semantics, thereby using a classifying fact type that can explicitly be used in the definition of (non-subtype defining) derivation rule(s). We have also shown that (a) the 'derivation-logic induced' classifying fact type(s) can coincide with the sub-type classifying fact type(s). If the classifications do not coincide or can not be generalized into the same (set of) classifying fact type(s) we simply add (an) additional classifying fact type(s) for the 'under what condition' question when multiple 'derivation logics' are applicable for the derived fact type.

References

1. Halpin, T., Morgan, T.: Information Modeling and Relational Databases; from conceptual analysis to logical design, 2nd edn. Morgan-Kaufman, San Francisco (2008)
2. Hoffer, J., Prescott, M., McFadden, F.: Modern database management, 7th edn. Pearson/Prentice-Hall (2005)
3. Curland, M., Halpin, T., Stirewalt, K.: A role calculus for ORM. In: ORM 2009, Springer, Vilamoura (2009)
4. Vermeir, D.: Semantic hierarchies and abstractions in conceptual schemata. Information Systems 8, 8 (1983)
5. Halpin, T., Proper, E.: Subtyping and polymorphism in object-role modelling. Data & Knowledge Engineering 15, 251–281 (1995)
6. Halpin, T.: Subtyping Revisited. In: Halpin, T. (ed.) EMMSAD 2007, Academic Press, Trondheim (2007)
7. Halpin, T.: Object-Role Modeling: an overview (2001),
   http://www.orm.net/pdf/ORMwhitePaper.pdf
8. Halpin, T.: Information Modeling and Relational Databases; from conceptual analysis to logical design. Morgan Kaufmann, San Francisco (2001)

Information Grammar for Patterns (IGP) for Pattern Language of Data Model Patterns Based on Fully Communication Oriented Information Modeling (FCO-IM)

Fazat Nur Azizah[1], Guido P. Bakema[2], Benhard Sitohang[1], and Oerip S. Santoso[1]

[1] School of Electrical Engineering and Informatics, Bandung Institute of Technology
Jln. Ganesha no. 10, Bandung, Indonesia
{fazat,benhard,oerip}@stei.itb.ac.id
[2] Faculty of Engineering, Institute of Information Technology, Media and Communication,
HAN University of Applied Sciences
Ruitenberglaan 26, 6802 CE, Arnhem, The Netherlands
guido.bakema@han.nl

Abstract. The use of patterns in a design process, including data modeling, is an attempt to create a better solution to a problem. We propose the use of data model patterns, organized in a pattern language, and based on Fully Communication Oriented Information Modeling (FCO-IM) as the modeling approach, as a standard to produce high quality data models. We introduce the concept of Information Grammar for Pattern (IGP) which works as a kind of template to generate FCO-IM's Information Grammar (IG). IGP is also used to define the relations among patterns. Based on how they are abstracted, we also define 3 types of IGP. The IGP provides the basic idea for the pattern language of data model patterns based on the relations among patterns.

Keywords: data model pattern, pattern language, FCO-IM, IGP, IG.

1 Introduction

The use of patterns in a design process, including data modeling, is an attempt to create a better solution that is reusable for more than one instantiation of a problem. It is generally accepted that creating a high quality data model is not an easy task. This problem can be reduced if data modelers are acquainted with standards which ensure that the data models both meet business needs and be consistent [15]. Data model patterns are expected to become such standard in data modeling.

Most current works on data model patterns focus on providing data model patterns, especially the so-called domain-specific data model patterns, using either Entity Relationship Modeling (ERM) or Object Oriented Modeling (OOM) (see e.g. [6]-[10], [14]). In this research, we propose the use of conceptual data model patterns organized in a pattern language as a standard to produce high quality conceptual data models. We use the concept of pattern and pattern language by Christopher Alexander [1],[2] with Fully Communication Oriented Information Modeling (FCO-IM) [5], one of fact

R. Meersman et al. (Eds.): OTM 2010 Workshops, LNCS 6428, pp. 522–531, 2010.

oriented modeling (FOM) method, as the modeling approach. It is expected that the use of FCO-IM will give more insights and provide a more powerful concept for the data model patterns and the pattern language. A preliminary work on data model patterns based on FCO-IM can be found in [3]. In our proposal, the pattern language is used to generate an FCO-IM conceptual data model which is also called the *Information Grammar (IG)*.

2 The Concept of Data Model Pattern

Our definition of data model pattern is based on classical definition of pattern by Christopher Alexander. According to Alexander, each pattern is a three-part rule, which expresses a relation between a certain context, a problem, and a solution [1]. Thus, we define: a *data model pattern* (π) is a triplet consisting of *problem* (P), *context* (C), and *solution* (S); each applies to a pattern:

$$\pi \equiv (P, C, S) \tag{1}$$

According to [1] and [2], a *problem* (P) describes the intent of the pattern, i.e. the goals/objectives that it wants to reach within a *context* (C) as well as a system of forces which is required to be balanced by a *solution* (S). In an FCO-IM based conceptual data model patterns, the goal is in general to provide an IG (FCO-IM conceptual data model) which works for particular situations (*context*). *Context* (C) defines a set of situations in which the *problem* (P) recurs and the *solution* (S) is desirable. In an FCO-IM based conceptual data model patterns, it defines a set of situations in which a particular data modeling problem recurs.

Solution (S) is the configuration that balances the system of forces in order to achieve the intent within the given *context* (C). In FCO-IM based conceptual data model pattern, we employ a kind of *template* to produce FCO-IM IG that can solve the problem within a given context. An IG stores in type level the facts related to a specific UoD [9]. In other words, it stores a higher level of abstraction of the facts. The template to produce FCO-IM IG stores an even higher level of abstraction of the fact types stored in IGs. We call this template as *Information Grammar for Pattern (IG_P)*. This template will not contain only the template to generate IG, but also the rules to generate other patterns. See section 3 for further explanation on the IG_P.

The *solution* contains other elements which are used to give further explanation about the IG_P. They are called *rationale* and *resulting context*. *Rationale* is used to explain how the IG_P can be used to achieve the intent of the pattern by balancing the system of forces, while the *resulting context* is used to explain the consequences that follow the application of the pattern.

Problem, context, and *solution* are the main elements of a conceptual data model pattern. There are other elements that support the description of a conceptual data model pattern: *example, known uses*, and *name*. *Example* and *known uses* of conceptual data model patterns are other elements that provide clearer description of the pattern by giving instances of the application of the pattern. While *example* explains in full detail how a pattern is used in a typical case (it can be a real or a made-up case), *known uses* explain real world cases in which the problem is found. Every pattern must be given a *name* that embodies the knowledge described within the pattern. It is used to introduce a pattern and to give the first glimpse of what the pattern might be.

We introduce the concept of *pattern category*. Some data model patterns with the same problem characterizations are grouped together into a *category*. We defined 4 pattern categories as shown in Table 1. Table 1 also shows the data model patterns which belong to each category. Some brief descriptions on several of these patterns can be found in [4]. Pattern G4P1 is created based on our work described in [12].

Table 1. List of pattern categories and related data model patterns

Pattern Category	Data Model Pattern	
	Code	**Name of Pattern**
Code: G1 Patterns on the identification of an object	G1P1	Single Identification Pattern
	G1P2	Recursive Identification Pattern
	G1P3	Set Identification Pattern
	G1P4	Generalized Identification Pattern
	G1P5	Synonymy Pattern
	G1P6	Homonymy Pattern
	G1P7	Subtype Pattern
Code : G2 Patterns on collection of objects	G2P1	Graph Pattern
	G2P2	Sequence Pattern
	G2P3	Parent-Child Pattern
Code : G3 Patterns on the relation between two objects	G3P1	Attribute Pattern
	G3P2	Mapping Pattern
	G3P3	Assembly-Part Pattern
	G3P4	Supertype-Subtype Pattern
Code : G4 Patterns on the architecture of the objects	G4P1	Viewpoints to A Dataset Pattern

3   Information Grammar for Pattern (IG$_P$)

Information Grammar for Pattern (IG$_P$) is the central element of the *solution* of a pattern and therefore, its structure is required to be explored. As in IG, IG$_P$ is mainly presented in text format. New notations are introduced in addition to FCO-IM notations (see [5]).

3.1   New Notations

Table 2 lists the new notations used in IG$_P$. Consider the following example of an IG$_P$ of Single Identification Pattern (code G1P1, see Table 1):

```
(object)

[F1 : "There is a|an (object) [<(object-id-
1#1)|(G1#1)>[ <(object-id-2#2)|(G1#2)>]*."

O1 : '(object) <(object-id-1#1)|(G1#1)>[ <(object-id-
2#2)|(G1#2)>]*'

UC1 : "(object) is uniquely identified by <(object-id-
1#1)|(G1#1)>[[,] <(object-id-2#2)|(G1#2)>]*."
```

Table 2. List of notations in IG_P

No.	Notation	Meaning
1.	(x#a)	x can be replaced by a term or can be a pattern to be generated, or pattern category from which a pattern of the category can be chosen to be generated. a is the number of role or the alias of the role in which the term, pattern, or pattern category must be generated. #a is optional.
2.	[α]	α is generated 0 or 1 time.
3.	[α]*	α is generated 0 or n times.
4.	[α]+	α can be generated 1 or n times.
5.	{α}	α generates the members of a set.
6.	α‖β	Either α or β are to be generated and can be both.
7.	α|β	Either α or β are to be generated, but not both.

Information stated in the example is the following:

- Terms to be replaced with meaningful terms from the UoD are object, object-id-1, and object-id-2.
- F1 are optional. It means that it can appear in the resulting IG or can be omitted. The IG_P will be equipped with notes when to use or to omit the fact type expressions.
- Patterns of category G1 are expected to be generated according to the roles mentioned.

An IG_P is equipped with a diagrammatic version of it. The concept of the diagram is also based on the concept of FCO-IM Information Grammar Diagram (IGD). The diagram of IG_P is called the IG_P Diagram (IG_PD). We add the following symbols from the concept of IGD:

- Dashed-lined boxes or lines to indicate that something can be generated or not.
- Double-lined boxes to indicate that the pattern or term inside it must be generated.

The corresponding IG_PD for the IG_P example is shown in Fig. 1.

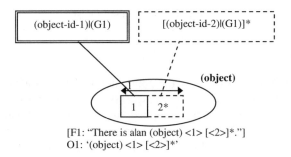

[F1: "There is a/an (object) <1> [<2>]*."]
O1: '(object) <1> [<2>]*'

Fig. 1. An example of an IGPD

3.2 Types of IG$_P$

The IG$_P$ stores an abstracted form of IGs by doing parameterization on some parts of the IGs to form the IG$_P$. Thus, the concept of IG$_P$ is closely related to the concept of IG. Based on the parts abstracted, we define 3 types of IG$_P$: type 0 IG$_P$, type 1 IG$_P$, and type 2 IG$_P$.

3.2.1 Type 0 IG$_P$

Type 0 IG$_P$ parameterizes only the population (concrete examples) of IGs. It means that the user of the pattern with type 0 IG$_P$ is required to put concrete examples of a UoD in order to create an IG to the UoD. Type 0 IG$_P$ provides already the structure of the IG that is ready to be used as a model.

An example of a type 0 IG$_P$ is as the following:

```
Name of Product
F1 : "The name of product <Product : O1> is <product
name>".
O1 : "product <product code>"
UC1 : "Name of Product is uniquely identified by
Product."
UC2 : "Product is uniquely identified by product code."
```

A type 0 IG$_P$D will look exactly like an FCO-IM IGD without the population part. The IG$_P$D for the above example is shown in Fig. 2.

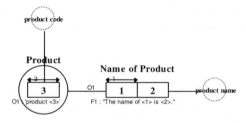

Fig. 2. An example of IG$_P$D

3.3 Type 1 IG$_P$

Type 1 IG$_P$ parameterizes not only the population of IGs, but also some parts of Fact Type Expression (FTE), Object Type Expression (OTE), or Label Type Expression (LTE) of an IG. When the pattern is applied, the parameterized parts of FTE, OTE, or LTE can be replaced with some terms appropriate for the UoD by the users. Once these terms are given, it works just as type 0 IG$_P$ in which the population can be placed in order to form a complete IG.

An example of a type 1 IG_P is as the following:

```
Name of (object)
F1 : "The name of <(object) : O1> is <(object-name)>".
O1 : '(object) <(object-id)>'
UC1 : "Name of (object) is uniquely identified by
(object)."
UC2 : "(object) is uniquely identified by (object-id)."
```

The corresponding IG_PD for the IG_P is shown in Fig. 3.

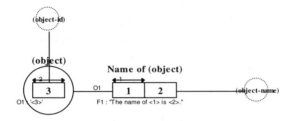

Fig. 3. IG_PD for 'Name of (object)' example

The bold parts (which also are inside brackets) are the parts of the FTE, OTE, and LTE as well as constraints that are required to be replaced by specific terms when the pattern is used. A type 1 IG_P contains a set of fact types and constraints in which some terms within the fact types and constraints are required to be defined further. The model is structurally correct, but semantically not meaningful. Thus, the user needs to provide the correct terms in order to deliver a meaningful IG.

The result of the assignment of the specific terms into the type 1 IG_P is a type 0 IG_P. For example, we can create the following type 0 IG_P based on the IG_P:

```
Name of Person
F1 : "The name of <Person : O1> is <person name>".
O1 : "person <person id>"
UC1 : "Name of Person is uniquely identified by
Person."
UC2 : "Person is uniquely identified by person id."
```

We can put some concrete examples to the IG_P in order to get a complete IG that is ready to be used to resolve the problem to model the name of a person.

3.3.1 Type 2 IG_P

Type 2 IG_P parameterizes not only the population and some parts of FTE, OTE, or LTE, but also a whole FTE, OTE, or LTE. The FTE, OTE, or LTE are replaced by applying other pattern(s). In this way, type 2 IG_P provides the relation between patterns. The position in which a pattern should be generated can be replaced by a pattern category. This means that one of the patterns in the category can be generated.

An example of a pattern called Attribute Pattern (code G3P1, see Table 1) is as the following:

```
(attribute) of (object)
F1 : "(attribute) of <(G1#1)> is <(attribute's-
name)|(G1#2)>."
UC1 : "(attribute) of (object) is uniquely identified
by (G1#1)."
[UC2 : "(attribute) of (object) is uniquely identified
by (attribute's name)|(G1#2)."]
[TC1 : "All (G1#1) must have (attribute) of (object)."]
[TC2 : "All (G1#2) must have (attribute) of (object)."]
```

The bold parts of the IG$_P$ are the parts on which the user of the pattern must replace it with something. Some parts such as (attribute) and (object) must be replaced by some terms appropriate for a certain UoD. So, they work just as type 1 IG$_P$. Nevertheless, other parts must be replaced by generating other patterns. In this case, for example: (G1#1) shows that a pattern from category G1 must be generated in order to create an object type that plays role #1 of fact type F1.

The corresponding IG$_P$D is shown in Fig. 4.

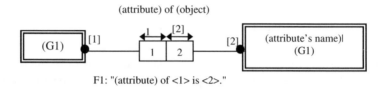

F1: "(attribute) of <1> is <2>."

Fig. 4. IG$_P$D of Attribute Pattern

An example of the use of the pattern is the following:

```
Gender of Person
F1 : "Gender of <Person : O1> is <Gender : O2>."
Person
F2 : "There is a person <firstname> <surname>."
O1 : 'person <firstname> <surname>'
Gender
O2 : '<gender-name>'
UC1 : "Gender of Person is identified by Person."
UC2 : "Person is uniquely identified by firstname,
surname."
UC3 : "Gender is uniquely identified by gender-name."
TC1 : "All Person must have Gender of Person."
TC2 : "All Gender must have Gender of Person."
```

The fact type 'Gender of Person' is generated from Attribute Pattern, while the nominalized fact type (object type) 'Person' and 'Gender' are generated from a pattern from category G1 called Single Identification of Pattern (code G1P1, see Table 1). UC1, TC1, and TC2 is generated from Attribute Pattern, while UC2 and UC3 are generated from Single Identification Pattern.

4   A Pattern Language of Conceptual Data Model Patterns

IG$_P$ provides the basic idea for the pattern language because it contains the parts that are required to be "generated". It can be a term, or a pattern, or a category of pattern (from which a pattern must be chosen to be applied).

We use formal grammar theory [11] to define our pattern language. A formal grammar G is formed by the following quad-tuple:

$$G = (V, T, P, S) \tag{2}$$

in which: V is a finite set of variables; T is a finite set of terminals; P is a finite set of productions; and S is the starting symbol in which $S \in V$. A language L(G) is defined as the language that can be generated by grammar G.

Applying the theory to data model patterns, we have the following definitions of the elements of the grammar for the pattern language:

1. *Variables (V)*: consists of a starting symbol (D), the data model patterns and a category of patterns (usually denoted by the codes of the pattern or the category), etc.
2. *Terminals (T)*: consists of the final terms to be generated in an IG$_P$.
3. *Productions*: the rules to generate a language over the variables and terminals.
4. *Starting symbol*: denotes a valid string that can be generated by the grammar. It is indicated with the variable D.

The productions are defined based the IGp. The translation from IG$_P$ notations to productions are shown in Table 3.

Table 3. Translation from IG$_P$ notations to Productions

No.	Notation	Productions	No.	Notation	Productions
1.	(α)	$\rho \to \alpha$	6.	[(β)]*	$\rho \to \varepsilon \mid \beta+$ $\beta+ \to \beta \mid \beta\ \beta+$
2.	(α) (β)	$\rho \to \alpha\ \beta$	7.	(α) [(β)]+	$\rho \to \alpha\ \beta+$ $\beta+ \to \beta \mid \beta\ \beta+$
3.	(α) [(β)]	$\rho \to \alpha \mid \alpha\ \beta$	8.	[(β)]+	$\rho \to \beta+$ $\beta+ \to \beta \mid \beta\ \beta+$
4.	[(β)]	$\rho \to \varepsilon \mid \beta$	9.	X ‖ Y	$\rho \to X\ Y \mid X \mid Y$
5.	(α) [(β)]*	$\rho \to \alpha \mid \alpha\ \beta+$ $\beta+ \to \beta \mid \beta\ \beta+$	10.	X ∣ Y	$\rho \to X \mid Y$

Consider the example of IG$_P$ in section 3.1.3. Suppose the code of the pattern is G3P1, then some of the productions based on the IG$_P$ are as the following:

```
G3P1 → attribute object G1 attribute's-name | attribute
object G1 G1
G1 → G1P1 | G1P2 | G1P3 | G1P4 | G1P5 | G1P6 | G1P7
```

G1 is a category of pattern in which pattern with the code G1P1, G1P2, G1P3, P1P4, G1P5, G1P6, and G1P7 belong to (see again Table 1). There will be other productions based on these patterns as well which we exclude in this discussion for conciseness.

5 Conclusions

In this paper, we present the concepts of Information Grammar for Pattern (IG$_P$) and its position within the concept of data model pattern as well as how a pattern language can be formed based on the concept of IG$_P$. The concept of IG$_P$ is based on the concept of Information Grammar (IG) in FCO-IM. These results provide the foundation for a new approach in data modeling using FCO-IM as the modeling approach in which standards of best practices in modeling is put forward. The use of such standards is expected to provide more high quality conceptual data models which provide better supports to organization's activities.

We have carried out some experiments to test the quality of the IGs resulting from the use of pattern language of data model patterns on several case studies. The quality are measured based on 3 aspects: *syntactic quality*, *semantic quality*, and *pragmatic quality* [13]. These experiments will be a subject for another paper.

Further research can be carried out to test whether the new methodology provide a more efficient and effective way of modeling in comparison to traditional way of modeling. Based on the concepts, we can also create a CASE (Computer Aided Software Engineering) tool which will help the use of the pattern language of data model patterns in data modeling activity.

References

1. Alexander, C.: The Timeless Way of Building. Oxford University Press, USA (1979)
2. Appleton, B.: Pattern and Software: Essential Concepts and Terminology,
   http://www.cmcrossroads.com/bradapp/docs/patterns-intro.html
   (accessed on 19/04/2006)
3. Azizah, F.N., Bakema, G.: Data Modeling Patterns using Fully Communication Oriented Information Modeling (FCO-IM). In: ORM Workshop 2006 (part of OnTheMove Federated Conferences and Workshops 2006), working papers, Montpellier, France (2006)
4. Azizah, F.N., Bakema, G.P., Sitohang, B., Santoso, O.S.: Generic Data Model Patterns using Fully Communication Oriented Information Modeling (FCO-IM). In: Proceeding in International Conference on Electrical Engineering and Informatics ICEEI 2009, Kuala Lumpur, Malaysia (August 2009)
5. Bakema, G., Zwart, J. P., van der Lek, H.: Fully Communication Oriented Information Modeling (FCO-IM), The book can be downloaded for free in (2002),
   http://www.casetalk.com/php/index.php?FCO-IM%20English%20Book
6. Coad, P., North, D., Mayfield, M.: Object Models: Strategies, Patterns, and Applications. Prentice Hall, Englewood Cliffs (1997)
7. Fowler, M.: Analysis Patterns Reusable Object Models. Addison Wesley, Reading (1996)
8. Gamma, E., Helm, R., Johnson, R., Vlissides, J.: Design Patterns: Elements of Reusable Object oriented Software, 1st edn. Addison-Wesley Professional, Reading (1995)
9. Hay, D.C.: Data Model Patterns: A Convention of Thought. Dorset House Publishing, New York (1996)
10. Hay, D.C.: Data Model Patterns: A Metadata Map. Morgan Kaufmann Publishers, San Fransisco (2006)

11. Hopcroft, J.E., Motwani, R., Ullman, J.D.: Introduction to Automata Theory, Languages, and Computation, 2nd edn. Addison Wesley, Reading (2001)
12. Liem, I., Azizah, F.N.: Metadata Approach in Modeling Multi Structured Data Collection Using Object Oriented Concepts. In: Proceeding in International Conference on Networking and Information Technology ICNIT 2010, Manila, Philippines (June 2010)
13. Lindland, O. I., Sindre G., Solvberg A.: Understanding Quality in Conceptual Modeling. IEEE Software (March 1994),
    http://csdl.computer.org/dl/mags/so/1994/02/s2042.pdf
    (accessed on 14/7/2008)
14. Silverston, L.: The Data Model Resource Book: Revised edn., vol. 1,2. John Wiley & Sons Inc., Chichester (2001)
15. West, M.: Developing High Quality Data Models;
    http://www.matthew-eest.org.uk/documents/princ03.pdf
    (accessed on 04/07/2008)

Literacy and Data Modeling

Ron McFadyen and Susan Birdwise

University of Winnipeg, Winnipeg, Manitoba, Canada
r.mcfadyen@uwinnipeg.ca
University of Manitoba, Winnipeg, Manitoba, Canada
s.birdwise@mts.net

Abstract. Reading and assimilating information in documents is a necessity of modern life. Literacy was once considered to be just the ability to read and write; but the term has evolved today to mean the ability to understand and employ printed information in daily activities, at home, at work and in the community. As used today, literacy involves many scales including prose, document, and quantitative; literacy testing involves the completion of several tasks designed for each scale. What is of interest to us here is the concept of document literacy and how that fits into the development of an information model. When developing an information system the data analyst designs a conceptual schema using a process such as the Conceptual Schema Development Process. In this paper we focus on non-continuous matrix documents as known for document literacy and their counterparts in Object-Role Modeling's conceptual model.

Keywords: document literacy, matrix documents, lists, object-role model.

1 Introduction

At one time being literate meant being able to read and write. Literacy is seen to be an important factor when it comes to the economic well-being of individuals and countries. Many surveys have been run and continue to be run to assess literacy levels. As such the meaning of literacy has evolved; the definition given by the International Adult Literacy Survey (IALS) [1] is

> *Literacy is using printed and written information to function in society, to achieve one's goals, and to develop one's knowledge and potential.*

For measurement purposes, the IALS considers 3 scales for measuring literacy: prose, document and quantitative. Documents are classified as: continuous (prose) or non-continuous text. Continuous documents typically comprise sentences structured into paragraphs and organized with typographic features such as headings and indentation to signal the organization of the text. Non-continuous documents (e.g. tables, graphs, charts, forms) explicit certain typographic features to organize information in a matrix structure. This view of documents has been used in many literacy surveys [2].

Modern literacy surveys comprise a number of tasks where the participant is presented with some information and must answer a question that will be evaluated for

R. Meersman et al. (Eds.): OTM 2010 Workshops, LNCS 6428, pp. 532–540, 2010.

correctness. Tasks and documents are derived from a broad range of contexts such as: home and family, health and safety, community and citizenship, consumer economics, work, leisure and recreation. For the purpose of assessing the complexity of survey tasks document types are considered to be of increasing complexity: 1 for simple lists, 2 for combined lists, 3 for intersecting lists and 4 for nested lists. Other factors related to document and task complexity are discussed in [3].

Non-continuous texts are organized differently than continuous texts and so allow the reader to employ different strategies for entering and extracting information from them. On the surface, these texts appear to have many different organizational patterns or formats, ranging from tables and schedules to charts and graphs, and from maps to forms.

The matrix structure of non-continuous text is covered in a series of articles [4], [5], [6], [7] by Mosenthal and Kirsch. In this series they present an organizational structure for non-continuous documents based on the elementary notion of a list. Four basic structures are developed: simple list, combined list, intersected list, and nested list. Together, these four types of documents comprise *matrix* documents. Matrix documents have clearly defined rows and columns. Continuing in this series Mosenthal and Kirsch discuss other documents such as graphic, locative, and entry documents and how they relate to matrix documents.

Object-Role Modeling (ORM) is an approach to data modeling that views the world in terms of *objects* (things) playing *roles* (parts in relationships). Other popular approaches include entity-relationship modeling [10] and UML-based modeling [11]. From an object-role model one can develop an entity-relationship model, a unified modeling language model, and/or a relational database [12].

As discussed in [13] ORM begins with a multi-step process called the Conceptual Schema Development Process (CSDP). CSDP prescribes the analyst begin a conceptual design with data use cases that involve data used by the system under development. These data use cases involve familiar examples of information output by, or input to, the information system.

In this paper we examine this organizing structure of documents and present mappings of these structures to an object-role model. In the following section we present the organizing structure of documents developed by Mosenthal and Kirsch. Then we briefly discuss ORM, followed by a description of how to transform knowledge of documents to ORM constructs. Finally, we present our summary and suggest areas of further research.

2   The Study of Documents

There are four types of increasingly complex matrix documents: simple lists, combined lists, intersecting lists, and nested lists. We will refer to this representation as the Literacy Model for documents. The simple list is the basic unit upon which the others are built.

As the Literacy Model has its origins in educational research and as it is used in evaluating literacy, it would be expected that an education curriculum would involve such an approach. Hence, students could arrive at university with this viewpoint. We would also expect that a data analyst should have no trouble understanding this viewpoint.

However, it may be easy for a professional to underestimate the readability of various document forms or the comprehension of the same by others. Kirsch reports [3] many university students (approximately 40%) including graduate students have significant difficulty grasping the most complex type, nested lists.

The *simple list* [4] comprises a label and a set of items. The label identifies the nature of the items, and the items belong to the grouping identified by that label. The association or connection between label and list items may be shown vertically or horizontally. Figure 1 (based on an example in [8]) shows a list organized vertically with the label *Provinces* and 5 items.

Provinces
Alberta
British Columbia
Manitoba
Ontario
Quebec

Fig. 1. A Simple List

Each simple list leads to a predicate or statement of meaning. For example, for the Provinces list we can make statements: *Alberta is a province*, and *British Columbia is a province*. For each simple list we can construct a *document sentence* that describes an item relative to the label, e.g. *X is a province*.

Simple lists tend to be lists that identify persons, places, or things; these lists are called *subject* lists. Other simple lists are referred to as *modifying* lists; these serve to qualify objects in some way in a subject list. Modifying lists are typically arranged with subject lists to form combined lists.

Combined lists [5] comprise a title and two or more simple lists where each list has the same number of items. When two or more simple lists are placed together and ordered in a similar fashion, the resulting combined list is richer in information than the constituent lists separately. In a vertically-oriented combined list, we find not only a vertical connection between list item and label, but also between items in one list and items on the same row of other ordered lists. By convention the first list determines the ordering of the other lists and is referred to as the subject list; but of course this is not mandatory. Figure 2 shows a combined list (appears in [8]) comprising four lists (Provinces, Pig Population, Farmland, and Human Population) ordered by province.

The connection between items in any row of a combined list is one of *predication*. Predication adds details to a subject. In the table shown, each item in the row adds information about a province. A number of sentences can be constructed from one combined list using the subject-predicate model. For example: *Newfoundland has a pig population of 5,000* or *Ontario supports a human population of 10.76 million*. The document sentence would be the conjunction of such statements: *The province W has a pig population of X, has Y hectares of farmland, and supports a human population of Z million*. In Figure 2, the subject list is Provinces and the other lists are modifying lists.

Provinces	Pig Pop x 1,000	Farmland x 1,000 ha	Human Pop x 1,000,000
Newfoundland	5	35	0.55
Prince Edward Island	118	259	0.13
Nova Scotia	133	397	0.91
New Brunswick	84	375	0.74
Quebec	3,410	3,430	7.14
Ontario	3,330	5,451	10.76
Manitoba	1,869	7,724	1.14
Saskatchewan	907	26,855	0.91
Alberta	2,115	20,811	2.70
British Columbia	213	2,392	3.73

Fig. 2. A combined list

The third type of document is the *intersected list* [6] that comprises exactly three simple lists in its basic form. There are two intersecting lists and one intersected list. One of the intersecting lists holds row labels, the other list holds column labels. If we were looking at a typical conference program like the one in Figure 3 (appears in [8]), we see a list of locations intersecting with a list of times. The cells at the intersection of these two lists comprise a third list of presentations. A particular presentation occurs at the intersection of a time in the times list and a location in the locations list.

In Figure 3 we can consider the intersected list the subject list and that the intersecting lists contain the modifying information. However this is not always the case.

The fourth and most complex type of matrix document is the *nested list* [7] which in its basic form consists of four simple lists combined appropriately. The basic nested list comprises an intersected list, two intersecting lists, and one simple list nested within an intersecting list. In order to economize on space, as well as to display comparative information, designers sometimes arrange lists to form a nested list structure. Figure 4 (appears in [9]) illustrates the sightings of ring-necked pheasants. We say that seasons are *nested* within states and so the seasons are repeated for each state item.

Time	Locations			
	Regency	**Colonial**	**Oak**	**Centennial**
09:00	Household pets equal business opportunities.	New developments in animal medicine.	Hookworms and your ferret.	Training and using guard cats.
10:30	Feline angst; truth or fiction?	Avoiding hip dysplasia in large breed dogs.	Raising pythons for fun and profit.	Communicating with pet owners and their pets.
13:00	The contented hamster: a focus on environment.	Pet nutrition in stressful times.	The essential of running an obedience school.	The well-tended salt water aquarium.
14:30	Postpartum: caring for queen and kittens.	Selling additional grooming for small dogs.	Canine arrhythmia in older dogs.	Financing of horribly expensive pet surgery.

Fig. 3. An intersected list

Year	Washington		New York	
	Spring	**Fall**	**Spring**	**Fall**
1938	30	100	3200	6585
1939	90	425	4679	8594
1940	300	825	7896	9253
1941	600	1520	8509	10,376
1942	1325	1900	9502	10,939

Fig. 4. A nested list

Figure 4 has one nested list; of course, a document could contain more than one level of nesting and in either rows or columns. It is left as an exercise for the reader to consider Figures 3 and 4 and how the same information would appear in combined lists.

Other document categories [3] such as pie charts, bar charts, time lines, and locative documents (maps) contain visual features that help to display quantitative information. An entry document is a form used for supplying data. On the surface these other document categories appear to be very different from matrix documents, but they can all be shown as derivable from combined, intersected, or nested lists and assigned a complexity rating accordingly.

3 Object-Role Modeling (ORM)

Our discussion of ORM is limited here; if necessary the reader is referred to [13] for more detail. ORM views the world in terms of *objects* (things) playing *roles* (parts in relationships). To determine these objects and roles, the ORM methodology recommends *data use case* analysis. A data use case is an example of how data is used, such as in an output report or a data entry form. It is expected that relationships existing in data will be expressed in natural language sentences. From such statements, and with objects replaced by ellipsis, the ORM analyst constructs *verbalizations*. Verbalizations express the semantic relationship of objects and the roles they play. ORM uses diagrams to express verbalizations in graphical format. For example, consider that a report leads us to express the verbalizations:

Province ... supports a human population of ...
Province ... has a pig population of ...

Then we can equivalently express these in diagram form as shown in Figure 5.

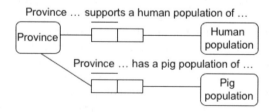

Fig. 5. An object-role model

Bars above a role box express a uniqueness constraint; in this case that a province instance has associated with it exactly one human population value, and also, one pig population value. The interested reader is referred to [13] for more details. We give further examples in our next section on the transformation of structured documents to an object-role model.

4   From Document Structures to Information Modeling

Documents are an important source of information pertinent to the development of an information model. In this section we consider that an analyst understands structured documents as given for the Literacy Model defined in [3], [4], [5], [6], [7], and we consider how this understanding maps to ORM constructs.

With ORM objects of interest are not divided into different categories (e.g. entity/attribute in ERM or class/attribute in UML), and so we say that an object-role model is attribute-free. Because of this we can map a document to an object-role model, whereas one cannot directly map a structured document to an ER or UML model unless you make further assumptions or have knowledge of how to map labels to entities or classes. Because of the attribute-free nature of ORM, Mosenthal's and Kirsch's classification of documents is easily adapted.

Transforming documents known as simple lists, combined lists, intersected lists or nested lists to object-role models follows the general principles:

1. A document sentence becomes an ORM verbalization: A document sentence is expressed with variables representing the various lists. These variables are simply changed to ellipses in an ORM verbalization. For example, the document sentence *The province W has a pig population of X, has Y hectares of farmland, and supports a human population of Z million* becomes *The province ... has a pig population of ..., has ... hectares of farmland, and supports a human population of ... million.*
2. Labels become object types: A label describes or identifies a list of similar items. These labels then can be used as the names of object types in an object-role model.
3. Document predicates become roles: Lists are related through predicates expressed in document sentences. These predicates define the roles in an object-role model.
4. A list L with labels $L_1, L_2, \ldots L_n$ and document sentence S maps to the basic ORM construct in Figure 6 where v represents the list's verbalization. This basic construct may be modified as discussed later.
5. The document is the source for any fact or object populations.

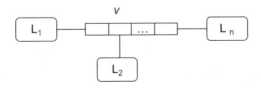

Fig. 6. Transformation of a list to an object-role model

4.1 Simple List

The transformation for Figure 1 is simple and shown in Figure 7.

Fig. 7. Transforming a simple list

4.2 Combined List

The initial transformation for Figure 2 is shown in Figure 8. Note that Provinces is a subject list which leads to a uniqueness constraint based on Province. The ORM construct is broken down into elementary facts; in ORM terminology the model is *splittable*, and we obtain the model in Figure 9. More detail on splittable models is found in [13].

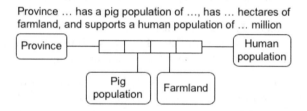

Fig. 8. Initial transformation of the combined list

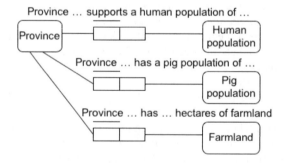

Fig. 9. Model splits into elementary facts

4.3 Intersected List

The basic intersected list implies a uniqueness constraint involving the intersecting lists. Consider Figure 3 where we have two intersecting lists, Times and Locations. Figure 10 shows the transformation to an object-role model. It is left to the reader to consider if there are other uniqueness constraints that apply.

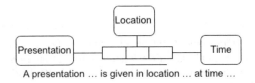

A presentation ... is given in location ... at time ...

Fig. 10. An object-role model for an intersected list

4.4 Nested List

The nested list is a variation on an intersected list and so the considerations for uniqueness apply again but with the inclusion of the nested list(s). The transformation of Figure 4 is shown in Figure 11.

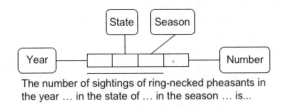

The number of sightings of ring-necked pheasants in the year ... in the state of ... in the season ... is...

Fig. 11. A nested list as an object-role model

5 Summary

In this paper we have reviewed a document modeling approach that has its origins in educational and literacy research. A student of literacy who has studied document structure from a reading comprehension perspective has a view of documents based on the notion of a simple list and combinations thereof. Because ORM is attribute-free it is relatively straightforward to represent matrix documents as object-role models.

The Literacy Model can be leveraged to instruct students in data modeling. We are not aware of any database or analysis text that discusses data modeling in the context of the Literacy Model. We are currently examining the use of the Literacy Model to introduce students to data modeling. This includes more comprehensive examples for combined, nested and intersected lists and with various uniqueness constraints.

Literacy surveys measure the complexity of tasks based on two elements: the complexity of the document and the complexity of the processing model for a given document. In subsequent work we intend to explore the processing model and its relationship to conceptual query languages such as Conquer [14] and Constellation Query Language [15].

Acknowledgments. The authors thank the referees for their constructive comments.

References

1. Kirsch, I.S.: The International Adult Literacy Survey (IALS): Understanding What was Measured, Research Report, Educational Testing Service, Princeton, NJ (2001)
2. Group, P. E.: PIAAC Literacy: A Conceptual Framework. OECD Education Working Papers, No. 34, OECD Publishing (2009)
3. Mosenthal, P.B., Kirsch, I.S.: A New Measure For Assessing Document Complexity: The PMOSE/IKIRSCH Document Readability Formula. Journal of Adolescent and Adult Literacy 41(8), 638–657 (1998)
4. Mosenthal, P.B., Kirsch, I.S.: Lists: The Building Blocks of Documents. Journal of Reading 33(1), 58–60 (1989)
5. Mosenthal, P.B., Kirsch, I.S.: Building Documents by Combining Simple Lists. Journal of Reading 33(2), 132–135 (1989)
6. Mosenthal, P.B., Kirsch, I.S.: Intersecting lists. Journal of Reading 33(3), 210–213 (1989)
7. Mosenthal, P.B., Kirsch, I.S.: Nested Lists. Journal of Reading 33(4), 294–297 (1990)
8. Evetts, J., Gauthier, M.: Literacy Task Assessment Guide. National Literacy Secretariat, Human Resources and Skills Development Canada. (2005),
   http://www.ibd.ab.ca/files/
   Literacy-task-assessment-guide.pdf
9. Mosenthal, P.B., Kirsch, I.S.: Information Types in Nonmimetic Documents: A Review of Biddle's Wipe-Clean Slate. Journal of Reading 34(8), 654–660 (1991)
10. Chen, P.: The Entity-Relationship Model - Toward a Unified View of Data. ACM Transactions on Database Systems 1(1), 9–36 (1976)
11. Booch, G., Rumbaugh, J., Jacobson, I.: The Unified Modeling Language User Guide, 2nd edn. Addison-Wesley, Reading (2004)
12. Codd, E.F.: A Relational Model of Data for Large Shared Data Banks. CACM 13(6), 377–387 (1970)
13. Halpin, T., Morgan, T.: Information Modeling and Relational Databases. Morgan Kaufmann Publishers, San Francisco (2008)
14. Bloesch, A.C., Halpin, T.: Conceptual Queries using ConQuer-II. In: 16th International Conference on Conceptual Modeling, ER 1997(1997)
15. Heath, C.: The Constellation Query Language. In: Meersman, R., Herrero, P., Dillon, T. (eds.) On the Move to Meaningful Internet Systems OTM 2009 Workshops. LNCS, vol. 5872, pp. 682–691. Springer, Heidelberg (2009)

MONET'10 & P2PCDVE'10 - PC Co-chairs Message

The research areas of mobile technologies, social networking and mobile services applications are receiving wide interest from private and public companies as well as from academic and research institutions. The mobile and networking technologies, the new generation of wireless local area networks and ad hoc networks are devoted to playing an important role in many areas of social activities, predominantly in those areas where having the right data at the right time is a mission-critical issue. Mobile and networking technologies for social applications serve groups of people "on the move", sharing activities and/or interests; in particular these technologies involve geographically distributed groups who are collaborating on some task in a shared context or independently from their location. By their real nature, mobile technologies can be considered multidisciplinary technologies involving social aspects; indeed, they often involve personal, group and ubiquitous issues, supporting inter-personal connections and involving human-technology interaction in different, and dispersed, contexts. Mobile technologies also play an essential role in personalizing working and interaction contexts, while supporting experimentation and innovation, and the advancement of the field is fundamental for developing social networking. Moreover, mobile technologies are the base for Collaborative Distributed Virtual Environments (CDVE) enabling geographically distant users to echange information, communicate and collaborate. A special session of the workshop was organised on them. Social networking technologies bring friends, family members, co-workers and other social communities together. These technologies are convergent, emerging from a variety of applications such as search engines and employee evaluation routines, while running on equally diverse platforms from server clusters to wireless phone networks.

Social networking and its connection with the use of mobile devices represents one of the most relevant phenomena related to the networking technologies and their emerging problems of use, robustness, vulnerabilities to reliability and performance due to malicious attack.

The fifth International Workshop on Mobile and Networking Technologies for social applications (MONET 2010) was held in October 2010 in Hersonissou, Crete, Greece. The workshop allowed researchers, experts from academia and industry, and practitioners to discuss new mobile and networking technologies, social networking and mobile applications; this debate has represented a stimulus to identify challenging problems in the social applications of those technologies and to show results and experiences connected with social networking, business applications and, mobile applications and services. This year, after a rigorous

R. Meersman et al. (Eds.): OTM 2010 Workshops, LNCS 6428, pp. 541–542, 2010.
© Springer-Verlag Berlin Heidelberg 2010

review process, eight papers were accepted for inclusion in the conference proceedings related with the following issues:

- Improving Social Networking: service-oriented architectures, location-based services, and multimodality;
- P2P- Collaborative Distributed Virtual Environments (CDVE);
- Applicative Issues and Solutions in Networking and Mobile Applications.

The success of the MONET 2010 workshop would not have been possible without the contribution of the OTM 2010 workshops organizers, PC members and authors of papers, all of whom we would like to sincerely thank.

August 2010

Fernando Ferri
Patrizia Grifoni
Irina Kondratova
Arianna D'Ulizia
Laura Ricci
MONET'10

Black-Hole Attacks in P2P Mobile Networks Discovered through Bayesian Filters*

Jorge Hortelano[1], Carlos T. Calafate[1], Juan Carlos Cano[1],
Massimiliano de Leoni[2], Pietro Manzoni[1], and Massimo Mecella[3]

[1] Departamento de Informática de Sistemas y Computadores
Universidad Politécnia de Valencia, Spain
[2] Department of Mathematics and Computer Science
Eindhoven University of Technology, The Netherlands
[3] Dipartimento di Informatica e Sistemistica
SAPIENZA Università di Roma, Italy

Abstract. MANETs (Mobile Ad-hoc NETworks) are an example of Peer-to-Peer (P2P) mobile networks in which security attacks, as black-hole ones, may cause serious dangers to the whole system. The watchdog is a well-known sensor usually adopted for detecting black-holes in such networks, but typical watchdogs are characterized by a relatively high number of false positive and negative cases, which can affect the effectiveness and efficiency to deal with intrusions.This paper proposes a novel approach for detecting black-hole attacks and selfish nodes in mobile P2P networks by using a watchdog sensor and a bayesian filtering. We demonstrate the validity of the approach through testing.

1 Introduction

Peer-to-Peer (P2P) mobile networks, such as Mobile Ad hoc NETworks (MANETs), are distributed systems composed by wireless mobile nodes that can freely and dynamically self-organise into arbitrary and temporary topologies [8]. These networks have origins in military missions and recovery operations but, in the recent years, a wide range of possible civil applications emerged, e. g., vehicular networks (a.k.a. VANETs), a form of P2P mobile networks used for communication among vehicles and between vehicles and roadside equipment.

The main characteristic of such networks is that they allow different kinds of devices to easily interconnect in areas with no pre-existing communication infrastructure; there exist several protocol specifications, such as AODV [4], that aim to find routing paths between pairs of devices. These allow non-neighbouring nodes to communicate by using intermediate nodes as relays. But the majority of these protocols assume a friendly,

---

* The work of Hortelano, Calafate, Cano and Manzoni was partially supported by the Ministerio de Educación y Ciencia, Spain, under Grant TIN2008-06441-C02-01, and by the "Ayudas complementarias para proyectos de I+D para grupos de calidad de la Generalitat Valenciana (ACOMP/2010/005)". The work of de Leoni – performed while he was at SAPIENZA Università di Roma – and Mecella was partly supported by SAPIENZA Università di Roma through the grants AST 2009 "METRO" and FARI 2008, and by the EU through the project SM4All.

R. Meersman et al. (Eds.): OTM 2010 Workshops, LNCS 6428, pp. 543–552, 2010.
© Springer-Verlag Berlin Heidelberg 2010

reliable and cooperative environment. Therefore, a single malicious node can easily prevent a mobile network from working, and therefore the emerging need for research focused on the provision of practical proposals for securing them [5].

In this context, intrusion detection systems (IDSs) aim at monitoring the activity of the various nodes in the network in order to detect misbehaviours. A basic brick of some IDSs is the watchdog, a collective name for special sensors that can detect selfish nodes and black-hole attackers.

In few words, a black-hole is a type of attack to the network in which a node intends to disrupt the communication with its neighbourhood by attracting all traffic flows in the network and then dropping all packets received without forwarding them to their final destination.

A watchdog is continuously listening neighboring devices for verifying that they, when they are not the final expected recipients, forward packets/messages toward the final destinations. Indeed in MANETs every node is able to analyse the packet headers and learn whether neighbouring nodes are the actual receivers or, conversely, they should forward it to another node on the path to the destination. Devices that do not forward packets for which they are not recipient are considered as misbehaving.

Malicious nodes' detections of current-day watchdogs are affected by several errors due to nodes' mobility and signal noises. This work aims at reducing the number of false positives and negatives by integrating watchdogs with bayesian filtering techniques. Bayesian filters can partly fade the problems by using historical information obtained by the watchdog in the previous time. The technique proposed is independent of the underlying routing protocols and, hence, is widely applicable in several different scenarios of P2P mobile networks. The general approach here proposed, even if demonstrated in the context of MANETs, is in general applicable to a wide spectrum of P2P networks, not only mobile, but also application overlay networks, etc. In a few words, the proposed approach can be summarized as follows:

1. Every node installs a watchdog, thus allowing for detecting misbehaviors (e.g., the number of packets that nodes should forward but that they do not do).
2. The percentage of packets that nodes do not correctly forward is used as input for the bayesian filters in order to predict the percentage of non-forwarded packets in the near future. If such a percentage is higher than a certain threshold, then the node is considered as malicious since it does not behave correctly. Please note that it is not possible to assume that "good" nodes forward correctly all packets because of radio noises, packet losses and other similar characteristics of the aerial medium, which cause some delivery attempts to fail.
3. Every node that detects this malicious behaviour enables consequently appropriate actions to avoid malicious nodes to influence the right network's functioning. Every device can take its own recovery actions, or, conversely, all nodes can reach a consensus on the collaborative actions to deal with the situation. However, this point is out of the scope of this paper: we focus on signalling malicious nodes, assuming another component to take care of mitigating the consequences of such attacks.

The rest of this paper is organised as follows. Section 2 summarises relevant work and the motivation of our work. Section 3 introduces bayesian filters, whereas Section 4 presents our adaptation of the bayesian filters for detecting black-hole attacks.

Section 5 complements our development proposal by explaining the different implementation trade-offs that should be taken into account. Section 6 shows the evaluation performed to validate our mechanism. Finally, Section 7 outlines possible future work.

2 Related Work

The concept of watchdog is not a novelty in the literature. Due to the effectiveness of this methodology and its relatively easy implementation, several proposals use it as the basis of their IDS solutions. Similarly to our approach, Obimbo et al. [3] implement a watchdog that listens neighboring nodes and checks whether they misbehave as they do not forward the packets they are supposed to. In the Pathrater approach [10], each node uses the information provided by watchdogs to rate neighbours. The Routeguard mechanism [6] combines the watchdog and Pathrater solutions to classify each neighbouring node as Fresh, Member, Unstable, Suspect or Malicious. Other approaches like Patwardhan [11] extend the detection capabilities provided by the watchdog with public key encryption and signatures. Marti et al. [12] uses watchdogs in order to prevent malicious nodes from breaking the routing protocols.

But as already pointed out in [10], the problem of all of these solutions is that the used watchdogs report a lot of false detections. Hence, they consider malicious nodes that really are not or, vice versa, actual malicious nodes are not detected as such. The approach we are proposing is more precise as it integrates techniques to mitigate the causes of erroneous detections, that are radio noises and the packet losses.

The appropriateness of bayesian filtering for our intent has been previously confirmed in several fields, such as to implement reputation systems [2] or to predict the nodes' disconnections [9].

3 Bayesian Filtering

Bayesian filters [1] probabilistically estimate a dynamic system's state from noisy observations. At time t, the state is estimated by a random variable θ, which is unknown and this uncertainty is modelled by assuming that θ itself is drawn according to a distribution that is updated as new observations become available. It is called *belief* or $Bel_t(\theta)$. To illustrate this, let's assume that there is a sequence of time-indexed observations $z_1, z_2, ..., z_n$. The $Bel_i(\theta)$ is then defined by the posterior density over the random variable θ conditioned on all sensor data available at time t:

$$Bel_t(\theta) = p(\theta | z_1, z_2, ..., z_t)$$

In our approach, the random variable θ belongs to [0,1]. Then we use for the *belief* the distribution $Beta(\alpha, \beta)$ that is suitable for this interval:

$$Bel_t(\theta) = Beta(\alpha_t, \beta_t, \theta)$$

where α and β represent the state of the system, and it is updated according to the following equations:

$$\begin{cases} \alpha_{t+1} = \alpha_t + z_t \\ \beta_{t+1} = \beta_t + z_t \end{cases}$$

The Beta function only needs two parameters that are continuously updated as observations are made or reported. In our approach, the observation z_t represents the information from the watchdog obtained in time interval $[t, t+1]$ about the percentage of non-forwarded packets.

4 The Bayesian Watchdog

Our approach is based on the information of the incoming packets that devices have not forwarded, nonetheless they should have done so. Our bayesian watchdog relies on some basic assumptions:

1. Every device is equipped with a wireless card that allows for promiscuous mode: any device can listen the packets traversing its neighbourhood and, hence, monitor the activity of one-hop distant nodes.
2. Each node has an implementation of a watchdog sensor, let's indicate as i. The i-th watchdog of a given node monitors the incoming and outgoing traffic of every neighbouring node. In this way, analysing the packet headers, it is able to count the packets that nodes did not forward.
3. Each node has at least three neighbours. We assume a density of the network that makes different paths possible for reaching a destination, and each node is monitored by different neighbours.

The watchdog of device i is in charge of listening the packets' traffic in its neighborhood and verifying whether the fraction of packets that are not correctly forwarded by every neighboring device j. If a given j forwards less than a given fraction of packets than it should, the watchdog considers j as misbehaving. Device i does not know a priori such a fraction for each neighbouring node j and, therefore, it defines a random variable $\theta_i(j)$ to estimate it for j. In fact, $\theta_i(j)$ is the viewpoint of device i for what concerns device j. It is worthy highlighting that taking only the last observation is not sufficiently reliable since this could be effected by noise. So the old observations should be considered.

Therefore our watchdog makes use of bayesian filtering, as described in Section 3. Variable $\theta_i(j)$ complies with the Beta distribution with parameters $(\alpha^{(i,j)}, \beta^{(i,j)})$. These parameters are continuously updated with new incoming observations of the fraction of non-forwarded packets. Node i makes periodical observations each t seconds (with t constant) of the behaviour of node j. Let s be the fraction of packets observed by i that are not forwarded by node j in this observation period. Parameters $\alpha^{(i,j)}$ and $\beta^{(i,j)}$ are updated as follows:

$$\begin{cases} \alpha^{(i,j)} := u \cdot \alpha^{(i,j)} + s \\ \beta^{(i,j)} := u \cdot \beta^{(i,j)} + (1-s) \end{cases} \tag{1}$$

Values $\alpha^{(i,j)}$ and $\beta^{(i,j)}$ are initially set to 1.

The variable u is a fading mechanism for past experiences. This fading mechanism allows for redemption of a neighbour if its behaviour changes to a correct one along the time. This fading mechanism will be useful if there are false positives due to the environmental noise. Greater values for u corresponds to consider the old observations more significantly.

With the beta function defined previously we can define the reputation function of node j on node i $R_i(j)$ using the estimated distribution $Beta(\alpha_i(j), \beta_i(j))$ of variable $\theta_i(j)$:

$$R_i(j) := \begin{cases} 1 & P(\theta_i(j) < \gamma) \\ 0 & P(\theta_i(j) \geq \gamma) \end{cases} \tag{2}$$

where, according to the Probability Theory, the probability that $\theta_i(j)$ is less than γ is computable as the integration of the distribution of $\theta_i(j)$ between $-\infty$ and γ, i.e. in our case between 0 and γ:

$$P(\theta_i(j) < \gamma) = \int_0^\gamma Beta(\alpha_i(j), \beta_i(j))$$

If $R_i(j) = 0$, node i reputes j as malicious. This means that node j is malicious if the estimated fraction of packets that are not correctly forwarded is more than a given value γ, named *tolerance threshold*. This tolerance threshold may be depending on the environmental noise and must be defined for each scenario.

5   Tuning of the Bayesian Watchdog

The bayesian filtering used in our watchdog approach is based on some parameters that need in several cases to be tuned for the specific scenarios through a previous training procedure. In particular, the bayesian filtering depends on the following parameters:

Tolerance threshold γ. An higher value for the tolerance threshold requires more time for the watchdog to detect an attack, as an higher value of alpha is needed on function 2 to set the reputation as malicious; to achieve this higher value of alpha, the bayesian filter needs to perform more observations. But, on the other hand, the watchdog is more robust against environmental noise (less false positives). Conversely, if we set a low value for gamma, some nodes affected by noise would be declared as malicious ones and false positives would appear.

Fading value u. This parameter indicates the weight of the old information obtained by the bayesian watchdog. When closer to 1, the old observations weight similarly to the new ones. In case of the change of the behavior of a given node, since the misbehavior detected in the latest observation periods is mostly as relevant as the good behavior observed in the past, the bayesian filters require more time to learn that the node has changed to a bad behavior. On the other hand, the effects of noise onto the filter become less relevant and they are mitigated by the past observations. Therefore, the percentage of false positives is lower. Clearly, for smaller u's value, the opposite behavior should be observed.

Updating time. This is the period between two subsequent updates of parameters α and β according to the observations harvested about the packets that, wrongly, are not forwarded. Too frequent updates can cause problem to the bayesian filters if the noise is relatively high. If the the filter's parameter is updated frequently and the packet losses are high, it is likely that the number of packets received in the update period is nearly 0%, thus causing nodes to be wrongly considered as malicious. Conversely, if the observation time is too long, parameters are updated too infrequently and, hence, the time to detect a malicious node may become unacceptable.

6   Evaluation

We have performed several tests using the NS-2 simulator [13] in order to evaluate the approach and to tune some of the parameters of the bayesian filters used inside the watchdog. In our simulation we considered a network of 50 nodes in an area 870x870 meters wide.

We have performed our experiments both considering static and dynamic scenarios. The channel has been modelled in NS-2 as a noisy IEEE 802.11 wireless affected by the fading effect. In the scenarios where nodes have been moving, we have used random way point model provided by the NS-2. As a matter of fact, the mobility affects the accuracy of the watchdog for two main reasons: *(i)* routes used for the traffic flow need to be recalculated each time the topology changes, causing packet losses; and *(ii)* if the attacker is moving, there is a possibility that the malicious node moves outside the watchdog's signal range before it is detected. Both characteristics of these scenarios cause false negatives and false positives to be increased.

6.1   Static Scenario

We use random scenarios for validating the implementation of our bayesian watchdog. In the first place we perform several tests to evaluate the behaviour of the watchdog's module in a static scenario. Figure 1 shows how the bayesian watchdog detects the 100% of the attacks independently of the number of attackers that there are in the network, and therefore a 0% of false negatives. The absence of mobility makes the number of false positives negligible. But, that is not a realistic setting.

6.2   Dynamic Scenario

The experiments described below are targeted to find the best tuning of parameters in order to improve the effectiveness. The experiments have been conducted for different motion speeds of the MANET devices, thus verifying how the speed can affect the detection of malicious nodes.

Evaluation of the Tolerance Threshold γ. We perform different tests in scenarios with different mobility speeds and changing the tolerance threshold. Figure 2 shows the results measured. For both of diagrams, the x axis represents the various thresholds tested. In Figure 2(a) and Figure 2(b), the y axes measure respectively the percentage of actual attacks detected and false negatives. For the results' analysis, it seems any

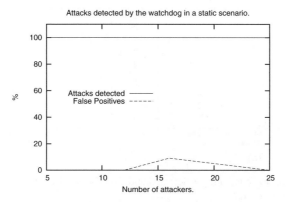

Fig. 1. Actual detections and false positives in a static scenario

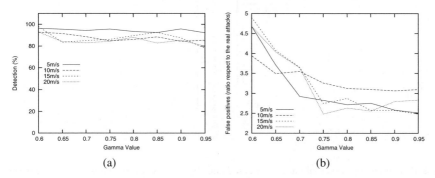

Fig. 2. Percentage of (a) actual attacks detected and (b) false positives for different tolerance threshold and for different devices' speed

threshold between 0.75 and 0.85 decreases the false positives while keeping a good rate detection.

A survey of the NS-2 trace shows that an higher value of gamma (closer to 1) causes the bayesian watchdog to be more strict when detecting an attack, decreasing the false positives but also decreasing the percentage of detection. This is caused by the fact that, as discussed in Section 5, the watchdog needs an higher value of alpha to decide if a neighboring node is malicious, and therefore, more time is needed to detect it.

Evaluation of the Fading Value u. The next step is to evaluate what is the influence of the fading value upon the accuracy of detection. Figure 3 shows the results obtained when varying the fading value of the bayesian watchdog. We use a gamma value of 0.85 for these tests, as it seemed the most suitable according to the results of the previous experiments for the tolerance threshold.

As shown in Figure 3, we can see how an high value of fading is more robust against false positives. But, when a node starts behaving maliciously, it takes longer to detect that. Therefore, such a longer time decreases the accuracy of detecting actual attacks. As a result, the optimal fading value may be depending on the needs of the network.

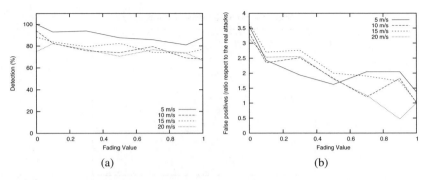

Fig. 3. Percentage of (a) actual attacks detected and (b) false positives for different fading values and different mobility speeds

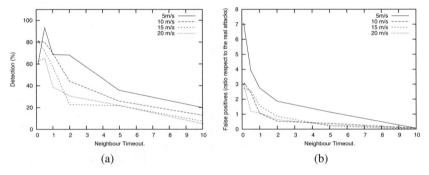

Fig. 4. Percentage of (a) actual attacks detected and (b) false positives when varying the updating time

E.g., if the routing protocol needs to recalculate new routes frequently due to a high value of the node's speed, a higher value of fading is recommended. Or, if a malicious node performs intermittent attacks, a lower value of fading is needed.

Evaluation of the Update Time. Figure 4 confirms what stated in Section 5: shorter update time of the parameters of the bayesian filter increments the detection of false negatives but also decrements the accuracy for what concerns the false positives.

6.3   Comparing the Bayesian Watchdog with a Standard One

The section proposes a comparison between the standard watchdog and the bayesian watchdog in order to judge whether bayesian filters can really be supportive in the accuracy of the detection of malicious nodes. Specifically, we have used a standard watchdog that was previously implemented [7] (with tolerance threshold of 20%). As far as the bayesian watchdog, the tolerance has been set to 0.85, the fading u to 0.5 and the updating time to 2 seconds.

Figure 5 shows a comparison between the bayesian watchdog and the standard watchdog in a set of scenarios where the degree of mobility is varying. As far as the

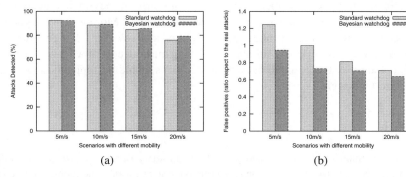

Fig. 5. Comparison between both watchdogs with different degrees of mobility: (a) actual attacks detected and (b) false positives

percentage of actual attacks detected, Figure 5(a) shows that the bayesian watchdogs perform mostly at the same level as the standard. Some small improvements have been measured for scenarios where nodes were moving faster. In fact, the bayesian watchdog is less affected by the problem of the mobility as explained at the beginning of this section.

The best improvement has been measured for what concerns false positives that have been decreased of 20%. Indeed, the bayesian filter deals very well with noisy environment such as MANETs. A smaller influence of the noise in the measurement of the non-correctly forwarded packets has resulted in a lower number of false positives.

In addition to a significant decrease of false positives, the bayesian watchdog is also able to detect malicious behaviors more quickly that standard ones.

7   Conclusions and Future Work

The work described in this paper is aimed at increasing the accuracy of the detection of malicious nodes' behaviour in P2P networks, as MANETs. One of the most significant problems of the standard watchdog are concerned with the influence of the noisy observation upon the accuracy. Here we have proposed a new class of watchdogs that rely on bayesian filters. Bayesian filters are broadly used in several scenarios due to their ability to reduce the influence of the noise on the measurements.

In the standard watching, most of the false positives and negatives are caused by the erroneous measurements of the packets that nodes should forward but actually they do not. The erroneous measurements are mostly caused by the unreliability of the wireless medium. Nothing can be done on reducing that. But bayesian filtering deal very well with preventing this node from influencing the judgement of the maliciousness of given devices.

We have devised a technique to integrate bayesian filtering techiques inside the watchdogs and we have conducted some experiments inside an ns-2 implementation to verify the approach. The integration of bayesian filtering inside the watchdogs has decreased the number of false positives detected while the percentage of the detection of the actual attacks has been kept quite high (or, even, slightly improved). As future work, we intend to provide a concrete implementation of our bayesian watchdog and to perform a deeper experimental phase on the real devices. Moreover, we argue that the approach to detect malicious nodes can be applied also to other P2P networks (e.g., application overlay networks) by suitably modifying the concepts of what it is observed and what is the noisy (transmitted packets in MANETs, could be application messages in overlay networks, etc.)

References

1. Berger, J.O.: Statistical Decision Theory and Bayesian Analysis. Springer, Heidelberg (1993)
2. Buchegger, S., Boudec, J.Y.L.: A robust reputation system for p2p and mobile ad-hoc networks (2004)
3. Obimbo, C., Arboleda, L.M., Chen, C.Y.: A Watchdog Enhancement to IDS in MANET. In: IASTED conference on Wireless Networks (July 2006)
4. C. Perkins, E. Belding-Royer, S. Das: Ad hoc on-demand distance vector (AODV) routing. Request for Comments 3561, Network Working Group (July 2003), http://www.ietf.org/rfc/rfc3561.txt experimental
5. Yang, H.: Security in mobile ad hoc networks: challenges and solutions. IEEE Wireless Communications 11(1), 38–47 (2004)
6. Hasswa, A., Zulkernine, M., Hassanein, H.: Routeguard: an intrusion detection and response system for mobile ad hoc networks. In: Wireless And Mobile Computing, Networking And Communications, 2005 (WiMob 2005), vol. 3, pp. 336–343. IEEE Computer Society Press, Los Alamitos (August 2005)
7. Hortelano, J., Ruiz, J.C., Manzoni, P.: Evaluating the usefulness of watchdogs for intrusion detection in VANETs. In: ICC 2010 Workshop on Vehicular Networking & Applications, Cape Town, South Africa (2010)
8. Chlamtac, I., Conti, M., Liu, J.J.: Mobile ad hoc networking: imperatives and challenges. Ad Hoc Networks 1(1), 13–64 (2003)
9. de Leoni, M., Humayoun, S.R., Mecella, M., Russo, R.: A bayesian approach for disconnection management in mobile ad-hoc network. In: Ubiquitous Computing and Communication Journal (2008)
10. Marti, S., Giuli, T.J., Lai, K., Baker, M.: Mitigating routing misbehavior in mobile ad hoc networks. In: Proceedings of the 6th Annual International Conference on Mobile Computing and Networking, MobiCom 2000, pp. 255–265. ACM, New York (2000)
11. Patwardhan, A., Parker, J., Joshi, A., Iorga, M., Karygiannis, T.: Secure Routing and Intrusion Detection in Ad Hoc Networks. In: Proceedings of the 3rd International Conference on Pervasive Computing and Communications. IEEE Computer Society Press, Los Alamitos (March 2005)., main Conference
12. Marti, S., Giuli, T.J., Lai, K., Baker, M.: Mitigating routing misbehavior in mobile ad hoc networks. In: 6th MobiCom, Boston, Massachusetts (August 2000)
13. UC Berkeley, LBL, USC/ISI, and Xerox PARC researchers: Network Simulator - ns (Version 2) (1998), http://www.isi.edu/nsnam/ns/

Improved Load Balancing on Distributed Massive Simulation Environments

Cristoforo Caponigri, Gennaro Cordasco,
Rosario De Chiara, and Vittorio Scarano

ISISLab, Dipartimento di Informatica
ed Applicazioni "R.M. Capocelli",
University of Salerno,
Fisciano 84084, Italy
{cordasco,dechiara,vitsca}@dia.unisa.it

Abstract. In this paper, we report the findings we gathered in designing and implementing a system that provides a distributed massive simulation environment. Massive Battle is a system capable of simulating historical battles for the purpose of learning and to carry out historical researches (e.g. what-if scenarios). We present a distributed implementation of Massive Battle and some early tests. We report and discuss some analysis of the problems related to the workload distribution in this particular environment. We report how is possible to measure a better load balancing by adopting a more general scheme of computation that generalize the assignments that each peer has to complete together with simulation.

Keywords: Massive Simulation, Peer–to–Peer systems, Load Balancing.

1   Introduction

Distributed Virtual Environment (DVE) is an emerging research field which combines 3D graphics, networking and behavioral animation with the purpose of simulating realistic and immersive virtual environments offering a high degree of interactivity. The distributed nature of these systems widened the scenarios of use that now ranges from online videogames to serious games for training including online cooperative systems for learning and problem solving.

In this paper we will discuss the design of a Peer-to-Peer (P2P) system for Distributed Virtual Environments. In particular we will report our experiences in implementing it and we will discuss some experimental results, as well. Distributed Virtual Environments (DVEs) constitute a challenging research area in the wider area of the Distributed Systems. DVEs are designed with the intent to convey and highly interactive experience to a number of users widespread geographically [17]. An architecture based on a single server, or even a small number of servers, is not able to handle the load generated by such systems, on the other hand a centralized server architecture allows to target serious problems like accounting and security.

R. Meersman et al. (Eds.): OTM 2010 Workshops, LNCS 6428, pp. 553–562, 2010.
© Springer-Verlag Berlin Heidelberg 2010

A motivation supporting the adoption of P2P architectures is that the most of the DVEs intend to develop Massively Multiuser Virtual Environment (MMVE). Videogames are particular MMVEs, and their success is directly proportional to the number of subscribers they have. For example *World of Warcraft* and *Second Life* have reached around 10 million subscribers worldwide and roughly 1 million of active users [13]. Indeed, during last years, a lot of interests has raised for the development and research of novel platforms for next-generation MMVEs. The idea is to use the P2P architecture to let peers to communicate with other peers through the overlay network, without going through the server. Furthermore each peer may also alleviate the server work by sharing some of the tasks such as maintaining game state. The division of such responsibilities between peers is an interesting research topic.

1.1   Massive Simulation Environments (MSEs)

The simulation of groups of characters moving in a virtual world is a topic that has been investigated since the 1980s with the purpose of simulating a group of entities, dubbed *autonomous actors*, whose movements are related to social interactions among group members.

A classical example of use of this approach is the simulation of a flock of birds in the most natural possible way. Elements of this simulated flock are usually named *boids* (from *bird-oid*) and got instilled a range of *behaviors* that induces some kind of *personality*. A widespread approach to this kind of simulations has been introduced in [15]. Every boid has its own *personality* (e.g. the trajectory of its flight) that is the result of a weighted sum of a number of *behaviors*. The simulation is performed in successive steps: at each step, for each boid and for each behavior in the personality, the system calculates a request to accelerate in a certain direction in the space, and sums up all of these requests; then the boid is moved along this result. The behaviors are, in the most of cases, simply geometric calculations that are carried out for each boid considering the k-neighbors it is flying with: for example the behavior called *pursuit* just let the boid to pursuit a moving target (e.g. another boid). Each boid reacts to its k-neighbors, which constitute its neighborhood. Given a certain boid out of a flock of n boids, the most simple way of identifying that boid's neighborhood is by an $O(n^2)$ proximity screening, and for this reason the efficiency of the implementation is still to be considered an issue.

1.2   Designing a P2PMSE

In [7] we presented Distributed Massive Battle, a DMSE that is able to simulate historical battle from the past. The purpose of our system is to expand the number of simulated actors in a MSE by distributing the computational load to various PCs (peers) connected to the system. In Distributed Massive Battle the functionality of a peer are divided into two categories, Simulation and Rendering. Each of the workers participate to the simulation while one single peer is devoted to the visualization of the simulation.

We also provided some tests to assess the performances of such DMSE. Tests revealed that the architecture presents a quite good scalability and the communication overhead due to the peers interaction is dominated by the computational power provided by the peer.

Our result. In this paper we present a generalization of Distributed Massive Battle where each peer provides CPU power, to contribute to the simulation, and, in exchange, it can visualize a part of simulation. As we said before, the most reasonable scenario of use of such systems are MMVEs. In a MMVE, on each peer, together with the simulation, several other complex tasks needs to be carried out (e.g. artificial intelligence, social interactions, complex user interfaces interaction etc...), in this paper we will refer to such computations with the name "assignments". We intend to take into account assignments tasks by generalizing the model. The rationale behind this decision is to let the uneven load distribution in the simulation, we measured in [7], be balanced, with no particular effort by the system, by a randomization of the assignments. For further details see Section 3.

2 Distributed Massive Battle: The Architecture

In this Section we describe the architecture of Distributed Massive Battle. Massive Battle is a MSE capable of animating autonomous actors with the purpose of reconstructing interactive scenes from a battlefield showing a number of platoons fighting each others [2].

2.1 Background

Peer–to–Peer systems. Peer-to-peer (P2P) is a class of network applications that takes advantage of existing computing power, computer storage, and networking connectivity, which are available at the edges of the Internet. Hence P2P allows users to leverage their collective power to the benefit of all. After the initial popularity of centralized Napster and flooding based networks like Gnutella, several research groups have independently proposed a new generation of P2P systems which are completely distributed and use a scalable Distributed Hash Table (DHT) as a substrate. A DHT is a self–organizing overlay network that allows to add, delete, and lookup hash table items. One of the most important benefits provided by P2P systems is the scalability. In a P2P system, each consumer of resources also donates resources.

Typically, DHTs are based on similar designs, while their search and management strategies differ; they include Chord [16] (based on the hypercube), CAN [14] (based on the torus), P-GRID [1] (based on trees), Pastry [8], or Tapestry [18]. One of the reasons for the success of the DHT approach is that DHTs provide a generic primitive that can benefit a wide range of applications.

Massive Battle. Massive Battle is an example of *serious game* system that offers an effective way of simulating historical battles for the purpose of learning (e.g. providing new insights for battles to engage students) and to carry out historical researches (e.g. what-if scenarios). The simulation of historical battles also imposes some constraints on the number of agents the system is capable of simulate: as an example the Waterloo Battle involved $\approx$ 250000 soldiers, while Massive Battles, running on an off-the-shelves PC, is capable of simulating only $\approx$ 5000 units, at an interactive rate ($\approx$ 25 frames-per-seconds). Massive Battle is implemented in C++ and is based on Ogre3d, a rendering engine, for this reason Massive Battle can be considered a reasonable approximation of a real DVE as a Massive Multiplayer Online Role-Playing Game (MMORPG).

2.2   Design Issues

The design of Distributed Massive Battle has been carried out by addressing four main issues: world partitioning, world state propagation, self-synchronization and load balancing [6].

World Partitioning. A scene in Massive Battle is defined by a map, platoons and checkpoints: each platoon pass through the checkpoints assigned to it. To achieve scalability, we adopt a Geographic decomposition approach: the environment map is partitioned into a set of static Regions. The peer which is responsible for a region is dubbed *Region Master*. The granularity of the world decomposition (that is, the region size and, consequently, the number of regions, which a given map is partitioned into) determines a trade-off between load balancing and communication overhead. The finer is the granularity adopted, the higher is the degree of parallelism that, ideally, can be reached by the system. However, due to regions' interdependency and system synchronizations, fine granularity usually determines a huge amount of communication. Our system is designed to be used with different granularity.

World State Propagation. We adopted a simple Publish/Subscribe mechanism: a multicast channel is assigned to each region; users then simply subscribe to the channels associated with the regions which overlap with their AOI to receive relevant message updates.

Self-synchronization. One of the goal of the design is to implement a *self-synchronizing* system. Each simulation is decomposed in time slots (henceforth steps). Each step is associated with a stable state of the simulation. The number of steps is used as a *wall-clock* so that each event can be associated with a timestamp. Regions are simulated on a step base. Since the step i of region r depends on the states $i-1$ of r's neighborhood (the regions which confine with region r), the step i of a region cannot be executed until the states $i-1$ of its neighborhood have been computed and delivered. In other words, each region is synchronized with its neighborhood before each simulation step. The peer in charge for each region has a double buffer in which it stores the state of the region neighbors. One buffer is used for even steps states while the other one for odd steps. When the simulation of a even (resp. odd) step is terminated, the region master waits until the odd (resp. even) buffer is full. Using this synchronization approach, we have that the timing of two closed region may differ by at most 1. So two buffers are enough to realize the synchronization barrier.

Load Balancing. One of the motivations of the P2P infrastructure described here is to address the needs for more computing power. In order to better exploit the computing power provided by the peers of the system, it is necessary to design the system so that the simulation always evolves in parallel, avoiding bottlenecks. Since the simulation is synchronized after each step, the system advances with the same speed provided by the slower peer in the system. For this reason it is necessary to design the system in order to balance the load between the peers. We addressed this problem by relying on three factors: (i) the node id on a DHT are distributed uniformly; (ii) it is possible to tune the granularity of world decomposition. This decision allowed us to implement a totally decentralized system without introducing too much communication overhead; (iii) we split the duties of each region in assignments that are carried out by different peers in such a way to improve load balancing.

2.3 System Architecture

In Distributed Massive Battle [7] we adopted FreePastry, the open source version of Pastry [8], as the underneath network infrastructure and we used Scribe [5], the multicast infrastructure built on top of Pastry, to disseminate the simulation state and, at the same time, synchronize the system.

It is worth annotating here how we addressed the problem of distributing the simulation which is carried out by Massive Battle. Massive Battle has been designed and implemented as a simulation written in C++ to be executed on a single PC and this needed to be adapted for the network infrastructure that was implemented in Java. To address this problem we used Java Native Interface (JNI) that allowed us to invoke Java method from C and vice-versa. Once the technological issues have been worked out, we had to take a decision on how to distribute the computational load of the simulation. We just added a World State Propagation step after the Simulation and Rendering steps: each region r publishes the updates to all regions that are subscribed to r and (ii) r waits for the updates from all the regions r is subscribed to (r's neighbourhood). The World State as well as the self-synchronization logic is implemented in the Java part, while the Simulation methods are invoked once the buffer contains all the necessary information to perform a step. The P2P infrastructure is totally agnostic respect to the payload that is propagated among regions: upon receiving/transmitting the updates are handled (marshalling/unmarshalling) in the Simulation engine.

3 Improved Load Balancing

The main finding of our previous paper was that even if Distributed Massive Battles showed a good scalability, the general load balancing of the system, which relied on the distribution of IDs on the DHT, was not enough. Hence an enhanced load balancing strategy is needed. Several approaches have been proposed to balance the workload across the peers, for instance a dynamic partitioning can be used, but on the other hand, the management of dynamic regions requires a large amount of communication between peers that consumes bandwidth and introduces latency [3,9].

As we said before in a MMVE each peer will carry out a number of different assignments, each of this assignments will consume CPU time. Together with the Simulation, part of the CPU time will be employed in performing, for example, high quality visualization of the simulated scene, gathering input from user, implement a voice chat system. For sake of the clarity of the description we will consider how the Rendering can be performed in such MMVE, without loss of generality. In our experiments every region will have two different assignments: Simulation and Rendering. At the very beginning of the execution, each peer will be Region master for a number of region, the coupling will be performed by the IDs in the DHT. The Region master will publish the updates it calculates and will received updates from border regions.

What we have just described until now is the situation we depicted in the previous paper. We now intend to take into account a variation: we split each computation step into a set of assignments. Besides the Simulation assignment, a range of other assignments shall be considered, for instance the Rendering of some regions. Each peer, that actually is a PC with a user, will be interested in visualizing a number of regions in the map, to see how the Simulation is running. For this reason such peer will subscribe to updates from the regions it means to visualize, so, together with the updates it will use to carry on the Simulation, it will also receive the updates from the region whose it perform the Rendering. The workload of the Rendering assignment will depend on a number of factor like quality of rendering, screen resolution, complexity of the model, and, is proportionally to the number of agents it intends to render: the more agents are present in the regions the peer intend to visualize, the higher will be the workload, and larger will be the portion of CPU time subtracted to the Simulation and absorbed by the Rendering.

In the most general case, together with Simulation and Rendering we can consider other tasks, as we said above. For this reason, in our experiments, each peer will be Region master for a number of cells and will also subscribe to a number of cells for what we have defined assignment. For the purpose of the testing, after performing a Simulation step, each peer spend an amount of idle time proportional to the number of agents that belongs to the regions it is interested to. This time consumption is performed by using a `sleep()` system call, for a number of milliseconds proportional to the number of agents present in the region managed by the peer.

In Figure 1 we have summarized the whole process we have described above: in the Figure is depicted a single step of computation as it is performed on a single peer. Each peer is actually made by two parts, one written in C++, that is in charge for the Simulation and the other assignments, and a Java part that handles the communication on the P2P overlay network. The Simulation assignments executes the Distributed Massive Battle engine with the purpose of animating the agents. Other assignments are executed in C++ and corresponds

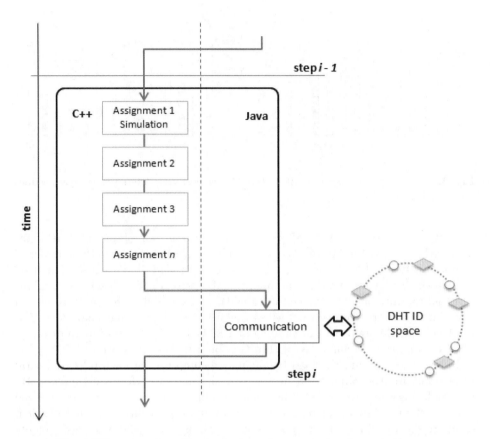

Fig. 1. The execution of a single step of computation for a single peer

to a `sleep()`. The communication task is where the synchronization takes place and the double buffers mechanism is used. It is worth noting that the Java part is agnostic respect to the data it actually handles, and this allows to independently expand and modify the C++ part to add new functionalities.

3.1   Tests

We performed a number of tests of the system in order to evaluate the load balancing improvement obtainable by decomposing, on each peer, the computation task into two components: Simulation and Assignments.

Test setting. Tests were conducted on a scenario consisting of 64 regions (a 8×8 grid). On each run the distribution of the regions to peers, both for the simulation and for the assignments, is decided by randomly associating DHT identifiers to both regions and peers (each peer is given two IDs, one is used for the simulation and one for assignments). Sixteen platoons of 100 soldiers (overall 1600 actors) were placed on the map. Each platoon follows a prefixed

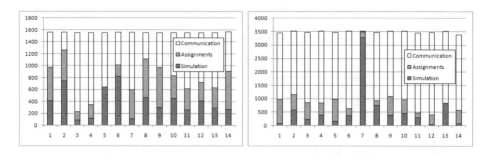

Fig. 2. Two runs of the system 1000 steps: (left) best case (right) worst case. Times are expressed in seconds.

path which guarantees that all the regions become non-empty at least once during the simulation. We ran the simulation with 14 peers while the number of simulation step is 1000. Since the performances of the system are also influenced by some arbitrary factors (for example, the allocation of ID to peers and regions can lead to more or less balanced workload), we executed each test 10 times All experiments are performed on 14 mid-range PC having similar characteristics: Intel Xeon dual-core processor running at 2.80 GHz, with 2 GB of main memory. All the PCs are interconnected with a Gigabit Ethernet network.

In order to evaluate the load balancing we compute, for each peer, the total time spent for the Simulation and the total time spent for Assignments. By extrapolating these times from the whole running time, we obtain the idle time (that is, the time spent for both communication and synchronization). We then compare the variability of this results with a similar test where no Assignments take place. Since the two data sets provide quite different means (the tests with no Assignments are shorter) we can not use neither the standard deviation nor the variance to compare the variability of these results. Both standard deviation and variance are strictly dependent to the mean of the data. We compare the variability of our data set by using the coefficient of variation, which is the ratio between the standard deviation and the mean. The coefficient of variation is a dimensionless number and is independent from the mean, so it fits our purpose.

Discussion. In Figure 2.(left) we report the time distribution among the peers, for two executions which correspond to the best (left) and the worst case (right). The results are encouraging, decomposing the computation task into two tasks meaningfully reduce the variability of the results. The improvement ranges from 43% to 65%. For instance, in Figure 2.(left), the amount of computation peer number 6 carried out for the simulation has been counter balanced by a small amount of computation for the assignments; the opposite happened to peer 14. Even in the worst case, Figure 2.(right), the balancing is improved since the most loaded peer (number 7) received an extremely small amount of assignments.

4   Conclusion

The rationale behind our research is to design a system for Distributed Virtual Environments in which work distribution, synchronization and load balancing are implemented in a totally distributed manner. Plenty of works that address each of this aspects are available in literature, but we intend to study them in an integrate manner, in order to verify how they interact.

In this paper, in particular, we addressed the load balancing problem we scoped in a previous research, by considering how, in a more general case of a Distributed Virtual Environment where each PC was not only busy in Simulation but was also employed in more general assignments (rendering, social interactions, user interaction, etc...). In the situation where the computational load is heavier, tests say it is possible to obtain a better load balancing because the unbalancing we measured when peers were busy only in Simulation of certain regions, was balanced by the execution of assignments (e.g. Rendering) of other regions.

References

1. Aberer, K., Cudré-Mauroux, P., Datta, A., Despotovic, Z., Hauswirth, M., Punceva, M., Schmidt, R.: P-grid: a self-organizing structured p2p system. SIGMOD Rec. 32(3), 29–33 (2003)
2. Boccardo, A., De Chiara, R., Scarano, V.: Massive Battle: Coordinated Movement of Autonomous Agents. In: Proc. of the Workshop on 3D Advanced Media In Gaming And Simulation (3AMIGAS) (2009)
3. Buyukkaya, E., Abdallah, M., Cavagna, R.: VoroGame: A Hybrid P2P Architecture for Massively Multiplayer Games. In: Proc. of the 6th IEEE Consumer Communications and Networking Conference (CCNC 2009), pp. 1–5 (January 2009)
4. Castro, M., Jones, M.B., Kermarrec, A.-M., Rowstron, A., Theimer, M., Wang, H., Wolman, A.: An Evaluation of Scalable Application-Level Multicast Built Using Peer-to-Peer Overlays. In: Proc. of the 22nd Annual Joint Conference of the IEEE Computer and Communications Societies, INFOCOM 2003 (2003)
5. Castro, M., Druschel, P., Kermarrec, A.-M., Rowstron, A.: SCRIBE: A large-scale and decentralized application-level multicast infrastructure. IEEE Journal on Selected Areas in Communications (JSAC) 20, 100–110 (2002)
6. Cordasco, G., De Chiara, R., Erra, U., Scarano, V.: Some Considerations on the Design of a P2P Infrastructure for Massive Simulations. In: Proceedings of International Conference on Ultra Modern Telecommunications (ICUMT 2009), St.-Petersburg, Russia (October 2009)
7. Caponigri, C., Cordasco, G., De Chiara, R., Scarano, V.: Experiences with a P2P Infrastructure for Massive Simulations. In: Proceedings of the second International Conference on Advances in P2P Systems (AP2PS 2010), Florence, Italy, October 25-30 (2010) (to Appear)
8. Druschel, P., Rowstron, A.: Pastry: Scalable, Decentralized Object Location, and Routing for Large-Scale Peer-to-Peer Systems. In: Proc. of the 18th IFIP/ACM Inter. Conference on Distributed Systems Platforms (Middleware 2001), pp. 329–350 (November 2001)

9. Kang, H.-Y., Lim, B.-J., Li, K.-J.: P2P Spatial Query Processing by Delaunay Tri-angulation. In: Kwon, Y.-J., Bouju, A., Claramunt, C. (eds.) W2GIS 2004. LNCS, vol. 3428, pp. 136–150. Springer, Heidelberg (2005)

10. Karger, D., Lehman, E., Leighton, F., Panigrahy, R., Levine, M., Lewin, D.: Con-sistent hashing and random trees: Distributed caching protocols for relieving hot spots on the world wide web. In: Proc. of the 29th Annual ACM Symposium on Theory of Computing (STOC 1997), pp. 654–663 (1997)

11. Knutsson, B., Lu, H., Xu, W., Hopkins, B.: Peer-to-Peer Support for Massively Multiplayer Games. In: Proc. of the 23rd Annual Joint Conference of the IEEE Computer and Communications Societies (INFOCOM 2004), p. 107 (2004)

12. Nandan, A., Parker, M.G., Pau, G., Salomoni, P.: On index load balancing in scalable P2P media distribution. Multimedia Tools and Applications 29(3), 325–339 (2006)

13. Pittman, D., GauthierDickey, C.: A Measurement Study of Virtual Populations in Massively Multiplayer Online Games. In: Proc. of the 6th ACM SIGCOMM workshop on Network and system support for games (NetGames 2007), pp. 25–30. ACM, New York (2007)

14. Ratnasamy, S.P., Francis, P., Handley, M., Karp, R., Shenker, S.: A scalable content-addressable network. In: Proc. of ACM Special Interest Group on Data Communication (ACM SIGCOMM 2001), San Diego, CA, US, pp. 161–172 (Au-gust 2001)

15. Reynolds, C.W.: Flocks, Herds, and Schools: A Distributed Behavioral Model. Computer Graphics 21(4), 25–34 (1987)

16. Stoica, I., Morris, R., Liben-Nowell, D., Karger, D., Kaashoek, M., Dabek, F., Balakrishnan, H.: Chord: A Scalable Peer-to-Peer Lookup Protocol for Internet Applications. IEEE/ACM Transactions on Networking (TON) 11(1), 17–32 (2003)

17. Waldo, J.: Scaling in games and virtual worlds. Commun. ACM 51(8), 38–44 (2008)

18. Zhao, B., Kubiatowicz, J., Joseph, A.: Tapestry: An infrastructure for fault-tolerant wide-area location and routing. Tech. Report No. UCB/CSD-01-1141, Computer Science Division (EECS), University of California at Berkeley (April 2001)

EI2N'10 & SeDeS'10 - PC Co-chairs Message

After the successful fourth edition in 2009, the fifth edition of the Enterprise Integration, Interoperability and Networking workshop (EI2N'2010) has been organised as part of the OTM'2010 Federated Conferences and is supported by the IFAC Technical Committee 5.3 "Enterprise Integration and Networking", the IFIP TC 8 WG 8.1 "Design and Evaluation of Information Systems", the SIG INTEROP Grande-Rgion on "Enterprise Systems Interoperability" and the French CNRS National Research Group GDR MACS. Collaboration is necessary for enterprises to prosper in the current extreme dynamic and heterogeneous business environment. Enterprise integration, interoperability and networking are the major disciplines that have studied how to do companies to collaborate and communicate in the most effective way. These disciplines are well-established and are supported by international conferences, initiatives, groups, task forces and governmental projects all over the world where different domains of knowledge have been considered from different points of views and a variety of objectives (e.g., technological or managerial). Enterprise Integration involves breaking down organizational barriers to improve synergy within the enterprise so that business goals are achieved in a more productive and efficient way. The past decade of enterprise integration research and industrial implementation has seen the emergence of important new areas, such as research into interoperability and networking, which involve breaking down organizational barriers to improve synergy within the enterprise and among enterprises. The ambition to achieve dynamic, efficient and effective cooperation of enterprises within networks of companies, or in an entire industry sector, requires the improvement of existing, or the development of new, theories and technologies. Enterprise Modelling, Architecture, and semantic techniques are the pillars supporting the achievement of Enterprise Integration and Interoperability. Internet of Things and Cloud Computing now present new opportunities to realize inter enterprise and intra enterprise integration. For these reasons, the workshop's objective is to foster discussions among representatives of these neighbouring disciplines and to discover new research paths within the enterprise integration community. After peer reviews, 6 papers have been accepted out of 12 submissions to this workshop. Prof. Michael Sobolewski (Polish-Japanese Institute of IT, Poland) has been invited as EI2N plenary keynote on "Exerted Enterprise Computing: from Protocol-oriented Networking to Exertion-oriented Networking". In addition to the presentations of the accepted papers, groups have been organised into what E2IN traditionally calls "workshop cafs", to discuss and debate the presented topics. This year discussion enabled putting forward new research related to "interoperability issues in collaborative information systems". These groups reported the results of the respective discussions during a plenary session that was jointly organised with the CoopIS'2010 conference, in order to share the vision for future research on this top domain. The papers published in this volume of

R. Meersman et al. (Eds.): OTM 2010 Workshops, LNCS 6428, pp. 563–564, 2010.

proceedings present samples of current research in the enterprise modelling, systems interoperability, services management, cloud integration and, more globally, systems engineering and enterprise architecture domains. Some new architecting principles that has gained currency in the recent past is semantic technique, service oriented architecture and cloud computing with their principles, reference models and technology, and if applied correctly can be an important contributor to the future of interoperable, networked and collaborative enterprises. The success of this complex field also depends on the maturity and coherency of the management of the involved enterprises, a topic covered by the second workshop caf. As a special track of EI2N'2010, SeDeS'2010 is the first international workshop on Semantics & Decision Support. The call for papers saw 12 submissions, among which the Programme Committee has selected 4 papers to be presented at EI2N'2010. The selected papers cover the topics of ontology-based decision making applications in the fields of eGovernment, eLearning, business rule management and Human Resource Management.

It has been a great pleasure to work with the members of the international programme committee who dedicated their valuable effort for reviewing the submitted papers; we are indebted to all of them.

We also would like to thank all authors for their contribution to the workshop objectives and discussions.

August 2010

Qing Li
Herv Panetto
Giuseppe Berio
Kemafor Anyanwu
EI2N'10 & SeDes'10

Re-engineering Business Rules
for a Government Innovation Information Portal

Peter Spyns[1,2] and Geert Van Grootel[1]

[1] Vlaamse overheid – Departement Economie, Wetenschap en Innovatie
Koning Albert II-laan 35, bus 10, B-1030 Brussel, Belgium
Geert.VanGrootel@ewi.vlaanderen.be
[2] Vrije Universiteit Brussel – STAR Lab
Pleinlaan 2, Gebouw G-10, B-1050 Brussel, Belgium
Peter.Spyns@vub.ac.be

Abstract. For any information system the quality of the underlying data is crucial for the quality of the information offered to a user. Quality control when
uploading data into a portal is essential. In this paper we describe a practical
case of how existing business rules are re-engineered into semantically
grounded business rules that validate data before being uploaded into a government innovation information portal. Some practical experiences and lessons
learnt are presented. The case has shown that not only a substantial gain in engineering time can been achieved but also that the support of related stakeholders is more easily obtainable.

1 Background

1.1 The Flanders Research Information Space

An information portal unlocking scientific technological knowledge is an important
asset for government policy and strategic decision making by industry and research
organisations. Needing a new system for managing research information, the Flemish
department of Economy, Science and Innovation launched the Flanders Research Information Space programme (FRIS)[1]. The term is used to refer both to the virtual environment of research information and the program that is being set up in order to
create this research information space. The FRIS concept creates a virtual research information space covering all Flemish players in the field of science and innovation.
Within the space, research information can be stored and exchanged in a transparent
and automated way – see [14] for more details. A first realisation is the FRIS research
portal (www.researchportal.be) to provide up to date research information on projects,
researchers and organisations of the Flemish universities.

A key feature is that data can be collected at the point of creation, in the operational
processes of data providers (e.g., universities). For example, information on a research
project can be found in the assessment process for a funding application. Collecting
information at the operational process level at the source offers major advantages.

---

[1] www.ewi-vlaanderen.be/fris

R. Meersman et al. (Eds.): OTM 2010 Workshops, LNCS 6428, pp. 565–574, 2010.

The data, collected bottom up, are accurate and up-to-date because they are being used in an operational process. Also, it is not necessary to establish a parallel, usually top down, data gathering process, so data providers are spared a lot of administrative work. Nevertheless, it is essential to check the quality of the incoming data.

1.2   The Common European Research Information Format

A basic problem is that the information in repositories, information systems or virtual information spaces comes from various sources or suppliers, is represented in various formats, is of varying quality, inconsistent or redundant (and sometimes even contradictory in its meaning). For information interchange and integration across systems, however, a common meaning between the integrated sources has to be defined and declared, to which the different information sources can be mapped. CERIF stands for Common European Research Information Format. It is a recommendation to EU-members for the storage and exchange of current research information [4].

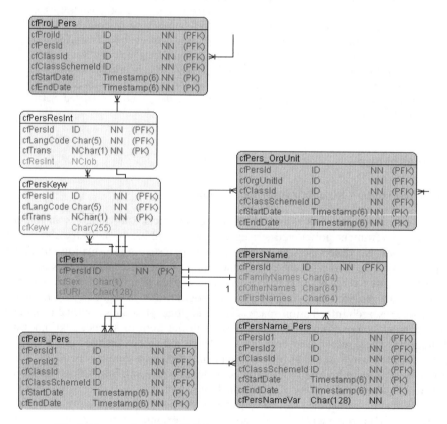

Fig. 1. Excerpt from the CERIF E-R scheme (focused around Person)

CERIF is built on a limited set of basic concepts:

- The business objects or entities of the research and innovation domain: project, person, organisational unit, publication, event, ...
- The multiple relations through time that exist between these objects
- Support for multilingualism for textual attributes
- A separate semantics storage layer

Traditionally, CERIF has been modelled by using Entity-Relationship (E-R) modelling techniques. CERIF is powerful with respect to modelling time-stamped, typed relationships. A CERIF relationship is logically represented as an entity in an E-R scheme, linking two entities (represented by square rectangles on Fig. 1). A link entity can be recognised by its two identifiers that refer to the two linked entities. In addition, relationships are situated in time ('cfStartDate' and 'cfEndDate').

Fig. 1 shows the CERIF core entity 'cfPerson' and some of its relationships (linked by the two identifiers of the linked entities: 'cfProj_Pers' and 'cfPers_OrgUnit'. The core entity 'cfPerson' with (language neutral) attributes 'cfSex' and 'cfURI' has in addition 'cfPersKeyw' and 'cfPersResInt' as translatable attributes. A language code 'cfLangCode' specifies the language concerned. E.g., a Flemish researcher can be active in scientific domains (topic keywords) for which the labels can be translated in English, French and Dutch. Also a reflexive relationship exist ('CfPers_Pers'). The exact nature of the relationships (or roles) is fixed through relationship classes and classicification schemes (identified by means of 'cfClassId' and 'cfClassSchemeId'). Classes and classicification schemes are managed in the CERIF Semantic Layer [5] (not shown here). The semantic layer allows associating translated definitions and translation terms to relationships as well as putting type constraints on the entities participating in a relationship.

2   Problem Statement

Table 1 is an excerpt of the spreadsheet in actual use that contains all the business logic of the FRIS research portal. All rules related to the core entity 'Person' have been listed. When browsing through Table 1, one can detect some flaws or potentially problematic issues. In some rules, the modality is not explicitly included: e.g., is a name obligatory or not ?. In addition, the description of some rules is ambiguous: e.g., the rule 'sex of a person is known' implies a yes/no value but contains a male/female value. Also this rule "hides" the modality. Other rules are composite rules that should be split for the sake of clarity. E.g., the rule 'is connected or has been connected with at least one organisation unit' can be divided into two rules indicating that (i) a person (c.q. researcher) has to be associated during his/her current activities with at least one organisational unit and (ii) (s)he can be associated with more than one organisational unit during the span of his/her entire career. Combinations of "person-organisational unit" instances complying with the first rule are a subset of instance combinations complying with the second rule (logical implication relationship). In natural language, it means that an active researcher must always be associated with at least one research group (synchronically) but in the course of his/her career can have worked for several ones (diachronically).

Table 1. FRIS business rules involving the core entity 'Person'

Rule description	Type	Entities/attributes
Has a unique identifier for each supplier *		cfPersonId
Has a name *		cfPersonName.cfFamilyNames
Has one or more surnames *		cfPersonName.cdFirstNames
Can have other names *		cfPersonName.cfOtherNames
The sex of a person is known *		cfPerson.cfSex
Can have a URI *		cfPerson.URI
Has at least one electronic address	Relation	cfPerson_ElectronicAddress
Is connected or has been connected with at least one organisational unit	Relation	cfPerson_OrgUnit
Can have associated keywords*	Related language dependent entity	cfPersonKeyw
Can have associated science domains	Relation	cfPerson_Classification

* included in the E-R scheme – cf. Fig. 1

Other rules are rather cryptic: e.g., 'can have associated keywords' could mean that a person can be associated with any kind of tag. It is not clear how this rule is to be distinguished from the following one 'can have associated science domains'.

And, most importantly, it is not clear whether or not the rule vocabulary is related to domain concepts that have been clearly defined. E.g., one can assume that the natural language term 'keyword' corresponds to the entity attribute 'cfPersonKeyw', but is 'supplier' related to some well defined domain entity ? This problem explains why a column called 'entities/attributes' is included next to the rule description. Without this column, the rules 'has a name' and 'can have other names' would be highly confusable. Furthermore, it is not really clear what is an 'other name'. The table column labelled 'type' indicates what kind of type the core entity 'Person' is linked with. It shows that some rules involve CERIF E-R link entities. The third possible type is calculation (not shown in Table 1): e.g., a project has to last at least for one day and at maximum for 40 years. The exact duration is calculated by comparing starting and ending dates.

In short, one can easily see that the FRIS business rules can modelled in a clearer way leaving less room for interpretation and ambiguity. In addition, the business rules could be expressed on a level that makes abstraction of the CERIF E-R scheme while relying on the semantics of the overall domain model. After all, one cannot require all the stakeholders to become experts in the intrinsics of the CERIF E-R scheme and express their business logics and rules in terms of a specific implementation (c.q., the CERIF E-R schema) of a conceptual model (the research domain model). In fact, as happens all too often when designing database applications, the domain model has been constructed at the same time as the CERIF E-R scheme. Afterwards, any extension or modification of the domain model has been applied directly in the E-R scheme. The fact that the semantic layer is actually included in the same E-R scheme illustrates this point. Clearly, there is a lack of *meaning independence*: semantic knowledge is not separated from how it is used in an application [10] – cf. the by now classic principle of data independence in the database world. Hence, it is difficult to semantically ground the related business rules.

3 Work in Progress

3.1 Re-engineering the Domain and Business Rules

Expressing the semantics of the FRIS business rules in an easily understandable way for domain experts has become a major concern. This aligns with the positions of some academics who consider the issue of agreeing on business rules more difficult than agreeing on domain concepts and relationships [8]. In the same way as an ontology serves to ground the concepts and relationships of a domain, the same ontology can be used to ground the business rules vocabulary making them much more unambiguous. Additionally, business rule operators, connectives and qualifiers that are formally defined (see e.g., [13]) can be executed by rule engines. Also creation and

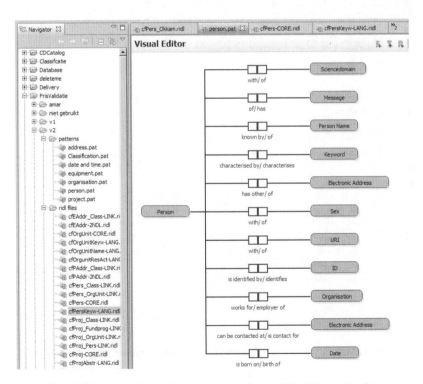

Fig. 2. Representation of the semantic patterns of the '*Person*' entity

maintenance by humans of semantically grounded business rules can be greatly improved using development environments based on formal standards – e.g., semantics of business vocabulary and business rules (SBVR)[2]-based tools.

Therefore, efforts are currently undertaken to develop a FRIS/CERIF business semantic glossary. To each CERIF entity an entry in the glossary explaining their intended meaning will correspond. This effort addresses the problem of diverging interpretations of the business rules vocabulary. EWI developers have created a common conceptual model for CERIF and established a consensus amongst the involved parties (here: Flemish university data centres' information analysts) following the Business Semantics Management (BSM) method [1] and using development tools of Collibra NV[3], namely Collibra Studio. The method strongly relies on fact oriented modelling [3], ontology engineering [11] and the OMG standard SBVR.

Once the CERIF entity labels have received their respective definition, they are, according to the Business Semantics Management methodology of Collibra [1], used to create semantic patterns (corresponding to binary fact types) – see Fig. 2, which are

Fig. 3. Mapping data tags on domain entity labels and defining constraints

---

[2] Semantics of Business Vocabulary and Business Rules,: http://www.omg.org/spec/SBVR/1.0/
[3] www.collibra.com

then semantically restricted by constraints expressing specific business rules. Business rules, i.e. specific constraints on the relationships, have been separated from the semantics of the domain concepts and relationships. Stated in a simplified way: the domain model, the conceptual dictionary and the semantic patterns – e.g., "keyword characterises/is_associated_with a publication" – are distinguished from the application constraints – e.g., a publication can have at maximum five keywords. The CERIF business rules vocabulary (e.g., publication, key word) can be re-used. Its meaning stays the same even if the nature of the relation between the vocabulary changes in other rules for the same application (or even for other applications). Adding a constraint can easily be performed by a domain expert using the development environment.

Before the business rules can be actually used in some application, it is necessary to relate the variable names of the application with to the definitions of the domain ontology. In the FRIS context, the tags of the CERIF XML [6] data sets have to be mapped to the appropriate entry of the FRIS business glossary (see the mapping section of Fig. 3). This is called "committing an application to an ontology" [2].

The business rules are stored in XML (see the 'constraints' section in Fig. 3) to profit from existing XML tools for the actual validation step. When publication data are uploaded, all the data are automatically checked against the business rules. Note that very complicated constraints can be handcrafted in the XML code if needed.

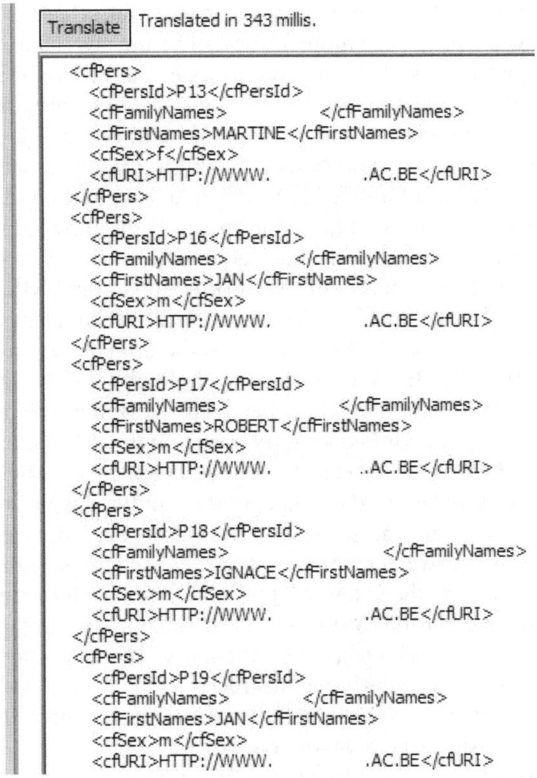

3.2 Testing

An experiment has been organised to test the domain model and re-engineered business rules. It tested the validity of the harvested publication data and metadata by universities that maintain publication repositories compliant with the Open Archives Initiative[4] Protocol for Metadata Harvesting (OAI-PMH).

Fig. 4. Validation output

If the experiment proves to be successful, publications should be correctly attributed to authors and research organisations even if coming from data sets of different

---

[4] Open Archives Intitiative (OAI): http://www.openarchives.org/

providers. Only publications with at least one and at most five associated keywords may be uploaded. Harvesting and upload scripts had to be implemented as well as specific subsequent data cleaning scripts. Nevertheless, an important gain in time (compared to the "old" way of processing incoming data) and hence cost reduction was realised. Additional advantages include the re-usability of the semantic patterns, the repeatability at little costs of the entire upload process, and an increased robustness and scalability of the upload and verification procedures. More details can be found in [14].

4 Discussion and Future Work

The lack of data quality control processes at the source repositories remains a serious problem. Nevertheless, re-engineering the business rules proved to be positive – also for the quality of the information offered in the FRIS portal. Stated in information retrieval terms, the precision is higher (information available is more correct), while the recall is lower (more information not available due to data not passing the quality control process). Potential users of the FRIS portal might consider such a portal more reliable when only correctly aggregated information is presented instead of a near exhaustive list containing errors. Usability studies should be organised to quantitatively support this hypothesis. In addition, from a maintenance point of view, gradually enlarging a knowledge base while safeguarding its correctness and consistency is easier than turning a large but inconsistent knowledge base into a consistent one. By collecting and entering the data closer to the source with more rigid upload validation checks, the quality of the information at the FRIS portal has been improved.

The fact that discussions with the stakeholders were held while avoiding technical E-R parlance and focussing on the domain was an important "trump card" to gain the effective "buy-in" of the stakeholders (mainly data providing universities). It did facilitate communication between the domain experts and alleviated substantially the process of coming to agreements on the domain and business rules vocabulary.

Currently, the entries in the business vocabulary glossary entries are not yet directly linked to the concept labels in the development environment (see Fig. 2). Work on defining the semantics has partly been done in parallel as not all facilities of the glossary were available when the meetings with the stakeholders took place. However, it is the intention to "feed" the development environment directly from the semantic business glossary. The stakeholders are positive regarding the approach and way of working as they recognise the advantages. They have accepted the overall principles underlying the FRIS and the methods to realise it. Stated a bit provocatively, the stakeholders have involved their domain specialists and information analysts instead of their software engineers or database modellers. In addition, the stakeholders appreciate the apparent promise on scalability and better maintainability of the data and knowledge in the FRIS portal.[5]

In the future, following the philosophy of the model driven architecture efforts will go into separating the domain conceptual model (and semantic descriptions) better from the platform independent model (the CERIF E-R representation) and on an automatic transformation of the former in the latter.

---

[5] In [0], more details on the (meta-)data harvesting experiment mentioned about are given.

5 Conclusion

In this paper we have presented a concrete case of re-engineering existing business rules into semantically grounded business rules. The latter are used to validate data from various sources and origins before upload into a government innovation information portal. The rules and domain model have been created and validated by domain experts (also from stakeholder organisations), not by software engineers, thanks to applying a collaborative business semantics management method. Many hurdles still wait to be overcome but the opportunities of a system like FRIS are apparent, in particular when set up to apply appropriate scientifically validated methods and standards to model the business logics.

Acknowledgements

We'd like to thank all our colleagues of the EWI FRIS team (Namik Akyel in particular), Brigitte Jörg (DFKI Berlin) and Stijn Christiaens (Collibra NV) for their collaboration and input.

References

1. De Leenheer, P., Christiaens, S., Meersman, R.: Business Semantics Management with DOGMA-MESS: a Case Study for Competency-centric HRM. Journal of Computers in Industry: Special Issue about Semantic Web Computing in Industry (2009) (to appear)
2. Guarino, N.: Formal Ontologies and Information Systems. In: Guarino, N. (ed.) Proceedings of FOIS 1998, pp. 3–15. IOS Press, Amsterdam (1998)
3. Halpin, T.: Information Modeling and Relational Databases: from conceptual analysis to logical design. Morgan-Kaufmann, San Francisco (2001)
4. Jörg, B.: The Common European Research Information Format Model (CERIF). In: Asserson, A. (ed.) CRISs for the European e-Infrastructure Data Science Journal (2009) (to appear)
5. Jörg, B., Jeffery, K., Asserson, A., van Grootel, G.: CERIF2008 - 1.0 Full Data Model (FDM) - Model Introduction and Specification. euroCRIS (2009)
6. Jörg, B., Krast, O., Jeffery, K., van Grootel, G.: CERIF2008XML - 1.0 Data Ex-change Format Specification, euroCRIS (2009)
7. Jörg, B., Jeffery, K., Asserson, A., van Grootel, G., Rasmussen, H., Price, A., Vestam, T., Kar-stensen Elbæk, M., Houssos, N., Voigt, R., Simons, E.J.: CERIF2008-1.0 Seman-tics, euroCRIS (2009)
8. Meersman, R.: An essay on the role and evolution of (data)base semantics. In: Meersman, R., Mark, L. (eds.) Database Application Semantics, Proceedings of the Sixth IFIP TC-2 Working Conference on Data Semantics (DS-6), IFIP Conference Proceedings 74, pp. 1–7. Chapman and Hall, Boca Raton (1996)
9. Nijssen, M., Lemmens, I.: Verbalization for Business Rules and Two Flavors of Verbalization for Fact Examples. In: Meersman, R., Tari, Z., Herrero, P. (eds.) OTM-WS 2008. LNCS, vol. 5333, pp. 760–769. Springer, Heidelberg (2008)

10. Spyns, P., Meersman, R., Jarrar, M.: Data modelling versus Ontology engineering. In: Sheth, A., Meersman, R. (eds.) SIGMOD Record Special Issue, vol. 31 (4), pp. 12–17 (2002)
11. Spyns, P., Tang, Y., Meersman, R.: An ontology engineering methodology for DOGMA. Journal of Applied Ontology 1-2 (3), 13–39 (2008)
12. Spyns, P., Van Grootel, G., Jörg, B., Christiaens, S.: Realising a Flemish govern-ment innovation information portal with Business Semantics Management. In: Proceedings of CRIS 2010, pp. 45–53 (2010)
13. Tang, Y., Spyns, P., Meersman, R.: Towards Semantically Grounded Decision Rules using ORM+. In: Paschke, A., Biletskiy, Y. (eds.) RuleML 2007. LNCS, vol. 4824, pp. 78–91. Springer, Heidelberg (2007)
14. Van Grootel, G., Spyns, P., Christiaens, S., Jörg, B.: Business Semantics Management Supports Government Innovation Information Portal. In: Meersman, R., Herrero, P., Dillon, T. (eds.) OTM 2009 Workshops. LNCS, vol. 5872, pp. 757–766. Springer, Heidelberg (2009)
15. Verheyden, P., De Bo, J., Meersman, R.: Semantically Unlocking Database Content Through Ontology-Based Mediation. In: Bussler, C.J., Tannen, V., Fundulaki, I. (eds.) SWDB 2004. LNCS, vol. 3372, pp. 109–126. Springer, Heidelberg (2005)

A Personalized and Collaborative eLearning Materials Recommendation Scenario Using Ontology-Based Data Matching Strategies

Ioana Ciuciu and Yan Tang

Semantics Technology and Applications Research Laboratory,
Department of Computer Science, Vrije Universiteit Brussel, Pleinlaan 2,
B-1050 Brussels, Belgium
{iciuciu,yan.tang}@vub.ac.be

Abstract. We propose a virtual teacher for the evaluation of students' competencies. It aims to improve learning by making personalized suggestions on the learning materials. It is based on three main components: 1) a semantically enriched content management system (CMS), playing the role of knowledge base, 2) a 3D anatomy browser and 3) an ontology-based matching strategy called Controlled Fully Automated Ontology Based Matching Strategy (C-FOAM), providing the evaluation methodology. Together with the collaborative knowledge base, which allows knowledge to be represented in natural language and to be further reused, the evaluation methodology becomes the main contribution of the paper. The approach is demonstrated on a learning scenario illustrated around 3D anatomical structures.

Keywords: Ontology, Ontology-based Data Matching, Evaluation Methodology, Knowledge Management, E-learning.

1 Introduction

The present study focuses on semantically rich medical data annotations for eLearning. The goal is to create an intelligent system that evaluates students based on the Controlled Fully Automated Ontology Based Matching Strategy (C-FOAM) developed in the EC FP6 Prolix project and on the evaluation methodology for the evaluation. The intelligent system makes personalized suggestions on the learning materials according to the similarity scores found by C-FOAM when comparing the students' answers with the knowledge base.

This paper focuses on a collaborative knowledge base in natural language and the evaluation methodology. The study begins with a background on ontology engineering in Section 2, it continues with the three components of the virtual teacher: the CMS - introduced in Section 3, the visual framework - introduced in Section 4 and the matching strategy - introduced in Section 5. The learning scenario and the interpretation of the results are presented in Section 6. Section 7 is the related work of the paper. Section 8 concludes on the presented work and discusses future research ideas emerging from it.

R. Meersman et al. (Eds.): OTM 2010 Workshops, LNCS 6428, pp. 575–584, 2010.
© Springer-Verlag Berlin Heidelberg 2010

2 Backgrounds

The knowledge in this study (e.g., learning materials) is grounded in natural language, following the paradigm of Developing Ontology Grounded Methodology and Applications (DOGMA) [1, 2]. In DOGMA, the ontology is two-layered, in order to make the reuse of facts easier. It is separated into 1) a *lexon* base layer and 2) a *commitment* layer.

A lexon is a quintuple $\langle \gamma, t_1, r_1, r_2, t_2 \rangle \in \Gamma \times T \times R \times R \times T$, where T is a finite set of terms; t_1 and t_2 represent two concepts in a natural language (e.g., English). R is a finite set of roles; r_1 and r_2 (r_1 corresponds to "role" and r_2 corresponds to "co-role") refer to the relationships that the concepts share with respect to one another; γ is a context identifier and refers to a context, which serves to disambiguate the terms t_1, t_2 into the intended concepts, and in which they become meaningful. For example $\langle human\ anatomy, lower\ limb, part, part\ of, muscle \rangle$ means the fact that "in the context of human anatomy, the lower limb has as part the muscle and muscle is a part of the lower limb". This example is depicted in Fig. 1.

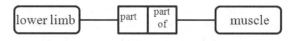

Fig. 1. A lexon example

A commitment contains a constraint of a set of lexons. For instance, we can apply the constraint on the above lexon: "each muscle belongs to at most one lower limb". The commitment language is specified in a language such as OWL [3] or SDRule [4].

3 Collaborative Semantic Data Annotation

The collaborative CMS [5, 6] provides the communities with a framework for knowledge sharing and storage platform based on ontologies. The data - images, videos, publications, etc. - stored in the CMS is assigned meaning through annotations. The annotation of the data models is a social, collaborative process. The tool we propose is highly suitable for these social processes. It collects different parts of knowledge - expressed in natural language - from domain experts in the form of on-line templates. The knowledge captured by the templates can be made machine-readable by transforming it in the corresponding RDF(S) classes and properties.

In this study, the CMS serves as knowledge base for the visualization framework and for the ontology-based matching strategies, providing a way of representing, communicating and sharing knowledge for learning purposes. C-FOAM processes the knowledge in the lexon format. Therefore, we derive lexons from annotations and input them into C-FOAM in order to find the scores.

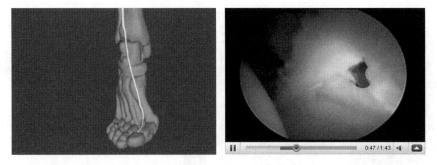

Fig. 2. Learning materials stored in the CMS: an image (left); a video (right)

Table 1 and Table 2 provide (partially) a conceptualization in terms of lexons of the two anatomical structures represented in Fig. 2. The lexons are inferred from the annotations of the learning materials (scientific publications, books, etc.) associated to these anatomical structures in the CMS.

Table 1. Lexons derived from the learning materials for the Extensor Hallucis Longus Tendon

Extensor Hallucis Longus Tendon	part of	part	Tendons Of Lower Leg
Extensor Hallucis Longus Tendon	affected by	affects	Rupture
Extensor Hallucis Longus Tendon	reconstructed with	reconstructs	Gracilis Tendon Autograft
Extensor Hallucis Longus Tendon	repaired by	repairs	Surgery
Extensor Hallucis Longus Tendon	replaced by	replaces	Accessory Tendon

Table 2. Lexons derived from the learning materials for the Acetabular Labrum Cartilage

Acetabular Labrum	part of	part	Cartilage of Hip
Acetabular Labrum	stabilizes	stabilized by	Hip Joint
Hip Arthroscopy	repairs	repaired by	Acetabular Labrum
Hip Arthroscopy	is a	is	Surgery
Arthroscopy	diagnoses	diagnosed by	Acetabular Labral Tear

The user can visualize the anatomical structures and in the same time retrieve semantic information thanks to the knowledge interaction framework, presented in the next section.

4   3D Anatomy Browser

We setup an interaction framework for the examination of the knowledge describing the musculoskeletal system of the human lower limb. The user can browse the anatomical structures which are of interest for him using the anatomy browser [7] and in the same time query the CMS to retrieve information on the selected structures.

Every time new structures are added to the anatomical browser resources, related information (text, images, associated publications, etc.) are updated on the collaborative CMS and annotated. Then a link is created between the application and the online data, enhancing the application with semantic information (see Fig. 3).

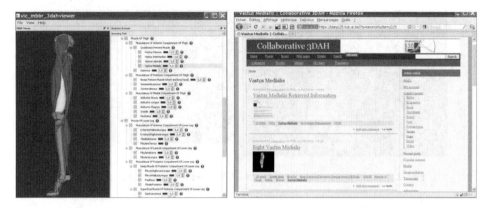

Fig. 3. Knowledge interaction: anatomy browser (left) and the corresponding annotation via the collaborative CMS (right)

In the scenario presented in this study, the anatomy browser is used only for visualization of the anatomical structures during the tests. All the semantic information related to those structures is hidden from the user. The following section introduces the ontology-based matching strategy algorithms used for competency evaluation.

5 C-FOAM Ontology-Based Data Matching Strategy

The ontology-based data matching framework (ODMF, [8]) contains matching algorithms originally for: 1) matching strings, such as the ones for SecondString [9], in particular UnsmoothedJS [10, 11, 12], JaroWinklerTFIDF [10, 11, 12] and TFIDF (term frequency-inverse document frequency [13]); 2) matching lexical information, such as using WodNet [14] and 3) matching concepts in an ontology graph. There are several ontology-based data matching strategies in ODMF. Each strategy contains at least one graph algorithm.

5.1 C-FOAM

In this study, we applied Controlled Fully Automated Ontology Based Matching Strategy (C-FOAM), developed within ODMF. C-FOAM contains two modules: 1) the *Interpreter* and 2) the *Comparator*. The interpreter module makes use of the lexical dictionary, WordNet, the domain ontology and string matching algorithms to interpret end users' input. Given a term that denotes either (a) a concept in the domain ontology, or (b) an instance in the ontology, the interpreter will return the correct concept(s) defined in the ontology or lexical dictionary, and an annotation set.

There are two penalty values in the interpreter module. The first one is the threshold for the internal output using string matching. The filtered terms will be the input for the lexical searching components. The second penalty value is to filter the output of the lexical searching components. For instance, when a user enters a string "hearty" or "warmhearted", C-FOAM finds a defined concept "heart" in the domain ontology and its annotation using JaroWinklerTFIDF (the string matching algorithm) and WordNet (the lexical dictionary).

The comparator can as well use any combination of the different graph algorithms to produce a composite score.

5.2 C-FOAM Applied to an eLearning Scenario

Let Ω be the musculoskeletal ontology and C_i a labeled concept, i.e., "Patella". We denote L as a lexon set defined in Ω; L_i describes C_i. Similarly, we denote L' as a lexon set of the learning materials. Each $L_i{}'$ corresponds to a learning material, e.g., "Imaging of the dysplasia". Let $q(L_i, L_i{}')$ be a function that calculates the overlapping rate of L_i and $L_i{}'$: $q(L_i, L'_i) = 1 - |L_i - L_i{}'|/|L_i \cup L_i{}'|$

It means that$\{\forall L_i, L'_i | 0 \leq q(L_i, L'_i) \leq 1, L_i, L_i{}' \subseteq L\}$.

Let $\alpha_i \in \alpha$ be a natural language string provided by a student. Let $\alpha_i{}' \in \alpha$ be the concept label that is linked to the interpretation of α_i. We denote S_i as a synonym set of $\alpha_i{}'$.

Below are three possible situations:

Situation 1: $\alpha_i = \alpha_i{}'$

The similarity score $SIM(\alpha_i, L'_i) = q(L_i, L'_i)$.

Situation 2: $\alpha_i \neq \alpha_i{}'$ and $\alpha_i{}' \notin S_i$

In this situation, α_i needs to be mapped into a set of $\alpha_i{}'$.

The similarity score $SIM(\alpha_i, L'_i) = q(L_i{}'', L'_i)$, where $L_i{}'' \in L$ is a lexon set defined for $\alpha_i{}''$.

Situation 3: $\alpha_i \neq \alpha_i{}'$ and $\alpha'_i \in S_i$

In this situation, we use a he lexical dictionary, such as WordNet, to define S_i. The similarity score is calculated by finding a synonym or hypernym of α_i, which is equivalent to C_i.   The similarity score $SIM(\alpha_i, L'_i) = q(L_i, L'_i) \times W$ iff $C_i \neq \emptyset$ and $SIM(\alpha_i, L'_i) = 0$ iff $C_i = \emptyset$, where W is a weight that satisfies the following conditions: $0.5 \leq W \leq 1$ if C_i is the synonym of α_i; $0.2 \leq W \leq 0.5$ if C_i is the hypernym or hyponym of α_i.

Note that in this paper $q(L_i, L_i{}')$ is calculated by the LeMaSt algorithm (simple version), which is a kind of graph similarity algorithm. We can as well use other graph algorithms for the calculation [8].

6 The eLearning Scenario

6.1 Scenario

We have tested our approach on a learning scenario, as follows : Step 1) the computer shows a highlighted zone in the anatomy browser; Step 2) the student gives text input - the anatomical structure he considers to be highlighted; Step 3) the matching engine finds the similarity scores (between student input and knowledge base); Step 4) the evaluator calculates the matching score; Step 5) repeat Step 1, 2 and 3 as many times as wanted; Step 6) the evaluator calculates the final score; Step 7) the evaluator shows the correct answers for the answers with final score $\neq 100\%$; Step 8) the computer

580   I. Ciuciu and Y. Tang

finds and suggests the learning materials to the student, based on the annotations in the CMS.

Five anatomical structures (see Fig. 4) have been considered for the test, with the corresponding learning material in the CMS: "Patella", "Gluteus Medius", "Acetabular Labrum", "Extensor Hallucis Longus Tendon" and "Popliteus". The learning materials for the five anatomical structures consist of scientific publications and books, images and videos (see Fig. 2). The annotations corresponding to the learning materials are transformed into lexons (299 lexons in total in the lexon base) in order to be processed by the C-FOAM algorithms. The final goal is to find the final score and to make suggestions for the learning material.

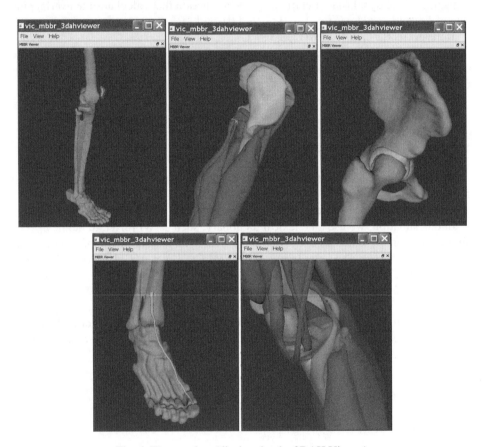

Fig. 4. The test data (displays by the 3DAH Viewer)

6.2 Results and Interpretation

We simulated a test composed of five questions with correct and wrong answers to analyze the behavior of the system. In order to test the different matching algorithms, the answers range from correct ("patella"), correct with typo error ("patela"), correct synonym ("kneecap"), partially correct ("labrum"), partially wrong ("plantaris", "disease").

The typo error case is solved using a string matching algorithm. For the last two questions, the answer was supposed to be wrong, that means 0% matching. However, the results found by C-FOAM are different from 0% (we obtained 0,30% for "plantaris" and "0,11" for disease). This is due to the fact that the matching algorithms found in the ontology (graph) that even if the two concepts are different, they are somehow related. Actually, "plantaris" and "popliteus" are both muscles of the "Posterior Compartment of the Lower Leg". Whilst for "disease", there are many annotated learning materials related to the diseases of the "popliteus", so even if the concepts do not match, the score if different from zero. The test data and the scores are given in Fig.5.

Image (correct answer)	Student's input	Score	Message	Suggested materials	Remarks
patella	patella	1	perfect	-	String matching
patella	patela	0,98	[TYPO] typo error	-	String matching
patella	kneecap	0,75	[SYNONYM] patella	Publ1, publ2,...	Lexical matching
patella	knee	0,69	[SYNONYM+TYPO] kneecap	Publ1, publ2,...	Lexical matching
gluteus medius	gluteus	0,71	[TYPO] typo error	Video1, publ1, publ2,...	String matching
acetabular labrum	labrum	0,71	[TYPO] typo error	Video1, Publ1, Book1,...	String matching
tensor hallucis longus tendon	hallucis longus tendon	0,87	[TYPO] typo error	Publ1, Publ2,...	String matching
popliteus	plantaris	0,30	[ONTOLOGY] is-a	Video1, Publ1, Page1, Web1,...	Role-co-role matching
popliteus	disease	0,11	[ONTOLOGY] lexon term	Video1, Publ1, Page1, Web1,...	Lexon matching
Total score		73			
Maximum score		100			

Fig. 5. The results of the eLearning scenario and remarks

For "patella", four situations have been tested: 1) correct answer – score 1; 2) error spelling – score 0,98; 3) correct synonym – score 0,75; 4) correct synonym and error spelling – score 0,69. These results have been calculated by an advanced C-FOAM version, which combines JaroWinkler and WordNet. Both of them use LeMaSt, which is a graph algorithm. For "patela", LeMaSt performed a string matching to find the matching with the correct term "patella" and then a lexon matching in order to find the matching in the ontology graph. Whilst for "kneecap", LeMaSt performed a lexical matching using WordNet to find the correct term and then a lexon matching to search it in the ontology.

Based on these results, the system can recommend learning materials that can provide missing competencies or improve the existing skills. For instance, in the case of "knee" or "kneecap", the system can infer that the student understands the concept, but he doesn't remember the correct terminology for that particular structure.

7 Related Work

A number of works have been done lately in the field of personalized delivery of learning materials for eLearning. They mainly focus on capturing the user context in order to be able to recommend the right content, in the right form, to the right learner. Examples are as follow, just to name a few:

Baloian [15] proposes a recommender system, which suggest multimedia learning material based on the learner's background preferences and available software/hardware. This approach faces the inconvenient of information overloading. Schmidt [16] proposes an approach for capturing the context of the learner based on the semantic modeling of the learner's environment. Yu [17] proposes a method for context-aware learning content provisioning for ubiquitous learning.

Our approach is slightly different in that it focuses on capturing and evaluating the user knowledge. The evaluation and the delivery of the learning materials are based on the ontology-based data matching methodology.

A general evaluation methodology for ontology-based data matching does not exist. Evaluation methods are trivial and application specific. Related work on the types of evaluation methods is described as below:

Program evaluation is the systematic collection of information about the activities, characteristics and outcomes of programs to make judgments about the program, improve program effectiveness, and inform decisions about future programming [18].

Utilization-focused evaluation [19, 20] is a comprehensive approach to doing evaluations that are useful, practical, ethical and accurate.

Purpose oriented evaluation methodologies [21] contain three kinds of evaluation methodologies – formative evaluation, pertaining evaluation and summative evaluation. Formative evaluation focuses on the process. Pertaining evaluation focuses on judgment of the value before the implementation. Summative evaluation focuses on the outcome.

8 Conclusion

The paper presents an ontologic approach to improve eLearning by finding the similarity score between the student's knowledge and the learning materials available in the knowledge base. The approach is based on collaborative semantic data annotations, on visual interaction and on ontology-based data matching strategies.

The learning score is used to evaluate the students' competencies and also to make suggestions on the learning materials for further improvement of the students' skills. Different strategies exist to find the similarity score and a methodology has been developed to evaluate these strategies.

The knowledge (i.e., the learning materials) is modeled using the DOGMA ontology, which has the advantage of being grounded in natural language.

For the present, the suggestions on the learning materials are only done by the system, based on the similarity scores given by the different matching algorithms. A work in progress emerging from this study is to submit the results to the human expertise for verification and improvement. Different contexts/factors will have to be considered in the recommendation, to capture and understand the learner's individual characteristics and learning behavior. For example, how often did the student take the test, how much time is needed for the student to acquire new knowledge, the learning context, etc.

A future research direction is to apply the ontology-based data matching strategies on annotated anatomical data for the purpose of medical diagnosis.

Acknowledgments. This work is supported by the EU FP6 Marie Curie project 3D Anatomical Human (MRTN-CT-2006-035763) and by the EU FP7 TAS3 project. The work has also been partly supported by the EU ITEA-2 Project 2008005 "Do-it-Yourself Smart Experiences", founded by IWT 459.The authors would like to thank Jerome Schmid from the University of Geneva and Jose Antonio Iglesias Guitian from CRS4, Visual Computer Group, Sardinia, Italy for the permission to use their anatomy browser for this study.

References

1. Meersman, R.: Ontologies and databases: More than a Fleeting Ressemblance. In: Raś, Z.W., Skowron, A. (eds.) ISMIS 1999. LNCS, vol. 1609. Springer, Heidelberg (1999)
2. Meersman, R.: Semantics Ontology Tools in Information System Design. In: The Proceedings of OES/SEO 2001 Rome Workshop, Luiss Publications (2001)
3. Web Ontology Language (OWL), http://www.w3.org/TR/owl-ref
4. Tang, Y., Meersman, R.: SDRule Markup Language: Towards Modeling and Interchanging Ontological Commitments for Semantic Decision Making. In: Handbook of Research on Emerging Rule-based Languages and Technologies: Open Solutions and Approaches, , IGI Publishing, USA (2009) ISBN: 1-60566-402-2
5. Collaborative 3DAH, https://starpc25.vub.ac.be
6. Ciuciu, I., Kang, H., Meersman, R., Schmid, J., Magnenat-Thalmann, N., Guitian, J.A.I., Gobbetti, E.: Collaborative Content Management: an Ongoing Case Study for Imaging Applications. In: Proceedings of the 11th European Conference on Knowledge Management, Famalicao, Portugal (2010)
7. http://3dah.miralab.ch/index.php?option=com_remository&Itemid=78&func=fileinfo&id=394
8. Tang, Y., Meersman, R., Ciuciu, I.G., Leenarts, E., Pudney, K.: Towards Evaluating Ontology Based Data Matching Strategies. In: Proceedings of the Fourth IEEE International Conference on Research Challenges in Information Science, Nice, France, pp. 137–145 (2010)
9. Cohen, W.W., Ravikumar, P.: Secondstring: An Open Source Java Toolkit of Approximate String-matching Techniques.(2003), Project web page, http://secondstring.sourceforge.net
10. Jaro, M.A.: Advances in Record-linkage Methodology as Applied to Matching the 1985 Census of Tampa, Florida. The Journal of the American Statistical Association 84, 414–420 (1989)
11. Jaro, M.A.: Probabilistic Linkage of Large Public Health Data Files (disc: P687-689). Statistics in Medicine 14, 491–498 (1995)
12. Winkler, W.E.: The State of Record Linkage and Current Research Problems, Statistics of Income Division, Internal Revenue Service Publication R99/04 (1999), http://www.census.gov/srd/www/byname.html

13. Jones, S.K.: A Statistical Interpretation of Term Specificity and its Application in Retrieval. Journal of Documentation 28(1), 11–21 (1972)
14. Fellbaum, C.: WordNet: An Electronic Lexical Database, Massachusets Institute of Technology (1999) ISBN 0-262-06197
15. Baloian, N., Galdames, P., Collazos, C.A., Guerrero, L.A.: A Model for a Collaborative Recommender System for Multimedia Learning Material. In: de Vreede, G.-J., Guerrero, L.A., Marín Raventós, G. (eds.) CRIWG 2004. LNCS, vol. 3198, pp. 281–288. Springer, Heidelberg (2004)
16. Schmidt, A., Winterhalter, C.: User Context Aware Delivery of E-Learning Material: Approach and Architecture. Journal of Universal Computer Science 10(1), 28–36 (2004)
17. Yu, Z., Nakamura, Y., Zhang, D., Kajita, S., Mase, K.: Content Provisioning for Ubiquitous Learning. IEEE Pervasive Computing 7(4), 62–70 (2008)
18. Patton, M.Q.: Qualitative Research and Evaluation Methods, 3rd edn. Sage Publications, Inc., London (2002) ISBN 0-7619-1971-6
19. Stufflebeam, D.L., Madaus, G.F., Kellaghan, T.: Utilization-Focused Evaluation. In: Book Evaluation in Education and Human Services, 2nd edn., vol. 49, pp. 425–438. Springer, Netherlands (2006)
20. Blundell, R., Costa Dias, M.: Evaluation methods for non-experimental data. Fiscal Studies 21(4), 427–468 (2000)
21. Bhola, H.S.: Evaluating "Literacy for development" projects, programs and campaigns: Evaluation planning, design and implementation, and utilization of evaluation results. Hamburg, Germany: UNESCO Institute for Education; DSE [German Foundation for International Development], 306 pages (1990)

Ontological-Based Model for Human Resource Decision Support System (HRDSS)

Rohayati Ramli, Shahrul Azman Noah, and Maryati Mohd Yusof

Faculty of Information Science & Technology,
Universiti Kebangsaan Malaysia 43600 UKM Bangi, Selangor, Malaysia
rohayatir@gmail.com, {samn,mmy}@ftsm.ukm.my

Abstract. This research concerns the development of Ontology-based model as an input to Human Resource Decision Support System (HRDSS) and to assist in the efficient and effective data analysis and leveraging the semantic content of ontology. These are to give intelligence support in decision-making and to proposed and develop suitable system architecture of the intelligence DSS model for the Human resource planning at national level. The initial model was developed based on the literature review on issues related to Human resource planning complex unstructured decision making process. We have been working on ontology to manage knowledge in human resource and integrate multiple data resources in order to support decision making in forecasting and projection for supply and demand in Human Resource Development.

Keywords: Decision support System, Ontology, Human resource planning, Supply and demand.

1 Introduction

Labour environment and employment trend change constantly due to domestic and global influence. Creating, establishing and maintaining job opportunities in conducive investment climate is important in ensuring healthy working environment and thus benefits the manpower. Globalization and economic liberalization has created a borderless labour market. Thus, planning of national development has to consider global and regional development. The Government's role in analyzing the national employment market situation and identifying labour policy will create job opportunities effectively. Human Resource planning or manpower planning is crucial to address the problem of imbalance between demand and supply.

The goal of this research is to leverage the semantic content of ontology to provide intelligence support in forecasting job opportunities based on supply and demand. We proposed an DSS model for the Human Resource Planning (HRP) which represents a new, interdisciplinary approach to the management of knowledge in a problem-solving process and to improve human resource decision-support systems (HRDSSs) that employ model-based module approaches. Even if the application studied is specific, it can serve as a basis for any human resource planning whether at organizational level or industry level. This vision is achieved by managing knowledge in human resource and integrates multiple data resources of data and information

R. Meersman et al. (Eds.): OTM 2010 Workshops, LNCS 6428, pp. 585–594, 2010.
© Springer-Verlag Berlin Heidelberg 2010

from internal and external organization. Based on the identified data requirement, we develop an ontology-based model for supply and demand. We show and explain how the addition of ontologies and semantics results in a more reliable and practical management of complex problems.

This paper is structured as follows. The next section provides general background on Human Resource planning, and on the needs for forecasting using DSSs, ontologies and its application in DSS and HR. Section 3 focuses on the Framework of DSS model for Human resource planning decision support system (HRDSS) proposed and, finally, Section 4 presents the conclusions.

2   Theoretical Background

2.1   Human Resource Planning (HRP)

The Human resource planning (HRP) provides annual projections of the major macroeconomic and industry dimensions of the economy and detailed analysis of the labour requirements and labour supply. HRP is a complex unstructured decision making process [1, 2] because information related to manpower problems is inadequate[2] and issues on business environment are dynamic and uncertain [3, 4]. Quantifiable data is limited because developmental and evolutionary nature of manpower process itself impact human resource planning decisions [5] and allocations [6].

2.2   Need for HRP Forecasts

Forecasts must be developed to identify the mismatch between HR supply and HR demand. The basic rationale for making HRP forecasts is the long gestation lags in the production of skilled professional people. HRP forecasts made well in advance, facilitate planning of education/training is the effort to ensure that manpower required and job opportunities are available at the time when they are needed. This is important especially for development country.

The basic rationale for making HRP forecasts are to identify the mismatch between HR supply and HR demand and to reduce the cost of job loss and associated loss. This also to overcome the reliance on foreign labour and the long gestation lags in the production of skilled professional people. Advanced HRP facilitate the planning of education/training by ensuring that manpower required and job opportunities are available in a timely manner. This is important especially for country development.

The second major reason is the observed imperfections in the labour market. Markets for manpower with long lead time for production are characterised by cobweb cycles, because of long lags in the supply side and short lags, on the demand side. If the event supply is not planned to meet the requirement, cobweb cycles [7] in the labour market may ultimately lead to distortions in occupation-education correspondence, the fallout of which could either result in huge educated unemployment or with people taking up occupations for which they are not adequately prepared or both. HR forecast is expected to facilitate correction of labour market distortions.

The third major reason is that in the short-run at least, elasticities of substitution among various skills have been observed to be either zero or near zero. Production of goods and services, therefore, requires various categories of skilled manpower in fixed proportion. Shortage of any skilled category of manpower, in such a situation would adversely affect the production of goods and services within the economy. HRP forecasts would help avoid such a situation by facilitating anticipation of skill shortages and planning skill supplies accordingly.

2.3 Ontology

Hopkins [8] highlighted that data availability for HRP is poor at the national level in developing countries. There is much confusion over the meaning of employment and unemployment mainly to suit the interests of one political party or another [8]. However, with global interconnectivity we now need to deal with more heterogeneous information resources consisting of a variety of digital data. Data from HR information systems has a number of limitations including in availability, lack of consistency, and not expressed in a general way to be shared between systems, ambiguous terminology, and semantic integration of information does not exist. Furthermore, there are no standard understanding on the structure of knowledge for a domain for certain term in HR [9, 10]

Ontology can facilitate knowledge sharing and reuse. In this research, ontology can provide: (1) a shared and common understanding of the knowledge domain that can be communicated among agents and application systems, and (2) an explicit conceptualization that describes the semantics of the data [11]. Ontology is a formal specification of domain knowledge and has been used to define a set of data and their structure for experts to share information in a domain of interest. It is well suited for the representation and utilization of relations among data, and is efficient in knowledge reasoning. Ontology-based method is a new and promising approach to manage knowledge in HR, integrate multiple data resources, and facilitate the consideration of the complex relations among concepts and slots in decision making [12].

Decision support System (DSS) applications can be used to extract information to structure data and readable machine format [13]. The current challenges of HR planning model is the need of domain experts to extract the input manually from unstructured text. Based on that research on automated development of ontologies from texts [14, 15] has become increasingly important because manual construction of ontologies is labour intensive and costly, and, at the same time, large amount of texts for individual domains is already available in electronic form.

Hence, it is the interest of this research to explore the usefulness of ontology-based model as an input to DSS and as an aid to analyse data efficiently and effectively as well as leveraging the semantic content of ontology. These features are meant to provide intelligence support in decision-making for the Human Resource Development Planning.

2.4 Ontology-Based DSS

Ontology-based implementation to support decision making process has been addressed in a number of research involving various domains such as financial, product design, Geographical Information System (GIS), plant treatment and medical.

OntoWEDSS decision-support system for waste water management design by [16] helps to improve the diagnosis of faulty states of a treatment plant, provides support for complex problem-solving and facilitates knowledge modelling and reuse. Meanwhile [17] developed ontology-based approach to structure information in order to support management system audit in gathering, translating and consistency checking to generic management system standard. Ontology-based approach used to parse semantic query in order to do data integration of product design from different heterogeneous format. and decision support environment for e-Design [12]. [18] explores the of use ontology as a technical solution to integrate heterogeneous systems and subsequently to support decision-making in Engineer-To-Order (ETO) products design phase. Similar research by Shue et al. (2009) apply ontology model to assess financial quality of an enterprise. In dealing with the complexity of financial statement analysis, this approach separates knowledge content into domain knowledge of financial statements and operational knowledge of analysts' analytical process [19]. While Niararki and Kim (2009) studies on ontology-based architecture using a multi-criteria decision making technique to design a personalized route planning system using information system such as geographic information system (GIS) in order to identify the best route for travelling based on user preferences stored on mobile appliances [20].

Thus the need to anticipate and integrate ontologies to DSS in order to improve decision-support systems and forecasting is crucial in HRP. Many researches focus on human resource development based on competency ontology without anticipate it with DSS [21-26].

2.5   Ontologies in Human Resource

Knowledge based automation in the domain of HR faces some daunting challenges. Information technology scientists and practitioners involved in the HR domain have to quantify and qualify the common knowledge that underlies meaningful conversations about human resources. The common language used to describe jobs, functional roles and staff vacancies is generally well understood and formalised, at least within specific enterprise domains or regional scopes. Models and emerging standards for the description of tasks and responsibilities have been used with various degrees of success.

Various standardisation efforts also support capturing the combination of tasks and responsibilities that make up a typical job description or job vacancy. The existing ontologies in HR has been built such as : ProPer Ontology [27] on skills management, KOWIEN Ontology [28] on competence and skills management, Knowledge Nets [29] on national and international classifications for jobs and branches, "ePeople" [30] on Skills, Skill Profiles of Employees and Job Skill Requirements, LIP Ontology [31] for on-demand learning support, CommOnCV [32] on competencies from CV descriptions, TOVE (Toronto Virtual Enterprise Ontologies) which is an integrated ontologies for the modelling of commercial and public enterprises, PROTON (PROTO-Ontology) upper-level ontology for a number of tasks in different domains, and COKE [33] a three-level ontology containing a top-level HR ontology (representing employees and their social groups), a middle-level Business Process ontology and a lower-level Knowledge Objects ontology which are related to organizational entities.

In summary, there are several approaches to elaborating ontologies in the HR domain, each of them with a different focus. These researches try to combine the strengths of different approaches like the Professional Learning Ontology, the TOVE ontologies, and the HR-XML initiative.

3 The Approach

In this section, the proposed HRDSS framework and ontological-based model are reviewed.

3.1 Overall Framework of HRDSS

The proposed framework of DSS model for Human resource planning is depicted in Figure 1. This framework is made up of ontological-based model, modules of model based (HRD modelling), and user interface. The Ontology will be used for interpretation and extraction of information from heterogonous resources for the development of its knowledge structure. The knowledge produced from such a process will be used as an input to HRD Modelling System. The model base module is the core of the system; it consists of balancing of labour supply and labour demand (HBF), system control of input and outputs (HSC) and Market and Policy.

3.2 Ontological-Based Model

In the following, an ontological-based model is discussed to demonstrate the application of the ontology to HRDSS.

3.2.1 The Domain and Scope of the Ontology

The aim of this research is to integrate ontology in the process of decision making for HR planning. As HR planning relies on various forms of heterogeneous data and information, the ontology will act as a mediator between the HRD modelling system and the heterogeneous data resources as illustrated in Figure 1. In this case the data and information will be mapped and integrated into the ontology and serves as dynamic knowledge bases for supporting the forecasting and projection for supply and demand in HRD system.

3.2.2 Design of Ontology Model

In order to reuse of (parts of the) existing domain knowledge in HR this research will adopt an ontological approach, in which we plan to use levels of increasing specialization [34]. The classic ontological approach consists of an ontological structure with concepts and relations and instances of the concepts, which contain the knowledge content. The approach will provide an ontological framework, in which the more generic ontological levels can be reused easier. The proposed levels are as follows:

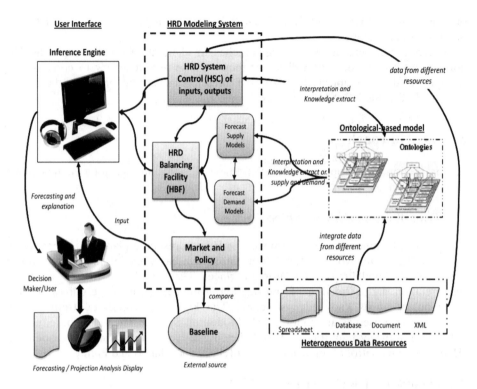

Fig. 1. Proposed framework of DSS model for Human Resource Development (HRP)

- Level 0: Upper-level ontology with basic terminology (*ontology*, *concept*, *relation*, *instance*, *property*, *process*);
- Level 1: generic process knowledge (*steps*, *task*, *activity*, *method*, *user type*, *domain*, etc.);
- Level 2: specialized process knowledge (in the Human Resource: generic modelling knowledge with a generic description of what to do and methods on how to do it);
- Level 3: domain specific process knowledge (in the HRP Modelling system: modelling knowledge specialized for specific HR domains);

A stepwise ontology specialization with the modelling ontology expanded to some more particular ontological concepts. The top (Upper-level ontology) is the most generic ontological level and the concepts at the bottom the most specialized ones.

3.2.3 Competency Questions

In developing the domain ontology, the TOVE [39] ontology engineering approach will be adopted. This approach consists of six phases: motivation scenario, informal competency question, terminology, formal competency question, axioms, and completeness theorem. The six phases encompass the identification of problem domain, the analysis of knowledge content, and the development of relationships and related reasoning processes.

Since the major reasoning part of the completed system, which is the diagnostic process, will be handled by the rule-based module, hence the development of reasoning process will be excluded, which includes formal competency question and axioms. It is common however to design informal competency questions in such a way that the ontology developed fulfil the systems requirements. These questions are initially expressed in the motivation scenario and later become informal competency questions. Among the competency questions for this research are as follows:

i)   What is the population by gender by age by citizenship?
ii) What is the labour force projection by education by citizenship?
iii) What is the forecast of the labour force by occupation and the explanation for the projection?
iv) What are the forecasts of Gross Domestic Product (GDP), interest rates, and price and wage inflation?
v)   What is the forecast of employment by industries?
vi) What is the forecast of employment by occupation?

3.2.4 Domain Knowledge of Supply and Demand

In this research, the ontology will be used to demonstrate the analysis of the domain knowledge and the development of its knowledge structure from heterogeneous resources such as databases, XML file and textual document as well. Extraction knowledge from databases, document and XML file will be use the facilities provided in protégé - importing data from files or spreadsheets. In fact Protégé will be the tool used for modelling the ontology for supply and demand. Available ontologies [40] relating to demographic, education and temporal will also be used and integrated as they contain non-trivial knowledge for supporting the decision making process. An ontology model containing relationships between inputs of forecast supply model is as depicted in Figure 2.

The Forecast Labour Supply Model consists of three components; which are the demographic component (HDM) for projecting the population by age group and gender; the educational attainment component (HEM) for projecting the labour force by educational attainment; and The occupational supply component (HOSM) for converting the projection from HEM of the labour force by educational attainment to a projection of the labour force by occupation. Meanwhile, the Forecast Labour Demand Model consists of two components: (i) Macro-models (HMM) for projecting labour demand by industries, following the industry classification used in the national accounts and later will constructed to initially project labour demand by industries; (ii) the occupational demand model (HODM for converting the forecasts of labour demand by industry to labour demand by occupation.

The second model, the HSC, is a control centre where scenario inputs are provided and scenario outputs are collected from the system. The HSC models introduce and examine the effects of alternative policies. The HSC mode; then collects the results for these alternative policy scenarios and compares them with the baseline scenario. Meanwhile, the HBF model takes the labour demand and supply predictions from the respective models and identifies any structural shortages and surpluses for labour markets.

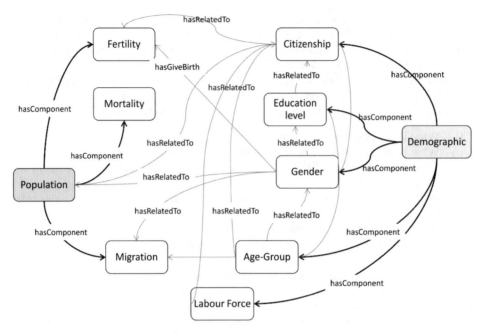

Fig. 2. An ontology model containing relationships between inputs of forecast supply model

4   Conclusions

Efficient and effective decisions are largely supported by sufficient and relevant data from heterogeneous resources. The domain knowledge produced from ontology will be used as input in as proposed in HRDSS framework.

The framework of the HRDSS proposed in this research can be useful in providing guidelines for Human resource planners to consider when developing a HRDSS. The need for automated computerised tools is paramount with respect to improving decision making processes. This will be useful when planners need to carry out forecasting and other statistical analysis of the required decision. Furthermore, it also provides information for DSS developers on managing quantitative model in the HRDSS system. Prototype will be developing to validate the proposed framework and the output of HRDSS will be compared against the output from other similar systems to evaluate the performance. For the future, the framework can be improved by automatically extracting all the knowledge from each level of HR planning to support the decision making.

References

1. Shih, H.S., Huang, L.C., Shyur, H.J.: Recruitment and Selection Processes Through an Effective GDS. Computers and Mathematics with Applications 50(10-12), 543–1558 (2005)
2. Kolehmainen-Aitken, R.: Human Resources Planning: Issues and Methods. Department of Population and International Health. Harvard School of Public Health, Massachusetts (1993)

3. Bennet, A., Bennet, D.: The decision-making process in a complex situation. Handbook on Decision Support Systems: Basic Themes 1, 3–20 (2008)
4. Trust, B.: Nursing workforce planning: mapping the policy trail (2005)
5. Mohanty, R.P.,, S.G.D.: Evolution of a decision support system for human resource planning in a petroleum company. Internatinal Journal of Production Economics 51, 11 (1997)
6. Murphy, G., O'Brien-Pallas, L.: How Do Health Human Resources Policies And Practices Inhibit Change?: A Plan For The Future. Ottawa Queensland Health (2002), Health, 2002 (2020)
7. Rothschild, K.W.: Cobweb cycles and partially correct forecasting. The Journal of Political Economy 72(3), 300–305 (1964)
8. Hopkins, M.: Manpower Planning Revisited, Ph. D. thesis. Geneva, Switzerland: Faculté des Sciences Économiques et Sociales de L'Université de Genève (2000)
9. Wache, H.: Semantic mediation for heterogeneous information sources, PhD thesis, Univeristy of Bremen (2004) (in German)
10. Marinoni, C., et al.: HR-Semantics Roadmap (2007)
11. Fensel, D., et al.: OIL in a nutshell. Knowledge Engineering and Knowledge Management Methods, Models, and Tools, 137–154 (2000)
12. Chang, X., Terpenny, J.: Ontology-based data integration and decision support for product e-Design. Robotics and Computer-Integrated Manufacturing 25(6), 863–870 (2009)
13. Woods, J.F., et al.: Conceptual Framework for an Optimal Labour Market Information System Final Report, Kalamazoo, Michigan: WE Upjohn Institute for Employment Research (2006)
14. Agichtein, Y.E.: Extracting relations from large text collections, Citeseer (2005)
15. Lee, C.S., et al.: Automated ontology construction for unstructured text documents. Data & Knowledge Engineering 60(3), 547–566 (2007)
16. Ceccaroni, L., Cortés, U., Sànchez-Marrè, M.: OntoWEDSS: augmenting environmental decision-support systems with ontologies. Environmental Modelling & Software 19(9), 785–797 (2004)
17. Ishizu, S., et al.: Ontology-Driven Decision Support Systems For Management System Audit. (2008)
18. Pandit, A., Zhu, Y.: An ontology-based approach to support decision-making for the design of ETO (Engineer-To-Order) products. Automation in Construction 16(6), 759–770 (2007)
19. Shue, L.-Y., Chen, C.-W., Shiue, W.: The development of an ontology-based expert system for corporate financial rating. Expert Systems with Applications 36(2, Part 1), 2130–2142 (2009)
20. Niaraki, A.S., Kim, K.: Ontology based personalized route planning system using a multi-criteria decision making approach. Expert Systems with Applications 36(2, Part 1), 2250–2259 (2009)
21. Hirata, K., Ikeda, M., Mizoguchi, R.: Total resolution for human resource development based on competency ontology. In: ICCE 2001 (2001) (in print)
22. Trichet, F., Leclère, M.: A framework for building competency-based systems dedicated to human resource management. In: Zhong, N., Raś, Z.W., Tsumoto, S., Suzuki, E. (eds.) Foundations of Intelligent Systems 2003. LNCS (LNAI), vol. 2871, pp. 633–639. Springer, Heidelberg (2003)
23. Sim, I., Olasov, B., Carini, S.: An ontology of randomized controlled trials for evidence-based practice: content specification and evaluation using the competency decomposition method. Journal of Biomedical Informatics 37(2), 108–119 (2004)

24. Ahmad, S., Simonovic, S.P.: An intelligent decision support system for management of floods. Water Resources Management 20(3), 391–410 (2006)
25. Kunzmann, C., Schmidt, A.: Ontology-based Competence Management for Healthcare Training Planning: A Case Study. In: Proceedings of I-KNOW 2006, pp. 143–150 (2006)
26. Tarasov, V., et al.: Ontology-Based Competence Management for Team Configuration. In: Mařík, V., Vyatkin, V., Colombo, A.W. (eds.) HoloMAS 2007. LNCS (LNAI), vol. 4659, pp. 401–410. Springer, Heidelberg (2007)
27. Hepp, M., Bachlechner, D., Siorpaes, K.: OntoWiki: community-driven ontology engineering and ontology usage based on Wikis. ACM, New York (2006)
28. Dittmann, L., Zelewski, S.: Ontology-based skills management (2004)
29. Bizer, C., et al.: The impact of semantic web technologies on job recruitment processes. In: Wirtschaftsinformatik 2005, pp. 1367–1381 (2005)
30. Cain, M.M., Sarasohn-Kahn, J., Wayne, J.C.: Health e-people: the online consumer experience. Institute for the Future (2000)
31. Schmidt, A.: Enabling learning on demand in semantic work environments: The learning in process approach. Emerging Technologies for Semantic Work Environments: Techniques, Methods, and Applications, IGI Publishing (2008)
32. Schmidt, A., Braun, S.: Context-aware workplace learning support: Concept, experiences, and remaining challenges. In: Nejdl, W., Tochtermann, K. (eds.) EC-TEL 2006. LNCS, vol. 4227, pp. 518–524. Springer, Heidelberg (2006)
33. Gualtieri, A., Ruffolo, M.: An ontology-based framework for representing organizational Knowledge. In: Proceedings of I-KNOW 2005 (2005)
34. Scholten, H., Kassahun, A., Beulens, A.J.M.: Use and reuse of an ontological knowledge base framework. In: International Institute for Applied Systems Analysis Laxenburg, Austria (2006)
35. Gruninger, M., Fox, M.S.: Methodology for the Design and Evaluation of Ontologies (1995)
36. Gómez-Pérez, A., Ramírez, J., Villazón-Terrazas, B.: Reusing Human Resources Management Standards for Employment Services. Citeseer (2007)

SWWS'10 - PC Co-chairs Message

The Web has now been in existence for quite some time, and it has produced a major shift in our thinking on the nature and scope of information processing. It is rapidly moving towards an application deployment and knowledge deployment that requires complex interactions and properly structured underlying semantics. There has been a sudden upsurge of research activity in the problems associated with adding semantics to the Web in the last few years. This work on semantics will involve data, knowledge, and process semantics. The International IFIP Workshop on Semantic Web & Web Semantics (SWWS 2010), which is in its sixth year, provides a forum for presenting original, unpublished research results and innovative ideas related to this voluminous quantity of research. This year we accepted 8 high quality papers for presentation at SWWS with an acceptance rate of 46%.

Each of these submissions was rigorously reviewed by at least two experts. The papers were judged according to their originality, significance to theory and practice, readability and relevance to workshop topics. Papers for the SWWS workshop mainly focus on the areas of ontology development, ontology evaluation, semantic interoperability, semantic support for human computer interaction and process semantics. We feel that SWWS 2010 papers will inspire further research in the areas of Semantic Web and its applications. We would like to express our deepest appreciation to the authors of the submitted papers and would like to thank all the workshop attendees. We would also like to thank the program committee members and external reviewers for their efforts in maintaining the quality of papers and turning the SWWS 2010 workshop into a success. Thank you and we hope you enjoyed participating in SWWS 2010.

August 2010

Ernesto Damiani
Elizabeth Chang
SWWS'10

R. Meersman et al. (Eds.): OTM 2010 Workshops, LNCS 6428, p. 595, 2010.
© Springer-Verlag Berlin Heidelberg 2010

Enabling Access to Web Resources through SecPODE-Based Annotations

Quentin Reul and Gang Zhao

VUB STARLab,
Vrije Universiteit Brussel,
Pleinlaan 2, 1050 Brussels, Belgium
{quenreul,gang.zhao}@vub.ac.be

Abstract. The annotation of resources with policy metadata enables
the enforcement of security and privacy policies in open and distributed
environments. In this paper, we present the Security Policy Ontology for
Distributed Environment (SecPODE), which is capable of representing
different types of security policies. This ontology differs from existing
security policy ontology by being grounded in natural language rather
than complex paradigms. As a result, SecPODE is both easy to use and
intuitive to extend by security experts and data subject alike. Finally,
we show how SecPODE can be used to gain access to Web resources.

1 Introduction

With the advent of the Semantic Web [3], the Web has shifted from simply
storing documents to enabling the consumption of resources by *distributed* and
autonomous services. For instance, a recruitment agency could gather data
about a job seeker by crawling distributed data repositories (e.g. Monster[1] and
LinkedIn[2]) on the Web. Although these data repositories guarantee some form of
privacy, the data subject[3] may not always have control over how their personal
information is processed and stored by third-party services.

As a result, resources need to be sufficiently annotated with policy metadata so
that these security and privacy policy can be correctly enforced by services trying
to gain access to them. For instance, the actions and resources that are subject
to access control policies can be given meaning through the use of ontologies.
An ontology is commonly defined as: *"a formal, explicit specification of a shared
conceptualization"* [16]. More specifically, an ontology is an engineering artifact
composed (i) of a vocabulary specific to a domain of discourse, and (ii) of a
set of explicit assumptions regarding the intended meaning of the terms in the
vocabulary for that domain.

In this paper, we extend on the work by Reul et al. [12] by using the security policy ontology to define different types of policies, such as access control,

---

[1] http://www.monster.be/
[2] http://www.linkedin.com/
[3] A data subject is an individual whose personal information is stored.

R. Meersman et al. (Eds.): OTM 2010 Workshops, LNCS 6428, pp. 596–605, 2010.

obligation, and delegation policies. The Security Policy Ontology for Distributed Environment (SecPODE) is based on the DOGMA (Developing Ontology-Grounded Methods and Applications) framework [10] and defines not only the structure of policies, but also the meaning of their content. This ontology differs from existing security policy ontology by being grounded in natural language rather than complex paradigms, such as description logic. By grounding knowledge in natural language, security experts and data subjects can use ordinary language constructs to communicate security policies, and thus facilitating semantic interoperability across distributed services. SecPODE is intended to be accompanied and enhanced by application-specific ontologies covering the meaning of the content.

The rest of the paper is organised as follows. Section 2 describes the DOGMA framework, while section 3 presents the Security Policy Ontology for Distributed Environment (SecPODE). In section 4, we show how SecPODE can be used to access resources on the web. We review some related research in section 5, while the final section outlines future work.

2   Background

DOGMA [10] is a formal ontology engineering framework that makes a distinction between the lexical representation of concepts and their semantic constraints. This strict separation is known as the *double articulation* principle, and facilitates the potential for reuse as it is much easier to reach an agreement on the conceptualization rather than on domain rules [11].

Consequently, the DOGMA framework consists of two layers; namely the *lexon base* and *the commitment layer*. The lexon base layer stores plausible binary fact-types, called *lexons*. A lexon is formally described as a 5-tuple $<\gamma$, Head, *role*, *co-role*, Tail$>$, where the context identifier (i.e. γ) is used to group lexons that are logically related to each other in the conceptualization of a domain. Intuitively, a lexon may be read as: within the context γ, Head may have a relation with Tail in which Head (resp. Tail) plays a *role* (resp. *co-role*). For example, the lexon $<$Employability, Student, *seeks*, *sought by*, Placement$>$ can be read as: in the context Employability, Student plays the role of *seeks* Placement and Placement plays the role of being *sought by* Student. The goal of the lexon base is to reach a common understanding about the ontology vocabulary and is thus aimed at human understanding. Note that lexons are bi-directional statements, and thus each lexon can be converted into two sets of triples in RDF [4] or OWL [2].

The commitment layer consists of a set of lexons from the lexon base that approximate well the intended conceptualization, followed by the addition of a set of constraints and/or rules. An important difference with the lexon base layer is that commitments are semantically unambiguous and consistent. For example, MAND([Employability, Student, *seeks*, Placement]) express that a student seeks at least one job placement. Moreover, the commitment layer provides mappings between the ontology and the data layer. Note that the set of logical constraints (e.g. cardinality restrictions and mandatory constraints) and the mappings are defined at the application level and are thus not included in this paper.

3   Security Policy Ontology for Distributed Environment

In this section, we first describe the core elements of SecPODE. We then show how these elements can be used to represent different types of security policies; namely access control, obligation, and delegation policies.

3.1   A Broad Notion of Security Policy

A *security policy* imposes constraints governing the behaviour of a system [15]. More specifically, a security policy implements *countermeasures* defined to address *vulnerabilities* that could be exploited by threat agents.

Table 1. Lexons representing the concept of security policy

Context	Head term	role	co-role	Tail term
SecPODE	Countermeasure	*addresses*	*addressed-by*	Vulnerability
SecPODE	SecurityPolicy	*implements*	*implemented-by*	Countermeasure
SecPODE	SecurityPolicy	*specifies*	*specified-by*	Condition
SecPODE	SecurityPolicy	*controls*	*controlled-by*	Action
SecPODE	SecurityPolicy	*protects*	*protected-by*	Resource
SecPODE	SecurityPolicy	*has*	*of*	Effect
SecPODE	SecurityPolicy	*has*	*of*	Identifier
SecPODE	SecurityPolicy	*has*	*of*	Description
SecPODE	SecurityPolicy	*written-by*	*writes*	Person

Table 1 provides the conceptualization of security policy in terms of lexons. A security policy specifies a set of *conditions*, which are evaluated to determine whether a set of *actions* may be performed on a set of *resources*. For example, an access control policy could state that only placement advisors (i.e. condition) have the right to consult (i.e. the action) the CV of a student (i.e. resource). The *effect* of a security policy provides a statement committing the system to enact the action articulated in the policy. For example, the effect of an access control policy would be to grant or deny access to a resource. In distributed systems, every security policy is given an *identifier* to uniquely refer to it within an information system as well as a natural language *description* of what the policy actually does. A security policy is written by a *person* (e.g. system admin) and is recorded to provide provenance. The rest of this section describes the concepts of *condition, action,* and *resource* in more detail.

Condition. A *condition* is a statement that can be evaluated to either TRUE or FALSE [14]. A security policy may specify a number of conditions that need to be met before executing an action. For example, the access to a student's CV (i.e. the action) could be restricted to a placement coordinator trying to find an appropriate placement for the student (i.e. the condition).

Table 2. Lexons representing the concept of condition

Context	Head term	role	co-role	Tail term
SecPODE	Condition	*has*	*of*	Environment
SecPODE	Environment	*has*	*of*	Descriptor
SecPODE	Descriptor	*subsumes*	*is-a*	Time
SecPODE	Descriptor	*subsumes*	*is-a*	Location
SecPODE	Descriptor	*subsumes*	*is-a*	Attribute

Each condition defines some variable that is associated with the *environment* of the request (Table 2). The environment is described in terms of *descriptors* such as *time, location,* or other *attributes.*

Action. An *action* determines the operation that an *agent* must perform once the conditions of the policy have been met (Table 3). Note that an action can either be a simple operation, or a bundle of complex operations provided as an integrated set.

Table 3. Lexons representing the concept of action

Context	Head term	role	co-role	Tail term
SecPODE	Action	*performed-by*	*performs*	Agent
SecPODE	Action	*performed-on*	*under*	Resource
SecPODE	Action	*has*	*of*	Parameter
SecPODE	Parameter	*is-a*	*subsumes*	Attribute

Each action may be associated with a list of *parameters* (i.e. *attributes*) describing how the action must be executed. In this framework, actions are defined in application-specific ontologies to provide semantics to its content.

Resource. A *resource* represents an entity, which is protected by the security policy (Table 4). More specifically, it states which entity can be acted upon once the conditions of the policy have been fulfilled. In our framework, we identify two main types of resources; namely *tangible* and *abstract* entities. A tangible entity is something that has a physical existence. We further separate tangible entities into two categories. Firstly, a *document* is something in which information is recorded. Examples of documents are pictures, curriculum vitae, medical records, and even security policies. Secondly, an *instrument* is a device with which some actions can be performed. For example, a printer enables people to print digital documents on paper.

An abstract entity refers to an intangible entity or a concept. In this paper, we aim to facilitate the enforcement of privacy when *personal information* is shared across autonomous and distributed services. By personal information we refer to any *information* relating to an identified or identifiable *person* (see art. 2 (a) in EU directive 95/46/EC[4]). For example, a CV contains different types of personal information including address, qualifications, and past experiences.

---

[4] http://ec.europa.eu/justice_home/fsj/privacy/index_en.htm

Table 4. Lexons representing the concept of resource

Context	Head term	role	co-role	Tail term
SecPODE	Resource	described-by	describes	Descriptor
SecPODE	Resource	of	performed-on	Action
SecPODE	Resource	subsumes	is-a	Tangible
SecPODE	Tangible	subsumes	is-a	Instrument
SecPODE	Tangible	subsumes	is-a	Document
SecPODE	Document	subsumes	is-a	SecurityPolicy
SecPODE	Resource	subsumes	is-a	Abstract
SecPODE	Abstract	subsumes	is-a	Information
SecPODE	Information	contained-in	contains	Document
SecPODE	Information	subsumes	is-a	PersonalInformation
SecPODE	PersonalInformation	identifies	identified-by	Person

3.2 Representation of Specific Security Policies

In the previous section, we presented the basic concepts required to define a security policy. We are now going to show how these basic concepts can be used to represent different types of security policies; namely access control, obligation and delegation policies.

Access Control Policy. An *access control* policy [13] determines the *conditions* to be fulfilled by a *subject* to gain *access* to a *resource* (Table 5). More specifically, a subject is assigned one or more *permissions*, which grant or deny her the right to perform an *action* on a resource. In the employability domain, for example, a placement coordinator (i.e. subject) may be able to consult (i.e. action) the content of a student's curriculum vitae (i.e. resource) after gaining access to it. In general, the conditions of the access control policy are assessed by a policy decision point, while a policy enforcement point carries out the actions if the conditions have been met.

There exists different types of access control policies. For instance, the attribute-based access control (ABAC) model [18] controls the access to resources based on the security attributes assigned to a subject. More specifically, *permissions* are assigned to *security attributes*, and those security attributes are assigned to one or more *subjects*. In a distributed environment, a security attribute may describe any property of the subject, such as its network address or its identity (e.g. passport number, login ID, or email address).

Obligation Policy. An *obligation policy* specifies the *actions* that have to be performed by the policy enforcement point of the service provider when a given *event* occurs providing the associated *condition* is fulfilled (Table 6). For example, an obligation policy could state that an e-mail notification has to be sent every time a request to access a particular resource (i.e. event) has been denied (i.e. condition). An obligation policy may also include *fallback* actions that should be performed if the original obligation fails to be enacted.

Table 5. Lexons representing the concept of access control policy

Context	Head term	role	co-role	Tail term
SecPODE	AccessControlPolicy	*controls*	*controlled-by*	Access
SecPODE	Access	*is-a*	*subsumes*	Action
SecPODE	Access	*enables*	*enabled-by*	Action
SecPODE	AccessControlPolicy	*has*	*of*	Subject
SecPODE	Subject	*has*	*assigned-to*	Permission
SecPODE	Subject	*is-a*	*subsumes*	Agent
SecPODE	Permission	*grants*	*granted-by*	Action
SecPODE	Permission	*denies*	*denied-by*	Action

Table 6. Lexons representing the concept of obligation policy

Context	Head term	role	co-role	Tail term
SecPODE	ObligationPolicy	*triggered-by*	*triggers*	Event
SecPODE	ObligationPolicy	*defines*	*defined-by*	Action
SecPODE	ObligationPolicy	*defines*	*defined-by*	Fallback
SecPODE	Fallback	*is-a*	*subsumes*	Action

Delegation Policy. A *delegation policy* defines whether an agent, called *delegator*, is able to delegate her *permissions* to another agent, called the *delegatee*, for a period of time, called *validity*. A permission allows the delegatee to perform an action on a resource in the name of the delegator. For example, a delegation policy could state that the manager (i.e. delegator) can transfer her permissions to a trusted employee (i.e. delegatee) whilst she is on holiday (i.e. validity).

Table 7. Lexons representing the concept of delegation policy

Context	Head term	role	co-role	Tail term
SecPODE	DelegationPolicy	*delegates*	*delegated-by*	Permission
SecPODE	Permission	*from*	*has*	Delegator
SecPODE	Permission	*to*	*has*	Delegatee
SecPODE	DelegationPolicy	*has*	*of*	Validity

4   Annotation-Based Access Control

In this section, we describe how SecPODE can be used to gain access to Web resources. Figure 1 shows how a service requester tries to access a resource from a service provider via a Web browser. The browser sends the request to the service provider and checks whether the information received from the service requester are sufficient to gain access to the resource. Note that we assume that both services commit to SecPODE as a upper ontology even though they may commit to different domain ontologies.

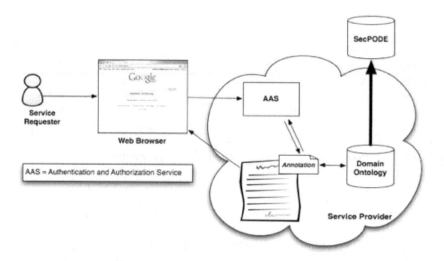

Fig. 1. Access to Web Resources through Annotations

In some universities, taught courses are combined with an industrial placement to achieve a degree. An industrial placement provides the opportunity to students to put into practice knowledge gained from taught courses. A placement coordinator would need to access students' personal information from different data repositories to match students to appropriate placements based on their competencies and qualifications. In this scenario, each data repository is considered to be a service provider, which is governed by access control policies.

Suppose Bob is a placement coordinator and requests access to a student's personal information from a repository with the following annotations:

- Subject=PlacementCoordinator,
- Action=Read,
- Resource=CV

where Subject, Action and Resource are defined in SecPODE, and PlacementCoordinator, Read and CurriculumVitae are defined (and published) in the service requester's domain ontology. Moreover, Anna is a student who has secured her personal information with the following annotations:

- Condition=(Subject=UniversityStaff),
- Permission=(Action=Read),
- Resource=CV,
- Effect=Grant

where Condition, Subject, Permission, Action, Resource, and Effect are defined in SecPODE, and UniversityStaff, Read, CV and Grant are defined in the service provider's domain ontology. Note that in this example we assume that both Bob and Anna commit to the same domain ontology $\mathcal{O}$, which extends SecPODE.

Let us now show whether Bob can access Anna's personal information to match her to appropriate placements. The authentication and authorization service (AAS) from the service provider receives Bob's request (and his annotations) and checks whether his credentials are sufficient to gain access to Anna's data. This process entails assessing the similarity between pairs of annotations of the same type. For instance, Anna's security policy states that access should only be granted to members of her university. In the ontology $\mathcal{O}$, the concept PlacementCoordinator is defined as a subclass of UniversityStaff and thus Bob fulfils the condition for subject. AAS then checks whether the action is permitted by Anna on the resource. As the Bob's request attempts to carry out an action allowed by Anna's policy, the service provider allows the request and the information is displayed in the Web browser. Suppose now that Bob and Anna commit to different domain ontologies, then AAS would require a mapping service to asses the similarity between the concepts in the two ontologies. Note that this mapping service is not the focus of this paper and the authors refer to [6] for more detail on the subject.

5   Related Work

Kim et al. [9] present the NRL Security Ontology, which complements domain ontologies, to annotate resources and services on the Web. These annotations define the security capabilities and requirements of resources (and services) and are used to discover resources (and services) that meet the requirements. More specifically, Kim et al. have developed a matching service that matches the requirements of a service with the capability of a resource, and vice-versa. However, the NRL Security Ontology does not provide semantics for specific types of security policies.

Alternatively, Damiani et al. [5] describes an approach to annotate traditional security policy languages (e.g. XACML [1]) with semantic content. More specifically, they use a *resource* and *subject* domain ontology to define domain-specific terms to refer to resources and subjects respectively. Concepts in these ontologies are then used to assess whether the subject and resource satisfy the conditions defined in the policy. However, they rely on the user to have a knowledge of these security policy language, which are rather difficult for data subjects to use.

Several security policy ontology (e.g. Rei [8], KAoS [17], and ROWLBAC [7]) have been proposed to allow policies to be described over heterogeneous domain and to promote a common understanding among participants who might use different vocabularies. For instance, the KAoS Policy Ontology (KPO) consists of several ontologies representing basic security concepts, such as conditions, actions, subjects, places, situations, etc. These ontologies have been developed to be used within proprietary framework, which supports policy specification, analysis and reasoning in distributed systems. However, these ontologies rely on security experts and data subjects alike to understand complex paradigms, such as description logic.

6 Conclusion

In this paper, we have described the SecPODE ontology based on the DOGMA framework. Due to its grounding in natural language, the DOGMA approach provides a framework to define security policies that can be understood not only by technical experts, but also by data subjects and auditors. The ontology provides unambiguous building blocks not only to define the structure of security policies, but also to convey the meaning of their content. Note that the meaning of the content is provided by enhancing SecPODE with domain- and application-specific ontologies.

We have also shown how the building blocks could be used to define a different types of security policies, such as access control, obligation, and delegation policies. As a result, we have demonstrated that the SecPODE ontology was flexible and extensible. Note that this security policy ontology is intended to be further enhanced by application-specific ontologies covering the meaning of its content. Based on this framework, security experts and data subjects alike are able to annotate existing resources with policy metadata to facilitate the semantic interoperability across services.

Acknowledgements

The research leading to these results has received funding from the EC's FP7 programme under grant agreement n 216287 (TAS^3 - Trusted Architecture for Securely Shared Services). We would like to thank D. Chadwick and L. Shi from the University of Kent for their expertise on security policies.

References

1. EXtensible Access Control Markup Language (XACML). Standard version 2.0, OASIS (2005), http://docs.oasis-open.org/xacml/2.0/
2. Bechhofer, S., van Harmelen, F., Hendler, J., Horrocks, I., McGuinness, D.L., Patel-Schneider, P.F., Stein, L.A.: OWL Web Ontology Language Reference. W3C Recommendation, World Wide Web Consortium (2004), http://www.w3.org/TR/owl-ref/
3. Berners-Lee, T., Hendler, J., Lasilla, O.: The Semantic Web. Scientific American, 34–43 (May 2001)
4. Brickley, D., Guha, R., McBride, B.: RDF Vocabulary Description Language 1.0: RDF Schema. W3C Recommendation, World Wide Web Consortium (2004), http://www.w3.org/TR/rdf-schema/
5. Damiani, E., De Capitani di Vimercati, S., Fugazza, C., Samarati, P.: Extending Policy Languages to the Semantic Web. In: Proc. International Conference on Web Engineering (2004)
6. Euzenat, J., Shvaiko, P.: Ontology Matching. Springer, Berlin (2007)
7. Finin, T., Joshi, A., Kagal, L., Niu, J., Sandhu, R., Winsborough, W.H., Thuraisingham, B.: ROWLBAC - Representing Role Based Access Control in OWL. In: Proc. 13th Symposium on Access control Models and Technologies (2008)

8. Kagal, L., Finin, T., Joshi, A.: A policy based approach to security for the semantic web. In: Fensel, D., Sycara, K., Mylopoulos, J. (eds.) ISWC 2003. LNCS, vol. 2870, pp. 402–418. Springer, Heidelberg (2003)

9. Kim, A., Luo, J., Kang, M.: Security ontology for annotating resources. In: Meersman, R., Tari, Z. (eds.) OTM 2005. LNCS, vol. 3761, pp. 1483–1499. Springer, Heidelberg (2005)

10. Meersman, R.: Semantics ontology tools in information system design. In: Raś, Z.W., Skowron, A. (eds.) ISMIS 1999. LNCS, vol. 1609, Springer, Heidelberg (1999)

11. Meersman, R.: Web and Ontologies: Playtime or business at the last frontier in computing? In: Proc. NSF-EU Workshop on Database and Information Systems Research for Semantic Web and Enterprises (2002)

12. Reul, Q., Zhao, G., Meersman, R.: Ontology-based access control policy interoperability. In: Proc. 1st Conference on Mobility, Individualisation, Socialisation and Connectivity, MISC 2010 (2010)

13. Samarati, P., De Capitani di Vimercati, S.: Access Control: Policies, Models, and Mechanisms. In: International School on Foundations of Security Analysis and Design on Foundations of Security Analysis and Design, FOSAD 2001, (2001)

14. Schulzrinne, H., Tschofenig, H., Morris, J., Cuellar, J., Polk, J. Rosenberg, J.: Common policy: A document format for expressing privacy preferences. Technical Report RFC 4745, Internet Engineering Task Force (2007), http://www.rfc-editor.org/rfc/rfc4745.txt

15. Sloman, M., Lupu, E.: Security and management policy specification. IEEE Network Special Issue on Policy Based Networking 16(2), 10–19 (2002)

16. Studer, R., Benjamin, R., Fensel, D.: Knowledge Engineering: Principle and Methods. Data & Knowledge Engineering 25(1), 161–197 (1998)

17. Uszok, A., Bradshaw, J.M., Lott, J., Breedy, M.R., Bunch, L., Feltovich, P.J., Johnson, M., Jung, H.: New developments in ontology-based policy management: Increasing the practicality and comprehensiveness of KAoS. In: Proc. IEEE Workshop on Policies for Distributed Systems and Networks, POLICY 2008 (2008)

18. Yuan, E., Tong, J.: Attribute Based Access Control (ABAC) for Web Services. In: Proc. 3rd International Conference on Web Services, ICWS 2005 (2005)

Reflecting on a Process to Automatically Evaluate Ontological Material Generated Automatically

Peter Spyns

Vrije Universiteit Brussel - STAR Lab, Pleinlaan 2 Gebouw G-10, B-1050 Brussel - Belgium
Tel.: +32-2-629.1237; Fax: +32-2-629.3819
Peter.Spyns@vub.ac.be

Abstract. Ontology evaluation is a labour intensive and laborious job. Hence, it is relevant to investigate automated methods. But before an automated ontology evaluation method is considered reliable and consistent, it must be validated by human experts. In this paper we want to present a meta-analysis of an automated ontology evaluation procedure as it has been applied in earlier tests. It goes without saying that many of the principles touched upon can be applied in the context of ontology evaluation as such, irrespective of it being automated or not. Consequently, the overall quality of an ontology is not only determined by the quality of the artifact itself, but also by the the quality of its evaluation method. Providing an analysis on the set-up and conditions under which an evaluation of an ontology takes place can only be beneficial to the entire domain of ontology engineering.

1 Introduction and Motivation

Following the growing importance of ontologies for information systems interoperability and overall business semantics in the context of the semantic web, the need gradually arises to assess ontologies irrespectively of the way they have been created, adapted or extended. How can ontology engineers in the course of building and adapting an ontology get an idea whether their modifications are actual improvements or not compared to a previous version ? Another context that involves ontology assessment is that of experimenting with various ontology mining methods: how to determine when one method performs better than another? Ontologies can be assessed or evaluated from many angles [5]. In many cases, human experts are still needed, which constitutes a crucial bottleneck. And, more often than not, a reference standard is not available.

A way out is to use the corpus[1] itself as a source of a gold standard if one wants to avoid bringing in human experts who are costly and rapidly bored by tedious evaluation exercises. Therefore, we discuss the evaluation of a method that automatically measures to which extent ontological material contains the important domain notions and relationships. However, it still remains necessary to have humans assess the quality of the ontology mining results first. Often neglected in (ontology) engineering is the way in which an evaluation has been set up. The quality of the evaluation process determines the "value" of an evaluation as much as the quality of the items evaluated.

---

[1] Of course, this only applies to situations in which a corpus is available.

R. Meersman et al. (Eds.): OTM 2010 Workshops, LNCS 6428, pp. 606–615, 2010.

The remainder of this paper is organised as follows. A short section (2) presents a short overview of earlier experiments. The method is elaborated on in section 3, where we present in detail the meta-evaluation framework which we have applied to our automated ontology evaluation procedure. Subsequently, we analyse how the experiments that have been set up comply or not with the meta-evaluation framework (section 4). In the discussion section (5) we provide some comments on the analysis and how this kind of research could contribute to advancing the state of the art. Related work is outlined in section 6. Indications for future research are given in section 7. Some final remarks (section 8) conclude this paper.

2   Material

As this paper concerns a meta-evaluation, it is not the data (two EU directives) and tools (an unsupervised ontology miner [14] and automated ontology evaluation procedure) used in the experiments that are of importance, but rather the way how they have been used. Therefore, we mention only shortly the purpose of these earlier tests and refer the reader to the references for more technical details. Different stages can be identified in the past course of our experiments:

- exploring the initial idea of an automated evaluation procedure [15,23]
- refining the method and enhancing its repeatability [16,24]
- applying the method to another domain [22]
- repeating the same tests as in the previous two steps [17,18,19]
- testing the suitability of the method for regression like tests [20,21]
- analysing and reflecting on the entire process [20, and this paper]

As in the early stage both the ontology miner and the evaluation procedure still underwent modifications, we do not take this phase into account. As soon as the tools have been tested on their repeatability and applied to a new domain, they remained unchanged to maintain the comparability of the outcomes across the various tests.

3   Methods

In essence, in the following sections we discuss how the human experts have executed the evaluation in order to demonstrate that the evaluation process has been performed with a high concern of objectivity and with an effort to avoid as much as (practically) possible all kinds of biases. In that respect, the work of Friedman and Hripcsak [9] consisting of 21 criteria, summarised in Table 1, has been our main source of inspiration. Their paper demonstrates the substantial impact the conditions under which an evaluation happens can have on the reliability of the outcomes of an evaluation exercise.

4   Meta-evaluation

In this section, we explain how our earlier experiments have been organised and analyse their set-up according to the 21 criteria of Friedman and Hripcsak. The analysis is organised along the five main groups of Table 1.

Table 1. Issues to address to avoid bias during evaluationn (reproduced from [9, p.335])

	Minimising Bias
1	The developer should not see the test set of documents.
2	If domain experts are used to determine the reference standard, they should not be developers of the system nor designers of the study.
3	The developer should not perform the evaluation.
4	The NLP system should be frozen prior to the testing phase.
5	If generalisability of the processor is being tested, the developer should not know the details of the study beforehand.
6	Ideally, the person designing the evaluation study should not be a developer of the system.
	Establishing a Reference Standard
7	If domain experts are used to determine the reference standard, there should be a sufficient number to assess variability of the reference standard.
8	The test set should be large enough in that there is sufficient power to distinguish levels of performance.
9	The choice of the reference standard should be based on the objectives of the study (e.g. extraction capability vs. performance in an application).
10	If domain experts are used to determine the reference standard, the type of expert should be appropriate.
	Describing the Evaluation Methods
11	The methods used to determine the reference standard should be clearly described, particularly if domain experts were used.
12	The manner in which the test documents were chosen should be described.
13	Methods used to calculate performance measures should be clearly presented and if non-standard measures are used, they should be described.
	Presenting Results
14	Performance measures should relate to the complete test set.
15	If human experts are used, inter-rater and intra-rater agreement should be given.
16	Confidence intervals should be for all measures.
	Discussing Conclusions
17	Limitations of the study should be discussed.
18	Results should be presented in light of requirements of the target application.
19	Overgeneralisation of the results should be avoided.
20	An analysis of system failures should be presented along with a discussion that describes the degree of difficulty of corrections.
21	The types and possible causes of disagreements among the experts should be analysed.

4.1 Minimising Bias

The ontology miner nor the automated evaluation procedure have been modified in the course of the experiments (*criterion 4*). In addition, the developers of the core parts of the ontology miner have not at all been involved in the experiments (*criterion 5*). Only one member (linguistic engineer) of their team became slightly knowledgeable of the test corpora and results when performing the batch runs of the ontology miner (*criterion 1*). She has not been involved in the evaluations at any other point. Nor had the domain experts performing the evaluation experiment anything to do with the ontology miner, the automated evaluation procedure and the design of the experiments in general (*criterion 2*). They only knew they had to assess ontological material and were unaware of the related purposes. The computer scientist responsible for the automated evaluation procedure had no knowledge of the internals of the ontology miner. A minor drawback is that the computer scientist who developed the automated evaluation procedure also designed the evaluation studies (*criterion 6*). But he was not involved in the actual assessment by the domain experts (*criterion 3*). He merely distributed and collected the files (corpora to linguistic engineer, mining results from linguistic engineer and to domain experts, assessments from experts) and implemented and ran the automated evaluation procedure.

The domain experts were unaware of the scores of the automatic validation procedure as well as each other's scores (so there was no mutual influence at all). As a result of a first round of experiments, one expert suggested to manually preprocess the corpus before ontology mining (they thought removing irrelevant parts would improve the quality of the ontology miner output). In order to avoid a learning bias (= experts remembering, and sometimes improving, their "answers" of the first round - a criterion not mentioned by Friedman and Hripcsak), a follow-up experiment (second round of ontology mining) was not held earlier than about one year later. In addition, during the second round the experts had no access to their scores of the first round[2]. The separation of roles was thus well observed. It guarantees that the various persons involved did not influence each other or had no insights that would allow them to "bend" the system or procedures into their advantage.

4.2 Establishing a Reference Standard

Ontology mining rounds combined with the automated evaluation procedure have been applied in two domains: VAT and privacy EU regulation. The privacy and VAT corpora (two separate documents) consist of 72,1K resp. 49,5K words. They consist of two *directives* (English version), namely the 95/46/EC of 18/12/2000 (privacy) and the 77/388/EC of 27/01/2001 (VAT), which EU member states have to adopt and transform into national legislation. The size of both texts however is not that big, when compared to other machine learning experiments (*criterion 8*). A possible workaround would be to include unofficial documents that provide comments on the official directives.

Unfortunately, for the VAT domain, no expert was available for participation in the evaluation experiments. As a substitute, 900 domain specific terms manually selected constitute the reference vocabulary. It has not been communicated how agreement on these terms has been reached. Even if not ideal from a scientific point of view, this corresponds to real life situations where lists of terms generally accepted by a community are put forward as a de facto standard. From a methodological point of view, one can argue that the list of terms collected by experts does not necessarily adequately reflect the important terms in the text(s) submitted to the ontology miner. On the other hand,

---

[2] In theory, they could have stored their earlier assessment file and consulted it during the second round without anybody else knowing it. However, the intra rater agreement scores clearly allow to discard this possibility.

in many cases such term lists are compiled by several representative domain experts (or other stakeholders) on behalf of (standardisation) sector committees and are (publicly) available. Thus, even if not ideal, it is as close as one can get to some objective and qualitative source for a standard reference if experts are otherwise not available.

As the ontology miner outputs lexical triplets, and the automated evaluation procedure processes these triplets and attributes a numerical score to them, it is logical to create a reference standard for a domain that consists of triplets, labeled with a unique identifier, that are qualified as (entirely) fit or not. It becomes rather easy then to (automatically) compare a set of triplets resulting from ontology mining with the reference standard built by domain experts, and subsequently to compare that set of triplets evaluated by the automated procedure with the same reference standard (*criterion 9*).

For the privacy domain, two experts in the matter independently validated the list of privacy triplets as produced by the ontology miner. One has been a privacy data commissioner and still is a privacy legal consultant while the other is a knowledge engineer and researcher specialised in privacy and trust. Ontology engineering involves experts of various background and affiliations to come to a commonly agreed upon conceptualisation. Hence, we consider them as appropriate for the experiments. Unfortunately, we did not receive precise information on the VAT experts who compiled the VAT terms list. Friedman qualifies this as a source of potential bias [9, p.336]. However, the vocabulary list originates from an organisation that specialises in these VAT matters, so we are quite confident that the list is appropriate and suited (*criterion 10*).

4.3   Describing the Evaluation Methods

The two experts have assessed twice all the privacy triplets output by the ontology miner. The experts have marked the list of triplets with '+' or '-' indicating whether the entire triplet is valid or not, i.e. useful or not in the context of the creation of a privacy ontology. Their assessments have been merged subsequently. Only those triplets positively scored by both privacy experts have been retained as the privacy reference standard. Regarding the VAT case, a vocabulary list (see above) has been used as a source to simulate a reference standard built by human experts (a set of VAT triplets marked with '+' or '-'). In both cases, it has been clearly described how the reference standard has been built (*criterion 11*).

It would have been better if more than two human (privacy) experts had been involved [9, p.335], but unfortunately many experts are quite reluctant to perform this kind of validation as it is quite tedious and boring. This source of bias (variability of the reference standard - *criterion 7*) should even be stressed more in the context of ontology engineering as have shown our experiments: experts - even if appropriate ones - having a different point of view on the ontology behave differently when assessing and rating output from an ontology miner. Not involving a sufficient number of human experts (or stakeholders in the broadest sense) definitely constitutes a flaw in our experiments. As a consequence, the automated evaluation procedure runs the risk of not having been adequately assessed.

The VAT and privacy directives (see above) are the sole official legal reference text for their domain. Including other related documents might distort the legal status of the outcomes (an ontology representing each directive) content-wise as these additional texts do not necesarily represent the official EU legislation. For the second test round, the two experts manually removed passages from the privacy corpus deemed irrelevant or superfluous. These two "cleaned" versions of the privacy directive have been concatenated and constituted the test corpus for the second round of ontology mining. Hence, the test corpus has been chosen for an objective reason (*criterion 12*).

All the performance measures (lexical precision, recall, coverage and accuracy as well as triplet precision, recall (or sensitivity) and specificity) used during the tests with the automated evaluation procedure have been defined and explained [22,24] (*criterion 13*). Regarding the human reference standard, it was impossible to calculate the amount of triplets missed (=false negatives) by the ontology miner. The experts did not first independently produce a list of triplets themselves as this would definitely demand too much from them. Hence, the current way of the experts assessing the miner's results may introduce a bias in the evaluation procedure: the experts only judged what the miner has produced ignoring potential misses - this is also called "leading the witness" [3] [9, p.336]. The automated evaluation procedure uses the lexicometric scores mentioned above as a workaround.

4.4 Presenting Results

The performance measures mentioned above have been applied to the entire sets of triplets (*criterion 14*). Inter and intra rater agreement scores [24,21] have been calculated (*criterion 15*). When presenting the results, we did not compute confidence intervals as it did not seem worthwhile seen the low kappa scores (*criterion 16*).

4.5 Discussing Conclusions

When presenting and discussing the outcomes of our experiments, we have openly addressed the limitations of the tests: the main problem being the absence or an involvement too limited in number of domain experts. Also the other elements mentioned so far allow a reader to easily discover the limits of our experiments (*criterion 17*). In particular, the involvement of VAT experts might have provided additional support for (or at the contrary casting extra doubt on) certain findings that are now only applying to the privacy case. E.g., an additional round of tests and comparisons would have become possible involving a privacy term list.

The applications targeted are on the one hand an ontology miner and on the other an automated procedure for ontology evaluation. The basic requirement for the former is to produce as many as possible good triplets while the basic requirement of the latter is to detect as many as possible of these good triplets. We are convinced that the outcomes of the experiments have been presented from this point of view (*criterion 18*).

By involving two different domains in the evaluation experiment, we tested to which extent the outcomes can be generalised over several application domains. It is clear from the analysis above that one should not overgeneralise the findings (*criterion 19*).

Depending on the exact topic of the papers mentioned in section 2, we have mentioned flaws and errors of the involved software components and reasons for their

---

[3] Without a golden reference, evaluators show a tendency to agree with the system output - unless there is a glaring error.

"failure". In some occasions, we have suggested ways for potential improvements or workarounds (*criterion 20*).

The very low inter rater agreement scores show that the privacy experts adhere to a different point of view on the concepts and relationships to be included in a privacy ontology, and perhaps have a different conceptualisation of the domain. In addition, one expert even behaved inconsistently over the two rounds (very low intra rater agreement score), which we cannot explain for the moment (*criterion 21*). These findings confirm the statement by Friedman and Hripcsak that two experts are not enough [9, p.335] to establish a gold standard. The consensual and collaborative aspects [6] of ontology engineering make the criteria related to human experts all the more relevant.

5 Discussion

Contrary to other experimental set-ups (e.g. clinical tests) where the experts are not that disparate, in the context of ontology engineering it is important that stakeholders of diverse backgrounds and with different goals are represented. Inevitably, this entails that these experts will show a behaviour much more prone to differences when rating ontological material resulting from ontology mining. Hence, the issue of (dis)agreement amongst experts needs an adaptation to the ontology engineering and evaluation context, which constitutes an interesting avenue for further research.

However, as happens often in this kind of evaluation experiments, practical constraints of daily life are balanced with scientific correctness and principledness, in particularly concerning the workload requested from the available experts. A low number of available experts is a problem to guarantee the scientific generality of some of the findings. As involvement of a sufficient number of experts is needed to validate automated evaluation methods but remains very hard to obtain, we have called this earlier on a catch-22 or deadlock situation [19].

Currently, research on ontology evaluation in general does not pay sufficient attention to the conditions under which evaluations happen. Many reference standard ontologies are the work of a single ontology engineer without any stakeholder intervention. Often developers of ontology learning applications also perform the evaluation - sometimes as a sole evaluator. If a more formal evaluation has been organised, the conditions under which this has happened are rarely detailed to such an extent that one can be confident about biases having been consciously avoided. And even if details are given, they do not always inspire confidence. E.g., sometimes master class students participate in evaluations as modelling or domain experts in order to have a sufficient number of evaluators. This can be justified in some cases, but in other situations one can question with reason the appropriateness of students as experts. Also, one rarely finds inter and intra rater agreement numbers. All in all, it is justified to wonder how many (positive) evaluations of ontological material or ontologies reported in the literature will survive an analysis of the evaluation set-up as scrutinous as the one presented here.

We strongly believe that the criteria of Friedman and Hripcsak, even if originally defined for medical language processing, are very relevant to ontology evaluation (and probably to evaluation knowledge engineering efforts in general). This is why we have chosen their set of 21 criteria as a framework to evaluate how we have organised our ontology evaluation experiments. We hope that our experiences, which unfortunately are not always positive, will stimulate the field in applying a more rigourous way to evaluate ontologies. The least that researchers could do in the future is adding more practical details. Providing an analysis on the set-up and conditions under which an evaluation of an ontology takes place can only be beneficial to the entire domain of ontology engineering.

6 Related Work

Various researchers are working on different ways to evaluate an ontology from various perspectives. Good overviews of the recent state of the art that also contain a comparison of the characteristics of the different methods are [2,3,4,5,8,11,13], the most recent one being [1]. However, to our knowledge no other related work treats the issue of evaluating, or at least reflecting on, the conditions under which an ontology is evaluated. If details are provided, in many cases, the developer of the evaluation method is also the main evaluator (or, which is slightly better, one of his/her students). In the same way as the attention for the community and collaborative aspects of ontology engineering is rather recent, the idea that also (automated) ontology evaluation efforts should take into account the (different) points of views of (various) stakeholders is rather novel.

Gangemi [10] provides in his impressive overview (and ontology) of ontology evaluation metrics and measures some elements and insights that come close to some of our findings. We have rather focused on a meta-analysis of how content material for an ontology can be assessed by means of a gold standard approach and which pitfalls are to be avoided to obtain methodologically sound outcomes. To some degree our approach can be related to work of *Dellschaft and Staab* [7], who continue earlier work of Maedche and Staab [12], or *Zavitsanos* et al. [25]. They all compare a learnt ontology with a reference ontology, while we compare automatically generated ontological material with the text corpus it was generated from. The former one makes additional use of the hierarchy to calculate similarities between a new ontology and a reference standard ontology. The reference ontology however has been created by a single ontology engineer. In addition, no domain experts have been involved in the evaluation process. The latter one uses a corpus as a direct point of comparison. However, this method implies that the concept instances (also of the reference ontology) are annotated in the (new) source corpus text. This condition might be difficult to transpose to any source corpus of any ontology being learnt and automatically evaluated.

Even if the method of Dellschaft and Staab could be easily applied in a cycle of incremental ontology engineering, they have not attempted to include multiple human experts - or at least they do not provide details on it - in the assessment of their method. In that sense, our initiative remains rather unique, which we consider nevertheless as unfortunate.

7 Future Work

When considering the meta-evaluation level, additional sources of potential bias and pitfalls for ontology evaluation could be detected. In that sense, the work of Burton-Jones and Gangemi [5,10] can be a source of inspiration. What is also not yet explored are factors related to the communal and consensual aspects of ontology evaluation. We are convinced that new and relevant insights can be discovered in those areas.

8   Conclusion

We have illustrated, by means of our experiments on automated ontology evaluation, that there is more to ontology evaluation than currently meets the eye. We have tried, as far as practically possible, to organise these experiments in such a way that many of the potential pitfalls in evaluation in general have been avoided. In order to do so, we have used an existing framework of 21 criteria. We can only apply and promote this framework, and hope that other researchers active on ontology evaluation will use it as well to enhance the overall quality of the ontology evaluation process.

References

1. Almeida, M.: A proposal to evaluate ontology content. Journal of Applied Ontology 4, 245–265 (2009)
2. Brank, J., Grobelnik, M., MladenićOntology, D.: evaluation. SEKT Deliverable #D1.6.1, Jozef Stefan Institute, Prague (2005)
3. Buitelaar, P., Cimiano, P. (eds.): Learning and Population: Bridging the Gap between Text and Knowledge of Frontiers in Artificial Intelligence and Applications, vol. 167. IOS Press, Amsterdam (2008)
4. Buitelaar, P., Cimiano, P., Magnini, B. (eds.): Ontology Learning from Text: Methods, Applications and Evaluation. IOS Press, Amsterdam (2005)
5. Burton-Jones, A., Storey, V., Sugumaran, V.: A semiotic metrics suite for assessing the quality of ontologies. Data and Knowledge Engineering 55(1), 84–102 (2005)
6. de Moor, A., De Leenheer, P., Meersman, R.: DOGMA-MESS: A meaning evolution support system for interorganizational ontology engineering. In: Schärfe, H., Hitzler, P., Øhrstrøm, P. (eds.) ICCS 2006. LNCS (LNAI), vol. 4068, pp. 189–203. Springer, Heidelberg (2006)
7. Dellschaft, K., Staab, S.: On how to perform a gold standard based evaluation of ontology learning. In: Cruz, I., Decker, S., Allemang, D., Preist, C., Schwabe, D., Mika, P., Uschold, M., Aroyo, L.M. (eds.) ISWC 2006. LNCS, vol. 4273, pp. 228–241. Springer, Heidelberg (2006)
8. Dellschaft, K., Staab, S.: Strategies for the Evaluation of Ontology Learning Ontology Learning and Population: Bridging the Gap between Text and Knowledge. IOS Press, Amsterdam (2008)
9. Friedman, C., Hripcsak, G.: Evaluating natural language processors in the clinical domain. Methods of Information in Medicine 37(1-2), 334–344 (1998)
10. Gangemi, A., Catenacci, C., Ciaramita, M., Gil, R., Lehmann, J.: Ontology evaluation and validation: an integrated formal model for the quality diagnostic task. Technical report (2005), http://www.loa-cnr.it/Publications.html
11. Hartmann, J.,Spyns, P.,Maynard, D., Cuel, R., de Carmen Suarez Figueroa, M., Sure, Y.: Methods for ontology evaluation. KnowledgeWeb Deliverable #D1.2.3 (2005)
12. Maedche, A., Staab, S.: Measuring similarity between ontologies. In: Gómez-Pérez, A., Benjamins, V.R. (eds.) EKAW 2002. LNCS (LNAI), vol. 2473, pp. 251–263. Springer, Heidelberg (2002)

13. Obrst, L., Ashpole, B., Ceusters, W., Mani, I., Ray, S., Smith, B.: The Evaluation of Ontologies: toward Improved Semantic Interoperability. In: Semantic Web: Revolutionizing Knowledge Discovery in the Life Sciences, pp. 139–158. Springer, Heidelberg (2007)

14. Reinberger, M.-L., Spyns, P.: Unsupervised text mining for the learning of DOGMA-inspired ontologies. In: Buitelaar, P., Cimiano, P., Magnini, B. (eds.) Ontology Learning from Text: Methods, Applications and Evaluation, pp. 29–43. IOS Press, Amsterdam (2005)

15. Reinberger, M.-L., Spyns, P., Johannes Pretorius, A., Daelemans, W.: Automatic initiation of an ontology. In: Meersman, R., Tari, Z. (eds.) OTM 2004. LNCS, vol. 3290, pp. 600–617. Springer, Heidelberg (2004)

16. Spyns, P.: Evalexon: assessing triples mined from texts. Technical Report 09, STAR Lab, Brussel (2005)

17. Spyns, P.: Validating a tool for evaluating automatically lexical triples mined from texts. In: Meersman, R., Tari, Z., Herrero, P. (eds.) OTM-WS 2007, Part I. LNCS, vol. 4805, pp. 11–12. Springer, Heidelberg (2007)

18. Spyns, P.: Validating EvaLexon: validating a tool for evaluating automatically lexical triples mined from texts. Technical Report x6, STAR Lab, Brussel (2007)

19. Spyns, P.: Evaluating automatically a text miner for ontologies: a catch-22 situation? In: Meersman, R., Tari, Z. (eds.) OTM 2008, Part II. LNCS, vol. 5332, pp. 1403–1421. Springer, Heidelberg (2008)

20. Spyns, P.: Regression testing for an automated ontology evaluation procedure. Technical Report x1, STAR Lab, Brussel (2009)

21. Spyns, P.: Assessing iterations of an automated ontology evaluation procedure. Technical Report x1, STAR Lab, Brussel (2010)

22. Spyns, P., Hogben, G.: Validating an automated evaluation procedure for ontology triples in the privacy domain. In: Moens, M.-F., Spyns, P. (eds.) Proceedings of the 18th Annual Conference on Legal Knowledge and Information Systems (JURIX 2005), pp. 127–136. IOS Press, Amsterdam (2005)

23. Spyns, P., Johannes Pretorius, A., Reinberger, M.-L.: Evaluating DOGMA-lexons generated automatically from a text. In: Cimiano, P., Ciravegna, F., Motta, E., Uren, V. (eds.) Proceedings of the EKAW 2004 Workshop on Human Language Technology and Knowledge Management, pp. 38–44 (2004)

24. Spyns, P., Reinberger, M.-L.: Lexically evaluating ontology triples automatically generated from text. In: Gómez-Pérez, A., Euzenat, J. (eds.) ESWC 2005. LNCS, vol. 3532, pp. 563–577. Springer, Heidelberg (2005)

25. Zavitsanos, E., Paliouras, G., Vouros, G.: A distributional approach to evaluating ontology learning methods using a gold standard. In: Proceedings of the third ECAI Ontology Learning and Population Workshop (2008)

A More Specific Events Classification to Improve Crawling Techniques

David Urdiales-Nieto and José F. Aldana-Montes

University of Málaga, Department of Computer Languages and Computing Sciences
Boulevar Lois Pasteur 35, 29071 Malaga, Spain
{durdiales,jfam}@lcc.uma.es
http://khaos.uma.es/

Abstract. Nowadays the popularity of data quality is increasing notably in linked data. Linked data consuming applications need to be aware that changes in a dataset. Changes such as update, remove or creation links may occur for a time so is necessary to detect them to update local data dependencies where this annotation is made by detecting changes systems. Updated or removed links can be detected using a syntactic change similarity measure, and it can be done simply using the Levenshtein distance measure. However, a specific event subclassification of *updated event* and *removed event,* which is created by detecting changes systems developed, does not exist based on content analysis. A semantic signature and Maximum Similarity Measure (MaSiMe) combination approach is developed to create a more specific subclassification of the initial *updated* and *removed event* when its meaning has been changed. It is used to enrich the resources, annotating the new subclassification of the initial *updated event* and *removed event*, and will be annotated the author who created this annotation, adding provenance information. Annotations on the modification time are made in linked data resource, and making an average time study about when these specific events changes, could be improved the crawling techniques for a domain.

Keywords: Linked data, Crawling, Versioning, Semantic Signature, Similarity.

1 Introduction

Linked data is a movement which has increased during last years. Currently there are hundred data sets published, providing a huge amount of RDF triples interlinked by hundreds of millions of RDF links [1]. Generally this information is static, but a new approach is recently emerging in which links are not static, appearing changes in this dataset. Due amount of data that exist in the Web, such data may change by adding new resources or by deleting old one. In this sense, to avoid wasting resources is necessary the availability of different resource states.

Various aspects related to linked dataset are studied, such as the change frecuency of data in the Web and change volume, and it is seen as a great bulk of updates that affect many resources [2].

There are certain frameworks that use crawling techniques to detect data in the Web, such as Multicrawler framework [3]. Using this crawling framework, it allows for a measure on a dynamic data set.

R. Meersman et al. (Eds.): OTM 2010 Workshops, LNCS 6428, pp. 616–625, 2010.

Other approach to avoid linked-less is creates a resource versioning. In this case previous information together with new information is stored. Some version of a resource is given, and it is needed to create an annotation with a particular timestamp, looking for during navigation to the previously archived version.

Therefore, tracing the data provenance is interesting in this versioning system and it could be also obtained by crawling technique. Then in this sense, detecting links in linked data set and change frecuency of them are interesting. However, nowadays detecting changes systems developed only detects *created event*, *updated event* and *removed event*. *Create event* occurs if some representation for a resource was not available in the past. *Update event* occurs if the representation of resource changes. Finally, *removed event* occurs if some representation was available in the past but is not available any more.

However, in these detecting changes systems there is not made any specific event classification based on content analysis, which could allow us to enrich the data provenance and it can also be used to improve Crawling Techniques in Linked Data.

In this context, with a resource versioning system approach, and using a semantic signature combined with a similarity measure approach can be decided what kind of specific changes have been produced in an incoming resource against an archived resource. In general, a representation of a resource can change, and it would be detected as *Updated event*, however if it changes so much in content, could be it only classified as *Updated event*? For this reason a content analysis is introduced when representation of a resource does not change enough. Therefore, the content changes could be high or it could only change a bit, and then how is classified this general *Updated event*? In this sense, a similarity measure threshold to compare semantic signature is defined, and can be decided if an incoming resource is subclassified as *updated event* when only bit content changes are produced or subclassified as *modified event* when high content changes are done. Thus, a new event subclassification is made in an updated event defined for the detecting changes systems developed, and a more specific annotation will be done. In same context, *removed event* is defined as a representation that was available in the past but it is not available any more. Following with our approach, if new incoming resource and archived resource have high same representation, and they have different URL, they could have a different content. Then, could it be classified only as *removed event*? Then, in this case, using the content analysis can be decided two events. A resource is a *removed event* when only bit content changes are produced or *deleted event* when high content changes are done.

Our main contributions are:

- Create a more specific event subclassification based on content analysis for *updated event* and *removed event* which are defined by detecting changes systems developed. *Updated event* is subclassified as *modified event* when high content changes are done, or it will be maintained as *Updated event* when only bit content changes are produced. In the same way, *removed event* is subclassified as *deleted event* when high content changes are done, or it is maintained as *removed event* when only bit content changes are produced.
- Enrich data provenance, using annotations of this specific events created. For instance, who has *modified* the resource, when is *modified*, etc. This time event annotation can also be used to improve Crawling Techniques in Linked

Data, to drive crawling detecting phase which depends of frecuency changes annotated in this more specific even classification.

-    Create a customized resource versioning to a specific domain in which we have always stored last resource version to be managed, together with the previous resource version and which we want to keep with provenance annotation and with this specific event annotation produced during time.

Finally the rest of paper is structured as follows. Section 2 describes the state of art of the actual detecting changes systems describing briefly in these tools their advantages and limitations. In Section 3, is described in detail the algorithm created to make a subclassification of *Updated event* or *removed event,* and how they are created. Examples of this new events subclassification for Sensor, Web Services resource and HTTP resource are also described. And finally, Section 4 concludes with a summary and future work.

2   State of the Art

In this section, a presentation about actual applications is made, describing them, and doing emphasis in the main differences with our purpose.

Currently there are many approach presented in the context to discover, detect changes or transform data as RDF.

First, in the context of *Change detection* there are some systems developed, like **Triplify** [4] which is a system that exposes data from relational databases as Linked data in RDF. It is based on mapping HTTP request to RDBMS queries and the result is shown as RDF. Triplify also includes a system to detect changes in linked dataset, this is *Linked Data Upadate Log* that groups updates to a RDF model within timespan into nested collection which is accessible via HTTP. This notification focus is well defined but requires that clients often go to this *log* and the update event does not contain specific information about if data is *moved*, or if a new event is *created* . It only informs about *update* and *deletion* events.

Peridot is a tool developed by IBM, and its main characteristic is that automatically allows us to fix links in the Web. This focus is centered in idea of calculate fingerprints of Web documents and repair broken links based on the degree of similarity. In this sense, this approach is similar to our contribution in which is compared the content of data based on similarity, but Peridot does not give us information about if data is *created*, *removed* or if it is an *update event.*

Other focus is a **Link Integrity Management tool** [5] which is focus on fixing broken links in the Web that occurs due to moved link targets. To do it inside this tool is developed a tool called *PageChase* which using a heuristic approach can find resources missed. An explorer component is included and using a search engines is possible to redirect information to find possible URIs of the resource moved. The main different with our approach is that in our approach is not necessary use a search engine mechanism to find URIs immediately. It will be included in a crawler component, and for an interesting domain, we have always stored last data version until new information will be found. In this sense, this important information for us is always available and does not appear any broken linked data.

In this last context, recently has been presented an annotated versioning mechanism, **Memento** [6] which is fully based on HTTP and uses datatime as a global version indicator. In this approach can be followed time-specific version resources using a timestamp, and it can match a version with other version data archived. This version mechanism based on a global notion of time can be used to navigate across versions, and it can be used as a versioning approach to be applied to Linked data. This approach is an annotated versioning mechanism for linked data, but it does not create a specific annotation about events produced. It only creates annotation about *created* or *modified* events in a general context.

This approach has in common with the our one that uses an annotated versioning mechanism, where is created a time annotation. However our approach includes a more specific event subclassification to create more specific data annotations, and these annotations will be used to improve the crawling technique.

Finally to complete a survey of the state of art about detecting broken linked data and versioning system, recently has appeared **DSNotify** [7] which is a generic framework able to assist in fixing broken links. It uses heuristic features to detect changes corresponding to resources, and a feature vector with this information is extracted. The feature vector is stores with the item's URI in an *item index (ii)*. Then, the item corresponding to resources that are not found are moved to other index, a *removed item index (rii)*. After a time, this item is moved to other index called *archived item index (aii)*. Therefore this process is always running by a local-house-thread that compares feature vectors and it tries to identify possible successors for removed items. A heuristic method is used to make comparison and a similarity measure for the features of vectors, using an exact string matching or using the Levenshtein distance.

This last point, similarity measure is common with our approach. However, it is only same in our first phase to detect if URI, generally URL, for an incoming resource and the archived resource are the same or if they are different. Our algorithm first the all, to detect it, make a similarity measure based on Levenshtein distance of the URIs. However once is known that URLs are the same or that they are different, our specific algorithm tries to identify, doing a content analysis, if content is the same or if it has changes. To make it, as it is said in introduction, a semantic signature is used and comparing through a Customized Similarity Measure, **MaSiMe** [8], which could be based on a combination of *Levhenstein [9]*, *B = BlockDistance [10]*, *M = Matching-Coefficient [10], and QGramsDistance [11]* distances algorithms, is also used before to decide if a content has changed. This is the main difference between our approach and the last one. We create a more specific event classification that make DSNotify and it will be used to create a more specific data annotation for events, and will be used to improve crawling technique depending of the frecuency that these events are produced in a domain.

3   Event Subclassification Algorithm

Main tasks of this algorithm are presented in this section. First, it is used to classify a general situation in which an incoming resource, detected using crawling technique, and that is classified by an actual detecting changes systems as *updated event* or *removed event*. It could have a more specific subclassification making a content analysis. As it is said in the introduction, in general, a representation of a resource can change, and a detecting changes systems will detected as *Updated event*, however if it does not change a lot, could be it classified as *Updated event*? A similar description was also done to describe *remove event* classification in introduction. Thus, to create this more specific event subclassification, first is done a similarity measure based on Levenshtein distance for URI incoming resource and archived resource one. If URIs is the same, a first whole subclassification can be done, being more specific that the classification made by the detecting changes systems as *updated event*. *Update event* could be subclassified as *Updated event*, *modified event* or *maintained event* (as special case if URL and content does change how will be explained later).

In the same way, in *removed event* to create this more specific event classification, is also made a similarity measure based on Levenshtein distance for URI incoming resource and archive resource one, and If URIs are different, *removed event* could be subclassified as *deleted event* or *removed event*. In **Figure 1** is shown this algorithm sequence, where **eight steps** are produced, and the first three steps were described in above paragraph. **Step 1**, detection using crawling technique of an *updated event* or *removed event* for an incoming resource, and using the last archived version of same resource. **Step 2**, similarity measure based on Levenshtein distance for URI incoming resource and archive resource one. **Step 3,** possible subclassified events when URIs are same in *Updated event*, and a possible subclassified events when URIs are different in *removed event*. **Step 4,** use of a semantic signature combined with a similarity measure approach to decide what kind of specific changes have been produced in an incoming resource against an archived resource for each case.

On focus semantic signature, it could be thought as a content concentration about a resource expressed with a string value. This simple representation about content represents the global mean about resource content as an image can represent it, or a simple heading summarizes the content about a text. In this context, **textwise API** [12] is used in our algorithm to construct this signature summary string about a resource. It expresses the string content together a percentage bar. The highest string percentage is used as the semantic signature.

An example about how it could be used is, for example, the next one. If a URL for a computer company where today its content is about some computer components biddings, then its semantic signature could be computercomponnetsoffer. If a week later, the URL for the same computer company has computer components binding again but it has included other bidding as electronic devices biddings, its content will be changed. This URL will have other semantic signature, for example, computercomponentdeviceoffer. Strings like these are used by MaSiMe to make content similarity measure. As result MaSiMe return a similarity measure of semantic signature URI content for incoming resource and it is compared with semantic signature URI content of last archived resource.

Thus, this combination, similarity measure and semantic signature will allow us to know what kind of subclassification event will be produced in each case. *Modified event* or *updated event* for *updated event* classification made with actual detecting changes systems, and *removed event* or *deleted event* for *removed event*.

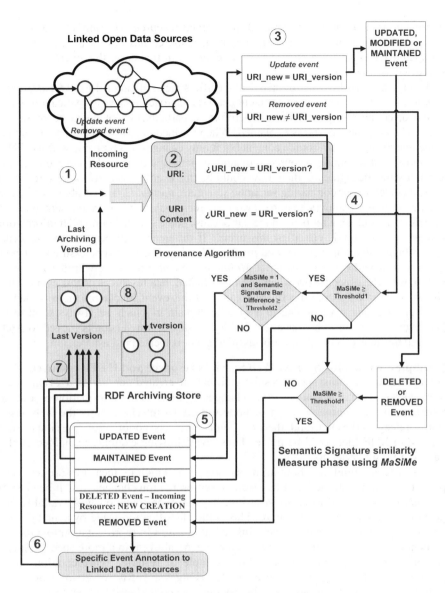

Fig. 1. Event Subclassification Algorithm

If incoming resource has a high content change compared with the last archived version content, this event will be subclassified as *modified event*. A *threshold1* is defined to make this subclassification. On the other hand, if incoming resource has only a bit content change compared with last archived version content, this event will be subclassified as *Updated event*. The same analysis is made to create a subclassification of *removed event*. If incoming resource has a high content change compared with last archived version content, this event will be subclassified as *deleted event*, and this new incoming resource will be annotated as *created event*, and a new time and event annotation will be created in archived resource. *Threshold1* is also used in this subclassification. Therefore if incoming resource has only a bit content change compared with the last archived version content, in this case, this event will be sub-classified as *removed event*.

In Figure 1 can be seen, in step 5 a specific subclassification for *updated event* and *removed event* is made with our content analysis approach respect classification made by actual detecting changes systems. Therefore, a particular event could be produced in *updated event*, and the next is explained. When for incoming resource if its content is the same that the archived resource content but it only changes in a bit percent, if its URIs are the same, and incoming resource semantic signature is *exactly the same* that archived version semantic signature, then, how could be this event classified? Other threshold has to be included in our comparing semantic signature, *theshold2*. This is about a percentage bar that define semantic signature. Two resources could have the same semantic signature differing only in a bit percentage bar because some simple but no high information is changed, then, how is classified this event? If difference between this two percentage bars is higher than this new defined *threshold2*, it is maintained subclassified as *Updated* event, else it will be subclassified a *Maintained* event. Following with the Figure 1, in step 6, is made a specific event annotation in linked data resources of this event subclas-sification. In step 7, same specific annotation of this event subclassification is made in a customized resource versioning to a specific domain in which we always want to store last resource version to be managed. Finally, in step 8, last version is moved to Archiv-ing, and this new classified and subclassified event is located in Last Version.

Examples: Events for Sensor, Web Services resource and HTTP resource
An application of this specific subclassification created for *updated event* and *re-moved event* used in actual detecting changes systems, is the information produced by **Sensors.** In this approach, a sensor node reports its interface using the web descrip-tion language (WSDL), and then a content analysis about wsdl, previously trans-formed to RDF file, could be made. Thus, the following example explained could be able to a Web Service too.

For instance, thinking about an ozone sensor in which its measures are used as in-put for a geophysical model, if its resource representation changes, it will be classified as *updated event*, and as *removed event*, if some representation was available in the past but are not available any more. This is the classification made by actual detecting changes systems. However, if we think about changes in representation together with content changes, we could classify this more general event in a more specific subclas-sification following our approach. For example, if resource representation changes and content only change a bit, for example, changes in software version from version 1 to version 2, this event will be subclassified as *updated event*. Otherwise, if content changes are high, for example, modification of level ozone measure, this event will be subclassified as *modified event*.

In the same way, *removed event*, could be subclassified as *deleted event* if content is quite different, and *removed event* if content and resource representation change only a bit, but resource is located in other URL. For example, this ozone measure displaying is located in other URL. If content and representation do not change, the event will be classified as *Maintained event*. In Figure 2, a general schema of algorithm can be seen in which is made a specific study for wsdl file type. Time annotation for this specific event subclassification will be used to do an average time study of changes. It will be used to improve crawling technique and a resource will not be analyzed before this average time of event change.

Therefore, another application of this specific subclassification could be in HTTP resources. For instance, thinking about a Web page of a computer sale, it will be classified as *updated event* if its representation changes, and as *removed event*, if some representation was available in the past but are not available any more, made by actual detecting changes systems. *Updated event* will be subclassified as *modified event* if it content changes. For example, if it was about computer devices and now it is about components. Otherwise it will be subclassified as *updated event* if its contents only change a bit, for example now it sales another new computer devices.

In the same way, *removed event*, could be subclassified as *deleted event* if content is so different, and *removed event* if content and resource representation change only a bit, but resource is located in other URL.

Event Subclassification Algorithm
1. fetchURI (String uri)
2, ReadUri(uri);
3.   for (each element from the Uri)
4.   if (element is a link)
5.   file = get file(elemento);
6.   // Check what File_type it is
7.   File_type2Rdf wsdl2rdf = new File_type2Rdf(file);
8.   **File_type2rdf.transform();**
9.   **File_type2rdf.processRdf();**
10.   end if
11.   end for
File_type2Rdf (String uri)
12.   File_typeUri = uri;
13.   **transform()**
14.   **processRdf()**
15.   int idRdfFile = existObjectWithProperty(tablaNew,   File_typeUri);
16.   if (idRdfFile!=-1)   //
17.   if (equalRdfContent(idRdfFile, tablaNew, tempFile)) // **Content is the same**
18.   newDescription = get Documentation from new Wsdl;
19.   oldDescription = get Documentation from stored Wsdl;
20.   barNew = get highest bar label from TextWise (newDescription);
21.   barOld = get highest bar label from TextWise (oldDescription);
22.   t1 = MaSiMe (barNew, barOld);
23.   t2 = 1.0;   ///   *threshold_1=0.05; threshold_2=0.8*
24.   if (t1==1.0)
25.   t2 = diferencia(barNew, barOld);
26.   if (t2 < *threshold_1*)
27.   // *Maintained event*
28.   else
29.   // *Update*
30.   end if
31.   else if (t1 > *threshold_2*)
32.   // *Update*

Fig. 2. Event Subclassification Algorithm for wsdl files

```
33.                    else
34.                        // Modified
35.                    end if
36.                    if (t2 >= threshold_1) updateStoredRdf(idRdfFile);
37.                else
38.                    // Content has changed
39.                    updateStoredRdf(idRdfFile);
40.                end if
41.            else
42.                int idFileEqualContent = someEqualRdfContent(tablaNew, tempFile);
43.                if (idFileEqualContent!=-1)
44.                    newDescription = get Documentation from new Wsdl;
45.                    oldDescription = get Documentation from stored Wsdl;
46.                    barNew = get highest bar label from TextWise (newDescription);
47.                    barOld = get highest bar label from TextWise (oldDescription);
48.                    t1 = MaSiMe (barNew, barOld);
49.                    t2 = 1.0;
50.                    if (t1 > threshold_2)
51.                        // Removed
52.                    else
53.                        // Deleted  →  Insert Creation Event
54.                    end if
55.                    updateStoredRdf(idFileContenidoIgual);
56.                else
57.                    storeRdf;
58.                end if
59.            end if
```

Fig. 2. (*continued*)

4   Conclusions and Future Work

In this paper is presented an algorithm to create a more specific subclassification for *updated event* and *removed event* made by actual detecting changes systems. In these detecting changes systems do not exist any specific event classification based on content analysis.

This more specific subclassification for *updated event*, as *modified event* or maintained as *updated event*, will be used to enrich the resources. In the same way, for *removed event* it will be subclassified as *deleted event* or maintained as *removed event*. Thus, a new subclassification annotation for *updated event* and *removed event* will be done, and therefore, will be annotated by who created this annotation, adding provenance information. About time modification annotation, it is made in linked data resource, and doing an average time study about when this specific event changes, could be improved the crawling techniques for a domain. As it is described, together with linked data annotation, a customized resource versioning to a specific domain in which we have always stored last resource version is created. This resource version which we want to maintain with provenance annotation is stored in local.

Then, an improved and optimized archiving phase together with improve of the crawling techniques, using a change frecuency study for this new event subclassification for a domain, is a future work.

Acknowledgements

This work has been funded: ICARIA: From Semantic Web to Systems Biology (TIN2008-04844) and Pilot Project for Training and Developing Applied Systems Biology (P07-TIC-02978).

References

1. Tim Berners-Lee. Linked Data. World Wide Web Consortium (2006),
   `http://www.w3.org/DesignIssue/LinkedData.html`
   (retrieved August 08,2008)
2. Umbrich, J., Hausenblas, M., Hogan, A., Polleres, A., Decker, S.: Toward Dataset Dynamics: Change Frequency of Linked Open Data Sources. In: LDOW 2010, Raleigh, USA (2010)
3. Harth, A., Umbrich, J., Decker, S.: MultiCrawler: A Pipelined Architecture for Crawling and Indexing Semantic Web Data. In: Cruz, I., Decker, S., Allemang, D., Preist, C., Schwabe, D., Mika, P., Uschold, M., Aroyo, L.M. (eds.) ISWC 2006. LNCS, vol. 4273, pp. 258–271. Springer, Heidelberg (2006)
4. Auer, S., Dietzold, S., Lehmann, J., Helmann, S., Aumülle, D.: Triplify: light-weight linked data publication from relational databased. In: WWW 2009. ACM, New York (2009)
5. Morishima, A., Nakamizo, A., Iida, T., Sugimoto, S., Kitagawa, H.: Bringing your dead links back to life: a comprehensive approach and lessons learned. In: Proceedings of the 20th ACM conference on Hypertext and hypermedia, HT 2009, pp. 15–24. ACM, New York (2009)
6. Van de Sompel, H., Sanderson, R., Nelson, M.L.: An HTTP-Based Versioning Mechanism for Linked Data. In: LDOW 2010, Raleigh, North Carolina, USA. ACM, New York (2010)
7. Popitsch, N.P., Haslhofer, B.: DSNotify: Handing Brokeb Links in the Web of Data. In: WWW 2010, Raleigh, North Carolina, USA. ACM, New York (2010)
8. Urdiales-Nieto, D., Martínez Gil y, J., Aldana-Montes, J.F.: MaSiMe: a customized similarity measure and its application for tag cloud refactoring. In: Meersman, R., Herrero, P., Dillon, T. (eds.) OTM 2009 Workshops. LNCS, vol. 5872, pp. 937–946. Springer, Heidelberg (2009)
9. Levenshtein, V.: Binary Codes Capable of Correcting Deletions, Insertions and Reversals. Soviet Physics-Doklady 10, 707–710 (1966)
10. Ziegler, P., Kiefer, C., Sturm, C., Dittrich, K.R., Bernstein, A.: Detecting Similarities in Ontologies with the SOQA-SimPack Toolkit. In: Ioannidis, Y., Scholl, M.H., Schmidt, J.W., Matthes, F., Hatzopoulos, M., Böhm, K., Kemper, A., Grust, T., Böhm, C. (eds.) EDBT 2006. LNCS, vol. 3896, pp. 59–76. Springer, Heidelberg (2006)
11. Ukkonen, E.: Approximate String Matching with q-grams and Maximal Matches. Theor. Comput. Sci. 92(1), 191–211 (1992)
12. `http://textwise.com/api/semantic-signatures`

EPICA: Easy Persistent Identifier Common Architecture

Paolo Ceravolo[1] and Emanuele Bellini[2]

[1] SErvice-oriented Secure software ARchitectures Laboratory
Università degli Studi di Milano - Dipartimento di Tecnologie dell'Informazione
Crema, Italy
paolo.ceravolo@unimi.it
[2] Distributed Systems and Internet Technology Laboratory
University of Florence, Department of Systems and Informatics
Firenze, Italy
bellini@dsi.unifi.it

Abstract. Nowadays the World Wide Web has become the most important platform for publishing scientific materials. The first advantages of online publication are instant access and easy, low-cost, distribution and duplication. But of great impact in middle term success of electronic publication is the availability of systems that support citation and metrics to evaluate the performances of the different actors in the scientific sector. EPICA is an new infrastructure technology supporting integration of uniform and persistent naming systems and declarative expression of metrics used to asses performances. This way independent actors are allowed to cooperate in a common infrastructure. The key element to support this integration is the semantic mapping between metrics and scientific publications available in the Web. This paper discusses this vision and proposes preliminary results related to the definition of a Metrics Assessment Data Model to express this semantic mapping.

Keywords: Digital Libraries, Declarative Metrics, Uniform and Persistent Identifiers.

1 Introduction

Electronic and online publishing has become common in scientific domain. The main motivation is related to dissemination as electronic publishing is lowering the time from submission to publication and increasing the visibility and retrievability of resources. The positive impact of electronic publishing on dissemination was furthermore proved by statistical evidence [34]. Nevertheless, it is clear that the transition to full development of online publishing is far to be coplete. In many instances, the resources uploaded to online repositories are still intended as a simple digital copy of hard version of peer-reviewed journal. In fact, the electronic version of a journal is mostly considered only as a smart access interface to the hard version while the process of selection, evaluation and distribution of resources still remains the same.

R. Meersman et al. (Eds.): OTM 2010 Workshops, LNCS 6428, pp. 626–634, 2010.

The idea that this paradigm will shift is implied by the advent of online publishing linked to the Open Access (OA) approach. OA is an initiative that proposes to foster the development of knowledge making easily the access to relevant scientific literature. The adoption of OA on large scale can have deep effects on the business process behind scientific publication. Several points of innovation can be introduced acting both on the technical infrastructure and on license restrictions. For example we can mention the use of copyright not to restrict access but to ensure permanent open access to the articles published. Since the price is one of barriers to access, OA proposes to do not charge subscription or access fees, but to cover expenses by asking authors to pay in order to be published.

Several important initiatives has been undertake at national and European level based on the standardization initiative called Open Archive Initiative (OAI [14]) with OAI-PMH for harvesting metadata and OAI-ORE for describing sematinc relationship among digital objects. These initiatives are mainly with the purpose of providing discover and access to resource by implementing infrastructure to aggregate open archives behind a unified web portals (DRIVER [5]) or service provider (OAIster [13]), studying new business models of Open Access publishing (SOAPs [16]), but at the moment the main issue that prevent the impact of OA publication on scientific domains is the missing of a standard bibliometric based evaluation process for OA resource. Bibliometrics is a set of methods used to measure the relevance of scientific publication. Since 1950s, when linguist Eugene Garfield [28] began indexing the scientific literature using punch cards the development of ever more sophisticated measures has accelerated rapidly. Initially it was all done manually with tremendous impact on scalability; but electronic databases has radically changed the matter making indexing a widespread service, available from an archive and more and more easy to integrate. Today the Web of Science from Thomson Reuters, Scopus from Elsevier and Google Scholar are the most important databases providing a Citation Index. The metrics adopted to make use of citation in order to asses scientific production are of a big variety and today a community of scientists is debating on their implications and significance. In [23] correlations between 39 measures was compared, attempting to tease out what different aspects they capture. The most important factor seems to be whether a metric measures rapid or delayed impact. But the relevance assigned to a metric strongly depend on the actor that is willing to measure performances. For instance co-authorship can be considered positively, under specific circumstances, as an indicator of the level of cooperation within a community or negatively when evaluating the impact of the production of a single scholar. In the OA domain the bibliometric evaluation is still an open issue. In fact, starting from Borgmann and Furner bibliometric analysis [24], we know that the evaluation systems influence the authors behaviours. In fact, even if the digital paradigm in general and the OA in particular are growing, many of authors seems to prefer hard copy paper publications. The transaction to digital publication is characterized by the production of new type of document like blogs, research report, technical report, articles and

Ph.D. theses archived in institutional deposit; new archive models like library, institutional archive and institutional deposit; new tools of information retrieval and new business model like pay per view, authors payment, pay per click, etc.

In the literature, there are some interesting initiatives to evaluate the scientific articles build upon the Open Access paradigm. For instance, Open Commentary [15] is based on a sort of peer review but performed by a wide number of externs that can annotate comments, votes and justices. Another important initiative is Open Linking [27] where a evaluation process is performed on the base of the number of links to a resource and their weight. Citeseer [3] provides an index based on a citation index analysis built by the authors. The success of these apporaches are strictly related with the quality of OA implementation. In [22] it is discussed the last state of art of OA world wide implementation and the results show that the OA domain is a very fragmented landscape where each institution tends to adopt its own policies for workflow, publication, access, descriptive metadata adoption, type and format of contents, distribution, etc. The scenario of the OA applied to the scientific community is based on the assumption of interoperability among archive but, de facto it is hard to be massively viable. The number of different metadata schemas like Dublin Core [6], METS [11], MARCXML [9], MPEG21 DIDL[18], Uketd_dc [17], etc, are used to describe and classify OA resources, suggests that an international and community oriented policy for repository and related resource evaluation is missing. This status prevents a trustable qualitative and quantitative evaluation of research production, putting out the OA publications form official evaluation system like ISI. Moreover, many institution do not use any standard and community oriented identification system making impossible a trustable retrieval, comparison, citation, etc.

In order to face these issues, our research aims at defining a meta-model interconnecting information about (i) digital resources (ii) authors and institutions (iii) citation indexes (iv) assessment metrics. This is achieved through a metadata mapping system built upon a unique distributed multi-level persistent identification system (as shown in fig 1). In fact every measurement starts from a trustable identification of digital resources. In particular a trustable identification system is the infrastructure needed to link the resource with their institution responsible for its quality and preservation. In particular the EPICA meta-model requires a trustable global infrastructure that allows:

- High level of descriptive metadata completeness and accuracy according to the schema adopted by the institutions.
- Flexible and distributed infrastructure for persistent identification and certification for open access resources to in order to avoid duplication or IPR violation and at the same time to guarantee authority, reliability and wide dissemination.
- Responsibility delegation system for institutions.
- Declarative metrics that take into account the differences of institution publication policies.
- Declarative mapping layer to harmonize the metadata coming from service and data providers.

The second element that characterizes our model is related to the development of a Metrics Assessment Data Model that describes metrics, providing the mathematical formulation and the scope of application. In fact, assuming the requirements as constraints, EPICA designs upon this infrastructure a meta-model that can be adopted by single institution in order to set up the condition for an automatic evaluation according with metrics.

The structure of this paper is as follow: A review of related works is conducted in Section 2 to demonstrate that an innovation in representing metrics is needed; in Section 3 we present a brief analysis on persistent identifier infrastructures available and in particular the Italian NBN system; in Section 4 the EPICA approach is discussed; Section 5 is devoted to present the mapping formalization; Section 6 is presented the early Metrics Assessment Data Model; the conclusions are outlined in the last section.

2   Related Works

As we are proposing a meta-model for handling the assessment of scientific publication let us compare our proposal with existing systems in the domain of online publishing systems, commonly named *digital libraries.*

Digital libraries are complex information systems where interoperability issues are central. For example, the community of data providers take part to an overall business process and can benefit form information sharing. In addition preserving digital resources along the technological changes is of paramount importance. One of the most notable sources of orientation in the definition of digital libraries is The Reference Model for an Open Archival Information System (OAIS) [33]. The model is aimed at presenting terminology and concepts, for describing and comparing architectures and operations of digital archives; as well as different long term preservation strategies and the data models adopted to represent resources. Other formal frameworks include the DELOS Reference Model [26] and the Streams, Structures, Spaces, Scenarios, Societies (5S) formal framework [29]. DELOS attempted to integrate the research of several European teams working in digital library related areas. Its main objective and goal was to develop comprehensive theories and frameworks over the life-cycle of digital library; building interoperable multimodal and multilingual web services and integrated content management systems. 5S is as well aimed at providing a conceptual framework to design digital libraries rigorously. It proposes an integrated view on process, technologies, and data model to implement flexible and effective systems.

If the above mentioned standards pay attention mainly on process and architectures other proposals take a neutral point as to architecture and focus on data integration. The Common European Research Information Format (CERIF) standard [32] is developed by the European Union. It is intended to support storing and transferring data among databases and information systems. Knowledge Discovery Meta-Model [19] is a meta-model for representing information related to existing components of a system. The aim is to facilitate interoperability for exchange of data between systems based on different technologies or implementing adjacent operational processes to be integrated.

As seen none of the existing models is focusing on representing metrics and implementing their evaluation. Our model is intended to cover this lack. We propose it not as a new competitor among the digital library systems, but as the development of a specific focus that in the future could be integrated in a wider meta-model.

3   Trustable Identification Infrastructures

Presently, there are many persistent identifier infrastructures available for identifying digital resources on Internet like DOI [4], Handle System [7], ARK [2], Info URI [8] and several national implementation of NBN. Our analysis has shown that the Italian NBN infrastructure [12] seems to be more close to responsibility delegation, flexibility and authority requirements defined for the EPICA project. Moreover, the opening of the Italian NBN architecture allows an easy implementation of a metric evaluation layer upon this infrastructure. In fact the Italian NBN system defines a hierarchical distributed system, in order to face the criticality of a centralised system and to reduce the high costs of management for a unique resolution service preserving the authoritative control. As shown in [21] and [20], the hierarchical multi-level distributed approach for implementing persistent identifier architecture implies that the responsibility of PI generation and resolution can be recursively delegated to lower level sub-naming authorities, each managing a portion of the domain name space. In this sense, the assignment of an identifier to a resource by an institution linked to a common infrastructure means that this resource is certified and has to be take into account for harvesting and the consequent evaluation process.

4   EPICA Approach

EPICA moves in a general background were a decentralized architecture supports all tasks related to the assessment of the scientific production. Looking at the current standards and technologies we identified a precise lack in languages and standards to specify metrics and their scope of application. To develop such a standard two main elements must be considered:

1. how to express the semantics of the mathematical expressions used to specify metrics;
2. how to express the semantics of the metric's scope, i.e. the objects to be measured.

First point is addressed referring to declarative format to express mathematical expressions. For example MathML is an XML vocabulary that allows to combine presentation and content markup [10]. Presentation markup captures notational structure to support rendering of the mathematical object to various media. Content markup captures mathematical structure. It encodes mathematical structure in a sufficiently regular way in order to facilitate the assignment of

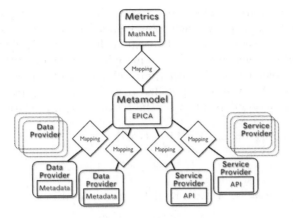

Fig. 1. The EPICA architecture

mathematical meaning to an expression by application programs. Second point is addressed thanks to a meta-model that maps the schemata used by data and service provider. Figure 1 illustrates the relations among the different components involved in the global picture addressed by EPICA. The EPICA meta-model is related both with different sources of data and with metrics. Source of data are distinguished among data providers, such as any institution that is archiving research products, and service providers such as citation index databases or uniform and persistent identifier handlers. Mappings are expressed by an XML vocabulary that was used for data integration purpose [35] and that can associate the records of two models specifying the constraints and the functions to be implemented in order to use data from a source record within a target record. The meda-model is a global view on the different sources integrated and can be considered as the union of the source data models considered.

5 Mapping

The mapping between the EPICA meta-model and the data sources allows to construct an integrated view on the resources we want to measure. Several works in literature describe Data Integration System (DIS) dividing them in two main categories: *declarative* and *procedural* approach [31]: the procedural approach creates ad-hoc integration with respect to a set of predefined needs or requests (queries) [1]. According to [36], we can define a declarative DIS as the following triple:

$$DIS = < G, L, M >$$

Where G is the global representation, L the set of local representations (the data sources) composed by n single representations $s_1, s_2, ..., s_n$ and M is the mapping

---

[1] When the queries to be applied on the sources cannot be predetermined, a declarative approach is required.

of G over L. A declarative DIS can be classified in two more categories: *Local As View* and *Global As View* approach ([25], [30], [37]) that refers to the definition of the common representation G. The system that we consider in this paper is based on *Global as View* approach: the mapping between G and L is given by associating each element in G with the combination of the correspondent set of elements in L. This way it is possible to define the mapping M as a tuple, generated by a function dependent on the set of matching relations M_t:

$$M = f(M_t) \tag{1}$$

where:

M_t - *Matching Relations:* M_t can be defined as a set of relations:

$$e_g^j \cong e_{s_k}^i \tag{2}$$

or

$$e_{s_k}^i \cong e_{s_h}^j \tag{3}$$

Where $\cong \in \{=, \bot, \subset\}$ respectively: *equality, disjointness,* and *inclusion* binary operators.

The definition we provided is quite general. For example the SolR [1] framework that is largely adopted in web based applications is a specification of our mapping system where only relation of equality among elements is supported.

6   Metrics Assessment Data Model

In this section we illustrate the Metrics Assessment Data Model introduced by EPICA. This model represents metrics and their scope and can be described as the combination of (i) the mathematical operations to be applied on data to compute a metric, (ii) the links between the variables in the mathematical expression and the data in the meta-model that instantiate these variables. Figure 2 illustrates our model. A metric is composed by a presentation and a content markup. The content describes the mathematical operations, the constants

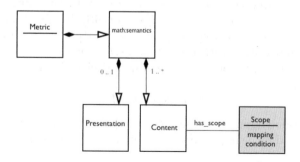

Fig. 2. An overview on the EPICA Metric Assessment Data Model

and the variables characterizing a metric. In our extension content markup is associated to a scope markup containing an element describing the mapping and an element defining the conditions making active this mapping.

7   Conclusions

In this paper, we have discussed the issues related to the implementation of a decentralized architecture supporting all tasks related to the assessment of the scientific production. The nature of this business process is characterized by a variety of actors that take on the evaluation process different view points and are interested in different results. This underlined the need of increasing the effectiveness of the process of definition of the metrics adopted in assessing performances. A declarative approach to express metrics and their scope of application was drafted. Further works will proposed a formal specification and technical implementation details.

Acknowledgments

The EPICA project is funded by Università degli Studi di Milano, Italy.

References

1. Apache solr, http://lucene.apache.org/solr/
2. Archival resource key (ark), http://www.cdlib.org/inside/diglib/ark
3. Citeseer, http://citeseer.ist.psu.edu/
4. Digital object identifier (doi), http://www.doi.org
5. Digital repository infrastructure vision for european research (driver), www.driver-repository.eu
6. Dublin core metadata initiative. dublin core metadata element set, version 1.1, http://dublincore.org/documents/dces/
7. Handle system, http://www.handle.net
8. Info uri, http://info-uri.info
9. Marcxml, http://www.loc.gov/standards/marcxml/schema/MARC21slim.xsd
10. Mathematical markup language (mathml) version 2.0, http://www.w3.org/TR/MathML/
11. Mets, http://www.loc.gov/standards/mets/
12. Nbn italy, http://www.rinascimento-digitale.it/indexEN.php?SEZ=531
13. Oaister, www.oaister.org
14. Open archive initiative, www.openarchives.org
15. Open commentary, www.opencommentary.org/
16. Study of open access publishing (soaps), http://project-soap.eu/
17. Uketd-dc, http://naca.central.cranfield.ac.uk/ethosoai/2.0/uketd_dc.xsd
18. Mpeg-21, information technology, multimedia framework, part 2: Digital item declaration, iso/iec 21000-2:2003 les/did/didl.xsd (March 2003), http://standards.iso.org/ittf/PubliclyAvailableStandards/MPEG-21_schema_fi
19. Knowledge discovery metamodel (kdm) 1.1. Technical report, OMG (2009), http://www.omg.org/spec/KDM/1.1

20. Bellini, E., Cirinnà, C., Lancia, M., Lunghi, M., Puccinelli, R., Saccone, M., Sebastiani, B., Spasiano, M.: Persistent Identifier Distributed System for Digital Libraries
21. Bellini, E., Damiani, E., Fugazza, C., Lunghi, M.: Semantics-aware resolution of multi-part persistent indentifiers. In: WSKS, vol. 1, pp. 413–422 (2008)
22. Bellini, E., Deussom, M.A., Nesi, P.: Assessing open archive oai-pmh implementations. In: The 16th International Conference on Distributed Multimedia Systems (2010)
23. Bollen, J., Van de Sompel, H., Hagberg, A., Chute, R.: A principal component analysis of 39 scientific impact measures. nih.gov (2009) ncbi.nlm.nih.gov
24. Borgman, C.L., Furner, J.: Scholarly communication and bibliometrics. Annual Review f Information Science and Technology 36, 3–72 (2002)
25. Schatz, H., Braun, B., Lotzbeyer, P.: Consistent integration of formal methods, pp. 48–62 (2000)
26. Candela, L., Castelli, D., Ferro, N., Ioannidis, Y., Koutrika, G., Meghini, C., Pagano, P., Ross, S., Soergel, D., Agosti, M., Dobreva, M., Katifori, V., Schuldt, H.: The DELOS Digital Library Reference Model. Foundations for Digital Libraries. ISTI-CNR (2007)
27. Cronin, B.: Semiotics and evaluative bibliometrics. Journal of Documentation 56(4), 440–453 (2000)
28. Garfield, E., Sher, I.H.: In Research Program Effectiveness, pp. 135–146 (1966)
29. Gonçalves, M.A., Fox, E.A., Watson, L.T., Kipp, N.A.: Streams, structures, spaces, scenarios, societies (5s): A formal model for digital libraries. ACM Trans. Inf. Syst. 22(2), 270–312 (2004)
30. Hakimpour, F., Geppert, A.: Global schema generation using formal ontologies. pp. 307–321 (2002)
31. Hammer, J., Garcia-Molina, H., Widom, J., Labio, W.: The stanford data warehouse project. IEEE Data Eng. Bulletin, Specail Issue on Materialized Views (1995)
32. Jeffery, K.G., Lopatenko, A., Asserson, A.: Comparative study of metadata for scientific information: The place of CERIF in CRISs and Scientific Repositories. In: CRIS 2002, pp. 77 (2002)
33. Lavoie, B.F.: The open archival information system reference model: Introductory guide. Microform & Imaging Review 33, 68–81 (2004)
34. Lawrence, S.: Online or invisible? Nature 411, 521 (2001)
35. Leida, M., Ceravolo, P., Damiani, E., Cui, Z., Gusmini, A.: Semantics-aware matching strategy (sams) for the ontology mediated data integration (oddi). Int. J. Knowl. Eng. Soft Data Paradigm. 2(1), 33–56 (2010)
36. Lenzerini, M.: Data integration: a theoretical perspective. In: Proceedings of the twenty-first ACM SIGMOD-SIGACT-SIGART Symposium on Principles of Database Systems, PODS 2002, pp. 233–246. ACM Press, New York (2002)
37. Parent, C., Spaccapietra, S.: Issues and approaches of database integration. Commun. ACM 41, 166–178 (1998)

Knowledge Representation with Autonomic Ontologies

Stainam Brandao[1], Jonice Oliveira[2], and Jano Souza[1]

[1] COPPE/UFRJ, Graduate School of Engineering
[2] DCC-IM Dept. of Computer Science, Institute of Mathematics
Federal University of Rio de Janeiro (UFRJ), Rio de Janeiro, Brazil
{stainam,jonice,jano}@cos.ufrj.br

Abstract. The important role given to domain ontologies for knowledge representation implies increasing need for development and maintenance of them. However, we have a scarcity of tools supporting the life cycle from creation to management and adaptation. Our research group focuses on developing an autonomic process for knowledge representation through a systematic evaluation and redesign of ontologies. This autonomic behavior intends to specify a self-management repository for domain ontologies with an evolution strategy to make adjustments to optimize and protect against undesirable scenarios. In this article, we present the repository with embedded autonomic features to perform the abstraction action of knowledge upon documents collection, using the background knowledge already specified in the domain ontologies.

Keywords: Ontologies, Autonomic Computing, Knowledge Representation.

1 Introduction

Ontologies are defined in this work as a representation of the conceptualization [14] and thus, a symbolic representation of world concepts taking an epistemological view of reality and therefore a possibility of consistent world [4]. Also, the language and common sense influence the ontology building, because our mind filters out this reality, where a concept is used in different contexts and its meaning depends on context.

Ontologies have proven beneficial to the representation of domain knowledge [6], and its importance in the semantic web [11]. In this case, ontologies often support the process of indexing resources content, which is called semantic annotation and can result in the representation of explicit knowledge that cannot be assessed and managed due to the independent environment like the Web, where there is no restriction on the information being published, which can damage their quality.

However, ontologies as a conceptual model for a business domain should react to any changes in business environment, without affecting the intended model and also incorporating additional functionality in accordance with changes in the user's needs, organizing information in a better way, providing an abstract view based on the documents set of domain, etc. If the ontology update or semantic annotation is performed in an inconsistent, redundant or incomplete way, then reliability, accuracy and efficiency of the system decrease significantly [1]. According to these authors, to avoid these real problems, ontologies-based applications may support mechanisms for changes detection, analyze and resolve it in a consistent way.

R. Meersman et al. (Eds.): OTM 2010 Workshops, LNCS 6428, pp. 635–644, 2010.
© Springer-Verlag Berlin Heidelberg 2010

Within this context, we define autonomic ontology as domain ontology with autonomic features to capture and analyze data related to use of ontology. After, it also plans and performs actions to ontology evolution that leads to optimal configuration based on the represented knowledge, on existing instances and user queries performance.

In this paper, our goal is to incorporate autonomic features in domain ontologies to monitor assessment criteria and quality metrics, detects events through environmental data analysis and performs solution applicable to a particular context. The detection of events are made by active rules to evaluate criteria and quality metrics defined within the repository and associated with the ontology that does not need to be modified to incorporate features of autonomic.

Likewise, we propose a repository that will support the lifecycle of the ontology from creation to evolution, adaptation and management. Our research focuses on developing semi-automated ontology evolution to determine the side effects of any development or use of ontology. Always aiming to preserve the intended model already specified by the ontology engineer. For this repository will give the name Onto-CHOP.

2   Autonomic Framework for Knowledge Representation

Below, we describe a repository with autonomic features to enrich domain ontologies through indexed web documents and user queries performed on them. It will allow self-management of domain ontologies to treat the dynamism of the Web environment by identifying events that demands new configuration, correction, optimization and protection. The monitoring of events is associated with actions to reduce the need for human intervention and they are identified through guard expressions with ontology-based metrics already defined in the literature. Notice that ontology engineers remain responsible for auditing the autonomic actions, confirming or revoking the evolution proposed for the domain ontology.

To achieve this, the first step was to define the categories of metrics that will be monitored by the repository. Any changes in metrics values of ontologies are detected and reported to the module responsible for analyzing this event. Event in this research is defined as any change in metrics values specified in the ontology repository. The metrics currently used are into three categories: Natural Language Application, Taxonomic Structure and Instance Structure.

Any changes in the metrics value can point out a self-configuration, protection, healing, optimizing to the ontologies saved on the framework. Thus, guard expressions are defined for values that trigger autonomic actions. The figure 1 shows an example, where some metrics have guard expressions, that are triggered when are represent by a (x) on the columns: Configuration (C), Healing (H), Optimization (O) and/or Protection (P). On the other hand, when the guard expression exist and do not achieve the value to be triggered, then they represent by a (v) on the columns. Notice that more than one expression can be defined for each metric.

Therefore, when actions are triggered after an event, a planning may be build to define the execution script of this actions avoiding endless shots and unexpected results for the evolution of ontology.

Category	Metric	Value	C	H	O	P
Natural Language Application	Precision	0.59	✓			
	Recall	0.65		✓		
	Coverage	0.81	✓			
	Accuracy	0.72	✓			
	Cost-Based Evaluation	0.0				
	Lexical Comparison Level	0.0				
Taxonomic Structure	Width	1.76				
	Depth	50.0				
	Specificity	50.0				
Instance Structure	Completeness	0.0				
	Importance	0.59				
	Average Population	0.65				
	Class Richness	0.3				

Fig. 1. Guard expressions for metrics: 'x' means expressions triggered and 'v' metrics values in accordance

The challenge related to the capture, modeling, storage and monitoring events justifies the need for an appropriate architecture for this purpose. The system architecture was developed using the approach of autonomic computing to provide capacity for self-management, hiding from the user complexity of programming and providing a system that works 24 / 7 [7], [8], [9], [10].

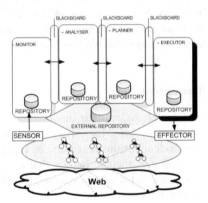

Fig. 2. Framework Architecture

The figure 2 shows the architecture with the following four modules and a brief description, which will be detailed in the next section:

- Monitor has sensors that detect events in domain ontologies. We defined as an event any changes related to user queries, new documents associated on the ontology and manual evolution performed by the ontology engineer. When an event is identified, the framework recalculates the metrics and publishes the changes to the Analyzer module;
- Analyzer has active rules to verify guard expression that are activated after the occurrence of correspondent event and triggered an autonomic action;

- Planner is responsible to orchestrate multiple expressions triggered simultaneously to avoid endless shots and unexpected results;
- Executor manages the action specified by the Planner module to be executed, generating the expected result for ontology enrichment (with intervention of the ontology engineer).

For communication between the modules the blackboard approach is used for modules register all the ontologies events. Blackboard is defined as an area of knowledge where loosely coupled entities share information [12]. In the next section we present the autonomic actions in the form of standard to facilitate understanding.

2.1 Monitoring: Capturing Metrics

The monitor module is one that is aware of events on the ontologies, recalculating the metrics and reporting when any values changes. The quality metrics consolidated in the literature and presented in the framework are classified into three (3) categories: Intentional Size, Taxonomic Structure and Natural Language Application.

The Natural Language Application category provides metrics to evaluate the semantic annotation of the documents content. Seven measures have been defined to express how well the ontology represent the domain documents annotated. Also, the Taxonomic Structure category evaluates the structure of the ontology. And finally, the Intentional Size category evaluates the instances of ontologies and its distribution on them.

With these metrics, the repository monitor and report any change that occurs in their values to other modules through the blackboard to determine whether the new value trigger an action.

2.2 Analysis: Quality Assessment

The Analyzer module is responsible to evaluate any change in the ontological metrics values available on the blackboard. Also, the Analyzer module maintains a database with the rules and its correspondent actions that must be triggered when the condition of the rule is satisfied by ontologies metric. Notice that all triggered actions will be forwarded to the Planner module before been executed in order to be orchestrated, avoiding endless shots and unexpected results.

An action is defined as a pattern that specifies the autonomic behavior. The action presented in this paper is the Abstraction of the domain ontologies for documents set when (1) the NLP metrics achieve undesirable values defined in the guard expression or when (2) the ontology engineer input any documents collection and desire an abstraction view of the ontology.

For the first case, guard expressions are created with Precision, Recall, Coverage and Accuracy metrics from NLP category that trigger an action when at least one of this four metrics achieve the minor value specified. These guard expressions identify register in the blackboard the necessities of the action perform.

In Figure 3, we see an guard expression for Precision metric that is triggered when its value is less than a value defined by the user and load in *'?precision'* variable. This value is configured on the graphical user interface of the repository as shown in Figure 4. Every guard expression is associated with an autonomic action and every action can be associated with more than one guard expression.

```
(defrule PRECISION
    ?o <-(OntologyVO  (precision  ?precision))
    ?mCon <-(MetricaVO ( nomeMetrica "precision") {vlMinSelfCon > ?precision } )

  =>

    (save-problem "CONFIGURATION" "PRECISION")
    (printout t "Self-configuration -> ontology availability: " ?availability
        " vlMinSelfCon: " ?mCon.vlMinSelfCon crlf)
)
```

Fig. 3. Active Rule in Jess

Autonomic Rules: Precision

0.00	CONFIGURATION	0.55
	HEALING	
	OTIMIZATION	
	PROTECTION	

Fig. 4. Interface gráfica para a configuração da guard expression

For the second case, the abstraction action can be triggered by the user to obtain an ontology view for any documents collection. The figure 5 shows the domain ontology abstraction with the selected concepts highlighted in yellow color with the possibility to be export as a independent domain ontology.

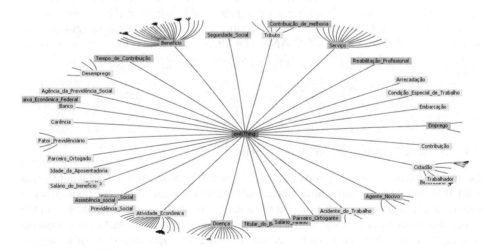

Fig. 5. Ontology resulted after the Abstraction

2.3   Planner: Orchestrating the Abstraction Action

Even within a domain, the knowledge to be represented through ontologies can have a different view depending on the documents collection to be represented and processed.

Domain ontology cannot be static and may provide functionalities to deal with knowledge representation, even when the domain is the same but the focus differ based on the documents collection.

The Abstraction action is triggered when a guard expression associated with it and controlled by the Analyzer module is enabled. When it occurs, the action uses the External Repository that contain the metrics and the current location of the ontology and the internal Repository that maintain the metrics that must be addressed by the set of documents involved in Abstraction, the Function name to be used in action and where the ontology abstraction will stored before engineer validation.

Upon receiving an event initiator of the Abstraction action (ABSTRACTION), the first step (IDENTIFY DOCUMENTS) is to select sub-set of documents that will define the view to be considered. If the user does not specify the documents collections, then all the documents indexed by the repository will be taken into account. The next step (RETRIEVE SUB-ONTOLOGY) is the recovery of the ontology concepts associated with documents presented in the previous step and, also in parallel the extraction of domain vocabulary from the documents collection identified on the previously step (GET IDF). As describe below, the IDF (inverse document frequency) is retrieved from the Semantic Annotation repository that is populated before any autonomic action. The next step (GET MORE FREQUENT TERMS) retrieves the most frequent terms (the minimum value pre-defined by the ontology engineer), which will be the candidate terms for the ontology. In possession of these terms, the next step (IDENTIFY RELATIONS) is the identification of relations between the candidate terms in the Web documents collection. This step uses taxonomy of natural language (Wordnet) [5] and the domain ontology. On the next step the taxonomy built with candidate term and the relations identified is showed for the ontology engineer responsible for integrating this with the sub-ontology selected from the documents collection (WAIT APROVALE). After the engineer finish the manual integration, the last step (PERFORM SEMANTIC ANNOTATION) is executed to perform semantic annotation up on the documents collection selected and the ontology defined for this abstraction.

Accordingly, if the engineer has done some integration between the sub-ontology extracted and taxonomy defined autonomically, we can deem that a new abstraction was defined form the ontology and the documents collection selected.

2.4 Executor: Autonomic Actions Modeling

Domain ontologies are the specification of conceptualization [14] and we want to deal with different abstractions views about any documents collection. For this reason, the ontologies cannot be static and we have to guarantee the accuracy in deal with the conceptualization [11] through ensuring that ontology abstraction view occurs on the conceptualization, but that the intended model remains as the original. In other words, we must keep the focus on relevant conceptual relationships to a specific context.

In this context, the Executor module is responsible for ontology changes presented by Planner module, performing the action requested on the ontology and finally generates a label with the new version of it. This, however, has the annotation semantic action as a preliminary step to associate documents to the domain ontologies. Indeed, the documents are associated with the ontology and their contents indexed to be used for further ontology enrichment through ontology abstract action, where new concepts are identified when the precision and accuracy metrics point to this necessity or, when the user wants to view an abstract for a specified documents collection.

The semantic annotation action analyzes the content and indexes on the proposed repository to provide semantics to the documents without these be aware of this and even been modify. Which we consider an annotation "top down", which is different of annotation manual, known in the literature, where the user insert annotation with a markup (tag) language in the content using an ontology (or vocabulary) to give semantic to the Web document.

3 Case Study

The Brazilian Social Security domain ontology was developed within our project with the short-term objective to represent the vocabulary and a long-term goal of mapping the services, laws and norms of Brazilian Social Security available online libraries. Currently, the ontology has 200 concepts and is available in the repository implemented.

3.1 Objective

The case study goal was to evaluate the approach presented in this article to generate an ontology abstraction based on documents collection provided by the user in the ontology repository. For this, the first step was to define the URLs that contains the documents source:

- Social Legislation System (SisLex): *http://www81.dataprev.gov.br/sislex/;*
- National Institute of Social Security (INSS): *http://www-inss.prevnet/;*
- Official Brazilian Social Security site: *www.previdenciasocial.gov.br/*

3.2 Preliminary Results

Following the execution of Semantic Annotation Methodology proposed, approximately 600 documents were crawled and about 400000 words were analyzed, processed and their documents associated to the ontology concepts and the results presented in the table below.

Table 1. Results obtained from the Case Study

Goals	Values
Ontology concepts identified	42 concepts
Terms candidate to Ontology	35 words
Precision	59%
Recall	65%
Coverage	81%
Accuracy	72%

The next Case Study step was to analyze the vocabulary produced, where two specialists from Social Security Administration evaluate the documents summaries and ontology concepts to which they are associated and identified the concepts that should have been associated, as well as the concepts they should not, but were mistakenly associated with the document. A module developed exclusively for this study has used this information to calculate the Precision, Recall, Accuracy and Coverage metrics for the vocabulary produced. Within this work, accuracy is considered the relationship between the number of items correctly identified and the number of items identified. Recall measures the relationship between the number of items correctly identified and the total number of correct items. Accuracy is the average frequency of coverage on classes that include at least 60% of the relevant words. And finally, Coverage is computed as the average of the overlap between the vocabulary of the triples and the input text for each frequency class.

The figure 8 show the interface, where we can view the documents associated with each concept or candidate term domain.

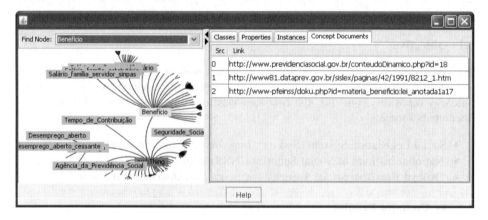

Fig. 8. Screen capture with the documents associated with the 'Benefício' concept

In the same figure 8, we have the concept 'Benefit' (in Portuguese) on the left side with three links (right side) from where this concept has been identified.

4   Conclusions and Future Works

This paper proposes a repository for domain ontologies that encompasses guidelines for capturing and analyzing data related to their use and also, planning and execution of behaviors to ontology evolution that leads to an optimal configuration based on the represented knowledge, on existing concepts instances and user queries performance. The proposed autonomic ontology repository has shown to be simple, yet powerful. However, we do know that challenges still exist regarding:

- Action quality, since, as an autonomic system, it should be able to distinguish trustworthy from untrustworthy action;
- Analysis of document content indexed in the ontology;
- Summarization through autonomic aggregation of content in heterogeneous format;
- Specification of new action patterns related to other metrics defined in the literature.

One future work is the development of a Context-Sensitive Search based on the documents content analyzed, when a systematic to analysis of web content was defined. Another future work will be allow navigation through documents by the domain ontology, deeming the correlation of documents already defined with the Vector Model (TF-IDF) approach from Lucene [14] to calculate the similarity between documents.

A future target is the integration with Formal Ontology to establish formal meanings for domain vocabulary allowing axiomatization and integration of domain ontologies from different sources. We notice that domain ontologies consist of specialized terminology and a particular vision of reality. But the meaning remains dependent on the context. The use of Formal Ontology to integrate the domain ontology can promote the reuse, integration and management through the construction of ontologies from web documents.

Acknowledgments. We thank CAPES, CNPq and IBM for supporting this work.

References

1. Maedche, A., Motik, B., Stojanovic, L., Studer, R. and Volz, R.: An infrastructure for searching, reusing and evolving distributed ontologies. In: WWW, pp. 439–448 (2003)
2. Omelayenko, B.: Learning of Ontologies for the Web: the Analysis of Existent Approaches. In: Proceedings of the International Workshop on Web Dynamics, held in conj. with the 8th International Conference on Database Theory (ICDT 2001), London, UK (2001)
3. CLIPS: http://clipsrules.sourceforge.net/
4. Guizzardi, G.: Ontological foundations for structural conceptual models. Doctoral Thesis (2005)
5. Miller, G.A.: WordNet: A Lexical Database for English. Communication of the ACM 38, 39–41 (1995)
6. Alani, H., Brewster, C.: Ontology ranking based on the analysis of concept structures. In: Proceedings of the 3rd International Conference on Knowledge capture, pp. 51–58. ACM, Banff (2005)
7. Huebscher, M. C., McCann, J.A.: A survey of autonomic computing-degrees, models, and applications. In: ACM Computing Surveys (2008)
8. IBM: An architectural blueprint for autonomic computing. In: Autonomic Computing White Paper, 3 edn. (June 2005)
9. Kephart, J.O., Chess, D.M.: The Vision of Autonomic Computing. IBM Thomas J. Watson Research Center (2003)
10. Miller, B.: The autonomic computing edge: Can you CHOP up autonomic computing? IBM Corporation (2005)

11. Guarino, N.: Formal Ontology and Information Systems. In: Proceedings of the International Conference on Formal Ontology in Information Systems, pp. 3-15 (1998).
12. Shaw, M., Garlan, D.: Software Architecture: Perspectives on an Emerging Discipline. Prentice Hall, Englewood Cliffs (1996)
13. Berners-Lee, T., Hendler, J., Lassila, O.: The Semantic Web A new form of Web content that is meaningful to computers will unleash a revolution of new possibilities (2001)
14. Lucene, http://lucene.apache.org/

Semantic Support for Computer-Human Interaction: Intuitive 3D Virtual Tools for Surface Deformation in CAD

Ioana Ciuciu[1], Robert Meersman[1], Estelle Perrin[2], and Frédéric Danesi[3]

[1] STARLab, Department of Computer Science, VUB, Brussels, Belgium
{iciuciu,meersman}@vub.ac.be
[2] ERT Gaspard Monge, CReSTIC, URCA, Charleville-Mézières, France
{estelle.perrin}@univ-reims.fr
[3] DINCCS, MICADO, Charleville-Mézières, France
{frederic.danesi}@dinccs.com

Abstract. Decision making is tightly related to the understanding of the design and manufacturing practices. In our previous work, we proposed an intuitive approach for geometric modeling in CAD, based on the integration of the user's knowledge with virtual design tools. This approach facilitates the design of the CAD models using deformations. Deformations are done by the bias of a layered architecture which captures and represents the user's knowledge at five semantic levels. The idea of using semantics was to provide high level modeling primitives for the data model in order to facilitate the design for a non-expert user. This paper discusses the natural language representation of the user-specific knowledge by means of ontologies and its major contribution to the computer-human interaction. The approach is demonstrated on an industrial example of surface deformation for the design of a car parcel shelf.

Keywords: Knowledge Engineering, Semantic Data Modeling, Ontology Engineering, Decision Support, Computer Aided Design, Surface Deformation, Man-Machine Interaction.

1 Introduction

Knowledge management is of tremendous importance in the field of Computer Aided Design (CAD) today. It consists of a series of actions – create, derive, expose, share, use – applied to knowledge resources. Knowledge management helps agents make better decisions during the production chain, helping companies to increase their competitiveness.

In our previous work [1], we proposed a collaborative and social approach which takes into account the user knowledge during the design process in CAD. We argued that this would benefit a non-expert user in order to produce better results in shorter times.

Even though powerful from a geometrical point of view, current CAD systems do not take into account the functional aspect of the designed object. Several models

R. Meersman et al. (Eds.): OTM 2010 Workshops, LNCS 6428, pp. 645–654, 2010.
© Springer-Verlag Berlin Heidelberg 2010

have been proposed, aimed at preserving the design intent (function and behavior) throughout the product lifecycle [2,3]. Moreover, these systems are based on complicated interfaces, which can be confusing for a novice user.

To overcome these problems, we proposed a new, intuitive, methodology, based on 3D user-friendly virtual tools. This technique includes semantics into the model and allows visualizing the model in order to help the user make the right design decisions using his knowledge. Yet, semantic models are application-specific, making it difficult for users with different background knowledge to understand and use these highly abstracted models. Consequently, the shareability and usability aspects are poorly satisfied within this approach.

As a solution, this paper proposes the use of ontology for representing knowledge related to surface deformation. Ontology provides relatively generic knowledge that can be shared and reused in different applications. One of the ontology engineering approaches is the DOGMA (Developing Ontology-Grounded Methods and Applications) paradigm [4,5,6], grounded in natural language. Using DOGMA, the knowledge can be represented in natural language to be accessible to users and then transformed into RDF machine-readable triples.

The main motivation of this paper is to express knowledge in natural language to make it accessible to users in a distributed and collaborative context and to make this knowledge reusable by representing it using ontology.

The article is organized as follows: Section 2 introduces our previous work around a CAD system based on intuitive deformations. A new approach of knowledge representation for intuitive surface deformation is discussed in Section 3. A case study is discussed in Section 4 and related work is presented in Section 5. Section 6 concludes on the presented approach and discusses new research directions emerging from this work.

2 Knowledge Representation in DIJA

In [1], the authors argue that in order to provide both expert and neophyte CAD users with an intuitive and easy-to-use system, this one has to capture the user's background knowledge and to follow the user's synthetic thinking along the design process. From this idea, the DIJA project [7] emerged – whose purpose is to provide any kind of user with a functional, distributed, collaborative and intuitive CAD system. As opposed to actual modeling techniques, DIJA's "synthetic" approach places the user in his habitual working environment thanks to adapted deformation tools which capture the user's know-how. The design is based on deformations applied on visual entities on the surface of the object, called dialog elements. Modeling using deformations is a well-known and efficient technique largely used in 3D graphics and animation. We aim at using this technique coupled with an interaction technique based on user's business domain concepts. The interaction between the user and the system can be done at multiple levels thanks to the system's multi-layered internal architecture: 1) low-level interaction (purely geometric); 2) interaction on visual elements; and 3) high-level semantic interactions (business domain-oriented techniques and interactions). This architecture is described in the following section.

2.1 System Architecture

DIJA system is based on a top-down approach for modeling. Going from global to local reasoning shows the way the user thinks along the design process: he focuses his attention on more and more refined areas of the designed object. This leads to a progressively focused vocabulary. It will be, at the beginning, domain-oriented but still vague (e.g. "embossing" or "stretching") and it will evolve into more and more geometrical vocabulary (e.g. "smoothing" or "remeshing"). Designing this way leads to several levels of thinking, represented by the system's architecture: the design vocabulary is more or less full of semantics, depending on the abstraction level. There are five semantic levels under DIJA:

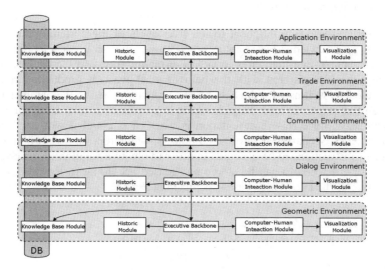

Fig. 1. DIJA system architecture

1) the "Application" level, the uppermost semantic level, where the knowledge specific to a certain application is configured; 2) the "Trade" level, associating the knowledge to a specific domain (user's business domain); 3) the "Common" level, which is an intermediary level, containing generic knowledge applying to all the domains; 4) the "Dialogue" level, where each term of the vocabulary represents a visible entity on the surface of the object; and 5) the "Geometric" level, containing the knowledge necessary for representing geometric models.

DIJA architecture is based on a modular approach, making it possible to decompose and to transmit the knowledge between the five abstraction levels, from the uppermost ("Application") level to the lowest ("Geometric") level. The modular approach also ensures that the result is sent back to the appropriate module and level in order to be visualized. As described in Fig.1, five modules are identified in the DIJA architecture: 1) the "Computer-Human Interaction" Module (CHIM), which manages the human-computer interactions; it also creates the interfaces according to the user domain; 2) the "Visualization" Module (VM), managed by the preceding module, and which displays the CAD object being modeled; 3) the "Historic" Module (HM), which stores the different actions regarding the modeling process; 4) the "Executive Backbone" Module (EBM), managing the data flow between the different modules; it executes the scenarios sent by the KBM; and 5) the "Knowledge Base" Module (KBM), containing all the data necessary to guide the modeling process; when this module receives an instruction from the EBM it returns a script which explains how to execute the instruction.

Each abstraction level is composed of five modules regrouped under the name of "environment", as illustrated in Fig.1. As the architecture of the DIJA CAD system is out of the scope of this paper, we refer to [8] for details. We focus, in the next section, on the knowledge representation via the "Knowledge Base" Module.

2.2 Knowledge Base Module

The knowledge base is orthogonal to the five levels of the system architecture. At each level, the knowledge base captures the know-how both in a declarative and in a procedural manner, and integrates it with deformation tools. At the declarative level, the knowledge is registered with the help of what we call production rules ("IF-THEN" rules) as well as with the help of constraints (applied to the parameters of the model). At this stage, the knowledge is stored in a structure similar to an encyclopedia or a dictionary. Since this representation is weak, it is coupled with scenarios at a procedural level. Scenarios are structured objects, which represent algorithmically the sequence of instructions to be executed in order to obtain a solution for a design process. This way, a scenario can be stored and reused according to the design context. The structure of the knowledge base is depicted in Fig.2.

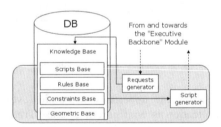

Fig. 2. The components of the "Knowledge Base" Module

Until present, the knowledge was represented using XML schemas whose structure is specified by a particular grammar, stored by XML files as well. The five hierarchical levels of DIJA are interchangeable: we could change the geometric modeler without changing the rest. In the context of the system's evolution, the knowledge management has evolved. This article is linked to this evolution.

We claim that the use of ontologies with the presented approach would result in an important degree of reusability and shareability of the represented knowledge. Therefore, we propose to represent the semantics of the model at each level by DOGMA ontology. This approach is presented in the next section.

3   Knowledge Representation Formalized with DOGMA Ontology

One of the premises of successful work today is to be collaborative. Nowadays, people group together around collaborative projects. This often implies heterogeneous knowledge and background from the part of each partner. In order for the collaboration to be successful, the knowledge has to be shared between people, and interoperability has to be assured between all the agents (users, information systems, processes, etc.). The goal of the ontology is to make possible the knowledge sharing and the interoperation among agents.

Tom Gruber defines ontology as "an explicit specification of a conceptualization" [9]. Guarino [10,11] further refines the definition of conceptualization as the intended models, with which a set of logical axioms are designed to account for the intended meaning of a vocabulary. In other words, ontology explicitly defines a set of real world objects and the relations between them, in such a way that it is understandable by both humans and machines. Ontologies are widely used for communication between machines (e.g. Semantic Web [12]). Yet, ontologies can also be used to improve the interoperability between multiple human actors and between humans and computer systems [13], which is the case of the DIJA CAD system.

Based on the above definitions of Tom Gruber and Nicola Guarino, the DOGMA paradigm for ontology engineering was introduced, summarized in the next section.

3.1   DOGMA Approach to Ontology Engineering

DOGMA is a formal ontology engineering framework based on the idea of applying the principles of database design methodology (NIAM/ORM2 [14]) to ontology engineering. DOGMA creates reusable resources (ontologies), not only for a specific application, but for as many applications as possible within a specific domain. DOGMA ontology is grounded in natural language and based on the "double articulation" [6] principle, which separates the concepts with their relations (facts) from their semantic constrains. This results in two layers of the ontology, with the intention to make the reuse of facts easier: 1) the *lexon* base layer that contains a vocabulary of simple binary facts called lexons; and 2) the *commitment* layer that formally defines rules and constraints by which a set of applications may make use of the lexons. We will detail the two layers in the next paragraphs.

Lexon layer. A lexon is formally defined as a quintuple ⟨γ, *headterm, role, co-role, tailterm*⟩, where γ is a context identifier used to disambiguate the terms (*headterm, tailterm*). For example, the lexon ⟨*Geometry, Function, induces, is induced by, Shape*⟩ explains that in the context *Geometry*, *Function* plays the role of *induces Shape* and *Shape* plays the role of *is induced by Function*. The goal of the Lexon base is to reach a common agreement on the understanding of the ontology terminology and is therefore aimed at human understanding.

Commitment layer. Ontological commitments are "agreements to use the shared vocabulary in a coherent and consistent manner" [9]. A commitment in the Commitment layer is a finite set of constraints, rules and axiomatized binary facts that specify how lexons in the Lexon base are interpreted in the committing application.

The next section demonstrates our approach on applying DOGMA ontology to the knowledge base of the DIJA system for the creation of a car parcel shelf.

3.2 Surface Deformation Represented by DOGMA Ontology

DIJA incorporates a surface modeler for CAD which integrates domain knowledge with virtual deformation tools. We propose to reorganize the structure of the knowledge base at each semantic level by introducing two layers: the Lexon layer and the Commitment layer, following the DOGMA principles, in order to enhance reusability and shareability of the knowledge. An ontology is created at each level of the system's architecture. At the "Trade" level, a domain ontology, corresponding to the vocabulary related to a specific domain is created, whose terms are further matched to more specialized terms at the lower levels. The refinement of the ontology terms between the semantic levels is done at run time by the EBM. We illustrate this approach with an industrial application for the design of a car parcel shelf, in the context of surface deformation. The design of a parcel shelf is realized by applying the "Thermoforming" deformation tool. For each level, we first create the Lexon base and then we describe the commitment rules for the chosen example.

Lexon layer. The formal representation of the deformation tools at each level of the architecture (starting from the "Trade" level) is as follows:

Table 1. Lexons representing the 3D surface deformation tools

Context	Head Term	role	co-role	Tail Term
Trade	Thermoforming	deforms	is deformed by	Surface
Trade	Thermoforming	has	characterizes	Height
Trade	Thermoforming	produces	is produced by	Loading Zone
Common	Die Stamp	deforms	is deformed by	Surface
Common	Die Stamp	has	characterizes	Shape
Common	Die Stamp	has	characterizes	Height
Common	Die Stamp	has	characterizes	Volume
Dialogue	Deformation	affects	affected by	Surface
Dialogue	Deformation	has	characterizes	Contour
Dialogue	Deformation	has	characterizes	Initial Point
Dialogue	Deformation	has	characterizes	Target Point
Dialogue	Deformation	has	characterizes	Height
Dialogue	Deformation	has	characterizes	Volume
Geometric	Deformation	affects	affected by	Surface
Geometric	Surface	contains	is part of	Zone
Geometric	Zone	contains	is part of	3D Points
Geometric	Deformation	has	characterizes	Shape
Geometric	Shape	is induced by	induces	Function
Geometric	Deformation	has	characterizes	Initial Point
Geometric	Initial Point	represented by	represents	3D Point
Geometric	Deformation	has	characterizes	Target Point
Geometric	Target Point	represented by	represents	3D Point
Geometric	Deformation	has	characterizes	Height
Geometric	Deformation	has	characterizes	Volume

Commitment layer. Based on the above Lexon base, we present in Table 2 the rules that compose the Commitment layer. These rules represent application axiomatizations, where the application is the insertion of a parcel shelf using a "Thermoforming" deformation tool.

Table 2. Commitments based on the lexons (in *Italic*) from Table 1

Abstraction Level	Rule
Trade level	Every *thermoforming* has a maximal *height*.
Common level	Every *die stamp* has a maximal *height*.
Common level	Every *die stamp* has a maximal *volume*.
Dialogue level	The *contour* of the *deformation* lies on the *surface*.
Dialogue level	The *contour* of the *deformation* delimits the *deformation* from the rest of the *surface*.
Dialogue level	The *initial point* lies on the *surface*.
Dialogue level	The *initial point* lies inside the *contour*.
Geometric level	The *deformation* is applied locally on a *zone* of the *surface*.
Geometric level	The deformable *3D points* are inside the *zone* of the *deformation*.
Geometric level	The *initial point* lies in the center of the *zone*.
Geometric level	The *target point* lies either inside or outside of the *surface*.
Geometric level	The *target point* determines the displacement of the *3D points* of the *zone* of *deformation*.
Geometric level	For every *3D point* inside the *deformation zone*, the displacement is computed by the *deformation function*, according to the position of the *target point*.
Geometric level	Every *deformation* has a maximal *height*.
Geometric level	Every *deformation* has a maximal *volume*.

4 Case Study

The "Thermoforming" deformation tool represented by DOGMA is applied to a surface in order to obtain a parcel shelf. The process is depicted in Fig.3. It shows how the deformation tool and its characterizing parameters are refined at each level by the EB who interprets the user's actions and reflects them on the surface of the object. The user interacts with the system by means of ontologies who describe the deformation tools in terms of the user's domain knowledge.

The Lexon base can be further reused in other applications. Both the Lexon base and the Commitment layer can be enriched by expert users and reused by all the other users. Fig.4 shows examples of die stamps inserted using the above constraint rules.

The refinement (matching) of the knowledge (ontologies) between the levels is done using scenarios and scripts from the knowledge base. We refer to [8] for details.

The system accepts any geometric model as long as the points of the surface can be extracted from it in order to be submitted to the deformation algorithms. Imagine now that several users work together to design an object collaboratively, each on his station. Let us suppose that each user uses a different format to represent and store the

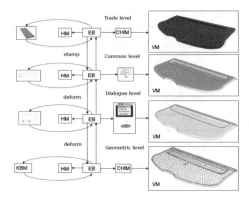

Fig. 3. Representation of the 3D deformation tools at different architectural levels

data. In order for them to be able to collaborate and share the model, they need to commit to a central format, i.e an ontology. Therefore, besides the reuse of the knowledge, the system makes it possible now to share knowledge collaboratively, thanks to the ontological approach.

Fig. 4. Design of a car parcel shelf (different stages)

5   Related Work

The application of ontology engineering in industry is gaining more and more terrain nowadays. In CAD, ontologies are mainly used for interoperation purposes in collaborative work and for describing the different parts and functions of the designed product. Depending on the context, the purpose of ontologies in CAO is to share knowledge collaboratively, to retrieve information and to facilitate modeling and simulation. An ontological approach to integrating CAD and computer-aided process planning is discussed in [15]. [16] discusses the difficulties arising in case of distributed knowledge and misunderstanding and communication faults among partners. The authors propose an ontology to model the totality of constraints related to the object structure.

Several Human-computer interaction models based on ontologies exist in the literature. Park [17] used OWL to facilitate the mapping between the components of different models under the same environment. Toro [18] embedded semantics into virtual reality tools in a commercial CAD system to improve the user workflow and to help him focus on the design task.

Other efforts have been done to support the virtual reality interaction with engineering knowledge in CAD. The SEVENPRO [19] project developed tools to improve the product engineering process by means of semantically, ontology-based, supported acquisition, formalization and support of knowledge. Lavbic [20] proposed a user friendly approach to capture knowledge represented in enterprises. The approach uses interfaces based on constraints and predefined templates. A rather similar approach to ours is the approach of Parisi [21] to create 3D animations for training purposes using ontologies. It uses ontology to understand generic natural language requests to help non-expert designers to create animations used for industrial workers in a "learning by doing" approach.

To our knowledge, none of these approaches use natural language to formalize the user knowledge in order to integrate it with user-friendly 3D virtual tools to support deformation-based design in CAD.

6   Conclusions and Future Work

This paper presents a new approach to knowledge representation and knowledge sharing for a CAD system based on intuitive deformations. This was achieved by means of DOGMA approach to ontology engineering that has its groundings in natural language. As compared to the previous approach, based on semantics, this approach has the advantage of knowledge reuse and collaborative sharing. This naturally results into better decision support to improve human productivity.

Future work will focus on redefining the production rules by semantic decision tables. Another research direction would be to annotate – textually and geometrically – the model in order to capture the user knowledge and to enrich the ontology base. Non-expert users could be further assisted in the design process by a geometry browser, which would identify and retrieve information for each geometrical feature visually on the model.

Acknowledgments. We would like to thank FAURECIA Acoustics and Soft Product Line Mouzon R&D Center for the permission to use their parcel shelf CAD model for this study.

References

1. Ciuciu, I.G.: A Proposal for Integrating Trade-based Deformations into a Computer Aided Design System. PhD thesis, University of Reims Champagne-Ardenne (2009)
2. Fenves, S., Foufou, S., Bock, C., Sriram, R.D.: A Core Model for Product Data. Journal of Computing and Information Science in Engineering 5, 238–246 (2005)
3. Gero, J.S., Kannengiesser, U.: The Situated Funtion-Behavior-Structure Framework. In: Artificial Intelligence in Design 2002, pp. 89–104. Kluver Academic Publisher, The Nederlands (2002)
4. Meersman, R.: Ontologies and databases: More than a Fleeting Ressemblance. In: Raś, Z.W., Skowron, A. (eds.) ISMIS 1999. LNCS, vol. 1609, Springer, Heidelberg (1999)
5. Meersman, R.: Semantics Ontology Tools in Information System Design. In: The Proceedings of OES/SEO 2001 Rome Workshop, Luiss Publications (2001)

6. Spyns, P., Meersman, R., Jarrar, M.: Data Modeling versus Ontology Engineering. SIGMOD Record: Special Issue on Semantic Web and Data Management 31(4), 12–17 (2002)
7. Danesi, F., Denis, L., Gardan, Y., Perin, E.: Basic Components of the DIJA Project. In: The 7th ACM Symposium on Solid Modeling and Applications, Germany (2002)
8. Denis, L., Gardan, Y., Perrin, E.: A Framework for a Distributed CAD System. Computer-Aided Design 36, 761–773 (2004)
9. Gruber, T.R.: Toward Principles for the Design of Ontologies Used for Knowledge Sharing. In: Workshop on Formal Ontology, In book Formal Ontology in Conceptual Analysis and Knowledge Representation. Padova, Italy, Kluwer Academic Publishers, Dordrecht (1993)
10. Guarino, N.: Formal Ontology, Conceptual Analysis and Knowledge Representation. International Journal of Human-Computer Studies, Special issue: The Role of Formal Ontology in the Information Technology 43, 625–640 (1995)
11. Guarino, N.: Formal Ontology and Information System. In: Proceedings of FOIS 1998, pp. 3–15 (1998)
12. Berners-Lee, T.: Weaving the Web: Origins and Future of the World Wide Web. Texere Publishing, US (1999)
13. Uschold, M., Grüninger, M.: Ontologies: Principles, Methods and Applications. The Knowledge Engineering Review 11(2), 93–155 (1996)
14. Halpin, T.: Information Modeling and Relational Databases: From Conceptual Analysis to Logical Design. Morgan Kaufmann, San Francisco (2001)
15. Dartigues, C., Ghodous, P., Gruninger, M., Pallez, D.: CAD/CAPP Intergation using Feature Ontology. Concurrent Engineering 15(2), 237–249 (2007)
16. Colombo, G., Mosca, A., Palmonari, M., Sartori, F.: An Upper-level Functional Ontology to Support Distributed Design. In: 2nd International Workshop on Ontology, Conceptualization and Epistemology for Software and System Engineering, Milan (2007)
17. Park, M.: Ontology-based Customizable 3D Modeling for Simulation. PhD Thesis, University of Florida (2005)
18. Toro, C., Posada, J., Wundrak, S., Stork, A.: Improving Virtual Reality Applications in CAD through Semantics. The International Journal of Virtual Reality 5(4), 39–46 (2006)
19. SEVENPRO Annual Public Report (2008), http://www.sevenpro.org
20. Lavbic, D., Vasilecas, O., Rupnik, R.: Ontology-based Multi-agent System to Support Business Users and Management, Technological and Economic Development of Economy. Baltic Journal on Sustainability 16(2), 327–347 (2010)
21. Parisi, S., Bauch, J., Berssenbrugge, J., Radkowski, R.: Using Ontology to create 3D Animations for Training purposes. International Journal of Software Engineering and its Applications 1(1) (2007)

Towards Scalable Service Composition on Multicores

Daniele Bonetta, Achille Peternier, Cesare Pautasso, and Walter Binder

Faculty of Informatics, University of Lugano (USI)
via Buffi 13, 6900 Lugano, Switzerland
`first.lastname@usi.ch`

Abstract. The advent of modern multicore machines, comprising several chip multi-processors each offering multiple cores and often featuring a large shared cache, offers the opportunity to redesign the architecture of service composition engines in order to take full advantage of the underlying hardware resources. In this paper we introduce an innovative service composition engine architecture, which takes into account specific features of multicore machines while not being constrained to run on any particular processor architecture. Our preliminary performance evaluation results show that the system can scale to run thousands of concurrent business process instances per second.

1 Introduction

Service-oriented architectures promote the creation of new applications by orchestrating existing Web services by means of service composition languages [2]. Since compositions are themselves made accessible as Web services, composition runtime engines may have to handle a large number of concurrent service requests. Assuming that the composed services are designed to scale (e.g., they are hosted in a cloud environment), composition runtime engines can easily become performance bottlenecks. Existing engines rely on distribution and replication techniques in order to ensure scalability in peer to peer environments (e.g., OSIRIS [8]) or over clusters of computers (e.g., JOpera [6]). Other approaches (like Lu et al. [5]) propose an optimized architecture for service compositions based on event-driven patterns and message passing interactions.

Modern multicore machines offer a promising alternative to clusters or server farms, respectively allow to build a sufficiently powerful infrastructure with less machines. However, modern multicore architectures are fundamentally different from previous micro-processor architectures [4]. Since it has become difficult to further increase the clock rate of processors, nowadays chip manufacturers are delivering more processing power by increasing the number of cores per CPU. Recent chip multi-processors combine several cores with a hierarchy of caches on a single processor. Typically, each core has its own small L1 and L2 caches, while several or all cores on a chip share a larger L3 cache. Examples include Intel Nehalem, AMD Opteron, and IBM Power7 processors.

R. Meersman et al. (Eds.): OTM 2010 Workshops, LNCS 6428, pp. 655–664, 2010.

In order to take full advantage of the hardware resources on modern multicore machines, it becomes important to explicitly consider the characteristics of the multicore architectures in the design of the process execution engine.

In this paper we introduce the SOSOA process execution engine, an innovative service composition middleware based on a multicore-aware design. While we take into account the specifics of multiprocessor architectures in the design of process execution engines, we do not resort to any low-level implementation and optimization techniques. The resulting engine is thus platform-independent, but capable of adapting according to the actual hardware configuration.

The main contributions of this paper are to take emerging multicore architectures of modern processors into account for the design of process execution engines, and also to demonstrate the clear impact of multicore-awareness on their performance with some preliminary results.

The paper is organized as follows. Section 2 describes the main requirements and architectural characteristics of the process execution engine and how it has been designed to target multicore machines. Section 3 describes the evaluation testbed and presents the results of our first measurements. Section 4 concludes the paper and presents future research directions.

2   Architecture

This section gives an overview of the architecture of the SOSOA service composition engine and how it can adapt to run across different configurations of the underlying hardware resources.

2.1   Components

The logical architecture of the engine is designed following a multi-stage pipeline, comprising three components: the Request Handler, the Kernel, and the Invoker (Fig. 1). The Request Handler makes the composite Web services available to clients. The Kernel performs the actual execution of the processes and manages the state of multiple active instances of the running compositions. The Invoker takes care of interacting with the composed services.

The execution of a composition begins with a request from a client to instantiate a new instance (1). This request is forwarded by the Request Handler to a queue (2) which is read by the Kernel. The Kernel is in charge of retrieving pending requests from the queue (3) and then instantiating and executing the corresponding compositions, while keeping their state up-to-date. In order to interact with the composed Web services, the Kernel delegates the actual service invocations to the Invoker via a second queue (4).

The three components in the SOSOA process execution engine are decoupled using shared queues in order not to slow down the execution of compositions, due to the natural delay involved in the invocation of remote Web services. Once the Web service invocation completes (5), its results are enqueued by the Invoker into the queue shared with the Kernel, so that they can be used to

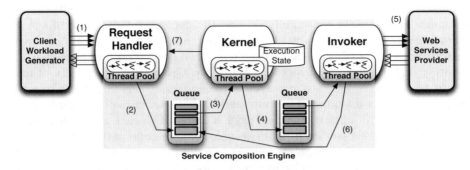

Fig. 1. Architecture of the SOSOA engine for Web service composition

continue the execution of the corresponding instance (6). Once the execution of an entire instance completes, the Kernel component notifies the Request Handler component which sends results to the client (7).

At this level of abstraction, the architecture does not yet define how its three execution stages are mapped to the available execution resources (i.e., OS threads). The goal is to define a scalable system architecture, where a limited number of operating system threads can be leveraged to execute a much larger number of composition instances. Thanks to the separation of the execution stage from the Web service publishing and invocation stages, this architecture makes it possible to use only three execution threads to run any number of process instances that may involve the parallel invocation of any number of Web services. Clearly, allocating at least one thread per component is necessary to make sure the system can operate and run its workload, but is not sufficient to provide an acceptable level of performance. If we need to implement parallel constructs commonly found in most service composition languages, we need to assign a larger number of threads to the Invoker component. Likewise, the Request Handler component needs a pool of worker threads to serve incoming concurrent requests from many clients. The same concerns also apply to the Kernel: as it acts as a bridge between two thread pools, it may become a performance bottleneck unless it can also rely on multiple threads to execute the composition instances.

This design thus adopts thread pools to assign more than one thread to each component. Thread pools not only have the potential to increase overall system throughput, but also provide a straightforward mechanism to leverage the underlying hardware parallelism [3]. In addition, thread pools provide a number of useful performance tuning knobs as well. For example, increasing the size of a thread pool may increase the system throughput for some workloads. In this way, the architecture can efficiently distribute work on the available cores to increase overall throughput.

2.2 Deployment on Multicore

The three-stage architecture characterizing the SOSOA engine should be flexible enough to be deployed on different hardware configurations, ranging from single-core single CPU machines all the way to multi-processor multicore environments. The main constraints driving the deployment decisions of the architecture concern data locality, cache sharing, and the minimization of thread migrations, as these have measurable effects on a system performance [7,9,10]. Another important design aspect is portability. Given the wide variety of multicore architectures that are appearing on the market, it is important to avoid making too many assumptions about specific characteristics of the hardware.

As previously discussed, a thread pool is assigned to each component in order to let the threads of each pool execute common code paths. Thread pools communicate through queues, reducing contention, as the number of shared data structures is reduced and can be specifically optimized for concurrent access. For example, only the threads of the Kernel can access the state of the running composition instances. Also, only a subset of the threads of the engine performs I/O operations (in the Invoker and the Request Handler components). This means that when some thread gets blocked (e.g., waiting for a remote Web service to reply), the rest of the engine continues the execution of other composition instances.

Concerning the mapping of threads to cores, we do not assume that each thread pool should simply run on a separate core. Instead, our deployment is based on a replication of the entire engine, where each replica runs on a different set of cores. Given an incoming request, the Request Handler locates an available replica of the engine. The replica manages then the execution of the newly created composition instance on its cores.

Based on this strategy, the engine scans the hardware configuration to determine the structure of the system memory, the total number of CPUs, and the number of available cores. In more detail, the engine identifies sizes and levels of processor caches, finding out (when available) cores under a common cache (usually a L2 or L3). In this way, the engine creates affinity groups composed by core IDs accessing the same last-level cache. According to the information collected, the engine replicates itself while forcing the OS scheduler to constrain the execution of all threads of a replica within a specific affinity group. The replication phase keeps the total number of threads and memory usage constant: the more replicas are instantiated, the less amount of threads and memory is assigned to each of them. Then, after all replicas have started, client requests are forwarded to each replica using a round-robin policy.

This adaptive deployment procedure, based on the ability to "pin" the threads of each replica to the corresponding cores, allows the SOSOA architecture to adapt to different hardware configurations, from a single-CPU setup to a multiprocessor multi-core deployment.

3   Preliminary Evaluation

In order to compare the performance of the different configurations of the SOSOA execution engine, we follow the approach presented in [1]. In this preliminary evaluation we focus on a limited set of workload types (based on 4 composition

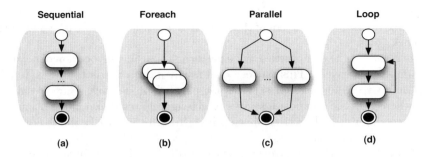

Fig. 2. Benchmark patterns executed by the service composition engine

patterns) and use the overall system throughput as the main evaluation and comparison metric.

3.1 Testbed Setup

The testbed environment has been configured to stress the service composition engine while minimizing the effect of the composed Web services running on the back-end. In this way, the components Workload Generator (WG) and Web Service Provider (WSP) never become performance bottlenecks and measurements are mostly influenced by SOSOA's behavior.

Workload Generator. Each test begins with the activation of the WG client component. This component drives the test generating a pseudo-random stream of service requests to the SOSOA engine. The component internally executes a specified number of clients, each one performing concurrent service requests according to a simple finite state machine composed of two states, "idle" and "busy". When "idle", a client sleeps for a random amount of seconds determined by a Gaussian distribution (fixed at $\mu = 1.0$ and $\sigma^2 = 0.5$). When the sleep time elapses, the client wakes up, moving to state "busy". In this state, the client makes a service request to the SOSOA engine, starting a new composition instance. The client then waits for the response message. Once the execution completion acknowledgement is received (or a timeout fixed at 30 seconds occurs), the client moves back to state "idle". This procedure is executed concurrently for the desired number of clients and repeated for a given number of iterations, in order to effectively measure the system throughput under reproducible conditions and to reduce the observed variance.

Benchmark Patterns. The second component of the testbed is the SOSOA service composition engine. The engine has been tested with four different composite Web services, chosen because each represents a common pattern used also in other benchmarking contexts (such as [1,5]). All compositions executed in the experiments contain the same number ($N = 6$) of service invocations and have the following control flow structures (see Fig. 2):

(a) *Sequential* — Each service invocation depends on the previous one, thus the engine invokes services sequentially. This is equivalent to a BPEL `<sequence>` block.

(b) *ForEach* — The composite service performs a parallel invocation of a variable number of services. This pattern occurs when data needs to be scattered to a number of independent services for parallel processing. Then, results are gathered by the composite service which aggregates them and continues the processing until all services have replied. In terms of BPEL, this is equivalent to a `<foreach>` block.

(c) *Parallel* — In this case, each service invocation is fully independent from the others and therefore they can be invoked in parallel. This is equivalent to a BPEL `<flow>` block without any control flow links between its child elements.

(d) *Loop* — The control flow of this composite service executes a loop for a fixed number of times (6 iterations), invoking a service at each iteration. It corresponds to a BPEL `<while>` block.

Web Service Provider. The third component of the testbed, WSP, is a common Web Server hosting the Web services invoked by the SOSOA engine. The component is deployed to an independent machine hosting $N = 6$ services. In order not to influence the overall execution time with delays caused by the Web Server, each service responds to any request with the same message after a controlled time interval. The size of each request and response message is negligible. In this way, we can ensure that the measured throughput is not limited by the WSP component.

Multicore Hardware and Software Environment. We measured the behavior of the SOSOA engine with different workloads and configurations by deploying it on a multicore machine equipped with 64GB RAM and two 2.6GHz Six-Core AMD Opteron processors, for a total of 12 cores. Each CPU comes with a high-capacity last-level cache (6MB L3 cache) shared by all cores. Each core also features 512KB L2 and 64KB L1 caches. This machine exploits a cache-coherent non-uniform memory access (cc-NUMA) architecture. To avoid interferences, the WG and WSP components are deployed on two additional dedicated machines with the following specifications: single-CPU Intel Core2-Quad desktop machine with a 3.0GHz processor (12MB L2 cache, 32KB L1 cache per core) and a total of 4GB RAM.

The whole testbed is connected through a private 100MBit LAN, with an average message round-trip time of 0.5 milliseconds. All machines in our testing environment run on the Ubuntu Linux Server 10.04 64bit distribution. We also used the standard Oracle Hotspot JVM 64bit Server version 1.6.20, since the SOSOA engine prototype is written in Java.

3.2   Test Configurations

For each machine, we first fix the total number of execution threads that are dedicated to run each replica of the SOSOA engine. Then we allocate the available

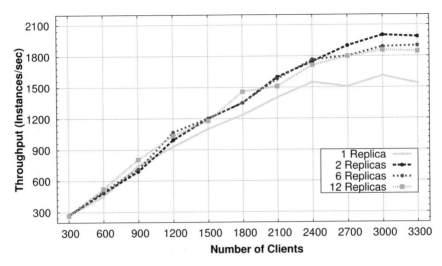

Fig. 3. Average throughput for an increasing number of clients

threads to the pools associated with each engine component. Since the Request Handler uses non-blocking I/O, we observed that it does not require a large number of threads to handle client requests. Thus, we kept their total amount fixed at 32. The remaining number of threads are allocated equally among the other engine components. For replicated configurations where we run multiple instances of the engine, we reduce the number of threads of each replica in order to keep the total amount of threads constant. The same policy has been adopted for memory allocation. Since the total amount of available memory is constant, we reduce each replica's JVM maximum heap size as the number of them increases.

3.3 Results

The results of our experiments show the average throughput scalability for the engine configurations summarized in Table 1. In order to minimize the noise introduced by the Java runtime, we repeated all test runs 10 times and show the average.

Table 1. Deployment configurations: the fixed amount of computational resources per machine (Total Threads) are allocated to a variable number of replicas of the engine's components

CPUs (cores)	Number of Replicas	Threads used by Kernel	Invoker	Total Threads
2 (12)	1	12	12	24
	2	6	6	24
	6	2	2	24
	12	1	1	24

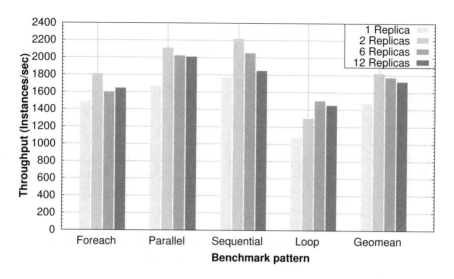

Fig. 4. Throughput for different patterns at the saturation point

Fig. 3 shows the average throughput (Y axis) of the four patterns for an increasingly large number of clients (X axis). The charts help to compare the scalability of the engine for different numbers of replicas. Fig. 4 shows a more detailed performance comparison, breaking down the average throughput obtained for each workflow and each engine configuration fixing the number of clients at the saturation point.

Different replicas increase the throughput by approximately 20% when compared to the baseline configuration. Results can ben explained considering the architecture of the machine: on NUMA systems, memory is allocated on the optimal RAM slot connected to the CPU where threads are running on. Hence, constraining the execution of each JVM to a specific CPU makes sure that threads do not migrate across different processors. This helps to reduce latency times due to unoptimized memory accesses. Among the several configurations tested, the best results are obtained when the number of replicas is equivalent to the number of physical CPUs available. Since the two CPUs share a large L3 cache among all cores, data confirm that two replicas make the most efficient usage of the available computing resources.

Overall, these preliminary results highlight the potential benefits of our replication based approach, where on the tested hardware configuration and for some types of patterns we observed performance gains of more than 20%. Our experiments support the validity of the multicore-aware approach under the following viewpoints. This improvement is due to the partitioning of a set of threads across multiple replicas, which have been tied to a specific CPU. Using a finer grained partitioning (where replicas are tied to individual cores) also provides better performance compared to the baseline, but does not improve over the configuration with two replicas.

4   Conclusion

Modern multi-processor machines have very heterogeneous and sophisticated architectures, featuring several cores aggregated into various hardware configurations with hierarchic, shared or privileged caches and memory access paths. These newer architectures offer higher computational power through improved parallelism but also require specific software optimizations to maximize performance gains.

In this paper we have presented the SOSOA process execution engine for service composition designed to scale on multi-processor multi-core machines. Our design allows the engine to adapt to the different processor architectures at deployment time. This is performed taking into account the number of available processors and the way cores and caches are physically mapped. This hardware analysis process is performed at startup to let the engine automatically decide if and how many replicas should be started.

Our results show that this approach is significantly faster (by about 20%) when compared to the baseline design, which uses the same number of execution threads, but keeps all of them within a single JVM. Our experiments also show that overhead introduced by the replication of the engine components is compensated by the speedup gains obtained on multi-processor architectures when replicas correctly exploit the locality of the underlying hardware.

We plan to extend our work to target other complex scenarios. Regarding future work, we plant to take QoS aspects into account. We also plan to perform additional experiments on a broader range of multicore architectures with different cache configurations in order to validate our claims of portability. Another important extension concerns the work sharing policy between the replicas. Adding a more sophisticated dispatching policy (e.g., based on work-stealing) could potentially improve the load-balancing among replicas and further increase performance.

Acknowledgment

We gratefully acknowledge the financial support of the Swiss National Science Foundation for the project "SOSOA: Self-Organizing Service-Oriented Architectures" (SNF Sinergia Project No. CRSI22_127386/1).

References

1. Bianculli, D., Binder, W., Drago, M.L.: Automated performance assessment for service-oriented middleware: a case study on BPEL engines. In: Proceedings of the 19th International Conference on World Wide Web (WWW 2010), Raleigh, NC, USA, pp. 141–150. ACM, New York (2010)
2. Dustdar, S., Schreiner, W.: A survey on web services composition. Int. J. Web and Grid Services 1(1), 1–30 (2005)
3. Goetz, B., Peierls, T., Bloch, J., Bowbeer, J., Holmes, D., Lea, D.: Java Concurrency in Practice. Addison-Wesley, Reading (2006)

4. Hill, M.D., Marty, M.R.: Amdahl's law in the multicore era. IEEE Computer 41(7), 33–38 (2008)
5. Lu, W., Gunarathne, T., Gannon, D.: Developing a concurrent service orchestration engine in ccr. In: Proceedings of the 1st International Workshop on Multicore Software Engineering, pp. 61–68. ACM, New York (2008)
6. Pautasso, C., Alonso, G.: JOpera: a toolkit for efficient visual composition of web services. International Journal of Electronic Commerce (IJEC) 9(2), 107–141 (Winter 2004/2005 2004), http://www.gvsu.edu/business/ijec/v9n2/
7. Rajagopalan, M., Lewis, B., Anderson, T.: Thread scheduling for multi-core platforms. In: Proceedings of the 11th USENIX workshop on Hot topics in operating systems, pp. 1–6 (2007)
8. Schuler, C., Weber, R., Schuldt, H., Schek, H.J.: Peer to peer process execution with OSIRIS. In: Orlowska, M.E., Weerawarana, S., Papazoglou, M.P., Yang, J. (eds.) ICSOC 2003. LNCS, vol. 2910, pp. 483–498. Springer, Heidelberg (2003)
9. Teng, Q., Sweeney, P.F., Duesterwald, E.: Understanding the cost of thread migration for multi-threaded Java applications running on a multicore platform. In: Proceedings of the IEEE International Symposium on Performance Analysis of Systems and Software, ISPASS 2009, pp. 123–132 (April 2009)
10. Zhang, E.Z., Jiang, Y., Shen, X.: Does cache sharing on modern cmp matter to the performance of contemporary multithreaded programs? In: Proceedings of the 15th ACM SIGPLAN Symposium on Principles and Practice of Parallel Programming, PPoPP 2010, pp. 203–212. ACM, Bangalore (2010)

Automatic Support for Product Based Workflow Design: Generation of Process Models from a Product Data Model

Irene Vanderfeesten, Hajo A. Reijers, Wil M.P. van der Aalst, and Jan Vogelaar

Technische Universiteit Eindhoven,
Department of Industrial Engineering and Innovation Sciences,
School of Industrial Engineering,
P.O. Box 513, 5600 MB Eindhoven, The Netherlands
{i.t.p.vanderfeesten,h.a.reijers,w.m.p.v.d.aalst,j.j.c.l.vogelaar}@tue.nl

Abstract. Product Based Workflow Design (PBWD) is one of the few scientific methodologies for the (re)design of workflow processes. It is based on an analysis of the product that is produced in the workflow process and derives a process model from the product structure. Until now this derivation has been a manual task and is therefore a time-consuming and error-prone exercise. Automatic support would enhance the use of the PBWD methodology. In this paper we propose several algorithms to automatically generate process models from a product structure and we present a software tool (implemented in ProM) to support this. Finally, the properties of the resulting process models are analysed and discussed.

Keywords: workflow product, process model, Product Based Workflow Design.

1 Introduction

In the field of Business Process Management (BPM) only a few scientific approaches exist that address the issue of how to actually *design* a process or, as in many companies processes are already in place, how to *redesign* one. The best-known references are situated in the domain of the popular management literature, e.g. [4,6]. Understandably, it is often said that process design is "more art than science".

One of the notable exceptions is Product-Based Workflow Design (PBWD) [15]. PBWD has been developed as a method for process redesign that is repeatable, objective, and effective. The focus of this method is on the design of processes that deliver informational products, the so-called *workflow processes*. The PBWD methodology takes the structure of the informational product, which is described in a Product Data Model (PDM), as a starting point to derive a process model.

PBWD has proven to be a valuable methodology used by various consultancy and service companies to improve the performance of various business

R. Meersman et al. (Eds.): OTM 2010 Workshops, LNCS 6428, pp. 665–674, 2010.

processes in the services domain, see e.g. [14]. However, the derivation of process models from a product structure has mainly been a manual task and therefore a time-consuming and error-prone exercise. Automatic support for this step would certainly enhance the use of the PBWD methodology.

Our contribution, presented in this paper, is focused on the automatic derivation of process models from a PDM. We propose a number of algorithms that generate a process model solely based on the structure of the product. These algorithms are implemented in ProM to show their feasibility and to provide automatic support. This paper shows that various process models may be derived from the same product structure. We analyse and discuss the differences between those process models based on their properties.

The paper is structured as follows. In Section 2, the notion of the PDM is explained and illustrated with an example. Next, the algorithms for the automatic generation of process models from a PDM are introduced and discussed in Section 3. Finally, related work is discussed in Section 4 and Section 5 concludes this paper.

2   The Product Data Model

The PBWD methodology takes the structure of the workflow product as a starting point to derive a process model. The product of a workflow process is an informational product, for example: an insurance claim, a mortgage request, or a social benefits grant. Similar to a Bill-of-Materials (BOM) from the manufacturing area [13], a product description for many informational products can be made. However, the building blocks of this product structure are not the physical parts that have to be assembled, but data elements (e.g. name, birth date, amount of salary, type of insurance and the amount of months that one is unemployed) that have to be processed to achieve new data. Such a product description, displayed as a network structure, is called a Product Data Model (PDM).

Figure 1(a) contains a small and simple example of a PDM. It describes the calculation of the maximum amount of mortgage a bank is willing to loan to a client. The figure shows that the maximum mortgage (element A in Figure 1(a)) is dependent either on a previous mortgage offer (E), or on the registration in the central credit register (H), or on the combination of the percentage of interest (B), the annual budget to be spent on the mortgage (C), and the term of the mortgage (D). The annual budget (C) is determined from the gross income of the client per year (G), the credit registration (H), and the percentage of the income the client is allowed to spend on paying the mortgage (F).

The *data elements* of the PDM are depicted as circles. The *operations* on these data elements are represented by (hyper)arcs: the arcs are 'knotted' together when the data elements are all needed to execute the particular operation. Compare, for instance, the arcs from B, C and D leading to A on the one hand, to the arc from H leading to A on the other in Figure 1(a). In the latter case only one data element is needed to determine the outcome of the process (A),

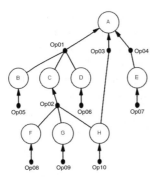

(a) The product data model (PDM) of the mortgage example.

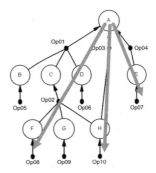

(b) A top-down order of walking through the PDM: starting from the root element walking to the leafs.

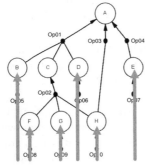

(c) A bottom-up order of walking through the PDM: starting from the leaf elements walking to the root element.

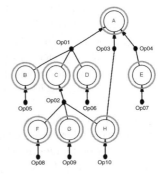

(d) A middle-out order of walking through the PDM: data elements and operations are selected arbitrarily.

Fig. 1. An example of a PDM (a), and a visualization of the different orders (see (b), (c), and (d)) in which an algorithm can translate the PDM of (a) to a process model

while in the case of B, C and D all three elements are needed to produce A. An operation is *executable* when a value for all of its input elements is available.

The mortgage example, which we discussed here, is very small. In industry the PDMs are much larger; typically containing hundreds of data elements (see for instance the case studies described in [14]). What is important to stress here is that PDMs typically allow for a wide variety of *alternative* ways to generate the desirable end product. This is in contrast to its manufacturing antipode, where the production process has fewer alternatives because of physical constraints.

3   Generation of Process Models

In the traditional PBWD methodology, the PDM is used as a starting point for designing process models. The design of a process model as a manual task is time-consuming and error-prone which illustrates the need for automatic support. In this section, we introduce a number of algorithms to generate process models based on a PDM. These algorithms only take into account the structural properties of the PDM, i.e. the data dependencies described by the PDM. It will be shown that only looking at these properties may already lead to various different process models for the same PDM. In this section we will first discuss the different ways to compose the process models, after which we will discuss the implications for the resulting models in Section 3.2.

3.1   The Algorithms

The algorithms presented here all build a process model step-by-step by 'walking through' the PDM. We have used three different strategies to walk through the PDM to build a process model: (i) a top-down strategy, (ii) a bottom-up strategy, and (iii) a middle-out strategy. These strategies will be explained in more detail below, including a short description of the algorithms and an illustration of the resulting process models. Due to space limitations not all process models are presented. Only those process models are shown that are necessary to analyse and discuss the results with respect to their different properties. A full explanation of the algorithms may be found in [8].

Top-down. With a top-down strategy to build the process model, we start at the top of the PDM and walk towards the leaf elements by following the data element dependencies in the PDM. Figure 1(b) illustrates this top-down order. We use *backward chaining* to 'climb down the tree'. This leads to the determination of all minimal execution paths of the PDM which contain no superfluous operations.

We have developed two algorithms with a top-down strategy: algorithm Alpha and algorithm Bravo. The process model for the mortgage example of Figure 1(a) resulting from algorithm Alpha is displayed in Figure 2. The difference between algorithms Alpha and Bravo is in the way in which data elements and operations are translated to activities in the process model. The process model generated by algorithm Alpha has a focus on data elements, i.e. the activities in the process model all relate to data elements, except for a few routing constructs. In contrast to that, algorithm Bravo focuses on the operations in the PDM to be translated to activities in the process model. This leads to two process models, with a similar structure but differences in the details.

Middle-out. In a middle-out strategy, data elements and operations are translated to transitions in the process model in an arbitrary order, not following the dependencies between data elements in a top-down or bottom-up manner (see Figure 1(d)). The dependencies between data elements and operations are added to the model later by checking the in- and output elements of an operation.

We have developed three algorithms with a middle-out strategy: algorithms Charlie, Delta and Echo. Figures 3 and 4 show the process models for the mortgage example generated by algorithms Charlie and Echo. Algorithm Delta uses

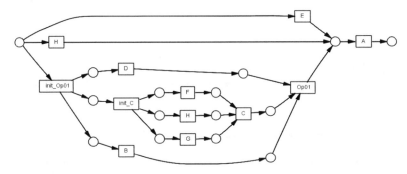

Fig. 2. The process model for the mortgage example generated by algorithm Alpha

the same basis as algorithm Charlie, but contains additional 'control places' and generates a YAWL [7] model instead of a classical Petri Net [12] to be able to use cancellation regions in the model. The difference between algorithms Charlie and Echo again is in the focus of the activities. Algorithm Charlie starts with an activity for each data element and links these activities when necessary through activities related to operations. In algorithm Echo, the focus is on translating operations to activities first. Next, these activities are linked through activities named after the data elements. This leads to two process models, with a similar structure but differences in the details (see Figures 3 and 4).

Bottom-up. Using a bottom-up strategy, we start with the leaf elements and walk towards the root element (see Figure 1(c)). Based on the data elements for which a value is available, it is determined which operations are executable as a next step in the process and which new data element values can be determined by these operations. Using this approach, we 'climb up the tree' from the input elements via the operations to their output elements. The determination of new steps is based on the availability of data element values. In general, the bottom-up order of walking through the PDM gives all possible execution paths of the PDM.

We have developed one algorithm with a bottom-up strategy: algorithm Foxtrot. A fragment of the resulting process model for the mortgage example of Figure 1(a) is displayed in Figure 5. Because the process model contains all possible execution paths, the model is very large.

3.2 Discussion of Results

Figures 2-5 all present a process model for the mortgage example. From these figures it may be clear that the process models are very different although they are generated from the same PDM. In this section, the main differences between the algorithms are discussed.

Concurrency. Concurrency means that parallel behavior during the execution of the process is allowed, e.g. several activities may be executed for the same case

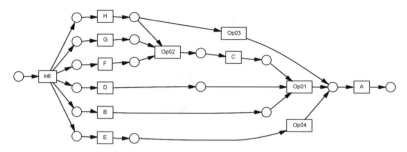

Fig. 3. The process model for the mortgage example generated by algorithm Charlie

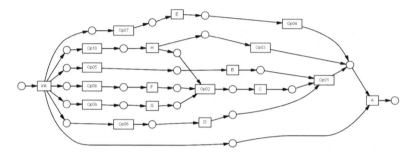

Fig. 4. The process model for the mortgage example generated by algorithm Echo. Note the differences in structure with the process model of algorithm Charlie: e.g. there are three different final transitions producing A (Op03, Op04, Op01 vs. A), and transition H has two output places instead of one.

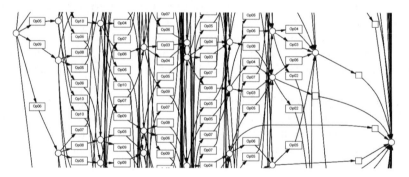

Fig. 5. A fragment of the process model for the mortgage example generated by algorithm Foxtrot. The complete process model contains 438 transitions.

at the same time. Algorithms Alpha, Bravo, Charlie, Delta and Echo all result in process models that allow for concurrency when the PDM contains an 'AND' construct such as the operation that produces a value for data element 'A' based on the values for data elements 'B', 'C' and 'D' in Figure 1(a). In contrast, the process model of algorithm Foxtrot only contains sequential behavior.

Moment of choice. With the moment of choice we indicate the point in time during execution at which a decision on alternative paths has to be made. When the PDM contains alternative paths to produce a value for a data element, this may be reflected in the process model by alternative branches ('XOR' constructs in the Petri Net) that have to be chosen 'early' or 'late' in the execution process. If the moment of choice in a process model is 'early', it has to be decided from the start which of the alternative branches is followed. If the moment of choice is 'late' this decision is deferred to a later point in time and the execution of the process is already started. Early choices in the process model are the case when using algorithm Alpha and Bravo. Figure 2 illustrates this by showing that the start place of the Petri net already is a choice for one of the branches to the end product. In the process models generated by algorithms Charlie, Delta, Echo and Foxtrot, choices are deferred, but this may also lead to the production of data element values that are not strictly needed.

Soundness. A process model is sound [1] if it can always terminate properly, i.e. it has a single token in the end place and all other places are empty. In addition, there must be no dead transition. Process models generated by algorithms Alpha, Bravo, Delta, and Foxtrot are sound per definition since this is enforced by the algorithm. Algorithms Charlie and Echo do not necessarily produce sound process models. Depending on the constructs in the PDM (e.g. duplicate use of a data element value, or alternative operations producing the same output element) the process models may contain possible execution traces in which deadlocks occur or tokens are left behind. In the process model in Figure 3 for example, tokens may be left behind after the end place is reached. This may eventually lead to several executions of transition 'A'. Also, in this process model $Op02$ may not be executable anymore if $Op03$ has fired. These situations are not possible in the process model of Figure 4 because of the different structure of the model. However, the process model of algorithm Echo is still not sound.

Table 1. This table contains a classification of the algorithms based on the criteria: (i) parallel execution, (ii) late choices, (iii) soundness

	Alpha	Bravo	Charlie	Delta	Echo	Foxtrot
Parallel execution	+	+	+	+	+	-
Late choices	-	-	+	+	+	+
Soundness	+	+	-	+	-	+

The above presented similarities and differences between the process models generated by the various algorithms are summarized in Table 1. Each of the process models has its own particularities and properties. Selecting the best algorithm to derive a process model from a PDM is therefore not trivial, but may be guided by the desired properties of the process model, e.g. if a sound process model is desired algorithms Alpha, Beta or Delta should be used, or the process model generated by one of the other algorithms should be adapted.

3.3   Tool Support

The algorithms presented in this paper are implemented as *conversion plugins* in
ProM. ProM [5] was initiated as a framework for *process mining*, but in recent
years it has evolved into a broad and powerful *process analysis* tool supporting all kinds of analyses related to business processes [5]. ProM has a plug-able
architecture. ProM 5.2 has 286 plug-ins, each realizing a particular type of functionality. Each PDM conversion plugin that we have developed takes a PDM as
input and produces the process model (represented by a Petri net or by a YAWL
model) as output. Figure 6 shows a screenshot of the ProM environment with an
example PDM, the list of conversion plugins that can be applied to this PDM,
and a number of process models generated by the different algorithms. Using the
basic functionality which is already present in ProM, these process models can
be converted to other languages, e.g. a Petri net can be converted to an EPC, or
exported to a file that can be loaded into another system. In addition, process
model analysis and verification can be done using the functionality of ProM.

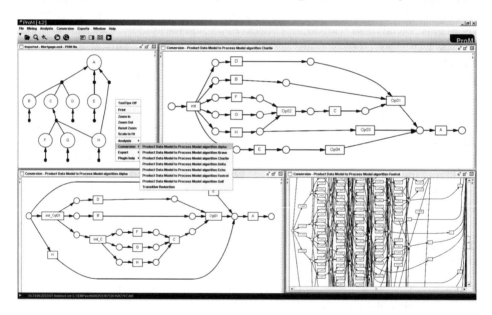

Fig. 6. A screenshot of ProM showing the conversion plugins available for a PDM

4   Related Work

The idea of using product structures to design a process model for a workflow
process was introduced in [2] and further detailed in [14,15]. The former article
also presents a (theoretical) algorithm for the derivation of a process model from
the product structure, but it was not implemented. This first algorithm has been
the foundation of the research presented in this paper and has served as a direct
basis for algorithm Alpha.

Related to this work is the research on object life cycles and business processes. Müller et al. [11] derive large process models based on the life cycle information of the elements in the (product) data structure. Each element in the (product) data structure has a subprocess that describes the life cycle of this element. Also, Küster et al. [9] present a technique to automatically derive compliant process models from given life cycles of the objects in the process.

Browne et al. [3] propose to use goal graphs to structure workflow processes in the healthcare domain. A goal graph describes the goals to be achieved to cure a patient with a certain disease. They define a mapping from the goal graph to a workflow process model in which every goal is translated to a sub process that is designed to achieve the specific goal.

Finally, a number of other approaches for modelling business processes based on products have been proposed, e.g. artifact centric design [10], and document centric modelling [16]. However, these approaches only focus on the manual task of designing a process model and do not provide (automatic) support nor any guidance for this task yet.

5 Conclusion

Automatic support is a necessary step towards the larger applicability of the PBWD method. This paper presents several algorithms for the automatic derivation of process models from a PDM and shows that a single PDM may lead to very different process models. The similarities and differences between the properties of the process models generated by these algorithms are discussed as a basis for selecting the most suitable algorithm in a certain situation.

The algorithms presented in this paper are only based on the structure of the PDM and do not take into account other information that can be added to the PDM, such as resource information, knock-out probabilities, costs, and duration of an operation. Considering these kinds of data when generating a process model would lead to an even larger variety of process models to support the execution of the process which would be worthwhile to explore in further investigations.

Acknowledgement

This research is supported by the Technology Foundation STW, applied science division of NWO, and the technology programme of the Dutch Ministry of Economic Affairs.

References

1. van der Aalst, W.M.P.: The Application of Petri Nets to Workflow Management. The Journal of Circuits, Systems and Computers 8(1), 21–66 (1998)
2. van der Aalst, W.M.P.: On the Automatic Generation of Workflow Processes based on Product Structures. Computers in Industry 39, 97–111 (1999)

3. Browne, E.D., Schrefl, M., Warren, J.R.: Goal-Focused Self-Modifying Workflow in the Healthcare Domain. In: Proceedings of the 37th Annual Hawaii International Conference on System Sciences (HICSS 2004), pp. 1–10 (2004)
4. Davenport, T.H.: Process Innovation: Reengineering Work through Information Technology. Harvard Business School Press, Boston (1993)
5. van Dongen, B.F., Alves de Medeiros, A.K., Verbeek, H.M.W., Weijters, A.J.M.M., van der Aalst, W.M.P.: The ProM framework: A New Era in Process Mining Tool Support. In: Ciardo, G., Darondeau, P. (eds.) ICATPN 2005. LNCS, vol. 3536, pp. 444–454. Springer, Heidelberg (2005)
6. Hammer, M., Champy, J.: Reengineering the Corporation. Nicolas Brealey Publishing, London (1993)
7. ter Hofstede, A.H.M., van der Aalst, W.M.P., Adams, M., Russell, N.: Modern Business Process Automation: YAWL and its Support Environment. Springer, Heidelberg (2010)
8. Kamphuis, J., Vanderfeesten, I., Reijers, H.A., van Hattem, M.: From Product Data Model to Process Model. BETA Working Paper Series, WP 238, Eindhoven University of Technology, Eindhoven (2008)
9. Küster, J.M., Ryndina, K., Gall, H.: Generation of Business Process Models for Object Life Cycle Compliance. In: Alonso, G., Dadam, P., Rosemann, M. (eds.) BPM 2007. LNCS, vol. 4714, pp. 165–181. Springer, Heidelberg (2007)
10. Liu, R., Bhattacharya, K., Wu, F.Y.: Modeling Business Contexture and Behavior Using Business Artifacts. In: Krogstie, J., Opdahl, A.L., Sindre, G. (eds.) CAiSE 2007 LNCS, vol. 4495, pp. 324–339. Springer, Heidelberg (2007)
11. Müller, D., Reichert, M., Herbst, J.: Data-Driven Modeling and Coordination of Large Process Structures. In: Meersman, R., Tari, Z. (eds.) OTM 2007, Part I. LNCS, vol. 4803, pp. 131–149. Springer, Heidelberg (2007)
12. Murata, T.: Petri Nets: Properties, Analysis and Applications. Proceedings of the IEEE 77(4), 541–580 (1989)
13. Orlicky, J.A.: Structuring the Bill of Materials for MRP. Production and Inventory Management, pp. 19–42 (December 1972)
14. Reijers, H.A.: Design and Control of Workflow Processes. LNCS, vol. 2617. Springer, Berlin (2003)
15. Reijers, H.A., Limam Mansar, S., van der Aalst, W.M.P.: Product-Based Workflow Design. Journal of Management Information systems 20(1), 229–262 (2003)
16. Wang, J., Kumar, A.: A Framework for Document-Driven Workflow Systems. In: van der Aalst, W.M.P., Benatallah, B., Casati, F., Curbera, F. (eds.) BPM 2005. LNCS, vol. 3649, pp. 285–301. Springer, Heidelberg (2005)

OTMA'10 - PC Co-chairs Message

We are very happy to organise the 7th OTM Academy (OTMA), the workshop for coaching promising PhD students. OTMA PhD students get the opportunity of publishing in a highly reputed publication channel, namely the Springer LNCS OTM workshops proceedings.

OTMA is not like the usual "PhD students' symposium" often found in many other conferences:

The OTMA faculty members, who are well respected researchers and practitioners, critically reflect on the students' work in a highly positive and inspiring atmosphere, so that the students can improve not only their research capacities but also their presentation and writing skills. Accordingly, we offer a complete coaching seminar. Crucial for the success of OTMA is the commitment of international researchers and experts of the permanent OTMA faculty. We sincerely thank:

- Erich J. Neuhold (University of Vienna, Austria), OTMA Dean
- Alfred Holl (University of Applied Sciences, Nuremberg, Germany)
- Maria Esther Vidal (Universidad Simon Bolivar, Caracas, Venezuela)
- Adam Wierzbicki (Polish-Japanese Institute of IT, Warschau, Poland)
- Josefa Kumpfmller (Vienna, Austria), OTM Integrated Communications Chair

This year new: an on-site reviewing exercise and the formation of the OTMA LinkedIn group. Together with the OTMA on-line community and the virtual 'Hall of Fame' we are proud that the network for our young participants grows continuously.

The OTM Academy reviews are performed by a highly reputed international pro-gramme committee of experts in the field. We gratefully thank for their effort and time:

- Galia Angelova (Bulgarian Academy of Science, Sofia, Bulgary)
- Christoph Bussler (Saba Software, Inc., USA)
- Paolo Ceravolo (Universitá degli Studi di Milano, Milan, Italy)
- Ling Feng, (Tsinghua University, Beijing, China)
- Avigdor Gal (Technion - Israel Institute of Technology, Haifa, Israel)
- Frédéric Le Mouël (University of Lyon, Lyon, France)
- Chengfei Liu (Swinburne University of Technology, Melbourne, Australia)
- Hervé Panetto (Nancy University, Nancy, France)

Seven submissions were independently assessed by three or four reviewers who finally accepted four papers (overall acceptance ratio of 57%). Two are technical papers from advanced PhD students wanting to discuss their achievements so far. The other two are position papers from junior PhD students presenting their

R. Meersman et al. (Eds.): OTM 2010 Workshops, LNCS 6428, pp. 675–676, 2010.
© Springer-Verlag Berlin Heidelberg 2010

research plans. We hope that you will find the papers of this next researcher generation promising and inspiring for your own research activities.

We also express our thanks to the ITW, the Institute for Technology Transfer and continuing Education of the University of Applied Sciences Augsburg, who generously sponsors the 'OTMA10 best paper award' and thus underlines the basic OTMA idea of continued education and research training.

August 2010   Peter Spyns
Anja Schanzenberger
OTMA'10

Context Semantic Filtering for Mobile Advertisement

Andrés Moreno[1,2] and Harold Castro[1]

[1] Universidad de los Andes, Carrera 1 N 18A 10 Bogotá, Colombia
[2] I3S, Université de Nice Sophia Antipolis, France
{dar-more,hcastro}@uniandes.edu.co

Abstract. Mobile advertisement causes an information overload problem that is addressed by information filtering systems. Semantical filtering systems stand out in comparison to traditional approaches thanks to their use of ontologies as knowledge model improving automatic user profiling and content matching processes in filtering. This position paper identifies some enhancement opportunities related to these two processes, manifold: The formulation of a semantic similarity metric that points out the importance of the relations and properties present in the knowledge domain and a extension in the contextual information included so far in filtering systems. The expected result of the work is to improve the overall effectiveness of semantic information filtering systems, tested in the mobile advertisement scenario.

1 Introduction

Nowadays users are bombarded with large streams of data from diverse sources such as social networks, rss feeds, or electronic mail. For example in advertisement, advertisers are interested in contacting their customers and sending them as much information as they can transmit. In order to avoid user frustration it is important that the process of filtering out the irrelevant information from a stream of advertisement messages takes into account the user interests, as well as other factors that can influence a user decision such as the context [1] of the user and the message.

The main goal of information filtering systems is to help users meet their needs of information by exposing them only to relevant information [2]. Semantical filtering systems are information filtering systems that base their knowledge model on ontologies [3] and enhance their filtering methods by using the conceptual reasoning that the information consigned in the ontology allows.

In this paper we will argue that the conceptual reasoning present in existing semantic filtering proposals is limited at a structural level analysis of the knowledge domain because the purpose of the inherent similarity metric that resides behind the automatic building profile and matching techniques is overlooked. We also plead for comprising the context of the user into these two processes in order to attain a more intimate understanding of the user interest and situation which is highly desirable in the mobile advertisement domain, in which we wish to test our findings.

R. Meersman et al. (Eds.): OTM 2010 Workshops, LNCS 6428, pp. 677–681, 2010.

2   Related Work

Information filtering for mobile advertisement is a type of publisher/subscriber system where the publisher is the advertiser and the event display occurs in the user's device. An intermediate broker is in charge of filtering the information for the subscriber based on the explicit information needs made available by the subscriber, and decoupling the publisher and subscriber in the time and space dimension. Requirements introduced by the mobile environment such as distribution and replication are well studied in literature [4]. We choose to focus on the problem of semantic filtering since no explicit requests of information will be made available to the broker, therefore it is important to implicitly understand the subscriber information needs. To our best knowledge no similar approaches exist using this approach in a mobile environment.

2.1   Automatic Semantical User Profile Generation

A user profile represents the user in the filtering system presenting his or her interests and situation. In a semantic filtering system, the user profile is represented as a set of concepts from the ontology, each concept has attached to it a user degree of interest for the concept. The user degree of interest is a numerical representation of the likeness or aversion towards a concept. Data items are represented also as instances or as a set of concepts. To represent properly this qualities, filtering systems use implicit information such as the observation of the user behavior or explicit information such as user feedback, or directly asking the users for their interests, this information is used to automatically build the user profile.

The concept reasoning applied for automatic building of semantical user profiles comes from the spreading activation theory [5]. Spread activation is used to spread the knowledge about one item to its neighbors depending on the type of relation between the items and the type of the item. At the beginning of the spreading process a fact known from the user (implicit or explicit information) updates the value of interest of a concept in the user profile, then this fact is spread through the network to neighbouring concepts by taking into account a loss factor based on the meaning of the relation between the activated item and its neighbor. This process is repeated for each node that is activated until a termination condition is reached. For example, in [6], the hierarchy structure is used to propagate interest value in the profile. Similar hierarchical reasoning was followed in [7] and [8]. Other proposals recognize the importance of using other relations and attributes present in the ontology, as well as the importance of the factor decay in the relations between concepts. Two main approaches exist in order to estimate this decay factor: the knowledge based that sets the factor as the result similarity measure between the two concepts [9] and the statistical approach that uses machine learning algorithms to learn the factor value based on the item frequency of the relation in the data items [10].

2.2   Matching Techniques between User Profile and Data Items

Traditionally, two approaches have been used in filtering systems: Content-based filtering and collaborative filtering. The content based strategy makes predictions based on the features of the items and the individual history of the individuals, the collaborative strategy makes predictions based on correlations between users with the similar history and behavior. Hybrid strategies between content and collaborative filtering are favored [11] in order to overcome perennial issues of pure content based or collaborative based strategies, therefore it is desirable that information filtering systems use both paradigms in order to achieve a better performance. We found two strategies for content based filtering in semantical systems: The first one is to represent the user profile and the data in a vector where cosine similarity between user profile and data item can be obtained [7] [12] [10]; the second one is to calculate a semantic similarity comparison between the concepts that describe both items [6] [8] [13]. Collaborative based strategies make use of collaborative filtering traditional approaches by the means of the a data vector inferred from the user profile [12] [8].

3   Proposal Approach

We identify the following enhancement opportunities on semantical information filtering:

A semantical similarity measure for spread activation. The use of the similarity measure is crucial for the conceptual reasoning of the spread activation applied on the user profile. Existing semantic metrics are based either on structural distance measures, fuzzy semantical distance or a function parameterized with the application purpose [14]. Because structural distance and fuzzy semantical distance motivation is used to find out the semantic closeness or relatedness between concepts, it doesn't always comply with the desirable behavior of the spreading activation theory where the semiotic of the relation is crucial in order to attain a correct propagation. For example if the relation "*antonym*" exists between two concepts in the knowledge model it would be desirable not to use the spreading algorithm through this relation; or even better to use it with the adequate semiotic, inverting the effect on the propagation. Structural distance measures, fuzzy semantical distance and statistical analysis of data items are vulnerable to assigning a decay factor to a relation that mismatches the semantics behind the spread activation. From the existing metrics, we found that [14] offers a formalization of the similarity measure that is sensible to the semiotic of the relations, however a modification of this proposal will have to be made in order to consider the cases when a opposite spread activation is desired.

The inclusion of contextual information into the filtering process. Based on the work already done by context aware applications that base their knowledge representation on ontologies [15], we believe that context integration from different domains such as location, role, time and activity can be included

into the user profile building process. Other proposals that claim to do a semantical context aware filtering like [12] limit the context reasoning to the disambiguation that can be achieved by using a controlled vocabulary in ontologies
and the task the user is performing. Our hypothesis is that the user context is
implicit information that has an influence over the user profile, such influence is
temporal and is directly related to the short term interest of the user, therefore
we propose to establish stereotypical user situations to activate or deactivate the
degree of interest of concepts present in the user profile. A properly represented
context using ontologies and controlling its impact on the user profile will allow the system to understand more closely the user interest, generating a more
accurate filtering system no matter which filtering paradigm is chosen.

4   Method for Validation

Validation of information filtering proposals is difficult since the size of the data
set and task of the user in the system greatly varies from one proposal to the
other, making it difficult to validate one system or to compare two different approaches, furthermore despite accuracy's wide acceptance as a tool in validation
of information systems, they are not the only factor related to measuring the
overall user satisfaction with the system [16]. From these works we have identified the factors that we will use to evaluate our work based on their influence on
user satisfaction and their pertinence to our information filtering proposal. We
plan to validate our system based on the quality of the filtering by measuring
the performance of our system using traditional metrics (precision, recall), and
to evaluate the user satisfaction we will take into account the learning rate and
coverage measures. This metrics will be obtained for different filtering systems;
first based on known information retrieval datasets to show the adequacy of the
proposed enhancements on semantical filtering, and another in the mobile advertisement scenario that shows the feasibility of including context information in
the filtering process taking into account the restrictions imposed by the mobile
environment.

5   Conclusion and Future Work

We have identified in this paper some enhancement opportunities in two semantic
filtering processes. We argue that some changes must be done into the calculation of the similarity measure to point out the importance of the relations and
properties present in the knowledge domain and extend the dimensions so far
considered as context in context-aware semantic filtering, also in order to avoid
the drawbacks of pure content based filtering is necessary to adopt an hybrid approach for filtering, taking into account the limitations linked to the scalability
requirements of collaborative based filtering algorithms and the computation and
the limitations of an agent running in a mobile device. In a publisher/subscriber
architecture, it would be reasonable to make available to the publisher or broker
some user profile information in order to do a coarse-grained filtering, reducing
network traffic and load on the filtering agent in the mobile device.

References

1. Dey, A.K.: Understanding and using context. Personal and Ubiquitous Computing 5, 4–7 (2001)
2. Hanani, U., Shapira, B., Shoval, P.: Information filtering: Overview of issues, research and systems. User Modeling and User-Adapted Interaction 11, 203–259 (2001)
3. Gruber, T.R.: A translation approach to portable ontology specifications. Knowl. Acquis. 5(2), 199–220 (1993)
4. Huang, Y., Garcia-Molina, H.: Publish/subscribe in a mobile environment. Wireless Networks 10(6), 643–652 (2004)
5. Crestani, F.: Application of spreading activation techniques in information retrieval. Artif. Intell. Rev. 11(6), 453–482 (1997)
6. Middleton, S.E., Shadbolt, N.R., De Roure, D.C.: Ontological user profiling in recommender systems. ACM Trans. Inf. Syst. 22(1), 54–88 (2004)
7. Sieg, A., Mobasher, B., Burke, R.: Web search personalization with ontological user profiles. In: Proceedings of the sixteenth ACM Conference on Conference on Information and Knowledge Management, CIKM 2007, pp. 525–534. ACM Press, New York (2007)
8. Blanco-Fernández, Y., Pazos-Arias, J.J., Gil-Solla, A., Ramos-Cabrer, M., López-Nores, M., García-Duque, J., Fernández-Vilas, A., Díaz-Redondo, R.P.: Exploiting synergies between semantic reasoning and personalization strategies in intelligent recommender systems: A case study. J. Syst. Softw. 81(12), 2371–2385 (2008)
9. Vallet, D., Cantador, I., Fernández, M., Castells, P.: A multi-purpose ontology-based approach for personalized content filtering and retrieval. In: Semantic Media Adaptation and Personalization, International Workshop on, vol. 0, pp. 19–24 (2006)
10. Jiang, X., Tan, A.H.: Learning and inferencing in user ontology for personalized semantic web search. Information Sciences 179(16), 2794–2808 (2009)
11. Adomavicius, G., Tuzhilin, A.: Toward the next generation of recommender systems: A survey of the state-of-the-art and possible extensions. IEEE Trans. on Knowl. and Data Eng. 17(6), 734–749 (2005)
12. Cantador, I., Bellogín, A., Castells, P.: Ontology-based personalised and context-aware recommendations of news items. In: Proceedings of the 2008 IEEE/WIC/ACM International Conference on Web Intelligence and Intelligent Agent Technology, WI-IAT 2008, pp. 562–565. IEEE Computer Society Press, Los Alamitos (2008)
13. Shoval, P., Maidel, V., Shapira, B.: An ontology- content-based filtering method. International Journal on Information Theories and Applications 15, 303–318 (2008)
14. Albertoni, R., De Martino, M.: Asymmetric and context-dependent semantic similarity among ontology instances. In: Spaccapietra, S. (ed.) Journal on Data Semantics X. LNCS, vol. 4900, pp. 1–30. Springer, Heidelberg (2008)
15. Strang, T., Linnhoff-Popien, C.: A context modeling survey. In: Workshop on Advanced Context Modelling, Reasoning and Management. In: Davies, N., Mynatt, E.D., Siio, I. (eds.) UbiComp 2004. LNCS, vol. 3205, Springer, Heidelberg (2004)
16. Herlocker, J.L., Konstan, J.A., Terveen, L.G., Riedl, J.T.: Evaluating collaborative filtering recommender systems. ACM Trans. Inf. Syst. 22(1), 5–53 (2004)

On the Social Dynamics of Ontological Commitments

Christophe Debruyne

Semantics Technology and Application Research Lab (STARLab)
Department of Computer Science,
Vrije Universiteit Brussel, Pleinlaan 2, B-1050 Brussels, Belgium
chrdebru@vub.ac.be

Abstract. The aim of my thesis is to provide a solution in which any stake-holder of a particular community (with a specific goal) can contribute to the ontology construction process, making the contribution of the "unproductive" long tail of the community relevant. Members in a community will describe their view and maintain a dialogue in natural language. I believe that granting the community first-class-citizenship within ontological commitments by (i) mapping those natural language descriptions and dialogues to formal descriptions and decisions within the ontology engineering process and (ii) exploiting the existing application commitments to that ontology improves the quality of ontological commitments by truly representing the community and their latest requirements.

1 Introduction

Modeling ontologies for the Semantic Web (SW) [4] is far from trivial: providing more rules that are important for effective and meaningful interoperation between applications may (and will) limit the generativity of an ontology [18] and lightweight ontologies that hold none or few domain rules, are not very effective for communication *between autonomously developed software agents*. Thanks to the Linked Data[1] (LD) initiative, we have access to billions of RDF triples ready to be exploited and even though the vast amount of data publicly available indicated a success in community effort, the absence of the so-called "killer application" indicates an issue. In LD, the primary reference scheme for concepts and their instances is a URI instead of a (more conceptually correct) reference scheme based on the attributes (literal or non-literal) of a concept. A conceptual reference scheme is necessary for applications with a specific purpose and is the reason why current popular SW technologies have a difficult uptake in "real" business.

My research aims to solve this issue by granting the community a more prominent role in the construction of ontological commitments on what and how things should be communicated. As a natural consequence, natural language (NL) will be used to reach consensus within community members for which we can draw inspiration from proved database techniques with groundings in linguistics [11,21]. As online communities' member-contribution follows the 80-20 Rule[2], stating that 80% of the people

---

[1] http://www.linkeddata.org/
[2] Which states that for many events, roughly 80% of the effects come from 20% of the causes.

R. Meersman et al. (Eds.): OTM 2010 Workshops, LNCS 6428, pp. 682–686, 2010.

are responsible for only 20% of the contribution. The technology used in those networks aims to exploit the 80% "unproductive" long tail and make their contribution significant.

2 Research Questions

What are the characteristics of a tri-sortal Internet? The Web is currently shifting from an information retrieval medium to a participatory medium spreading widely involving three types of actors: humans, computer systems and businesses. Three parallel and interconnected evolutions are simultaneously taking place on that Web, though unsynchronized [15]: (i) *Technology*, as exemplified by the SW; (ii) *Social forces* as manifested in the Social Web and (iii) *Economical forces*, the Internet now being the medium of choice for most content-based interaction of businesses or Enterprise 2.0. This shift changes the way how we should look at the Web.

Why is there a need for empowering organized communities in creating ontological commitments on a tri-sortal Internet? The introduction of business as an additional dimension motivates the need of making concepts such as group, community, etc. explicit. Community involvement is essential for interoperability as well as facilitating the uptake of LD. The LD initiative however relies on the URI mechanisms of RDF(S) to represent data and these are difficult to understand by non-technical people. Enabling communities to develop and maintain a representation of their (business) world needs a methodology since reaching a common agreement between many stakeholders proves to be difficult [7]. Appropriate methodologies for this can learn from database modeling principles.

What is a viable approach for empowering organized communities on a tri-sortal Internet? Social Web applications such as wikis and Content Management Systems (CMS) have already proven to be an appropriate tool for community participation on the Social Web and on-line communities will become the environment for meaning agreement, as it is key to achieve interoperability between systems and businesses. The result of such process of determining meaning by community agreement is called *Social Semantics*. This process hints a certain duality as two distinct and coexisting perspectives are needed. The first is the *Human perspective* characterized by high level reasoning about the shared concepts by and between humans in NL (through, for instance, dialogue). The second is the *System perspective* where agreement is made on the vocabulary used, the data access and room for simple, low level reasoning. This dual perspective forms the essence of *hybrid ontologies* [15] where concepts on the one hand are circumscribed linguistically and (mostly) declaratively by agreement within (human) communities, and on the other hand identified formally (and unambiguously) for use in computer-based information systems. Answering this question means looking for appropriate methods and tools for hybrid ontology engineering (OE).

How can (existing) ontological commitments guide the dialogue between the community members? Ontological commitments can be seen as software objects either manifested as agents or services that use these mappings to add semantics to their data. Even though a methodology supports an ontology to co-evolve with the communities' interoperability-requirements, doing so in an automated way still remains an open question. Members of a community might enter an observation while working on an ontology that might be true for their application, but not for the applications of other stakeholders. Counterexamples for such an observation result in the refusal of that observation, refinement of the ontology or the detection of mistakes in the data sets. I therefore investigate a method and tool to support an OE process by testing hypotheses on annotated data sets.

3 Related Work

Ontology Engineering. Before communities can use information and interoperability between information systems is established, a consensus on an ontology needs to be achieved among its different stakeholders. Various methodologies for OE have been developed to reach that consensus such as DOGMA-MESS [7], DILIGENT [17] and HCOME [12]. Application symbols are mapped onto concepts in that ontology once the community reaches an agreement.

DOGMA and DOGMA-MESS. DOGMA [14] is an ontology approach having some characteristics that make it different from traditional ontology approaches such as its groundings in the linguistic representations of knowledge and the methodological separation of the domain- and application-conceptualization [18]. The knowledge building blocks – called *lexons* [14] – only need in principle to express "plausible" facts (as perceived by the community of stakeholders) in order to be entered into the *Lexon Base*, a repository containing large sets of such lexons. A lexon is formally described as a 5-tuple ⟨γ, headterm, role, co-role, tailterm⟩, where γ is an abstract *context identifier* pointing to a resource such as a document on the Web. The context identifier is assumed to identify unambiguously (to human users at least) the concepts denoted by the term and role labels. The *Commitment Layer* contains ontological commitments that use a selection of lexons to annotate applications and specify constraints defining the use of the concepts in the ontology. DOGMA distinguishes two types of ontological commitments: *community commitments* and *application commitments*. The first denotes a meaningful selection of lexons and constraints that capture well the intended semantics of a domain. The latter extends the community commitments with mappings describing how one individual application commits to the ontology using Ω-RIDL [20].

Formalizing Dialogue. Knowledge management involves communication among loosely structured networks and communities of people with (complex) social practices and relationships that are happening in a particular context. Dialogue is one example for creating and communicating knowledge that can be supported by tools. Most work on the formalization of dialogue in computer science, however, is built around the multi-agent community [9,5].

Testing Hypotheses against Data Sets. By our knowledge, no-one has so far done work on incrementally extending ontologies by testing hypotheses to annotated databases, most existing work relates to manually or (semi-)automatically [19,1] mapping relational databases to RDF(S) and OWL. The latter often looks at the automatic transformation of database content and the schema. In [16], OWL is extended to cope with aspects of relational databases while reasoning over the data. In ontology matching [10], conflicting

Table 1. Examples of controlled sentences in Ω-RIDL: (1) depicts a lexon, (2) shows the mapping of a field in a table on a term of a lexon and (3) shows a constraint on that lexon

1	Person with / of First Name.
2	map "tblPerson"."fname" on First Name of Person.
3	Person has at most 1 First Name.

information resulting from schema/ontology mappings is used to improve the mappings. The annotations will be based on Ω-RIDL, whose application mappings (see Table 1) can be used to create the necessary queries to test the database for counterexamples.

Wikis for Ontology Engineering. Wiki technology has been put forward as a mean to reach agreement and share knowledge about different subjects over the past decade. The advantage of Wiki technology is that anyone can add content without much technical knowledge. Wiki technology has been adapted in the field of OE to enable non-technical users to create, visualize and maintain ontologies [3] or to semantically annotate the content [2,13].

4 Material and Setting

STARLab offers a dynamic and collaborative environment with quite a few international contacts and participates in a number of European and local projects in which my research is and will be applied, e.g., TAS^3 (Trusted Architecture for Securely Shared Services, EU FP7 216287). I have furthermore the unique opportunity to conduct experiments during the practical session of the Open Information Systems course taught to (primarily) 1st year MSc in Computer Science. The data obtained during such experiments already gave some interesting results published in [6]. The experiments with the students will be used to draw some first conclusions (e.g., via surveys) and its results as a benchmark for deployment within projects.

5 Conclusions and Future Work

The billions of triples given to us by LD are of little use for business applications as URIs are the primary reference scheme and some constraints are not possible nor imposed (e.g., identification constraints on multiple attributes). Popular Semantic Web technologies create a barrier for non-technical stakeholders, leaving them behind. My research aims to empower communities on the Tri-sortal internet by expressing their knowledge and thoughts in NL.

To this end, two prototypes are currently under development: GOSPL [8] and Ω-DIPPER. GOSPL stands for Grounding Ontology with Social Processes and Natural Language and tries to bridge the gap between the formal and informal descriptions of concepts. It is built on top of DOGMA and is currently being used within TAS^3 to allow end users (e.g., security and privacy experts) to easily develop conceptual models to provide security policy interoperability. Ω-DIPPER is a tool for testing hypotheses against annotated relational databases. Counterexamples found by Ω-DIPPER trigger various OE processes and guide the dialogue between the community members. The two next steps in my research are the formalization of dialogue and the social dynamics of commitments.

References

1. Astrova, Kalja.: Automatic transformation of SQL relational databases to OWL ontologies. In: WEBIST,vol. 2, pp. 131–136. INSTICC Press (2008)
2. Auer, Bizer, Kobilarov, Lehmann, Cyganiak, Ives: DBpedia: A nucleus for a web of open data. In: Aberer, K., Choi, K.-S., Noy, N., Allemang, D., Lee, K.-I., Nixon, L.J.B., Golbeck, J., Mika, P., Maynard, D., Mizoguchi, R., Schreiber, G., Cudré-Mauroux, P. (eds.) ASWC 2007 and ISWC 2007. LNCS, vol. 4825, pp. 722–735. Springer, Heidelberg (2008)
3. Auer, Dietzold, Riechert: Ontowiki - a tool for social, semantic collaboration. In: Cruz, I., Decker, S., Allemang, D., Preist, C., Schwabe, D., Mika, P., Uschold, M., Aroyo, L.M. (eds.) ISWC 2006. LNCS, vol. 4273, pp. 736–749. Springer, Heidelberg (2006)
4. Berners-Lee, Hendler, Lassila.: The Semantic Web. Scientific American 284(5), 35–43 (2001)
5. Besnard, Doutre, Hunter (eds.): Computational Models of Argument: Proceedings of COMMA 2008, IOS Press (2008)
6. De Leenheer, Debruyne: Peeters: Towards social performance indicators for community-based ontology evolution. In: CK 2008, collocated with ISWC 2009, CEUR-WS (2009)
7. de Moor, De Leenheer: Meersman: DOGMA-MESS: A meaning evolution support system for interorganizational ontology engineering. In: ICCS 2006, pp. 189–203. Springer, Heidelberg (2006)
8. Debruyne, Reul.: Meersman: GOSPL: Grounding ontologies with social processes and natural language. In: ITNG 2008, pp. 1255–1256. IEEE Computer Society, Los Alamitos (2010)
9. Dunne, Bench-Capon (eds.): Computational Models of Argument: Proceedings of COMMA 2006. IOS Press, Amsterdam (2006)
10. Euzenat, Shvaiko: Ontology matching. Springer, Heidelberg (2007)
11. Halpin: Information Modeling and Relational Databases. Morgan Kaufmann, San Francisco (2008)
12. Kotis: Vouros: Human-centered ontology engineering: The HCOME methodology. Knowl. Inf. Syst. 10(1), 109–131 (2006)
13. Krötzsch, V., Völkel, H.: Studer: Semantic wikipedia. J. Web Sem. 5(4), 251–261 (2007)
14. Meersman: Semantics ontology tools in information system design. In: ISMIS 1999, pp. 30–45. Springer, Heidelberg (1999)
15. Meersman, Debruyne: Hybrid ontologies and social semantics. In: DEST 2010. IEEE Press, Los Alamitos (2010)
16. Motik, Horrocks, Sattler: Bridging the gap between owl and relational databases. Web Semantics: Science, Services and Agents on the WWW 7(2), 74–89 (2009)
17. Pinto, Staab,Tempich: Diligent: Towards a fine-grained methodology for distributed, loosely-controlled and evolving engineering of ontologies. In: ECAI 2004, pp. 393–397. IOS Press, Amsterdam (2004)
18. Spyns, Meersman, Jarrar: Data modelling versus ontology engineering. SIGMOD Record Special Issue 31(4), 12–17 (2002)
19. Tirmizi, Sequeda, Miranker: Translating SQL applications to the semantic web. In: Bhowmick, S.S., Küng, J., Wagner, R. (eds.) DEXA 2008. LNCS, vol. 5181, pp. 450–464. Springer, Heidelberg (2008)
20. Trog, Tang, Meersman: Towards ontological commitments with Ω-RIDL markup language. In: Paschke, A., Biletskiy, Y. (eds.) RuleML 2007. LNCS, vol. 4824, pp. 92–106. Springer, Heidelberg (2007)
21. Wintraecken: The NIAM Information Analysis Method, Theory and Practice. Kluwer Academic Publishers, Dordrecht (1990)

Does IT Matter for Business Process Maturity?
A Comparative Study on
Business Process Maturity Models

Amy Van Looy[1,2]

[1] University College Ghent, Department of Management & Informatics,
Voskenslaan 270, B-9000 Ghent, Belgium
amy.vanlooy@hogent.be
[2] Ghent University, Department of Management Information Science & Operations
Management, Tweekerkenstraat 2, B-9000 Ghent, Belgium
Amy.VanLooy@UGent.be

Abstract. This article recalls the business process discussion between Carr, who stated that IT does not matter, and Smith and Finger, who proclaimed the opposite. In the end, both visions agreed that IT (or process deployment) counts, but must follow the business strategy (or process modeling). The present study broadens the discussion towards business process maturity, which is a more recent perspective within the literature on business processes. Various authors have proposed a maturity model to guide organizations on their journey to process excellence. However, to what extent do they rely on IT? A twofold approach is adopted, which starts by giving an overview of the academic and non-academic process maturity models. Afterwards, the components within each model are discussed to verify the impact of IT. This comparison suggests that IT-neutral models allow organizations to deal with organization-specific characteristics. IT does not matter after all, but it enables process maturity.

Keywords: business process maturity, business process management, business process orientation, business process integration.

1 Introduction

Today's customers have higher requirements than ever before. In a growing globalized market, organizations are striving to excel in order to gain competitive advantage or to outperform in their societal obligations. As a result, organizations are increasingly focusing on their business processes [1]. Business process management is expected to contribute to both process excellence and business excellence by assuring a uniform way of working and by continuously looking for optimizations. As the possibilities of IT continue to grow, business processes are enabled to cross the borders of departments and organizations [2,3]. Frequently used terms are e-business, virtual networks, or extended and seamless organizations. Likewise, cross-organizational collaboration is apparent in the public sector, albeit with a less stringent IT driver, e.g. public-private partnerships and multi-level governance.

R. Meersman et al. (Eds.): OTM 2010 Workshops, LNCS 6428, pp. 687–697, 2010.
© Springer-Verlag Berlin Heidelberg 2010

Since the journey towards process excellence is challenging, various authors have proposed step by step road maps with best practices. These road maps are called business process maturity models (BPMMs). They are evolutionary models for measuring (AS-IS) and gradually improving (TO-BE) process maturity, or *'the extent to which an organization consistently implements processes within a defined scope that contributes to the achievement of its business goals'* [4, p.2]. Business process maturity has received a great deal of attention in literature. Consequently, the proliferation of BPMMs prompts us to evaluate their usefulness in today's society. To our knowledge, few attempts have been made by [5,6,7,8]. Nonetheless, these studies lack a comprehensive review of both academic and non-academic frameworks. For this purpose, the PhD dissertation ultimately elaborates the topic of BPMM. Its objective is to present a BPMM for properly measuring (AS-IS) and improving (TO-BE) cross-organizational process maturity, which implies either an existing model with adjustments where needed, or a new one. Besides its scientific relevance, the final model will be of practical use for organizations that struggle with process integration. The research questions are:

(1) does a BPMM exist for cross-organizational collaboration?
(2) what is the importance of IT to achieve higher business process maturity?
(3) what is the impact of higher business process maturity on business excellence?

This study focuses on the second question, which is inspired by the debate between Carr [9], Smith and Finger [10]. The hypothesis is that a generic BPMM does not include IT to acknowledge organization-specific characteristics, such as size and type.

The subsequent section deals with the methodology. Next, the yielded results are presented and discussed. Afterwards the plans for future work are described. The last section concludes by summarizing the importance of IT for business process maturity.

2 Methodology

The research approach is twofold: (1) an overview of BPMMs, and (2) an elaboration of the IT impact within different perspectives. Before going into detail, we explain the data collection technique and the theoretical model components to validate the results.

2.1 Overview of Business Process Maturity Models: Data Collection

The research scope was set to generic business processes. Hence, it excludes BPMMs that are limited to specific process types, such as software engineering, product development or human resources. However, models that integrate various specific BPMMs were withheld to represent those specific topics.

Data was collected during the second quarter of 2010. First, we searched for articles in academic databases and search engines on the Internet by using the combined keywords of *'process'* and *'maturity'*. Secondly, we traced the references in the identified articles to get access to other relevant sources.

We acknowledge some restrictions regarding the accessibility of articles (in Ghent University engines), the language (English, Dutch, French or German), and the keywords. Notwithstanding these limitations, the technique turned out to be fruitful.

2.2 Comparison of the Model Components: Literature Study

During data collection, we experienced that the models emphasized different elements of a typical process life cycle. Some were limited to (1) modeling and (2) deployment, whereas others included (3) optimization and (4) management, or even considered the organization's (5) culture and (6) structure. In pairs, these six components respectively correspond to the definitions of '*business process*' (BP) [1], '*business process management*' (BPM) [11] and '*business process orientation*' (BPO) [12]. Consequently, they act as theoretical BPMM components to validate the results.

We will examine the prescribed use of IT per component, as well as the IT relationships among the components to jointly achieve higher process maturity.

3 Results

The yielded research results are discussed by following the twofold approach as presented in the previous methodology section.

3.1 Overview of Business Process Maturity Models

The data collection resulted in 37 BPMMs, of which 13 academic and 24 non-academic models. The overview is summarized in table 1.

Table 1. The overview of academic and non-academic business process maturity models

ID	Authors	Model	Ref.
(1) Academic			
AOU	Aouad et al.	Co-maturation model	[13]
ARM	Armistead et al.	BPM's degree of progress	[14]
DET	DeToro et al.	BP condition rating model	[15]
HAM	Hammer	BP and Enterprise Maturity Model	[16]
HAR1	Harrington	BP maturity grid	[1]
LEE	Lee et al.	Value-based BP maturity model	[17]
MAU	Maull et al.	BPR maturity model	[18]
MCC	McCormack et al.	BPO maturity model	[12]
ROH	Rohloff	BP management maturity assessment	[19]
ROS	Rosemann et al.	BPM maturity model	[8, 20]
SKR	Skrinjar et al.	BPO maturity model	[21]
SEI	SEI, Software Engineering Institute	Capability maturity model integration	[22, 23, 24]
WIL	Willaert et al.	Holistic BPO maturity framework	[25]

Table 1. (*Continued*)

(2) Non-academic			
BIS	Bisnez Management	BPM maturity model	[26]
BPM	BPMInstitute	State of BPM	[27]
BPT	BP Transformations Group & BPGroup	8 Omega ORCA	[28]
CAM1	CAM-I	BP-based management loop	[29]
CAM2	CAM-I	BPM assessment & implementation road map	[30]
CHA	Champlin	BP management maturity model	[31]
DEL	Deloitte	Business maturity model & scan	[32]
ESI	ESI, European Software Institute	EFQM/SPICE integrated model	[33]
FAA	FAA, Federal Aviation Administration	FAA integrated capability maturity model	[34]
FIS	Fisher	BP maturity model	[35]
GAR1	Gardner	BP improvement road map	[36]
GAR2	Gartner	BPM maturity & adoption model	[37]
HAR2	Harmon	BP maturity evaluation model	[38]
IDS	IDS Scheer AG	BPM maturity check	[39]
ISO	ISO/IEC	ISO/IEC 15504	[4, 40]
O&I	O&i	BPM scan	[41]
OMG	OMG, Object Management Group	BP maturity model	[42]
ORA	Oracle	BPM life cycle assessment survey	[43]
REM	Remoreras	BP culture maturity model	[44]
RUM	Rummler-Brache Group	BP Performance Index	[45]
SAP	SAP	Process maturity analysis	[46]
SCH	Scheer	BPM check-up	[47]
SMI	Smith et al.	BPM maturity model	[48]
SPA	Spanyi	BP competence grid	[49]

3.2 Comparison of the Model Components

Each table below presents one of the theoretical components. A distinction is made between models that: (1) are IT-neutral and do not mention IT in their road map to achieve higher process maturity, (2) generally suggest IT, e.g. tools, hard- and software or databases, (3) refer to specific technologies, or (4) promote specific tools.

Table 2. The use of IT in the maturity road map regarding business process modeling

IT-neutral (12)	General IT (9)	Specific IT (5)	Specific tools (6)
LEE, MCC, SKR, CAM1, CHA, DEL, ESI, FIS, GAR1, ISO, OMG, RUM	ARM, HAM, HAR1, MAU, ROS, SEI, GAR2, HAR2	AOU, WIL, BIS, IDS, SMI	ROH, BPM, O&I, ORA, SAP, SCH

First, the table above deals with process descriptions, procedures and flowcharting. Processes may be stored in a repository, such as a manual or a database [OMG]. The process architecture provides a hierarchical map of process levels, including value chains, (sub)processes and individual tasks or regional variations [MAU].

Two-third of the BPMMs propose electronic 2D or 3D design to improve maturity, e.g. [AOU]. Tools range from MS Office to advanced formats or BPM Suites, e.g. [ORA]. Examples of modeling languages are given in [BPM], e.g. BPMN and UML.

Table 3. The use of IT in the maturity road map regarding business process deployment

IT-neutral (5)	General IT (14)	Specific IT (9)	Specific tools (3)
LEE, CAM2, CHA, ESI, ISO	ARM, HAM, MAU, ROS, SKR, SEI, DEL, FAA, HAR2, IDS, O&I, OMG, RUM, SAP	AOU, WIL, BIS, BPT, FIS, GAR2, ORA, REM, SMI	ROH, BPM, SCH

As shown in table 3, the vast majority of BPMMs advise to use IT during deployment. Nonetheless, its extent depends on the strategy and organizational objectives.

In general, BPMMs refer to higher maturity with integrated databases, BPM Suites, workflow management systems and the link with a business rules engine for real-time, agile services, for instance [WIL, BIS, GAR2] (cfr. supra). IT architectures are suggested to use ERP, SOA or SaaS, e.g. [ORA, SCH]. Other specific concepts are relational databases [SCH], firewalls [FIS] and back-up tools for recovery [OMG].

Table 4. The use of IT in the maturity road map regarding business process optimization

IT-neutral (12)	General IT (14)	Specific IT (6)	Specific tools (4)
DET, HAM, LEE, MCC, CAM2, CHA, ESI, GAR1, ISO, O&I, RUM, SPA	ARM, HAR1, MAU, ROS, SKR, SEI, BPT, CAM1, FAA, HAR2, IDS, OMG, REM, SAP	AOU, WIL, BIS, FIS, GAR2, SMI	ROH, BPM, ORA, SCH

The third component is business process optimization (table 4). Metrics may concern (1) process and business parameters at (2) individual, process or enterprise level. BPMMs often suggest market surveys [FAA], Six Sigma, Lean, Value Stream Mapping, Statistical Process Control and simulation techniques [GAR2, HAR2, ORA, RUM]. KPIs are defined to measure the achievement of process objectives [WIL].

To facilitate reporting on past, present and future performance, most BPMMs use a performance management system, possibly with real-time dashboards and business activity monitoring [CAM1, HAR2, ORA]. For instance, [ROH] and [SCH] mention the ARIS tool as a BPM Suite. Other technologies to improve maturity are business intelligence, customer relationship management and virtual reality [AOU].

Table 5. The use of IT in the maturity road map regarding business process management

IT-neutral (23)	General IT (6)	Specific IT (6)	Specific tools (2)
ARM, HAM, HAR1, LEE, MAU, MCC, ROH, SKR, BPT, CAM1, CAM2, CHA, DEL, ESI, FIS, GAR1, GAR2, HAR2, IDS, ISO, RUM, SAP, SPA	ROS, SEI, FAA, O&I, OMG, REM	AOU, WIL, BIS, GAR2, ORA, SMI	BPM, SCH

We now focus on the management of previous components. Table 5 presents all BPMMs that rely on a process owner, who is supported by an improvement team. Among others, the owner is responsible for its resources, e.g. training and skills, and accountable for process performance, such as in [HAM]. He also manages the business rules, aligns with IT and liaises with stakeholders, for instance in [BIS, SEI].

Unlike previous components, most BPMMs are IT-neutral. However, IT may enable knowledge sharing, communication and collaboration through Intranet and Internet, e.g. mailing, portals and Electronic Data Interchange [AOU]. Some models require configuration or document management systems, management information systems and BPM Suites for planning and reporting on higher maturity levels, for instance in combination with the Balanced Scorecard technique [O&I, SEI, FAA].

Table 6. The use of IT in the maturity road map regarding the organization's culture

IT-neutral (19)	General IT (3)	Specific IT (3)	Specific tools (1)
ARM, HAM, LEE, MAU, ROS, WIL, BPT, CAM2, DEL, ESI, FAA, FIS, HAR2, O&I, OMG, RUM, SMI, SAP, SPA	SEI, CAM1, REM	GAR2, IDS, ORA	SCH

The previous components are frequently confronted with cultural barriers that impede process excellence. As a result, table 6 lists all BPMMs that contain: (1) attitudes and values for empowerment, innovation and multidisciplinary teamwork, (2) strategy alignment, (3) senior management involvement and (4) rewards.

Merely a quarter of the BPMMs recommend IT on higher maturity levels, e.g. for reusing common assets, such as lessons learned, success stories and templates [IDS]. Tools are also presented for planning and controlling strategic KPIs and rewards systems. Infrastructures like e-rooms, Web 2.0 communities or social networks facilitate cross-departmental and cross-organizational collaboration [GAR2, SCH].

Table 7. The use of IT in the maturity road map regarding the organization's structure

IT-neutral (11)	General IT (0)	Specific IT (0)	Specific tools (1)
ARM, HAM, MAU, WIL, BPM, CHA, FIS, GAR2, IDS, ORA, REM	-	-	SCH

The last component relates to the organization's structure, which frequently represents a matrix reconfiguration, as an alternative to a vertical or horizontal organogram. Most BPMMs propose a Center of Excellence, process office or council to coordinate process integration. Some BPMMs, such as [HAM], mention additional bodies, for instance a program management office and steering committees. In this case, the Center of Excellence is rather a senior management body than a competence center.

Although IT facilitates process integration and collaboration [SCH], table 7 is mostly IT-neutral . Due to the close link with previous components, in particular deployment and culture, no additional IT aspects are covered to improve maturity.

4   Discussion

Three findings are drawn from tables 2 to 7. First, most BPMMs do not include all components, e.g. [DET] aims to optimize. Culture and structure are often neglected.

Secondly, the components were derived from definitions to validate the results: BP<BPM<BPO. This hierarchy is translated into IT, since IT is most mentioned in the basic components to improve maturity: modeling<optimization<deployment. As a result, IT counts for the higher maturity levels. Typically, process modeling has an IT gradation: no design, manual design, design with MS Office, and BPM Suite design.

Thirdly, given this IT impact, we consider that if a BPMM requires IT on higher levels for one basic component, whether it does so for the other basic components.

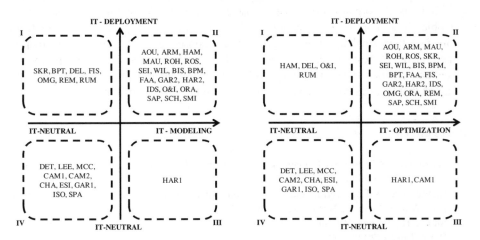

Fig. 1. The IT relationships among the modeling, deployment and optimization component

Figure 1 shows that most BPMMs have similar IT relationships among the basic components to improve maturity. The majority of models are situated in the second quadrants (fully with IT), and the fourth quadrants (fully without IT). Possible inconsistencies are situated in the first quadrants with models that mention automated deployment without electronic modeling and process engines, nor real-time metrics. However, we must note that those models may either intent to be generic for all organization sizes and types, e.g. [OMG, RUM], or that we didn't have access to all model information to appropriately assess the components in detail, e.g. [DEL].

5 Future Work

All BPMMs will be thoroughly compared with regard to other elements, such as the assessment (AS-IS) and improvement (TO-BE) method. Furthermore, the scope will be broadened towards supply chain integration and collaboration. Additional case studies will be conducted for the most comprehensive models. As introduced, the PhD dissertation will evaluate whether a new model design is appropriate for cross-organizational processes, considering the IT impact per component, e.g. cost-related. Gaps are expected to be identified in respect of a generic model for both products and services, and public and private organizations. Interestingly, multi-level governance or the mandatory collaboration among political levels, may be taken into account.

6 Conclusion

This study has compared 37 business process maturity models in respect of their use of IT to achieve higher business process maturity. Most models recommend IT to improve process modeling, deployment and optimization, with manual activities situated on lower maturity levels. IT can also facilitate managerial, cultural and structural aspects. Nevertheless, its extent strongly varies from general IT, to specific IT and specific tools. An organization must choose a maturity model that best fits its strategy and objectives. For instance, larger product organizations may benefit more from automation than smaller service organizations. Consequently, a generic road map is IT-neutral or, at best, general IT-focused. The initial hypothesis is thus partly accepted and broadened towards general IT. Similar to Carr [9], Smith and Finger [10], we agree that IT does not matter, but it enables higher process maturity.

References

1. Harrington, H.J.: Process Management Excellence. The Art of Excelling in Process Management. Paton Press, California (2006)
2. Champy, J.: X-Engineering the Corporation. Reinventing Your Business in the Digital Age. Warner Business Books, New York (2002)
3. Smith, H., Fingar, P.: Business Process Management: the Third Wave. Meghan-Kiffer Press, Tampa (2002, 2006)

4. ISO/IEC: Information Technology - Process Assessment - Part 7: Assessment of Organizational Maturity - ISO/IEC TR 15504-7:2008(E). ISO/IEC, Geneva (2008)
5. Hüffner, T.: The BPM Maturity Model - Towards a Framework for Assessing the Business Process Management Maturity of Organizations. GRIN, Munich (2004)
6. Lee, J., Lee, D., Kang, S.: An Overview of the Business Process Maturity Model (BPMM). In: Advances in Web and Network Technologies, and Information Management, Huang Shan, China, June 16-18, pp. 279–288. Springer, Heidelberg (2007)
7. Maier, A.M., Moultrie, J., Clarkson, P.J.: A Review of Maturity Grid based Approaches to Assessing Organizational Capabilities. In: Academy of Management Annual Meeting, 8-13 August, Academy of Management, California (2008)
8. Rosemann, M., de Bruin, T.: Application of a Holistic Model for Determining BPM Maturity. BPTrends (February 2005)
9. Carr, N.G.: IT Doesn't Matter. Harvard Business Review 81(5), 41–49 (2003)
10. Smith, H., Fingar, P.: IT doesn't matter-Business Processes Do. Meghan-Kiffer Press, Tampa (2003)
11. Gillot, J.-N.: The Complete Guide to Business Process Management. In: Business Process Transformation or a Way of Aligning the Strategic Objectives of the Company and the Information System through the Processes, Booksurge Publishing, South Carolina (2008)
12. McCormack, K., Johnson, W.C.: Business Process Orientation: Gaining the e-Business Competitive Advantage. St. Lucie Press, Florida (2001)
13. Aouad, G., et al.: Technology Management of IT in Construction: a Driver or an Enabler? Logistics Information Management 12(1/2), 130–137 (1999)
14. Pritchard, J.-P., Armistead, C.: Business Process Management - Lessons from European Business. Business Process Management Journal 5(1), 10–32 (1999)
15. DeToro, I., McCabe, T.: How to Stay Flexible and Elude Fads. Quality Progress, 55–60 (March 1997)
16. Hammer, M.: The Process Audit. Harvard Business Review, 111–123 (April 2007)
17. Lee, J., Lee, D., Kang, S.: vPMM: a value based Process Maturity Model. In: Roger, L., Gonzu, H., Huaikou, M. (eds.) Computer and Information Science 2009, pp. 193–213. Springer, Heidelberg (2009)
18. Maull, R.S., Tranfield, D.R., Maull, W.: Factors Characterizing the Maturity of BPR Programmes. International Journal of Operations & Production Management 23(6), 596–624 (2003)
19. Rohloff, M.: Case Study and Maturity Model for Business Process Management Implementation. In: 7th International Conference, BPM, September, pp. 128–142. Springer, Ulm (2009)
20. de Bruin, T., Rosemann, M.: Using the Delphi Technique to Identify BPM Capability Areas.. In: 18th Australasian Conference on Information Systems, 5-7 December, pp. 642–53. Toowoomba (2007)
21. Skrinjar, R., Bosilj-Vuksic, V., Stemberger, M.I.: The Impact of Business Process Orientation on Financial and Non-financial Performance. Business Process Management Journal 14(5), 738–754 (2008)
22. SEI: CMMI for Development, Version 1.2. Software Engineering Institute (August 2006), Online http://www.sei.cmu.edu/reports/06tr008.pdf
23. SEI: CMMI for Acquisition, Version 1.2. Software Engineering Institute (November 2007), Online http://www.sei.cmu.edu/reports/07tr017.pdf
24. SEI: CMMI for Services, Version 1.2. Software Engineering Institute (February 2009), Online http://www.sei.cmu.edu/reports/09tr001.pdf

25. Peter, W., et al.: The Process-Oriented Organization: a Holistic View. Developing a Framework for Business Process Orientation Maturity. In: 5th International Conference on Business Process Management, 24-28 September, p. 15. Springer, Brisbane (2007)

26. Bisnez Management: Business Process Management Onderzoek 2009-2010 (2010), Online http://www.bisnez.org/files/Rapport_BPM_volwassenheid_onderz oek_2009_2010_def.pdf

27. BPMInstitute: 2010 BPM Market Assessment Survey (2010), Online http://2010stateofbpm.surveyconsole.com/

28. BPT Group: Welcome to 8 Omega v2.0. BP Transformations Group (March 2008), Online http://bptg.seniordev.co.uk/8omega.aspx

29. Dowdle, P., et al.: The Process-based Management Loop. The Journal of Corporate Accounting & Finance, 55–60 (January 2005)

30. Dowdle, P., Stevens, J., Daly, D.: Process-based Management at Work in an Organization (2007), Online http://www.cam-i.org/docs/PBM_at_Work_in_an_organization.pdf

31. Champlin, B.: Dimensions of Business Process Change (June 25, 2008), Online https://www.bpminstitute.org/uploads/media/Champlin-6-25-08.pdf

32. Deloitte: Het Business Maturity Model (2010), Online http://www.deloitte.com/view/nl_NL/nl/diensten/consulting/ strategy-operations/business-maturity-model/index.htm

33. Ostolaza, E., Garcia, A.B.: EFQM/SPICE Integrated Model. The Business Excellence Road for Software Intensive Organizations. In: International Conference on Product Focused Software Improvement, June 22-24, pp. 437–452 Oulu (1999)

34. FAA: FAA-iCMM, Version 2.0, An Integrated Capability Maturity Model for Enterprise-wide Improvement (2001), Online http://www.faa.gov/about/office_org/headquarters_offices/ aio/library/

35. Fisher, D.M.: The Business Process Maturity Model. A Practical Approach for Identifying Opportunities for Optimization. BPTrends (September 2004)

36. Gardner, R.A.: The Process-Focused Organization. A Transition Strategy for Success. ASQ, Quality Press, Milwaukee (2004)

37. Melenovsky, M.J., Sinur, J.: BPM Maturity Model Identifies Six Phases for Successful BPM Adoption. Gartner Research, Stamford (2006)

38. Harmon, P.: Evaluating an Organization's Business Process Maturity. BPTrends Newsletter 2(3), 1–11 (2004)

39. IDS Scheer: BPM Maturity Check (2010), Online http://www.bpmmaturity.com/

40. ISO/IEC: Software Engineering - Process Assessment - Part 2: Performing an Assessment - ISO/IEC 15504-2:2003(E). ISO/IEC, Geneva (2003)

41. Tolsma, J., de Wit, D.: Effectief Procesmanagement. Procesgericht Sturen met het BPM model. Eburon, Delft (2009)

42. OMG: Business Process Maturity Model (BPMM) - Version 1.0 (1 June 2008), Online http://www.omg.org/spec/BPMM/1.0/PDF

43. Oracle: BPM Lifecycle Assessment (2008), Online http://bpmready.nvishweb.com/

44. Remoreras, G.: Achieving the Highest Level of Process Culture Maturity (August 23, 2009), Online http://mysimpleprocesses.com

45. Rummler-Brache Group: Business Process Management in U.S. Firms Today (March 2004), Online http://rummler-brache.com/upload/files/PPI_Research_Results.pdf

46. Scavillo, M.: Business Process Transformation in the Software Industry (30 June 2008), Online
    `http://www.sdn.sap.com/irj/scn/go/portal/prtroot/docs/`
    `library/uuid/70559771-c266-2b10-1499-8c36e668e0a6?QuickLink=`
    `events&overridelayout=true`
47. Scheer, A.-W.: BPM = Business Process Management = Business Performance Management (2007), Online `http://www.professor-scheer-bpm.com/`
48. Smith, H., Fingar, P.: Process Management Maturity Models. BPTrends (July 2004)
49. Spanyi, A.: Beyond Process Maturity to Process Competence. BPTrends (June 2004)

Detecting Near-Duplicate Relations in User Generated Forum Content

Klemens Muthmann[1] and Alexander Löser[2]

[1] Technical University Dresden
Chair for Computer Networks
klemens.muthmann@tu-dresden.de
[2] Technical University Berlin
DIMA Group
alexander.loeser@tu-berlin.de

Abstract. A webforum is a large database of community knowledge, with information of the most recent events and developments. Unfortunately this knowledge is presented in a format easily understood by humans but not automatically by machines. However, from observing several forums for a long time it seems obvious that there are several distinct types of postings and relations between them.

One often occurring and very annoying relation between two contributions is the near-duplicate relation. In this paper we propose a work to detect and utilize contribution relations, concentrating on near-duplication. We propose ideas on how to calculate similarity, build groups of similar threads and thus make near-duplicates in forums evident. One of the core theses is, that it is possible to apply information from forum and thread structure to improve existing near-duplicate detection approaches. In addition, the proposed work shows the qualitative and quantitative results of applying such principles, thereby finding out which features are really useful in the near-duplicate detection process. Also proposed are several sample applications, which benefit from forum near-duplicate detection.

1 Introduction

Today the internet and especially the world wide web is a huge collection of a large part of the knowledge available to humankind. In contrast to databases vast parts of this knowledge were never intended to be used for automatic information querying. This is particularly true for content created by often technically inexperienced users in the form of free text. Such content does not follow any consistent formal schema other than grammatical and lexical rules. Because there is so much of this unstructured user generated content available it is not an easy task to find out if a piece of information already exists or not.

A large part of unstructured user generated information is located in web forums. A forum is used to discuss current topics or ask questions to specific problems. Like the web, a forum is a growing collection of information and although it is possible to answer many questions instantly with available information, the

R. Meersman et al. (Eds.): OTM 2010 Workshops, LNCS 6428, pp. 698–707, 2010.

information overload often hides relevant discussions from their audience. To address this problem companies like Google or Microsoft created search engines, that crawl the web and try to point people to the information they seek. However since search engines - either the forums or global ones - usually only match keywords to documents they are not optimized to provide users with the answer they seek. So even though information might be available, users are not able to find it and thus create new discussion threads about similar topics again and again. Thereby the forums grow even faster and get more and more confusing, leading to more and more duplicate information - a vicious circle.

Although there are several algorithms to find similarity relations in databases or the web, these algorithms usually capture only very close, text similarity, without regarding the special features of forums or other domains. A special near-duplicate detection (NDD) approach on unstructured user generated forum content has many applications (See next section). Therefore this work is going to provide a general process for near-duplicate detection on user generated forum content.

1.1 Application Scenarios

To show the usefulness of NDD on forum content, this section presents some intended applications and stakeholders benefiting from these tools.

Answer Provider. When people use a forum they usually search answers, opinions or want to inform about some event or topic. If they cannot find threads covering their intention, they start creating new ones. When they use a forum's search engine to locate existing content, they usually can only enter a few key words that are matched against an inverted index. All threads containing these keywords are shown as results ordered by the number of keywords they contained.

In contrast to the keyword based query formulation provided by search engines, users provide much more information upon writing their new thread. During this step they describe their problem in whole sentences, in a way other people can understand. Therefore a tool could be created that analyses the new thread before it is actually created and proposes existing threads on the topic. If the user finds a solution he does not need to post his thread. If he finds no solution he can still create the already entered new discussion. Similar tools are already used on https://launchpad.net/ and http://digg.com/.

Subforum Advisor. Many forums contain a large list of subforums for several topic areas. This is helpful to structure the information but often also confuses new users. Since they do not know were to post their question, they just post were it seems appropriate - often in the wrong place. It is the moderators' job to move such threads to the correct place. Currently this is a hard manual work. One could imagine a tool that calculates the similarity between all threads and tells moderators which threads might be in the wrong place or a tool that tells a user which subforum his thread belongs to.

Thread Recommender. Often a user finds an interesting discussion and wants to know what else is discussed about this topic. Although there are some forums already supporting this feature, current implementations are insufficient.

Expert Assistant. A forum might contain questions that occurred often but never receive an answer because they are very complex. Usually it is in the interest of the forum community to solve such pressing questions. On the other hand experts should not waste time answering questions that were already answered in other threads. Using a duplicate detection system it is possible to detect such threads and support experts to find the threads they really need to answer.

Spam Detector. Sometimes users post their questions multiple times to heighten their visibility. It is usually possible to find such duplicates with existing techniques, but it becomes more complicated if one such thread actually gets an answer or is modified by its creator and thus changes one of the instances. A near-duplicate detection system is able to find such spam threads as well and shows them to a forum moderator. The moderator can delete the spam threads and warn the spamming user to stop doing this.

Table 1. Possible applications of near-duplicate detection on forum content

Functionality	Beneficiary	Scenario	Application
Answer Provider	Member Moderator Operator	"Before I ask... maybe there's already an answer?"	Tool to suggest existing answers to new threads.
Subforum Advisor	Member Moderator Operator	"Should post be into this forum?"	Tool to detect content in wrong forum.
Thread Recommender	Member	"Nice thread. Any others like it around?"	Tool to show related threads.
Expert Assistant	Expert Moderator Operator	"Which thread is most urgent to answer?"	Tool to detect most pressing questions.
Spam Detector	Member Moderator Operator	"Are there spam threads to delete?"	Tool to detect spam threads and show to moderators.

2 Related Work

Measuring similarity of web pages is carried out by many researches such as [3,4,10,8,5]. These approaches work quite well for pages with lots of equal text and only small changes like different banners, ads or headers. In [3,4,10] they use document fingerprints to decide whether two documents are near-duplicates or not. Chowdhurys I-Match algorithm uses bags of words filtering out words with no relevant information. These words are found using the well known TF/IDF measure. Unfortunately TF/IDF is only effective if the whole document collection is known in advance. Henzinger is doing work on improving existing algorithms. She proposes a combination of [3] and [4] and does research on how to reduce Broder's algorithm to the most relevant text n-grams [7]. However - although data in our work comes from web pages - we do not just compare the forums pages but the extracted entries themselves. This is more similar to near-duplicate detection in database records which was recently summarized by [6]. That work presents the common syntactical similarity measures for database entries. These are measures for the comparison of individual fields like edit distance (Levensthein distance), Q-Grams or soundex and classification algorithms to order database records to either be duplicates or non-duplicates. Even though these ideas are applicable for near-duplicate detection in forums, they are not optimized to capture the data fields provided by web forums.

As forums are a very useful source for cutting edge information, there is of course some work (see [14,15]) on structuring this content. The approach of [14] uses topical duplicate detection to improve on the PageRank [13] algorithm. It uses two feature types - discriminating words and forum internal links - to build a topical hierarchical clustering of all the pages in a forum. Yang et al. [15] in addition apply the user interaction graph within a forum to give more evidence for their clustering (DBSCAN) algorithm. However, these algorithms usually consider forum pages or whole threads - not contributions - as first class entities and assign each page to only one cluster, which are rather bad assumptions for the proposed use-cases (see 1.1). Another work [9] using contributions directly, proposes an algorithm to detect reply relationships between contributions. Even though it provides a coarse grained topical clustering of contributions, it is limited to relations inside of threads.

To summarize, one can see that there is work on clustering forum content, but it is constrained to very narrow use-cases. There also has been much work on near-duplicate detection, clustering of websites and topic detection but it is not optimized for the proposed use cases.

3   Research Theses

The work is based on two theses presented in this section. Both are structured into an antithesis and a thesis, were the antithesis states the deficiency and the thesis claims a solution.

Antithesis 1. It is not possible to find topically related near-duplicates in Forums with state-of-the-art near-duplicate detection methods, because user generated content shows heavy fluctuations in quality and most information pieces are very short.

Thesis 1. It is possible to improve on topical NDD by using forum specific features (structure) and semantical data (named entities, facts, ontologies).

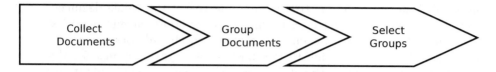

Fig. 1. Near-Duplicate Detection Process

Antithesis 2. Forum users are not happy with the way search engines in general and forum search engines especially present search results as result lists.

Thesis 2. By presenting groups of related contributions the information needs of forum users can be satisfied much more quickly and completely.

4   Near-Duplicate Detection Process

The most abstract process for NDD in forums consists of three distinct phases as presented in Fig. 1. An overview of these steps, the problems one faces and ideas on solutions are provided in the next paragraphs.

Phase 1: Collect Documents. The documents considered in the presented information retrieval problem are user contributions to a forum. Each contribution is posted by one user, has a title, a body text and often some rating of its quality provided by other users. To acquire these documents and especially the individual information entries, there are three ways available. If direct access to the forum's database is possible a simple database access layer is sufficient. However under most circumstances, direct access is not provided and so we either need to crawl the complete forum and retrieve the datasnippets by cutting them out the forum's webpage code or use a feed reader that provides the relevant information pieces for all new contributions published to the forum's RSS or ATOM feed. A crawler has the advantage that the whole forum is extracted in hours or minutes depending on the forum's size. The disadvantage is that a wrapper is needed to extract the information pieces. A feed reader in contrast is already provided with the correct datasnippets but gets no access to old contributions and needs very long to build up a reasonably sized document corpus.

Phase 2: Group Documents. Clustering of forum contributions requires a hierarchical soft clustering algorithm. Hierarchical means that clusters on one level of the hierarchy can contain clusters from a lower level forming a tree with the contributions at its leafs. Soft means that one contribution can contain information about several topics already discussed in other contributions and thus needs to be clustered into several clusters on the same level of the hierarchy (see Fig. 2).

To order documents to clusters a distance function between document pairs is required. This function compares document features that distinguish near-duplicate pairs from non-near-duplicate pairs. These features are extracted from

Fig. 2. Example of thread grouping

the raw data collected at Phase 1. As discussed in [12] features are basic elements forming a feature vector or profile for each document. A contributions profile is a data structure containing all information necessary for near-duplicate detection. Our observations so far revealed, that there are local, contextual and structural feature types. Some of them are evident from the raw data, others can be extracted using Information Extraction (IE) and Information Retrieval (IR) techniques. The following are some basic features organized by type:

- Local: PoS tags, named entities, external links, facts, keywords
- Contextual: publication date, author name, ratings, title, semantic data structure (ontology, taxonomy, ...) describing forums context
- Structural: Forum internal link graph, User graph, Subforum topic tree

As described by [11] hierarchical clustering has a complexity of $O(n^2)$ in contrast to the linear complexity of flat clustering. Therefore it is usually not usable on web scale. However since this work concentrates only on a small fraction of the documents from the web, hierarchical clustering will be applicable here.

Phase 3: Select Groups. Finally the grouped contributions are selected based on the use case as presented in Section 1.1. The spam detector might require to show only groups with very similar contributions, while the expert assistant presents groups containing many similar questions with no answers or clusters containing only one question for which no answer is available.

5   Evaluation and Current Results

Two areas are of interest for evaluating the near-duplicate detection system: quality of the results (effectiveness) and performance of the system (efficiency).

5.1   Current Experimental Setup

Until now we have already evaluated a very basic approach using three feature types - keywords, named entities and internal links. They were extracted from each thread from a set of around 2500 threads from the SAP Developer Network (http://forums.sdn.sap.com/). Similarity then was calculated using the overlap of the two keyword sets and entity sets for each pair of threads. Finally resemblance and containment [2] relations were used to group each thread together with all threads it contains or resembles. We ran several experiments evaluating the performance of only one of the three feature types and finally all three together with varying similarity thresholds. Our baseline was a simple SQL query returning only exact matches of the body of two contributions starting a thread. Results are shown in Table 2. The name of each experiment consists of the feature type and the threshold used.

Table 2. First experimental results

Experiment	Groups found	Duplicates	Precision	Groupsize		
				2	3 - 5	5+
Baseline	18	36	100%	18	0	0
External links	5	10	20%	5	0	0
Keyword-75	139	272	48,82%	96	29	14
Keyword-80	88	186	57,80%	76	9	3
Entity-50	142	501	28,14%	91	38	13
Entity-80	15	31	80,65%	14	1	0
All-34	126	194	74,33%	118	8	0

5.2   Effectiveness Evaluation

Result quality is investigated using the common measures of precision and recall. Precision is the ratio of correctly identified duplicates within all results, while recall is the ratio of actually found duplicates to all existing duplicates. To get these measures it is necessary to have an input set of forum contributions which was analyzed in advance and annotated with the expected results. This set is usually called gold standard. With such a dataset it is possible to compare the acquired results to the expected ones using precision and recall.

Unfortunately there is no existing gold standard for near-duplicates in forum content and it is quite costly to build one. To get a reasonably sized set one needs to compare $\frac{n^2}{2}$ threads manually and since reasonably sized means something around 1.000 or larger one would need to carry out $\frac{1000 \cdot 1000}{2} = 500.000$ comparisons manually. Therefore at first we concentrated on the evaluation of the precision of our first result set only. Surprisingly our precision was as high as 74,33% using all three feature types (keywords, named entities, external links). However for a really meaningful evaluation having a reasonably sized gold standard is essential. Therefore this work proposes a different approach, cutting down the number of required comparisons significantly. A gold standard need not to be one set, but could also be a collection of small sets that are processed independently. Each small set is annotated with the expected results, so precision and recall can be calculated as the mean value from the results for all the small sets. Small in this case means around 10 threads, which requires only $\frac{10 \cdot 10}{2} = 50$ comparisons each. This gold standard is also quite easy to be extended by new sets.

The complete gold standard consists of several subsets each designed to detect distributions and features of near-duplicates. They are created using the following principle. At first ten seed threads are chosen. We might for example choose the ten newest threads or the newest threads from the ten most active users and so on. Each seed thread title is used as a query to the forum's search engine and for each query the top ten results are collected. These top ten results should have an increased chance of actually containing near-duplicates, since they were found using a topic description that actually is used in the forum. Doing this for several seed threads should yield a corpus of evaluation sets each containing ten threads. These sets will be used as initial gold standard. As the work progresses they will be extended iteratively using results from new implementations.

5.3   Efficiency Evaluation

The second area for evaluation is performance. High quality results are worthless if not acquired in reasonable time. This means the analysis needs to be faster than the growth rate of the forum. In many cases it is of course possible to run near-duplicate detection on a larger machine or a cluster of machines. However this increases costs and thereby reduces productivity. The currently implemented algorithm has exponential complexity in the worst case: a forum were all threads are duplicates of each other. This is a very unlikely event, but our experiments show that it takes 21 minutes to group the 2500 threads from our input dataset.

Performance is analyzed measuring runtime, memory- and CPU consumption using a reasonable equipped computer or a cluster of computers.

6   Discussion and Future Work

Our initial experiments showed that forums can not be handled like common natural language texts. One of the greatest problems was the varying quality of the contributions, which makes it hard to apply established Natural Language Processing (NLP) methods, like Tokenization, Part of Speech (PoS) Tagging, Named Entity Recognition (NER) and link extraction.

For example we tried PoS Tagging with existing trained models, yielding quite bad results because of source code blocks and incomplete or grammatically incorrect sentences. Tokenization was hampered by missing or wrong separation characters like spaces or dots. Link extraction was hard because non valid characters are used, valid characters are used in the wrong locations or URLs where incomplete. In the future we plan to extract such unprocessable content in advance to improve on the quality of the examined contributions. This should also increase the quality of the keyword- and other local feature types. Ideas for finding low quality content were for example proposed by Agichtein et al. [1]

The problems with NER trace back to a lack of understanding for the forums content. Applying a western English NER system for example to a board like MSDN or SAP Developer Network, recognizes many of the East Indian author names as locations, while in programming forums code constructs like `Boolean` are recognized as names. In the future we will try to provide a context for each forum in the form of a semantical data structure like an ontology or a taxonomy. Many of these are available online (e.g. Freebase, WordNet, DBPedia, etc.) and can improve the systems understanding of the actual contents of a forum.

Another problem is the varying length of threads. Short threads provide very few information about their content while threads that are too long tend to divert into multiple topics that are hard to separate. When calculating similarity between a long and a short thread it often happens that the long thread "swallows" the shorter one, so that even though the whole topic of the short thread is discussed by the long one the similarity calculation does relate them.

We also observed that threads and contributions are assignable to different types and that we need to compare only types that can have a near-duplicate relation. So for example we do not need to compare answer and question.

7   Conclusion and Work Plan

This document shows ideas, on finding near-duplicate relations within forum content. It provided some possible applications. It shows how other people addressed NDD on the web and on databases and why these solutions are insufficient for web forum NDD. In addition it outlines a NDD process together with relevant features. Finally some early results and a methodology to evaluate further results is presented. This methodology is different to everything presented so far. The paper closes with a discussion on the problems and pitfalls encountered and proposes solutions on how to address these issues during the next experiments.

The Future work will concentrate in the following areas:

1. **Build gold standard.** At first we need to build the described (See Section 5.2) gold standard. Thereby investigating existing forum contributions
2. **Build typology of contributions and contribution relations.** With the knowledge on forum contributions gained from gold standard creation we categorize forum contributions and relations between them.
3. **Find features distinguishing contribution and relation types.** With the complete typologies, new features that are helpful to identify near-duplicates can be extracted and existing ones (See Section 4) verified.
4. **Improve similarity and grouping.** Two iterations are planned for improving and evaluating the existing similarity and grouping algorithms, building upon knowledge and requirements gained from the previous iteration.
5. **Develop Use Case.** Implementation of at least one of the use cases is intended when the next iteration on the similarity and grouping systems is available. Thereby we can show and evaluate the actual use of the work.

Acknowledgments

My thanks go to my colleagues and my advisor Professor Schill for careful prove reading.

References

1. Agichtein, E., Castillo, C., Donato, D., Gionis, A., Mishne, G.: Finding high-quality content in social media. Proceedings of the International Conference on Web Search and Web Data Mining, WSDM 2008, 183 (2008)
2. Broder, A.: On the resemblance and containment of documents. Proceedings. Compression and Complexity of SEQUENCES 1997 (Cat. No.97TB100171), 21–29 (1997)
3. Broder, A.: Identifying and Filtering Near-Duplicate Documents. In: DOM 2000: Proceedings of the 11th Annual Symposium on Combinatorial Pattern Matching, L, pp. 1–10. Springer, London (2000)
4. Charikar, M.S.: Similarity Estimation Techniques from Rounding Algorithms. In: Computer, pp. 380–388. ACM Press, New York (2002)
5. Chowdhury, A., Frieder, O., Grossman, D., McCabe, M.C.: Collection statistics for fast duplicate document detection. ACM Transactions on Information Systems 20(2), 171–191 (2002)
6. Elmagarmid, A.K., Ipeirotis, P.G., Verykios, V.S.: Duplicate Record Detection: A Survey. IEEE Trans. on Knowl. and Data Eng. 19(1), 1–16 (2007)
7. Hamid, O.A., Behzadi, B., Christoph, S., Henzinger, M.: Detecting the origin of text segments efficiently. In: WWW 2009: Proceedings of the 18th international conference on World wide web, pp. 61–70. ACM Press, New York (2009)
8. Henzinger, M.: Finding Near-Duplicate Web Pages: A Large-Scale Evaluation of Algorithms. In: SIGIR 2006: Proceedings of the 29th annual international ACM SIGIR conference on Research and Development in Information Retrieval, pp. 284–291. ACM, New York (2006)
9. Lin, C., Yang, J., Cai, R., Wang, X.: Simultaneously modeling semantics and structure of threaded discussions: a sparse coding approach and its applications. In: Proceedings of the 32nd, pp. 131–138 (2009)
10. Manber, U.: Finding similar files in a large file system. In: Proceedings of the USENIX Winter 1994 Technical Conference on USENIX Winter 1994 Technical Conference WTEC 1994, pp. 2–2. USENIX Association, Berkeley (1994)
11. Manning, C.D., Raghavan, P., Schütze, H.: An introduction to information retrieval. Cambridge University Press, New York (2009)
12. Muthmann, K.: Entwicklung eines Gruppierungs - Operators für Forenbeiträge. Diploma, Technische Universität Dresden (2009)
13. Page, L., Brin, S., Motwani, R., Winograd, T.: The pagerank citation ranking: Bringing order to the web. In: World Wide Web Internet And Web Information Systems, pp. 1–17 (1998)
14. Xu, G., Ma, W.Y.: Building implicit links from content for forum search. In: SIGIR 2006: Proceedings of the 29th annual international ACM SIGIR Conference on Research and Development in Information Retrieval, pp. 300–307. ACM Press, New York (2006)
15. Yang, C., Ng, T.: Analyzing Content Development and Visualizing Social Interactions in Web Forum. On Intelligence and Security Informatics (ISI&#39 (2008)

Author Index

Printing: Mercedes-Druck, Berlin
Binding: Stein+Lehmann, Berlin